ARMENIAN ART TREASURES OF JERUSALEM

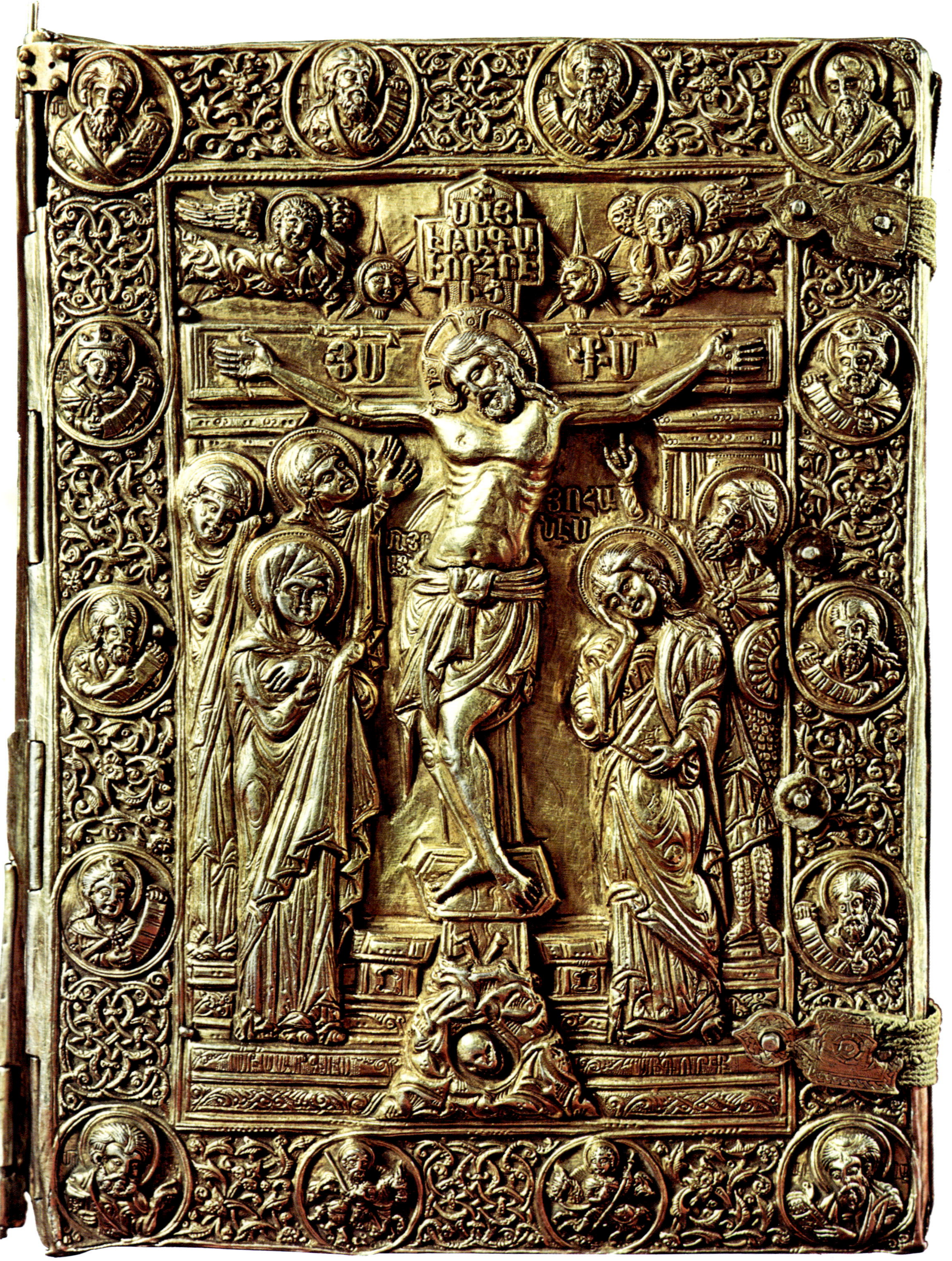

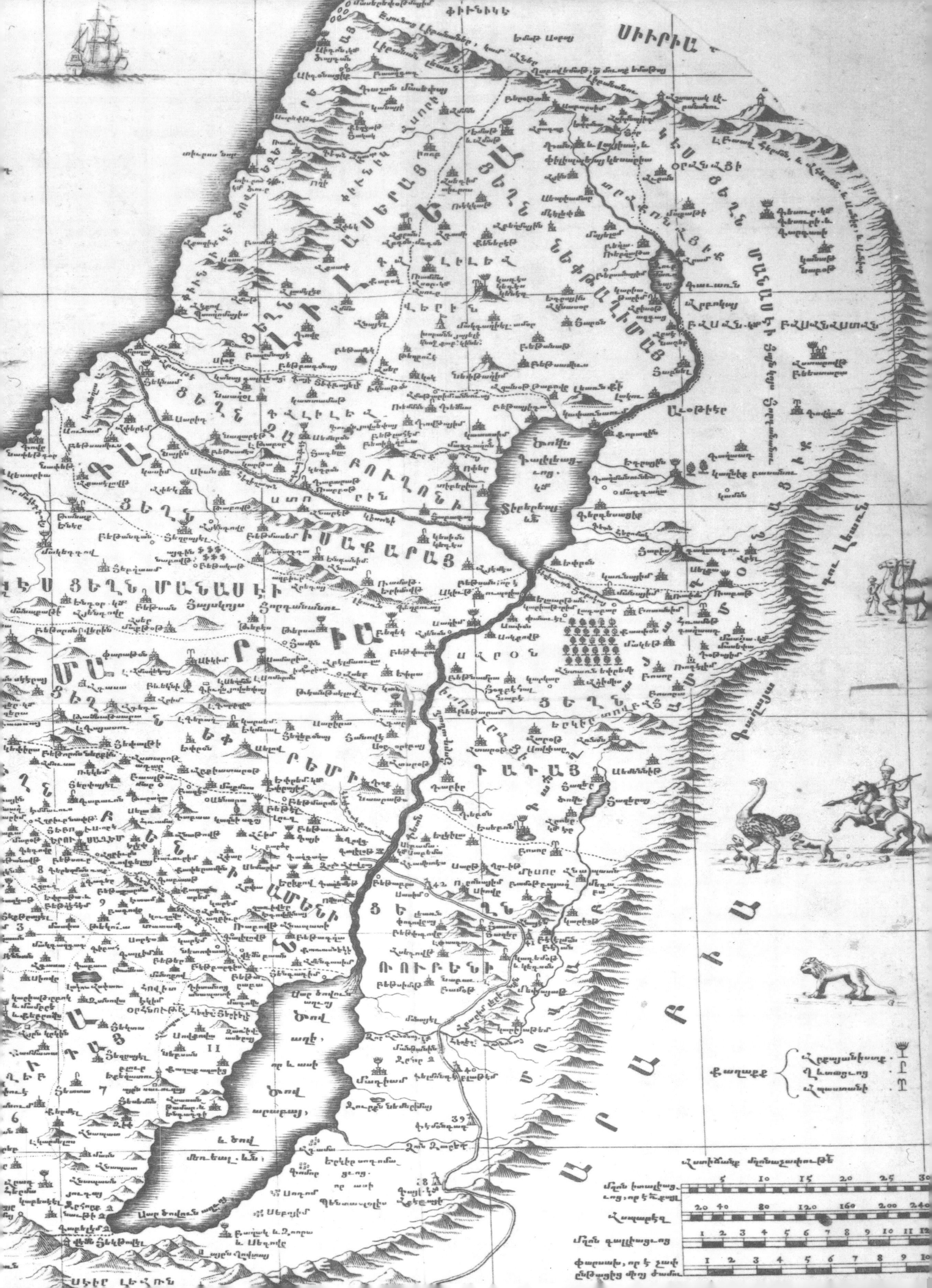

ՍԻՒՐԻԱ
ՓԻՒՆԻԿԷ
ԻՍԱՔԱՐԱՅ
ԳԱԴԱՅ
ՌՈՒԲԷՆԻ
Ծով աղի
Քաղաքք
5 10 15 20 25 30
20 40 80 120 160 200 240
1 2 3 4 5 6 7 8 9 10 11 12
1 2 3 4 5 6 7 8 9 10

To the Armenians in Jerusalem
for their Courage and Endurance

Frontispiece: *The Crucifixion. Silver-gilt, front binding of the Gospel of the Sea, executed by Yovhannes deacon at Sis (Cilicia) in 1334. Treasury of St. James No. 94 (Jerusalem ms. 2649).*

Front endpaper: *An Armenian map of the Holy Land, probably printed in Venice, 1746.*
Back endpaper: *Map of Armenia, Venice, 1751.*

ARMENIAN ART TREASURES OF JERUSALEM

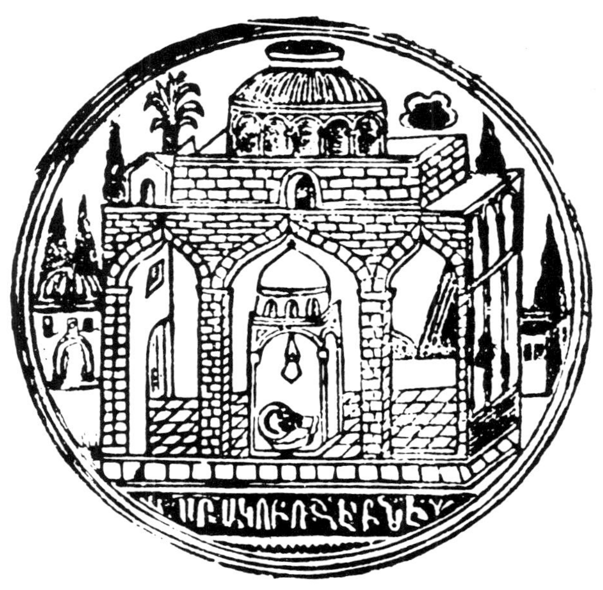

Edited by Bezalel Narkiss
In collaboration with Michael E. Stone
Historical survey by Avedis K. Sanjian
Managing editor: Alexander Peli

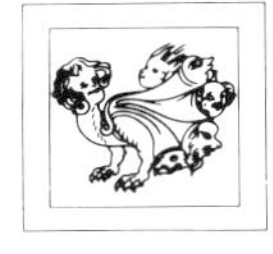

CARATZAS BROTHERS, PUBLISHERS
NEW ROCHELLE, NEW YORK
1979

Design Chava Mordohovich
Photography David Harris

Published in North America by

Caratzas Brothers, Publishers
481 Main Street, New Rochelle,
New York 10801 (U.S.A.)
(Mailing address: P.O. Box 210
New Rochelle, New York 10802)

ISBN 0-89241- 095-7

Colour Separation: Nefli b.v. - Haarlem
PRINTED IN THE NETHERLANDS by De Lang / Van Leer - Deventer

Table of Contents

Armenian Patriarchate Պատրիարքարան Հայոց

ELISHA II, Patriarch

The Armenian Patriarchate of Jerusalem is one of the most venerated of Holy Sees of the Christian Church. At the same time, it is a Holy Site, a spiritual center, a seat of religious learning and a great focus of pilgrimage. The Cathedral of St. James, which the Dominican Fathers have termed "Gem of Churches", stands out among the Holy Sites of Jerusalem not only as a sanctuary but also as a beautiful edifice. It has been the receptacle of miracles, and has withstood the trials of the ages. The arches do not bespeak the suffering of our people. The legion of saints, the Church Fathers, create a mystical atmosphere, hard to grasp humanly. The absence of gloom and the modest character of the Church single it out from other sanctuaries of Jerusalem. There, into the lap of the treasury of St. James have flowed our people's princely gifts; abundant gold, precious stones, gems big and small, dustlike and beads, of all color and shade, adorning the Church banners, crosses, chalices, the silver and gold covers of books. A true symphony of light and color. Muslins as thin as rose petals, as if to be blown away in your palm. Heavy vestments with embroidered folds which challenge the sturdiest of shoulders. Lamps, both of gold and silver, suspended from these mystic arches, twinkle in the dark to the point of repelling obscurity and death. Chasubles with embroidered roses peep at you like tongues of candles. Golden threaded curtains, which conceal the superb sculptures and beauty of altar paintings. Diamonds, emeralds, pearls, encrusted into crowns and crosses. Bunches of pearls embroidered into the body of muslin and velvet overflowing and pulsating with color and light. There are scepters too, omophorions which fire the most dormant imagination. There are embroideries as warm as kisses and as sweet as a prayer. It is a true joy to contemplate the parade of objects, the intense reflections of color, floating and genuine. All these works of art have been brought from Armenia and Cilicia by pious and princely souls. "Happy is he who has a memento in Zion" — the supreme desire and steadfastness of the Armenian spirit have brought art objects from far-off Armenia to Jerusalem and have stored here, together with the Treasures of Faith, the beauties of its Art. The great devotion of the Armenian people to beauty and good taste are best testified by these masterpieces of art, the contagious and commuting charm, which resolves in its depth all inconsistencies of form and color, coordinating them into an organic whole.

The illuminations have come to us in their thousands since the 13th century, after surviving the havocs of time. Painting is an art form native and true to the Armenian artistic temperament, occupying an important place in contemporary Oriental and Western painting. We lack words to describe the grace of this art. One must see them to enjoy the miracle of their splendor. It is exactly this immediate contact that we offer to the emotions of those who are sensitive to art. We consider it a privilege to reveal this, an art essentially religious, Christian in inspiration, Armenian in form, in Jerusalem, which we would desire to see in its blossoming as the Holy City of the great religions, cradle of great cultures and greatest of inspirations.

Preface

The Jerusalem Patriarchate owns one of the richest and the most important treasures of Armenian art in the world. Its wealth is due to the place of Jerusalem, the Holy City, in the minds and hearts of the Armenians throughout their existence as a Christian nation. As the first nation to accept Christianity, in 301 A.D., even before Constantine's Edict of Milan, the Armenians made the Holy Land their spiritual haven, and pilgrims with donations flocked to Jerusalem, beginning at this time. It is, therefore, not surprising to find such an important treasure of Armenian art in the Holy City. What is surprising is the fact that so little of this vast artistic material was made public, and apart from an exhibition which was held at the Armenian Compound in Jerusalem in 1969, accompanied by a catalogue, only some of the treasures were known from scholarly publications.

This is the first time that part of this artistic treasure is exposed to the general public to enjoy, and to students of mediaeval art to appreciate. This publication is by no means comprehensive. There are still more Armenian mosaic pavements, many more illuminated manuscripts, a wealth of ritual vessels and priestly vestments, which could not fit into this limited space. It is hoped, however, that the taste of what is reproduced and discussed will instigate more publications of art from Jerusalem and of Armenian art from other places.

It gives me and my colleague Professor Michael E. Stone great pleasure to thank those who helped and encouraged us in the pleasures and burdens of this book. Firstly, we would like to express our deep gratitude to the Armenian Patriarch of Jerusalem, His Beatitude, Elisha II Derderian and the instigator of the project, Archbishop Shahe Ajamian, without whose constant help the book would not have been possible. In addition we owe deep appreciation to Archbishop Norayr Bogharian, the Librarian of St. Thoros Manuscript library in Jerusalem, for his indispensable help, patience and good humor. Thanks are also due to the custodian of the Holy Sepulcher, Bishop Guregh Kapikian, for many fruitful discussions, Mr. Sahag Kalaydjian, the Librarian of the Gulbenkian Library, Mr. Ara Kalaydjian the former director of the Armenian Printing Press, and Mr. George Hintlian for their constant help.

Professor Stone has borne with me in the past four years, through planning, shifting, describing and discussing, as well as in endless sessions with our devoted photographer, Mr. David Harris. He, together with Mrs. Hava Mordohovich, Dr. Geoffrey Wigoder, Mrs. Elaine Varadi and Miss Jill Oster, formed part of the working team which helped to produce the book, and are heartily thanked for their participation. Thanks are extended to Professor Avedis Sanjian of UCLA, who kindly agreed to write the historical chapter, and was the first to be ready with his contribution. I am most grateful to the Director and Deputy Director of the Mashtotz Matenadaran in Erevan, Dr. Levon Khatchikian and Dr. Babken Levon Chookaszian who did their utmost to help me study some of their illuminated manuscripts during my visit in May 1977, and cordial thanks to Miss Jacqueline Boel who assisted me. Dr. V. Nersessian of the British Library was of much help in deciphering obscure passages and scenes. Gratitude is due to the Warburg Institute Library in London, where I pursued fruitful research and wrote most of this book.

I would also like to thank my colleagues who read parts of the text, and made valuable critical comments, among them Professor Hugo Buchthal, Dr. Ruth Mellinkoff, Dr. Michael Evans, Dr. Gabrielle Sed-Rajna, and Dr. Bianca Kühnel. My deepest thanks are also due to Mrs. Aliza Cohen-Mushlin, who critically read all the text, and to Miss Christine Evans, who made the book readable. I would also like to express special thanks to my wife Hillela and my daughter Irit, as well as to my publisher Mr. Alexander Peli, for their patience through long and hard times. Last but not least I would like to express my deepest appreciation to Professor Sirarpie Der Nersessian, the doyen of Armenian art studies, without whose extensive publications this book could not have been written. Let this be a tribute to her knowledge, devotion and personality.

Bezalel Narkiss
Princeton, October 1978

The Armenian Communities of Jerusalem

by Avedis K. Sanjian

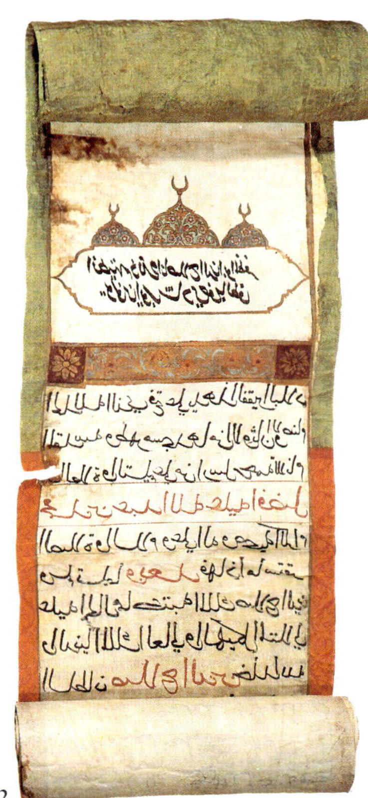

2

3

Figure 2: *The* Firman *attributed to the Prophet Mohammed, confirming the rights of the Armenians in the Holy Places of Jerusalem. Paper on silk backing, 327 × 21.5 cm.*

Figure 3: The Firman *attributed to Omar Ibn-al-Qattab, conqueror of Jerusalem in 638. Parchment, 65×* 43 cm.

The history of the Armenians in Jerusalem is, essentially, the story of the Armenian patriarchate in the Holy City, whose position of preeminence among the various sees of the Armenian church stemmed, primarily, from its unique association with the dominical sanctuaries. Indeed, the Armenian church has been and still is one of the three principal custodians of the Holy Places, the other two being the Greek Orthodox and Latin churches. Secondly, the patriarchate controlled a sizable number of privately owned monasteries in the Holy Land and in neighboring countries. And thirdly, it exercised administrative jurisdiction over several monastic and secular communities in Palestine, in the provinces of Beirut and Damascus, and in the bishoprics of Egypt and Cyprus.

1. *Early Christian Communities in Jerusalem*

In the earliest days of the Christian Church the sanctuaries in the Holy Places were used by all Christians. Along with other Christian groups, Armenians began to arrive in Jerusalem in substantial numbers as pilgrims and as residents after the proclamation of Christianity as the official religion of their country in the beginning of the fourth century. They at first shared the multiracial monastic facilities, but in due time, not unlike the others, they founded a number of private monasteries and churches throughout the Holy Land.

The wide breach occasioned by the Christological decisions of the Council of Chalcedon (451) did not seriously affect the religious harmony among the heterogeneous Christian communities in the Holy City; rather, for about a century after Chalcedon, all Christians remained under the spiritual authority of the patriarch of Jerusalem and, regardless of their ethnic origins, shared in common worship at the Holy Places. The schism came about after the persecutions of the monophysites, among them the Armenians, reached their climax during the reign of the staunch dyophysite Emperor Justinian I (527–565). Many monophysite clergy abandoned their monasteries at Jerusalem and sought refuge in other regions of the Holy Land and in neighboring countries. Those who remained established a distinct episcopal hierarchy independent of the Chalcedonian Greek patriarch. Henceforward, the see of Jerusalem was split into the Greek patriarchate exercising jurisdiction over the dyophysite Christians regardless of nationality or language, and the independent Armenian hierarchy having authority over the monophysite communities, that is, the Armenian, Jacobite Syrian, Coptic, and Abyssinian.

The actual extent of the Armenian religious establishments during the Byzantine period cannot be easily determined. A well-known document attributed to a seventh-century monk, Anastas *Vardapet*, contains a list of seventy monasteries and churches which the Armenians are said to have owned in that century in Jerusalem and its environs. The document asserts that an unspecified number of monasteries confiscated by the Greeks were eventually recovered by the Armenian princes after payment of a large sum of money to Emperor Justinian I. When subsequently the Byzantine authorities in Jerusalem warned the monophysites that unless they adhered to the Chalcedonian doctrine they would not be permitted to sojourn in the Holy City, some five hundred Armenian monastics were advised by Catholicos Yovhannes II (557–574) to abandon their monasteries rather than make doctrinal concessions to the Greeks. Although many of the monks are said to have left for Caesarea in Palestine and for Egypt, others remained in their institutions at Jerusalem, despite Byzantine coercions, until the Arab conquest in 638. The text also asserts that under Arab rule the Armenian monastic institutions gradually disintegrated and fell into ruins; some that had been left without administrators were occupied by the Greeks. This disintegration is ascribed to the failure of the catholicoses and princes to dispatch the revenues from the endowments in Armenia and to the heavy taxes imposed by the Arabs. The last section of the text, which appears to have been a much later addendum, asserts that there remained only fifteen monasteries in the hands of the Armenians. These were scattered on the Mount of Olives, in Bethlehem, on Mount Sinai, along the shores of the Sea of Galilee and Jordan River, on Mount Hermon, and on Mount Tabor. Even though the list is of doubtful authenticity, there is ample evidence that the Armenians did indeed have important religious institutions in the early Christian centuries.

The existence of these establishments at an early date is confirmed by the fact that in the mid-fifth century the Armenians had founded a scriptorium in Jerusalem, which also emerged as an important intellectual center where a significant number of religious, canonical, and patristic texts were

5

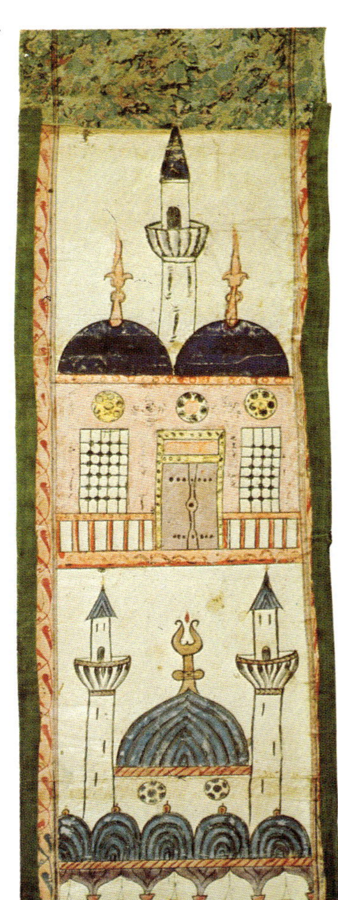

Figure 1: *"For the memorial and salvation of all the Armenians, whose names the Lord knows." An inscription in a mosaic in the apse of the sixth century funerary chapel in the Musrara Quarter of Jerusalem.*

1

rendered into Armenian. Evidence of a fully organized religious community there is also furnished by the extant Armenian Lectionary, a translation of the Greek liturgy as it was performed in the Holy City in the fifth century. More importantly, it is substantiated by the remains of mosaic pavements with Armenian inscriptions found in Jerusalem and on the Mount of Olives. Among these, the mosaics in the funerary chapel in the Musrara Quarter of Jerusalem are the most important *fig.1*. These artistic remains provide ample and most reliable evidence of the presence of Armenians in the Holy City and of the important religious institutions which they maintained there from the Byzantine period to the time of Arab rule *fig.2*.

With the Arab conquest in 638, the Armenian see of Jerusalem attained a stature which perhaps equaled the Greek patriarchate, whose associations with the Byzantine empire rendered it suspect in the eyes of the conquerors *fig.3*. Yet all Christian sects continued to enjoy the privilege of holding services in the dominical sanctuaries *fig.4*. In due time, the Greek coercions and the excessive taxes imposed by the Arab rulers resulted in the Armenians' loss of a substantial number of their private possessions.

2. Armenians in the Latin Kingdom of Jerusalem

The emergence of the Armenian kingdom in Cilicia (1080–1375), and its intimate associations with the Crusaders and the subsequently established Frankish principalities in the Levant and the Latin kingdom of Jerusalem (1099–1187), marked a significant turning point in the fortunes of the Armenians in historic Syria and in the Holy Land. To begin with, almost all the Latin queens and a substantial number of princesses were either Armenian or of Armenian blood. The kingdom had in its service an infantry corps of Armenians. In addition to a sizable number of ecclesiastics, there was a substantial secular community as well. These colonists had a number of private hostels and inns, and they also occupied several quarters in the city, one of which was known as "Ruga Armenorum" as late as the year 1222.

6

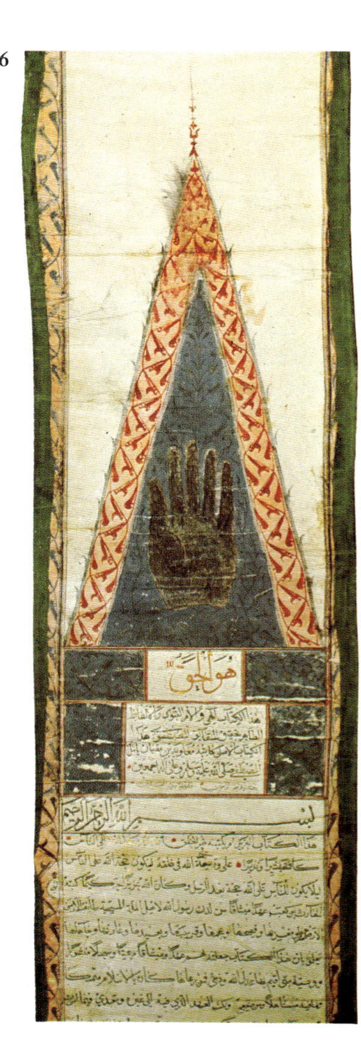

During the Latin rule, a number of Armenian princes and prelates from Cilicia visited Jerusalem; they left important memories of their munificence to the local community and also secured significant privileges for it from the Frankish authorities. Among these, Catholicos Grigor III Pahlavuni (1113–66) attended the Latin church council held at Antioch in 1141, and then accompanied the papal legate Albericus on a pilgrimage to Jerusalem, where he was given a place of honor at a second Latin council. Some twenty years later, King Thoros (1145–69) of Cilicia also visited the Holy City. In consequence of this close bond of friendship, the Armenians not only secured important privileges guaranteeing the continued prosperity of their institutions, but were also able to increase the number of their monasteries and hostels in the Holy City. The most enduring accomplishment of this period was the construction of the large Armenian cathedral of St. James consisting of a complex of sanctuaries which, besides the relics of the apostles James the Great and James the Younger, included the chapels containing the tombs of St. Makar and St. Minas.

Saladin's occupation of Jerusalem in 1187 marked another turning point in the fortunes of the three major custodians of the Holy Places. As an avowed enemy of the Latins and ever suspicious of the Greeks, Saladin found it expedient to endow the Armenians of the Holy Land with greater privileges *figs.5,6*. Indeed, the Armenian Patriarch Abraham (1180–91) and his leading clerical associates are said to have hastened to pledge their loyalty to the sultan and to pay the prescribed poll tax. Unlike other Christians, the Armenian population of the city, comprising some five hundred monks and one thousand families, were neither expelled nor taken as slaves by the lieutenants of the sultan. On the contrary, Saladin granted the Armenian patriarch a charter guaranteeing the community's security and freedom of worship throughout his entire domains, as well as the integrity of its possessions and prerogatives in the Holy Places *fig.7*. On the other hand, for a century or so, even after the fall of Jerusalem, Latin supremacy in the Holy Places was

Figure 4: *The* Firman *attributed to Caliph Ali (656–661). Parchment, 825 x 32.8 cm.*

Figures 5, 6, 7: *The* Firman *of Saladin, conqueror of Jerusalem from the Latins, 1187–88. Parchment on silk backing, 529 x 29 cm.*

7

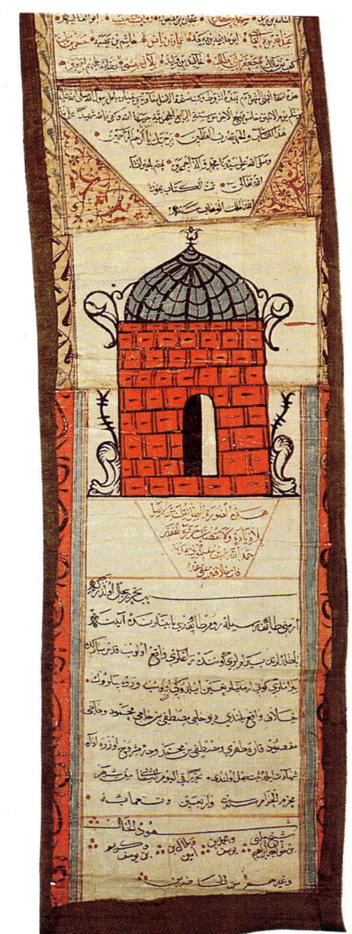

4

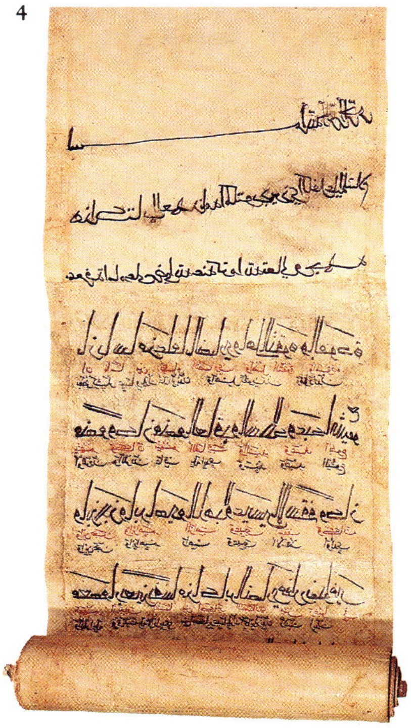

maintained. The ever deepening estrangement between Rome and the church of Byzantium, and particularly the sacking and plunder of Constantinople by Crusaders in 1204, accentuated the rivalry between the two parties in Jerusalem and, with the fall of Acre in 1291, undisputed Latin supremacy came to an end.

During the early period of Mameluke rule, the Armenians continued to enjoy relatively greater freedom in the exercise of their religious rites. The special privileges granted to them enabled not only the preservation but also the extension of their sanctuaries, monasteries, and other properties, after due payment of regular taxes and bribes. These were made possible through the generous contributions of Armenian pilgrims, who came to the Holy Land in ever increasing numbers, and through the munificence of the Armenian kings and royalty of Cilicia *fig.8*. In time, however, the increasing Mameluke intolerance toward the Christians in general and the tax collectors' constant harassment of the ecclesiastical institutions were responsible for the reduction of the Armenian populations into small enclaves in Greater Syria and in Palestine *fig.9*. This state of affairs continued until the Ottoman conquest of historic Syria in the beginning of the sixteenth century.

3. Armenians under Ottoman rule

The subsequent history of the Holy Places in Jerusalem and its environs has been a long story of bitter animosities and contentions among rival Christian churches, as well as the cause of much international conflict. As one of the principal custodians of the dominical sites, the Armenian church was frequently involved in these developments. The strongest and almost continuous challenge to the Armenians and their holdings in the Holy Land came from the Greek community, despite the fact that the charters issued in March 1517 to the Armenian and Greek patriarchates by the Ottoman conqueror of Jerusalem, Sultan Selim I, did no more than sanction the status quo.

On the basis of ancient edicts, among which special mention is made of those granted by the Caliph Omar and Saladin, the charter issued by Selim guaranteed the integrity of the Armenians' age-old possessions within and without the Holy City, as well as those of their dependent communities. The edict also prohibited members of the imperial family, government officials, and other Christian communities from disturbing the ecclesiastical rites of the Armenians and their dependents or molesting their monasteries, sanctuaries, and other possessions. The charter makes special mention of certain presumably major, institutions and sanctuaries owned exclusively by the Armenians, such as the monasteries of St. James *fig.10*, the Holy Archangels and the Holy Saviour, a church at Nablus, and unspecified monasteries, hostels, dwellings, cemeteries, orchards, and olive groves in and near Bethlehem. Among the principal shrines, the Holy Sepulcher, the church of St. Mary at Gethsemane, and the Grotto of the Nativity at Bethlehem are all considered Armenian possessions. Since the charter granted to the Greeks also mentions the same major shrines as Greek possessions, it must be assumed that the privileges to these sanctuaries were actually shared by the two communities. The charter which Selim I granted at the same time to the Greek patriarch secured the integrity of the Greek monasteries, churches, and other properties within and without the Holy City. These two edicts constituted the juridical bases of the two communities' status and holdings in the Holy Land; hence, time and again they figured prominently in the intercommunity controversies which followed the Ottoman conquest.

4. The Rival Custodians of the Holy Land

During the four centuries of Ottoman rule the paramountcy in the Holy Places alternated, although generally the Greek Orthodox secured the balance of power in their favor. Moreover, since the Latins were subjects of powers with whom the Ottoman empire was constantly engaged in war, the sultan's Greek and Armenian subjects in particular were treated with favor at the expense of the "Franks." During these centuries the possession of the Holy Places almost always remained in the forefront of international politics. The European Latin powers, especially France, supported Latin interests; the Orthodox cause was championed by the Ecumenical Patriarch and the Greek magnates of Constantinople and, beginning in 1774, by Russia. The Armenians, deprived of such political protection, had to rely on their own resources, particularly their patriarchate and influential secular magnates in the Ottoman capital.

Figure 11: *The scepter of King Hethum I of Cilicia (1215–1270). Amber and gold. Top part.*

Figure 12: *The scepter of King Hethum I of Cilicia. Amber and gold. Lower part.*

Figure 18: *Silver gilt chalice, given to the Cathedral of St. James in memory of Nazar, son of* Mahdesi *Arak'el and his wife Sarah, in 1733. Treasury of St. James.*

11

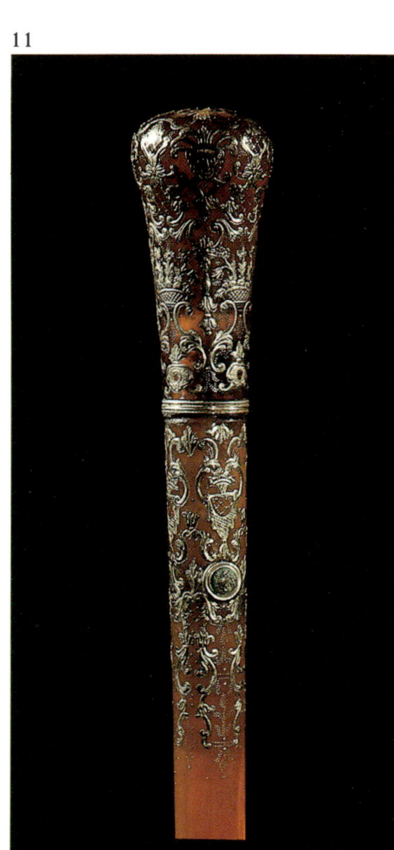

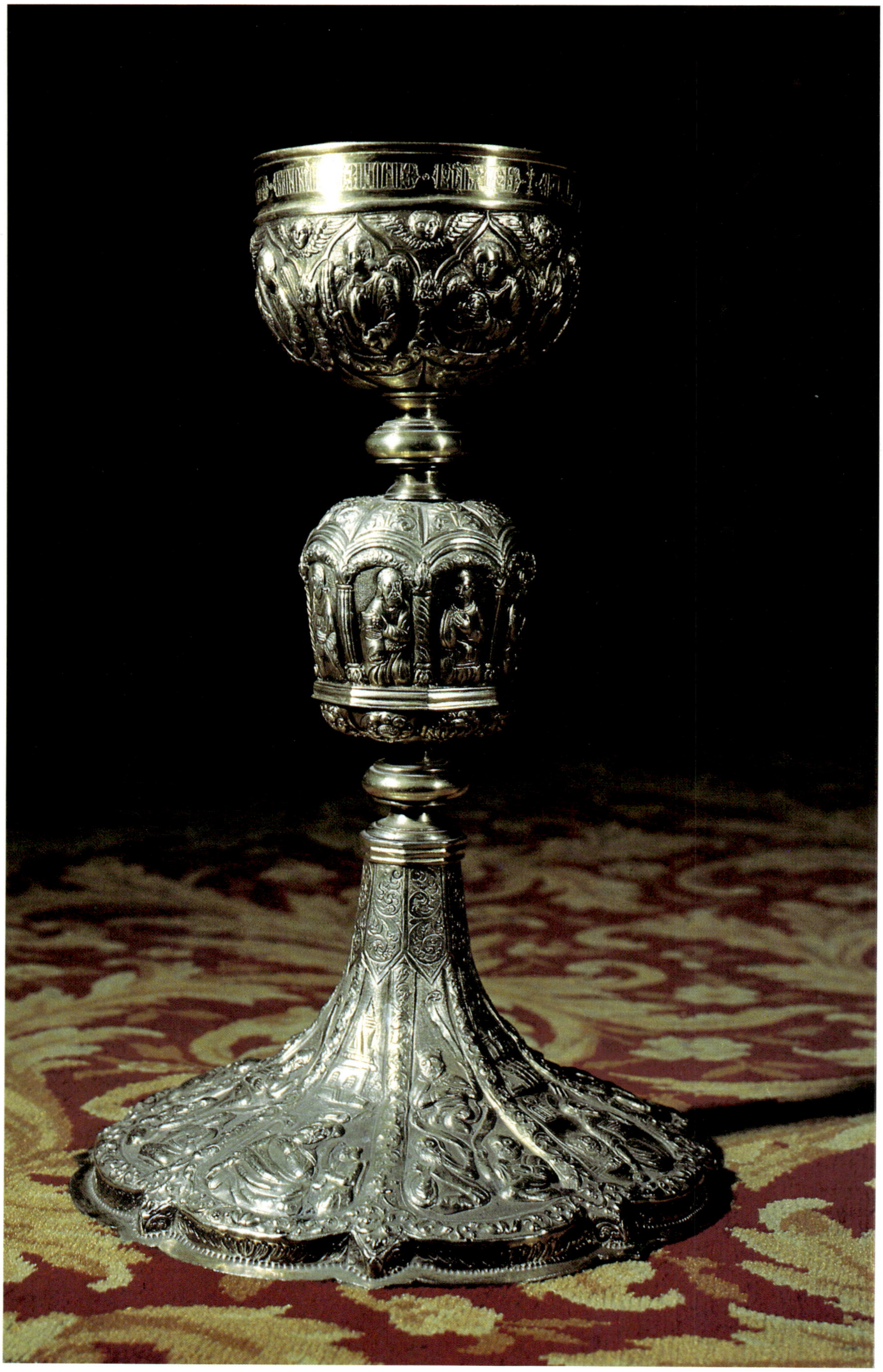

12

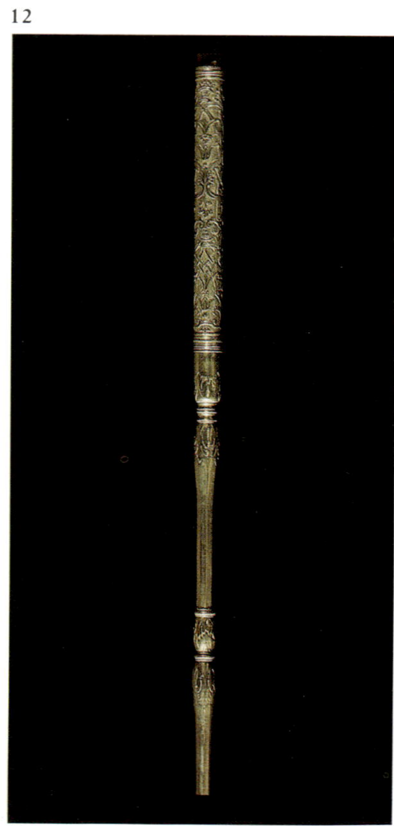

18

Figure 8: A khatchk'ar *of 1362 in the Church of the Archangels in a niche near the old font. Memorial stone cross of an Armenian pilgrim.*

Figure 9: *A fountain of 1900 at the entrance to the Armenian Compound. Behind, an Arabic inscription of 1437 by the Mameluke Sultan A-Zaher Abu Sayad Chakmak, abolishing all taxes imposed by his predecessors on the Armenians.*

8

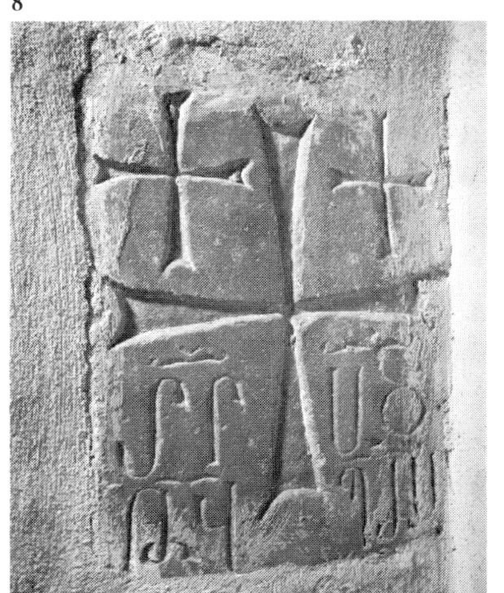

9

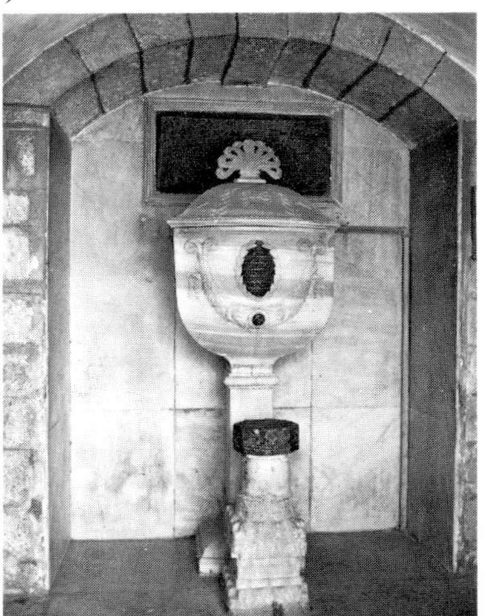

10

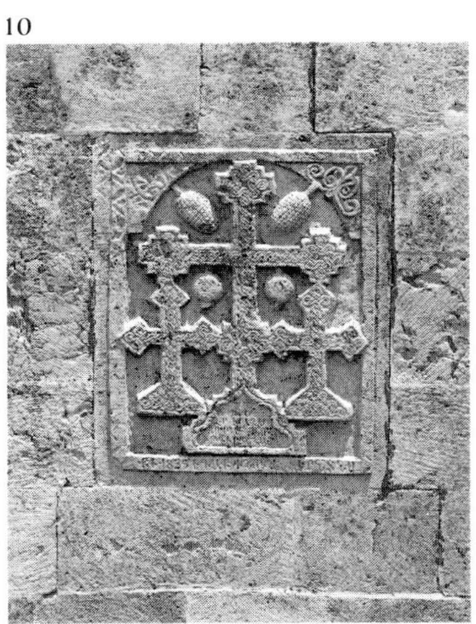

Figure 10: A khatchk'ar *(stone cross) of the eleventh century, set into the outer wall of St. James Cathedral in the nineteenth century.*

The rivalry and interminable struggles among the three major custodians of the Holy Places for aggrandizement at the expense of each other continued unabated under Ottoman rule until the 1850's.

With the revival in 1847 of the Latin patriarchate of Jerusalem which had been dormant since the fall of the Latin kingdom, there was an intensification of Roman Catholic attempts to control the commonly held dominical sanctuaries, particularly at the expense of the Greek Orthodox, with the aid of the Catholic powers The conflict that ensued was sparked by the Greeks' removal of a silver aureole affixed by the Latins to the altar of the Grotto of the Nativity, and the grave crises led to the Crimean War. Ironically, the Treaty of Paris of 1856 left the position of the contesting communities in the Holy Places as it had been before the conflict.

The status quo in the Holy Places, as enunciated in the 1850's and as reconfirmed time and again in subsequent years, was the sum of a historical evolution whose beginnings are traceable to the early centuries of Christianity, and as a result it established a most complicated network of rights and privileges. Even though controversies among the three major custodians of the Holy Places continued during the remaining period of Ottoman rule, no appreciable change in their holdings and privileges has occurred since the 1850's.

In 1929 L.G.A. Cust, then district officer of Jerusalem, catalogued the possessions and privileges of the Christian churches, including the Armenian, in a document known as "The Status Quo in the Holy Places," which was designed to serve as a guide for British mandate authorities concerned with the adjudication of disputes among the contending communities. This document still governs the relations of the principal custodians.

As head of the monastic congregation of St. James and as chief custodian, the primary function of the Armenian patriarch of Jerusalem was to safeguard not only the private institutions of his relatively small community but also its age-old privileges in the commonly held sanctuaries. In this most difficult task the patriarch relied upon the moral and material support of the local monastics and secular community, the other hierarchical sees of the Armenian church, pilgrims, and the Armenian people as a whole.

Tracing its origins to the traditional associations with the two apostles, SS. James, whose relics it has jealously guarded, the Armenian patriarchate occupies a truly prominent position in the Holy City. The extensive holdings in the dominical sanctuaries, which the Armenian church shares with the Greek and Latin rites, are impressive testimony to the Armenian role in the long and turbulent history of Jerusalem.

5. *The See of the Armenian Patriarchate of Jerusalem*

Throughout its long history, the patriarchate of Jerusalem also exercised administrative jurisdiction over the scattered Armenian ecclesiastical and secular communities in the rest of the Holy Land, in the Levantine coastal region, as well as in a number of towns in the Syrian hinterland. Armenian settlements in some of these localities can be traced back to the first century B.C. when Tigranes the Great (95–55 B.C.) carved out a short-lived Armenian empire. The Armenian colonies that existed under Byzantine and Arab rule were substantially augmented with the establishment of the Armenian kingdom in Cilicia, with the entrenchment of the Crusaders in the Levant, and with the founding of the Latin kingdom of Jerusalem. However, whereas under the Latins the Armenians were found almost everywhere from the Taurus Mountains to Egypt, under the Mamelukes and Ottomans they were represented by small enclaves in Cilicia, the Amanus, Jabal Musa, Jabal Aqra, the valley of the Orontes, Antioch and its environs, Aleppo, Damascus, Mount Lebanon, and in the Palestinian towns of Jerusalem, Bethlehem, Jaffa, Ramle, Gaza, and so forth.

Three factors were responsible for the extension of the patriarchate's administrative jurisdiction over these communities: the management of the local ecclesiastical institutions; the spiritual needs of the local secular communities; and, more importantly, the practical necessity of providing facilities and accommodations for the Armenian pilgrims who arrived annually in the Holy Land at Eastertime by land or by sea.

From time immemorial there had been in Bethlehem an Armenian community – ecclesiastic and secular – to oversee the Armenian interests in the Church of the Nativity. A carved wooden door

Figure 13: *Patriarchs Gregory Paronter (1613–1645) and Gregory the Chainbearer (1715–1749), who forged important links between Jerusalem and the Patriarchate in Constantinople. Mid-eighteenth century painting on paneling in St. James Cathedral, north wall.*

Figure 14: *A sun print of Patriarch Esayi III (1865–1885), one of the most active Patriarchs of Jerusalem, and himself a photographer, 1860.*

Figure 16: *The Holy Sepulcher from the south. A sun print taken by the Patriarch Esayi in 1861, while still a priest, and signed by him.*

Figure 17: *Priests, monks, and pilgrims at the entrance to St. James Cathedral in Jerusalem, 1860. A sun print by Patriarch Esayi.*

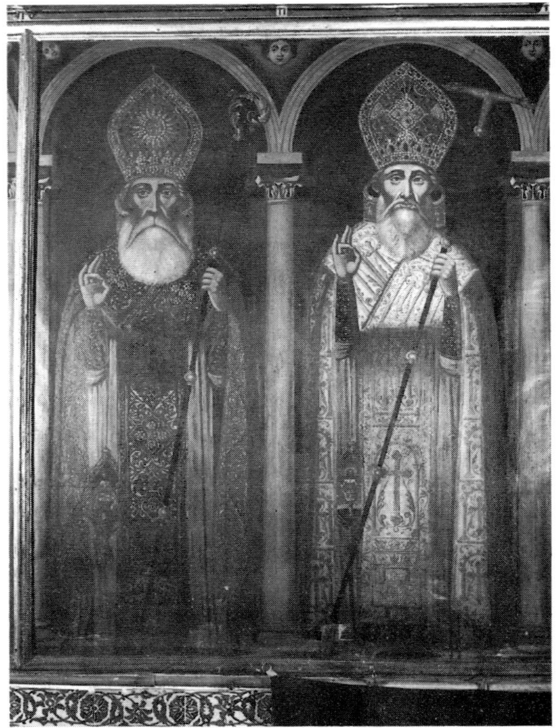

13

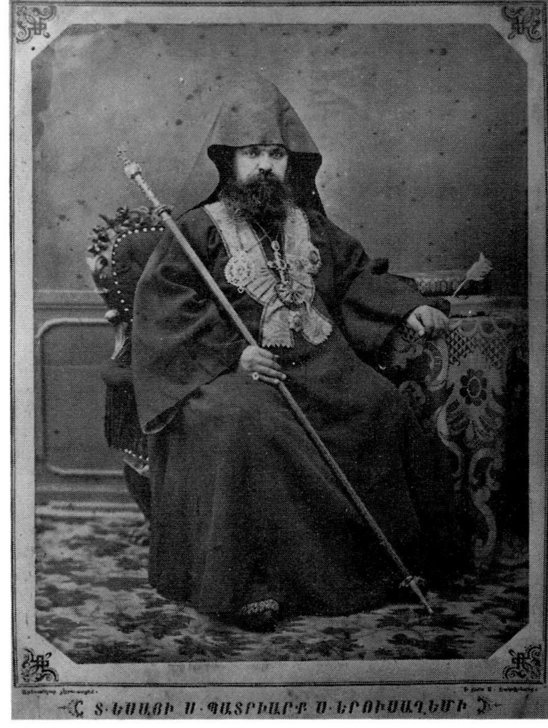

14

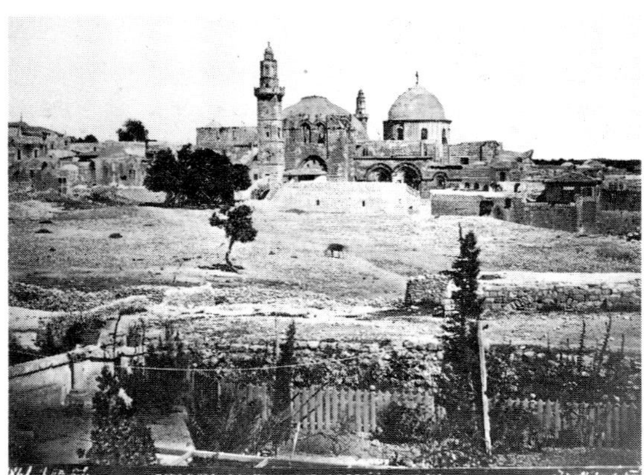

16

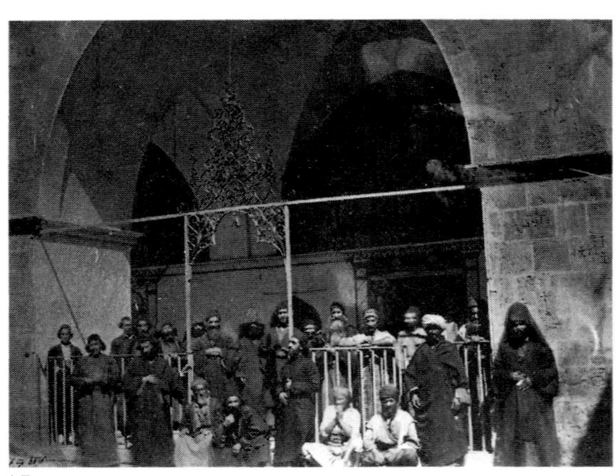

17

found in the church, executed in 1227 during the reign of King Hethum I (1226–70) of Cilicia and bearing inscriptions in Arabic and Armenian, attests to the important privileges which it enjoyed in this hallowed sanctuary. Whether or not the old and large Armenian monastery – which housed the monks and accommodated pilgrims – immediately adjacent to the basilica dates back to this period is uncertain *figs. 11, 12.*

Jaffa, the principal port of entry for pilgrims arriving by ship, had an Armenian monastery and a hospice. It is claimed that the monastery of St. Nicholas – which stood very close to the house of Simon the Tanner, where the Apostle Peter had his vision – existed as early as the time of the Arab conquest in the first half of the seventh century. The principal task of this institution was to lodge and care for the needs of the pilgrims en route to and from the Holy City. Equally ancient was the Armenian monastery at the town of Ramle, near Jaffa, which had always been an important pilgrim way station. Patriarch Eghiazar (1666–81) built the monastery's church of St. George; acquired dwellings and plots of land adjacent to it; and constructed additional facilities for pilgrims. At Gaza, too, there was the Armenian monastery and church of the Holy Archangels, as well as a hospice which accommodated pilgrims from Egypt. It is generally believed that these institutions were founded during the Latin kingdom of Jerusalem.

There were also ancient Armenian settlements and institutions in the Levantine coastal towns of Latakia, Beirut, Tyre, Sidon and Acre, all of which were important pilgrim stations. The hospice at Latakia was built in 1755, and the monastery's church in 1776. The importance of the colonies at Tyre and Sidon is attested by the fact that the Latin princes of these towns were married to Armenian princesses from Cilicia. Acre also had an Armenian population which in the middle of the twelfth century had its own hostel; and as late as 1248 Acre had an Armenian prince. To meet the spiritual needs of the community at Beirut and to provide facilities for pilgrims traveling via this port, a monastery with a small chapel was founded there in 1851.

By the mid-seventh century there was an Armenian cultural center at Damascus where monks engaged in intellectual pursuits. An ecclesiastical institution for the local community, with facilities for pilgrims, existed there before the Arab conquest. During the Ottoman period, the nucleus of the community was the monastery of St. Sargis built in the sixteenth century; it was restored in 1617 and a hospice was also constructed later to accommodate pilgrims. Although Aleppo was under the

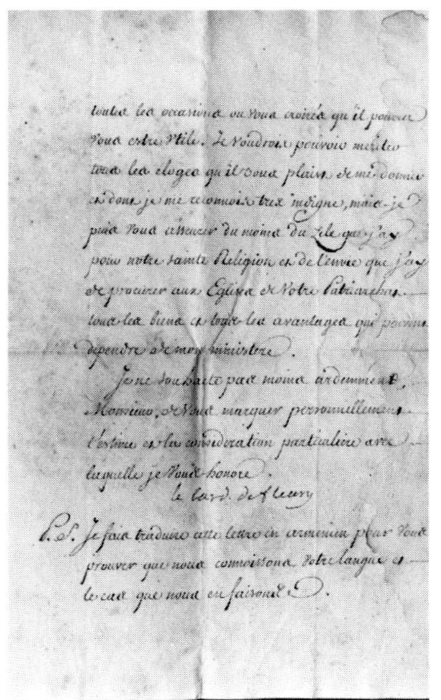

toutes les occasions ou vous croirés qu'il pourra
vous estre utile. Je voudrois pouvoir meriter
tous les eloges qu'il vous plaist de me donner
et dont je me reconnois tres indigne, mais je
puis vous asseurer du moins du zele que j'ay
pour notre sainte Religion et de l'envie que j'ay
de procurer aux Eglises de Votre Patriarchat
tous les biens et tous les avantages qui pourront
dependre de mon ministere.

Je ne souhaitte pas moins ardemment,
Monsieur, de vous marquer personnellement
l'estime et la consideration particuliere avec
laquelle je vous honore.

le Card. de Fleury

P.S. Je fais traduire cette lettre en armenien pour vous
prouver que nous connoissons votre langue et
le cas que nous en faisons.

15

Figure 15: *A hand-written letter to Patriarch Gregory the Chainbearer from Cardinal de Fleury, prime minister of Louis XV, dated from Versailles, 31 August, 1739.*

jurisdiction of the see of Cilicia, the patriarchate of Jerusalem had assumed responsibility for the accommodation of pilgrims by the fourteenth century; the hospice for pilgrims was built in 1624.

The Armenian community of Cyprus, whose origins can be traced back to the Byzantine period, was comprised of two bishoprics during the Armenian kingdom of Cilicia. Until 1775 the communities of Cyprus were under the jurisdiction of the Cilician see; from 1775 until World War I, the Jerusalem see appointed the Cypriot bishopric's prelates, and when the Cilician catholicosate was reconstituted in Syria and Lebanon in the early 1920's the bishopric came under the authority of the latter see. On the other hand, the bishopric of Egypt was administered by the Jerusalem see from 1311 until 1839, when by Ottoman imperial decree it was constituted as an independent bishopric within the see of Constantinople.

In each of the communities mentioned above, clerical representatives appointed by the patriarchate of Jerusalem attended to the spiritual needs and administrative affairs of the local communicants. They also administered the monastic and other ecclesiastical institutions, the parochial schools, as well as the hostels and revenue-yielding properties. These representatives also supervised the accommodations and attended to all the needs of the pilgrims en route to and from the Holy City. In compensation the pilgrims paid a prescribed fee, which generally was earmarked for the maintenance of the local monastic institutions.

The above-described administrative jurisdiction of the patriarchate of Jerusalem persisted until World War I. In 1929 the patriarchate voluntarily conceded its authority over the communities of Damascus, Latakia, and Beirut and placed its ecclesiastical holdings – the monasteries, churches, and schools – in those areas at the disposal of the catholicosate of Cilicia, which had been reconstituted in the French mandated territories of Syria and Lebanon, with the catholicosal seat at Antilias, near Beirut. In consequence the jurisdiction of the Jerusalem see has since been confined to the communities of the Holy Land, as well as to the community of Amman in Jordan.

6. *Relations of the Jerusalem Patriarchate and other Armenian Sees*

From the time of its inception in the sixth century, the patriarchate of Jerusalem has been an integral part of the hierarchical structure of the Armenian church, under the general authority of the "Supreme Patriarch and Catholicos of All Armenians" wherever his seat happened to be. When the political and religious authorities in the Armenian kingdom of Cilicia sought to compel the see of Jerusalem – which had always remained a bastion of Armenian orthodoxy – to adopt the pro-Latin decisions of the synod of 1307, the incumbent Patriarch Sargis and the Jerusalem clergy categorically refused to conform. With a view to enhancing his position Sargis even journeyed to Egypt in 1311 and secured an edict from Sultan Nasr Muhammad which recognized him as independent patriarch of the Armenians within the domains of the Mameluke sultanate. Nevertheless, the patriarchate remained within the framework of the pontificate at Sis until 1441, that is, so long as the latter represented the supreme authority of the Armenian church.

The history of the patriarchate in terms of its relations with the other hierarchical sees entered a new phase in consequence of the transfer of the supreme pontificate to its original site at Etchmiadzin in 1441, the revival of the hierarchy at Sis in 1446 as a regional catholicosate, and the establishment by the Ottoman Sultan Mehmet II of the Armenian patriarchate of Constantinople in 1461.

Under the Ottomans the individual religious communities, namely, the Greek Orthodox, Jews, and Armenians, were constituted into distinct entities known as *millets*, each of which was allowed to retain its own laws concerning matters of civil status and to enforce them under the general jurisdiction of a *millet bashi* (community head). Moreover, under this system, the Christians of the Ottoman empire were divided into two broad groups based on a profession of faith. Accordingly, all the Orthodox dyophysites of the empire were placed under the general authority of the Greek patriarch, though each still retained its religious head. The monophysites, on the other hand, comprising the Armenian, Jacobite Syrian, Coptic, and Abyssinian communities, while retaining their own autocephalic hierarchies, were made subject to the jurisdiction of the Armenian patriarchate at Constantinople.

The Armenian patriarch in the Ottoman capital enjoyed jurisdiction over his community's spiritual administration and officials, public instruction, and charitable and religious institutions, and the civil status of his coreligionists throughout the empire. This included the bishoprics dependent upon the regional catholicosates of Sis and Aghtamar and the patriarchate of Jerusalem *fig.13*. The patriarch of Constantinople also functioned as the deputy of the pontifical see of Etchmiadzin in its relations with the communicants of the Armenian church in the Ottoman empire.

Within this structure, however, the patriarchate of Jerusalem, because of its custodianship of the Holy Places, continued to enjoy a uniquely prominent position – second in importance, from the spiritual standpoint, only to the apostolic see of Etchmiadzin. Even after the adoption of the Armenian National Constitution of 1863, which established the machinery for a very elaborate democratic system of organization and administration of the Ottoman-Armenian *millet*'s ecclesiastical and civil affairs on the central, provincial, and local levels, the Jerusalem see still enjoyed a special relationship vis-à-vis the central authorities *fig.14*.

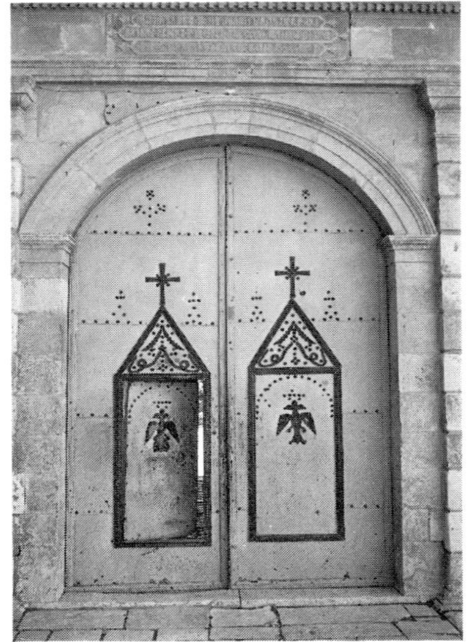

19

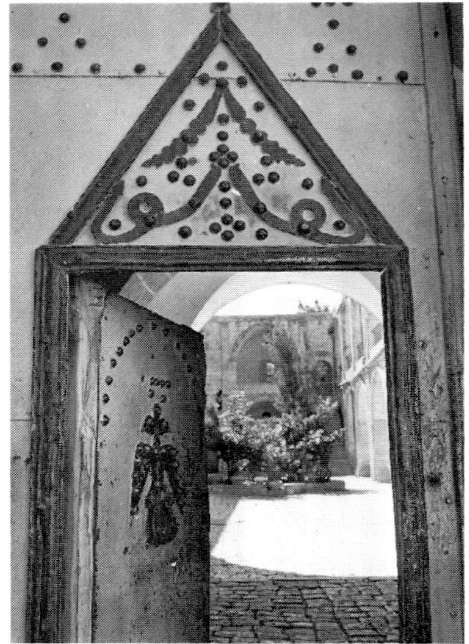

20

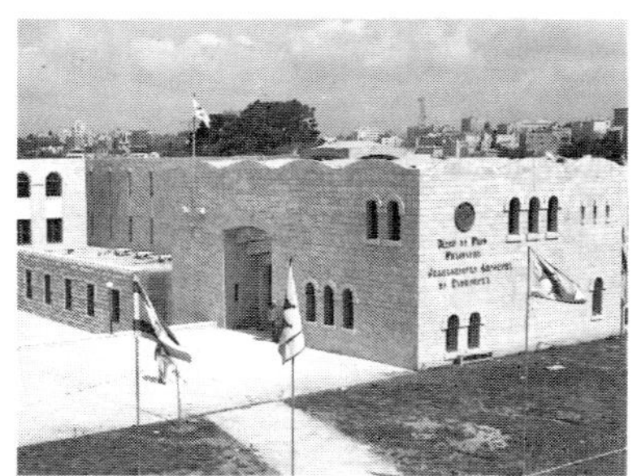

21

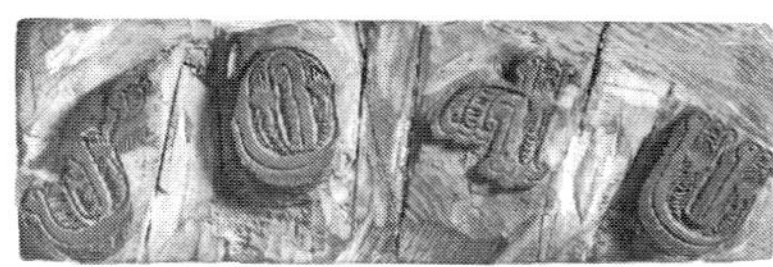

23

Figure 19: *Decorated gates of the old Theological Seminary in 1857.*

Figure 20: *Courtyard of the old Theological Seminary of 1857, seen through its wicket gate.*

Figure 21: *The new Theological Seminary. Benefaction of Marie and Alex Manoogian, Detroit.*

Figure 23: Sion, *journal of the Armenian Patriarchate. Woodblock of the first edition, 1866.*

For many centuries, the patriarchate of Jerusalem had maintained direct contacts with the local authorities and with the officials in the regions where the Armenian communities were under its jurisdiction. It had also had direct dealings with the imperial palace and the ministries at Constantinople, as well as with the pontifical see of Etchmiadzin and with foreign authorities *fig. 15*.

The Jerusalem see always maintained a special representative at Constantinople who served in a dual capacity: as liaison between the two Patriarchates, protecting the interests of his see; and as a representative of Jerusalem to the Sublime Porte, submitting various petitions of his see either independently or more often in consultation and cooperation with the Armenian leaders in the capital. The Jerusalem representative also had clerical and lay assistants: the *braviraks*, the title given to those clergy who were dispatched to the capital every year after Easter to make the necessary arrangements for and to accompany the pilgrims in the following year; and the nuncios who were sent on periodic fund-raising missions.

7. *The financial responsibilities of the Jerusalem Patriarchate*

The unique responsibilities of the patriarchate of Jerusalem placed very high demands upon its financial and material resources. Preservation of the patriarchal see and its monastic institutions in the Holy Land, and the protection of the Armenian interests in the Holy Places *fig. 16*, were very costly. Hence the see had to rely constantly upon the munificence of the Armenian people as a whole, who never failed to give ample evidence of their genuine concern for the historic institution by their generous support.

It had become an article of faith that every Armenian believer should, at least once in his lifetime, attempt to perform the sacred duty of visiting the dominical sanctuaries *fig. 17*. Concomitant with this was the tradition that each pilgrim should, as a sacred obligation, make a contribution to the see in accordance with his means. In addition to money many arrived in the Holy City with precious ecclesiastical vessels, ornaments, and vestments which they donated to the patriarchate as memorials *fig. 18*.

The second major source of revenue was the institutionalized system of the nunciatures, that is, the periodic visitation to the various communities of the Armenian Diaspora by duly authorized monastics of the see of Jerusalem to solicit contributions. As a direct result of these missions the patriarchate became the beneficiary of a substantial number of large bequests. When special circumstances prevented assistance from overseas and when the flow of pilgrims had stopped, the institution had no other recourse than to negotiate loans by mortgaging its properties or other assets to obtain needed cash. And frequently it was compelled to sell valuable gold and silver sacred objects in order to pay off the creditors.

The periodic economic insolvency of the patriarchate stemmed largely from the financial policy of the Ottoman state. At the root of this policy was the system of tax farming, which by its very nature encouraged corruption. Officials, whether on the central, provincial, or local level, aimed principally at deriving the maximum amount of revenues from the institutions and inhabitants under their jurisdiction. Insofar as the Holy Land was concerned, the Christian religious institutions were exploited not only by encouraging their intercommunity rivalries but quite frequently by precipitating crises with a view to securing bribes and gifts. Indeed, these Christian institutions expended enormous sums of money merely to guarantee their privileges and possessions, which they virtually purchased time and again from avaricious officials. It is remarkable that in spite of the prevailing political maladministration and widespread corruption the Armenian institutions were ever able to survive.

8. *Jerusalem as an Armenian Cultural Center*

The Christianization of Armenia and the adoption of a national alphabet, in the fourth and fifth centuries respectively, were the two most important historical factors which determined the essentially religious and national characteristics of Armenian intellectual, literary, and artistic history. Until the nineteenth century, this ethnic culture was developed almost exclusively by the clergy in the numerous monastic institutions in historic Armenia, Asia Minor, Cilicia, and elsewhere, and drew its inspiration from both the East and the West. In its long span of development, Armenian culture experienced several periods of revival and decline, culminating in the Armenian renaissance in the nineteenth century which ushered in the growth of secularism along European lines.

We have already seen that the Armenians had founded a scriptorium at Jerusalem in the mid-fifth century, which attests to the creation there of an important cultural center. Extant manuscripts confirm that this tradition persisted throughout the Middle Ages and in later times. Although the patriarchate of Jerusalem never distinguished itself as a major center of Armenian learning and scholarship, the institution nevertheless always sought to provide facilities for the educational and intellectual advancement of its young monastics at least sufficiently to enable them to perform adequately their ecclesiastical functions.

Until about the mid-nineteenth century the clerical candidates were customarily trained "at the feet" of some learned *vardapet* (doctor of theology). This pedagogue was often a resident monk;

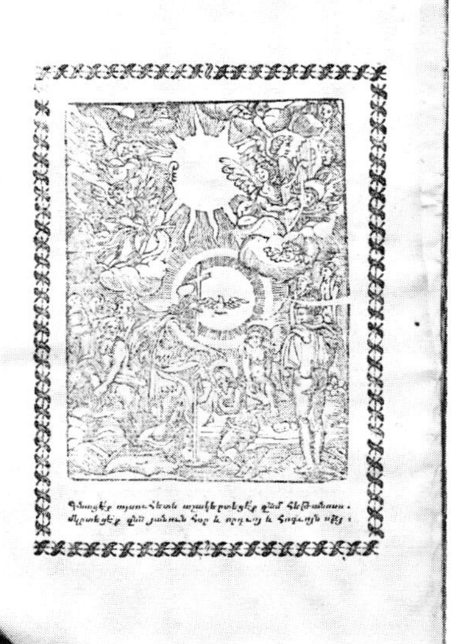

22

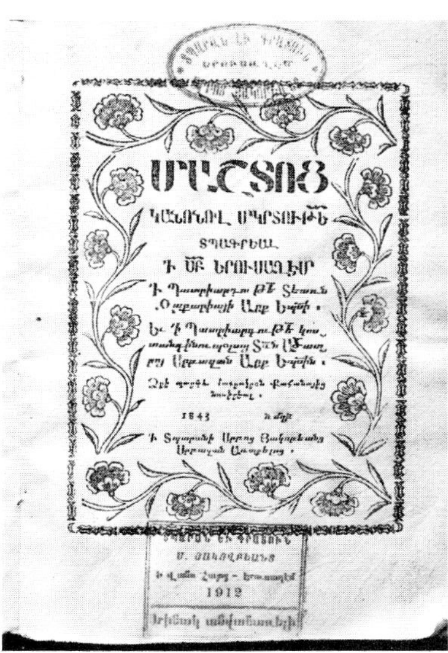

24

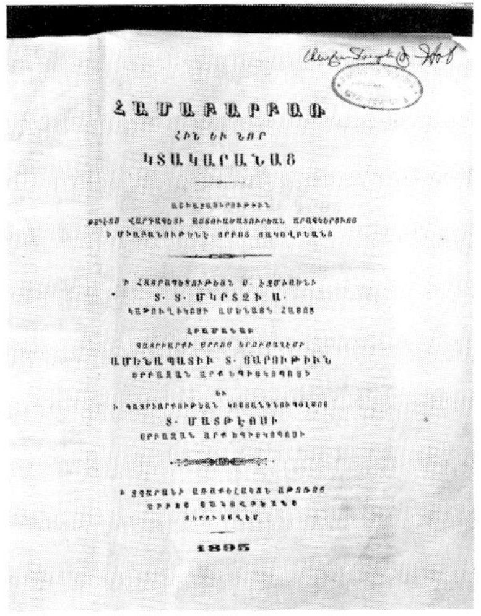

25

Figure 22: *Baptism of Christ. Frontispiece to a Prayer Book, the first book printed in Jerusalem, 1833. The wood block used to print the Baptism is modeled on the Oskan Bible (the first printed Armenian Bible, printed in Amsterdam in 1666) vol. II, p. 472, frontispiece to St. Mark.*

Figure 24: Mashtotz, *ritual book, title page. Printed in Jerusalem in 1843.*

Figure 25: *Th. Astuadzaturian's Concordance of the Armenian Bible, Jerusalem 1895.*

frequently, however, the patriarchate took advantage of some scholar's pilgrimage to Jerusalem and prevailed upon him to remain there for a number of years to instruct the novices in traditional religious subjects. It was not uncommon for ecclesiastics trained elsewhere in the Armenian Diaspora to join the monastic order of St. James. Conversely, young monks from the Holy City often journeyed abroad to study under some renowned scholar in another Armenian monastic institution.

The second half of the nineteenth century witnessed the phenomenal growth in the Armenian Diaspora of the printing industry, journalism, the national school system, the arts, and various genres of Armenian literature developed in the spoken vernacular. Albeit on a more modest scale, the Armenian patriarchate of Jerusalem also participated in this cultural revival.

The patriarchate's first regular seminary was founded in the monastery of St. George at Ramle in 1843. Some eighteen months later it was transferred to a building outside the monastic compound at Jerusalem. The move coincided with the pilgrimage of Murat Boyajian, a highly renowned pedagogue in the theological seminary of Armash, who was persuaded to assume the offices of dean and principal instructor. The task of constructing an adequate seminary building within the monastery of St. James was completed in 1857 *fig.19*. The seminary's course offerings were considerably extended in the 1860's with the appointment of Garegin Muratian, a Russian-born scholar and pedagogue, as dean *fig.20*. The institution's further progress was arrested due to lack of funds and difficulties stemming from the exacerbation of Turco-Armenian relations, which culminated in the Turkish genocide of the Armenians throughout the Ottoman empire during World War I. Indeed, the seminary was shut down in the summer of 1917, bringing to an end the first phase of its development. Since its reopening in 1920, the Jerusalem seminary has emerged, under the guidance of a number of outstanding clerical and lay pedagogues, as the leading institution dedicated to the training of clergy for the Armenian communities throughout the world. Thanks to the benefaction of Alex and Marie Manoogian of Detroit, Michigan, the seminary has recently been endowed with a magnificent new building with the most modern conveniences, *fig.21* and plans have already been drawn up to further expand the institution's instructional program.

The patriarchate also assumed the responsibility of establishing and maintaining parochial schools for the Armenian secular communities in Palestine, as well as in Syria and Lebanon. Before World War I, the parochial school system at Jerusalem consisted of three institutions, a coeducational kindergarten and two elementary schools. The Mesrobian boys' school was founded in the 1840's, and the Gayanian school for girls was established in 1862. Similarly, the patriarchate maintained elementary schools at Bethlehem and Jaffa, as well as at Damascus, Beirut, and Latakia. In the 1930's the schools at Jerusalem were combined into one institution, under the name of Holy Translators which has since been elevated to the status of a high school. In addition, the patriarchate currently maintains elementary schools for the communities in Jaffa, Haifa, and Amman.

9. The St. James Printing Press

The printing press established by the patriarchate at Jerusalem in 1833 was the first such Armenian establishment in Greater Syria prior to World War I *fig.22*. This press achieved its most noteworthy progress under Patriarch Esayi (1865–85). The equipment was modernized; the plant was reorganized, with separate departments for cutting type faces *fig.23*, for typesetting, and for printing; the bindery was improved; and the book-selling facilities were substantially augmented. It also has the distinction of being the first Armenian press to endow its plant with galvanoplastic and color-printing facilities.

Despite the Ottoman government's progressively more stringent censorship laws, as late as 1915 the Jerusalem printing press occupied an important position among Armenian ecclesiastical institutions possessing publishing establishments, not only because of the quality of its printing but especially as the publisher of unique works. During its first phase of operation (1833–1915) this press published some four hundred Armenian titles. Its most important contribution lay in multiple editions of practically the entire corpus of ritualistic, liturgical, and ecclesiastical books of the Armenian church *fig.24*. These included a number which appeared in print for the first time, and many bore the stamp of greater authenticity because they were based upon more ancient texts available in the rich manuscript collection of the patriarchate. The press' second contribution was its publication, in some cases for the first time, of a number of ancient and medieval classical Armenian texts, as well as Armenian translations of certain Greek works, from the patriarchate's manuscript holdings. The press also published some one hundred and fifty original scholarly studies *fig.25*, historical and religious books *fig.26*, creative literary works, travel books *fig.27*, guidebooks on the Holy Places and prayerbooks for pilgrims, and various textbooks. Beginning in 1867 it has also published an annual religious calendar, which supplies pertinent canonical information. After a hiatus of ten years, the printing press resumed its operations in 1925. With periodic modernization of its plant, as well as the continued publication of religious and other diverse works, it has since emerged as one of the foremost printing establishments in the Armenian dispersion.

The see of Jerusalem also published an official organ, the monthly *Sion fig.28*, from 1866 to 1877, which again had the distinction of being the only Armenian periodical published in Greater Syria before World War I. After a lapse of sixty years, its publication was resumed in 1927. While Tigran Savalaniants, the first editor of the earlier series, sought to transform the publication into a learned, scholarly journal of Armenian studies *fig.29* and, indeed, published a number of hitherto unknown textual materials, under his successors heavy emphasis was laid upon religious, ethical, and chronographic subjects. The current series has distinguished itself as one of the more important journals of Armenological studies in the Armenian Diaspora.

* * *

This brief survey has underscored the centuries-old unique role which the patriarchate of Jerusalem has played within the hierarchical structure of the Armenian church through its functions as one of the principal custodians of the Holy Places, its administration of a network of ecclesiastical institutions and secular communities throughout the Holy Land and in neighboring countries, and its creation and maintenance of a vital cultural center in the Holy City. In addition to the significant holdings and privileges in the dominical sites in Jerusalem and Bethlehem, the Armenian Quarter today occupies almost one-sixth of the entire area of the Old City of Jerusalem, in the southwestern elevation of Mount Zion, representing a vast complex of historic sites dominated by the cathedral of St. James, the elegant patriarchal residence, and the newly-constructed Manoogian Seminary building. The complex also includes the monastery of the Holy Archangels, the chapel of St. Theodorus, the Gulbenkian Library, the Holy Translators School, the printing press, and residential quarter for the members of the Order of St James and for the Armenian civilian population; outside the city walls, also on Mount Zion, are the monastery of the Holy Saviour (the House of Caiaphas), and the Armenian national cemetery.

The monastery of St. James is a veritable repository of Armenian cultural and artistic treasures, including: the collection of some 4,000 ancient and medieval manuscripts, with examples of outstanding miniature paintings and exquisite gold, silver and enameled covers, representing the second largest collection of Armenian manuscripts in the world *fig.30*, the Calouste Gulbenkian Library with over 50,000 books and one of the finest collections of Armenian periodical literature; the Kütahya ceramic tiles covering the walls of the St. James cathedral; and outstanding samples of gold and silver embroidered ecclesiastical vestments, vessels, and ornaments – all of which came to Jerusalem as pious gifts of pilgrims or munificent benefactors as living testimonials of their devotion to Armenian-Jerusalem *fig.31*.

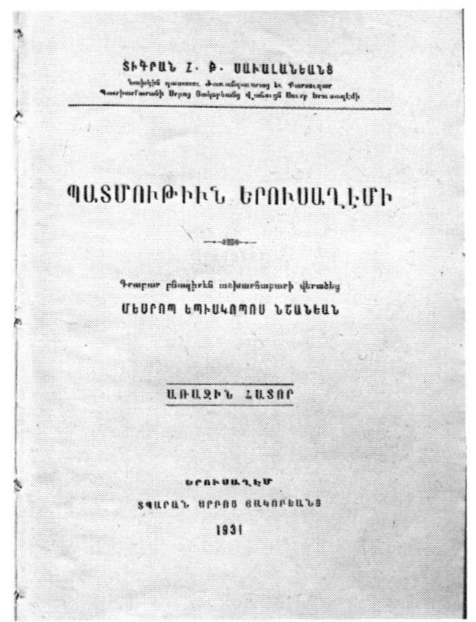
26

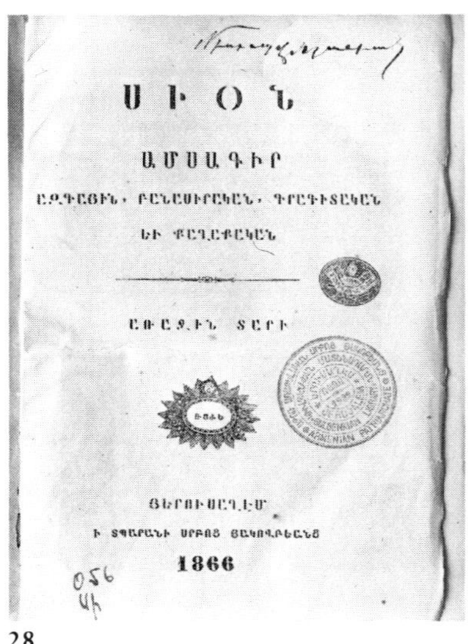
28

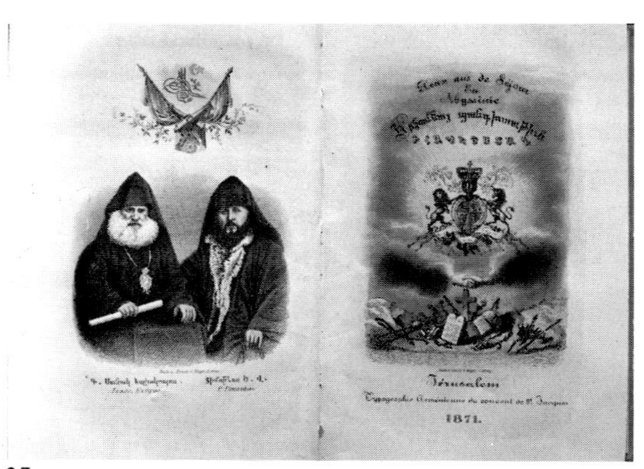
27

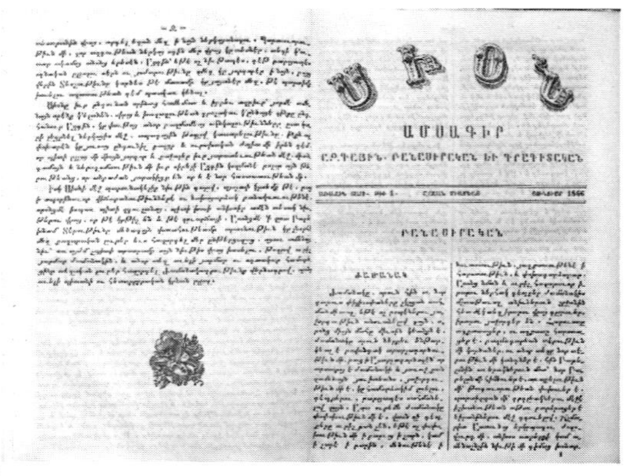
29

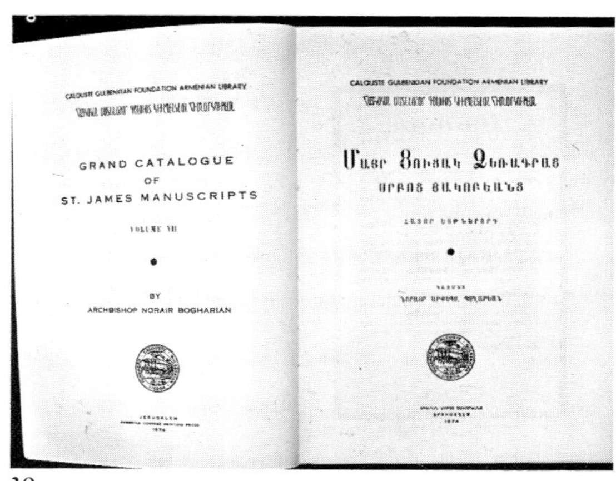

30

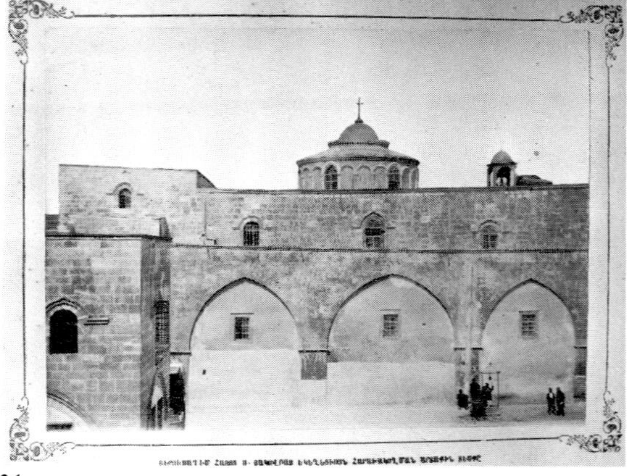
31

Figure 26: *Tigran Sawalaniantz,* History of Jerusalem, *1931.*

Figure 27: Two Years in Abyssinia *(in French), by Isaac and Timothy, two Armenian priests who were sent to secure the release of British prisoners. Jerusalem, 1871.*

Figure 28: Sion, *journal of the Armenian Patriarchate. Frontispiece of the first issue, Jerusalem, 1886.*

Figure 29: Sion, *vol. 1, p. 1, end of introduction and first article.*

Figure 30: *Norair Bogharian,* Grand Catalogue of St. James Manuscripts, *Vol. VII, Jerusalem, 1974.*

Figure 31: *St. James Cathedral from the south. A sun print of 1860 by Patriarch Esayi.*

The Armenian Treasures of Jerusalem

by Bezalel Narkiss

Chapter One: Mosaic Pavements

There was a time during the sixth century when Jerusalem and the surrounding area were filled with Armenian churches.[1] Seven surviving mosaic floors with Armenian inscriptions indicate the richness which must have characterized these Armenian sites that were destroyed through wars and persecutions, or as a consequence of constant use and rebuilding.[2] It is very probable that a large number of old churches and their mosaics were destroyed during the wars of the seventh century when the Persian conquest of the Holy Land was followed by the return of the Byzantines in 628, and the Moslem conquest of Jerusalem in 638.

There is no precise knowledge as to when the Armenians began to build in Jerusalem nor whether their fifth and sixth century churches were different from those established by the Christian Greeks. In fact, there is enough evidence to prove that the Armenian and Greek monks lived together in the same monastery, like the Armenian St. Euthymius and his Greek disciple, St. Saba, in the fifth century. Even a century after the Council of Chalcedon of 451, which was repudiated by the Armenians, the schism between the Armenian and Orthodox churches was not complete. The oppression of the Armenians, by regarding them as Monophysites, began only with Emperor Justinian I (527–565), as a consequence of his wish to unify the religion in the Empire. It is plausible to assume that until the middle of the sixth century, Armenian churches and their decoration were similar to those of the Greeks. Comparing the motifs and style of the surviving mosaics, it appears that during the fifth and sixth centuries, the Armenians of the Holy Land continued to decorate their churches in the contemporary Byzantine plan and style. The possibility that Armenian artists worked together with Greek artists for Armenian patrons may account for these common elements.

1. Mosaics with Armenian Inscriptions

During the second half of the fifth century, the Armenians were defining their national traditions and evolving special religious customs. The Armenian alphabet was invented, their special ritual developed, and the Bible was translated by Saints Mesrob and Sahak. The Armenians secured rights to certain churches, chapels, and areas in the Holy Land in order to be able to carry out their particular rites. They must have introduced some means of identification into the existing churches. The Armenian script, newly devised by Mesrob-Mashtotz, was no doubt an important means for expressing their possession of a place. Within the area which belongs to the Armenian Convent, two fragmentary floor mosaics have survived. In the border of one of them is a rural scene with a rabbit under a tree and remains of two other quadrupeds. Another fragmentary mosaic floor was found in an area belonging to the Armenian Patriarchate beyond the present city walls. It was discovered in 1971 in the enclosure of the cemetery near the chapel of St. Saviour within the complex of one of the traditional houses of Caiaphas, north of the Abbey of the Dormition of the Virgin, when the foundations for a new church were being laid. Neither in these nor in the three decorated floor mosaics discussed below is there a statement as to the exact date in which they were executed; only one mentions a day and a month, but no year. The Armenian calendar only dates from 551/2 A.D. but that era only came into use in the eighth century. The absence of a date on these pavements led J. Dashian to suggest that they must precede 551.[3] Paleographically, the oldest inscription is from Musrara *fig.39* and the latest that of the Artavan mosaic. However, this does not correspond to the stylistic chronology of the decoration of the floors, according to which the earliest is the Artavan mosaic.

2. The Artavan Mosaic

Of the seven surviving floor mosaics with Armenian inscriptions, only three merit artistic discussion. Two of these are on the Mount of Olives, and the third is in the Musrara Quarter near the Damascus Gate. The inscriptions on the Mount of Olives, within the present Russian Convent of the Ascension, cannot be identified with any of the three convents mentioned by Anastas as being on the Mount of Olives.[4] Most of the mosaic inscriptions belong to a group of funerary chapels, since they all mention deceased persons.[5] The earliest of the three decorated floors, the Artavan mosaic, preserved *in situ* in the hall of the Convent's Archaeological Museum, is a fragment of a larger, rectangular pavement *fig.33*. The floor is composed of interlacing bands forming roundels, semicircles, and a square centerpiece. Within the roundels and in the polygonal spaces between them are fish, a pearl, a hen, a Nile duck, clusters of grapes, and a citron. In the centerpiece is a lamb flanked by two opposed fan-shapes. Similar fan-shapes are placed along the border *figs.32, 33*. The interlacing bands are decorated with a guilloche, and the side border has an angular interlace. The background is composed of white tesserae, 12 ×8 tesserae in 10 square cm. The fish, birds, and fruit are made of smaller stones, have 15 ×13 tesserae in 10 square cm., executed in shades of yellow, ocher, red, green, gray, brown, black, and blue. A small rectangular panel is added on the west side, decorated with a single lozenge. The inscription along the north side of the pavement notes that "This is the tomb of the blessed Susannah, mother of Artavan" *fig.32*. A partial date is given as the 18th day of the month of *Hori* – actually the second month of the old Armenian calendar, corresponding to September.[6] No year is mentioned. The motifs in the mosaic certainly expose Christian themes; the lamb in the center symbolizes Christ, and the fish represents a mnemonic sign of His name. The birds recall Paradise *fig.33*, while the grapes are a sign of "grace" in the relation between God and the believer's soul and may also be an allusion to the Eucharist.[7]

The style of the Artavan mosaic recalls that of the ibex border of the House of the Phoenix from Antioch, now in the Louvre, Paris, which Doro Levi ascribed to the fifth century.[8] Like the ibex of the Antioch mosaic, the animals in the Artavan mosaic look statically monumental against their white background, laid to conform to the shape of the roundels and polygons. The bodies appear to be inflated, and the outlines are areas of gradual shading *fig.34*. The inflated plasticity is achieved by highlighted areas within the body which denote the closest plane to the spectator. Within this area, the tesserae are laid in the round – either in concentric circles or semicircles – with gradations in color from the dark on the outside to the light on the inside. Two rows of background tesserae usually outline the shape of the animals. On these stylistic grounds, the Artavan mosaic could be dated to the middle of the fifth century.

The later stage of this style in the mid-sixth century can be found in the mosaic pavement of the synagogue at Nirim.[9] The inflated plasticity becomes flat, the circular highlight areas formalized, and turn into a motif. The static monumentality of the Artavan mosaic is thereby lost. However, a new depth in composition is achieved in Nirim by the movement of the animal and its limbs against the background.

32

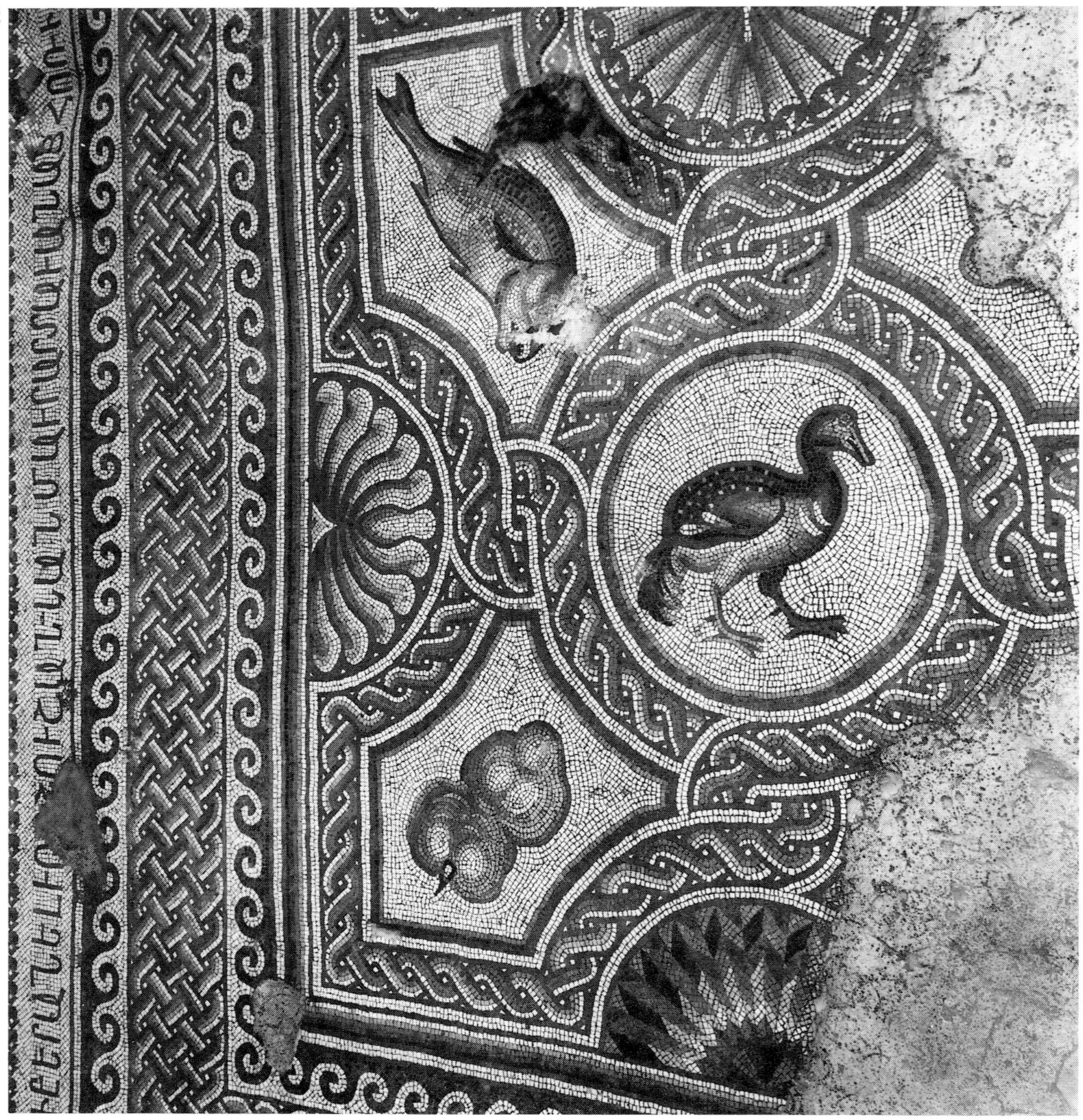

Figure 32: *Dedicatory inscription at the edge of the Artavan Mosaic pavement of the fifth century. From a funerary chapel on the Mount of Olives.*

Figure 33: *Birds, fish, lamb, and grapes. Part of the Artavan Mosaic pavement from the Mount of Olives.*

Figure 34: *A duck, fish, and fruit. Part of the Artavan mosaic.*

33

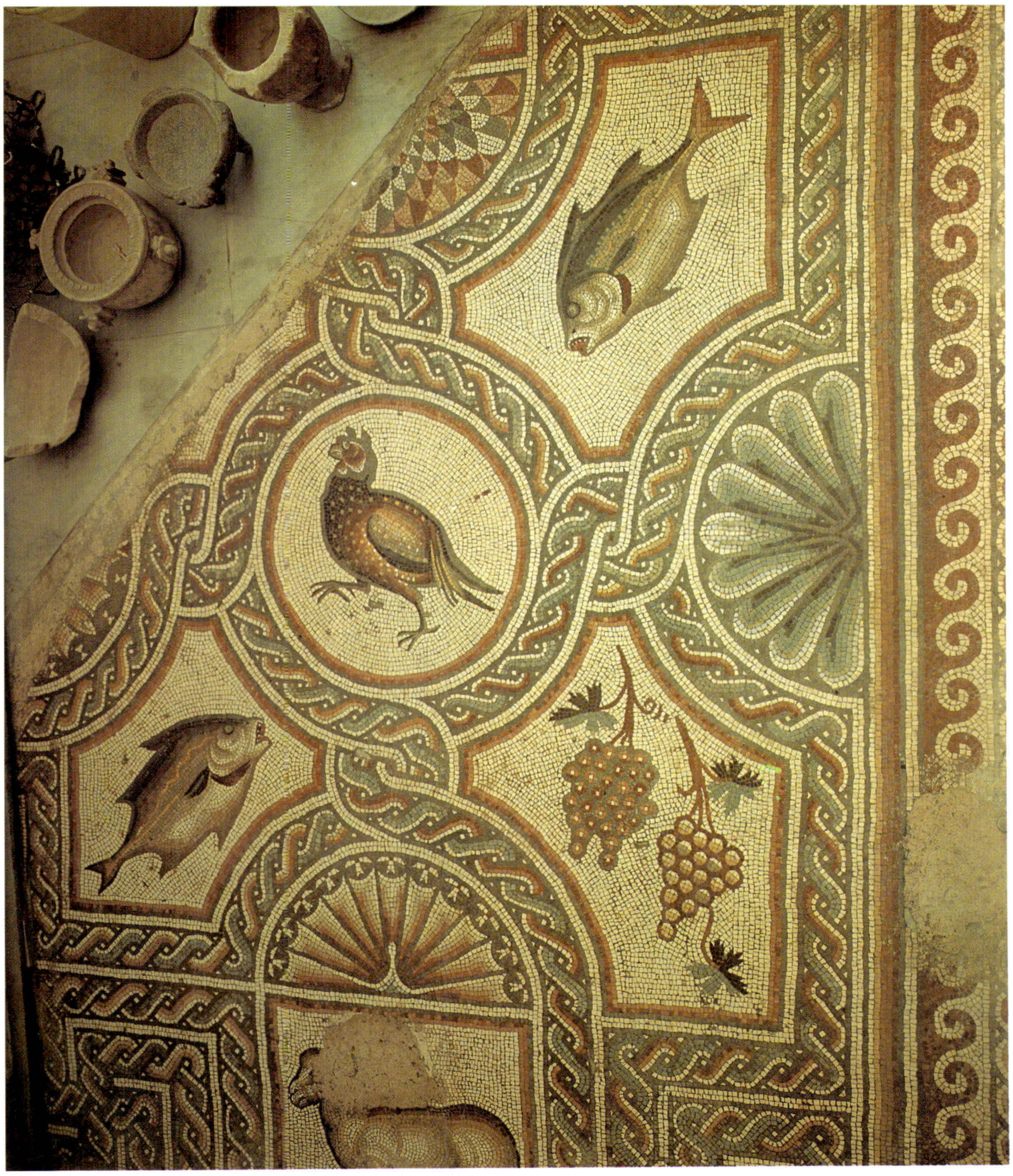

34

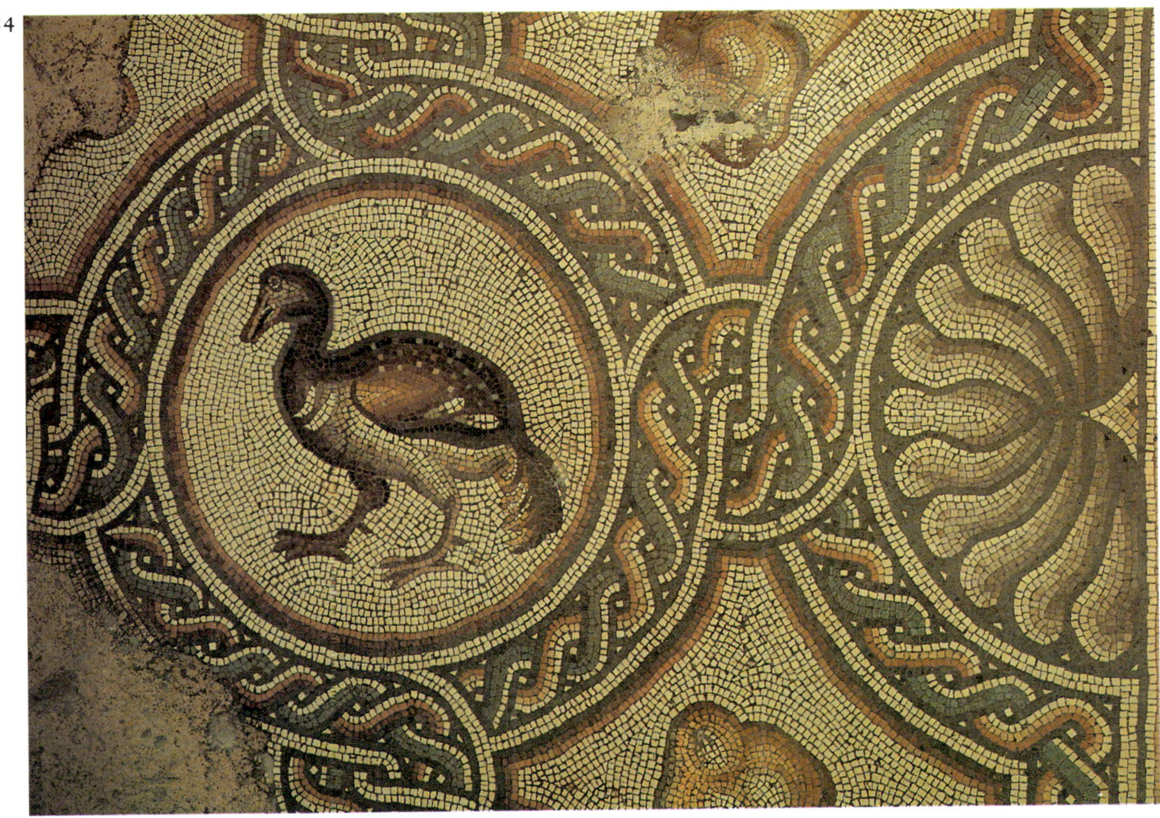

3. *The St. John's Mosaic*

The second mosaic within the Russian Convent adorns the Chapel of the Head of St. John the Baptist.[10] The mosaic is divided into three adjacent fields resembling carpets. The western field has an overall pattern of interwoven circles, crosslets within the circles, and a zig-zag and checkered border. On its east is a round concave recess, paved with mosaics, denoting the place of St. John's head.

The second field in St. John's Chapel is composed alternately of interlaced roundels and squares arranged horizontally and bordered by a braid motif *fig.35*. The compartments enclose many birds, among which are pheasants, flamingos, ibises, doves, ducks, parrots, and pearl hens. The central, third, horizontal row and the outer right-hand row are decorated differently with leaves and fruit such as figs, pomegranates, citrus, and grapes, and fish on a plate *fig.36*. A dog barking at a lamb is placed in the very center. Here too the birds, fruit, fish, and lamb may allude to a Christian meaning, although the arrangement within this context makes the symbolic element less obvious. The third field, to the east, has an Armenian inscription *fig.37*.

Although this triple mosaic pavement resembles the Artavan mosaic in color and technique, this too has 15 × 13 tesserae per 10 square cm. for the birds and fruit, but 10 × 11 for the background. Its workmanship is inferior, and its style is different. Birds and animals are in exaggerated movement, their outlines usually darkly delineated against the white background. Highlighted patches and color gradation are decorative, through being diffused, and therefore do not build up plasticity *fig.38*. The difference in style between the Artavan mosaic and the one in St. John's chapel can be explained by comparing the latter to the synagogue mosaic in Gaza dated 508/9.[11] The incomplete roundels of the Gaza mosaic are formed by vine scrolls, but the enclosed animals and birds leap in and out of their frames on to the first plane. Thus, compositional depth is enhanced, not only by the animals' movement against the white background, but also against the enclosing vine scroll. On the other hand, the empty abstract space surrounding the animals in St. John's chapel is void of the natural habitations and compactness which in the Gaza mosaic is achieved by filling the space with grape tendrils and vine leaves. The animals in Gaza have dark outlines, their various stages of plasticity being achieved by either color gradation and rounded highlight areas, recalling the Artavan mosaic style, or by diffused flat patches like the St. John's chapel mosaic. It can be assumed that the St. John's mosaic is somewhat later than the Artavan mosaic, but still dates from the fifth century, earlier than the Gaza mosaic of the beginning of the sixth century.

36

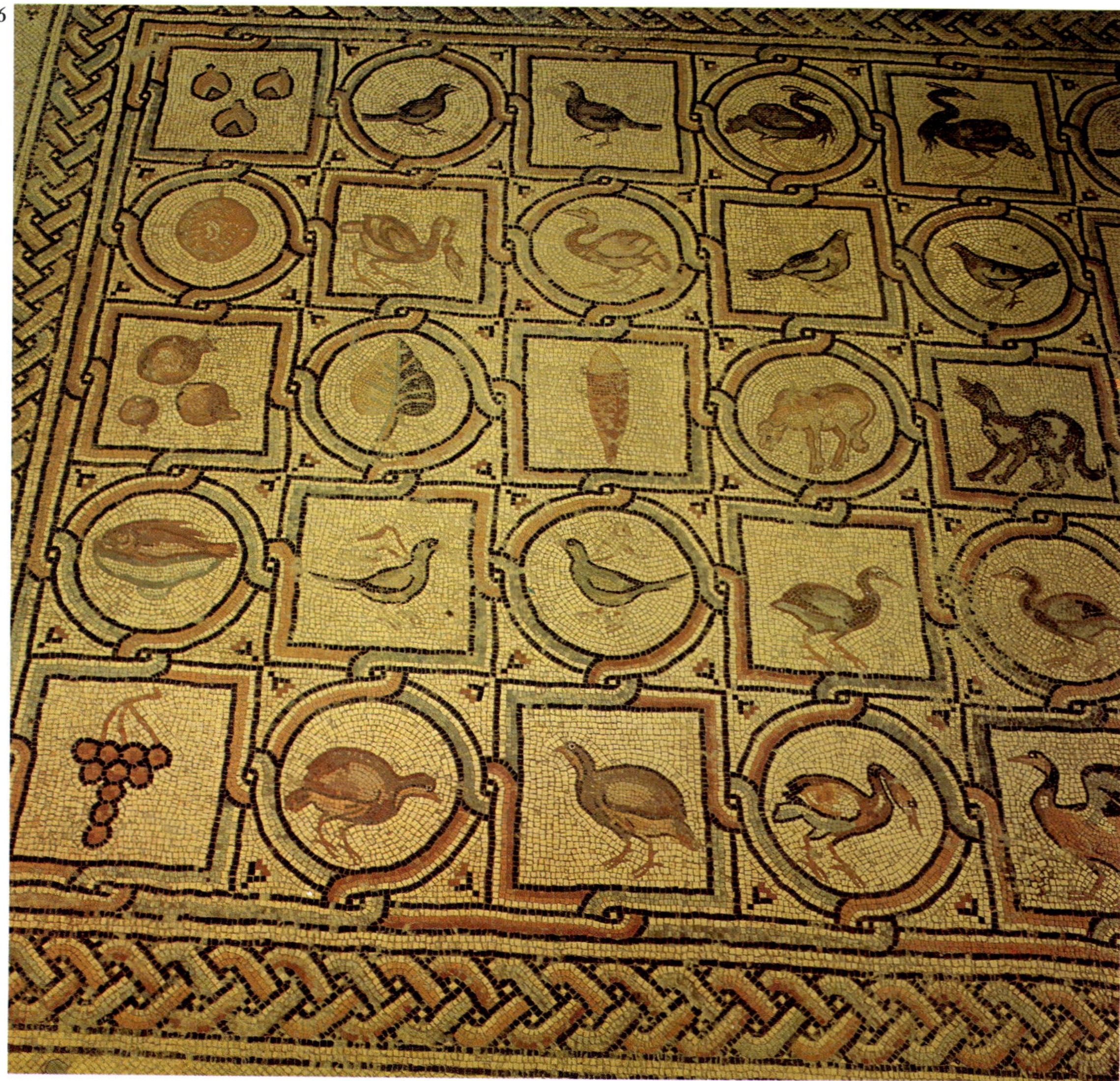

Figure 36: *Birds, fruit, fish, and a dog chasing a lamb. Northern part of the central field in the St. John Chapel on the Mount of Olives.*

Figure 35: *Overall view of the central and eastern fields in the Chapel of the Head of St. John the Baptist on the Mount of Olives, late fifth century.*

35

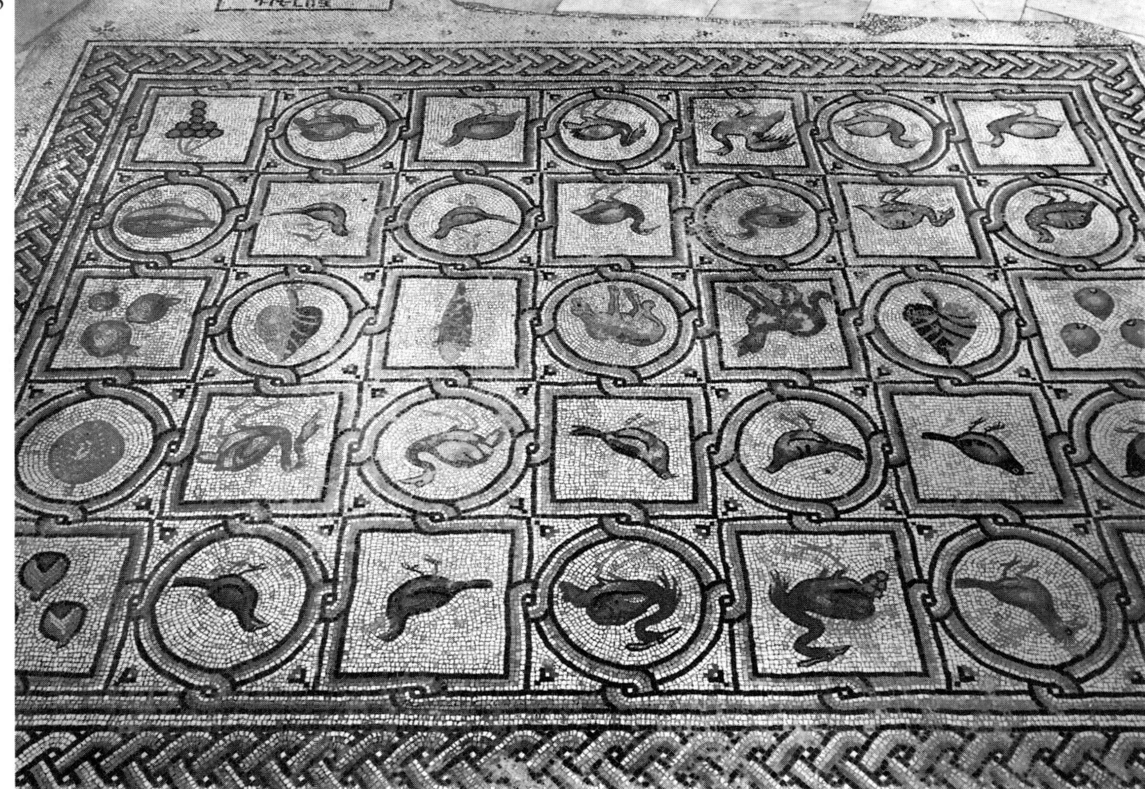

37

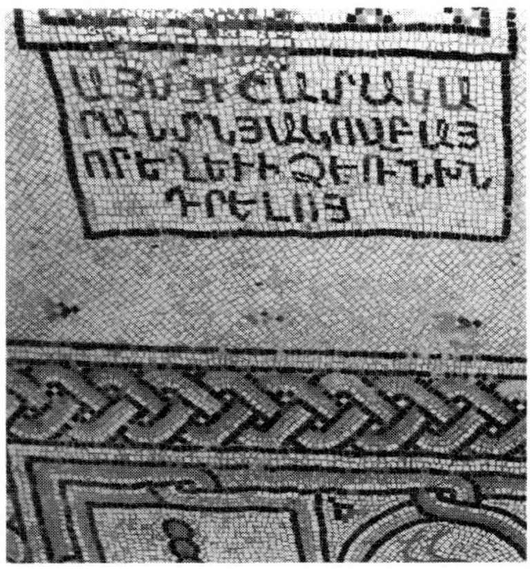

Figure 37: *Corner of the central field and the inscription in the eastern field of the St. John Mosaic: "This is the monument of the Lord Jacob, made at (his) request."*

38

Figure 38: *Four birds within medallions and squares. Section of the central field in the St. John Mosaic of the late fifth century.*

Figure 39 (pages 26–27): *The Musrara Mosaic, depicting birds within vine scrolls. Funerary Chapel of the middle of the sixth century.*

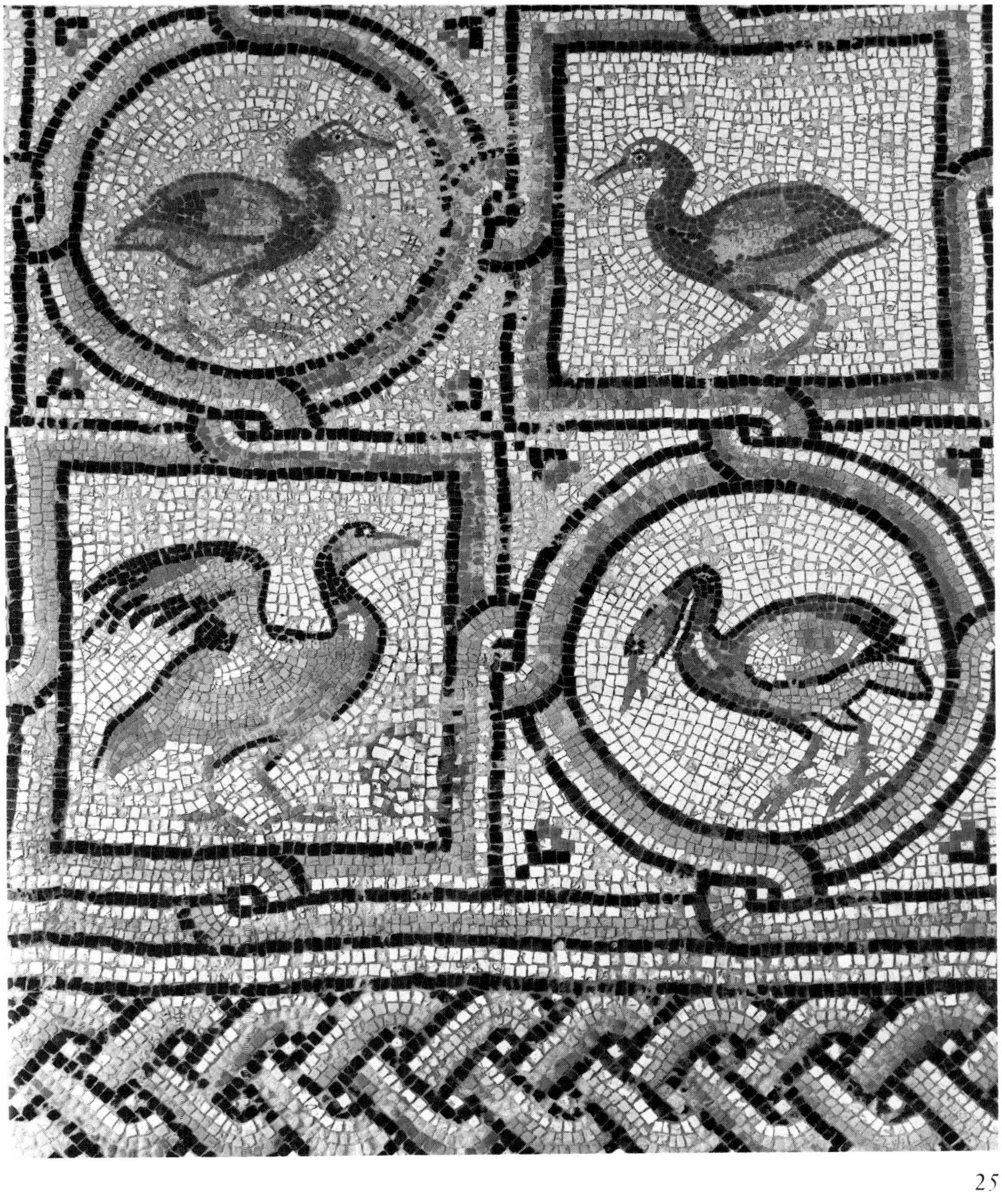

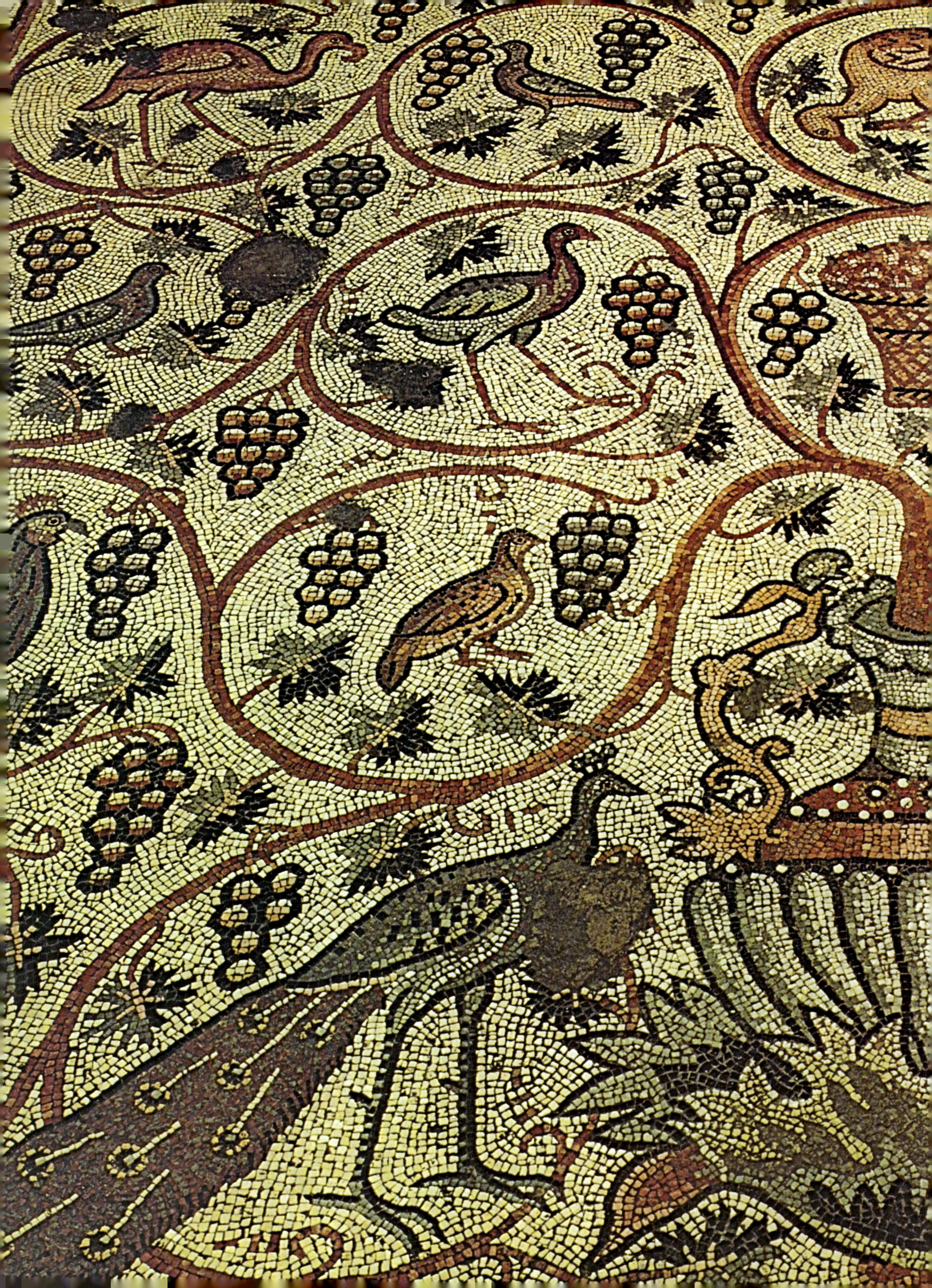

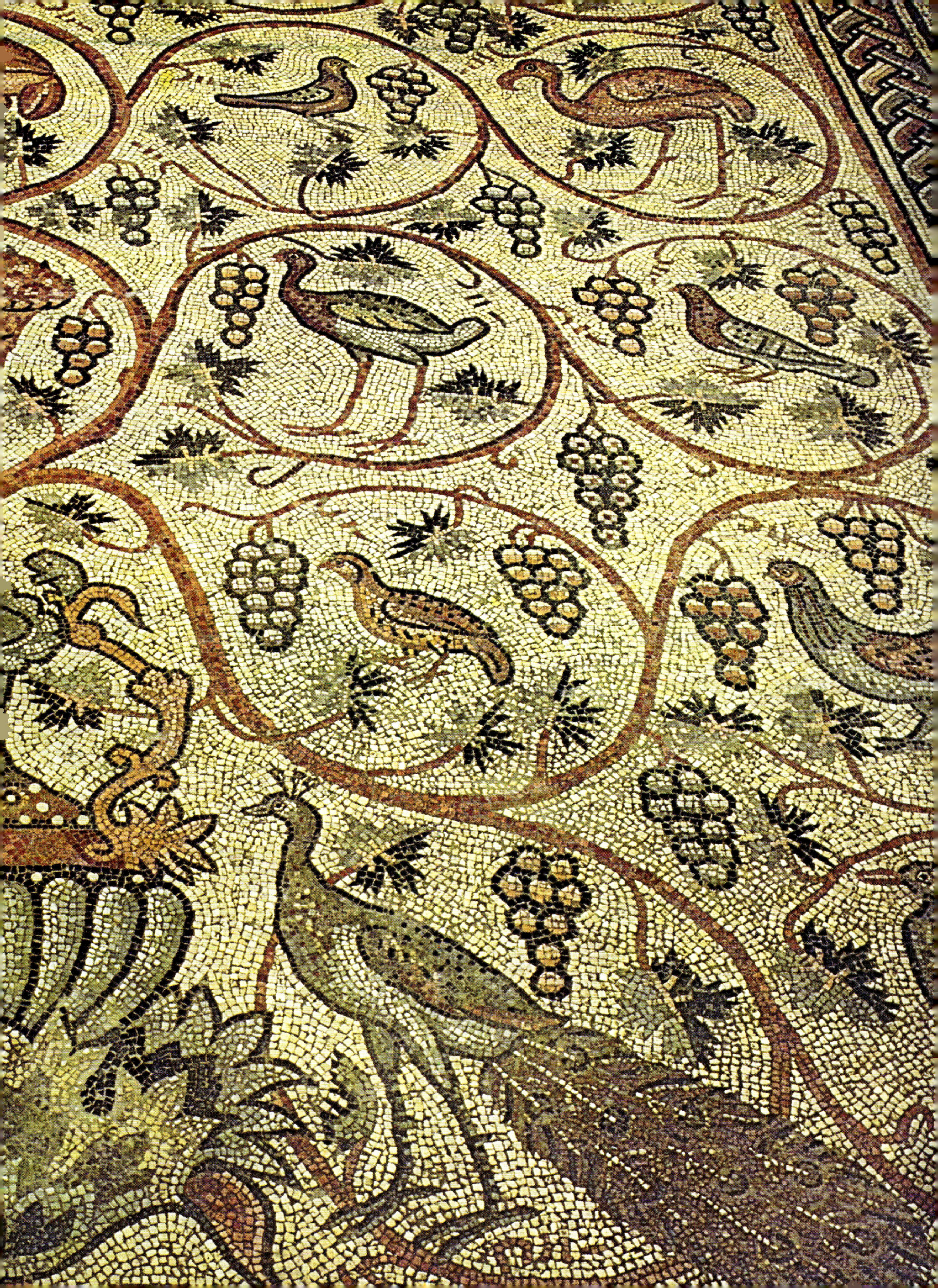

4. The Musrara Mosaic

The third sumptuous Armenian mosaic decorated the funerary chapel of St. Polyeuctos in the Musrara Quarter, near the Damascus Gate *fig.39*. It is mentioned by name in the list of Armenian churches attributed to Anastas, in the seventh century and can be dated in the middle of the sixth century.[12] It has an Armenian inscription *fig.1 above*. The colors used are different shades of red, gray, yellow, green, black, and white. The rectangular field is enclosed within a plaited border. Vine scrolls sprout from an amphora at the center of one end and divide the field into five vertical rows of nine medallions each, except for the center row, which acts as an axis to the bilateral, symmetrical composition. The amphora, partly covered by an elaborate acanthus leaf, is flanked by peacocks. Within the medallions, various birds are arranged symmetrically, almost heraldically, along the central axis, which encloses birds, baskets, kantharos, and a bird in a cage.[13]

The Christian motifs are stressed in this mosaic though most of them have their origin in Roman pagan art. The vine scrolls appear to imply life after death, possibly originating from the Dionysiac paradise, here converted to Christian symbols. The peacocks drinking the liquid of eternal life from an amphora are also a Christian symbol of life after death *fig.40*. The bird in a cage is another Christian symbol, conveying the incarnation of Christ within the human body.[14] This motif, which appears also in the mosaic pavements of the synagogues at Gaza and Nirim and the church at Shellal, is perhaps based on the Neoplatonic idea of the soul enclosed in the body, as a bird in a cage. The eagle which appears above it represents the dangers of evil to the soul. In Roman pagan art, the eagle is depicted as the messenger of Helios, who carries the soul of the deceased to Heaven.

The symmetrical composition of the St. Polyeuctos mosaic conveys a somewhat formal and symbolic approach, strengthened by the static, representational, position of the birds, which hardly ever cross the scroll medallions *fig.40*. The density in composition is evenly spread, by the added clusters of grapes and leaves in the more spacious medallions. The figures are outlined in black. The shading and highlights give the birds a plastic, natural feeling similar to that at Shellal and Gaza, and not like the bloated areas in Nirim, nor like the patches of St. John's mosaic. In its dense composition the Musrara mosaic is closer to that of the church at Shellal of 561 than to that of the Gaza synagogue of 508, which is more spacious, or that of the Kyrie Maria Monastery of 567,[15] which is more compact. Although the figure style is not identical to that of Shellal, the plan of decoration, and part of the iconography, may be of a similar origin. It can hardly be dated exactly on this basis, but a general date in the middle of the sixth century can be assumed.

The Armenian mosaic pavements of Jerusalem conform with the general Byzantine style of the fifth and sixth centuries. Armenian artists used techniques, plan, models, motifs and iconography similar to those used by the artists who decorated floors in Greek Orthodox, Iberian (Georgian), and Coptic churches, or Jewish synagogues in the Holy Land and in the neighboring countries. Often, their only means of identification are the Armenian dedicatory inscriptions, used in Jerusalem from the early period of the invention of the Armenian alphabet.

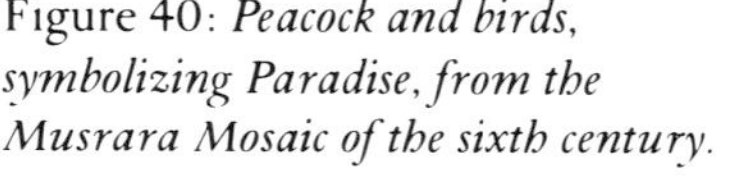
Figure 40: *Peacock and birds, symbolizing Paradise, from the Musrara Mosaic of the sixth century.*

40

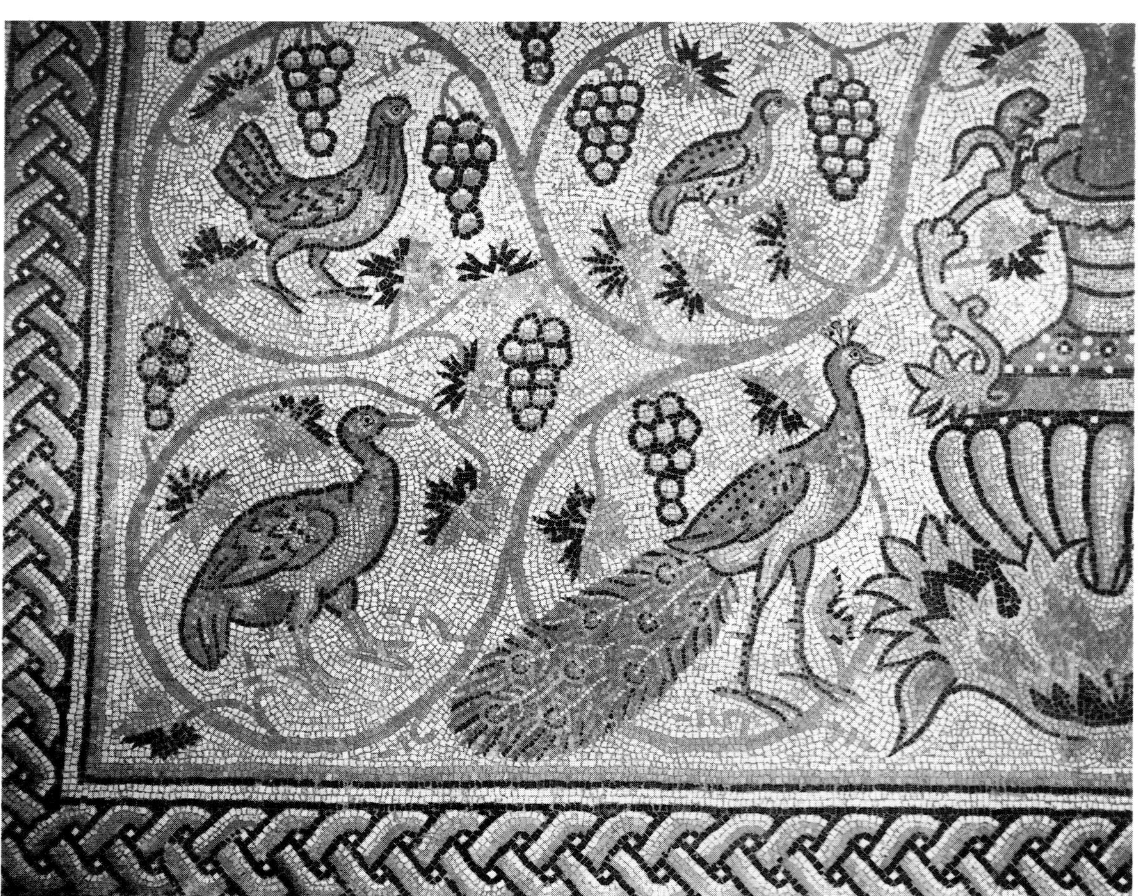

Chapter Two: Early Illuminated Manuscripts

The collection of Armenian illuminated manuscripts in the Library of St. Thoros in the Armenian Patriarchate of Jerusalem is one of the largest and most important in the world, second only to the Matenadaran Collection in Erevan.[1] It contains examples of illumination from the tenth to the eighteenth centuries, from all the provinces of Armenia, Asia Minor, Cilicia, New Julfa, Constantinople, Jerusalem, and Khizan. Most of these manuscripts were brought to Jerusalem and presented to the Monastery of St. James by the many pilgrims who visited the Holy City throughout the ages. They were donated to St. James in Jerusalem, because for a pious Armenian dedicating a manuscript to a church or a monastery is like dedicating the church itself, and this is thought to secure a place in heaven for him.

The history of Armenian illumination from the tenth to the eighteenth centuries can be studied to a large extent through the examination of the manuscripts treasured in Jerusalem.

1. Queen Mlk'ē and Etchmiadzin Gospels

In a survey of Armenian illumination based on the Jerusalem collection, it is necessary to refer to two important manuscripts, dating from before the eleventh century, not in the Jerusalem collection. These two manuscripts are considered to be the basis of Armenian illumination, and are the only survivors of the early schools, which have their origins in Eastern as well as Western Early Christian painting.

The earliest is the Queen Mlk'ē Gospel of 862 from Vaspurakan.[2] The second is the Etchmiadzin Gospel[3] which consists of two stages of illumination, one from the sixth or seventh centuries and the other of 989, from Noravankh in east Armenia. The earlier pictures of the Etchmiadzin Gospel, as well as its ivory covers, are remnants of the pre-Iconoclastic Controversy and preserve strong Byzantine elements in style and iconography.[4] This may illustrate the notion inferred from Vrthanes Kherthogh's description of illuminated manuscripts which "came from the land of the Greeks".[5] Armenian illumination from its beginning was predominantly influenced by Byzantium. Artistic activities in Armenia were a result of a social and political constellation, which a brief historical survey may elucidate.

2. History of Armenia during the tenth and eleventh centuries

During the tenth and eleventh centuries Armenia was still one of the areas fought over by the two great powers of the time, the Byzantine Empire and the Muslim Caliphate. The spheres of influence of these powers changed from time to time and the small Armenian states played a role here. The Abbasid Caliphs installed emirs in several places, most of whom recognized the local Armenian kings of the Bagratid family. The Byzantines, on the other hand, tried to annex more and more states and eliminate their rulers. Many small states developed in Armenia during the ninth and tenth centuries, since every king gave each of his sons a kingship, thereby dividing his state into several others.[6] It was perhaps because of the constant fighting between the two great powers that the small Armenian states were left to prosper at times. This, in turn, made it possible for some to become centers of great artistic achievement. The drawback of the division into small rival states was felt only later in the middle of the eleventh century, when the powerful Seljuk Turks conquered Armenia. The decline of the small states, however, began even earlier in the eleventh century, and one after another fell into the hands of the Byzantines. The King of Vaspurakan, for instance, surrendered his state to the Byzantine Emperor Basil II in 1022, and a similar fate befell the most important Bagratid kingdom of Ani.

After the long and prosperous reign of the Bagratid Gagik I (988–1020), who built and strengthened Ani as one of the most beautiful cities in the East, his two sons divided the kingdom between themselves. Fearing the Seljuk advance, John Smbat III, King of Ani, declared the Emperor Basil II his heir. But when the Byzantine army came to claim their rights after his death in 1042, the young King Gagik II put up a fight, and managed to hold out for three long years against the combined forces of the Byzantine army, those of the Moslem Emir of Dvin, and some pro-Byzantine citizens of Ani. It was only in 1045 that the brave king was lured to Constantinople, and Ani was annexed to the Byzantine Empire. King Gagik of Kars, whose reign began in 1029 and who became the chief king after Gagik of Ani was exiled, claimed the title of *Shahne Shah* (King of Kings) from

1045. He too surrendered his kingdom to the Byzantines in 1064, went into exile and received in exchange a kingdom in Asia Minor, where he reigned until his death in 1081. By 1064 only the kingdoms of Siunik and Lori remained independent. However, by this time the Seljuk invasion of Armenia, which started in 1048, was in full flood. The Seljuks conquered Ani and Kars in 1064, only a few months after the Byzantines occupied Kars, and by 1071 the entire land of Armenia was in the hands of the Seljuks.

Any artistic activities carried on by the royal houses of these kingdoms after the tenth century were no doubt executed by Armenian artists well trained in their traditional art. Most of their art survived in monumental buildings of churches and monasteries lavishly decorated with reliefs and sculpture. Their style is geometric, almost abstract, and very expressive and clear. There is some Byzantine influence in this decorative style, though more can be found in the iconography; but most of the elements which are not traditionally Armenian are of Eastern origin, Coptic, Syriac, Cappadocian, Persian or Sassanian.

3. *The Tyche Initial*

The earliest illumination in the Library of St. Thoros in Jerusalem is a headpiece for the book of St. Mark, painted on a single folio *fig.41*.[7] The headpiece frames Armenian and Greek inscriptions,[8] next to a bust of a crowned *tyche*, personifying a city, carrying two cornucopiae within the initial *sé* (= S in Armenian). The wide frame ending on the right with a stylized leaf resembles Sura openings in early Koran manuscripts.[9] The figure's flat, white painted, stylized face, very distinct features, and its ornamented though classicized drapery, can be related to the hieratic style of the images and drapery of the later stage of the Etchmiadzin Gospel dating from 989.[10] The face of the *tyche* is more elongated than those of the Etchmiadzin Gospel figures, but its facial features are quite similar. The drapery is comparable to the Virgin and Child panel of the Etchmiadzin Gospel with the exaggerated white highlights.[11] The fish-scale pattern in the frame and the deep blue and magenta colors are also related to the Etchmiadzin Gospel. The *erkathagir* (uncial) script of the folio is also characteristic of the late tenth or early eleventh century.

41

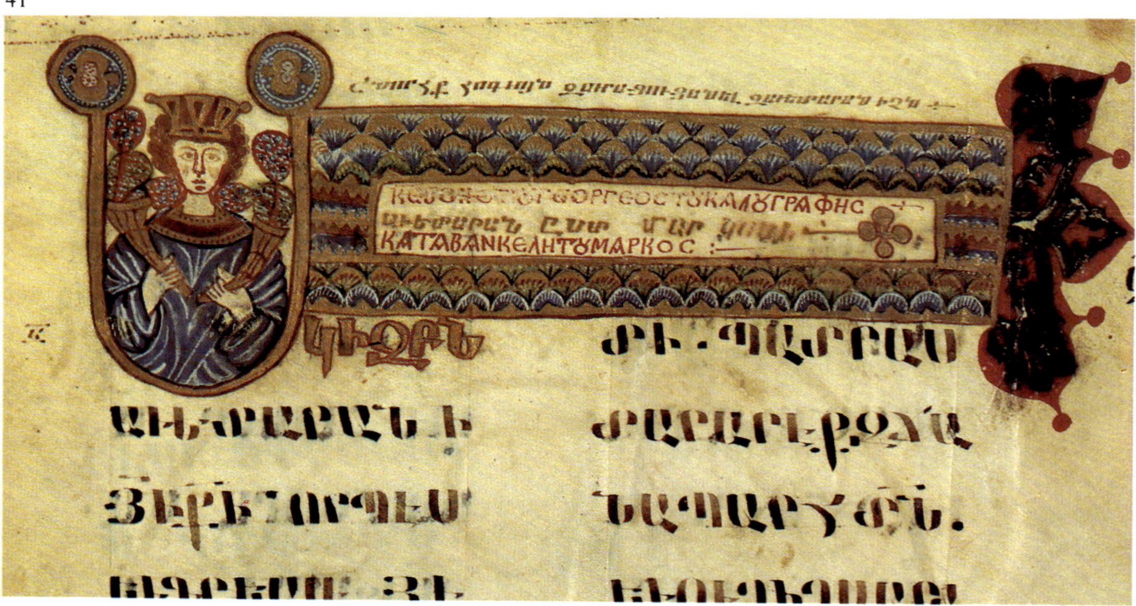

Figure 41: *The Tyche initial and headpiece for the book of St. Mark. Late tenth-century fragment used as binding material in a Gospel of 1312 (ms. 1949, fol. 390).*

Figure 42: *Sanctuary of the Holy Sepulcher in the form of a tempietto edifice, with hanging curtains. Frontispiece to the Second Etchmiadzin Gospel. Western Armenia, ca. 1000 A.D. (ms. 2555, fol. 7).*

4. *The Second Etchmiadzin Gospel*

The manuscript known as "The Second Etchmiadzin Gospel" also dates from the late tenth or early eleventh century.[12] It has somewhat primitive-looking paintings and is related to the Etchmiadzin Gospel mainly in its program and iconography. The portraits of the Evangelists standing in pairs under arches, the tempietto-like Sanctuary edifice representing the Holy Sepulcher *fig.42* and an orant Virgin, extending her arms in prayer, with the Christ Child in her lap at the top, and the Sacrifice of Isaac below *fig.43* resemble in detail the full-page illustrations of these same two scenes in the Etchmiadzin Gospel of 989.[13] The artist of the Second Etchmiadzin Gospel may not have fully understood the details, thus making the cushion of the Virgin's seat resemble a tub, and the steps of the altar on which Isaac is bound resemble a ladder. Next to the Virgin he added a cross-limbed Christ, who looks like the Angel of the Annunciation. This figure was taken from another source, since it does not appear in the Etchmiadzin Gospel. The decorated, full-page cross probably also came from another origin, possibly Syriac; similar examples are known from other tenth and eleventh century Armenian manuscripts.[14] In contrast to iconographic similarity, the style of each Etchmiadzin Gospel is pronouncedly different. The human figures, facial details, drapery, birds, beasts, and plants are much more stylized and linear in the Second Etchmiadzin Gospel, although the decorative motifs are similar. The resemblance between the two Etchmiadzin manuscripts suggests a common prototype, rather than a direct link between them.[15]

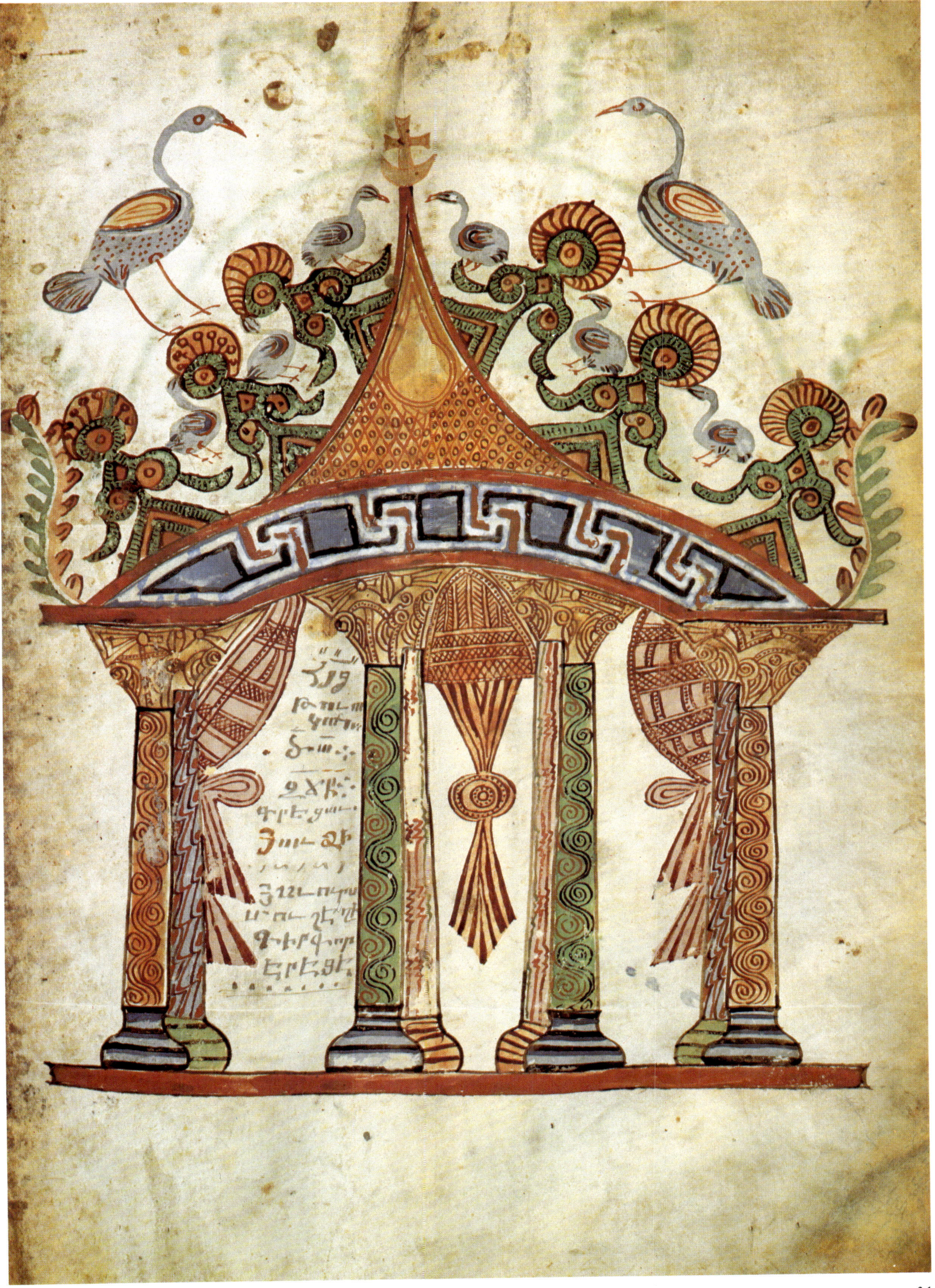

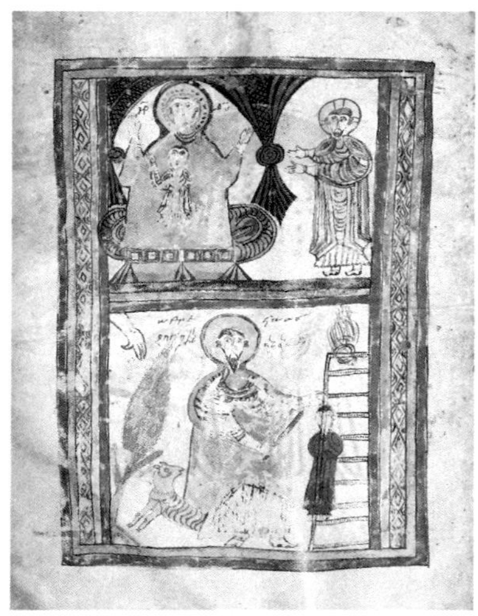

43

Figure 43: *Orant Virgin and Child, and the Sacrifice of Isaac, from the Second Etchmiadzin Gospel. Western Armenia, ca. 1000 A.D. (ms. 2555, fol. 8v).*

The frontal, orant Virgin with the Christ Child which appears in four tenth-century Armenian Gospels is known from Early Christian art. The wall painting in a niche in the Coemeterium Maius in Rome may, as a type, be the earliest surviving example.[16] The frontal, enthroned Virgin, holding a Child giving a blessing, is not usually portrayed in an orant attitude either in early Byzantine or in western art.[17] It becomes more frequent in later Byzantine wall painting, such as in the Vatopedi Monastery on Mount Athos of 1537,[18] and in later illuminated manuscripts, such as the late fourteenth-century Serbian Psalter in Munich, where the orant Virgin and Child appear seated, but in a tub-like fountain.[19] The tub in which the orant Virgin is sitting in the Second Etchmiadzin Gospel may therefore be a vestige of an earlier Byzantine representation of the Virgin in a fountain of life,[20] and not a misinterpretation by the artist. Whatever the origin may be, Early Christian, Byzantine, or a tenth-century invention, it has become a specific Armenian iconographical element in the Etchmiadzin Gospel and the late tenth-century manuscripts akin to it.

In the Sacrifice of Isaac, the high, burning altar with steps leading up to it is another detail which originates in Early Christian art; it is found in a fifth-century ivory pyxis in Berlin.[21] These special Armenian iconographical details may therefore reflect an earlier tradition, either from Early Christian times, or else from a later period but still before the tenth century.

The figural scenes of the Second Etchmiadzin Gospel seem to have been taken from a more sophisticated model. The elongated, oval-shaped faces, with eyes wide open above high cheekbones, are similar to the Gospel found in the Vienna Mekhitarist Monastery,[22] as well as to the Etchmiadzin Gospel.[23] The agitated drapery, close folds emphasized by parallel strokes, and enhancing the decorative element of the figures, also resembles those of the Vienna Gospel, although the style of the latter is more painterly. These facial types and dense drapery folds recall the wall paintings of the Armenian church at Aghthamar built by King Gagik I of Vaspurakan between 915 and 921 A.D.[24] The Second Etchmiadzin Gospel seems to represent a somewhat later stage in the development of this style at the end of the tenth century.

The search for a closer parallel in crude, linear style, expressive and colorful, leads to an examination of the style and iconography of some painted cave churches in Cappadocia. Among several churches closely related to Armenian illumination, nearest by far to the Second Etchmiadzin Gospel are the remains of the wall paintings in the *Ağaç Alti Kilise* (church under the tree) in Ihlara, south-west of Ürgüp.[25] The sketchy, decorative elements in the outlines of the human figure, the flat faces and large eyes with heavy shading under them, and the ornamental quality of the drapery, are fairly close to the Second Etchmiadzin Gospel. There are also some similarities in iconography and gesture. For instance, the angel's gesture in the Annunciation in *Ağaç Alti* is similar to that of the standing Christ next to the Virgin and Child *fig.43*; standing Apostles in Ihlara resemble the Evangelists in our Gospel book.[26] A comparison of the geometrical, decorative motifs of the two monuments would demonstrate a similar correspondence. The accepted date for the *Ağaç Alti* church is late tenth or early eleventh century, and its resemblance to the Second Etchmiadzin Gospel suggests a similar date for the manuscript.

The similarity in style and iconography of these and other Cappadocian wall paintings[27] to Armenian monuments has been explained by J. Lafontaine-Dosogne who assumes the artistic activity of an Armenian monastic community in Cappadocia during the ninth to eleventh centuries.[28] However, the iconographic similarity may be due to earlier common origins, but with elements peculiar to each. Their respective styles seems to have developed along parallel lines, revealing an individual manner with a similar decorative and linear vocabulary.

5. *The Gospel Book of King Gagik of Kars*

The decorative, linear tendency in the style of ninth to eleventh century Armenian illumination is commonly called provincial. This non-classical style appears in fact in the East as well as in the West throughout the early Middle Ages.[29] However, it exists side by side with the well-proportioned, classicizing figural style, which is usually considered more accomplished and therefore under courtly patronage. This combination is mainly based on similar dual styles which existed concurrently in the Byzantine Empire during the same period. This juxtaposition is not rare in Byzantium, and its use in Armenian art points to the immediate origin of both styles in Byzantine art proper.

The Byzantine classicizing style is most pronounced in some of the Armenian royal illuminated manuscripts. The sumptuous Gospel of King Gagik of Kars,[31] was lavishly decorated with text illustrations *fig.44*, some of which are framed in small panels *figs.45, 46*, mostly in the lower margins and across the double text columns and headpieces of books *fig.47*. The decoration program of closely related texts and illustrations resembles Greek illumination of the eleventh century,[32] such as the Gospel book in the Bibliothèque Nationale in Paris and the famous Imperial Lectionary in the Monastery of Dionysiou on Mount Athos. The extent of the text illustration in Gagik's Gospel is not entirely known, since many miniatures were unscrupulously cut out sometime before 1703 when it was rebound. The surviving miniatures, as well as the lacunae, indicate that the manuscript had some detailed and original text illustrations of the Gospel episodes. In one of the surviving illustrations Jesus is depicted teaching his disciples *fig.44* in a manner common to Byzantine art of the period. The unframed illustration on parchment depicts Christ seated on the ground with Peter next to him, most prominent. It is attached to the text of Jesus choosing his disciples (Mt. 4:18–21), but may represent the Sermon on the Mount (Mt. 5:1). Fairly conventional iconography occurs in the scene of the Risen Christ appearing to the Apostles in Galilee (Mt. 28:16–18), *fig.45* where Christ is shown standing on a hill as the text prescribes. The Three Temptations of Jesus by Satan are depicted twice in the Gagik Gospel. The extant fragments of the first series illustrate Matthew 4,[33] and show original iconography, especially in the depiction of Satan surrounded by the animals of the world on fol. 18. Its damaged condition does not allow its reproduction here. The second series of the Three Temptations on fols. 244, 244v, illustrating Luke 4, resembles the conventional Byzantine iconography *fig.46*, although even here the artist managed to introduce a new element by depicting a throne, to indicate the Kingdom of the World which Jesus refused to accept from Satan (Luke 4:5–8). Other unusual representations are the appearance of four women instead of two at the Empty Tomb (Mt. 28:1, fol. 132v), and the Pharisees examining the blind man who was healed by Christ (John 9:13–34, fol. 419v).

One interesting fragmentary panel, now attached to the lower part of fol. 135v, depicts King Gagik of Kars, his wife Gorandoukht, and their daughter Marem (although damaged and with the upper part of their faces cut out) seated in oriental fashion cross-legged, on a low bench *fig.48*. Their dresses and the carpet covering the bench are oriental textiles of Sassanian types, richly decorated with roundels containing lions and elephants. The panel certainly belongs to the manuscript, but definitely not to the end of St. Matthew where it is now bound. There may have been four such pictures, each at the end of a Gospel, since three have a dedicatory inscription at the top of their last page.[34] The dedicatory inscriptions, written in large red *erkathagir* script, states that King Gagik, King of Kings (*Shahne-Shah*), should be remembered by the Lord Jesus Christ. At the end of St. Luke on fol. 371v, the added names of Queen Gorandoukht and their daughter Marem imply that a similar panel with the family picture is now missing there.[35] However, it is quite clear that the existing family portrait was originally placed at the very end of the book after St. John, since the reverse side of the picture on fol. 135 bears part of the original scribe's colophon, in two columns, mentioning "the Holy Queen Gorandoukht and Marem their descendant."

The marginal decoration of the manuscript is sumptuous. It consists of floral, bird, and animal motifs attached to the initials; some of these such as a bull, a cock, or a round sanctuary, may be text illustrations. In addition, there are many small carpet-like panels, richly decorated and colored with Sassanian motifs. The style of the miniatures is influenced by Byzantine courtly art, but it is uneven, and at times crude in execution.

Sirarpie Der Nersessian suggested that although there is no exact relation between the Gagik Gospel and any Greek manuscript, there is some resemblance to the Imperial Lectionary of Mount Athos, already mentioned, from the middle of the 11th century.[36] However, the architectural settings in the Gagik Gospel and those in the Imperial Lectionary may derive from an earlier Byzantine style, such as the Constantinopolitan Menologium of Basil II, of about 1000.[37] The Menologium may have been the origin of the short, stocky figures of the Gagik Gospel and the lack of dramatic gestures, as compared with the Lectionary.

The similarity in style of the Gagik Gospel to the Menologium may indicate an earlier date for the royal Gospel. The dedicatory inscriptions referring to him as *Shahne-Shah* and the portrait of the royal family with the daughter, Marem, still young, suggests a date much earlier than his abdication in 1064, possibly around the middle of the century.[38]

47

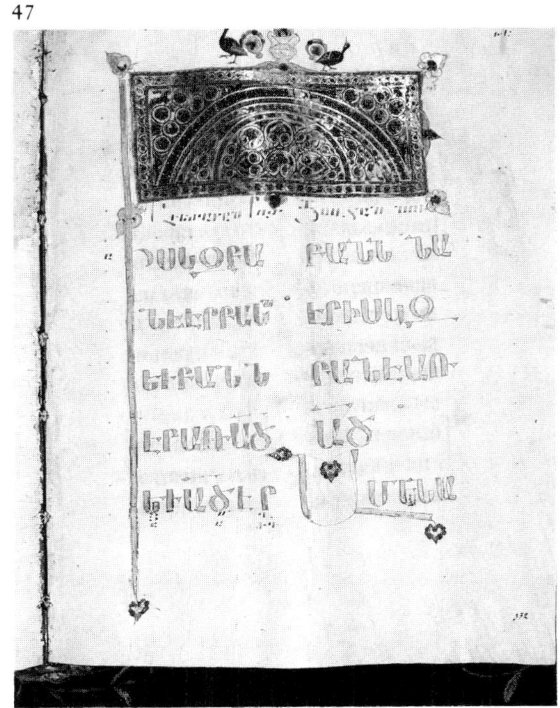

48

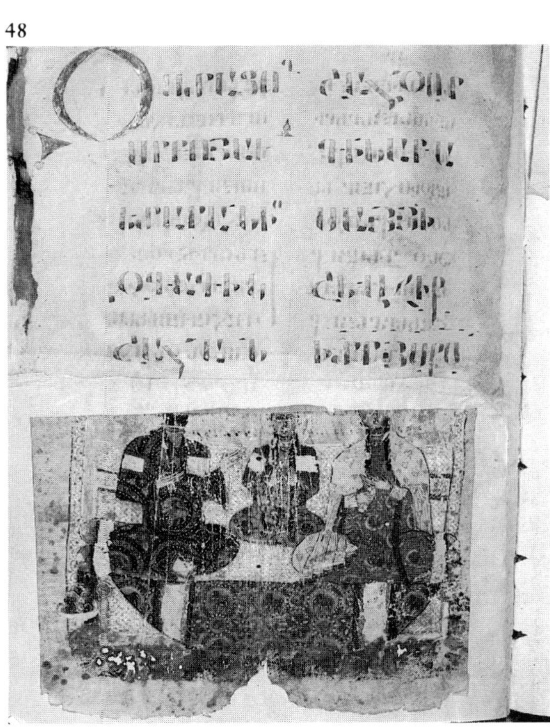

Figure 47: *Opening page with headpiece to the Gospel according to St. John in the Gagik Gospel (ms. 2556, fol. 372).*

Figure 48: *King Gagik of Kars, his wife Goradoukht, and their daughter Marem, one of four portraits of the royal family in the Gagik Gospel (ms. 2556, fol. 135v).*

Figure 49: *Arcaded canon table from the Melitene Gospel of 1041 (ms. 3624, fol. 5).*

Figure 50: *The Four Evangelists, from the Gospel of 1041 (ms. 3624, fol. 11).*

Figure 51: *The Transfiguration and the Raising of Lazarus, depicted in one panel as they are next to each other in Byzantine Feast icons, from the Gospel of 1041 (ms. 3624, fol. 7v).*

49

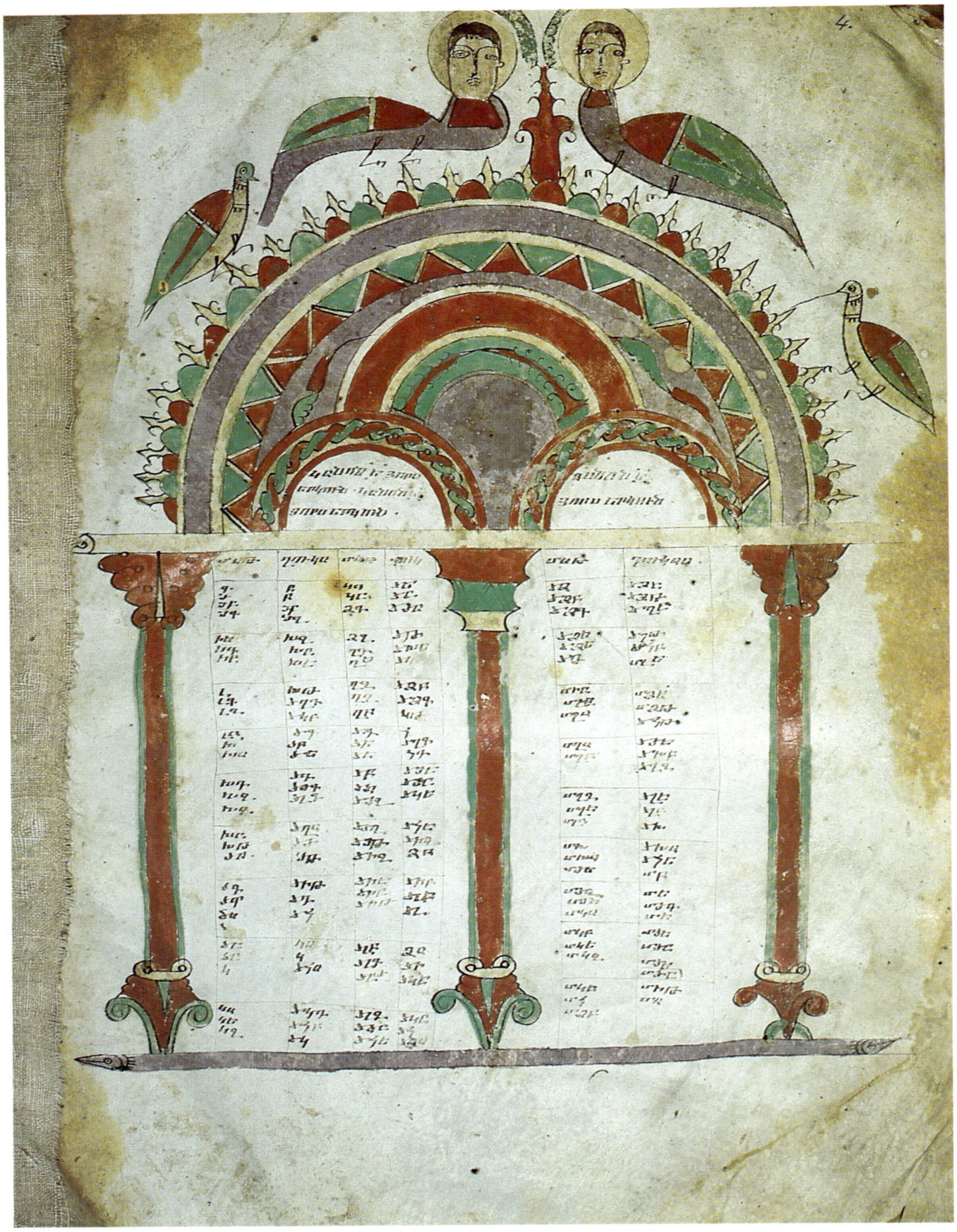

Figure 44: *Sermon on the Mount (Mt. 5:1ff), from the King Gagik Gospel of the middle of the eleventh century (ms. 2556, fol. 21v).*

Figure 45: *The Risen Christ appears to the Apostles in Galilee (Mt. 28:16–18), from the Gagik Gospel (ms. 2556, fol. 134v).*

Figure 46: *The last two Temptations of Christ by Satan, according to Luke 4, in the Gagik Gospel. On the left is a throne indicating the kingdoms of the world, which Christ refused to accept from Satan; and on the right Christ is refusing to throw himself off the pinnacle of the Temple (ms. 2556, fol. 244v).*

44

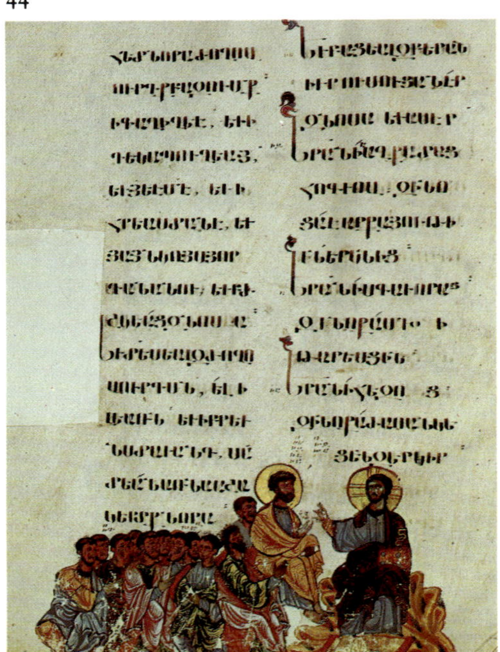

45

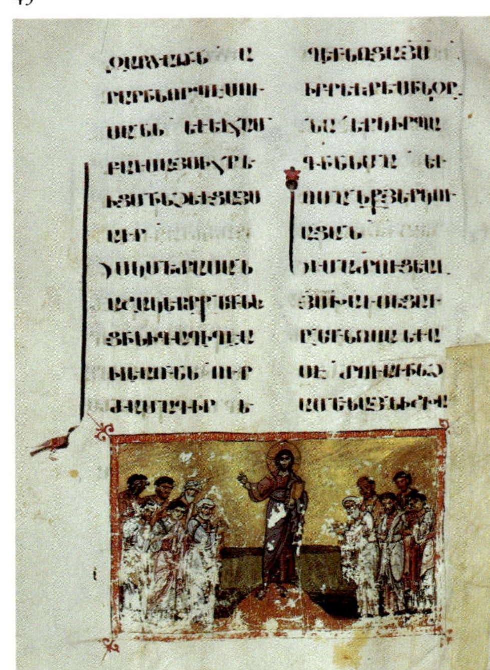

46

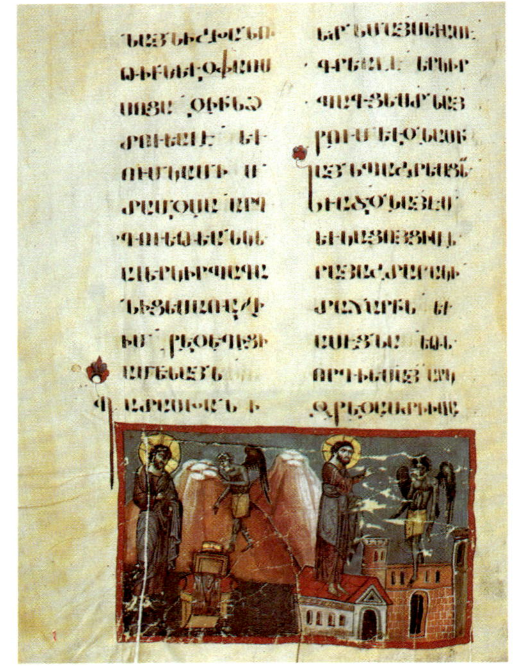

50

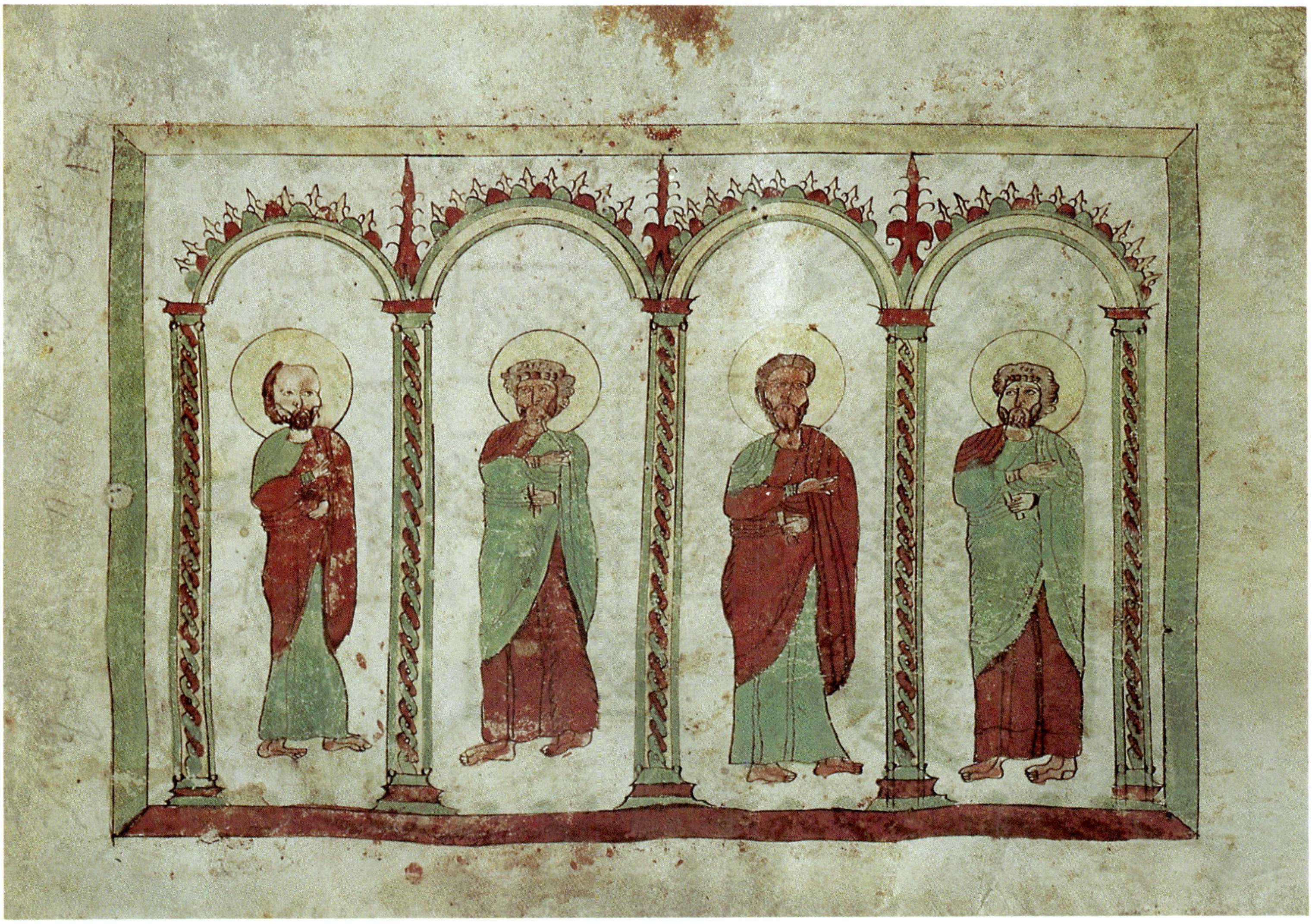

51

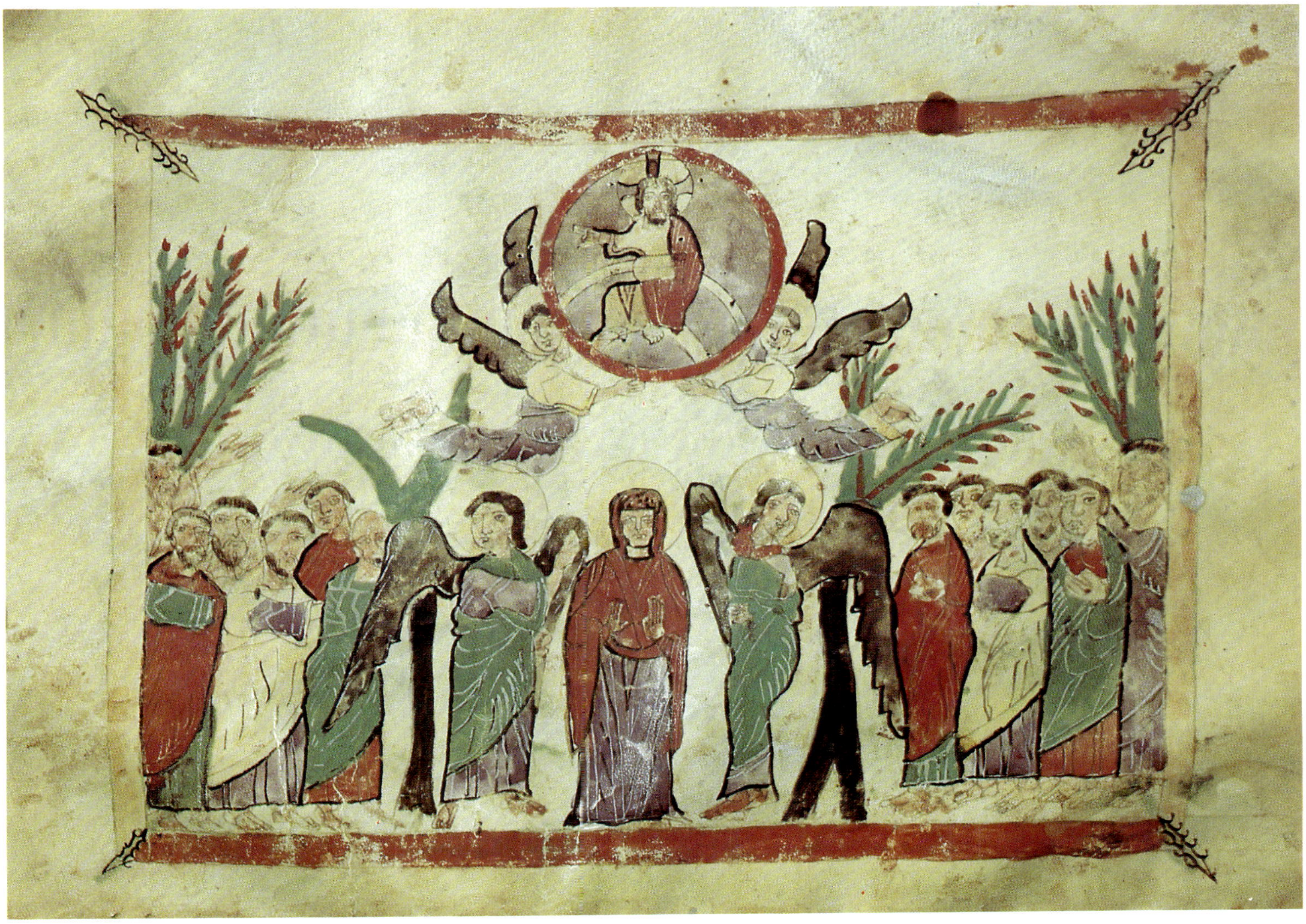

6. *The Eleventh Century Melitene Group*

This group consists of ten manuscripts, seven of which are dated. Nine of these were studied and listed by Sirarpie Der Nersessian.[39] The special features of this group are characterized by the choice, program, and type of the illustrations, as well as by the iconography, technique, composition, and style. They all originate from a similar prototype, which was available in the first half of the eleventh century in one school, possibly in or around Melitene, on the border between Cappadocia and Armenia. The Gospel in Jerusalem, which was copied by the priest Samuel in 1041,[40] and that in the Matenadaran of 1057[41] have the most extensive cycle in the group, and will therefore be used to establish the extent of the model cycle.

Each book begins with the letter of Eusebius to Carpianus,[42] and continues with the canon tables framed by arcades, decorated with geometrical and floral motifs, and crowned by birds[43] *fig.49*. These are followed by a series of full-page, framed scenes from the life of Christ, starting with the Annunciation to the Virgin and ending with the Ascension of Christ.[44] This is followed by the Four Evangelists *fig.50* and a decorated cross.[45] Each book of the Gospel has a decorative headpiece. Whereas the letter of Eusebius, the canon tables, and the cross extend across the width of the page, the artist painted the narrative illustrations and the Evangelists' portraits sideways on the page, with the heads to the outer margin. This peculiar manner, common to the entire group, makes it necessary to turn the manuscript round twice on each opening in order to understand it.

The illustrations for the cycle of the life of Christ vary from one manuscript to another.[46] It seems that every artist could choose the episodes he wanted to illustrate.[47] The wider cycle of episodes depicted in the 1041 Jerusalem Gospels corresponds only partly to the cycle of the Twelve Feasts of the Byzantine church.[48] Similar scenes are the Transfiguration and the Raising of Lazarus *fig.51* depicted in one panel and the Ascension of Christ *fig.52*. Two scenes are missing from the 1041 Jerusalem Gospel: the Women meeting the Risen Christ and Pentecost. The Women at the Empty Tomb with the Risen Christ appear in the 1038 Gospels at the Matenadaran[49], and Pentecost appears in the Shukhr Khandara Gospel of 1064 *fig.55*.[50]

Byzantine icons of the Twelve Feasts may have helped to determine the choice of episodes from the life of Christ in this group of manuscripts, but they were not the only source, since the cycles of the Melitene group go beyond the Twelve Feasts; for instance, the Gospel of 1041 has the Last Supper *fig.53*,[51] the Betrayal of Christ by Judas on fol. 9,[52] and the Deposition and the Entombment of Christ on fol. 9v.[53]

The relation of the cycle of some of the manuscripts in this group to the cycle of the Twelve Feasts of the Greek Church was discussed by T.A. Izmailova,[54] who maintains that the Melitene cycle is liturgical, not narrative in nature, and was adapted from the Cappadocian cave church cycles. Indeed, the ninth and tenth century wall-paintings in the Cappadocian churches have influenced the iconography of many scenes in our group.[55]

The similar iconography in the Melitene manuscripts and the Cappadocian churches is best exemplified in the Annunciation, Visitation, Baptism, Raising of Lazarus, Last Supper, and the Harrowing of Hell. In the Annunciation, both angel and Virgin are standing, the latter at times under an aedicule.[56] In the Visitation of Mary to Elizabeth, a maiden is standing on the threshold at the side, holding a curtain.[57] In the Baptism, the naked Christ is covered by a wave of water reaching up to his shoulders and is flanked by the Baptist and an adoring angel, with the hand of God sending down the Holy Spirit as a dove.[58] The Raising of Lazarus *fig.51* is depicted with Christ accompanied by Thomas, with both Mary and Martha kneeling, Lazarus in a shroud standing within an edifice, and an attendant covering his nose because of the stench.[59] In the Last Supper, the table is semi-circular, set with a large dish containing a fish, with Christ reclining on the left, and Judas not always distinguishable *fig.53*;[60] and in the Harrowing of Hell, Christ is within an aureole, stretching his hand out towards Adam and Eve, while David and Solomon, crowned, appear from behind a wall-like sarcophagus.[61] Nevertheless, some of the Cappadocian elements which are found in the Melitene group of manuscripts, are Early Christian in origin.[62]

Other iconographical elements in the Melitene group are Constantinopolitan, post-iconoclastic in origin, since they do not appear in the early Cappadocian cave churches. They could, therefore, stem directly from Constantinopolitan narrative cycles. To this group belong the scenes of the Nativity and the Magi, the Presentation in the Temple and the Transfiguration, the Entry into Jerusalem and the Betrayal, the Crucifixion, the Deposition, the Entombment, and the Descent into Hell.[63] Each of these scenes has a distinctive detail of post-iconoclastic Byzantine iconography, which include the round aureole encircling Christ, Moses, and Elijah in the Transfiguration *fig.51*; and the coupling of Mary with Longinus on the left of the picture of the Crucifixion with John and Stephaton on the right *fig.54*.

There are some other iconographical components in the Melitene group, which originate from Syria, and do not appear in Byzantine art of the eleventh century. For instance, the picture of the Descent of the Holy Spirit upon the Apostles at Pentecost (Acts 2:1–11), depicted in the Shukhr Khandara Gospel of 1064 *fig.58*, has all the Apostles standing in line, without the strangers in whose tongues the Apostles spoke, who are usually depicted in Byzantine art. The depiction of Pentecost resembles to some extent that in a Syriac Gospel of the twelfth or thirteenth century[65].

Figure 52: *The Ascension of Christ, from the Gospel of 1041 (ms. 3624, fol. 10v).*

Figure 53: *The Last Supper, from the Gospel of 1041 (ms. 3624, fol. 8v).*

52

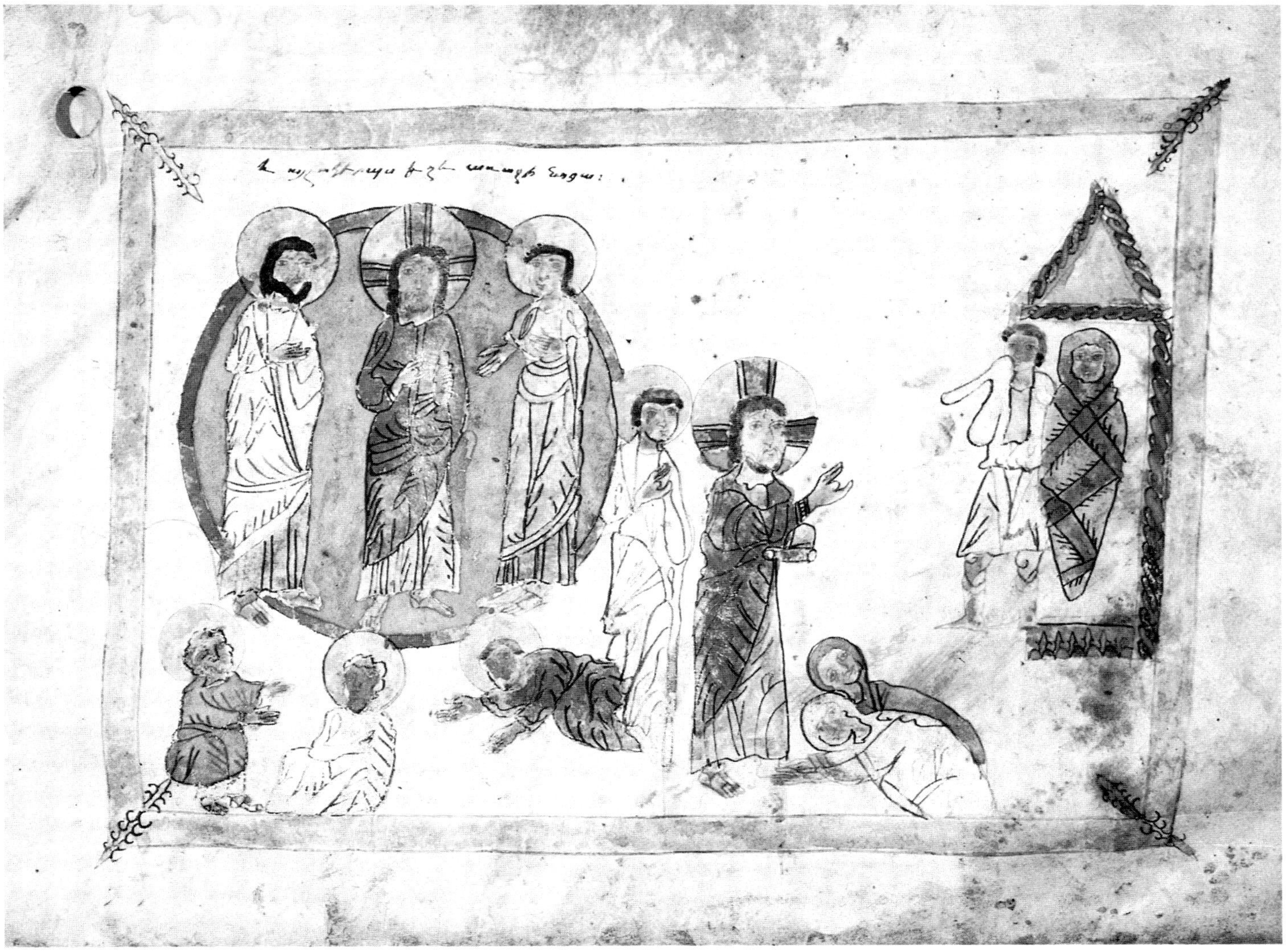

53

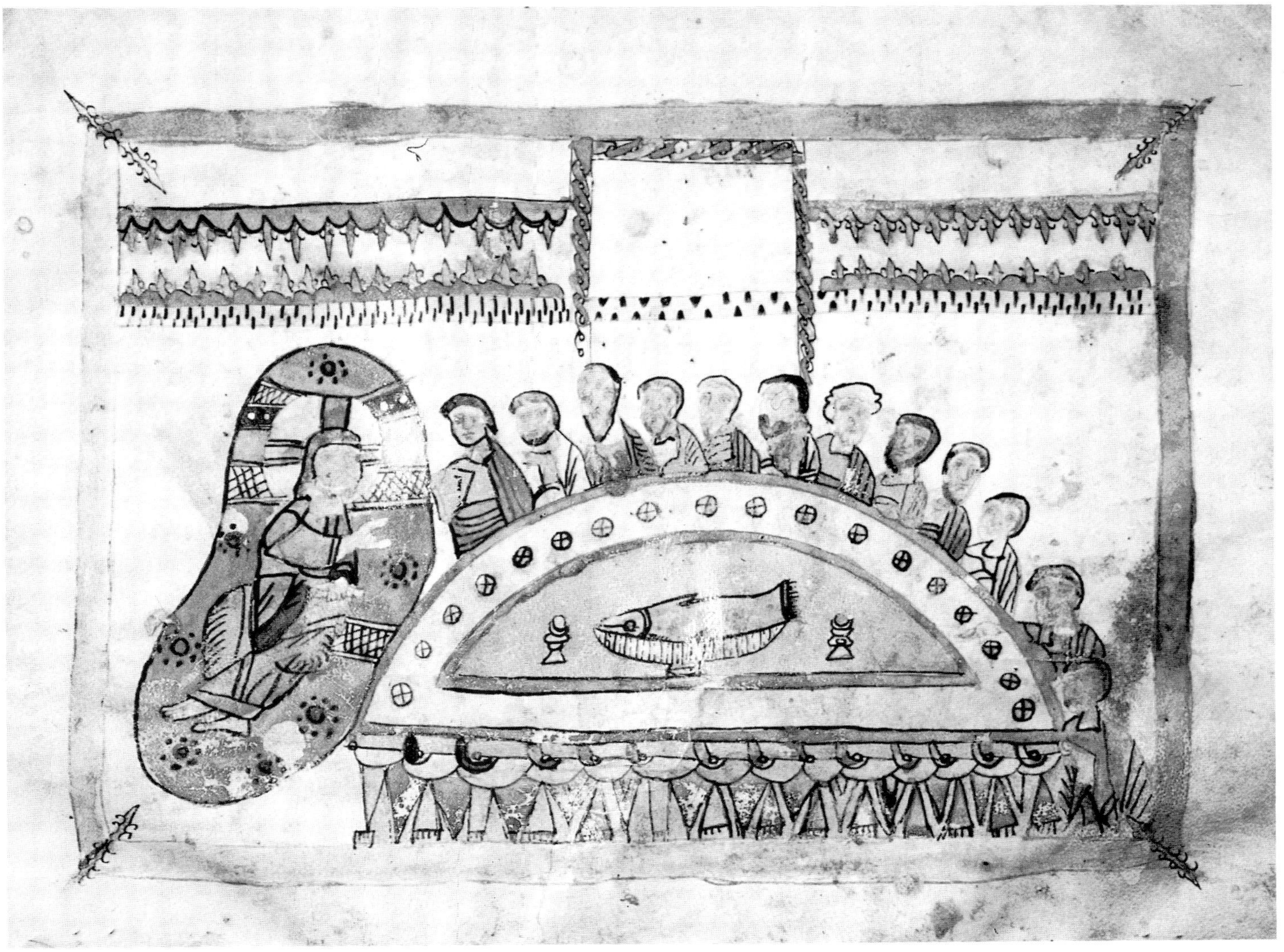

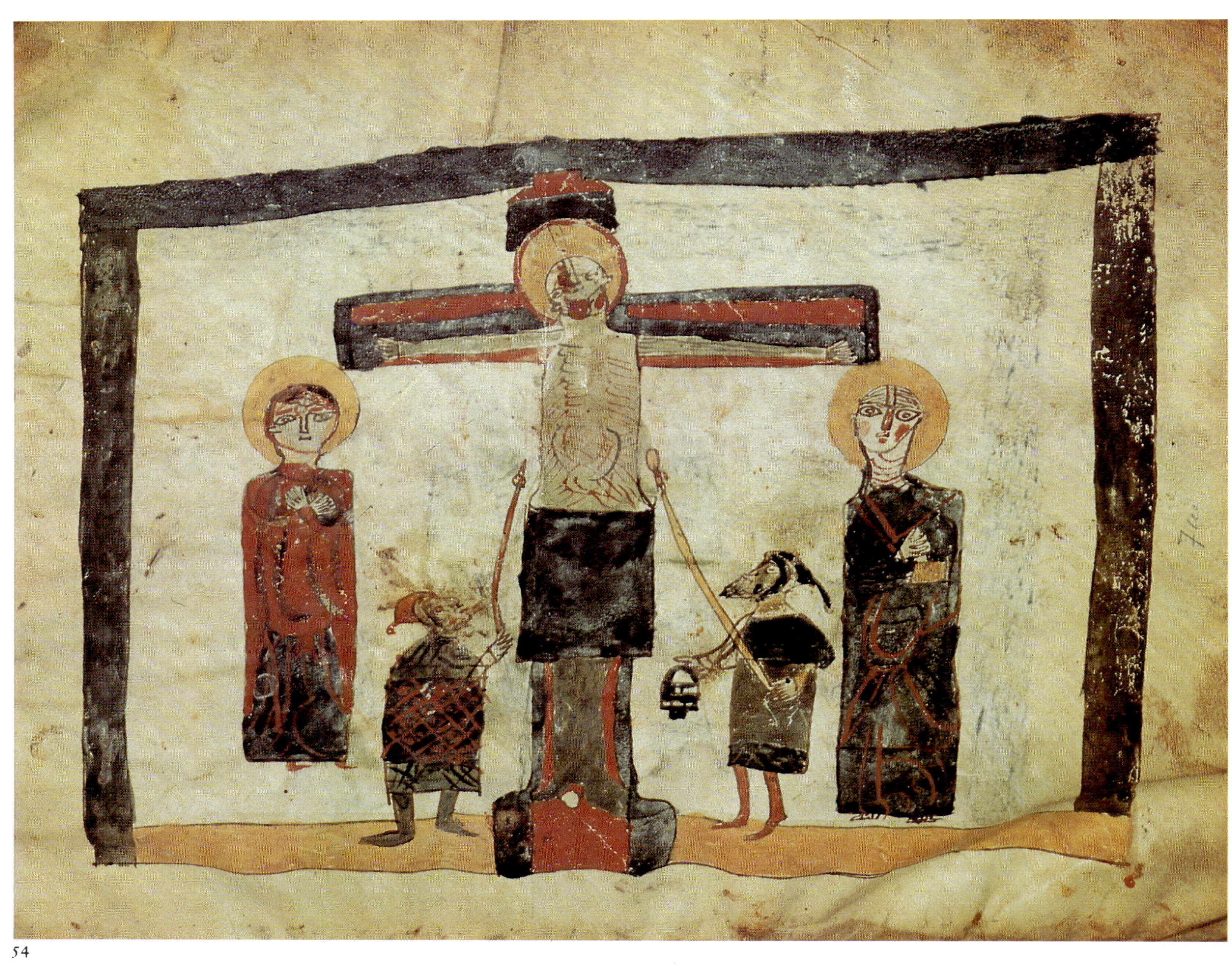

54

Figure 54: *The Crucifixion of Christ, from the Shukhr Khandara Gospel, written in the Taurus Mountains in 1064 (ms. 1924, fol. 7).*

Figure 55: *The Descent of the Holy Ghost to the Apostles at Pentecost, from the Shukhr Khandara Gospel of 1064 (ms. 1924, fol. 6v).*

Figure 56: *The Four Evangelists, from the Shukhr Khandara Gospel of 1064 (ms. 1924, fol. 6).*

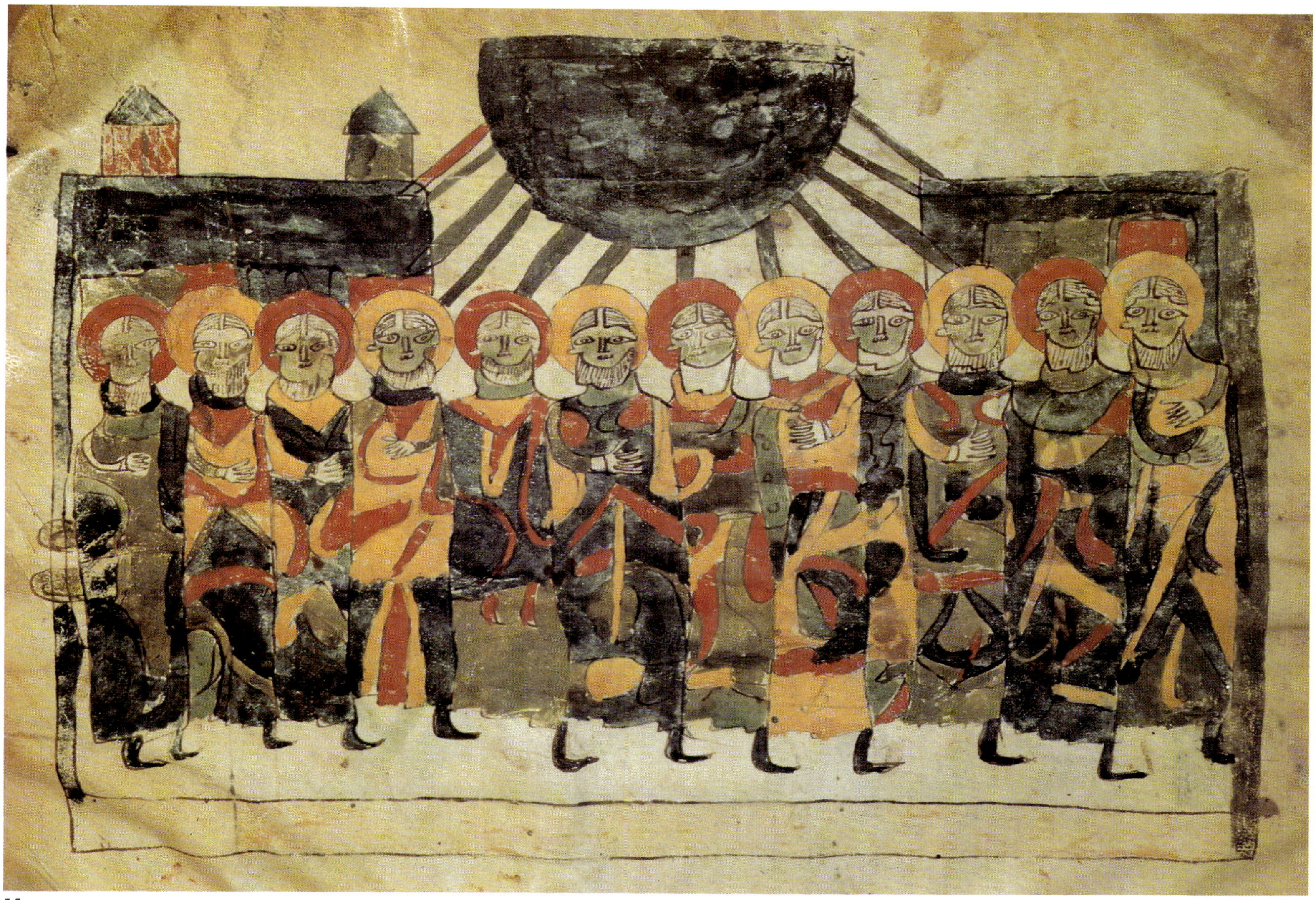

55

56

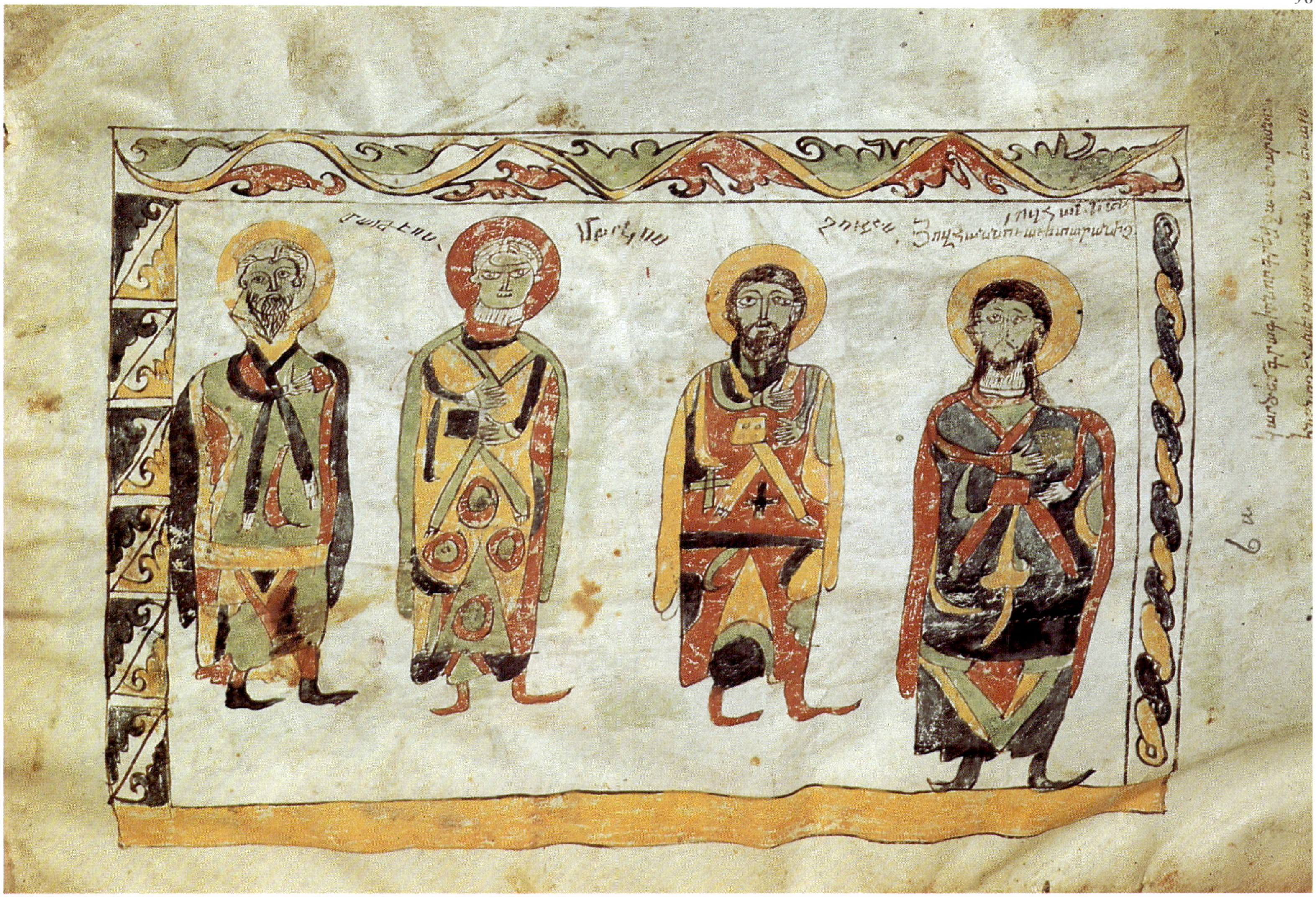

It is rather difficult to state categorically whether the eastern elements of the Christological cycle of the Melitene group are derived direct from Syriac sources or via Cappadocian monuments. It would be more plausible to assume that the Armenian, like the Syriac and Cappadocian, iconography, depended on Early Christian representations. This may explain how these three provincial schools have similar, unconventional iconography. However, to reach definite conclusions, further study is necessary.

The technique and style of the Melitene group is probably also of eastern origin. The scenes and single figures are drawn and painted on the parchment background, in a style similar to some of the early Cappadocian cave church paintings.[66] Outlined forms filled with single colors, hardly modeled at all, are part of the decorative technique and style of this group. The expressive heads and large eyes, at times the only outstanding features in the individual body, are common to many eastern schools from Coptic through Syriac to Cappadocian and Armenian art.

Melitene was regarded as an Armenian town during the eleventh century. After its capture by the Byzantines from the Arabs in 934, the Armenians inhabited the entire area east and west of the Euphrates, including Cilicia, Cappadocia, and Armenia Minor.[67] Four of the manuscripts in our group certainly belong to one atelier. These are the Gospels of 1041, 1045, and 1057 and the undated Matenadaran No. 974. Since the Gospel of 1057 is stated to have been copied at Melitene, there is good reason to attribute at least these four manuscripts to this provenance.[68] Because of its original iconography and composition, the Gospel of 1038 may belong to an atelier better acquainted with varied Byzantine sources.

The Jerusalem Gospel of 1064 was copied in the Monastery of Shukhr Khandara *fig.56* in the Taurus mountains south-west of Melitene. In this area many monasteries were engaged in artistic activity, which may have included the production of illuminated manuscripts. Since this Gospel, as well as the tenth-century Gospel Matenadaran 7739 and the Freer Gallery Gospel,[69] differ from the main Melitene group both in iconography and style, while preserving some Syriac rather than Cappadocian elements, these manuscripts can be grouped together. However, the Shukhr Khandara Gospel is more stylized than the other two, and possibly belongs to a different atelier, on the border of the Cilician region. The dispersion of the Armenians during the tenth century made possible the development of Armenian communities, monasteries, and culture during the eleventh and twelfth centuries. Armenian princes and kings, who were expelled from their home states when the Byzantines advanced in the eleventh century, established new principalities in the west. These included the new haven of Armenian culture, the Kingdom of Cilicia.

Chapter Three: Illuminated Manuscripts in the Kingdom of Cilicia

1. The Armenian Kingdom of Cilicia in the Twelfth Century

The Armenian kingdom of Cilicia became a haven for the dispersed Armenian nation after the Byzantine and Seljuk conquest of Greater Armenia in the third quarter of the eleventh century. The few Armenian communities that already existed in Cilicia as early as the tenth century facilitated the integration of their countrymen in the eleventh century. Former kings and princes became rulers of small states and baronies under the auspices of the Byzantine emperors. For Byzantium, the professional Armenian fighters served as a buffer against the attacking Arabs and Seljuks, and the Armenian rulers were rewarded with independence in exchange. There were basically two Armenian families who ruled large areas of Cilicia: the Hethumides, who dominated Western Cilicia with their capital in Lampron, and were most loyal to the Byzantine state[1]; and the Rubenides, their rivals, who reigned over the Eastern regions, with their principal city at Vahka. The latter's ambition was to establish a large, independent Armenian state, free of any Byzantine ties, which would encompass the whole of Cilicia. The arrival of the Crusaders helped the Rubenides to a certain extent in their attempt to gain control over all of Cilicia against the Byzantine regime. The Rubenides' first attempt to gain Cilicia culminated in the efforts of Lord Leo (1129–1137), who managed to occupy some of its most important cities. Soon afterwards, however, the Byzantine emperor, Johannes Comnenus, checked the campaign and led Leo, his wife, and two sons into captivity in Constantinople. But Thoros, Leo's younger son, managed to escape and within a few years established a new Armenian state in Cilicia. By playing off the Latins, the Moslems, and the Greeks against each other, both politically and militarily, and after being taken by surprise by the Byzantine army in 1158, he finally succeeded in becoming an independent ruler, Thoros II, under Byzantine suzerainty. The Armenian barony of Cilicia gradually expanded during the reigns of his successors, Ruben II (1175–1187) and his brother, Leo I (1187–1219). The latter cultivated relations with the Latin West to the uttermost, thereby strengthening his domestic power. In 1198, in the cathedral of Tarsus, the Armenian Catholicos, Gregory VI Abirad, crowned him King Leo I of Cilicia.

Until the fall of the capital, Sis, in 1375 and the captivity of the last Armenian king of Cilicia, Leo V, who fell into the hands of the Moslem ruler of Egypt, Armenian Cilicia was a power to be reckoned with in the political melting-pot of the Near East. The kingdom occupied a major strategic position between the Byzantine Empire and the Moslem Caliphates. With Western Europe's increasing interest in the East since the Crusaders and the appearance of the Mongols during the thirteenth century, Cilicia became an important crossroads. Maintaining good relations with Armenian Cilicia was essential for the Latin West, since Leo I was crowned after Crusader Jerusalem fell to Saladin in 1187. Through well-planned marriages, Leo I secured his relations with the Latin kingdom of Jerusalem as well as with the kings of Cyprus, and even with the rival Hethumide lords and the Byzantine Emperor of Nicaea. He also granted rights to the military orders of the Hospitalers and the Teutonic Knights, as well as to the merchants of Venice, Pisa, and Genoa. His only enemies were the Fatimids and the Seljuks. It is not surprising that Leo I and the kings who succeeded him were politically orientated towards the West. These ties resulted in the westernization of culture and even religion, to the extent that attempts were made to bring the Armenian Church under papal jurisdiction.

2. The Theodore Gospel and the Schools of Hromkla and Skevra

The art of Armenian Cilicia during the long reign of Leo II shows the gradual infiltration of Western European influence although it is still based on Eastern Byzantine elements. For instance, the scheme of decoration of a Gospel book, which differs from that used by the Armenians in the eleventh century, depends on new Byzantine programs. As already mentioned, the decoration program of a Gospel from the Melitene group was based on a full-page Christological cycle, preceded by the canon tables and followed by the four standing Evangelists and a decorated monumental cross. By contrast, in the eleventh century Byzantine Gospel books and lectionaries developed a system of decoration which depicts many Christological scenes in close relation to their text.[2] The Gospel of King Gagik of Kars, mentioned above, is an example of this Byzantine system of Gospel decoration, already in eleventh century Armenia. This early example was frequently followed by subsequent Armenian artists, who regarded it from the middle of the century as a model both for the text and the illumination.

One of these twelfth century illuminated Armenian manuscripts of this Byzantine type in the library of St. Thoros in Jerusalem is the Theodore Gospel, called after Theodore, the monk who painted the manuscript.[3] The patron, who dedicated it "to Christ", was Matthew, a monk whose portrait is preserved at the end of the manuscript *fig.57*. The seated Christ, holding an open book has his name in Greek letters, ĪC X̄P̄ above him. He is blessing the donor, Matthew, who holds a beautifully bound volume. Both figures are in Byzantine style, whereas the inscriptions have traditional Armenian formulae of dedication. The inscription on Christ's open book is based on Matthew 19:21, which implies that dedicating the Gospel to God is like giving one's entire fortune to the poor, and thereby one obtains a place in the Kingdom of Heaven.[4]

The decorative program of the Theodore Gospel is common to Byzantine and Armenian illumination of the twelfth century. It starts with the letter from Eusebius to Carpianus and the Eusebian canon tables, all under decorated arches. The portraits of the four Evangelists are painted in full-page panels, in their usual Byzantine posture, before the text of their Gospels. Each of the first three is seated, while St. John is standing, and dictating the Gospel to Prochoros, his scribe *fig.58*. Opposite each Evangelist's portrait is a decorative page with the opening verses of his Gospel. For example, the opening page of St. Luke's Gospel *fig.59* contains a decorated panel as headpiece with the initial *k'ē* (= k') surrounded by thin foliage scrolls which incorporate an ox, the symbol of St. Luke. In the outer margin and across the text column is a "living cross", depicted as a plant growing out of a foliage interlace.

Only one full page of Christological scenes was provided for the Theodore Gospel *fig.60*. It shows the two Marys meeting the angel at the empty tomb, and the risen Christ appearing to them (Mt. 28:1–10). The picture appears next to the text in St. Matthew which it illustrates and this may signify that the copyists used as a model a manuscript whose illustrations, framed in panels, were placed within the text columns. Our artist, Theodore, may have combined the two scenes in one page, although he left each scene framed in its own panel. The iconography of the two scenes, especially the two Marys prostrating themselves on either side of Christ, is mainly Byzantine, its sources dating back to the ninth century.[5] The fashion of placing Christological cycles together on full pages was already prevalent in Byzantium in the ninth century and influenced Armenian illumination almost immediately.[6]

Although not many survived, those Armenian Gospel books which are extant from the second half of the twelfth century in Cilicia have a similar decoration program. The place of execution of the ten most important Cilician Gospel books is either Hromkla or Skevra, between 1166 and 1197.[7] Eight of them were attributed by Der Nersessian to the school of Hromkla. The plan of decoration of all ten Gospel books must have been similar, although not all the components are extant. They all had full-page, arcaded Eusebian letters and canon tables, portraits of the Evangelists, sometimes accompanied by their symbols, some full-page panels with Christological scenes accompanying the text, and additional text illustrations in the margins. In addition, three, that of 1166, the Narek of 1173, and the Theodore Gospel, have the portrait of a suppliant donor before Christ.

The four undated manuscripts are related in iconography and motifs, and can be grouped together. Besides the Theodore Gospel, there are two in the San Lazzaro Monastery in Venice[8] and one in the Freer Gallery of Art in Washington.[9] Der Nersessian attributed this sub-group to Hromkla because of similar iconographical elements and because of a Syriac Gospel book from Hromkla with a similar style to the Freer Gospel.[10] All have similar canonical tables, portraits of the Evangelists, opening pages with a headpiece, and a "living cross". Most of their Gospel initials are adorned with delicate scrolls *fig.59*, and at times next to them with a full-figure winged Evangelist's symbol holding a book. This combination of an Evangelist's symbol and initial can be found sporadically in earlier Armenian illumination from Cilicia as in a Gospel book of 1113 in Tübingen University Library,[11] and another undated Gospel of the early twelfth century in the Matenadaran.[12] It also exists as a zoomorphic initial in an Armenian Gospel from Sebastia of 1066.[13] All three cases are isolated examples in Armenian schools, and their direct origin is rather obscure. The origin of this combination can hardly be Byzantine, since Evangelists' symbols appear very rarely in Byzantine illuminated Gospels before the eleventh century.[14] When they do appear, they are of western origin, related to the Evangelists' portraits and not to their initials.[15] From Early Christian times the symbols accompany the Evangelists in western illuminated Gospels, as half or full figures in the same panel.[16] Some Evangelists' symbols do appear in Early Christian Gospels, at the beginning of the texts.[17] Two Italian Gospels which have them are the St. Augustine of the sixth century, and the Valerianus of the early seventh century.[18] In the St. Augustine Gospel the lion of St. Mark is between the text columns, whereas in the Valerianus Gospel only the eagle of St. John is directly connected with its initial, and it is not holding a book. In the eighth century insular St. Cuthbert Gospel the symbol of St. John is placed next to its initial, holding a book.[19] This representation is similar to the type in the Armenian Theodore Gospel in Jerusalem, but the similarity does not mean that there is a direct relationship between the St. Cuthbert Gospel and Armenian manuscripts. It would, however, imply that the appearance of the Evangelist's symbol next to its initial in Armen an as well as in Byzantine art is of immediate origin, for there could hardly have been two identical inventions by coincidence. This juxtaposition became a popular feature in Armenian manuscript illumination, especially at the end of the twelfth century.

As in the Theodore Gospel, figurative full-page illustrations also appear in the other manuscripts of the Hromkla-Skevra group. The Christological illustrations in these manuscripts are not only on full pages: those of the Venice manuscripts 141 and 888 have also small panels within the text columns, and are closely attached to the text they illustrate.[21] Theodore and the artist of the Freer Gospel favored the full-page system, possibly because of its monumentality.

Of the four undated manuscripts forming this sub-group, the miniatures in the Theodore Gospel appear more monumental, with their figures filling the entire height of the panel. Their heavy, solemn figures, with large round faces, thick outlines and highlights, emphasizing the entire body, and the folds of drapery, have a quality characteristic of twelfth century Byzantine art of provincial origin. The monumentality of the figures in the Theodore Gospel may indicate that Theodore had another inspirational source. For the enthroned Christ with Greek initials, Theodore must have seen a large Byzantine wall mosaic of Christos Pantocrator. Using this scale, the artist painted the other scenes in a similar monumental manner. Apart from this monumentality, Theodore seems closer to the small figures of the Narek of 1173 than to the thin, elongated figures in the Hethum Gospel of 1193, from Skevra, now in Venice.[22] This may be a further indication of its origin in Hromkla, and possibly also of a date closer to the 1170s rather than the 1190s.[23]

59

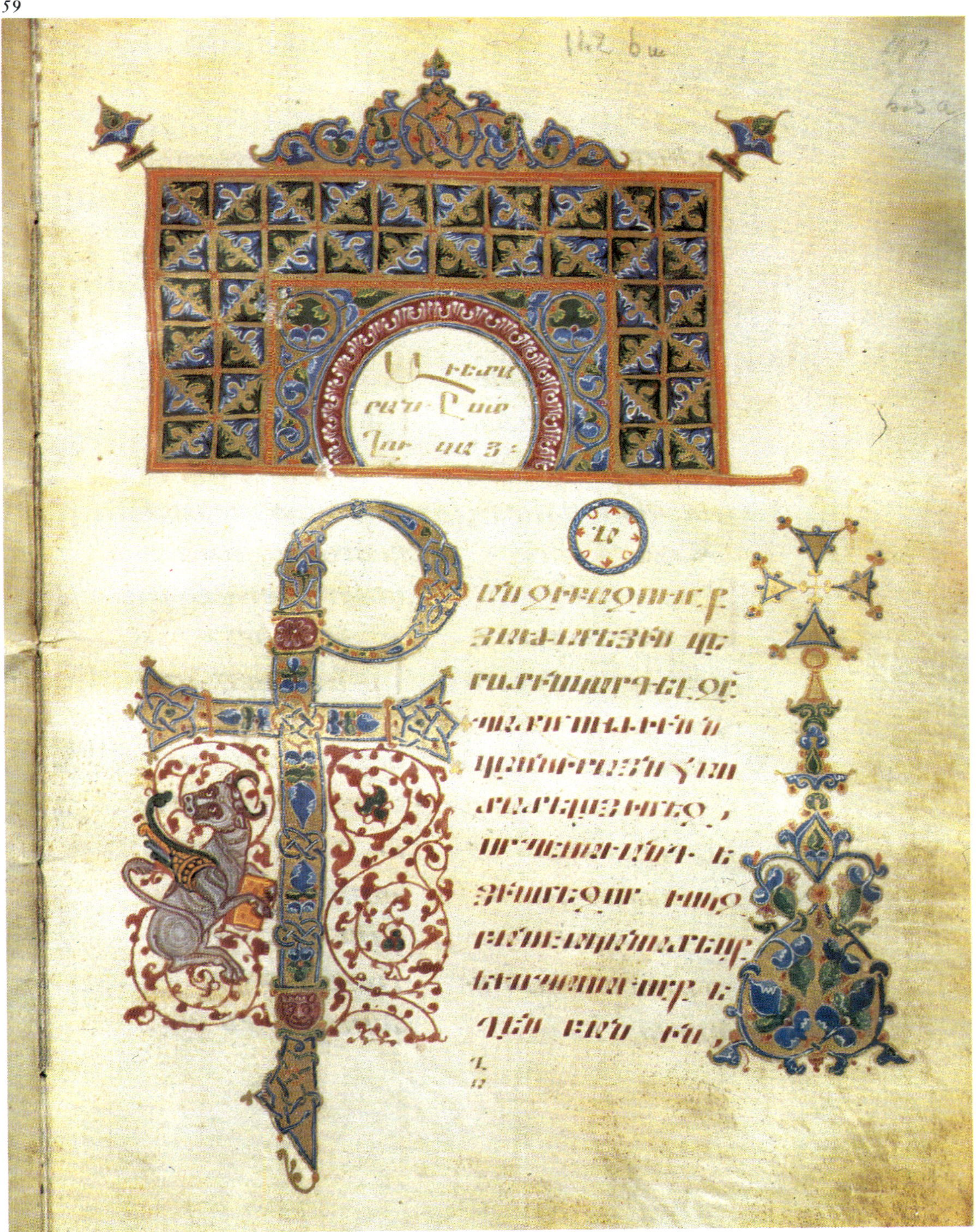

Figure 59: *Decorative opening page of the Gospel of St. Luke, including a headpiece, an initial with an ox as the Evangelist's symbol, and a living cross, from the Theodore Gospel (ms. 1796, fol. 142 bis).*

Figure 57: *The monk Matthew presenting a Gospel to Christ, from the Theodore Gospel of the late twelfth century. The inscription, based on Matthew 19:21, infers that this act is like giving one's entire fortune to the poor (ms. 1796, fol. 288v).*

Figure 58: *St. John receiving inspiration from the hand of God while dictating his Gospel to his scribe Prochoros, from the Theodore Gospel (ms. 1796, fol. 225v).*

57

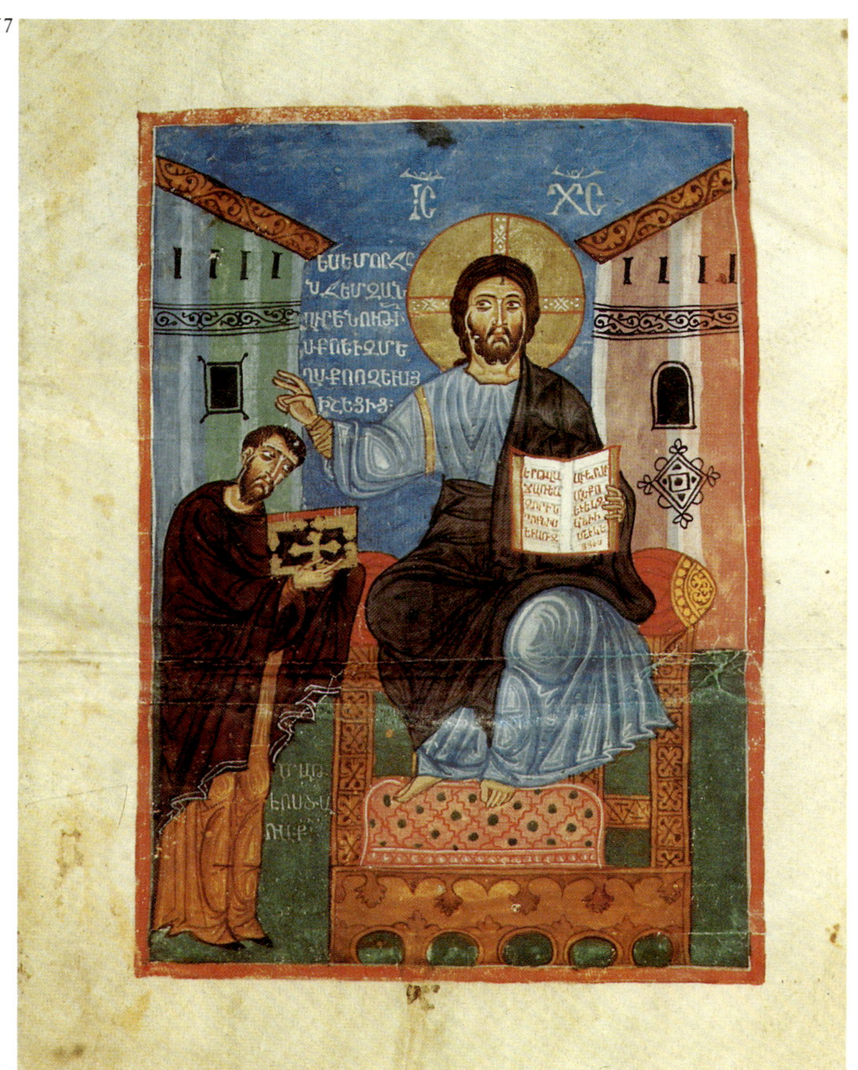

58

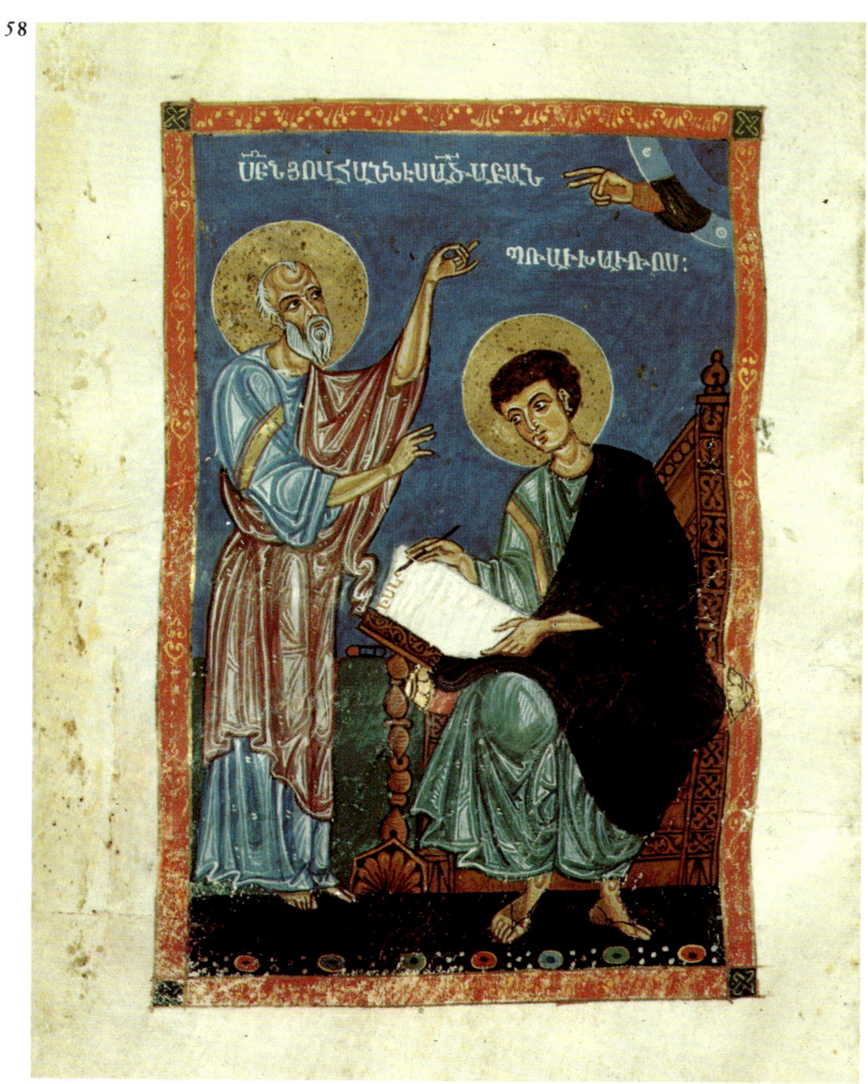

60

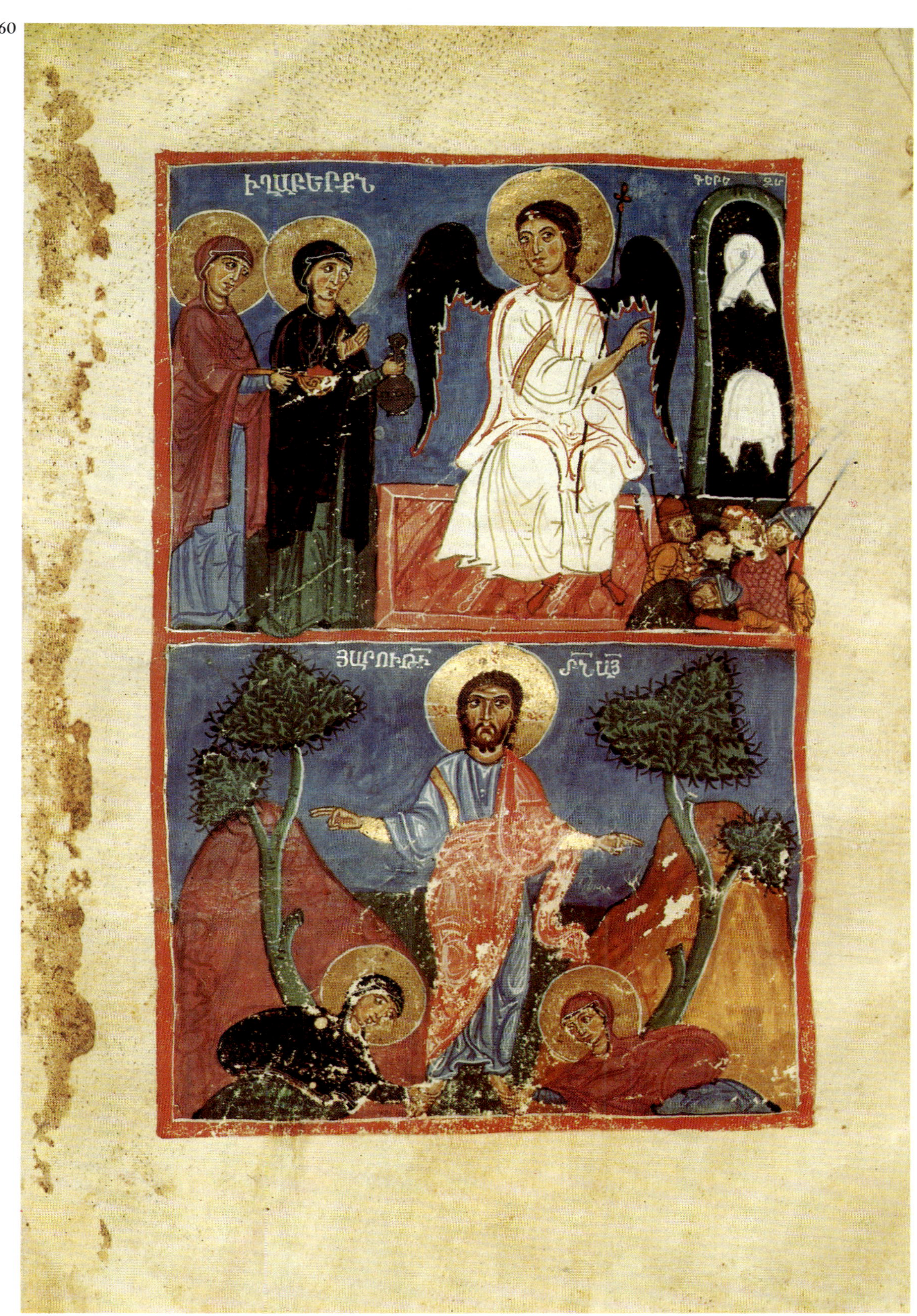

Figure 60: *The two Marys meeting the angel at the empty tomb, and the Risen Christ appearing to them (Mt. 28:1–10), from the Theodore Gospel (ms. 1796, fol. 88v).*

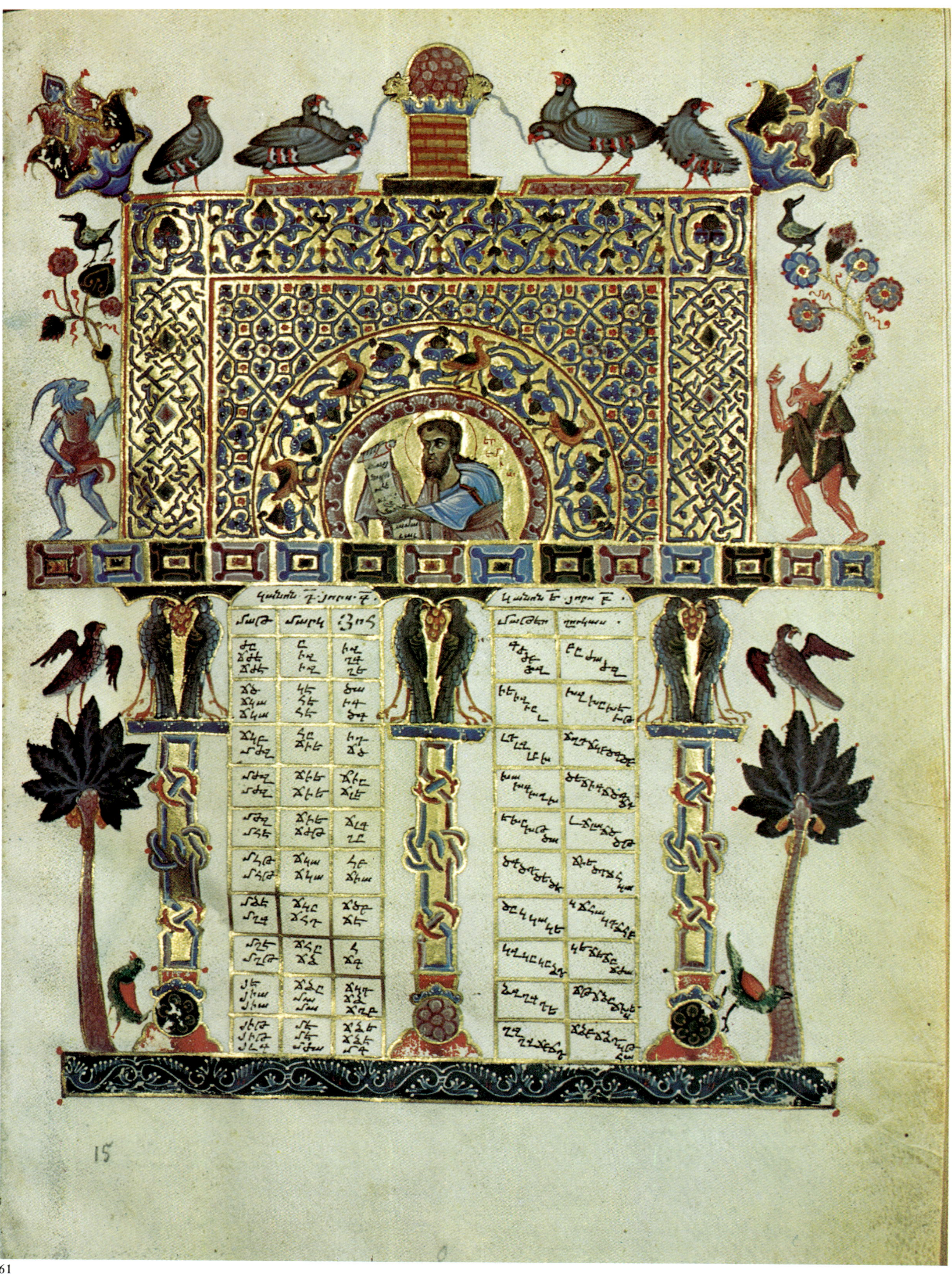

61

Chapter Four: Thirteenth Century Illuminated Manuscripts in Cilicia

63

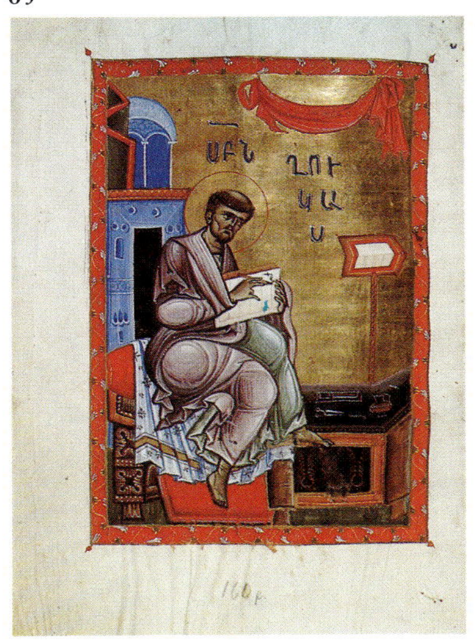

Figure 61: *Fourth and fifth canon tables, with portrait bust of Jeremiah, from the Second Constantine Gospel by Thoros Roslin, Hromkla, 1260 (ms. 251, fol. 8).*

Figure 63: *Portrait of St. Luke from the Second Constantine Gospel by Thoros Roslin (ms. 251, fol. 160v).*

1. Armenian Cilicia in the Thirteenth Century

The Armenian kingdom of Cilicia flourished throughout the thirteenth century, and centers like Hromkla, Sis, or Lampron were inhabited by rich princes, clergy, and courtiers who were patrons of art, literature, music, and philosophy. Being the largest kingdom between the Byzantine and Moslem empires, the Latin kingdom of Jerusalem in Acre, and Europe, it acquired knowledge, culture, and objects from the west as well as from the east – even from the Far East.

King Hethum I (1226–1269) was the main instigator of the growing interest in art. A son of the Hethumide Lord of Lampron, Constantine, Hethum gained the throne through his marriage to Zabel, the heiress of the Rubenid Leo I, founder of the Cilician kingdom.[1] Their joint rule was powerful, combining the forces of the Rubenid and Hethumide families and their countries. Their main enemies were still the Moslem Ayubid sultans of Egypt, but they managed to hold out against them, mainly through allegiance to the Mongol Khans of Karakorum.

By the end of the thirteenth century, when the power of the Mongols became weaker, and long after Hethum I was dead, the Moslems under the leadership of Baybars succeeded in conquering large parts of Cilicia, including Hromkla, the seat of the Catholicos, in 1292. The decline from then onwards was gradual and lasted almost a hundred years. Hethum II renewed the alliance with the Mongols, who in the meantime were converted to Islam, but this treaty did not stop the progress of the Egyptian Mamelukes, and in 1332 the important seaport of Ayas was destroyed. In despair Hethum II turned to the Latin kingdoms for help, giving rise to an internal conflict in Cilicia on political and religious grounds. The strong pro-Latin party was ready to submit to the Roman Catholic Church, and the Franciscan missionaries who roamed Cilicia managed to persuade Hethum II to don a Franciscan habit. When in 1342 there was no male heir to the throne, it passed to Guy de Lusignan, son of Amalric, King of Cyprus, and an Armenian princess; and when Guy was killed two years later, the throne remained in the Lusignan family until the fall of Sis into the hands of the Egyptians in 1375 and the capture of Leo V.

2. Thoros Roslin

The prosperous days of King Hethum I and the Catholicos Constantine I (1221–1267) form the setting for the appearance of a skilled and imaginative artist, Thoros Roslin. Thoros (the name is a diminutive of Theodoros) worked at Hromkla on the Euphrates during the third quarter of the thirteenth century, mainly on commissions from the Catholicos, and was deeply involved in the clerical life as well as in the political events and with the royal court. All the seven illuminated manuscripts which are known to have been painted by Thoros were dedicated to God by church dignitaries, kings, and princes. Thoros' first illuminated Zeytoun Gospel[2] of 1256 and his second Gospel of 1260[3] were commissioned by the Catholicos Constantine. His third Gospel[4] was ordered in 1262 by the priest Thoros, nephew of Constantine I. The fourth Gospel[5] was ordered by Prince Leo, later King Leo II, and Princess Keran in 1262 at Hromkla, and includes their portrait, while his fifth Gospel[6] of 1265 was for the noble Lady Keran, daughter of Constantine of Lampron and sister of King Hethum I. The only extant ritual book which Thoros painted, at Sis in 1266, was ordered by Bishop Vardan Nesepna.[7] His sixth and last Gospel was commissioned by the Catholicos Constantine I, and completed at Hromkla in 1268 after the latter's death, for Prince Hethum, son of King Leo II. This last manuscript, formerly in Jerusalem, was presented to His Holiness Vazkan I, the Catholicos of All the Armenians in Etchmiadzin, on the occasion of his visit to Jerusalem on June 28, 1975.[8]

During the thirteen years of his active life known to us (1256–1268), Thoros must have copied and illuminated more than the seven manuscripts signed by him. From the fact that in one year 1262 he completed the illumination of two magnificent manuscripts, it is evident that he must have worked very rapidly. Some of his manuscripts may have been lost during the political upheavals at the end of the century, which included the capture of Hromkla in 1292. There are a number of unsigned manuscripts ascribed to him, some of which may have lost their colophon. Der Nersessian attributes the unsigned Freer Gospel to his hand, as well as two other Gospel books in the Matenadaran.[9] Other works ascribed to Thoros obviously belong to a Cilician school, possibly to the next generation of artists at Hromkla, but not to the hand of Thoros himself.[10]

Figure 62: *Portrait of St. Mark, painted by Thoros Roslin in the Second Constantine Gospel (ms. 251, fol. 102v).*

Figure 64: *Portrait of St. Luke and the opening page of his Gospel, from the Leo and Keran Gospel of 1262 painted by Thoros Roslin at Hromkla (ms. 2660, fol. 140v–141).*

64

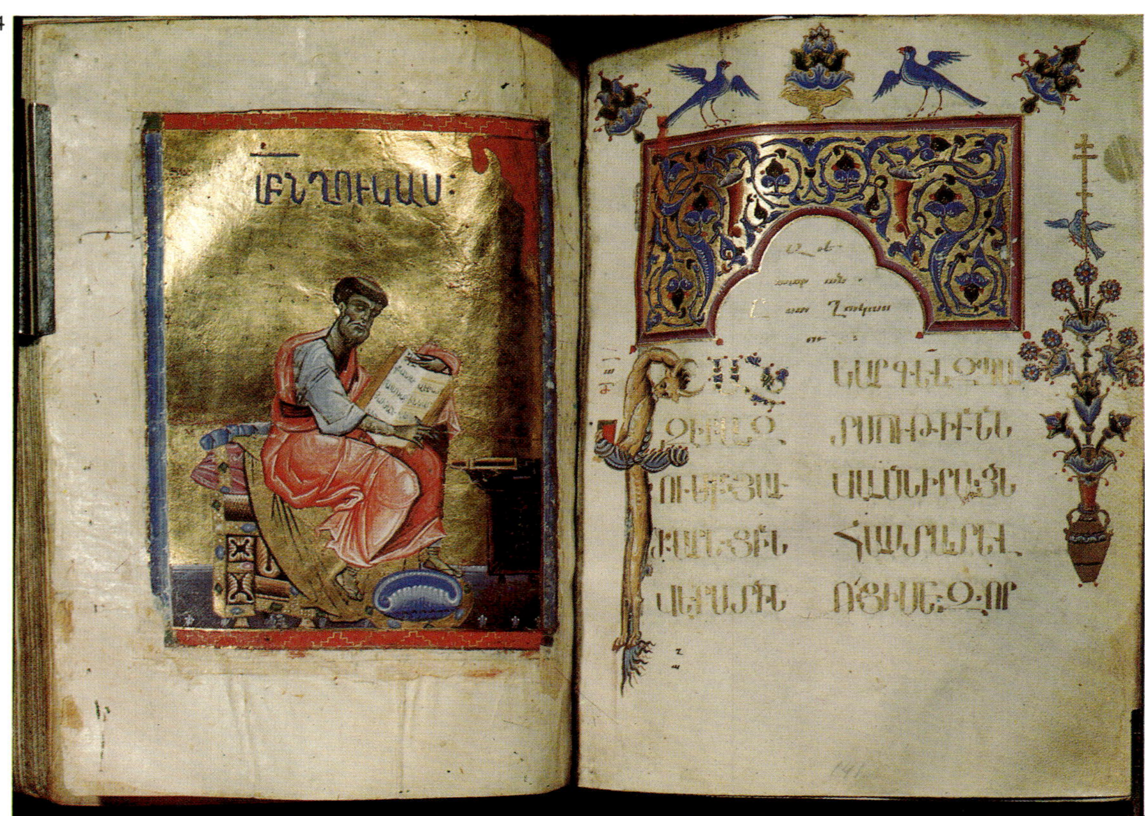

3. The School of Hromkla

From the first known manuscript which Thoros illuminated, the Zeytoun Gospel, he appears to have been a highly skilled artist who must have had a sound training in a well-established school in Hromkla. Indeed, there are a few illuminated manuscripts immediately preceding and contemporary with the work of Thoros, which point to the workshop where Thoros may have developed his skills as a scribe and painter. Besides Thoros Roslin, Der Nersessian counted three other scribe-illuminators who worked at Hromkla for Constantine I.[11] Two of them, Kirakos[12] and Yovhannes,[13] preceded Thoros in this work, and probably continued to copy and illuminate concurrently with him. The third, Kostadin, worked from 1263 until 1288.[14] These scribe-artists may have worked in one workshop, or at least in very close proximity to each other. They must have had access to similar models in order to use similar decoration programs, iconography, and detailed motifs, though each has his own individual style.

The closest in style and motifs to Thoros is Yovhannes' second Gospel of 1253 in the Freer Gallery. The scheme of decoration, which includes the Eusebian letter, canon tables, dedicatory inscription, Evangelists' portraits and decorated openings to books as well as the detailed motifs and most of the stylistic elements are so close to those of Thoros that it is evident that Yovhannes was Thoros' teacher.

The first striking similarity is the structure of the decorative framework in the Eusebian letter and canon tables, usually with similar decorations on opposite pages *figs.61, 65*. The main element is a large rectangular panel resting on two or three columns, some with animal or bird capitals. The panel is decorated with interlacing foliage scrolls, inhabited at times by animals and birds. The Eusebian letter has portraits of Eusebius and Carpianus within a lunette which serves as a tympanum. Surmounting the panel are birds or fantastic animals flanking a fountain, a vase, or an altar. On either side of the panel are stylized trees, large candles, bird- or animal-headed men, elaborate leaves, scrolls, and vases; on top of each of these elements a different bird is perched. Flanking the columns on either side of the text is a larger stylized tree with different birds perched on it or hovering above. Elaborate foliage, mainly a palmette motif, emerges from the top corners of the panel, and there is a decorative band under the columns and the panel.

4. Eusebian Letter and Canon Tables

This scheme of decorating the Eusebian letter and canon tables was, in fact, used by Thoros Roslin throughout his work on Gospel books, and it follows almost to the minutest detail that of the Yovhannes Gospel of 1253. The scheme is at times so formal that one can predict the decorative motifs for each canon table. For instance, the lay-out and decoration of the page with canon four and the beginning of canon five is almost identical in all of Thoros' Gospels as well as in Yovhannes'. It will suffice to compare the two examples reproduced here, one from the Second Constantine Gospel of 1260 *fig.61*, and the other from the Leo and Keran Gospel of 1262 *fig.65*.[15]

Sirarpie Der Nersessian suggested that the repetition of these decorative elements in the canon tables recalls the idea of the Catholicos Nerses the Graceful (1166–1173) that the ten canons, their detailed decoration, and even the colors should reflect the Church and its typological relations with

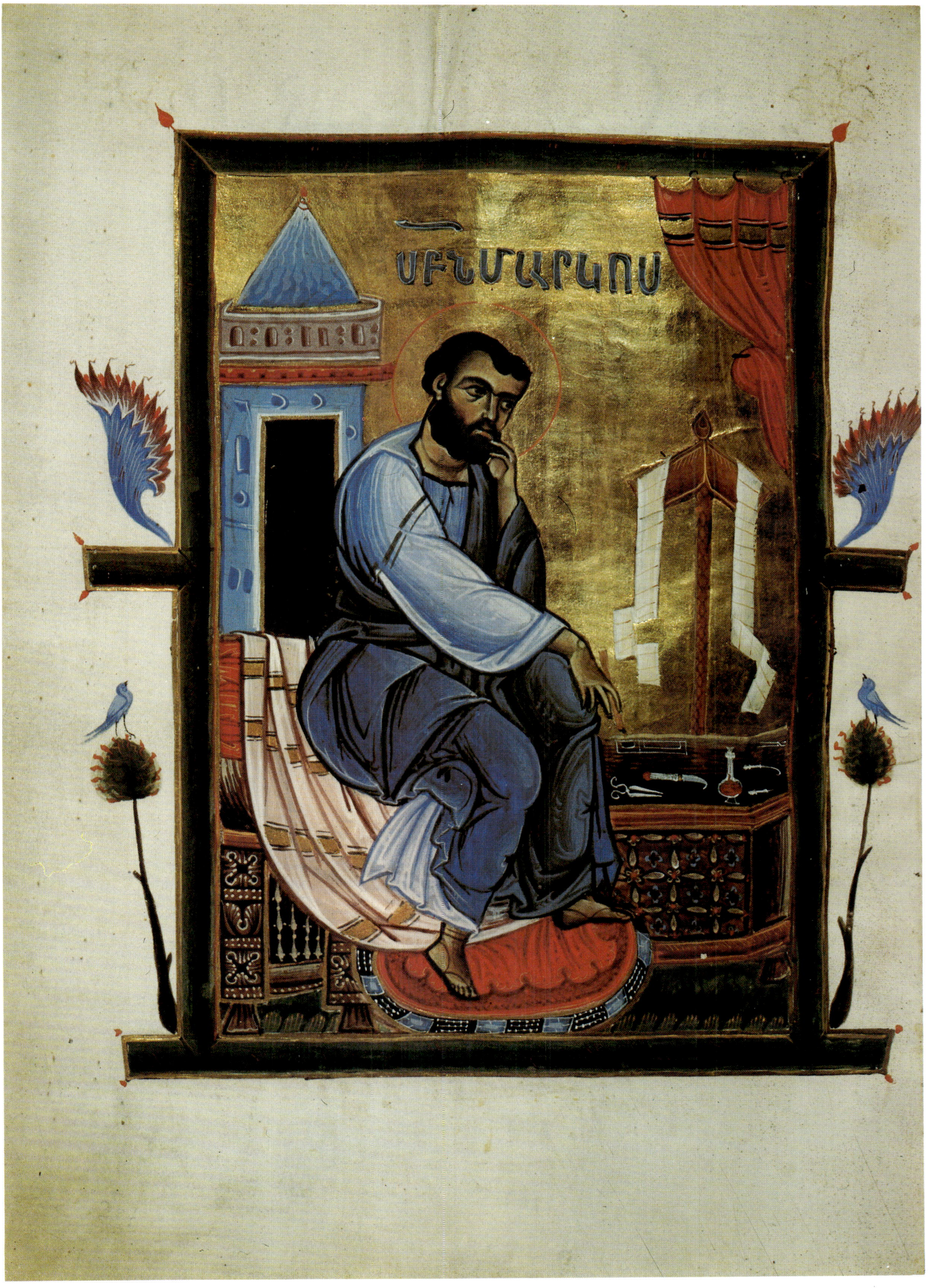
ՍԲՆՄԱՐԿՈՍ

the Old Testament. In his preface to a commentary on St. Matthew, Nerses gives the exact meaning of every detail. However, elements decorating contemporary canon tables from the second half of the twelfth century, such as the altar, the cóck, and other birds, express only by allusion some of the ideas put forward by Nerses.[16] In fact, these repetitious motifs round the square-topped canon tables and book openings had been used by Armenian artists since the eleventh century, as in the Trebizond Gospel,[17] the Mougna Gospel,[18] and the Sebastia Gospel of 1066.[19] They became common in Cilician illumination in the second half of the twelfth century, possibly because of Nerses' commentary. At that time the decorative elements were still interchangeable, and varied from one manuscript to another, to emerge in a fixed program just before the thirteenth century.

Though birds, flowers, and trees above arched canon tables are known from Early Christian times,[20] the decorated rectangular top originated in the late tenth century innovations in Byzantine Gospel decoration.[21] The Armenian artists of the period translated them into their own style by choosing their own elements, by adding to them, and by enlarging the flanking trees. Moslem and Iranian decorative motifs, such as palmettes and lotus buds, transmitted via Byzantium, were adopted as early as the eleventh century and added to harpies, sphinxes, and other fantastic animals.

One of the most important elements derived from Byzantine models are the portraits of Eusebius and Carpianus. They are to be found in all Thoros' Gospel books, as well as in the Gospel painted by Yovhannes before him. Contrary to earlier Byzantine representations, however, they are inserted as busts holding scrolls in the lunettes of the arches enclosing the letter of Eusebius to Carpianus, on confronting pages. The facial types of the two church fathers were adapted from eleventh-century illuminated Byzantine Gospels, where the figures are standing next to each other under an arch.[22] However, the portraits of Eusebius and Carpianus were not a novelty in Cilician Gospel illumination of the mid-thirteenth century. Precursors are known from late twelfth-century Gospel books, such as the Gospel of 1194 in Venice and that of 1197 in Lvov.[23]

65

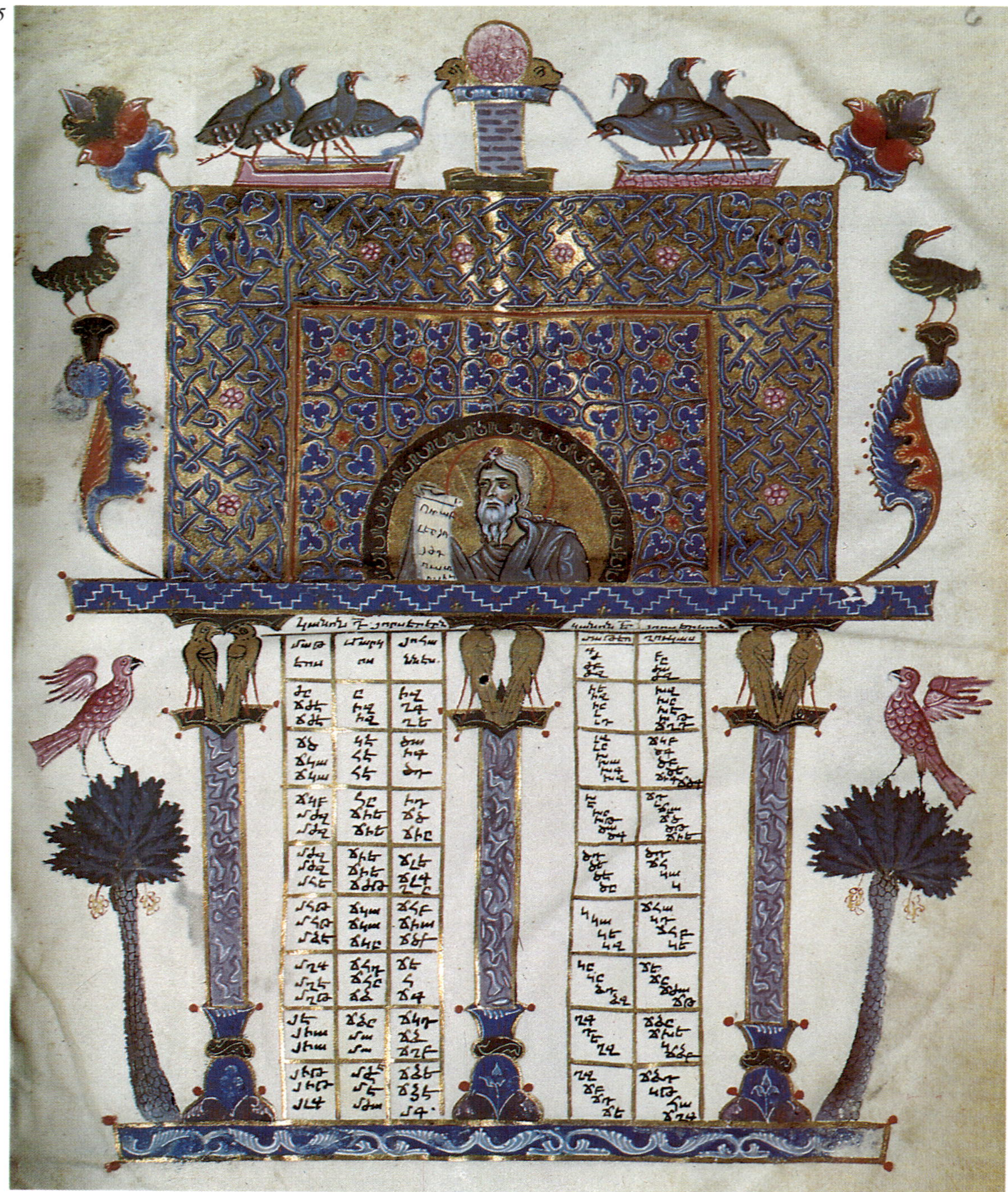

Figure 65: *Fourth and fifth canon tables, with the portrait bust of Zechariah, from the Leo and Keran Gospel by Thoros Roslin (ms. 2660, fol. 6).*

5. *Prophets' Portraits*

Thoros Roslin's innovation in the canon tables in Armenian Gospels is the introduction of Old Testament prophets holding scrolls. Most of them were inserted as busts in the lunettes above the canon tables, in a similar place to where the busts of Eusebius and Carpianus are traditionally found.

Two examples reproduced here are those of the prophet Jeremiah in the Second Constantine Gospel of 1260 *fig11*, and Zechariah in the Leo and Keran Gospel of 1262 *fig.65*. The prophets are holding scrolls with inscriptions from their prophecy relating to New Testament Christological events.[24] The Leo and Keran Gospel has full-length figures of Isaiah and Micah, standing on either side of the Eusebian letter, which also has the portrait busts of Eusebius and Carpianus in the lunettes.

The idea of texts from the prophets relating typologically to New Testament episodes no doubt underlies their representation in these canon tables. Moreover, this kind of typology is emphasized when Thoros introduces prophets holding scrolls near Christological scenes in his text illustrations.[25] It should be noted, however, that Thoros does not go so far as to paint scenes from the Old Testament to underline their relation to New Testament events.

Thoros' introduction of typology into Gospel books is an innovation in Armenian illumination which has parallels in Early Christian art in the east, as in the Syriac Rabbula Gospel of 586, and the Codex Rosannensis of the sixth century.[26] Apostles and Evangelists do appear as authors in illuminated western canon tables,[27] but these are not Old Testament typological figures. The two standing prophets flanking the Eusebian letter in the Leo and Keran Gospel of 1262 seem to be closest to Early Christian representations. However, the idea of placing the prophets in the lunettes could have occurred to Thoros by analogue with the portraits of Eusebius and Carpianus, who were placed there by his predecessors.

The concept of typology – joining Old Testament ideas or images with those in the New Testament – was commonly used during the Middle Ages in the west as well as in the east. Thoros must have been familiar with it from homilies and lections, if not from visual representations. The images of prophets and, above all, of David standing beside New Testament scenes gained new popularity in Byzantium during the twelfth century, and they may have been borrowed by Thoros from contemporary Byzantine illumination.[28] However, the prophets standing next to the Eusebian letter and the busts in the lunettes of the canon tables may have been Thoros' innovation, or a reintroduction fashioned after traditional Early Christian models.

6. *Evangelists' Portraits*

The portraits of the Evangelists in Thoros' Gospels do not differ from the iconographical types in the Greek Byzantine Gospels, *figs.62, 63, 64, 66*. They are similarly seated in front of desks and stands, and have the same facial types, though the details of their implements and the surrounding architecture may differ. This can be seen by comparing the two portraits of St. Luke from the Gospels of 1260 and 1262 reproduced here, *figs.63, 64* with similar Byzantine portraits.[29] A non-Byzantine element in Thoros' illumination is the use of the Evangelists' symbols on most of the opening pages of the Gospels as zoomorphic initials[30] *fig.64*. This is not an innovation by Thoros, for decorated zoomorphic initials were used in the Sebastia Gospel of 1066.[31] It is interesting to note that in his Gospel of 1253, the painter Yovhannes depicts the Evangelists' symbols above the protagonist, within the same full-page panel.[32] Thoros rarely places the symbol together with the Evangelist, and then inconspicuously, behind his chair, as in the Lady Keran Gospel of 1265 *fig.66*.

7. *Christological Scenes*

The most important of Roslin's innovations are his Christological text illustrations. The most elaborate of these, with the widest range of subjects, are undoubtedly in the Walters Gospel of 1262 painted for the priest Thoros, nephew of Constantine I. It has all the decorative elements mentioned so far prefacing the Gospel plus a profusion of illustrations of the text and of textual allusions. There are three types of text illustration: full-page panels, framed and unframed paintings within the text columns, and unframed marginal illustrations.[33] The Lady Keran Gospel of 1265 in Jerusalem has all three types of text illustration, though fewer in number than the Walters Gospel. Thoros' distinct way of rendering the different subjects posits a sound knowledge of Old and New Testament illustrations, including allusions to apocryphal text illustrations, some related to the lives of the Apostles and saints, others to apocalyptic and eschatological material, or even to contemporary events. In all of these Thoros seems to be a very imaginative and original artist, who invented much iconography, although he was undoubtedly acquainted with the common Byzantine and Greater Armenian Old and New Testament illustrations.[34] His reluctance to repeat his illustrations led to most of his iconographic innovations, which resulted either from conflating or abbreviating scenes. The conflated scenes are mainly in full pages or in large, framed panels, where he amalgamated several scenes into his own sophisticated composition. The abbreviated scenes are mainly in the margins and within text columns, but are not always due to lack of space. These abbreviations at times depict a single insignificant element taken from a more detailed description, which makes it difficult to identify immediately the episode it stands for.

8. The Second Constantine Gospel of 1260

It is typical of the Gospel illustrations in the four manuscripts by Thoros Roslin in Jerusalem that most of them are either full-page panels or marginal text illustrations. The smaller panels and unframed illustrations within the text columns, which are so profusely used by Thoros in the Walters and Freer Gospels, are here rather rare *figs.69, 71*. In the Second Constantine Gospel of 1260, all but one of the text illustrations are in the margins, and the full-page panels depict the Evangelists' portraits and the canon tables *figs.61, 62, 63*. The only other full-page panel, depicting the Nativity conflated with the Adoration of the Magi, replaces a full-page panel with a portrait of St. Matthew, who is nevertheless portrayed in the lower left-hand corner of the panel.[35] In this conflated picture Thoros refers to a contemporary event, which shows how his knowledge of political affairs was sound, though probably passive. In an inscription which he added within a quatrofoil at the top right, he states that this was "the day when the Tatars are coming".[36] This inscription seemed appropriate to Thoros, as he probably associated "the Magi who come from the East", the inscription on the left, with the Mongol Tatars.

Thoros' versatility is well illustrated by his various renderings of the Nativity.[37] That in the Walters Gospel of 1262 is the most basic, only the Adoration of the Shepherds being added, in the Byzantine manner. However, in the Freer Gospel, the Virgin and Child are seated in front of a cave and manger, with adoring Magi. In the Jerusalem picture this basic Adoration of the Magi is shown with an ox and ass at the manger, and the addition of adoring angels, shepherds, and townsmen. It also includes a star above and the washing of the Child next to St. Matthew in a strip below. A basic Adoration of the Magi, with no manger, is in Thoros' last Gospel of 1268, but in this same manuscript there is on folio 163v–164 another Nativity representation conflated with the Adoration of the Shepherds and the Magi.

Concentration of the depicted scenes, at times abbreviated to a mere hint, is characteristic of this Second Constantine Gospel of 1260. Joseph's second dream, with the three Magi standing above him (Mt. 2:1–13) on folio 18, is depicted without the angel at his side, and neither Herod nor the Virgin are next to them. The Massacre of the Innocents on folio 19v has only a soldier holding a sword and a child's head; the child's body is depicted below in the lower margin.[38] The Three Temptations of Christ are alluded to by the last episode of the devil fleeing[39] and the two blind men are healed with no Christ in sight.[40] The Temple of Jerusalem repeatedly appears in the shape of a small open tempietto; and in the Annunciation, the Archangel Gabriel stands at one end of two confronting pages, while the Virgin stands at the other end.

The style of the figures betrays the characteristics of Thoros' hand. The figures, usually squat with large heads, the dramatic though static gestures of the hands with somewhat bulky, almost deformed palms and fingers, the agitated but softly falling drapery, the intense gaze of narrow eyes, and the small, sensitive mouths are typical of Thoros, as are his bright colors, especially the reds, blues, and salmon pinks. His compact compositions can be seen not only in the full-page panel of the Nativity but also in the tight grouping of the figures in the margins.

9. The Leo and Keran Gospel of 1262

The Leo and Keran Gospel of 1262 has few marginal text illustrations, and the full-page panel comprises the elaborate canon tables, the Evangelists' portraits, and those of the patrons.[41] In this Gospel, as in the former, the marginal text illustrations are abbreviated allusions. The typical Byzantine John the Baptist appears as a preacher with a scroll instead of in a Baptism scene on folio 15v;[42] a devil issuing from a man's mouth on folio 55 refers to the healing of a possessed man;[43] the Apostles, heads covered and nimbed, are grouped compactly together in the address on the Mount of Olives, but without Christ foretelling his death (Mt. 26:1–2) on folio 79;[44] a dish with a lamb and three wafers above it alludes to the preparation of the Last Supper (Mt. 26:19–20) on folio 80; three men next to a palm tree allude to the Entry into Jerusalem;[45] and a few sheep and one horned goat recall Christ's parable of the Last Judgment (Mt. 25:31–34), although here they illustrate John 10:14–16 on folio 255, which stresses that sheep of different folds shall be gathered and kept by one shepherd.[46] This is undoubtedly one of Thoros' special renderings of minute details, illustrating obscure scenes by allusions to other biblical passages.

10. The Lady Keran Gospel of 1265

The Lady Keran Gospel of 1265 is undoubtedly the richest of Thoros' works now in Jerusalem.[47] Besides the four Evangelists' portraits *fig.66*, the Eusebian letter, canon tables and dedication,[48] it has many Christological scenes, six in full-panels, two smaller text panels and a few marginal text illustrations. Thoros' special iconography is evident in them all, and since he does not tend to repeat himself, he always finds an original way to represent a scene. In the Baptism of Christ on folio 21, he omitted the disciples but kept all the other elements, including Christ, the Baptist, the hand of God appearing from heaven, the dove, the adoring angels, and the personification of the River Jordan.

Thoros' compositions are less compact in the Lady Keran Gospel. In the Descent into Hell *fig.71*, spaciousness is expressed by the shiny gold background and enhanced by the flaring, wing-like garment.[49] Thoros created this same impression in the Transfiguration of Christ *fig.68* where the elongated composition is stressed by the gold mandorla. The Entry into Jerusalem in the Lady Keran Gospel, placed within the text columns *fig.69*, is a condensed version compared with the full-page representation in the Walters Gospels of 1262,[50] and not like the illustrations to St. Matthew's text in the Freer Gospel.[51] The Deposition from the Cross *fig.70* is very similar to that in the Walters Gospel, although the other women are missing from this picture.[52] The elongated composition makes it look more elegant. Here too the composition is not symmetrical but balanced.

Variations in composition and details were used by Thoros in the two last scenes represented in the Lady Keran Gospel: The Presentation in the Temple, *fig.71* and the Raising of Lazarus, *fig.72*. Compared with the Walters Gospel,[53] the composition of the Presentation in the Temple is reversed, similar to the Presentation in the last Thoros Gospel of 1268.[54] Since it occupies only part of one text column in the Lady Keran Gospel, it also lacks the baldachin above the altar. In its compactness, it resembles the scene of the Circumcision of Christ in the Freer Gospel. The Raising of Lazarus in the Lady Keran Gospel is painted on almost a full page, as in the Freer Gospel, but lacks the two sisters of Lazarus, who appear in the Gospel of 1268. The Jews witnessing the scene and the man carrying away the lid of the tomb are also missing from the last two manuscripts. In the Lady Keran Gospel, only Christ and two disciples appear on one side, with Lazarus and a man holding his hand to his nose (a familiar gesture in view of the stench issuing from Lazarus) on the other. The Evangelist, St. John (fol. 270v), is not accompanied by his scribe, Procopius, as is usual in most of Thoros Roslin's Gospels (apart from the Walters Gospel).

Thoros Roslin's system of illustrating a Gospel book is innovatory in all three types of illustration – full-page, part-page, and marginal – taking into consideration not only Armenian but Byzantine art as well. It was somewhat influenced by the Latin West, with which the Cilician Kingdom of Armenia had close ties. The very name Roslin may be of western origin. Intermarriages between Armenian women and westerners were common at the time.[55] However, his iconography and composition are mainly Armenian, with a certain Byzantine influence. The scenes he chose to represent in full pages are usually of the Twelve Byzantine Feasts. However, unlike the Byzantine custom, they are not arranged chronologically, but are usually attached to the relevant text.[56] Thoros was flexible enough to abbreviate the scenes when he did not paint them in a full page, and even to place them as a hinting reminder in the margin. His resourcefulness in this knew no bounds.

11. The Ritual of Thoros Roslin, 1266

The text of an Armenian ritual book usually contains daily and festival readings, with additional songs and canticles from the Old and New Testaments, as well as various other texts. Illustrating a ritual was for Thoros an opportunity to depict Old Testament episodes, which he executed in his usual innovative manner. The Ritual he painted at the commission of Bishop Vardan Nesepna in 1266 is the only one of his manuscripts known to have been executed in Sis. It has five full-page panels, three of which are Old Testament subjects: the story of Jonah *fig.73*, the Crossing of the Red Sea *fig.74*, and the three Children of the Hebrews in the Fiery Furnace *fig.75*. The first panel is divided horizontally into two compartments, with the first episode at the bottom, obviously a combination which Thoros made from two separate miniatures. The bottom compartment is a conflation of three scenes: Jonah being cast into the sea and a fish swallowing him; the third scene of the whale spewing Jonah out is implied by Jonah's head, and not his feet, sticking out of the fish's mouth. In the top compartment Jonah is seen lamenting his lot under the gourd, while the inhabitants of Nineveh, headed by the king, come towards him with gestures of condolence. These scenes are no doubt of Byzantine origin[57] which Thoros had in his repertory, and he combined them to form a new united composition.

The combination of three scenes can be found in the Story of Exodus *fig.74*: The Israelites crossing the Red Sea, the pursuing Egyptians being drowned, and Miriam with her maidens playing and dancing.[58] Thoros' literal knowledge of the Bible is evident, as he turns to the text to find new ideas for his iconography. This is the way to interpret the appearance of the hovering angel with raised sword, as the "angel of God, which went before the camp of Israel, removed and went behind them" (Exodus 14:19). Although an angel in the Crossing of the Red Sea is known from Early Christian art,[59] this may have been Thoros' own innovation evoked by the text. This literal interpretation is also responsible for Thoros' introduction of the segment of sky and a column from which "the Lord looked unto the host of the Egyptians through the pillar of fire and of the cloud" (Exodus 14:24).

The picture of the three youths in the Fiery Furnace *fig.75* shows only one episode from the book of Daniel (3:25), when King Nebuchadnezzar saw "four men loose, walking in the midst of the fire, and they have no hurt, and the form of the fourth is like the Son of God." Thoros constructed a monumental picture out of this episode, making the furnace rather small, with the angel of God dominating the scene.[60] This type of representation is also known from Early Christian art, though mostly without the angels[61] but Thoros no doubt had a Byzantine model for that.[62]

The Dormition of St. John the Evangelist is a rare scene in art *fig.76*. According to the legend,[63] St. John dug his own grave and lay in it asleep to await Christ's second coming. This is based on Christ's saying about the beloved disciple (John 21:22–23): "If I will that he tarry till I come...

Then went this saying abroad among the brethren that that disciple should not die." In our picture St. John is lying asleep in his grave surrounded by Apostles, including his brother St. James the Great (in bishop's attire) who is the patron of the Armenian Cathedral.[64]

The composition resembles the Byzantine representation of the Dormition of the Virgin, but Christ carrying a soul is missing. Other dying saints are similarly depicted in Byzantine art, lying in their coffin surrounded by their disciples.[65] This rare scene of the dormition of St. John was illustrated three years previously, in 1263, in a Gospel copied for Bishop John, the younger brother of King Hethum I, in the Monastery of Gerner in Cilicia by an unknown artist.[66] However, the latter does not correspond directly to the text, since the Evangelist is not lying in a trench but in a sacrophagus, surrounded by angels as well as Apostles, with two angels descending to receive his soul, and there is no man with a spade. This type of burial in an open sarcophagus is similar to earlier western representations of the scene, such as in the eleventh century wall paintings in the Sancta Sanctorum of the Lateran Palace in Rome,[67] and also in a choir book from the monastery of Zwiefalten of 1138–47.[68] The Byzantine representation of the dormition of St. John is quite different from either Thoros' or the Bishop John pictures.[69] In this scene too, Thoros Roslin has shown himself to be an original artist, who follows the text to the letter in rendering this illustration. Indeed, this picture illustrates the Armenian account of the dormition of St. John, which follows the usual readings of the Ritual in our manuscript.[70]

Thoros Roslin's iconographical innovations in renderings of Biblical, Christological, and hagiographical scenes as well as portraits of prophets constitute only part of his ingenuity. It is basically his sure hand and daring style which brought him fame for many centuries to come. His work became a model for other artists to follow, even during his lifetime, as can be seen from a Gospel book which was illustrated in 1263 for Bishop John.[71] Of the many Christological scenes which were painted by several artists in this Gospel, only some deviate from Roslin's iconography. Even at a much later date artists regarded Thoros' work as a model that cannot be altered. A seventeenth century scribe and artist, Michael, son of the scribe Borgham, obtained Thoros' Walters Gospels of 1262 and must have copied the Eusebian letter, the canon tables and the Evangelists' portraits in great detail.[72] Proud of the fact that he had such a good model to copy from, he asks the reader, in his colophon of 1670 related to the canon tables, "to remember the excellent scribe Thoros surnamed Roslin, the illuminator of the model."

Figure 66: *St. John the Evangelist with his symbol, from the Lady Keran Gospel of 1265, painted at Hromkla by Thoros Roslin (ms. 1965, fol. 270v).*

Figure 67: *Christ harrowing Hell and rescuing Adam and Eve from limbo, from the Lady Keran Gospel of 1265 (ms. 1956, fol. 110).*

66

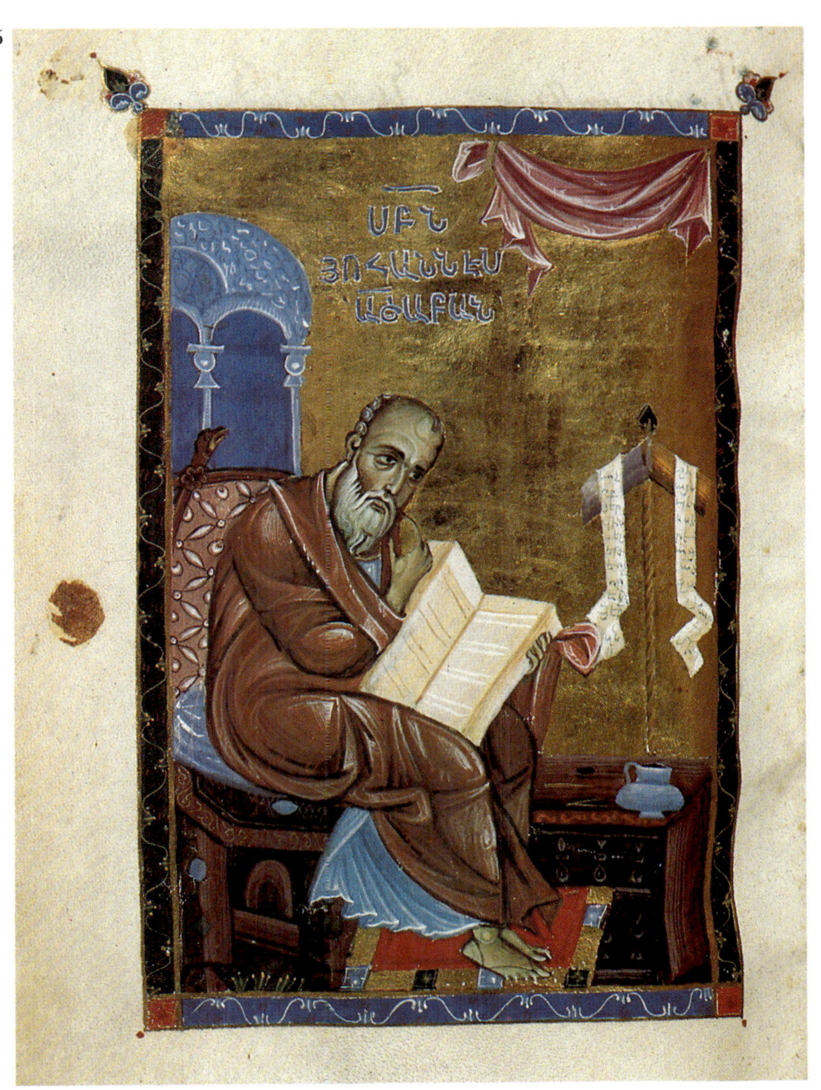

67

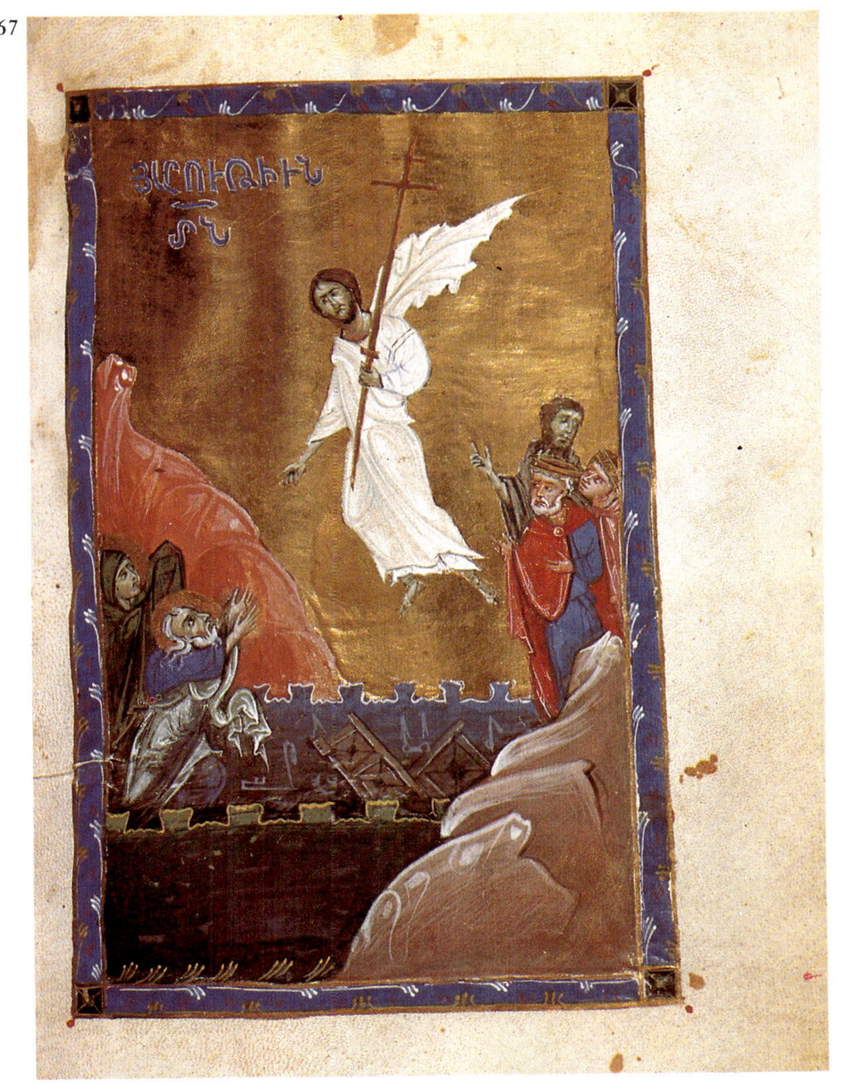

Figure 68: *Transfiguration. Christ in an aureole of light, with Moses and Elijah next to him, from the Lady Keran Gospel by Thoros Roslin, Hromkla, 1265 (ms. 1956, fol. 140v).*

Figure 69: *Entry of Christ into Jerusalem, from the Lady Keran Gospel by Thoros Roslin (ms. 1956, fol. 150v).*

Figure 70: *The Deposition of Christ from the Cross, with Joseph of Arimathea and Mary carrying his body, while Nicodemus pulls the nails out of his feet with tongs, from the Lady Keran Gospel (ms. 1956, fol. 171).*

70

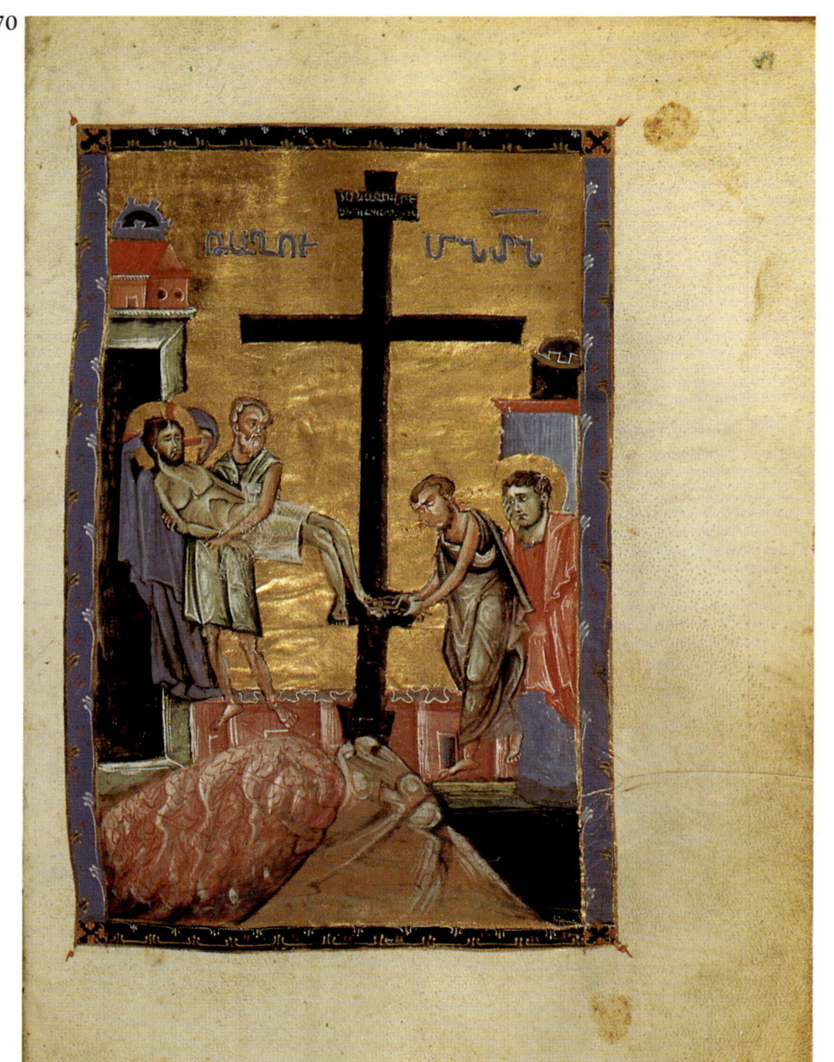

69

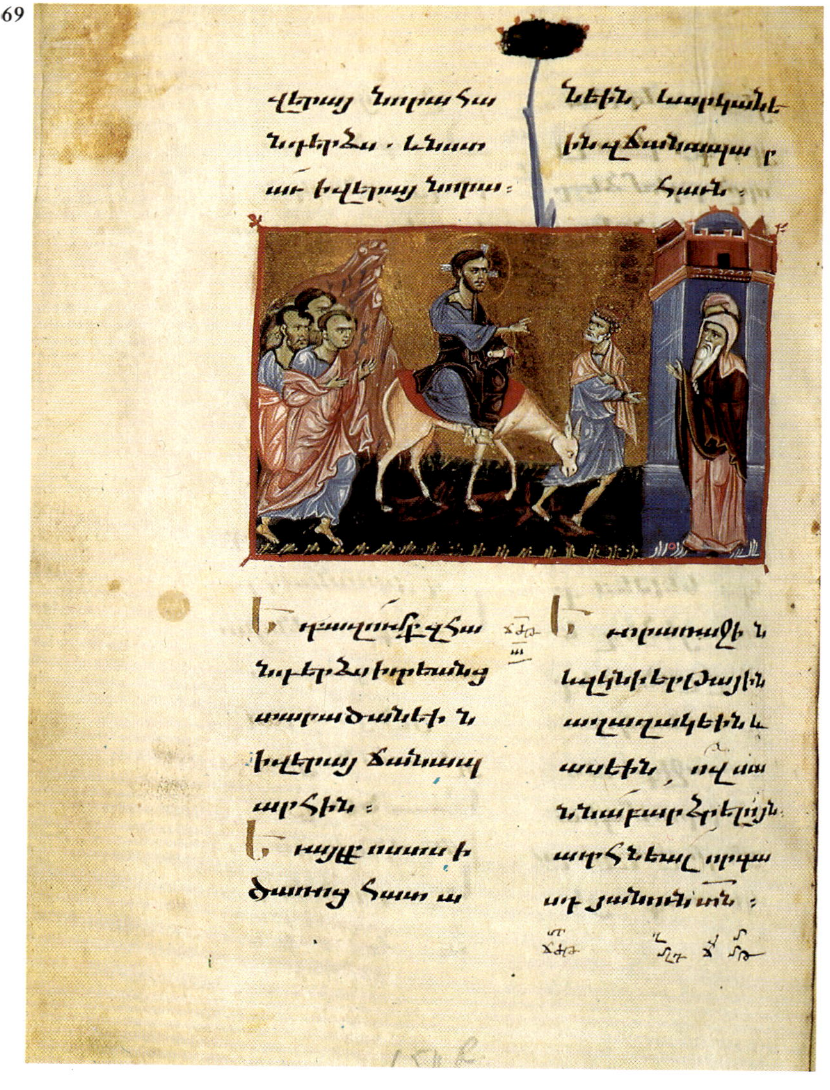

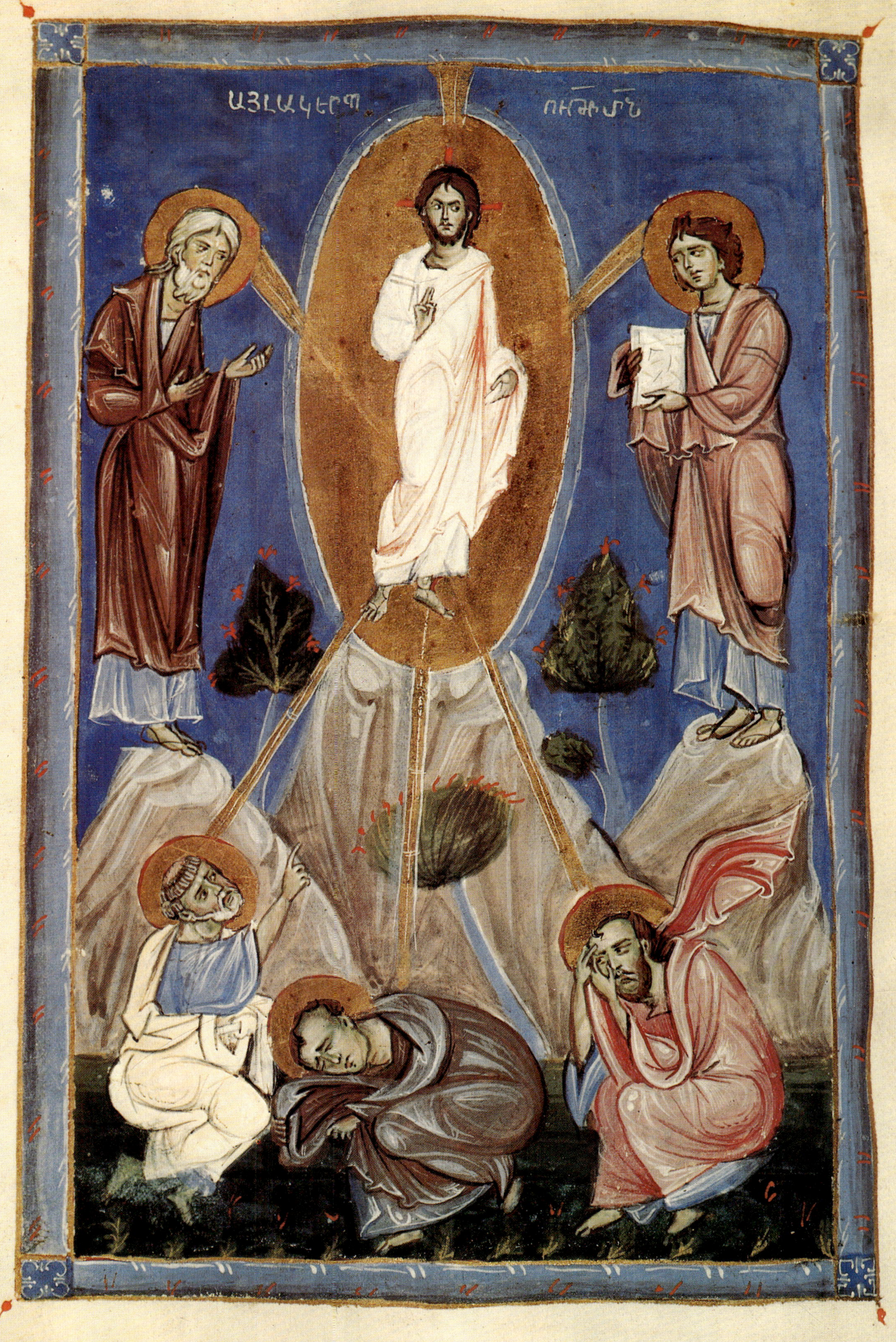
ԱՅԼԱԿԵՐՊ

Figure 71: *Presentation of the infant Christ in the Temple, from the Lady Keran Gospel painted by Thoros Roslin, Hromkla, 1265 (ms. 1956, fol. 183).*

Figure 72: *The Raising of Lazarus from the dead, from the Lady Keran Gospel by Thoros Roslin (ms. 1956, fol. 310v).*

71

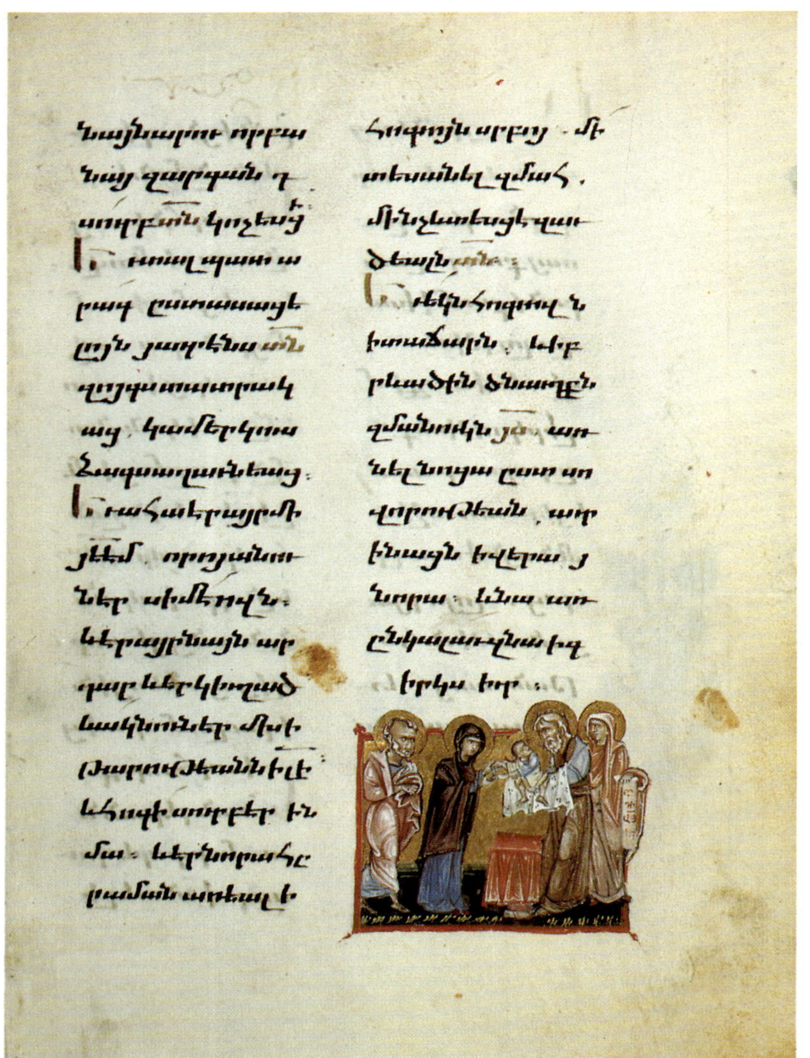

72

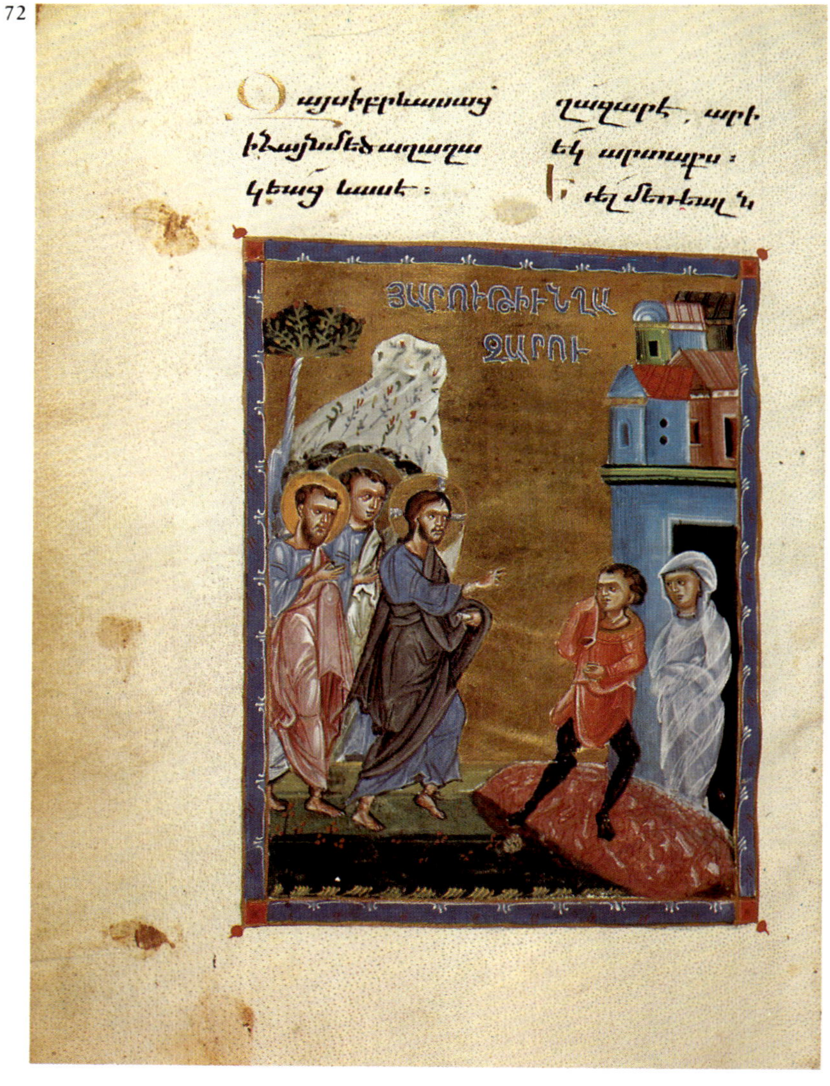

73

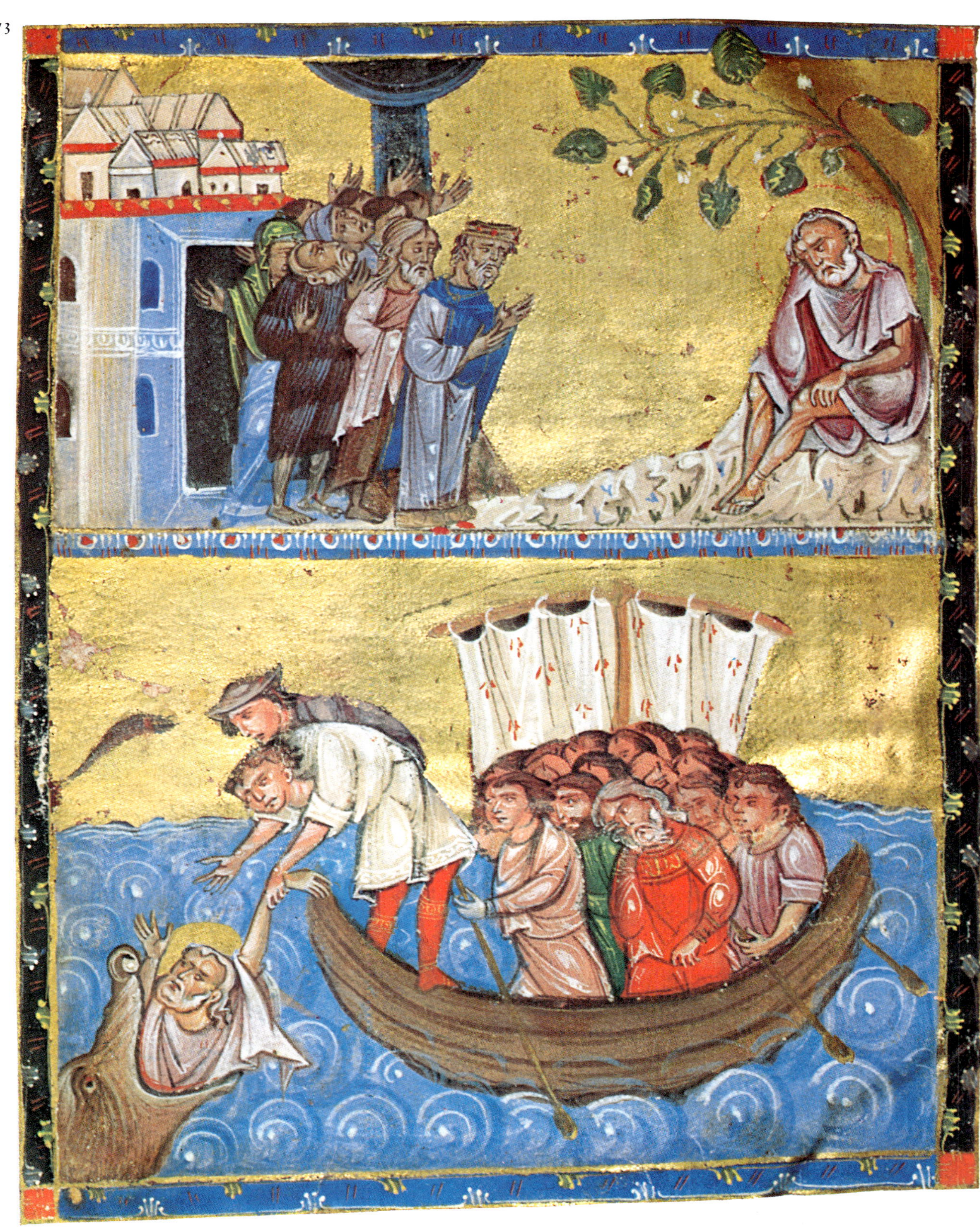

Figure 73: *Jonah being cast into the sea (bottom) and seated under the gourd while inhabitants of Nineveh approach him. Full-page panel from the Thoros Roslin Ritual of 1266, painted at Sis (ms. 2027, fol. 1v).*

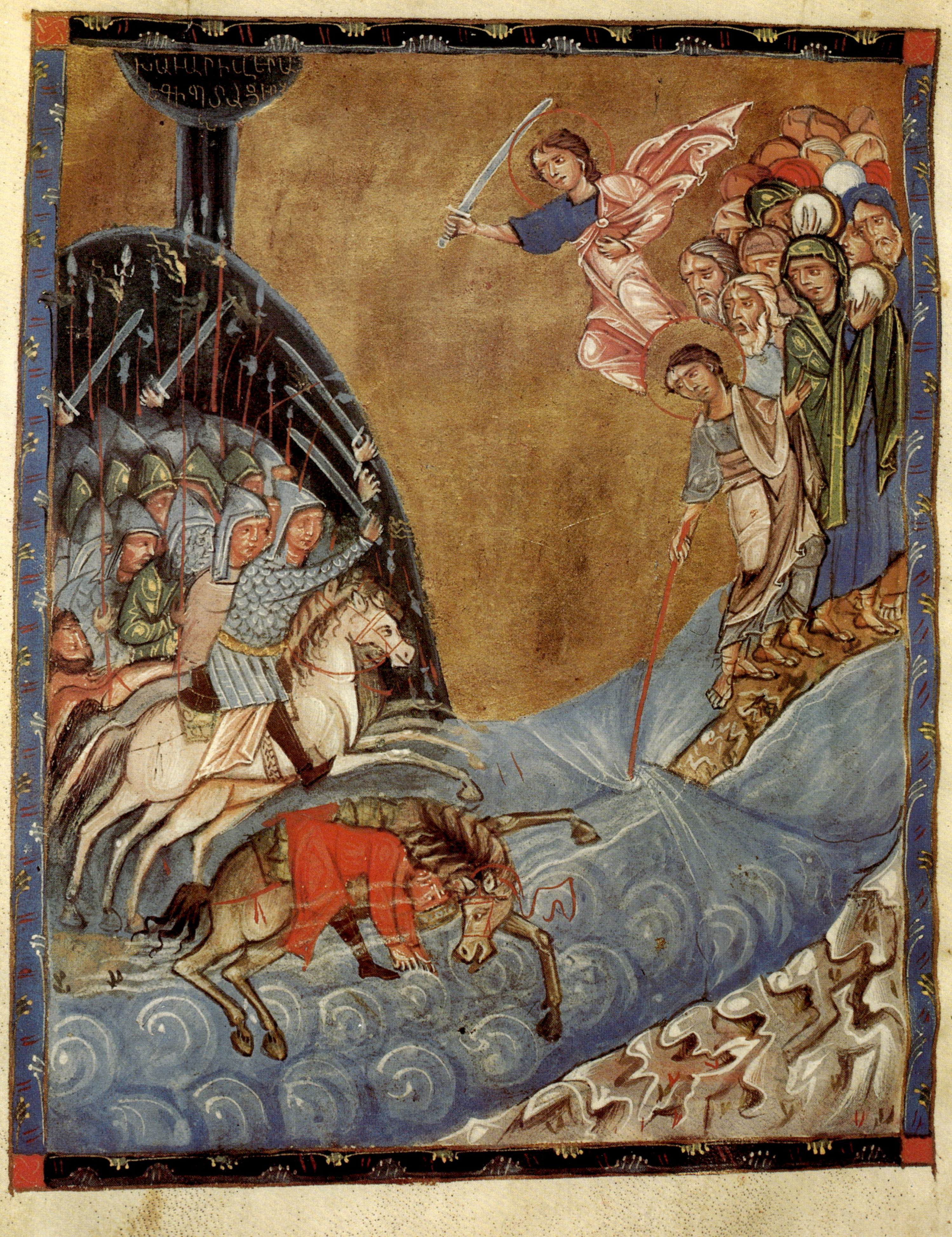

75

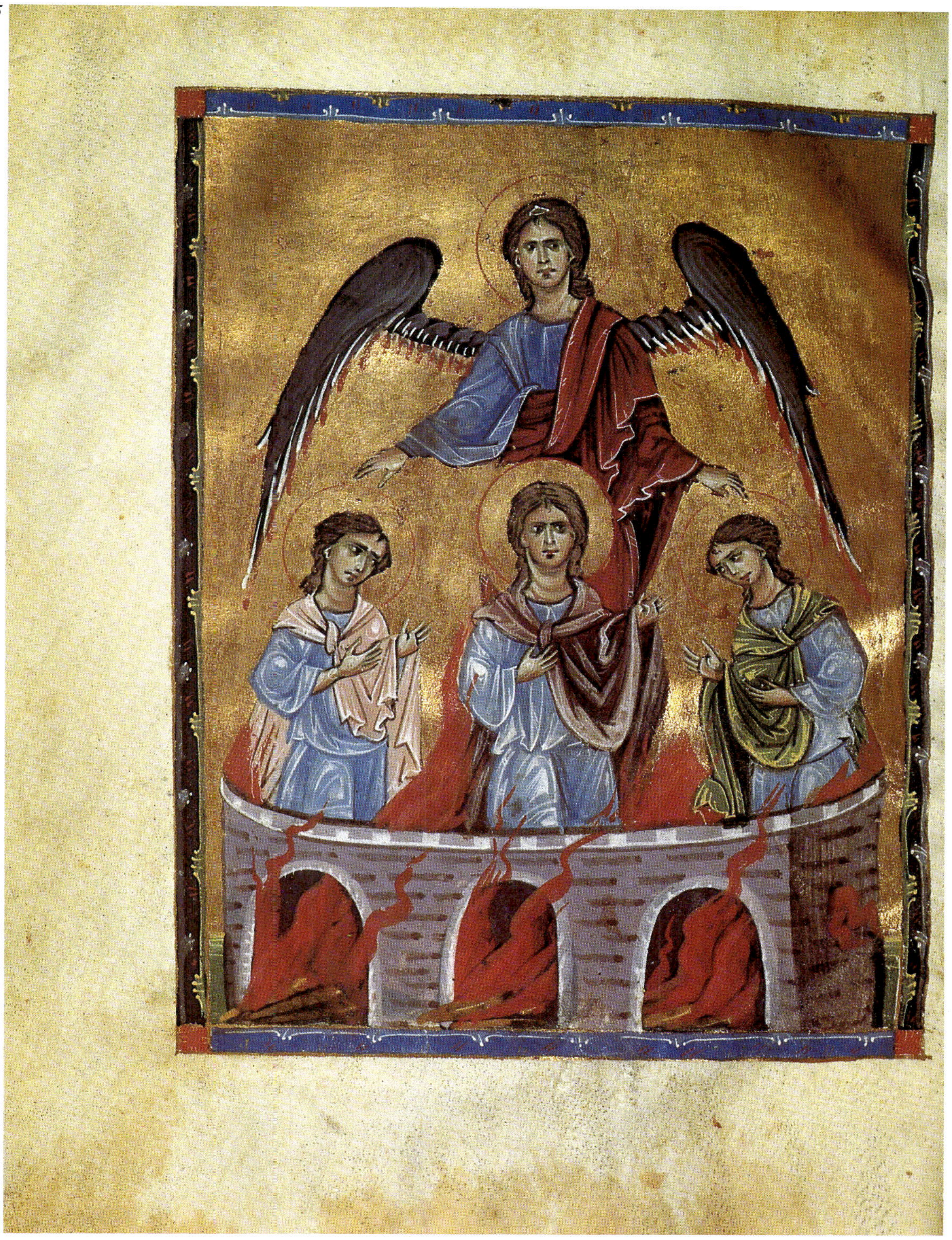

Figure 74: *The Israelites crossing the Red Sea, while the pursuing Egyptians drown, from the Ritual Book painted by Thoros Roslin at Sis in 1266 (ms. 2027, fol. 4v).*

Figure 75: *The three Hebrew youths, Shadrach, Meshach, and Abednego, being rescued by an angel from the fiery furnace into which they were thrown by Nebuchadnezzar, from the Ritual by Thoros Roslin, Sis, 1266 (ms. 2027, fol. 14v).*

Figure 76: *The Dormition of St. John the Evangelist, surrounded by his friends and disciples, preparing to live forever. A full-page panel from the Ritual Book of 1266 painted by Thoros Roslin at Sis (ms. 2027, fol. 224v).*

76

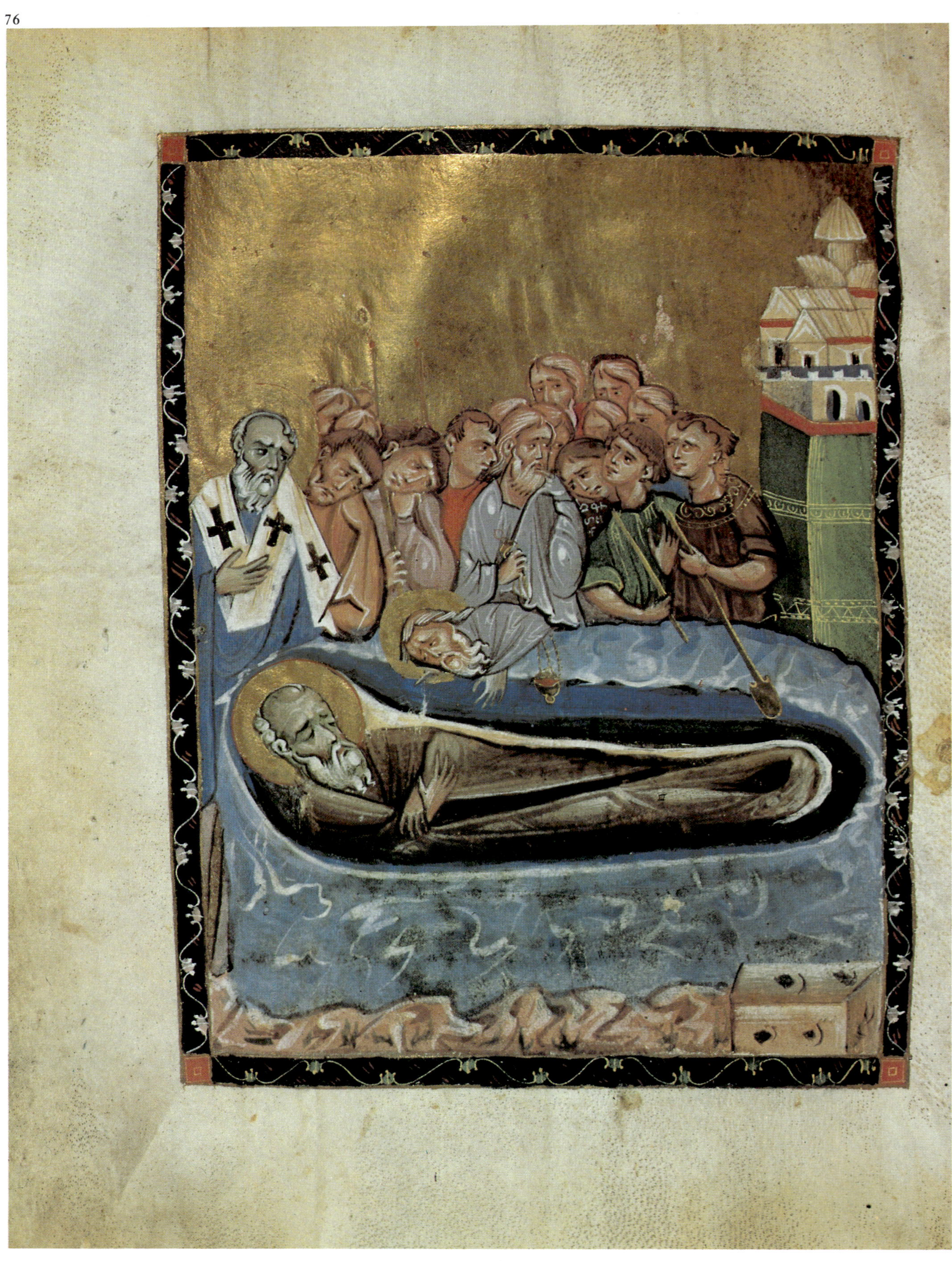

Chapter Five: Late Thirteenth Century Cilician Illumination

Concurrently with the activity of Thoros Roslin, manuscripts were being illuminated by other artists in Hromkla, in the capital, Sis, and in other centers in Cilicia. A second generation of artists evolved, each of whom developed his own individual style, dependent to some extent on Roslin's. Common to them all is the use of dramatic composition and an elegant figure style which, compared with that of Thoros, is manneristic. The exaggeration of gesture and movement is matched by the use of contrasting colors and a profusion of decorative motifs in the margins and round the frames.[1] Very few of these manneristic artists are known to us by name, as for some unknown reason no names were recorded in any of the colophons. In iconography these artists sometimes follow Thoros' innovations. However, in most cases they draw from traditional Byzantine iconography, of which they could have found many contemporary models.

Some of the most beautiful and sumptuous manuscripts were written and illuminated under royal patronage,[2] two of which are in Jerusalem. One was ordered by Queen Keran in 1272, after the accession of her husband, Leo II, to the throne in 1269. The second was dedicated by Prince Vasak, brother of King Hethum I and uncle to Leo II.

1. The Queen Keran Gospel

One of the most elegant and dramatic illuminated manuscripts of the late thirteenth century is the Gospel of Queen Keran.[3] The scribe, Awetis, states that it was copied by order of the Queen at Sis in 1272, and the dedicatory picture attests to this *fig.77*. The Queen is represented on one of the last leaves, together with her husband, King Leo II, and their five children – three sons and two daughters – kneeling piously in front of a *Deisis*. At the top of the panel Christ, enthroned in a heavenly sphere, is flanked by the two merciful mediators, the Virgin and John the Baptist. The grace of God emanates from the heavenly sphere in the form of seven rays directed at the royal family. The golden background of the panel heightens the majestic appearance of the *Deisis* and accentuates the distance between the heavenly and the terrestrial groups. The lofty, elongated figures in heaven are painted in contrast to the somewhat heavier, rounded figures of the worshiping family. This miniature can be regarded as the apogée of the elegant thirteenth-century Cilician style initiated by Thoros Roslin. The dramatic presentation in this picture is fully appreciated when it is compared to the dedicatory picture of Prince Leo and Princess Keran in the Gospel which Thoros Roslin painted for them in 1262, ten years earlier.[4] In the Thoros picture the prince and princess fill almost the entire space of the panel beneath the double arch, with a small bust of Christ and two hovering angels close above them, and their majestic, though static, bodies can hardly be discerned under the heavy, ornate garments; here, however, the *Deisis* is the dominant element in the picture. Moreover, the hand and head gestures of this later picture indicate movement, which is lacking in Thoros' very formal presentation.

These gestures in the Queen Keran Gospel, with sinuous figures in more clinging garments, create a greater sense of elegance. This feeling is also evident in the three surviving portraits of the Evangelists, as well as in the eleven full-page panels with Christological scenes in the manuscript. They are mostly taken from the twelve Byzantine feasts, and are on the whole rendered in Byzantine-type iconography, as for example the Descent of the Holy Ghost on the Apostles at Pentecost *fig.78*. The Holy Ghost, in the shape of a dove, is seen in the segment of sky at the top, radiating glory. Twelve rays of light, which include tiny flames, extend from the sky towards the twelve Apostles, who are seated in a semi-circle on thrones. Within the arched doorway encircled by the Apostles appear representatives of each of the countries converted by them and in whose languages they spoke after the descent of the Holy Ghost (Acts of the Apostles 2:1–12). Among those represented are a black man, an Arab wearing a turban, a Jew wearing a shawl, and a dog-headed man. The last is traditionally regarded as one of a nation dwelling beyond India. These images are a typical element of Byzantine iconography, as is the entire semicircular composition, and the inclusion of Paul as the twelfth Apostle, rather than Matthias as related in Acts (1:26). However, there are also some western elements in the style and iconography, for instance, the dramatic attitude of the fainting Virgin near the Crucifixion, supported by two women, suggests an Italian influence of the thirteenth century.[5]

The Eusebian letter, the canon tables, and the dedication pages are all executed in the traditional

Armeno-Byzantine style with a rectangular headpiece resting on columns, copying at times Thoros Roslin's decorative motifs in their most minute detail. For instance, the partridges in the two Roslin Gospel books of 1260 and 1262 *figs.61 and 65* drinking from a tower-like fountain, which is a specific motif for canons four and five, are depicted in Queen Keran's Gospel as well.

The fifteen full-page historiated panels and the preliminary arcaded pages were probably all executed by one artist, although there are at least two different scales of proportions by which the figures are composed. The difference can be demonstrated by comparing the round faces of the king, queen, and children on the dedication page, too heavy for their thin bodies to carry, with the elongated heads of Christ, the Baptist, and even the Virgin in the same picture. However, the rendering of the faces and drapery is so similar that it would be difficult to claim that two different artists worked on this page, or indeed on any other, including the Evangelists' portraits. Rather, one has to assume that the artist had a model for the *Deisis* and the Christological scenes, whereas the royal portraits had to be painted *ad hoc*.

2. *The Second Prince Vasak Gospel*

The Vasak Gospel is another sumptuous manuscript which was copied and illuminated by a fine artist[6] of the same school as the illuminator of the Gospel of Queen Keran. However, there are some differences. The compositions of the Vasak Gospel are more dense, thereby losing the effect of the empty gold spaces. The figures are elongated and more elegant than in the Keran Gospel. In most pictures one or two persons are brought to the fore by enlarging them unduly or by stressing their coloring. The smaller heads, with expressive gaze, are, however, of the same type as those in the Keran Gospel, but they lack the latter's delicacy and have bolder coloring.[7] Both manuscripts may be the product of one artist, at different, though close, periods. The dedication picture depicts the prince and his two sons kneeling before the enthroned Christ, introduced by the Virgin of Mercy, who protects them beneath her mantle *fig.79*. This strange element in iconography recalls the Mater of misericordia in western art, and was no doubt borrowed from it.[8] Since Vasak's wife is missing from this picture, it must have been painted after her death in 1268, but before Vasak's death in 1284.[9]

Quite different from the Queen Keran Gospel are the elaborate marginal decorations, which have multicolored, twisted foliage scrolls with sprouting leaves.[10] In some places there are abbreviated Christological scenes inserted within the foliage scrolls. Most profusely decorated are the margins of the opening pages of the books.

The four Evangelists' portraits (e.g., St. Matthew, *fig.80*) and the Christological pictures *figs.81, 82, 83* are all executed on separate, single pages, blank on the reverse and inserted into the volume near the text which they illustrate. Comparing these with the elaborate decorations of the opening pages of the text of the Gospels[11] and with other initials and marginal illustrations inserted within motifs, it is obvious that all were painted by the same hand in the same workshop.

A few full-page examples will help to demonstrate the style and composition as well as the iconography of the Prince Vasak Gospel. The Virgin in the Nativity scene *fig.81*, with her large body, dominates the composition, dwarfing all the other figures, including the Christ Child. The panel contains several episodes surrounding the Virgin and Child in the cave: the angels and shepherds, the Magi carrying gifts, the midwives washing the child, and Joseph sitting to one side. The compact composition resembles that of Thoros in the Second Constantine Gospel of 1260,[12] though the child is in the manger, as in traditional Byzantine iconography. The Baptism *fig.82* has all the usual elements of the naked Christ, John the Baptist, the adoring angels, and the Apostles looking on. However, the personification of the river god has turned into a tiny sea-horse, and the hand of God is missing. The Ascension, with Christ in a round aureole *fig.83*, has only two angels carrying him up. The Virgin in the front is flanked by the two angels dressed in white, and Peter and Paul. The elongated figures of the angels form the most compelling element in the picture because of their white color and elegant posture. One can see how this type of compact composition, with elaborate decorative motifs and colors, led to later illuminated manuscripts of this group, such as the Lectionary of King Hethum II of 1286,[13] and how it influenced later, fourteenth century illumination in Cilicia and abroad.[14]

Figure 77: *King Leo II, Queen Keran, their three sons and two daughters, kneeling in front of a* Deisis: *Christ enthroned, flanked by the Virgin and John the Baptist as mediators. The dedication picture from the Queen Keran Gospel, Sis, 1272 (ms. 2563, fol. 380).*

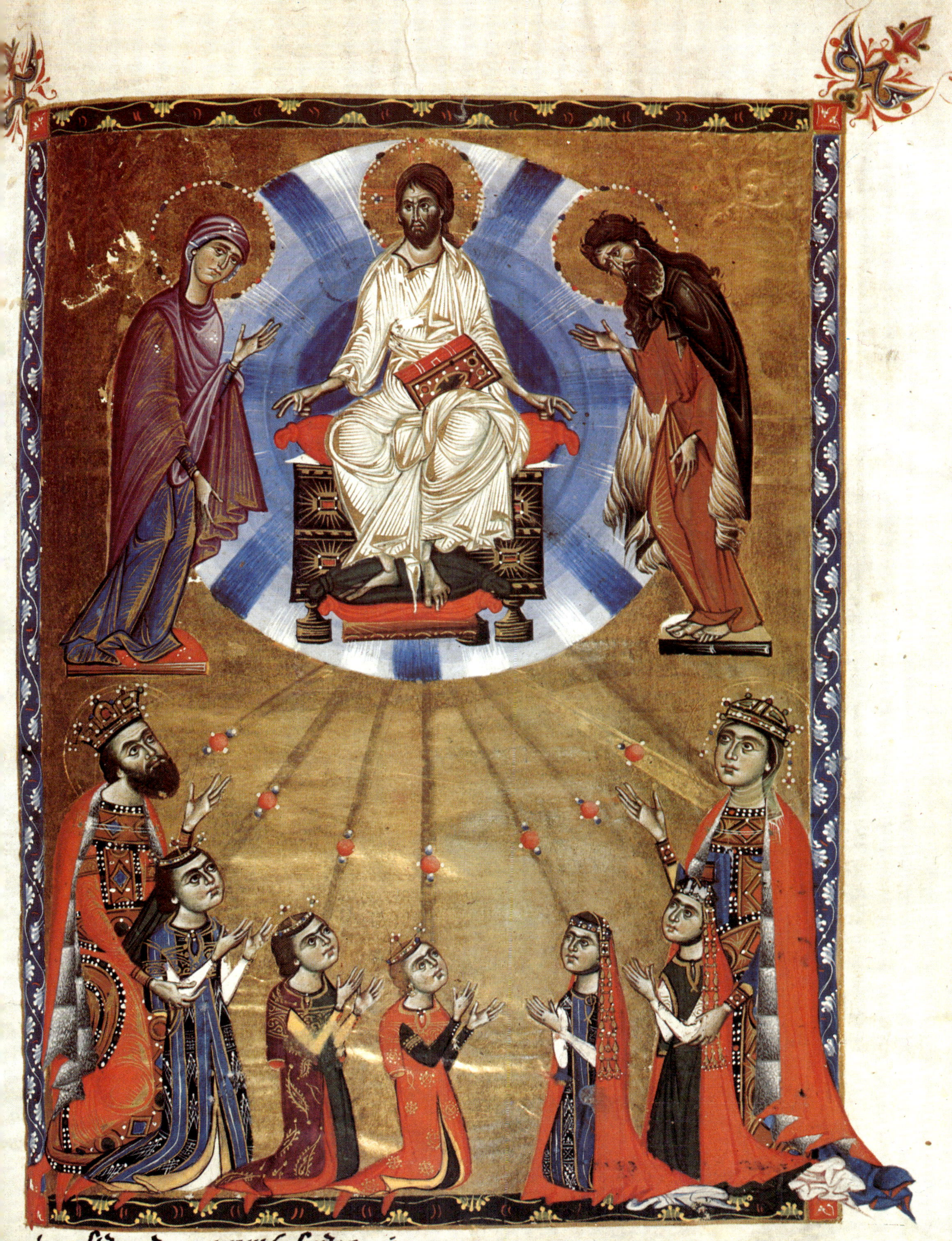

Եւ յամենայն պատուհասից ։

3. *The Erznka Bible*

According to its colophon the Erznka Bible of 1269–70[15] was copied by three scribes, Mkhithar, Yakob and Movses, in the city of Erznka (Erzinkan) on the Euphrates, east of the Cilician border, for Archbishop Sargis and his son, Yovhannes. No artist's name is given, but similarity in style to another manuscript which was copied by the scribe Mkhithar for the same Prince Yovhannes of Erznka seems to imply that Mkhithar was the painter of most of the illuminations in our manuscript.[16] Complete illustrated Bibles are scarce in Armenian illumination, unlike Gospel books and lectionaries, and this is the earliest extensive one known. The Erznka Bible reveals an extensive program for illustrating a Bible, possibly derived from an eastern plan such as Syriac illumination, which had a tradition of Old Testament illustration dating from Early Christian times.[17] Some books of the Erznka Bible have a portrait of the author sitting conversing or holding a book or scroll at the beginning of the text, next to a decorated opening panel (*khoran* in Armenian) and decorated initials. This is not consistently done for all books: for instance, the five books of the Pentateuch have only one frontispiece, for Genesis, while most of the prophets have their own author's portrait. Besides these portraits, there are at times additional narrative episodes added to openings of books, usually preceding them. Before the book of Genesis, for example, there is a full-page panel with Moses receiving the tablets of the law from the hand of God, in a common Byzantine iconography;[18] and preceding the book of Ezekiel his vision of God is depicted as described in the first and tenth chapters, *fig.85*. Sometimes an episode replaces the author's portrait. For example, above the opening of the book of Job, the latter is sitting on the ground, nimbed, with his three friends enthroned in front of him, while his wife, also nimbed, sits mourning behind him *fig.86*.

The idea of placing a portrait of the author at the beginning of his book is late Antique and early Christian in origin.[19] This tradition persisted in Byzantine and other eastern churches as well as in the West. In the Erznka Bible, Moses is sitting holding an inkwell and actually painting the first initial *fig.84*. In the opening panel above, Christ Pantocrator is seen in a medallion flanked by two six-winged seraphim and adoring angels. All the initial words in the frontispiece are decorated, and the last letter is filled in with a face, a tradition in Armenian illumination which goes back to the Etchmiadzin Gospel.[20] The Byzantine iconographical elements, such as Moses receiving the law and David playing the harp, are the exception in the Erznka Bible. The Syriac elements are also infrequent. One such Syriac element in the Erznka Bible is Joshua depicted as a standing soldier, similar to the Syriac representation in the sixth-seventh century Bible in Paris,[21] and not prostrate before the angel as in most Byzantine illumination such as the Joshua Roll and the Greek Octateuchs.[22]

The illustration of Ezekiel's Vision also seems to be taken from a prototype, probably of an eastern origin. The picture does not, in any case, illustrate the text of the first and tenth chapters of Ezekiel literally, but combines it with the Second Coming of Christ in the book of Revelation, chapter 4. The multi-colored, rainbow-like, oval frame and the fire within it seem to be based on Ezekiel (1:4, 28), as also are the wheels, one within the other, covered with eyes (1:15–18, 10:12). The enthroned Christ is also based on Ezekiel (1:26), although the blank scroll in his right hand is described in Revelation as a book written on both sides and relates to his Second Coming (5:1). The vision of the four-faced creatures covered with eyes is also Ezekiel's (1:5–11, 10:12–14), but the fact that they have six wings, rather than four, and that each has four identical, rather than different, faces relates it to Revelation (4:6–8). The hand emerging from the fire and grasping the shaft is a strange element in the composition, which may be related either to the creatures' hands mentioned in Ezekiel (1:8, 10:7), or to the hand which carried the scroll "written within and without" (2:8–10), similar to the apocalyptic book which God holds in His hand (Rev. 5:1). The undulating blue stripes under the vision represent the river Chebar, where the vision took place (Ezekiel 1:1), but the angel giving Ezekiel a scroll to eat is related to another stage of the vision (3:1). It may explain the appearance of the hand holding the shaft as related to this scene, a conflation which may have existed in the artist's unknown model.

Ezekiel's vision (chapters 1, 10), like that of Isaiah (chapter 6), no doubt helped to fashion pictures of theophanies (appearances of Christ as God), as in the Ascension (Acts 1:9–11), the Second Coming of Christ (Revelation 4, Mt. 24:30),[23] and Christ in Glory (Daniel 7), as well as the symbols of the Evangelists. The conflation of all these literary elements in visual representations had already occurred in Early Christian times. The four-winged, four-faced cherubim of Ezekiel were confused with the six-winged, single-faced seraphim of Isaiah and the similar creatures in Revelation, sometimes nimbed and carrying books, symbolizing the Evangelists. The result is that, even in Early Christian art, it is almost impossible to label a scene as a "pure" vision of Ezekiel. Even his appearance in a scene does not necessarily identify the other elements as pertaining purely to Ezekiel, as, for instance, in the fifth century mosaic in the apse of Hosias David in Thessalonika,[24] the Byzantine manuscript of Cosmas Indicopleustas in the Vatican,[25] and the so-called Roda and Farfa Catalan Bibles.[26] These representations have Ezekiel standing at the side, with cherubim of varying appearances either carrying or flanking Christ. Christ being carried by the four creatures is more commonly represented in the Ascension and the apocalyptic Second Coming than in the Vision of Ezekiel. Early eastern representations, for example in the Coptic chapels (Nos. 17, 26) in Bawit[27]

Figure 78: *The Descent of the Holy Ghost to the Apostles at Pentecost, from the Queen Keran Gospel of 1272, painted at Sis (ms. 2563, fol. 349).*

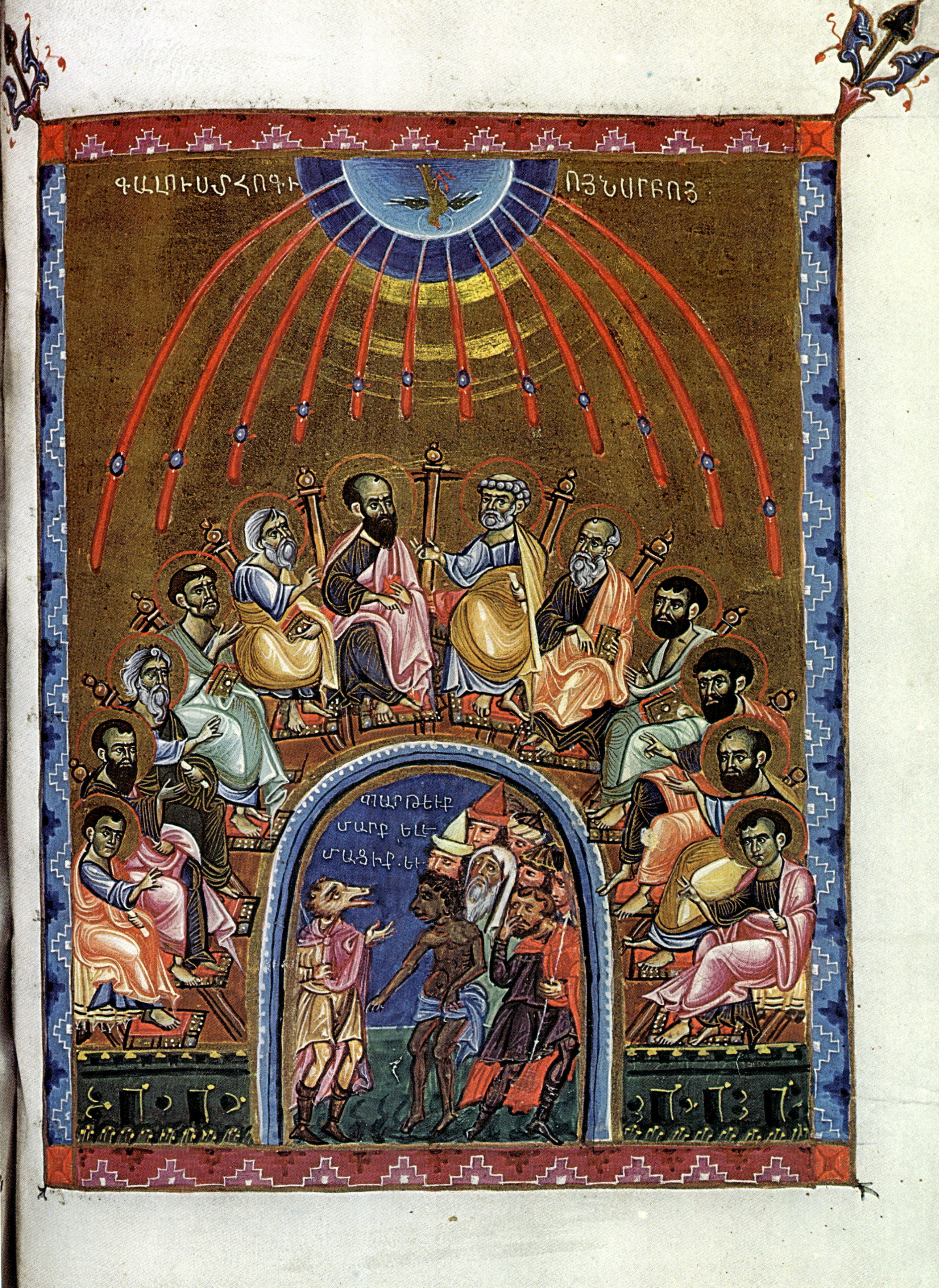
ԳԱԼՈՒՍՏ ՀՈԳՒՈՅՆ ՍՐԲՈՅ

Figure 79: *Prince Vasak and his two sons, presented by the Virgin of Mercy to the enthroned Christ. Dedication picture of the Second Prince Vasak Gospel, ca. 1270 (ms. 2568, fol. 320).*

Figure 80: *St. Matthew writing his Gospel, from the Second Prince Vasak Gospel (ms. 2568, fol. 4v).*

and in the Syriac Rabbula Gospel,[28] differ so much from each other that it is hard to establish a single tradition behind them.

The vision of Ezekiel in the Erznka Bible has four cherubim carrying Christ, each with four identical faces and six wings, unlike any other representation known to us, and may belong to another tradition. The oval frame of our picture resembles the aureole surrounding Christ in the Rabbula Gospel, though this is not sufficient to establish a link between them. Ezekiel lying under the representation of the vision may have been of western origin, for such a picture appears on the title page of the Sponheimer Gospel of the twelfth century, where an angel is handing a scroll to the reclining Ezekiel.[29]

The exact iconographical models for the Erznka Bible are not known to us, but they must have been early eastern Bibles, possibly Syriac, as well as later Byzantine and western prototypes. The style of the Erznka Bible is also ambiguous. It bears some relation to other contemporary manuscripts from Greater Armenia in the proportions of the figures, their dark outlines, somber faces, and the pipe-like folds of their garments. These resemble the Gospel of the Translators Monastery of 1232.[30] However, the clinging drapery falling more softly in undulating folds in the Erznka Bible and the more expressive faces must have been influenced by contemporary Cilician illumination, immediately preceding Thoros Roslin.[31] There were close contacts between the kingdom of Cilicia and Armenia, which was ruled by the Mongols at the time, and there was evidently artistic exchange between the two communities.[32]

Cilician illumination at the end of the thirteenth century was severely affected by the advance of the Moslems. The fall of Hromkla in 1292 undoubtedly put an end to this flourishing school of illumination. Manuscripts by the hundred were lost, mutilated, or destroyed, and only a few were saved. Many artists escaped from Cilicia to other Armenian centers, and continued through their work the tradition of Cilician illumination, although others adopted the art of their new environment.[33]

80

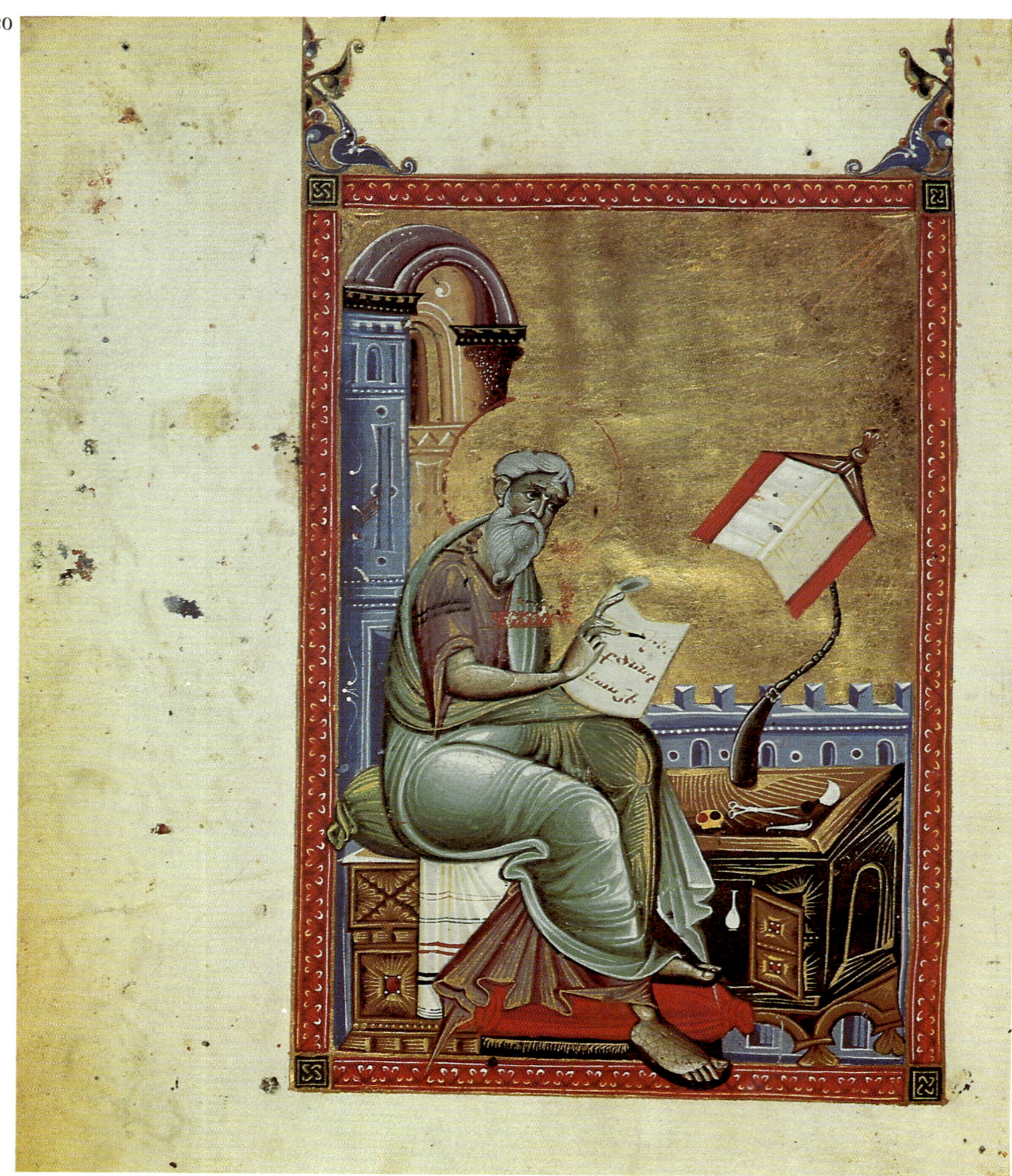

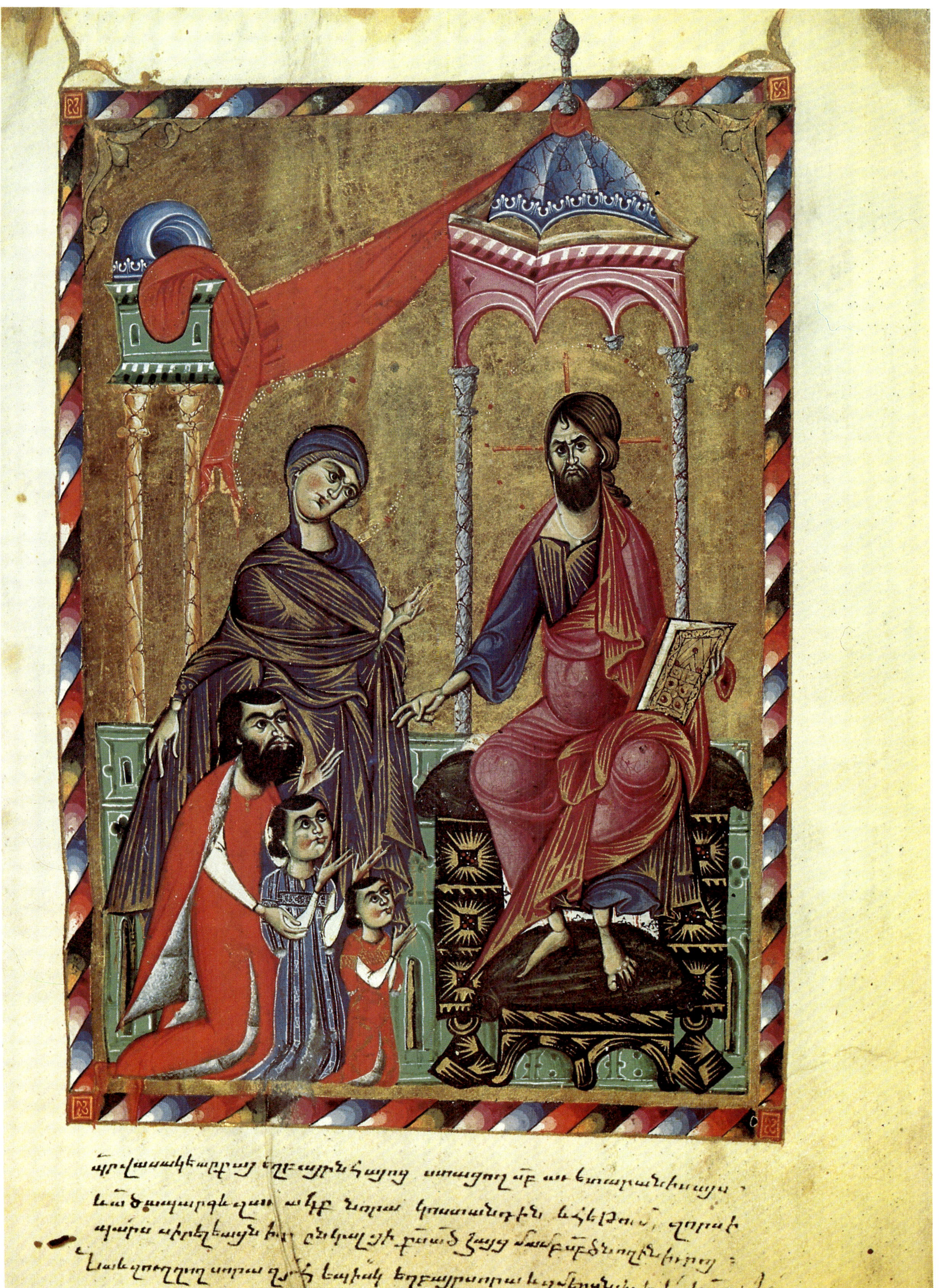

Figure 81: *The Nativity of Christ, with the Adoration of the Shepherds and the Magi, from the Second Prince Vasak Gospel, of between 1268 and 1284 (ms. 2568, fol. 8v).*

Figure 82: *The Baptism of Christ in the Jordan, from the Second Prince Vasak Gospel (ms. 2568, fol. 12v).*

Figure 83: *The Ascension of Christ, from the Second Prince Vasak Gospel, Cilicia, last quarter of the thirteenth century (ms. 2568, fol. 247).*

81

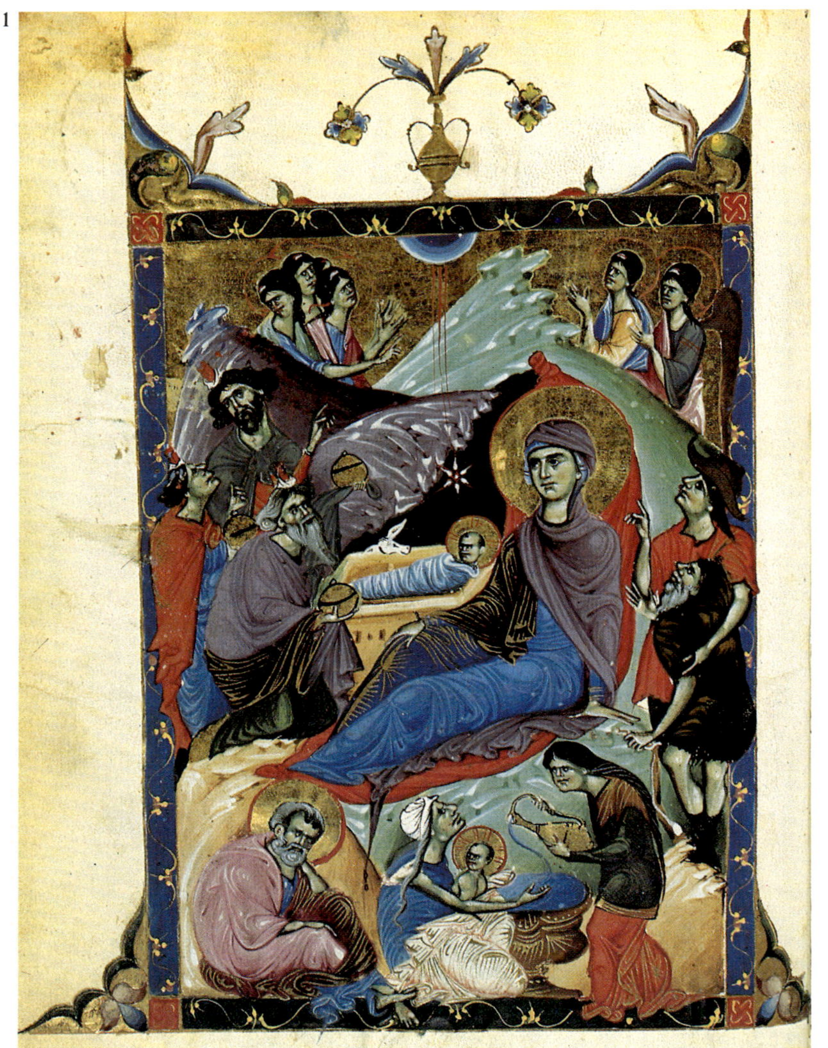

82

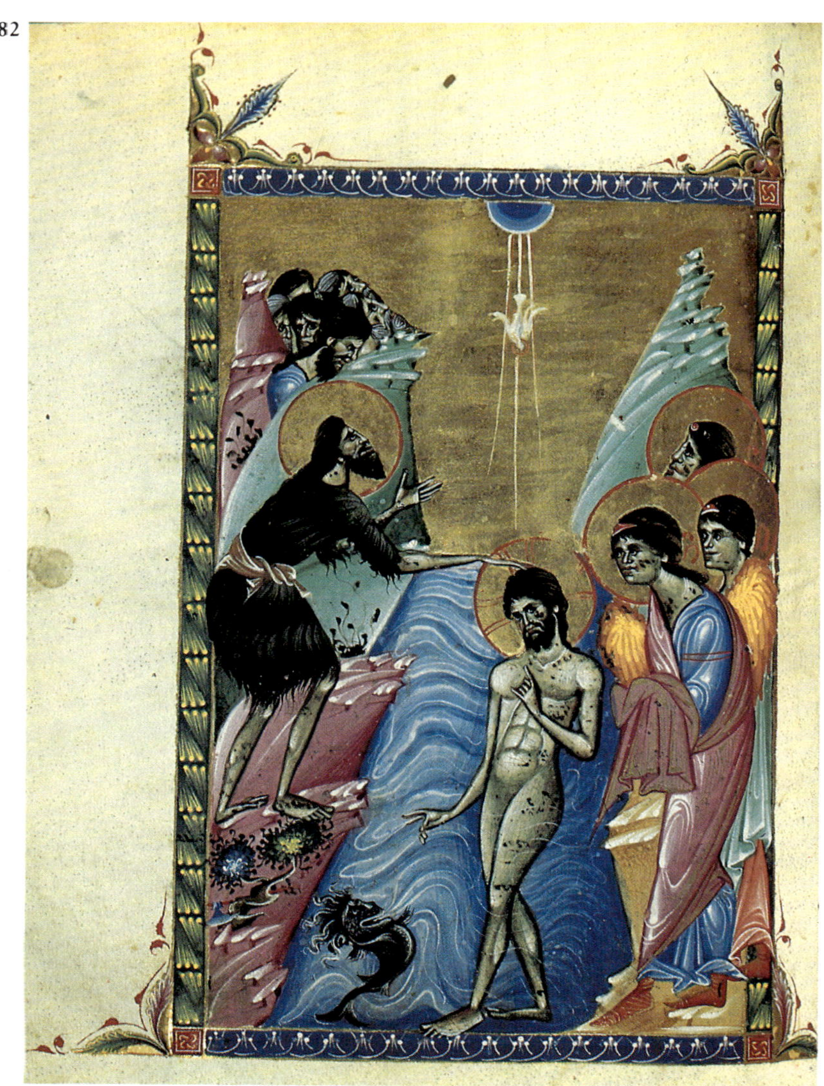

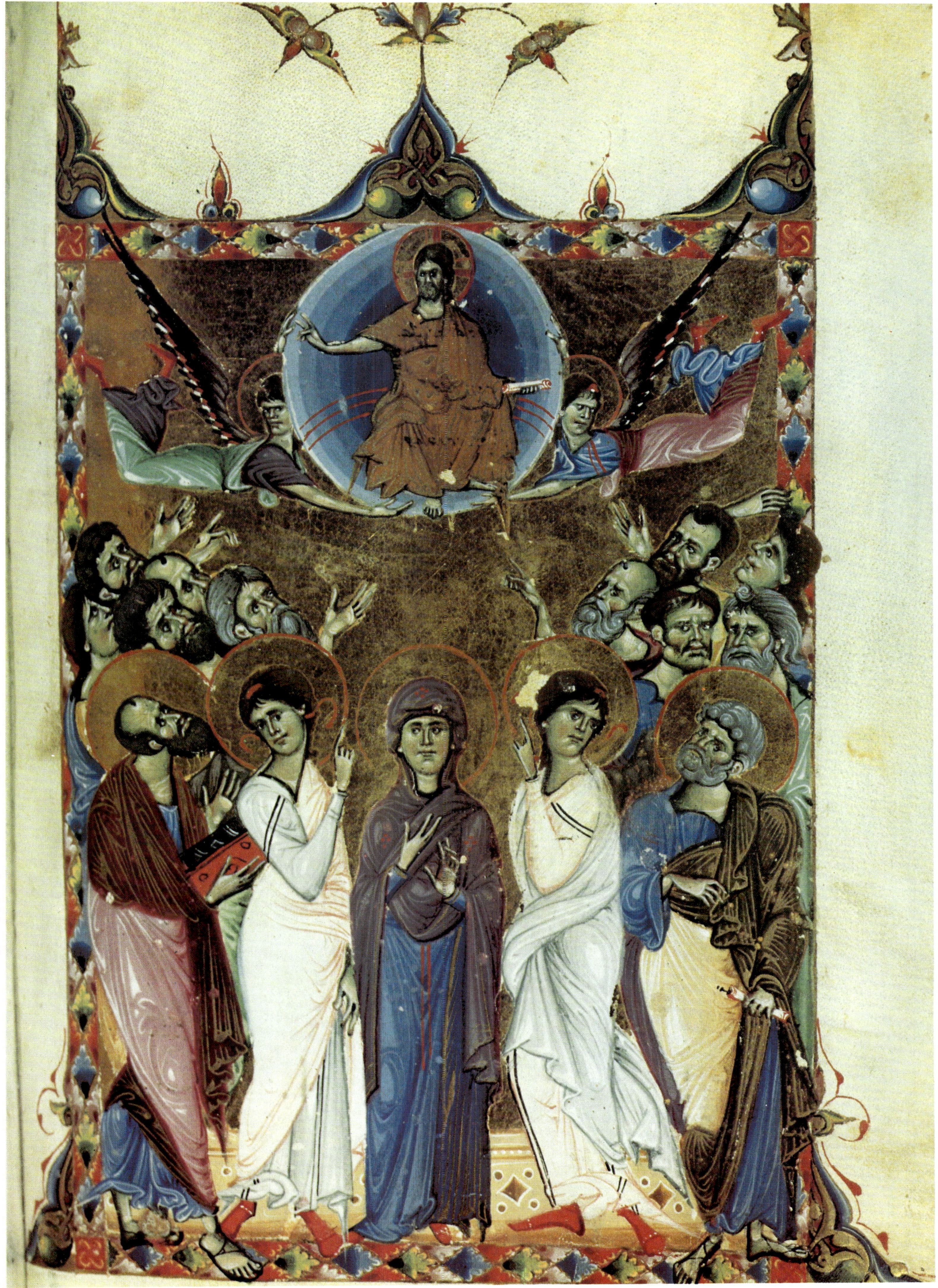

Figure 84: *Moses writing the initial of Genesis on the opening page of the Pentateuch, from the Erznka Bible of 1269 (ms. 1925, fol. 9).*

Figure 85: *Ezekiel's vision on the river Chebar. Four creatures carrying the chariot of God, and an angel feeding the prophet with a scroll, from the Erznka Bible of 1269 (ms. 1925, fol. 414v).*

Figure 86: *Job discussing his lot with his three friends, with his wife sitting behind him. Opening to the book of Job from the Erznka Bible of 1269 (ms. 1925, fol. 241).*

84

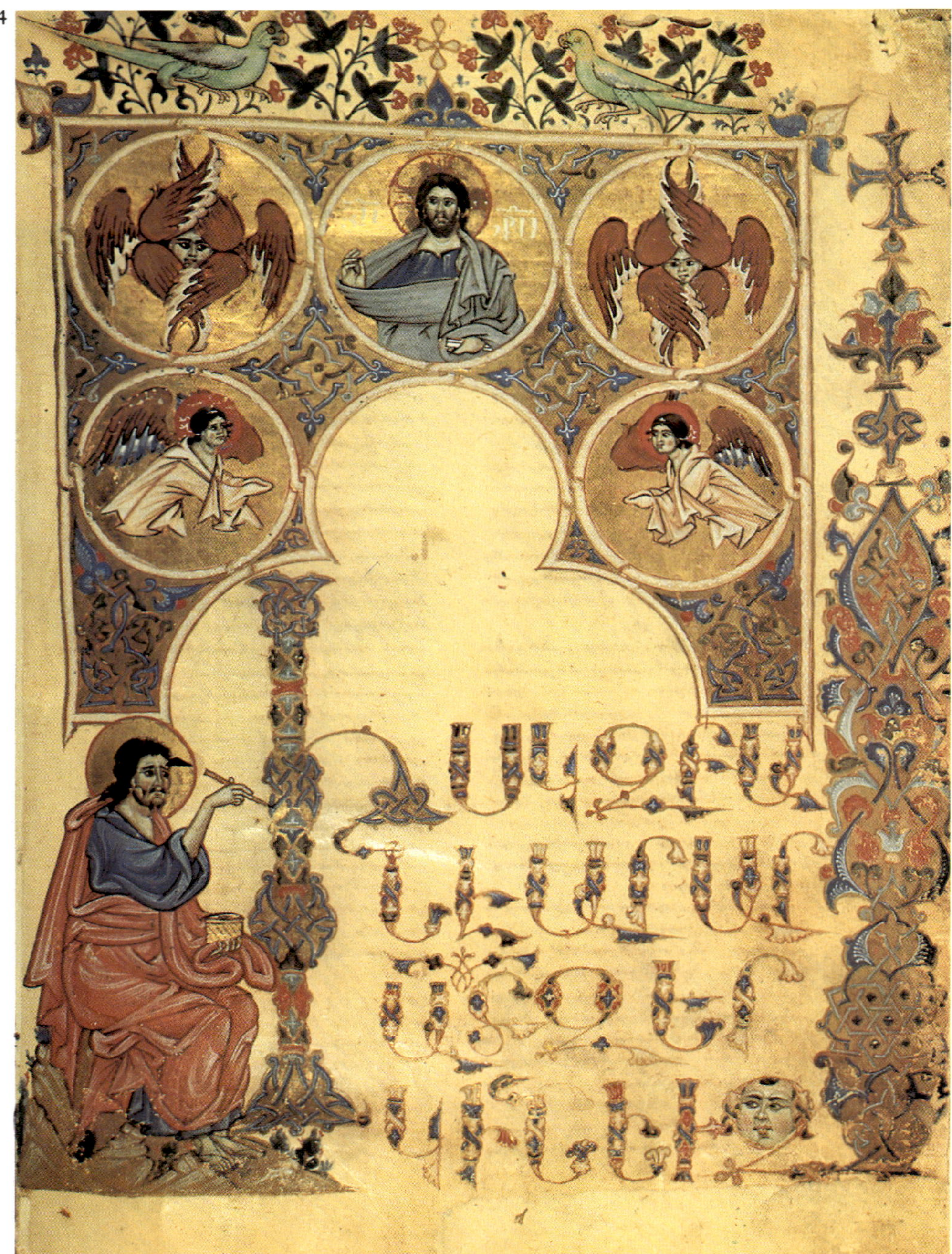

86

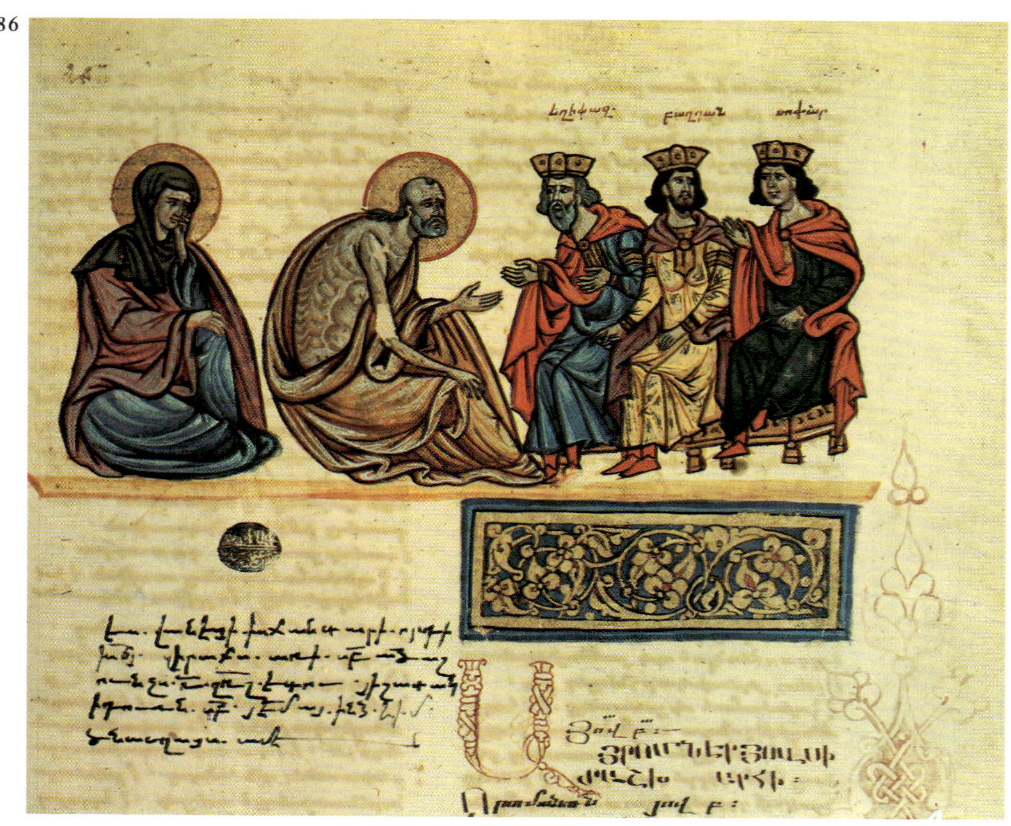

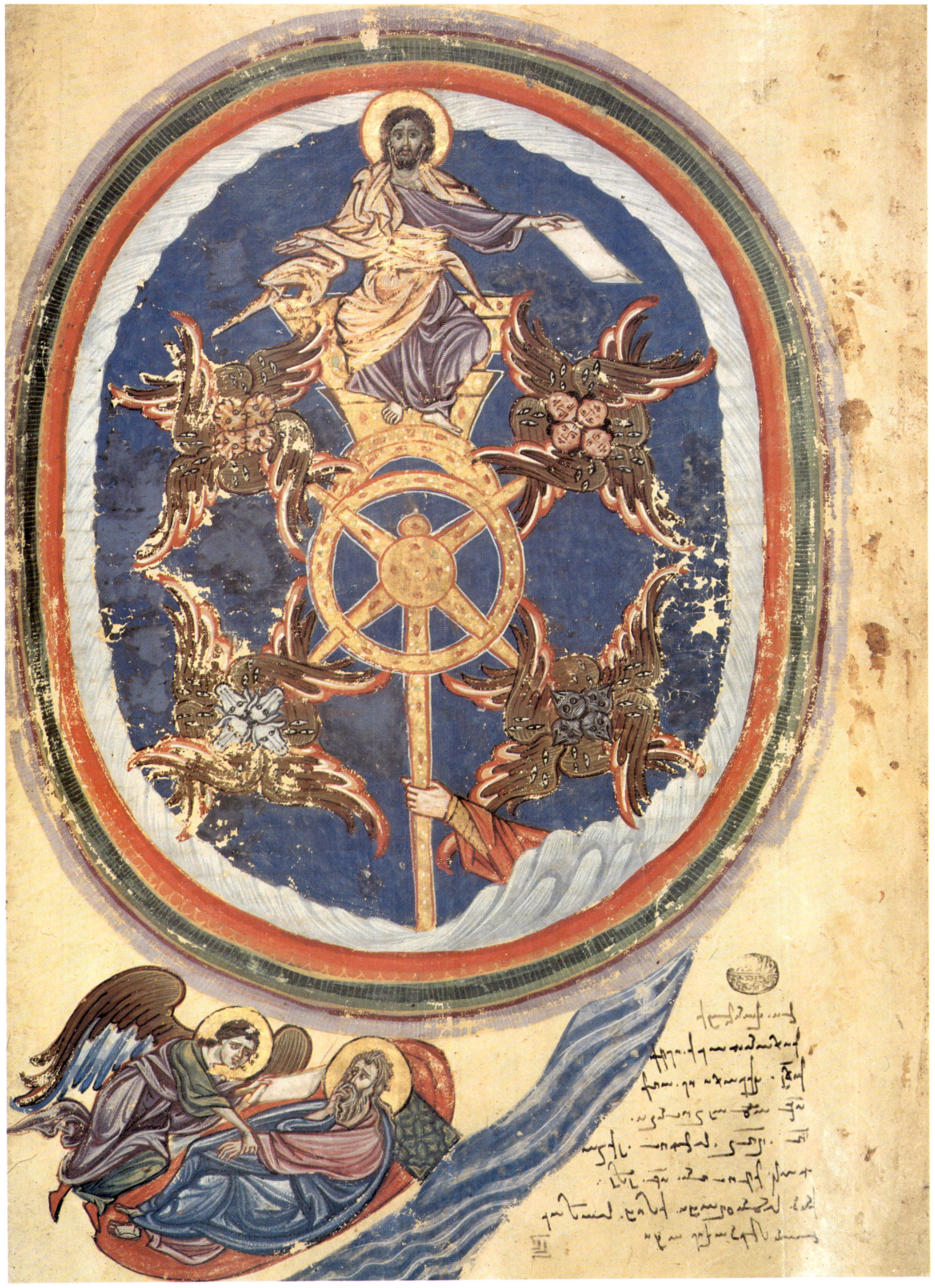

Figure 87: *St. Anthony in an Armenian monk's habit, surrounded by monsters and a snake as symbols of the temptations he overcame. From a religious Miscellany of 1273 from Greater Armenia (ms. 1288, fol. 142v).*

Figure 89: *St. John the Evangelist dictating his Gospel to Prochoros, with his symbol, a flying eagle, on the left. Opening page from the Khatchen Gospel of 1326 (ms. 1794, p. 290).*

87

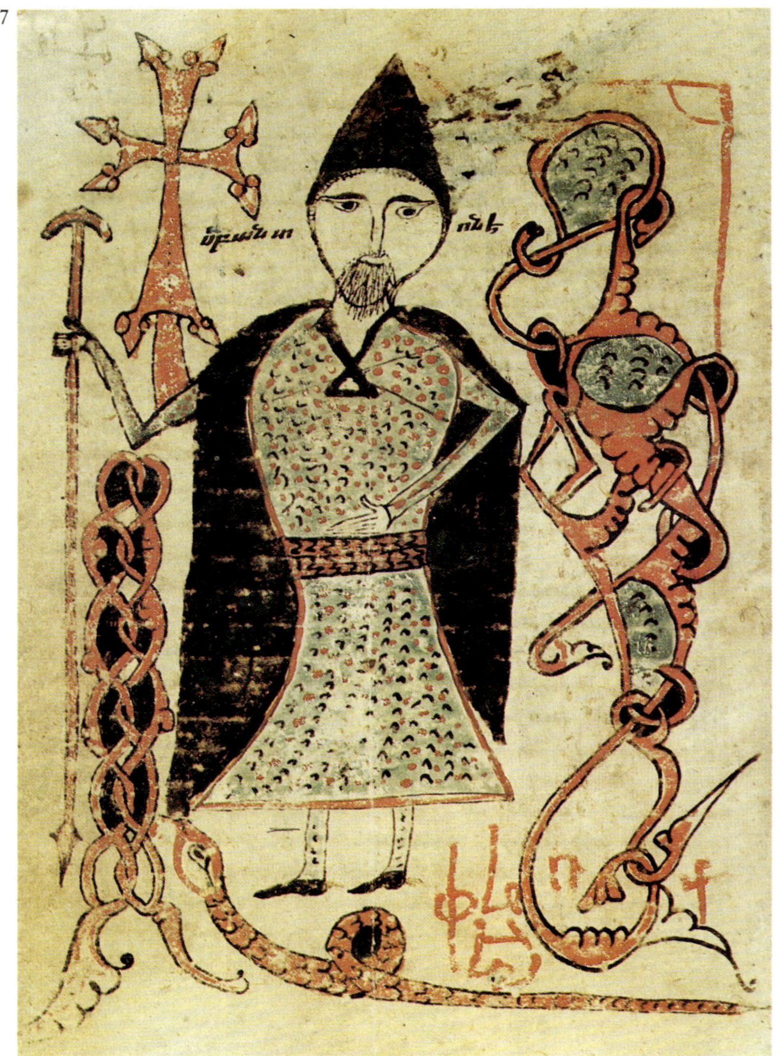

89

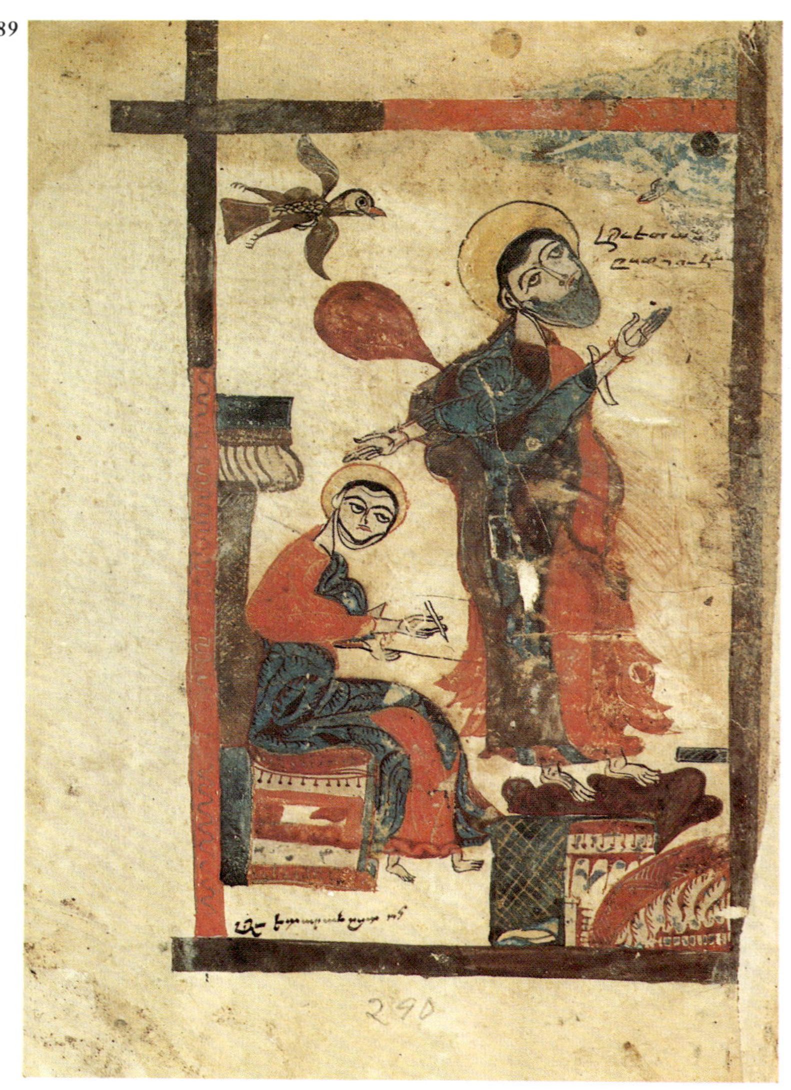

Chapter Six: Illuminated Manuscripts of the Thirteenth and Fourteenth Centuries in Greater Armenia

88

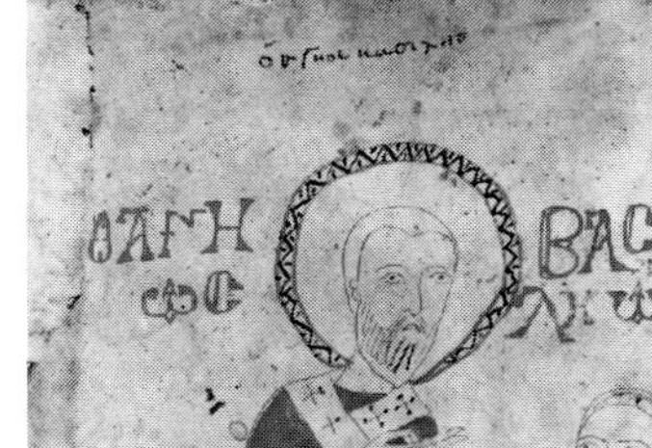

Figure 88: *St. Basil, in bishop's robes, blessing the scribe of the manuscript, Sargis, a deacon, while the donor stands behind him. Opening page from St. Basil's* Lives of the Christian Fathers *of 1298 (ms. 336, fol. 2v).*

During the long rule of the Mongols in Greater Armenia, no important schools of illumination developed until the beginning of the fourteenth century. In the middle of the thirteenth century, when the Cilician schools of illumination flourished at Hromkla and Sis, only a few artistic achievements could be numbered in Armenia proper, all of which were influenced by Moslem style. The so-called Homilies of Mush of 1204[1] and the Haghbat Gospel of 1211[2] are two early examples. Although their style and iconography are traditional Armenian with strong Byzantine influence, the Moslem elements are clearly distinguishable, mostly in the decorative motifs, but also in the rendering of garments and facial features such as turbans and narrowed eyes.[3]

During the last quarter of the thirteenth century and well into the fourteenth, similar types of illumination were practised. Most of the manuscripts of this period in the Jerusalem collection are more crudely executed than the Haghbat Gospel. Some of their stylistic elements are considered to be traditional in Greater Armenia, others are Moslem, and some reveal the use of Byzantine models at first hand. The three examples illustrated here are all dated, and well illustrate these stylistic tendencies in Armenian illumination. They are all written on eastern paper, probably because of lack of funds for vellum. The earliest of the manuscripts, dated to 1273, has a picture of St. Anthony in an Armenian monk's habit, surrounded by monsters and a snake symbolizing the temptations he overcame to the "glory of God,"[4] *fig.87*. It is the frontispiece to a Book of Questions on different religious matters of the thirteenth century. In style this Miscellany of 1273 resembles the Haghbat Gospel of 1211, and its crude quality emphasizes the Moslem influences.[5]

The second manuscript, the Lives of the Christian Fathers by St. Basil, was copied in 1298. The frontispiece to the entire work, *fig.88*,[6] depicts St. Basil as Bishop of Caesarea blessing the seated scribe Sargis, who wrote part of the manuscript, and a donor holding a Cross behind him. The Byzantine stylistic elements are recognizable in the more classicizing faces as well as in the drapery, especially when they are compared with the rather abstract style of the Miscellany of 1273 mentioned above. The Greek inscription, "St. Basil", clumsy though it is, also points to a Byzantine origin.

The third manuscript a Gospel from Khatchen, north-eastern Armenia, of 1326[7], is more traditional in its plan of decoration as well as in its iconography. The Eusebian letter and canon tables, which normally precede the Gospels, have been lost together with the portrait of St. Matthew. The other three Evangelists writing their books each form a frontispiece to their Gospel, all accompanied by their symbols. St. John *fig.89* stands on a hillock looking up to heaven, while placing his hands on Prochoros, who is seated writing. A bird in flight symbolizes his eagle. The decorative style is manifest in the drapery of the garments and in the coloring of the hillock and the chair. The crudeness is emphasized by the form of the hands, the thin necks, and the linear facial features. This simplified type of Evangelist's portrait is a tradition known from Armenian illumination of about a century and a half earlier.[8]

By this time, in the first quarter of the fourteenth century, this kind of illumination was archaic, though it helped to evolve the new, expressive style of the prolific artist, Thoros of Taron.

1. Thoros Taronatzi

Thoros of Taron was a scribe of great talent and imagination. He was active during the first half of the fourteenth century, in the monastery of Glatsor, under the auspices of Esayi of Netch, the archbishop who turned the monastery into a "second Athens", as it came to be praised. In her initial study on Thoros' earliest signed manuscript, in the Mekhitarist Monastery in Venice, Der Nersessian listed eight of his manuscripts, dating from between 1307 and 1332.[9] Since then, more manuscripts signed by or attributed to Thoros Taronatzi have been found. Although some of them are of doubtful ascription and others are lost, this brings Thoros' period of activity up to 1346.[10] Two of the manuscripts attributed to him are in the Jerusalem Collection, one a Gospel signed and dated 1321, and the other a Lectionary of 1331[11]. To these Archbishop Noraier Bogharian has suggested adding a frontispiece which was painted in a third manuscript of 1299.[12]

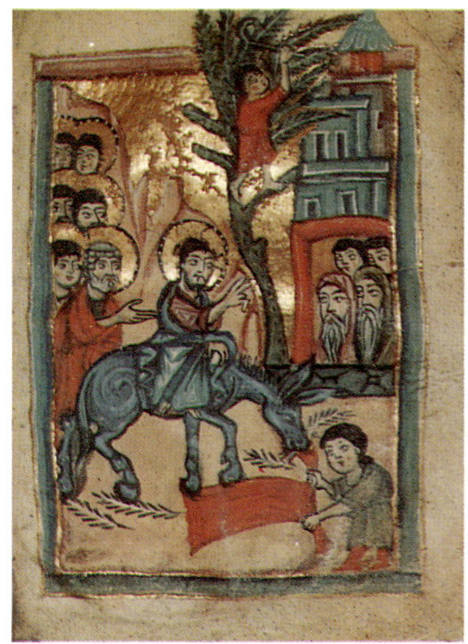

91

Figure 90: *Portrait of St. Matthew and opening of his Gospel, from the Thoros of Taron Gospel, Glatsor, 1321 (ms. 2360, fols. 18v–19).*

Figure 91: *Entry of Christ into Jerusalem, from the Thoros of Taron Gospel, Glatsor, 1321 (ms. 2360, fol. 127).*

2. *The Thoros of Taron Gospel*

Most of the illuminated manuscripts which Thoros painted are Gospel books. Their plan of decoration is quite common in Armenian art: Eusebius' letter and canon tables precede the Gospels, each of which has a full-page portrait of the Evangelist as a frontispiece, for example, St. Matthew *fig.90*. The opening pages have decorated headpieces, and the text is painted in zoomorphic letters with the first initial as the Evangelist's symbol. Full-page Christological scenes, mostly of the Twelve Greek Feasts, are painted on single leaves closely connected to the text, rather than arranged chronologically.

Thoros' iconography is very special, for he knows no bounds in borrowing from other sources or in creating new elements. His innovations stem from visual rather than literary sources, so that he must have had a vast repertoire at his disposal, which he repeated only rarely. A cock as a stand for St. Matthew's book *fig.90* resembles a live fowl rather than the carved wooden birds or fish which appear at times as lecterns in Evangelists' portraits. In the Entry of Christ into Jerusalem, reproduced here from this Gospel of 1321, *fig.91*, he depicts only the heads of the welcoming inhabitants, n a window-like gateway crowned with an Armenian-type church dome, which must have been familiar to him.

Thoros' style is very distinctive, both in his composition and in his figures and rendering of color. In all of these, Thoros is following the lead given by art in Greater Armenia a century before.[13] Thoros' compositions are extremely compact, with few empty spaces. All objects have thick, dark outlines singling out every detail. The figures are squat and stocky, with proportionately large heads, some round, others elongated. The facial features are distinctive and well articulated, Christ's head being most typical. They are composed of large, elongated eyes with the pupils in one corner, close to the upper lid; the eyebrows are thick, arching up and away from the eye, thereby creating a rather low brow. The delicate nose is straight, with the nostrils at right angles to it, the small mouth is sometimes connected to drooping side lines, thereby enlarging the cheeks. The hair is dressed closely round the head and is mostly dark, the hands large and expressive. The drapery, too, is bordered by dark outlines and shading, the folds arranged in parallel or spiral bands, with areas of highlight creating a restless impression.[14]

90

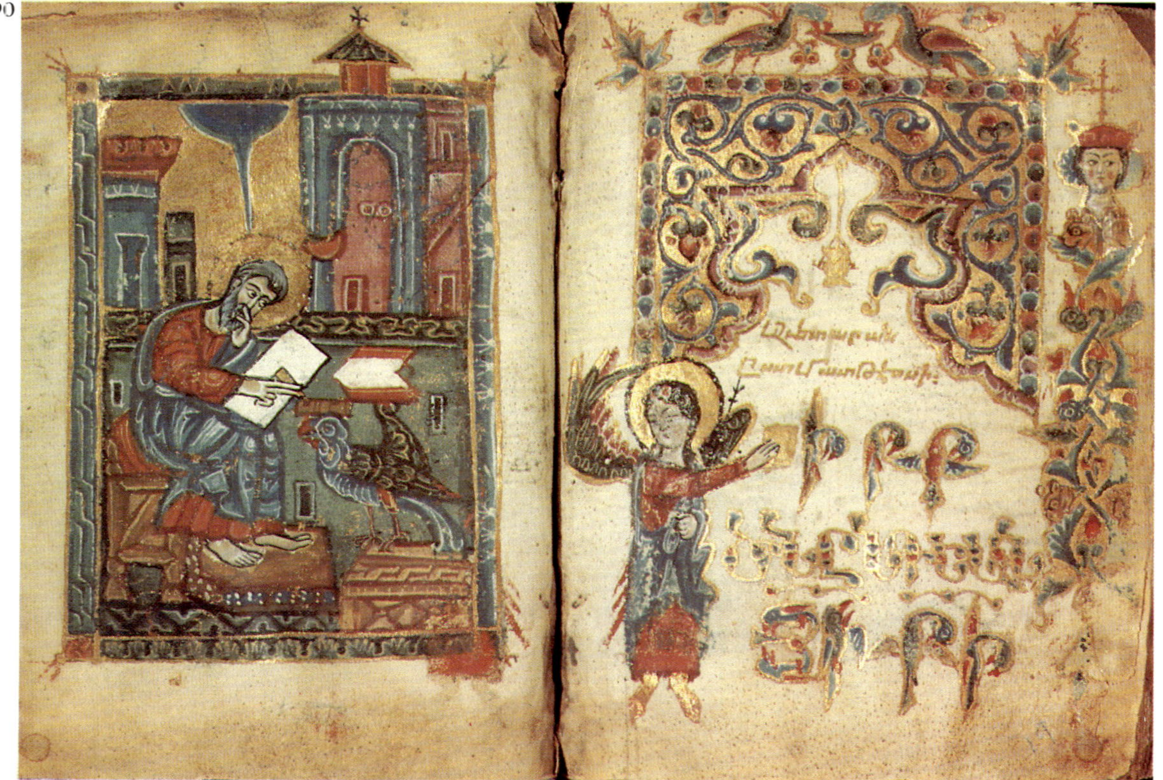

3. *The Isaiah Commentary of 1299*

The frontispiece to the commentary on Isaiah by George *Vardapet* of Skevra (?1245–1301) certainly does not belong to the manuscript with which it is bound.[15] It was copied in Cilicia by a scribe, Vardan, in 1299, and according to the colophon was shortly afterwards given, unbound, by Constantine, Bishop of Caesarea, to Esayi Ntchetzi at Glatsor. The frontispiece depicts Esayi of Netch surrounded by his pupils, who wear Armenian monks' hoods, *fig.92*, some holding books with the covers unwrapped, and one opening a book on a stand in the center. Light streams down to Esayi's head from heaven and diverges from his mouth towards his pupils. A large pomegranate tree, the symbol of knowledge, grows in the center of the picture, and there is a small kneeling figure of the painter or donor beneath the lower frame. Archbishop N. Bogharian, the custodian of St. Thoros' Library in Jerusalem, has suggested that no other artist could have portrayed this scene

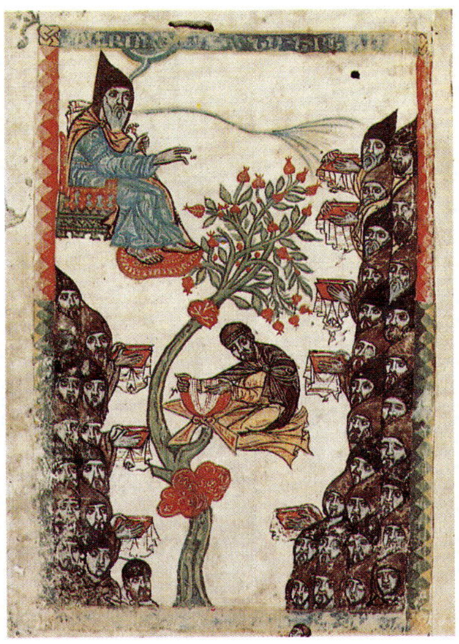

92

Figure 92: *Archbishop Esayi of Netch teaching his pupils in Glatsor. Frontispiece added in the first half of the fourteenth century to a manuscript of a commentary on Isaiah copied in Cilicia in 1299 (ms. 365, p. 2).*

of Esayi's Academy but Thoros of Taron, the almost official artist of Esayi at Glatsor.[16] Indeed, Esayi's large head, compared with his body, and the pronounced outlines are somewhat similar. However, the overall composition, the linear quality of the drawings, the coloring, as well as the figure style, are not those of Taronatzi. The composition of the Esayi Academy panel is very spacious, and the lack of colored background in the center of the picture makes it very different from any of Taronatzi's painted pictures. The grouping of the monks in two columns of heads, one above the other, is different from those in Taronatzi's Entry into Jerusalem *fig.91*. The linear style of the Esayi drawing, stressing the outlines rather than the shadings, and the white linear hatching of the drapery rather than areas of highlight, make it the work of a draughtsman and not of a painter of heavy gouache colors as was Thoros Taronatzi. This is stressed by the light coloring, which makes it possible to see the underdrawings. With only three full figures in the Esayi picture for comparison, it is difficult to find parallels. However, comparison of the seated Esayi with Taronatzi's seated St. Matthew *fig.90* reveals the differences in the proportions and posture of the figures. Esayi's large head is thrust forward somewhat from a hunched back, and his hands are longer, with upturned finger tips (best seen in the central figure).

The delicate facial features are also different from most of Taronatzi's work. Although the large, rounded eyes are similar, Esayi's picture lacks the elongation of the corner eye-line so typical of Taronatzi. The eyebrows are closer to the eye and slope down at the edges, the nose is composed of a downward pointing tip with two rounded nostrils, unlike the usual straight Taronatzi nose. Trifid noses and eyebrows closer to the eye can, however, be found in the earliest of Taronatzi's manuscripts, a Gospel of 1307.[17] Also, the little figure of the kneeling donor or artist is paralleled in Taronatzi's Gospel of 1307,[18] though there he is nimbed and kneels in the outer margin in front of the Virgin and Child. Despite these similarities, the Esayi Academy picture differs on the whole from the style of Thoros of Taron's illumination, and cannot be attributed to his hand.

Our Esayi Academy picture betrays, however, similar composition and draughtsmanship to another Gospel dated to 1311, a dispersed and fragmentary manuscript which was painted by another Thoros, a deacon.[19] This had eighteen full-page panels, which have been reconstructed by Der Nersessian.[20]

In all these panels the Deacon Thoros appears to be more of a draughtsman than a painter, even though all his panels are crudely painted in gouache. This becomes obvious not only in the rendering of rocks and ground, which are lightly colored,[21] but also in the overstressed outlines of the figures and the underdrawing revealed beneath the flaking colors. A good example is the picture of the Sacrifice of Isaac from the Berenson Collection in I Tatti,[22] where the details of the bark of the tree are to be seen beneath and not on top of, the light coloring. Even the gold background to some of the panels was painted after the drawings were completed, and not laid as gold leaf. Indeed, the heavy coloring laid in single areas and the gold backgrounds seem alien to the panels and may have been applied by an apprentice. However, the unmodeled colors, the blue faces, the pink ram, and the green tree do resemble to some extent the lightly colored drawing of the Esayi picture. The spacious compositions of Deacon Thoros' panels may have resembled the Esayi picture before the colored backgrounds were applied to them. The large figures have heads thrust forward on the necks; all facial features, including the large, rounded eyes, close eyebrows, trifid noses, and small mouths are similar. Particularly close are the garments and their draping. The figures with bent knees have long robes which flare from the knees in angular folds, for example Esayi and the kneeling figures in the center of the picture and beneath the frame, which resemble many figures in the Gospel of 1311. Abraham's garment in the I Tatti picture is similarly rendered, and part of his mantle is flapping on his back like that of Esayi. The drawn hatchings of the garments and the painted linear highlights can also be found in both manuscripts. The painter kneeling in front of Esayi and turning his head to look at the viewer is a common figure in Thoros the Deacon's pictures.[23] If the picture of Esayi's Academy is by Thoros the Deacon, it seems to conform more to his characteristic draughtsmanlike style.

4. *The Thonrak Lectionary of 1331*

The third manuscript in Jerusalem attributed to Thoros Taronatzi is a Lectionary copied by Yovhannes *k'ahanay* and painted by an artist called Thoros in the village of Thonrak in 1331.[24] Thonrak is in the canton of Apahunik', where Thoros of Taron was active, and the signature "Thoros" on folios 174 and 228v led Archbishop Bogharian to assume that it could have been Taronatzi who decorated the Lectionary.[25] The similarities in the large heads and some facial features are too common in this period to permit the identification with Taronatzi. Moreover, his characteristic features and heavy painting are missing in our Lectionary, even in the opening headpiece *fig.93*, which has the only painted figures, the Virgin and Child flanked by two angels. The pen-drawn trumpeter and the rest of the pen-drawn decoration on this page, obviously executed by the same hand, may illustrate how the coloring of a drawing can somewhat modify the style. The rest of the manuscript is pen-drawn *figs.94–99* in free compositions, with elegant and delicate figural and facial expressions.

It is difficult to compare the free marginal compositions of the Lectionary of 1331 with the full-

Figure 94: *The Sacrifice of Isaac, with the ram hanging from a tree-top, painted by Thoros in the Lectionary of Thonrak, 1331 (ms. 95, fol. 172).*

Figure 95: *Presentation of Christ in the Temple, from the Thonrak Lectionary by the painter Thoros (ms. 95, fol. 38v).*

Figure 96: *The Forty Martyrs of Sebastia who died of cold for their faith, depicted as a heap of winged heads, from the Thonrak Lectionary of 1331 (ms. 95, fol. 123).*

Figure 97: *St. George killing the dragon, from the Thonrak Lectionary of 1331 painted by Thoros (ms. 95, fol. 82v).*

Figure 98: *The Vision of Daniel of the first of the four beasts, with the Ancient of Days above (Daniel 7), from the Thonrak Lectionary (ms. 95, fol. 142).*

Figure 99: *Moses holding up the Tablets of the Law, from the Thonrak Lectionary (ms. 95, fol. 121).*

94

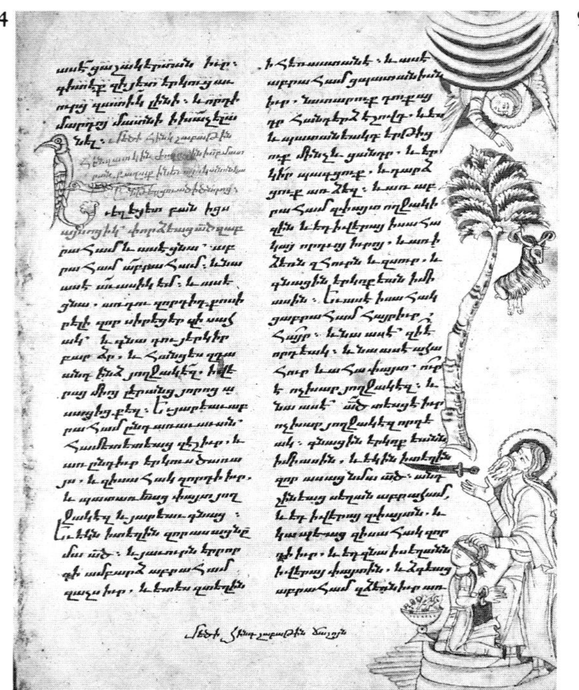

95

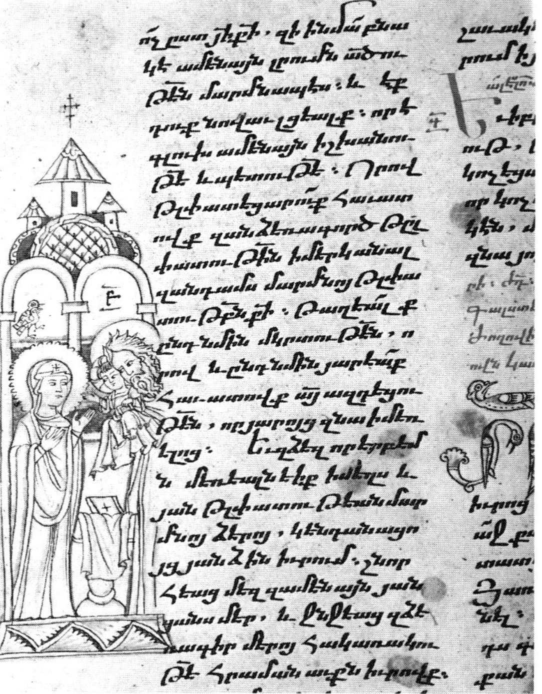

96

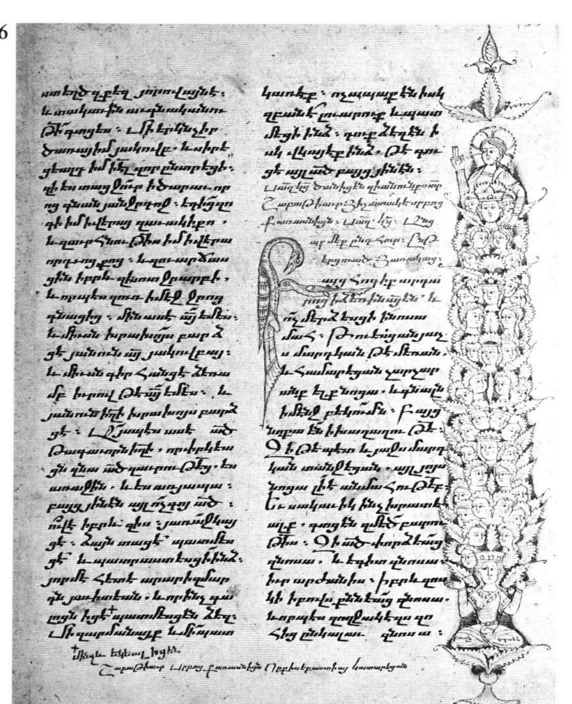

97

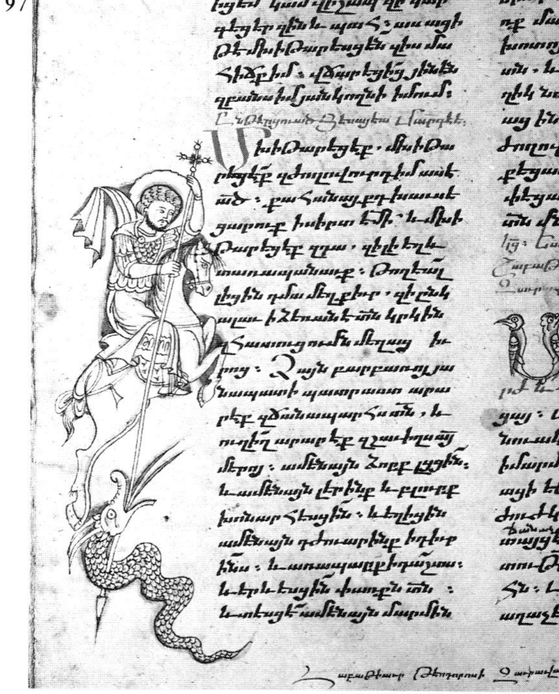

98

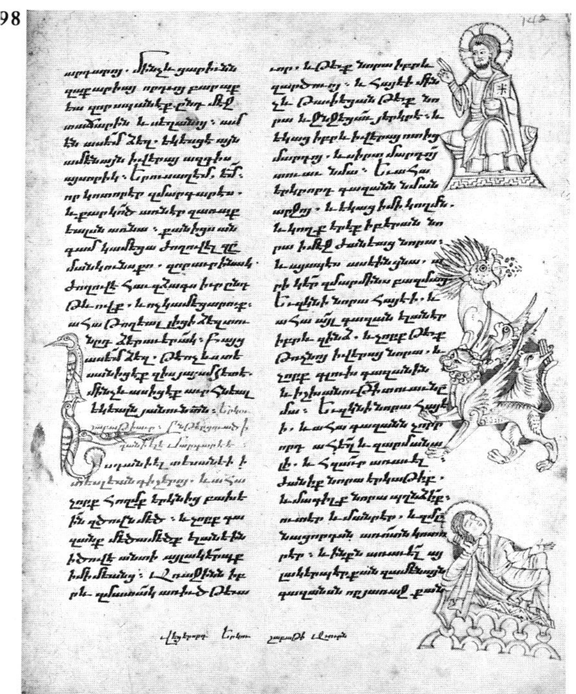

99

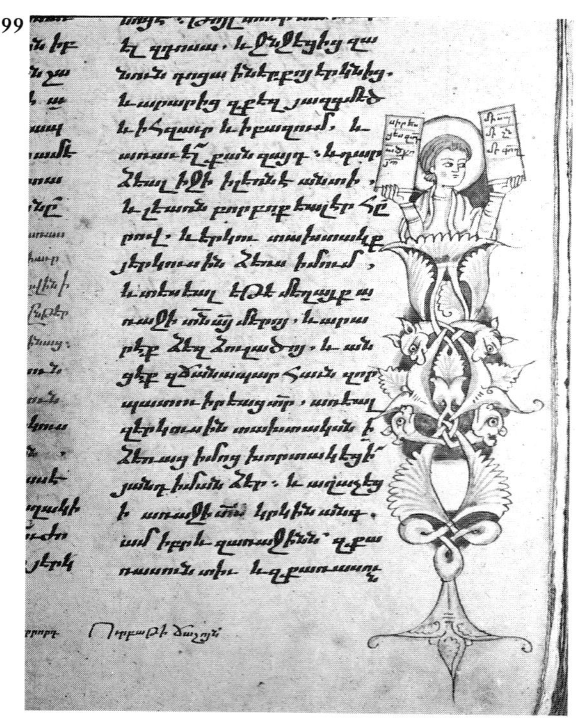

page panels of the Deacon Thoros Gospel of 1311, because of different lay-out and technique; but the figure style can be compared if one takes into account the lapse of twenty years between the execution of the two manuscripts and the possible development of the artist's style. The differences are not in the proportions of the figures or in their shape, nor in the position of the heads, but only in the more delicate facial features of shorter eyebrows, straight noses, and tiny mouths, and the expressive hands with upturned finger tips. The folds of Abraham's garment *fig.94* as well as those of St. George *fig.97* resemble to a large extent those of the Deacon Thoros Gospel of 1311, and also those of the Esayi Academy. The way Isaac's garment flares from the knees *fig.94* is also reminiscent of this element in the other two manuscripts. It is, however, difficult to make a complete identification between the style of the Deacon Thoros of the 1311 Gospel and that of the 1331 Thonrak Lectionary. They are certainly close enough to belong to the same school, which developed in Armenia at the beginning of the fourteenth century. This light, elegant style of drawing does not correspond to any painting by Thoros Taronatzi, who did not leave any tinted drawings known.

The technique of tinted drawing became a fashionable feature in Armenian illumination of the early fourteenth century, after appearing earlier in Cilicia, where several such manuscripts were executed in the late thirteenth century. The Vienna Gospel[26] is only one of those containing tinted drawings which were never meant to be colored. A 1306 Psalter from Cyprus, executed by an immigrant from Cilicia, is another example;[27] and there are several more.[28]

Striking in its similarity is a rare iconographical feature of the Sacrifice of Isaac in the Berenson panel and the Lectionary *fig.94*. The ram caught high up in the branches of a tree rather than in a bush is common to them both.[29]

Other similar elements in this picture are Abraham holding Isaac by his hair from behind, and the pointing angel. The feminine-looking servant remaining with the donkey in the Gospel is, on the other hand, missing from the Lectionary, possibly because of lack of space in the margin.[30] These peculiar iconographical elements in the two manuscripts need not, of course, be the exclusive vocabulary of one artist and may be derived from similar, earlier models.

Peculiar, abbreviated iconography appears in other scenes of the Thonrak Lectionary, whether for lack of space, since the illustrations are all drawn in the margins, or because it is the artist Thoros' manner. An example is the first Vision of Daniel (chapter 7) *fig.98*. Daniel is asleep on his bed, while above him are the four beasts grouped together with the winged lion in front, the bear with three ribs in its mouth and the four-winged leopard behind, and the ten-horned terrible beast with iron teeth towering above them. The enthroned Ancient of Days sits peacefully at the top, without the fiery stream or the thousands of ministers next to him.[31]

Other illustrations in the Lectionary seem to be of a decorative nature, although they still illustrate the text. Moses is shown emerging from an elaborate plant, holding up the two Tablets of the Law *fig.99*.

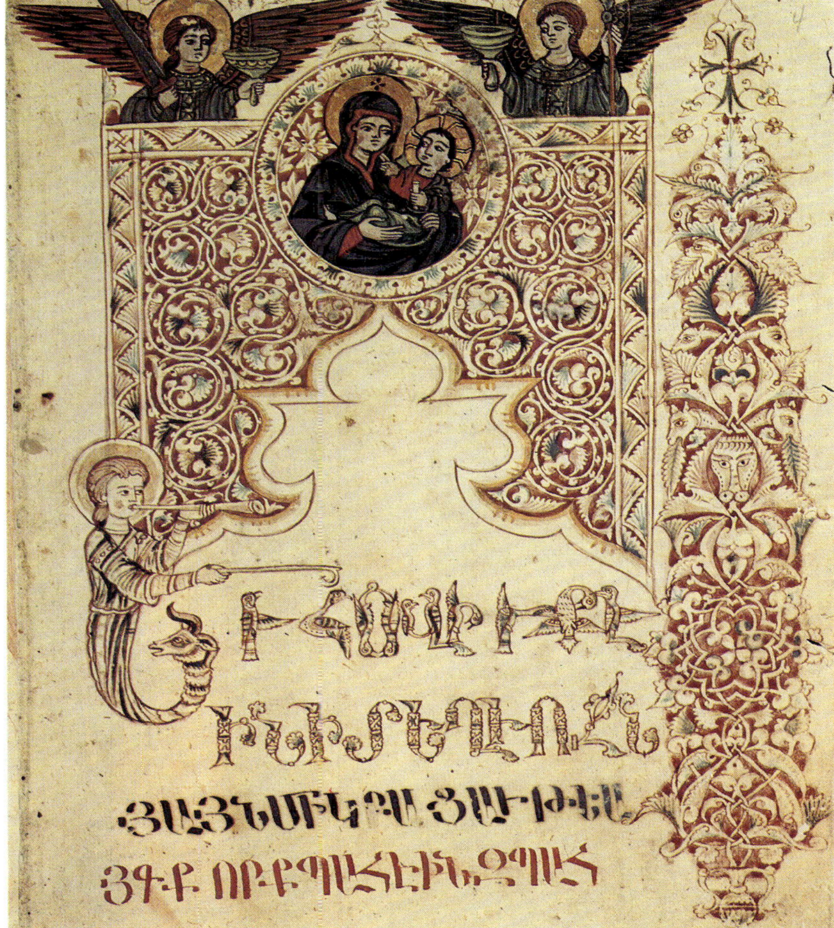

93

Figure 93: *Virgin and Child flanked by two angels. Headpiece to the Lectionary of Thonrak, 1331, painted by Thoros (ms. 95, fol. 4).*

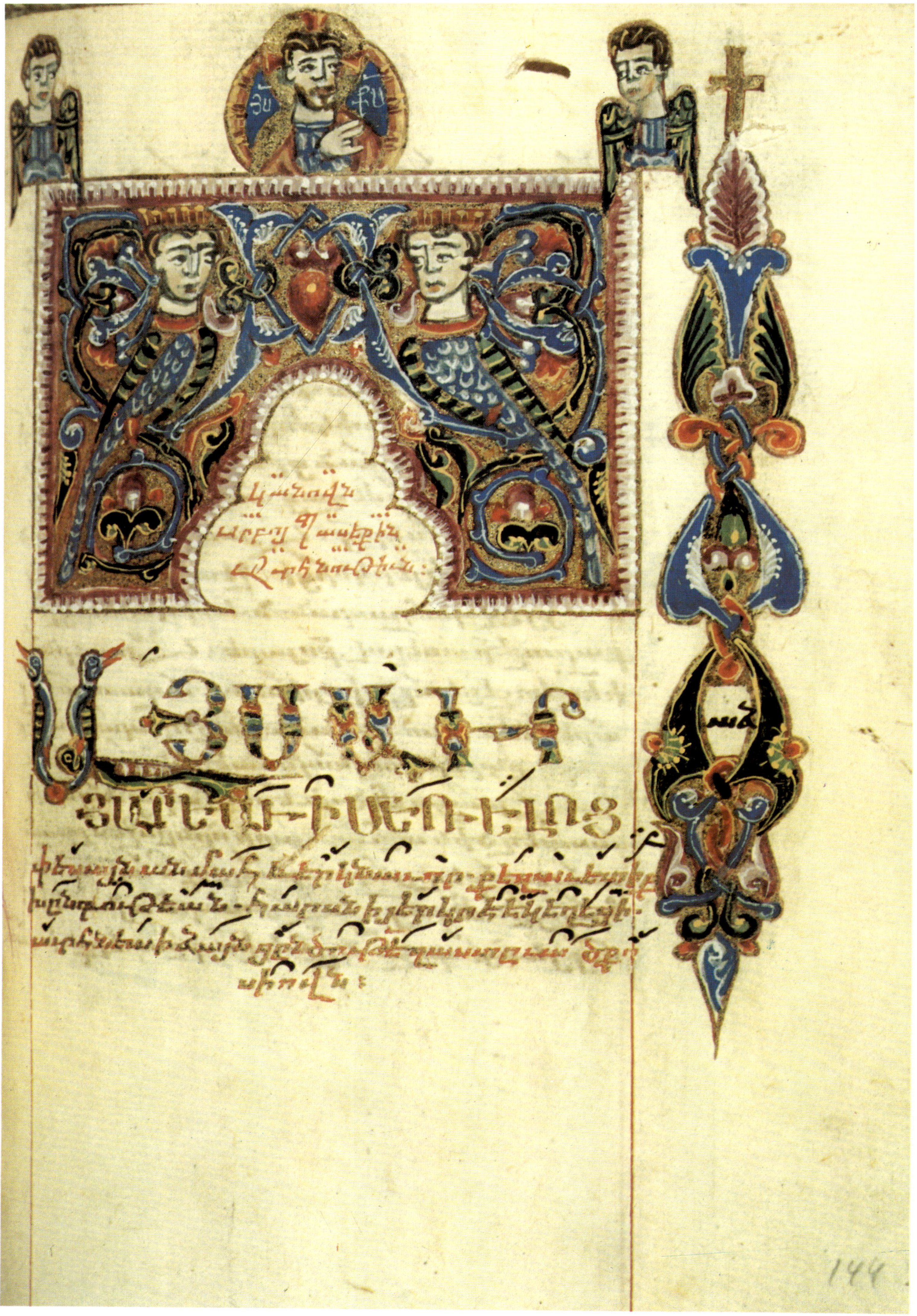

Chapter Seven: Cilician Illumination of the Fourteenth Century

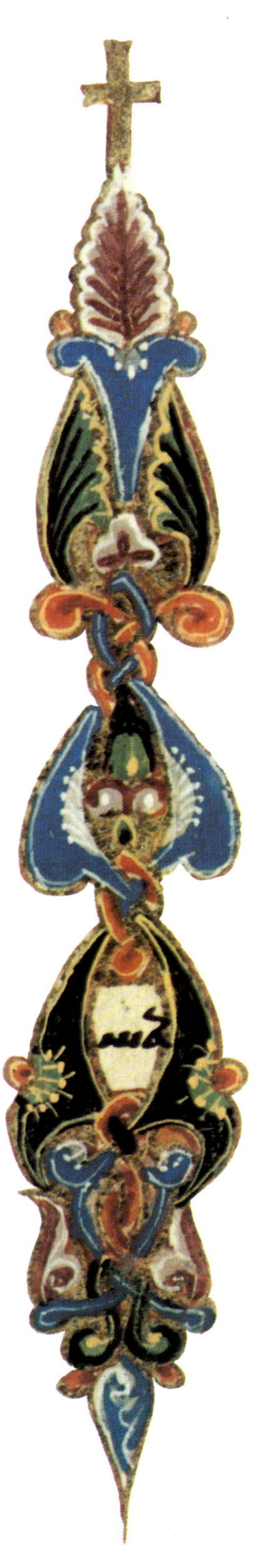

Figure 102: *St. John dictating his Gospel to Prochoros, from the Pidzak Bible of 1323 (ms. 1930, fol. 352v).*

Figure 102a: *Detail from Sargis Pidzak's Hymnal of 1322.*

1. Sargis Pidzak

At the beginning of the fourteenth century political and social conditions in Cilicia again became stable after the great upheaval of the late thirteenth century. With the improvement in conditions, new artistic centers developed in the capital, Sis, as well as in other cities and in monasteries throughout the kingdom. However, this was only a short flowering of less than a century before its decline and the end of the Cilician kingdom of 1375 with the exile of the last king, Leo V, to Egypt. During the first half of the fourteenth century Sargis Pidzak dominated the scene.[1]

The scribe and painter, Sargis *k'ahanay* (married priest), was the son of Gregor *k'ahanay*, himself a scribe and painter. His name is first recorded in 1301 by his father, who states that this Gospel[2] was copied with the help of his son Sargis, and he wishes him a long life as an artist. The wish of his father, who was probably his teacher, was fulfilled, because Sargis is known to have been still active as an artist more than fifty years later. Throughout his life he must have been a prolific scribe and painter, since we know of about thirty-three extant manuscripts painted by him.[3] In some cases two or three of the manuscripts were completed in a single year,[4] while others are very close to each other in date.

His diligence and productivity may have earned him his strange nickname of *Pidzak*, the bee. This name was also explained by a story illustrating his artistic talents.[5] It was said that one day, while he was painting flowers, a bee flew in through the window and settled on them. The people near him tried to chase it away, but then they realised that the bee on the flowers of which they were frightened was also painted by Sargis. It appears that the capital, Sis, and the Monastery of Drazark, where he mainly worked, provided him with ample material and clients. He was probably unable at times to meet the demand, since he did not copy all the manuscripts which he painted. For some Gospels, he painted the usual set of Evangelists' portraits on single vellum leaves, which were later attached to texts copied by other scribes on paper.[6] As an established artist, he acquired an apprentice, Yacob, whom he mentions in the so-called Gospel of the Sea, which he copied and illuminated in 1332.[7]

2. The First Pidzak Gospel of 1312

Sargis is known to have illustrated different types of manuscripts. Besides Gospel books and Bibles, he is thought to have worked on a Psalter and a Ritual; and he favored the fashionable hymnal, but also illustrated a Synaxarion in 1348[8] and a set of Assizes of Antioch in 1331.[9] For some illustrated Gospel books, Sargis painted just the four Evangelists' portraits. This is evident in his First Gospel of 1312[10] which was copied in the Monastery of Lazar in Taron, west of Lake Van in Armenia. The original artist of Taron is not known by name, but his red tinted, ink drawings reveal a talented draughtsman, flexible and imaginative in his decorative and figural motifs. In the letter of Eusebius, the original artist drew the portraits of Eusebius and Carpianus in the lunettes of the fully arcaded pages, with animals, birds, and grotesques in the canon tables as well as in the margins of some pages. The only painted parts executed by the original artist are the openings of the four Gospels[11] *fig.100*, which reveal the same decorative quality as the pen drawings. Sargis Pidzak's three surviving Evangelists' portraits[12] *fig.100, fig.101* also have a decorative style, but different, less busy and condensed than the headpieces. This becomes quite clear when they are juxtaposed, as in *fig.100*. The decorative motifs are also different, and the facial features in the headpiece are simplified compared to the more sophisticated St. Matthew.

3. Pidzak's style

Sargis Pidzak's style is very easily distinguishable because of several particular elements which are immediately noticeable. His compositions are fairly dense, but leave some gold background on which the interspersed objects with their dark outlines stand out clearly. Despite their elongated heads, the proportions of the figures are not exaggerated. The head widens at the top creating at times an unnaturally large forehead. The facial features are well proportioned and articulated: eyes and brows are rounded, with a downward stroke in the outer corners, and the pupils cling to the top center line of the upper lid, resulting in a distant gaze. The nose and mouth are small, and the lower

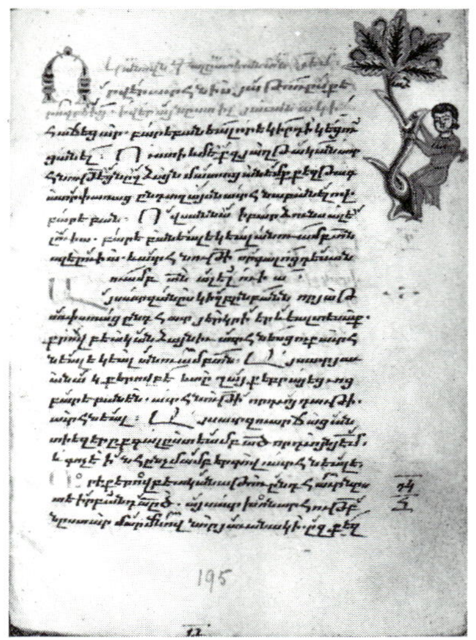

Figure 104: *A boy climbing a tree with an axe on his back. Text illustration from the Pidzak Hymnal of 1322 (ms. 1644, p. 195).*

lip is red and fleshy. The ears are large and distinctive, usually in the form of an isosceles triangle or like drooping, rounded cup handles. The hands are small, with thin, unmodeled fingers, which seem deformed when bent. The small feet are rendered flatly, one usually being seen from above. The drapery falls in geometrical folds outlined in dark tones, with distinct areas of highlight.

There is a gradual change in Sargis Pidzak's style throughout his period of activity, which is best seen by comparing his first Gospel of 1312 *figs.100, 101* with his later works reproduced here, such as the Nativity of John the Baptist in the Hymnal of 1335 *fig.107* and the panels of the Queen Mariun Gospel of 1346 *figs.108–111*. His own distinct stylistic elements are exaggerated and become manneristic. The composition becomes denser, the outlines and shadings are darker, the highlights more thickly applied, the decorative and abstract effects more pronounced, and the figures become shorter. This gradual change becomes more noticeable around 1330. The Chester Beatty Gospel of 1329[13] is more spacious and less manneristic than the Gospel of 1331 in Venice.[14]

4. *The Bible of 1323*

This change is, however, not yet noticeable in Pidzak's Bible of 1323[15] which belongs to the first stage of his development. The portrait of St. John dictating his Gospel to Prochoros is perhaps one of his best creations *fig.102*. In iconography, the Bible of 1323 has no innovations in the Evangelists' portraits, nor in fact in the rest of the illustrations. The Bible is incomplete, the first part – perhaps another volume – being missing. Commencing with Psalms, it has an almost full-panel with a pen-drawn portrait of King David, enthroned and playing a square psaltery. In the outer margins, next to the openings of the books of Job, the major and some minor prophets, the authors are depicted in red pen-drawing, either standing or as busts. Other illustrations in the Bible are abbreviated Christological scenes common in Sargis' Gospels, such as the dove for Pentecost, a temple, or a cock for Peter's denial.[16] The letter of Eusebius to Carpianus, copied on one page, has both busts drawn in the lunettes of a decorated headpiece above the two text columns. Their images are similar to those in Pidzak's Bible of 1319 in Venice[17] and in the Gospel of the Sea,[18] so called because it was salvaged from the sea.

5. *Pidzak's Hymnals*

Pidzak's illustrations to most of his Hymnals also lack innovation. The openings to the main divisions are decorated with headpieces, initials, and marginal ornaments, as in his Hymnal of 1322[19] *fig.103*. Other sections are decorated with painted marginal illustrations borrowed from his repertory of marginal Gospel illustrations. The two reproduced here are examples of the commonest. For the episode of the two blind men in Jericho (Mt. 20:29–34, *fig.104*) he painted a boy climbing a tree with an axe sticking out behind his back; and for the beheading of John the Baptist (Mt. 14:11, *fig.105*), a nimbed head appears above a platter.[20]

The Hymnal he painted in 1335[21] differs from the other Hymnals in having three full-page panels in addition to his usual sixteen marginal illustrations. The three panels depict the Annunciation to Joachim and Anne *fig.106*, the three women at the empty Tomb, and the birth of John the Baptist, *fig.107*. Most interesting of these is the first *fig.106*, which combines in one panel Anne's lament, its answer by an angel, and the meeting with her husband Joachim standing behind her.

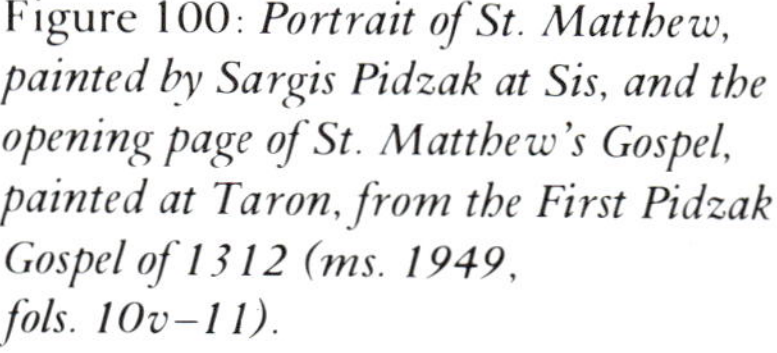

Figure 100: *Portrait of St. Matthew, painted by Sargis Pidzak at Sis, and the opening page of St. Matthew's Gospel, painted at Taron, from the First Pidzak Gospel of 1312 (ms. 1949, fols. 10v–11).*

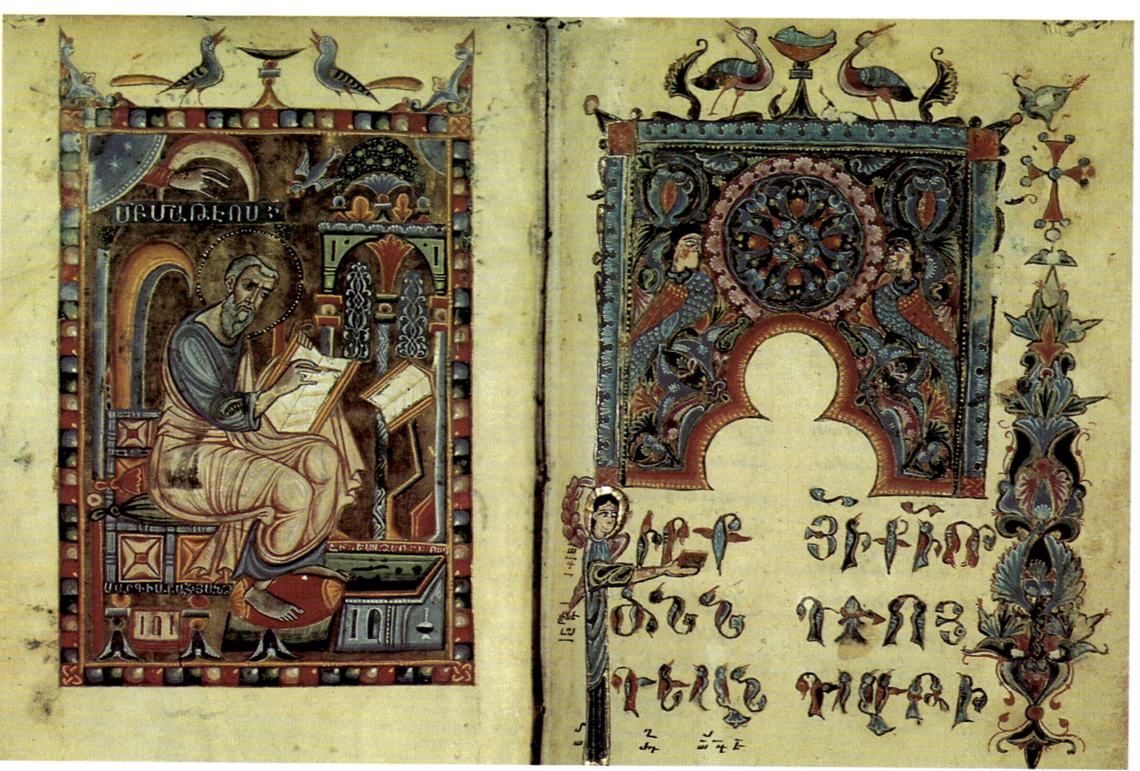

100

101

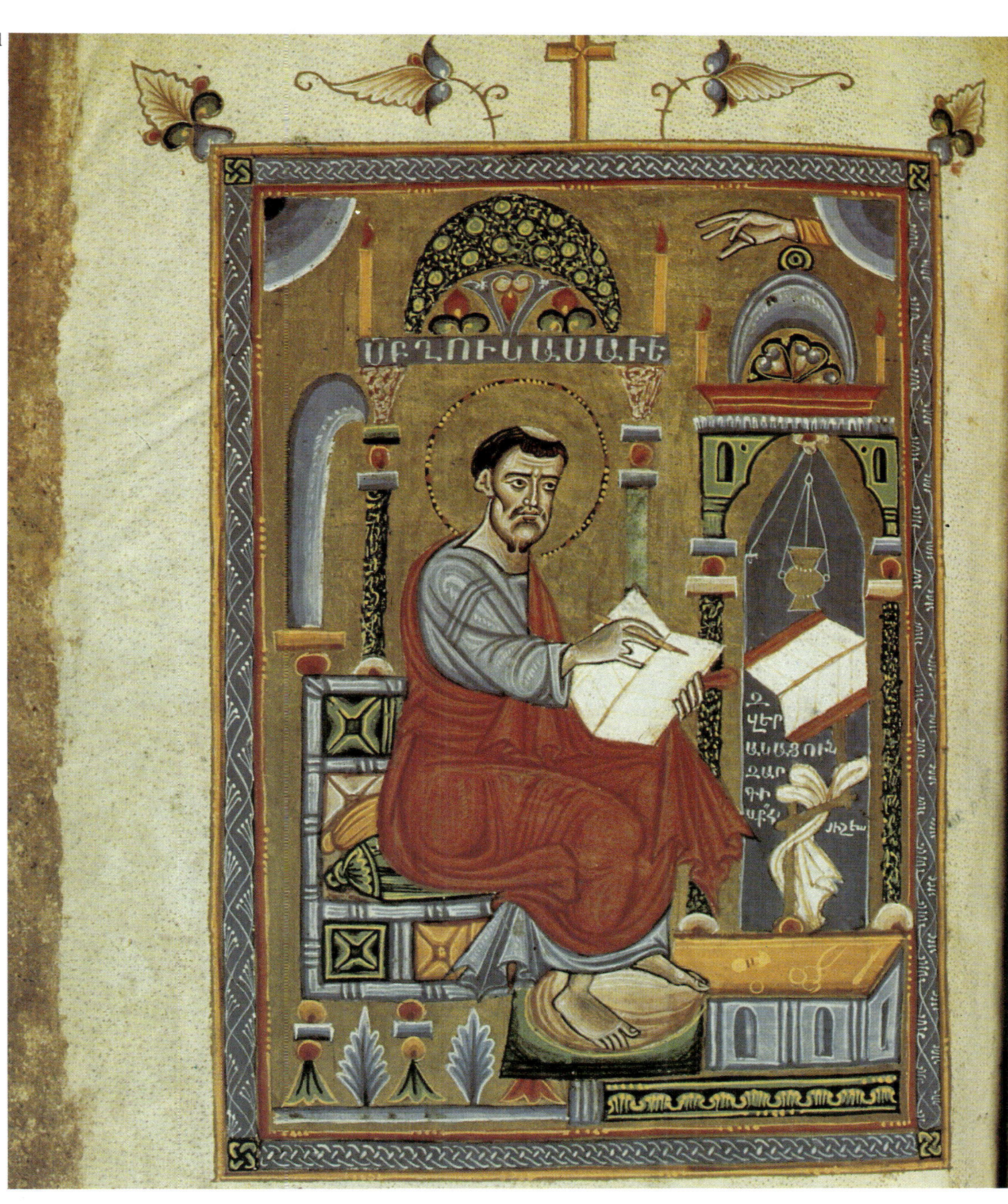

Figure 101: *Portrait of St. Luke, from the First Sargis Pidzak Gospel of 1312 (ms. 1949, fol. 183v).*

The story of the birth of the Virgin to Joachim and Anne is apocryphal and does not appear in any of the canonical Gospels. Anne's prayer and the Annunciation by an angel are related in two Early Christian Infancy Gospels: the Greek Proto-Evangelium of St. James (III:1–IV:1), and the Latin Gospel of Pseudo-Matthew (II:2–3). The picture in Pidzak's Hymnal is closer to the Pseudo-Matthew version, since only there is the serpent mentioned next to the birds, all of which have offspring, unlike Anne.[22] Both the Proto-Evangelium and the Pseudo-Matthew were fairly well known in the Middle Ages in several versions and languages. The Armenian version of the Infancy Gospels does not contain Anne's prayer in detail, although it is based on the detailed Syriac text of the Proto-Evangelium, but starts with Joachim's sojourn in the desert and the angel's annunciation to Joachim and Anne, followed by their meeting.[23] It is, however, certain that the text of Anne's prayer was known in Armenian from other collections of homilies.[24] These may have mentioned the serpent, as in Pseudo-Matthew, for Sargis Pidzak to have included it in his picture. This representation became a standard iconographical feature as a frontispiece to Armenian hymnals.[25] Early Byzantine representations similarly depict Anne in front of a tree with birds and an angel hovering above, usually with the fountain, for example in the eleventh-century mosaic of Daphni and the Homilies of Jacobus Kokkinobaphos.[26]

The birth of John the Baptist *fig. 107* is fashioned after the traditional picture of the Nativity of Christ, and combines other episodes with it. Elizabeth is reclining on a mattress on the left, pointing to the swaddled baby John, who lies in a manger-like crib. On the right is the priest Zacharias, struck dumb, writing his son's name "John" on a tablet (Luke 1:63). Elizabeth's neighbors and relations are standing behind pointing to Zacharias and to the hand of God in the gesture of blessing, an allusion to the Annunciation. A dove, representing the Holy Spirit, alludes to Zacharias' prophecy (Luke 1:67–79), which is written in the text under the panel.

All the canticles in the Hymnals are provided with musical numes above the text lines, as can be seen in the pages reproduced *figs. 103–107*.

Figure 103: Khoran *(headpiece) to the second division of Sargis Pidzak's Hymnal of 1322 (ms. 1644, p. 243).*

Figure 105: *The head of John the Baptist, a text illustration from the Pidzak Hymnal (ms. 1644, p. 254).*

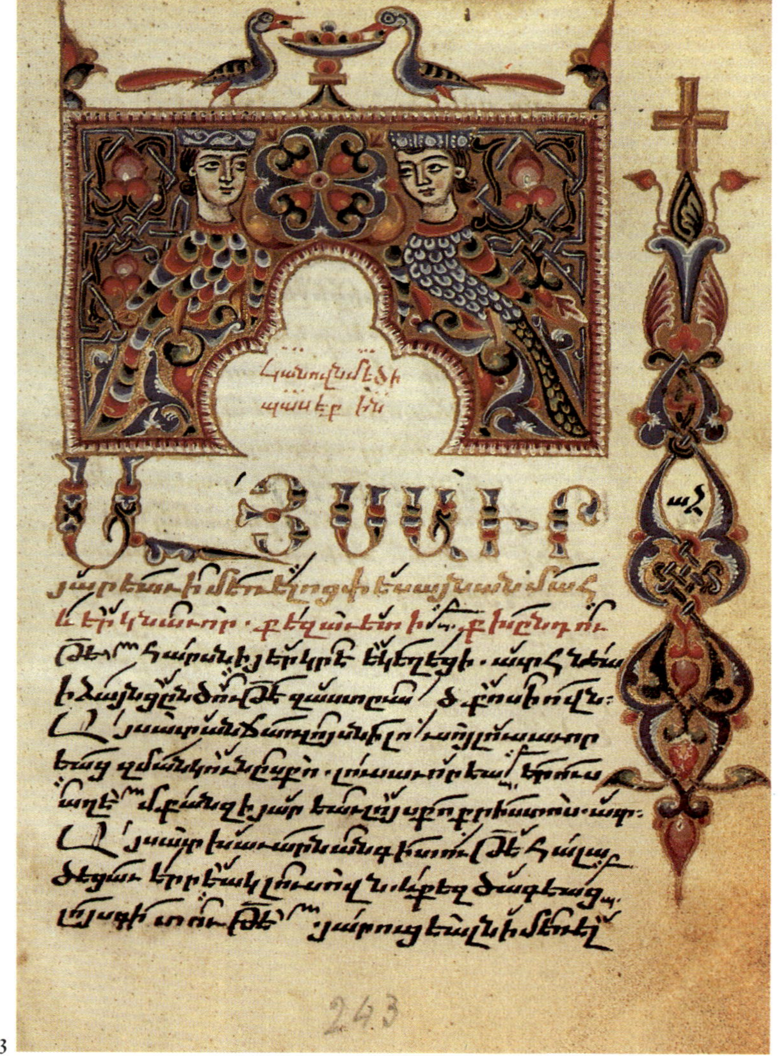

103

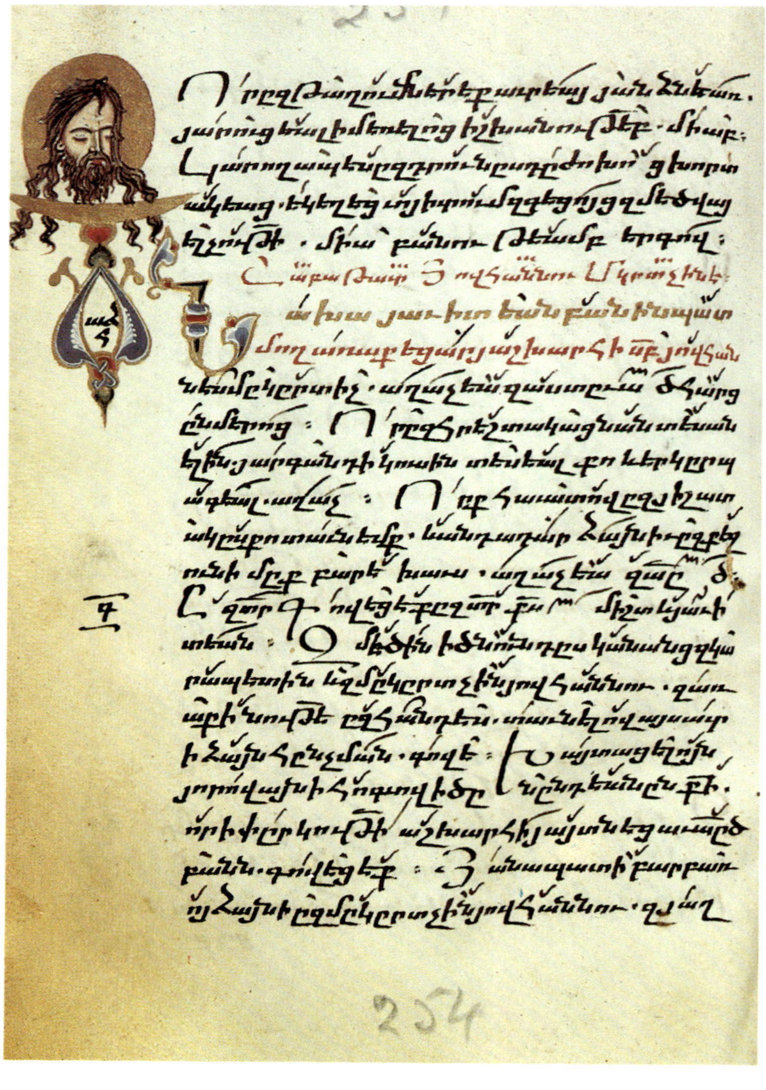

105

Figure 107: *Birth of St. John the Baptist, with his father, Zacharias, writing his name on a tablet, from the Pidzak Hymnal of 1335 (ms. 1578, fol. 179).*

Figure 108: *Nativity of Christ, with Queen Mariun washing the Child, from the Queen Mariun Gospel of 1346 by Sargis Pidzak (ms. 1973, fol. 8v).*

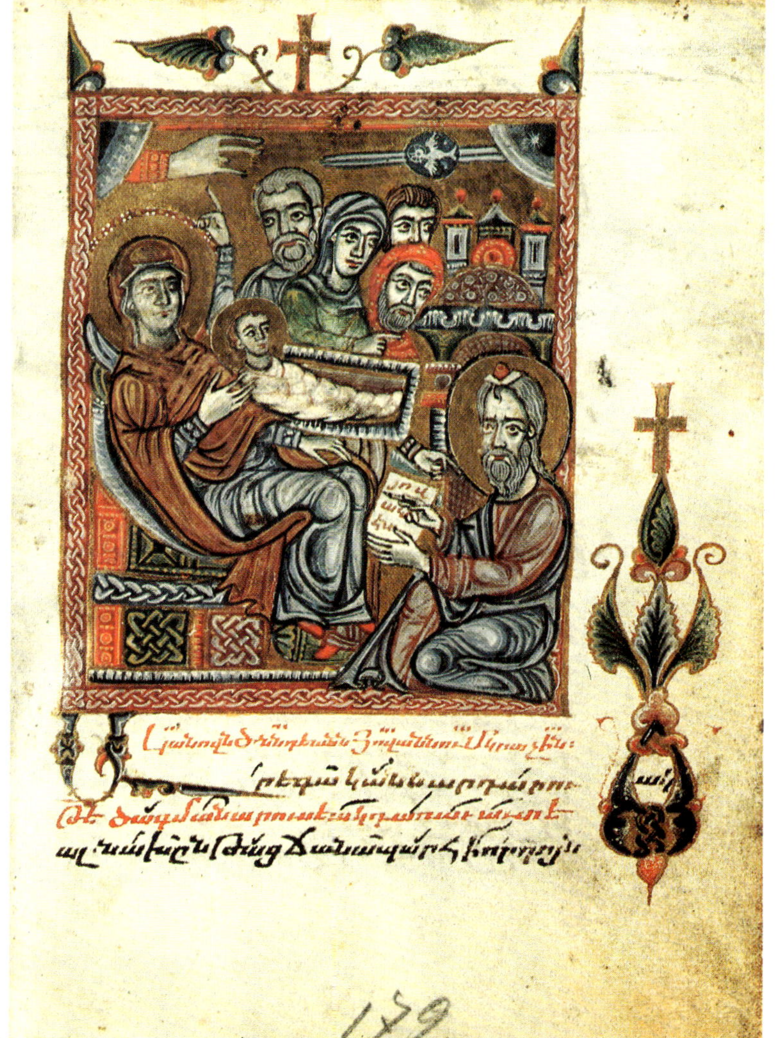

107

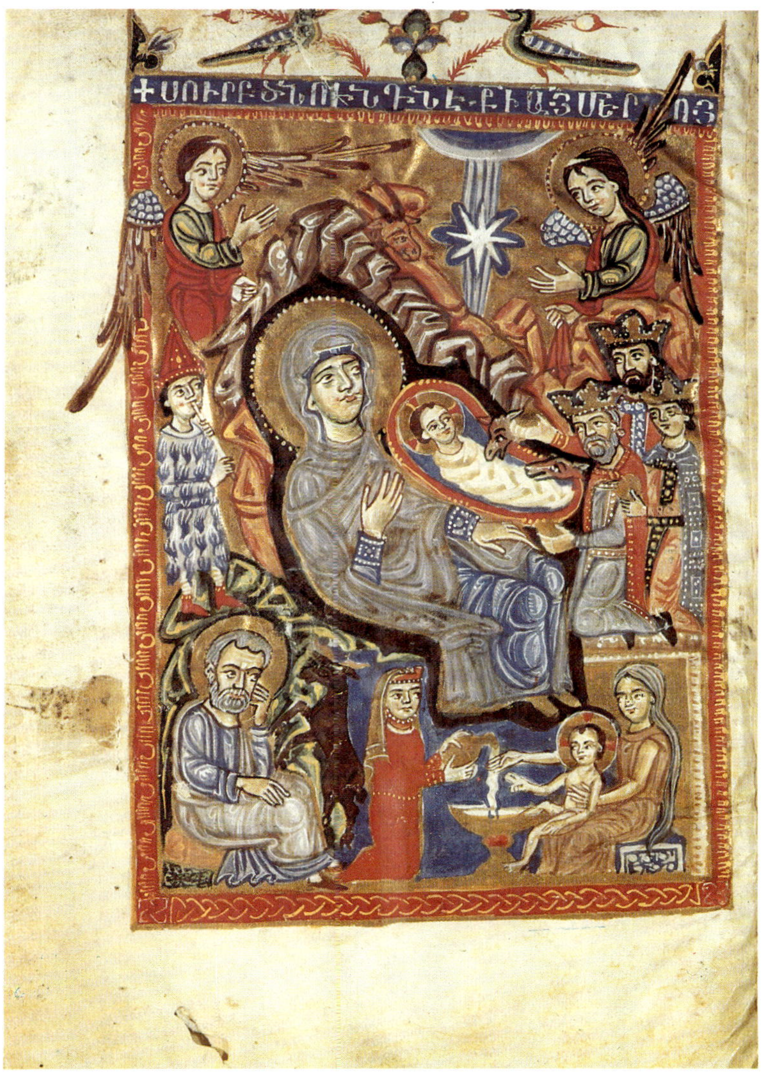

108

Figure 109: *Entry of Christ into Jerusalem, with Queen Mariun, from a Gospel dedicated to her by the scribe, Nerses, and the painter, Sargis Pidzak, Sis 1346 (ms. 1973, fol. 114).*

Figure 111: *Dormition of the Virgin, and the hands of a Jew who tried to prevent her burial, being severed, from the Queen Mariun Gospel by Sargis Pidzak in 1346 (ms. 1973, fol. 134).*

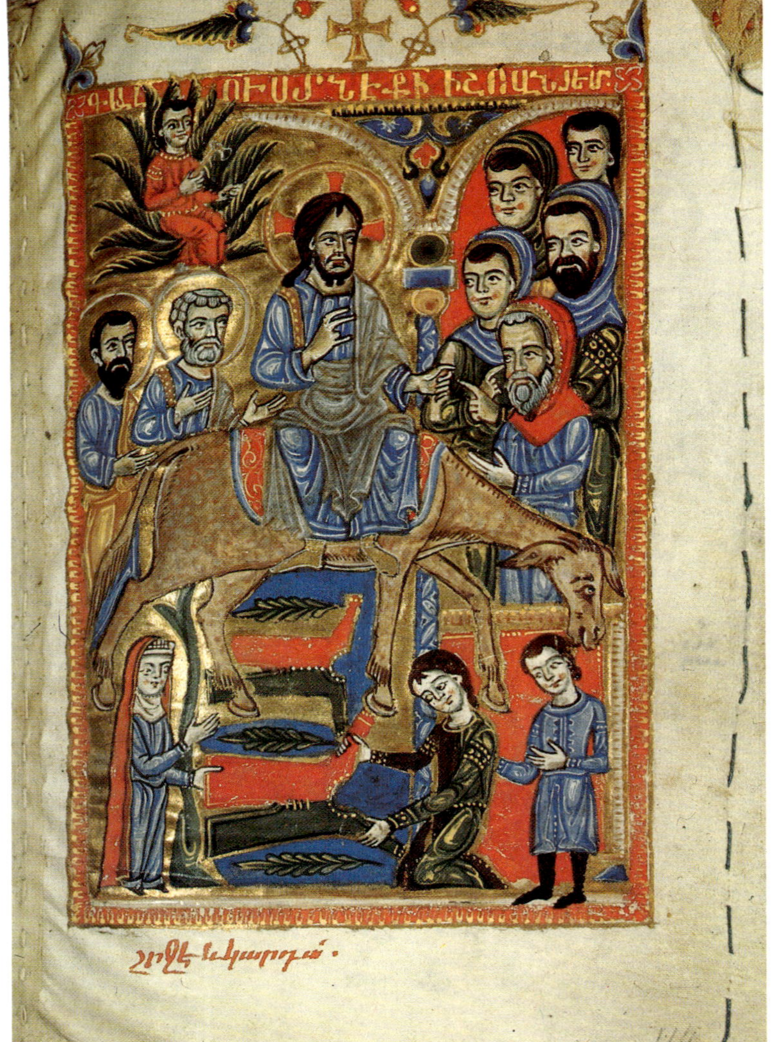

109

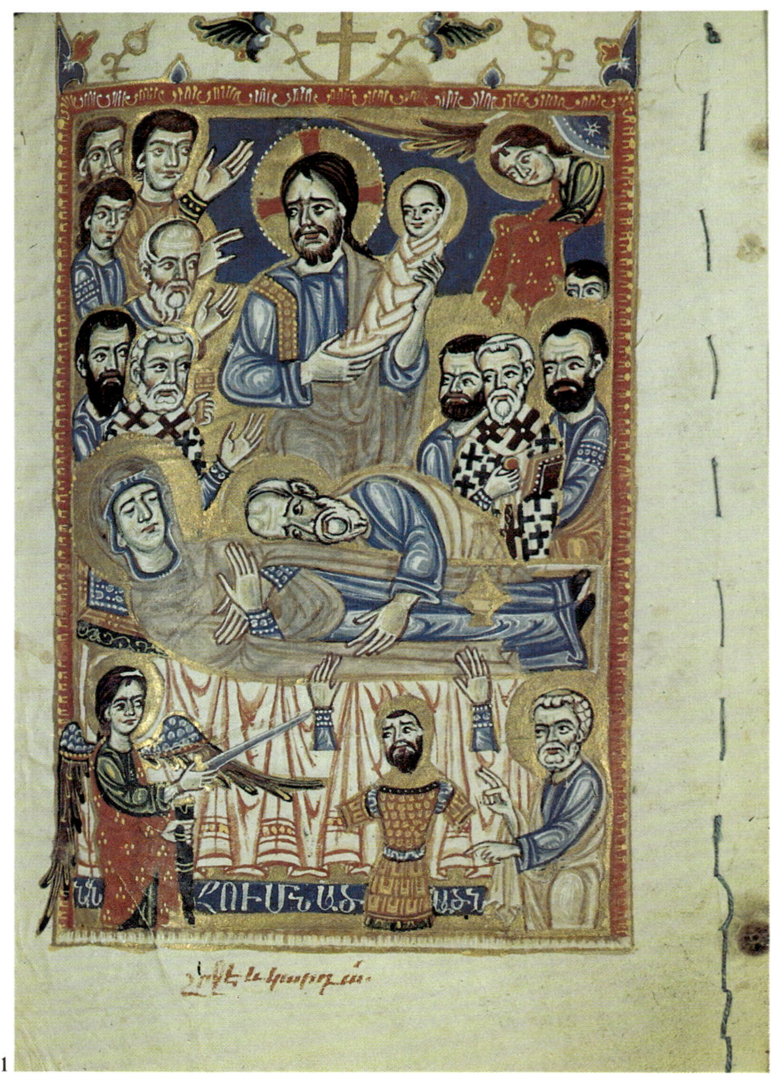

111

Figure 106: *Anne's prayer referring to birds and serpents having offspring, while she is barren, and the annunciation of the angel that she will conceive. Joachim, her husband, is approaching from behind to meet her. Frontispiece to Pidzak's Hymnal of 1335 (ms. 1578, fols. 1v–2).*

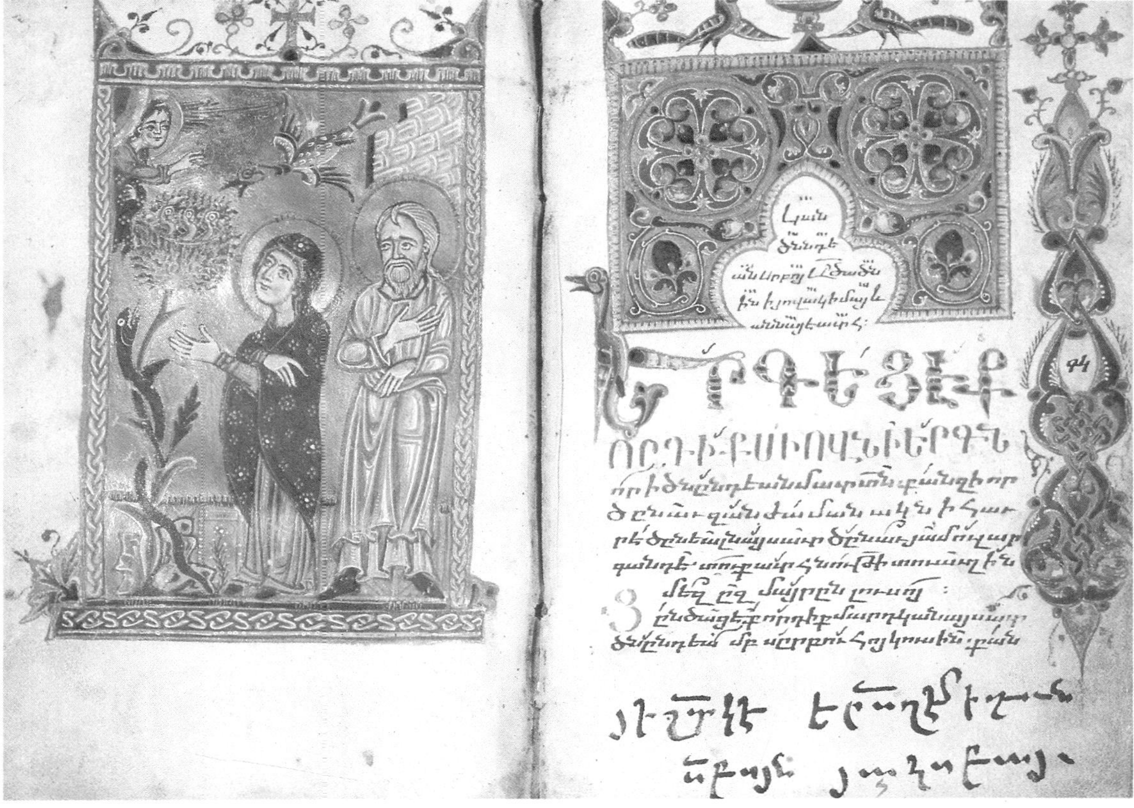

106

6. *Queen Mariun Gospel*

This Gospel was dedicated to Queen Mariun in 1346[27] by the scribe Nerses, and illuminated by Sargis Pidzak. It is one of the richest manuscripts painted by Pidzak, although here too he employed his system of painting full-page panels on single vellum leaves, which were then attached to the paper manuscript. It is, however, clear that these single leaves were expressly intended for the Mariun Gospel, since in most of the miniatures Sargis included the crowned Queen, at times taking an active part in the scene *figs.108, 109, 110*. The iconography of the episodes is traditional, and the composition somewhat compressed in accordance with Sargis Pidzak's special style. The Nativity of Christ *fig.108* incorporates the Adoration of the three Magi and a single shepherd. In the lower section, a midwife is preparing to wash the Child, while Queen Mariun, acting as a second midwife, kneels pouring water into the basin.

In the Entry into Jerusalem *fig.109*, Christ and the donkey dominate the picture, while the welcoming people are grouped within compartments. The smaller figures of the boys and Queen Mariun spreading garments are depicted in the lower part of the composition. The Descent from the Cross *fig.110* is also divided into differently colored compartments. Joseph of Arimathea, climbing a decorated ladder, holds Christ's body and Queen Mariun kneels in a separate compartment on the right. This is one of the panels to which Sargis Pidzak added his name; the other is the Crucifixion. The Dormition of the Virgin *fig.111* is depicted in the usual Byzantine manner, with Christ holding her soul, represented as a swaddled baby, above the body on the bier, which is surrounded by the Apostles. In the lower part of the picture another episode depicts Jephonias, a Jew who, to prevent her burial, held on to the bier; his hands were miraculously severed and remained clasping the coffin. On the left is the angel with a sword who performed the miracle, and on the right St. Peter is about to restore Jephonias' hands. This apocryphal episode[28] is not common in contemporary Byzantine art, though it is depicted in Cappadocian cave churches.[29]

During his long life Sargis produced scores of illuminated manuscripts, so many of which survived that he can be considered the best documented Armenian artist of the Middle Ages. He painted three self-portraits in three different periods of his life.[30] The political situation during the third quarter of the fourteenth century had already deteriorated, and it is quite understandable that no other artistic school developed there at that time. Sargis was the last of the great artists of the Armenian Kingdom of Cilicia.

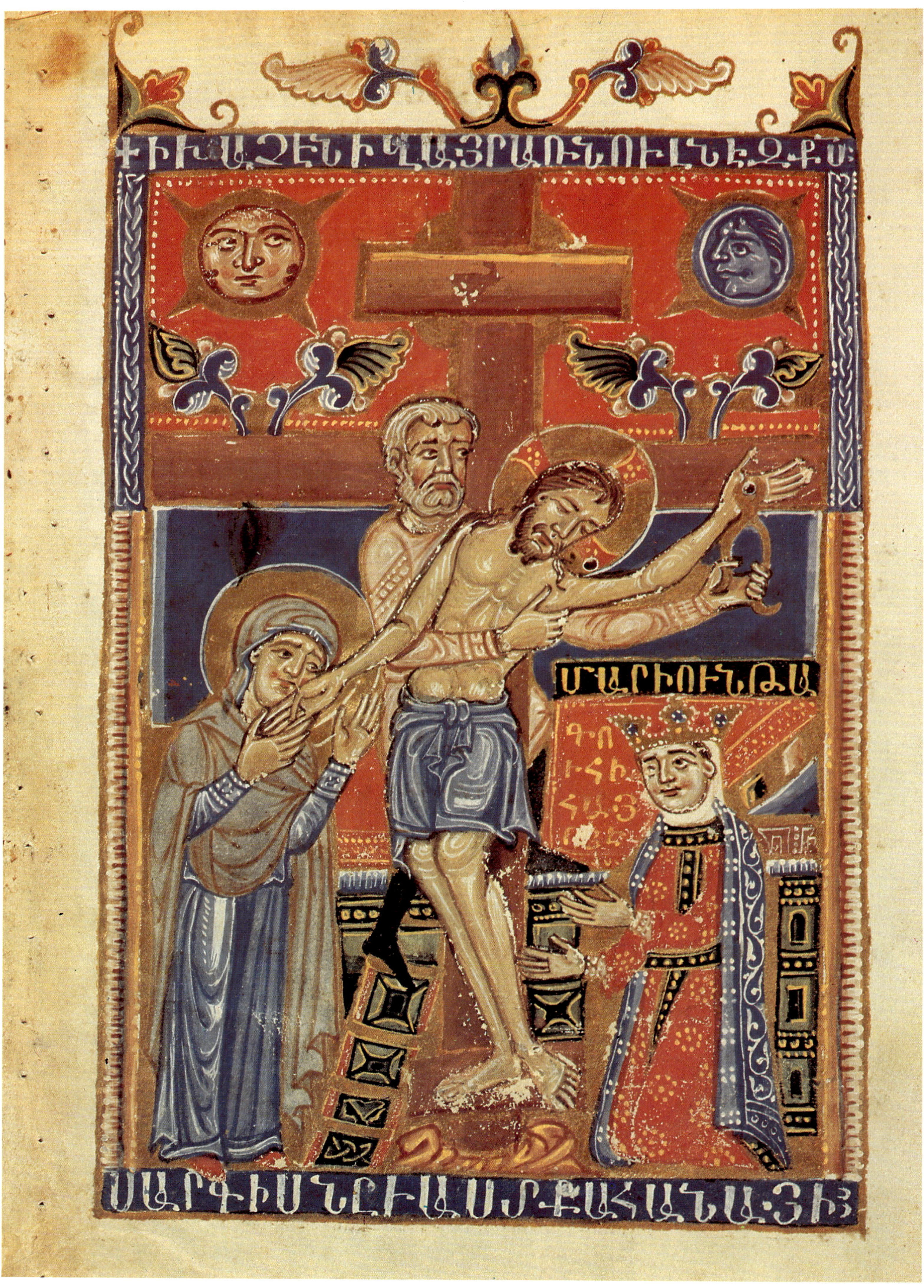

Chapter Eight: Later Armenian Manuscript Illumination

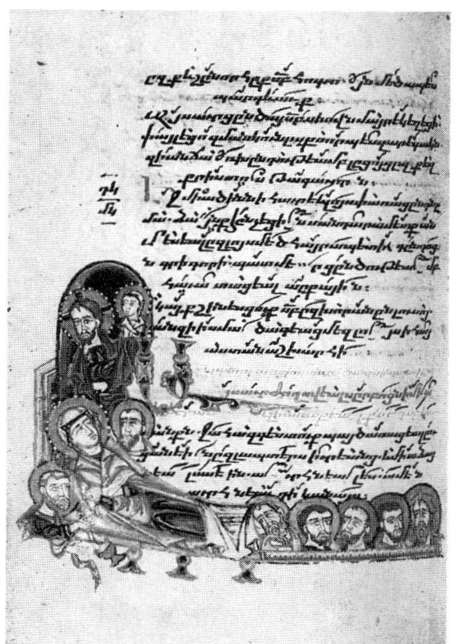

112

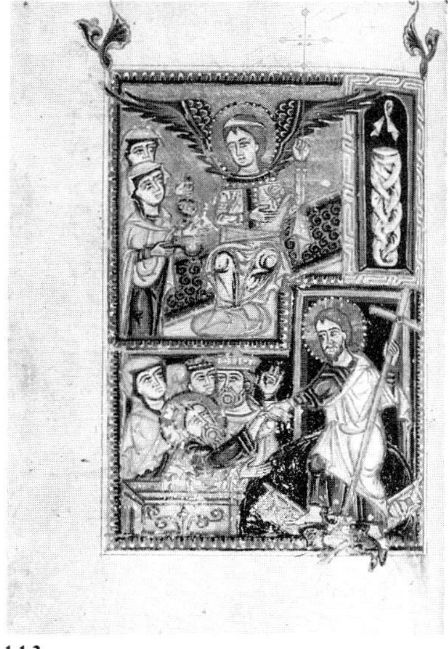

113

Figure 110: *Deposition of Christ from the Cross, with Queen Mariun worshiping, and with the signature of Sargis Pidzak, who painted her Gospel in 1346 (ms. 1973, fol. 258v).*

Figure 112: *Dormition of the Virgin, from the Thmok' Hymnal of 1426 (ms. 1534, p. 428).*

Figure 113: *The Women at the Empty Tomb and the Harrowing of Hell, from the Thmok' Hymnal (ms. 1534, p. 254).*

With the decline of the independent Armenian Kingdom of Cilicia, principalities with limited independence existed in Greater Armenia and helped to preserve Armenian culture. Indeed, all over Asia and Europe, wherever there were strong, rich Armenian communities, schools, churches, and, monasteries were built with workshops and scriptoria to copy and illuminate manuscripts. From the fourteenth century on, with the increasing importance of workmanship, more scribes' and artists' names are known.

Political conditions, however, became difficult in Greater Armenia at that time. The conversion of the Mongols to Islam, and the civil wars between rival tribes, followed by the advance of the Turks, brought about the destruction of monasteries and the massacre and dispersion of monks in northern Armenia by the end of the fourteenth century. Despite the worsening conditions, illuminated manuscripts were still being produced in the fifteenth century, for example the Hymnal of 1426,[1] copied in the fortress of Thmok' by the scribe Yovhannes of Ani. It was illuminated by another Yovhannes, a monk, with numerous marginal illustrations next to the openings of the different hymns, for instance the Dormition of the Virgin in abbreviated form *fig. 112*, but with only one full-page panel, of the two women at the Empty Tomb and the Harrowing of Hell *fig. 113*.

The development of better communications and of pilgrimages made it possible for scribes and artists, and not merely manuscripts, to reach Armenian communities, thereby disseminating their style and iconography throughout the Armenian world. The effect of these pilgrimages was certainly felt in Jerusalem, where a local school did not develop. Pilgrim artists, who worked in Jerusalem and signed their manuscripts to this effect, naturally used their native style. An example is a manuscript of Commentaries on the Epistles by Sargis *Vardapet*[2], copied by Sargis, Bishop of Jerusalem (1393–1412), and illuminated by the monk Tawnakan in 1399. The style of decoration is reminiscent of the early Khizan school, with headpieces in dense, interlacing scrolls, and two flanking animals *fig. 114*.[3] Another example of a manuscript copied by a pilgrim scribe is a Gospel of 1475 from the monastery near the Church of St. Saviour on Mount Zion. Copied by Solomon *abeghay* and illuminated by Yovhannes, it has a decorated Eusebian letter *fig. 115*, canon tables, and Evangelists' portraits *fig. 116*, all painted in the artist's native style, probably that of Khizan, and given as a present to St. James' in Jerusalem. There are many other examples of pilgrim artists from different schools in a later period, who painted manuscripts in Jerusalem in their own style and dedicated them to the church, some of which will be mentioned below.[4]

1. The main schools of later illumination

Some of the Armenian schools of illumination which flourished in the fifteenth century were already in existence in the fourteenth. Such centers were Constantinople before the Turkish conquest and the important school in the Crimea. In Greater Armenia several centers of illumination existed round Lake Van. Two of these developed into the most distinctive schools of Van and Khizan, and together with the school established at New Julfa in the seventeenth century, they constituted the three main streams of illumination in Armenia up to the eighteenth century. The school of Van was located to the east and north of Lake Van, spreading from the city of Van, whereas the Khizan school lay to the south and west of the lake. These schools had two developmental phases, one in the fifteenth and the other in the late sixteenth and early seventeenth century, with some changes in their style and iconography.[5]

The later school developed in New Julfa, a suburb of Isfahan, the capital of Persia, after the Shah Abbas in 1604–1605 transferred to his new capital over two thousand Armenian families from the town of Julfa in north-eastern Armenia. In memory of their old home, the settlers renamed their suburb New Julfa and with the aid of privileges accorded them, the Armenians turned Isfahan into one of the most important trade stations of the east, as well as a cultural and artistic center.

Other schools of illumination which developed among the Armenian diaspora were in Poland and Syria. The Turks granted the Armenians permission for a patriarchate in Istanbul in 1641, which encouraged the development of the school already existing there. It is impossible to enumerate here all the workshops and scriptoria which developed in the four hundred years from the fourteenth century on. The Library of St. Thoros in Jerusalem is particularly rich in illuminated manuscripts of these periods.

2. *Stylistic trends of later illumination*

The most pronounced element in all of these late Armenian illuminations is the tendency towards the abstract and the more colorful. There are, however, differences in each of the schools in the degree of abstraction and the construction of compositions. The school of the Crimea, for instance, is the most classical in the proportions of the figures and in the human gestures, probably being based on the Byzantine style. This classicizing, humanistic attitude is also noticeable in the Turkish schools in the sixteenth and seventeenth centuries, which are dependent on contemporary Greek or Russian icon painting.

The Van and Khizan schools of Greater Armenia are by far the most abstract, being dependent mainly on Persian Moslem illumination. They are related stylistically as well as iconographically, especially in their later stages, in the sixteenth and seventeenth centuries, but there are obvious differences between them. The school of Van created rather formal, symmetrical compositions, with almost geometrical colored areas, at times extremely decorative.[6] The proportions of the human figures are not overemphasized, and their gestures are subdued. The compositions of the Khizan artists, though symmetrical, tend to be more dramatic, with exaggerated figural proportions and gestures, as in the Gospel of 1455 in the Walters Art Gallery.[7] One of the most typical elements of the schools of Khizan and Van, which they share with that of New Julfa, is the lack of any architectural details and background. Most of the pictures are painted either on the vellum ground, on gold, or on a decorative floral ground. This enhances the dramatic effect on the one hand, and the decorative on the other.

The New Julfa style is influenced by Persian and Chinese, but also by European elements.[8] It is to a large extent stylized but, because of its heterogeneous models, some classicizing elements are also evident.[9] The New Julfa manuscripts are somewhat richer than the others in the use of gold leaf and lively colors.

The importance of these schools of illumination lies mainly in the iconographical innovations in rendering common subjects and in the plan of decoration of books. Each one of the schools mentioned above developed its characteristic plan of decoration and iconography, although once established they also borrowed freely from each other. During this later period, for certain texts not illustrated before, a new plan of illustration was devised; and in illustrated manuscripts the plan of decoration and iconography was either modified or furnished with new elements. A few examples of these changes will be discussed in the following pages.

3. *Lives of the Fathers*

One of the new illuminated texts is the *Lives of the Fathers*, which describes the early Egyptian hermits. The main text is an Armenian translation, probably made in Cilicia in the thirteenth or fourteenth century, based on a Greek version which was compiled during the Middle Ages. It thus differs from the earlier Armenian translations based on a fifth century Greek text.[10] The twenty-six chapters of this later version of the *Lives of the Fathers* were compiled as edifying stories, mainly based on events related to St. Anthony, the father of asceticism, and on his sayings and homilies. In our manuscript, the text is supplemented by the life-stories of many other saints, interpolated in the main text or following it. The illustration of some episodes from these lives became a tradition in later Armenian manuscripts of the fifteenth to seventeenth centuries.

Several illustrated copies of the *Lives of the Fathers* exist, the earliest being copied and illuminated by Thaddeus *abeghay* Avramentz in the monastery of St. Anthony at Caffa, in the Crimea, in 1428–30.[11] It starts with a full-page panel introducing St. Anthony *fig.117*, surrounded by demons in the guise of beasts of the desert. His elegant, dominating figure towers over the docile-looking animals, and the style is dependent on an earlier tradition, possibly from the monastery of Caffa itself.[12] The manuscript is profusely illustrated with over 500 small marginal and intercolumnar paintings next to initials of new paragraphs. Most illustrations are bust portraits of the saints, though some are narrative, for example, the busts of Sts. Basil and John, with Paul, the latter's disciple, who on his master's orders caught a bear and brought it to him, while searching for food, in *fig.118*. There are some part-page panels illustrating episodes from the lives of selected saints. An example is the detailed story of a follower of St. Anthony, St. Paphnutius (fourth century), with four panels depicting episodes from his life. Paphnutius[13] traveled in search of truth before embracing the ascetic life. During his journeyings in the desert, he met Timothy, leading a herd of buffalos, who told him the story of his life and why he lived in the even remoter desert *fig.119*.[14]

Our manuscript of *the Lives of the Fathers* of 1430 may have been the first to have been illustrated. The scribe and artist, Thaddeus Avramentz, edited and added to the text, which he annotated in the margins. He states in his colophon that he collected many manuscripts and compiled a more accurate recension, though his main exemplar was a manuscript copied by the monk Melk'izeth, which was given to him by the priest Stephanos. As an artist, he states that he "ornamented it with pictures and flowers in gold" in the hope that "perhaps because of the pictures they will read the book". This can lead to the assumption that just as he collected accurate texts, he could also have gathered pictorial models and illustrated his copy with the material he found, to which he may have added some original compositions of his own. The iconography of the individual saints with their attributes and of the episodes from their lives could derive from varied sources: Byzantium and other eastern schools, such as Cappadocia, Syria, Russia, Greece and other Balkan provinces. Western sources, mainly Italian, should also be considered, since the monastery was under Genoese rule in 1430. It was by then a highly important center, rich and cultured, and after Sargis *Vardapet*'s reform the monks had no need to live by begging. Once the series of illustrations was added to the newly compiled text, our manuscript became a model to be copied from, with few alterations to or omissions from either text or illustrations. The earliest extant copy is of 1615, now in the British Library, and was executed in Amida.[15]

Two later copies of our manuscript were executed in Jerusalem. A copy of 1651 has a colophon which mentions this fact,[16] but the colophon of the second copy, of 1623,[17] does not preserve the place of execution. However, since it was commissioned by Gregory Paronter, Patriarch of Jerusalem, and since our manuscript had been returned to Jerusalem from Amida by that time, there can be no doubt that the 1623 manuscript was copied in Jerusalem and illuminated there by the artist Kirakos. Its frontispiece depicts St. Anthony surrounded by the beasts *fig.120*. Other part-page panels depict 36 of the original episodes, and there are over 350 small busts and illustrations in the margins. The iconography is almost identical, but the illustrations differ in style. In contrast to the classicizing style of the Caffa manuscript, the 1623 *Book of Lives* is in the style of the school of Van, with drapery in decorative colored areas and tube-like folds, almost geometric in construction.

A somewhat later manuscript in Jerusalem is based, though not directly, on our model manuscript from Caffa. It was copied by a scribe from Poland fleeing persecution and illuminated at Aleppo in 1625, and its almost geometric stylization resembles that of the school of Van.[18] For example, St. Simon-Daniel of Antioch, one of the stylite ascetics, who lived on top of his high pillar until his death, is placed by the artist of this manuscript *fig.121* in an orant attitude within the colorful pillar. This almost abstract rendering, devoid of any landscape or background, is more stylized than the panel depicting St. Paphnutius *fig.122*, who came to visit the hermit St. Onuphrius shortly before his death. The naked Onuphrius, with a long beard and wearing a girdle of leaves, tells Paphnutius of the 60 years he has lived in the desert; he then dies, and is buried by Paphnutius with the help of two lions.[19] Though stylized, the elements of landscape in the picture, such as the tree, mountain, cave, and spring, are recognizable.

The later manuscript of 1651, copied in Jerusalem from the Caffa manuscript of 1430, has the same plan of decoration. Among its illustrations is the meeting between Theophilus, Patriarch of Alexandria (385–412), and Father Pambo, each heading a group of monks *fig.123*. Another picture shows St. Paphnutius being given communion by an angel *fig.124*, after he was found to be the most virtuous of many saints.

This group of illustrated copies of the *Lives of the Fathers* contributed greatly to the development and innovations of the later schools of Armenian illumination.[20]

4. *The Hymnal of Van, 1529*

Innovations in plans of decoration and iconography can also be found in the school of Van. The Gospel books of this school were illustrated with the traditional Christological cycle of pictures, and contrary to the plan of decoration in hymnals, mainly bound at the beginning of the book, with some Old Testament typological pictures appended. However, the depictions of the Sacrifice of Isaac and Isaiah's lips being purified by coal, as in the Deacon Thoros Gospel of 1311 (see above, pp. 77–78), are replaced in the sixteenth century Gospels of the Van School by the Tree of Jesse and Ezekiel's Vision.[21] A new iconography is devised for the latter, stressing the typological aspect of the Second Coming of Christ. Based on the composition of the painter Awak, it is quite different from that of the Erznka Bible *fig.85 above*. This new conception of the Vision of Ezekiel was not used by the Van artists solely for Gospels: a Hymnal of 1529 from the city of Van depicts this episode in a similar iconography[22] *fig.125*. Ezekiel kneels on the river bank, below a large central medallion of the enthroned Christ, surrounded by the four creatures, each with four different heads and six wings (Rev. 4:6–8; Ezek. 1:5–19) and with two hands below the heads; two diagonal shafts pierce the four golden wheels and separate the creatures from each other. An additional pair of crossed wings extends from the medallion above three creatures, and a blessing hand extending from below the medallion holds a written scroll for Ezekiel to eat (Ezek. 2:9–3:3), while a closed book is dangling from one of the reeds (Rev. 10:9–11).

Other pictures in this Hymnal are depicted in fairly conventional iconography, and all are placed next to the relevant hymns. The cycle commences with the Annunciation to Anne and Joachim, and ends with the representation of the Battle of Avarayr in 451. This depiction of Vardan Mamikonian fighting against the Persians with their elephants became traditional in the hymnals of the Van school from the sixteenth century on.[23] One of these illustrations, for the Monday in Holy Week, depicts the Temptation of Adam and Eve *fig.126*, who flank the Tree of Knowledge. Eve, encouraged by a two-legged, winged serpent, is plucking one fruit with her left hand and handing another to the crowned Adam with her right.[24] The cross as the sign of the Son of Man (Mt. 24:30–31), with the enthroned Christ surrounded by four angels blowing horns, is usually the penultimate illustration of a hymnal, preceding the battle of Vardanes,[25] though not in our manuscript. An additional Christological cycle, painted on different, smaller leaves, was inserted later, as described in the Catalogue below.

5. *The Alexander Romance of 1536*

The most important of all these manuscripts from the school of Van is the illustrated Romance of Alexander.[26] Its importance lies principally in the fact that through it the process of illuminating a manuscript can be traced, as well as the relation between scribe and artist.[27] The text is based on the Greek pseudo-Callisthenes, which was translated into Armenian in the fifth century. By the thirteenth century it had regained popularity, and was rendered with additional verses by Khatchatur *Vardapet* (1280–1320), after which many other verses were added to it, some the length of whole chapters.[28] Grigoris, the Catholicos of Aghthamar (1512–1545), the poet who illuminated our manuscript, revised the text afresh and improved on it.[29] He sent his verses from the island of Aghthamar in Lake Van to the scribe Markari *abelay*, who lived in the village of Varag and complained of the poor conditions there;[30] he copied the text he had received and sent it back to Grigoris. The instructions, indications, and remarks which the scribe wrote for the Catholicos beside the empty spaces left for illustrations are most interesting. All the inscriptions are in colloquial Armenian, some indicating that the scribe had at his disposal the older version of the *Life of Alexander* which at times he used by mistake.[31] His instructions are simple and clear, like: "Make a big, beautiful tortoise" (fol. 100); but some of his inscriptions are on a personal note: "On this page make the picture fill up the entire space, so that the dirt on the paper cannot be seen. They were shaking the bag out to-day, and the dirt came on to the page. Please forgive me" (fols. 85v–86).

The artist, Catholicos Grigor, must have exercised his imagination in order to fashion a secular iconography, probably based upon the traditional religious representations. For instance, the birth of Alexander *fig.118* is no doubt based on the Nativity of Christ: Olympias is reclining like the Virgin, and Alexander lies swaddled behind her, like Christ, with Nectanebos, his real father, adoring, like Joseph.[32] The story of the death of the Akarnanian king, Nicolaos *fig.119* in a chariot race in Pisa is probably a compilation from several representations of battle scenes. Nicolaos is seen lying dead next to his horse beneath Alexander, who is drawing his bow, accompanied by mounted soldiers. Of the chariot race in which, according to the Romance, Nicolaos dies, only the urn has survived.[33] The episode is depicted differently in other illustrated Armenian manuscripts of the *Romance of Alexander*, which are based on a different recension of the text. This and other episodes demonstrate Grigor's originality in text as well as in iconography.[34] Space was allocated for other illustrations which, for some unknown reason, were never executed.[35]

6. *The School of Khizan*

The school of Khizan was one of the most active schools from the fifteenth to the eighteenth century, producing hundreds of manuscripts, many of which have survived. The Jerusalem Patriarchate's collection contains a large number of them, from most periods in these centuries.[36] During the fifteenth century artists like Khatchatur and Mkrtitch illuminated Gospel books with the usual Christological cycles before the text, preceded by typological Old Testament scenes, like the Sacrifice of Isaac, which were borrowed from earlier traditions in Armenia; the Tree of Jesse and Ezekiel's Vision, when they appear, are taken from the school of Van.[37] The Khizan artists of the fifteenth century introduced some special iconographical elements, as for example an angel pouring the contents of a bottle of holy water over Christ's head in the Baptism.[38] They also added many scenes of Christ's miracles, pictures of the joys of the righteous in Paradise and the torments of the damned in hell *fig.134*, as well as an ornate Cross surrounded by four angels blowing trumpets representing the sign of the Son of Man in the Last Judgment (Mt. 24:30–31).[39] These innovations in the plan of decoration and iconography developed in the fifteenth century, continued in use up to the eighteenth century, and helped fashion the illustrations of other texts.

7. *Three generations of artists in a Khizan workshop*

During the second half of the sixteenth century and the first decades of the seventeenth, renewed interest in illuminated manuscripts led to a new phase in the development of the Khizan school. It was started by a scribe and artist named Sargis, who trained his two sons, Martyros and Sargis, and they in turn had their sons and several pupils working in the same scriptorium, the most important being Khatchatur and Kirakos.[40] The Jerusalem Patriarchate possesses some of the most significant illuminated manuscripts from this workshop, which demonstrate its development over three generations.

Sargis the Elder was trained by an artist from Aghthamar, which explains the influence of the school of Van on the decoration plan, composition, and iconography of his illustrations, as well as his tendency towards a schematic, abstract style. This is evident from a Gospel he painted in Jerusalem while on a pilgrimage during 1571–72.[41] Of the four Evangelists' portraits, only St. Luke's has survived *fig.129*, but the four decorated headpieces have several stylized figures similar to the portrait of St. Luke, as for instance that of St. Matthew *fig.130*. Sargis also decorated a hymnal,

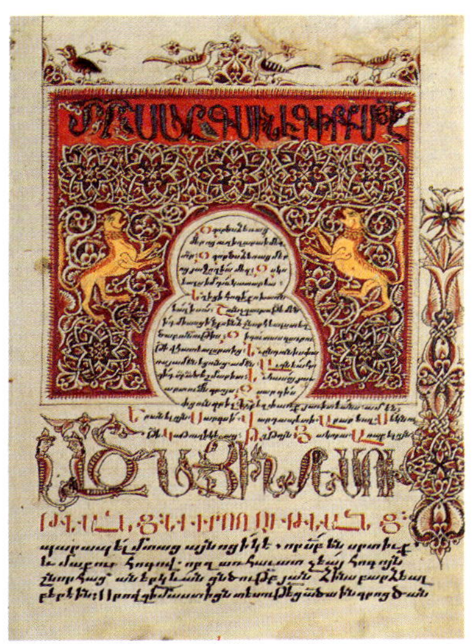

Figure 114: *Decorated headpiece at the beginning of a Commentary on the Epistles by Sargis* Vardapet *(1154), copied and illuminated at St. James in Jerusalem in 1399 (ms. 7, p. 1).*

which was copied at Pazentz, a village in the Khizan region, in 1553, now in Jerusalem.[42] The decorated headpieces resemble those in his Gospel of 1571–72, especially when the figure of Christ on the opening page of the Hymnal *fig.131* and the marginal decorative motif are compared with those of the Gospel. The figure style, however, is different, as can be seen in the full-page panel of Joachim and Anne *fig.131*, although it is derived from the same style. This is, as will be seen below *fig.137*, the work of Kirakos, a pupil of one of Sargis' sons.

8. *Martyros Khizantzi*

The most skilled of the two brothers was Martyros, about whose work and activities a considerable amount is known. The Jerusalem collection has a number of manuscripts illuminated by him.[43] The earliest illuminated manuscript attributed to Martyros is a *Gantsaran*, a collection of religious poems, which was copied in part at Khlath, north of Lake Van, in 1575.[44] Martyros' highly stylized, colorful drapery and figures, the latter with elongated bodies and small, expressive heads maintaining a calm symmetry, stem through his father from the School of Van. This is evident in the full-page panel of the Crucifixion *fig.132*, as well as in that of the Dormition of the Virgin *fig.133*. Some elements of western art were added to the traditional Armenian iconography of these representations, such as the pelican feeding its young with its own blood above the Crucifixion, symbolizing Christ's self-sacrifice.

Martyros Khizantzi illuminated a sumptuous Gospel at Khizan in 1577–79 which is now in Jerusalem.[45] It contains the usual portraits of the Evangelists and decorated headpieces, and a cycle of 29 full-page panels of Christological episodes, as well as 68 marginal text illustrations. He maintained close relations with the see of Jerusalem, and during his travels spent two years there, 1590–91, ordering a *khatchk'ar* (stone cross) to be carved commemorating his visit.[46] During his stay in Jerusalem, he copied part of a large Menologium for the Patriarch David, but did not illuminate it.[47] Patriarch David ordered from Martyros in 1596 an illuminated manuscript of selected books of the Old Testament, which he started to copy but left for his brother Sargis and his son Grigoris to complete.[48] He himself went in the same year to Istanbul, where he copied a Gospel now in the Chester Beatty Collection.[49] Another of his joint works with his brother Sargis and son Grigoris, which is now in Jerusalem,[50] is a selection of works by Gregory of Tathev. It was completed in Khizan in 1602, although begun in Sebastia, where there is evidence that Martyros was working in 1600. Martyros Khizantzi's life is typical of that of a wandering scribe and artist in the second half of the sixteenth century.[51] He must have been dead by 1609, when Grigor the scribe asks the reader to remember his master, Martyros, in the colophon to a collection of sermons which he copied.[52]

9. *Sargis Khizantzi*

Sargis, Martyros' brother, was neither as talented nor as famous as his brother.[53] He began working as a scribe and illuminator only in 1591, and the last manuscript known to be illuminated by him dates from 1610.[54] The most sumptuous illuminated manuscript to have survived from Sargis' pen and brush is the Hymnal from Khizan of 1601.[55] It contains 45 full-page panels illustrating Christological, Old Testament, historical, and hagiographical episodes, all depicted in great detail. The parable of Dives, the rich man, who ignored Lazarus, the beggar, and in consequence was tormented by thirst while being fried in hell, when Lazarus was being comforted in Abraham's bosom in paradise *fig.134*, is illustrated by Sargis with the naivety of a true believer. The iconography of both hell and heaven had been common in the school of Khizan since the fifteenth century, and there are numerous examples in the Gospels of the Jerusalem Collection.[56] The Israelites crossing the Red Sea and the Egyptians drowning are depicted in two facing pages *fig.135*. Above the drowning Egyptians, the regalia of Pharaoh, including his crown and scepter, is rising up to heaven, assisted by two angels.

10. *Sargis and Kirakos, Martyros and Khatchatur*

Sargis helped execute another hymnal, completed in 1602 in Khizan and now in Jerusalem,[57] of which he was the scribe and donor, while the illuminator was his pupil, Kirakos. The stylization of the figures resembles that of Sargis, though Kirakos has his own individual style. The dark outlines and the facial expressions can be seen in the frontispiece of the Annunciation to Joachim and Anne *fig.136*. As an artist of the third generation in the workshop, Kirakos has taken over the illumination of a hymnal which Sargis, the father of Martyros and Sargis Khizantzi, began to decorate. This manuscript,[58] which the scribe Stephanos copied in 1553, probably never had any full-page panels. Kirakos painted two, the Annunciation to Joachim and Anne, and Pentecost, on a different kind of paper from that of the manuscript and added them at the request of his pupil, Melk'izet, who owned the manuscript, as he states in the inscription under the panel page *fig.131*. However, the figure style is more expressive and sophisticated in Kirakos' Hymnal of 1602 than the stereotyped rendering of these two panels of 1623 *fig.137*, which were perhaps redrawn and colored by an apprentice.

Martyros, Sargis' brother, also had several pupils with whom he collaborated.[59] One of his pupils, Khatchatur of Khizan, collaborated with him in 1591, while in Jerusalem, in the illustration of a

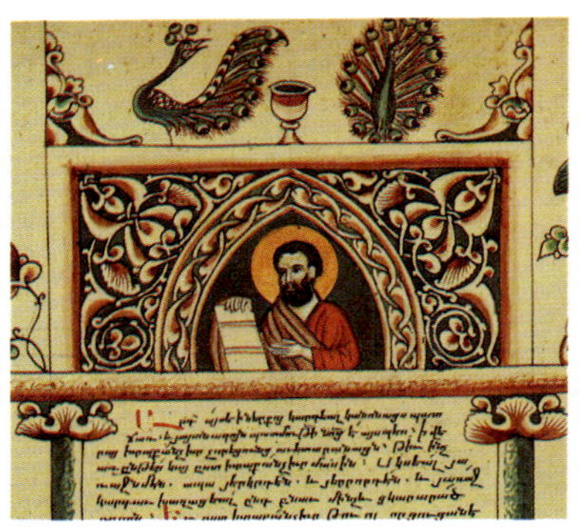

Figure 115: *Carpianus in the lunette of Eusebius' letter to him. Top part of a page from a Gospel copied in St. Saviour's, Jerusalem, in 1475 (ms. 1943, p. 13).*

large Menologium which Martyros, his brother Sargis, and Khatchatur himself copied.[60] The decoration of the Menologium consists of many marginal illustrations, two headpieces and one full-page panel of the Nativity of Christ *fig.138*. In an inscription under the panel the artist Khatchatur relates that he copied this picture from the Gospel of Queen Keran, which he found in Jerusalem.[61] The resemblance of the Khizan copy to its Cilician model is striking in its detail as well as in its composition, but Khatchatur's attempt to imitate the style is far from successful. The linear stylization of the Khizan school is readily discernible despite his attempts to simulate stylistic motifs such as hatchings in drapery and landscapes. Searching for good models and copying them was undoubtedly one of the aims of the artists of the late Khizan school, and Cilician models were in fashion, as were others of later periods.

The dispersion of the Armenians in the first quarter of the seventeenth century, as a result of the hostilities between the Persians and the Turks, resulted in the creation of new centers of manuscript illumination. Scribes and artists were forced to travel, but they continued to use their native style wherever they went. Martyros and Sargis Khizantzi, Yovhannes of Khizan, Sargis of Mokhs and their pupils were only some of these itinerant artists. Others settled in the New Armenian centers, mainly in New Julfa in Isfahan, where they were able to pursue their profession.[62]

11. The Bibles of the New Julfa School

The pupils of Martyros Khizantzi and Sargis of Mokhs were among the many scribes and artists who gathered at New Julfa from throughout the Armenian diaspora. This, together with the world-wide connections of the new capital, made New Julfa the melting-pot for many styles and a wide range of iconography. Evidence of this eclecticism in iconography is to be found in the Bibles from New Julfa, which contain the complete text of the Old and New Testaments, with some apocryphal additions,[63] lavishly illuminated with full- and part-page panels, decorated headpieces, and some marginal decoration.

Two main types of Bible developed in New Julfa during the seventeenth century. The earlier type, the New Julfa recension, is a compilation from Armenian and European models. In its first stage, only some illustrative frontispieces decorated the Bible, but about the middle of the century illustrations of Revelation were introduced, attached to the appropriate text. These were based on the woodcuts of the Apocalypse by Albrecht Dürer and his followers. The second type of New Julfa Bible is the De Bry recension. Most of its illustrations were selected about the middle of the century from a Bible illustrated by the engraver, Jan Theodor De Bry. This Bible also contains an apocalyptic cycle of pictures based on Dürer's woodcuts and similar to those of the New Julfa type in its later stage.

12. The De Bry Recension

One of the Bibles belonging to this group was copied by Stephanos between 1643 and 1646, and illuminated by an unknown artist.[64] The decoration of the Old Testament in this Bible consists of some full-page panels, each divided into four compartments, placed at the beginning of major sections. The four Gospels are sparingly illuminated with portraits of Eusebius, Carpianus, and the four Evangelists. The Apocalypse, however, is illustrated with 15 evenly distributed panels, concluding with the Heavenly Jerusalem.

The iconography of the pictures is strikingly dependent on a Bible illustrated by the Flemish-German engraver, Jan Theodor De Bry (Liège 1561–Frankfurt a.M. 1623),[65] and published at Mainz in 1609.[66] However, the choice of episodes depicted in our Bible is fortuitous. The iconography of the selected episodes at times follows the De Bry Bible down to the minutest detail of gesture and facial expression. Our New Julfa artist, with his stylized, painterly manner, did not render elements in the Renaissance style, and sometimes even omitted sections of the picture which did not fit his compressed compositions. Thus the animals in the background of the Fall are missing *fig.139*, as are the two boys with the donkey in the Sacrifice of Isaac *fig.140*. It is doubtful whether the New Julfa artist used the De Bry Bible as his direct and sole model. Some episodes appear in a different sequence, others have a different iconography, and some are missing altogether from De Bry. An example of the different sequence of episodes is Saul enthroned *fig.141*, which in De Bry, contrary to our Bible, follows the fight of David with Goliath. The very first picture provides an example of a different iconography, with God the Father hovering above the land in the act of creating the world *fig.139*; in De Bry's Bible, the composition is altogether different. The Heavenly Jerusalem, the final picture in Revelation, does not appear in the De Bry Bible. The direct model for our New Julfa Bible may not have been De Bry's, but another which served as a prototype for them both, with some of its pictures in a different order and some with a different iconography. It is, however, more plausible that our artist drew on other sources in those cases where his representations differ from De Bry's.

Figure 116: *St. Matthew from the St. Saviour Gospel of 1475, painted by Yovhannes, probably of Khizan (ms. 1943, p. 40).*

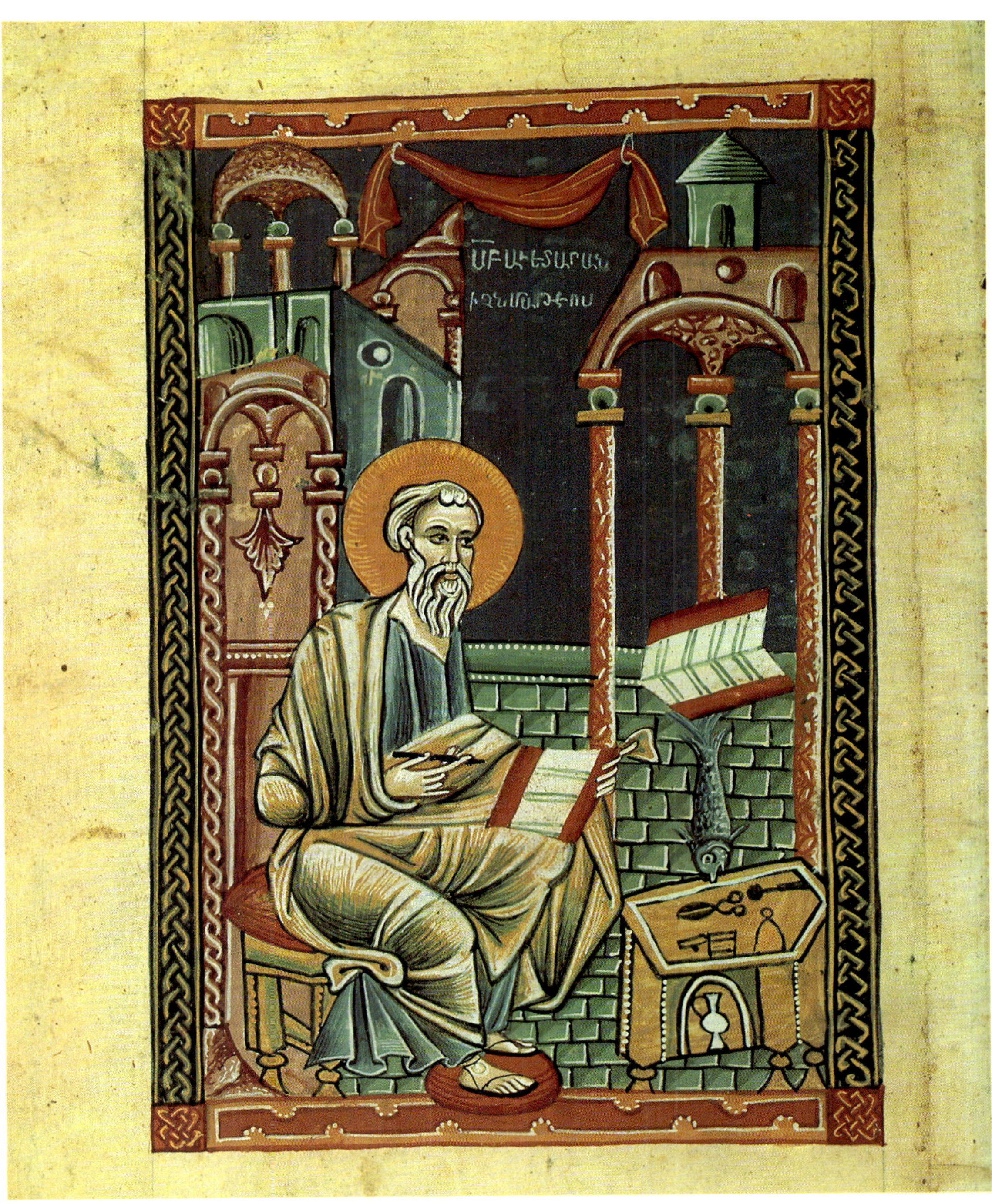

116

13. The Early New Julfa Bible Recension

The other Biblical recension, which developed in New Julfa, and became very popular throughout the Armenian diaspora in the seventeenth century, also has full- and part-page panels illustrating the Old and New Testaments. This recension must have developed on a limited scale at the beginning of the century, as it was already famous by 1620 when an unknown patron in Istanbul commissioned an artist from New Julfa to illustrate his Bible.[67] The name of the patron has been effaced, but the name of the artist, Khatchatur Isfahani, who traveled to Istanbul for this express purpose, remains.

The frontispiece illustrates the first chapters of Genesis *fig.142*, depicting the six days of Creation within medallions in the initial letter I of the book, as was usual in medieval western illumination, though the subjects and iconography are somewhat different. The Creator sits enthroned, surrounded by the four apocalyptic creatures of St. John. The first medallion, at the top, represents the situation before the Creation, with two angels acting as God's agents; behind them, in segments, are the four elements from which the world was created: fire, air, water, and earth. In the other medallions, the other days of Creation are depicted and in the main plane, the story of Adam and Eve is enacted.

The apocalyptic allusions are underlined on the confronting opening page *fig.142*. In the decorated headpiece, rays emanate from Christ's blessing hands with Moses, the author of the Pentateuch, and a dove representing the Holy Spirit within medallions. Under the rays are the faces of the twenty-four Elders of Revelation (4:4), prepared to sit in judgment. Above the headpiece is a lamb on an altar, flanked by two seraphim, and John the Baptist is carrying a lamb above a decorated marginal motif. The initial letter is formed by St. John the Evangelist lifting up his book, with the eagle, his symbol. These two facing pages represent the beginning and the end, Creation with the fall of man, and Redemption with the Last Judgment.

Figure 117: *St. Anthony surrounded by beasts. Frontispiece to the earliest* Lives of the Fathers, *Caffa (Crimea), 1430 (ms. 285, p. 14).*

These complementary frontispieces on confronting pages may not have been the innovation of the artist, Khatchatur, or of the scribe, Yakob. They could have been devised earlier in the century, soon becoming fashionable; they certainly constitute a tradition which persisted in New Julfa,[68] as well as in Jerusalem itself.

The Bible of 1640 copied by Mik'ayel was executed either in Istanbul or in Jerusalem "at the gate of St. James", as a later inscription states under the frontispiece.[69] The illuminations on both pages *fig.143* are similar to those of Khatchatur Isfahani and are related to the New Julfa prototype. The 1640 Bible has more text illustrations than Khatchatur's Bible of 1620, some of them related to the New Julfa Bible of the De Bry recension. However, a picture of Hannah sitting before Eli, which appears in a similar composition in the 1643–46 Bible, is missing from the De Bry Bible of 1609 from Mainz. All other copies of the New Julfa Bible contain the same iconography of Eli and Hannah. An undated copy in Jerusalem[70] similar to the 1620 Bible depicts them in a full-page *fig.144*. This example illustrates the eclectic nature of the New Julfa Bibles: once a new element was added to the repertory, it remained there, increasing the number of illustrations.

14. The Apocalypse illustrations

The richest of these Bibles in Jerusalem is a copy written by the scribe Astuadzatur and illuminated by the artist Hayrapet in 1645.[71] It contains 26 full-page panels, commencing with the Creation page[72] and concluding with St. John's vision of the Heavenly Jerusalem *fig.145*. Jerusalem is represented as a square city, as in the visions of Ezekiel (41:16–25) and St. John (Rev. 21:6), with twelve gates, each with an angel. In a cloud above the city is God the Father, crowned with the Holy Spirit as a dove beneath him. In front of the city is a Shepherd with his sheep.

The origin of the New Julfa representation of the Heavenly Jerusalem is not clear.[73] This iconography probably derives from the same source as the woodcut of the Dutch graphic artist, Christoffel van Sichem the Second.[74] To Dürer's basic Apocalypse cycle he added, in his Bible of 1646, a picture of the Heavenly Jerusalem which includes God the Father, the Dove, and the Good Shepherd in front of a square Jerusalem with angels in the gates.[75] This type of Heavenly Jerusalem could be an invention of van Sichem's for his Bible of 1646 for it carries only his monogram.[76] If so, the question remains of how this composition came to be copied in New Julfa in the Bible of 1645, a year before it was printed in Antwerp *fig.158*. One possibility is that this picture was cut by van Sichem, before its inclusion in his 1646 Bible, for an earlier impression of an entire apocalyptic cycle of the Dürer type, with other van Sichem additions, since all these pictures appear in the illuminated New Julfa Bible of 1645. A more plausible explanation, however, is that some of the New Julfa Bible pictures were added after 1646. Indeed, some full-page illustrations, among them the Heavenly Jerusalem, were painted on single leaves, and their style differs from the Genesis pictures which form an integral part of the manuscript.[77] The three early New Julfa Bibles in Jerusalem, two of which are dated 1620 and 1640 *figs.142, 143, 144*, do not have an illustrated Apocalypse. The illustrations for Revelation only appeared in Isfahan about 1645 in both the De Bry and the New Julfa recensions. Both are dependent on Dürer and his followers, such as Lucas Cranach the Elder. The Apocalypse in the illuminated New Julfa Bible of 1645 and the printed Oskan Bible of 1666 is based on the van Sichem Bible of 1646 or 1657.

118

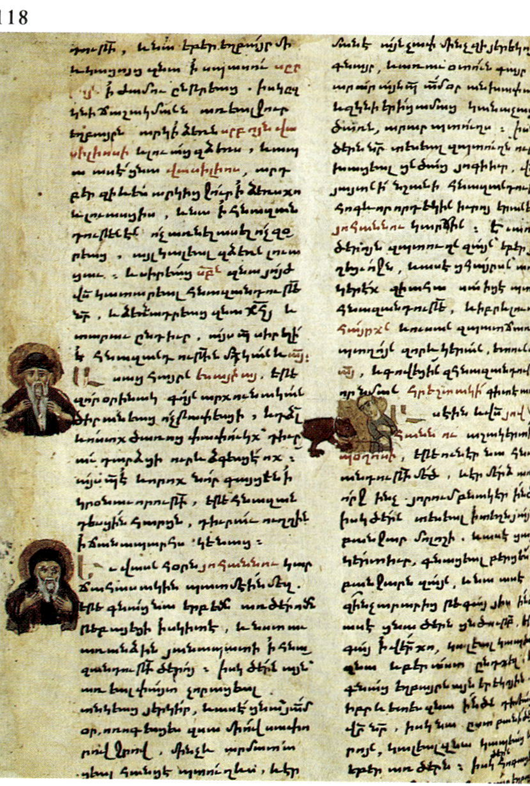

119

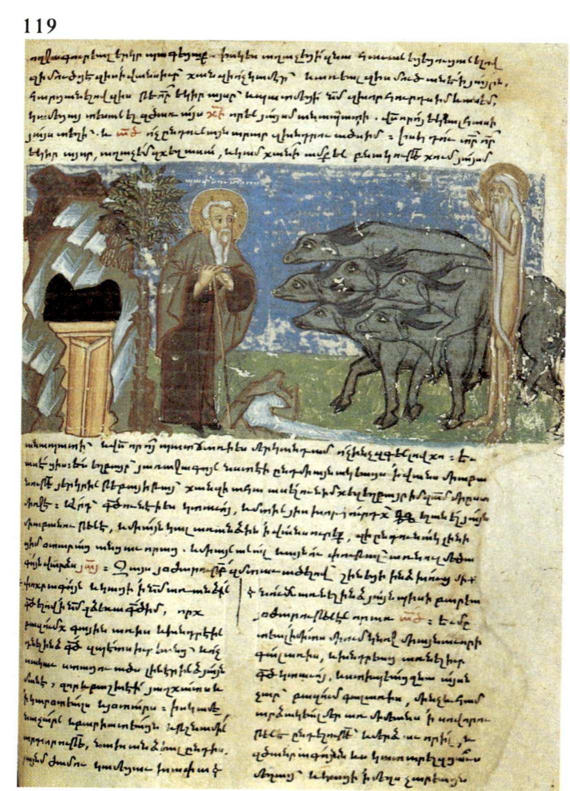

Figure 118: *Busts of Saints Basil, John the dwarf and his pupil Paul catching a bear, from the Caffa* Lives of the Fathers, *Crimea, 1430 (ms. 285, p. 412).*

Figure 119: *St. Paphnutius meeting St. Timothy and buffaloes in the desert, from the Caffa* Lives of the Fathers *(ms. 285, p. 573).*

Figure 121 (page 98): *St. Simon-Daniel, a Stylite of Antioch, on top of his pillar, from the 1625* Lives of the Fathers, *copied in Aleppo by a scribe from Poland (ms. 23, p. 541).*

Figure 122 (page 99): *St. Paphnutius listening to the life story of St. Onophrius shortly before his death, from the* Lives of the Fathers, *Aleppo, 1625 (ms. 23, p. 470).*

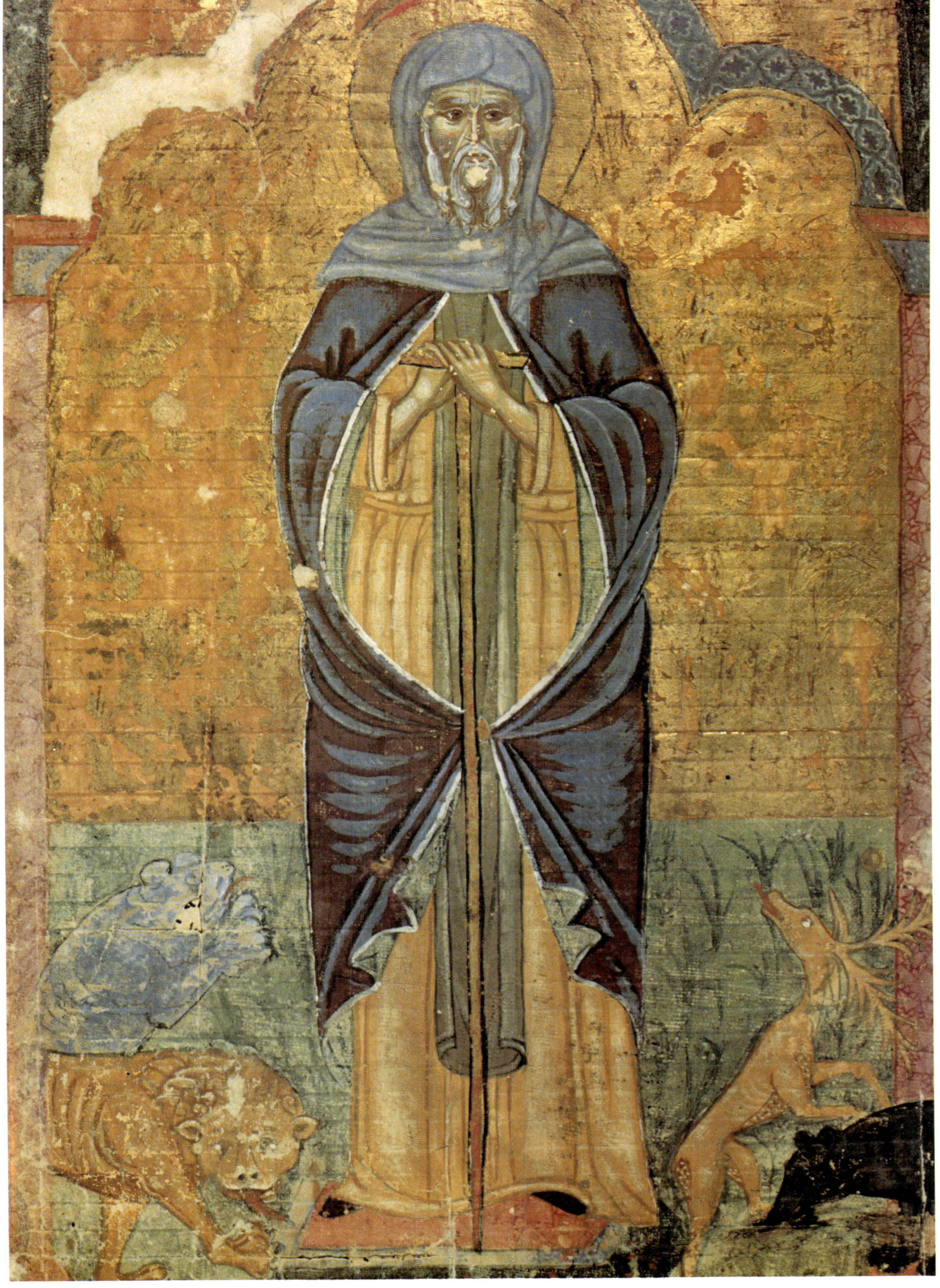

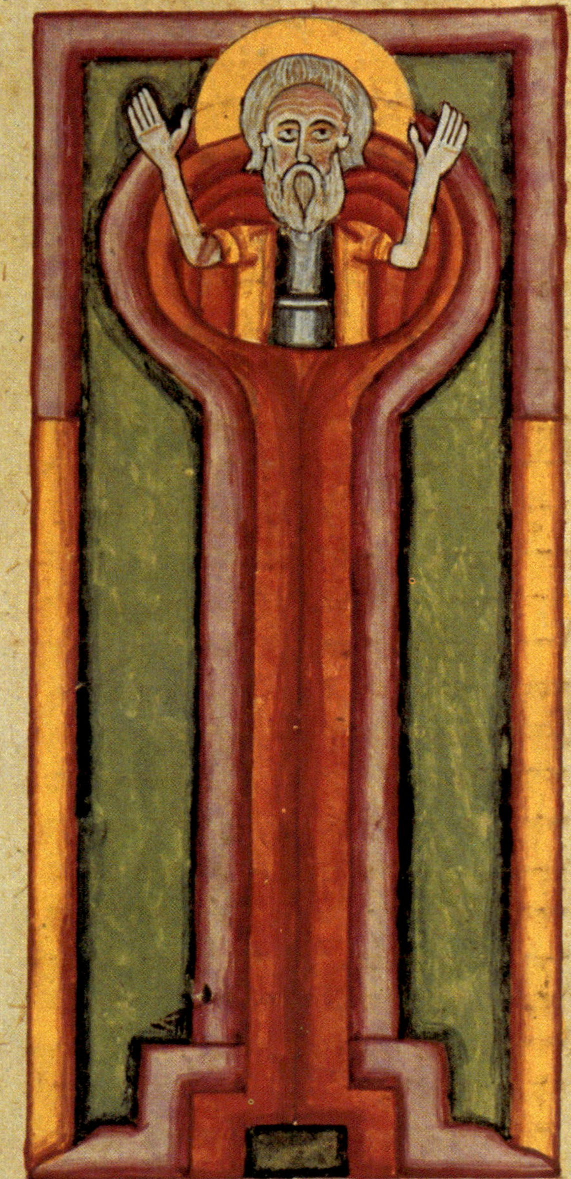

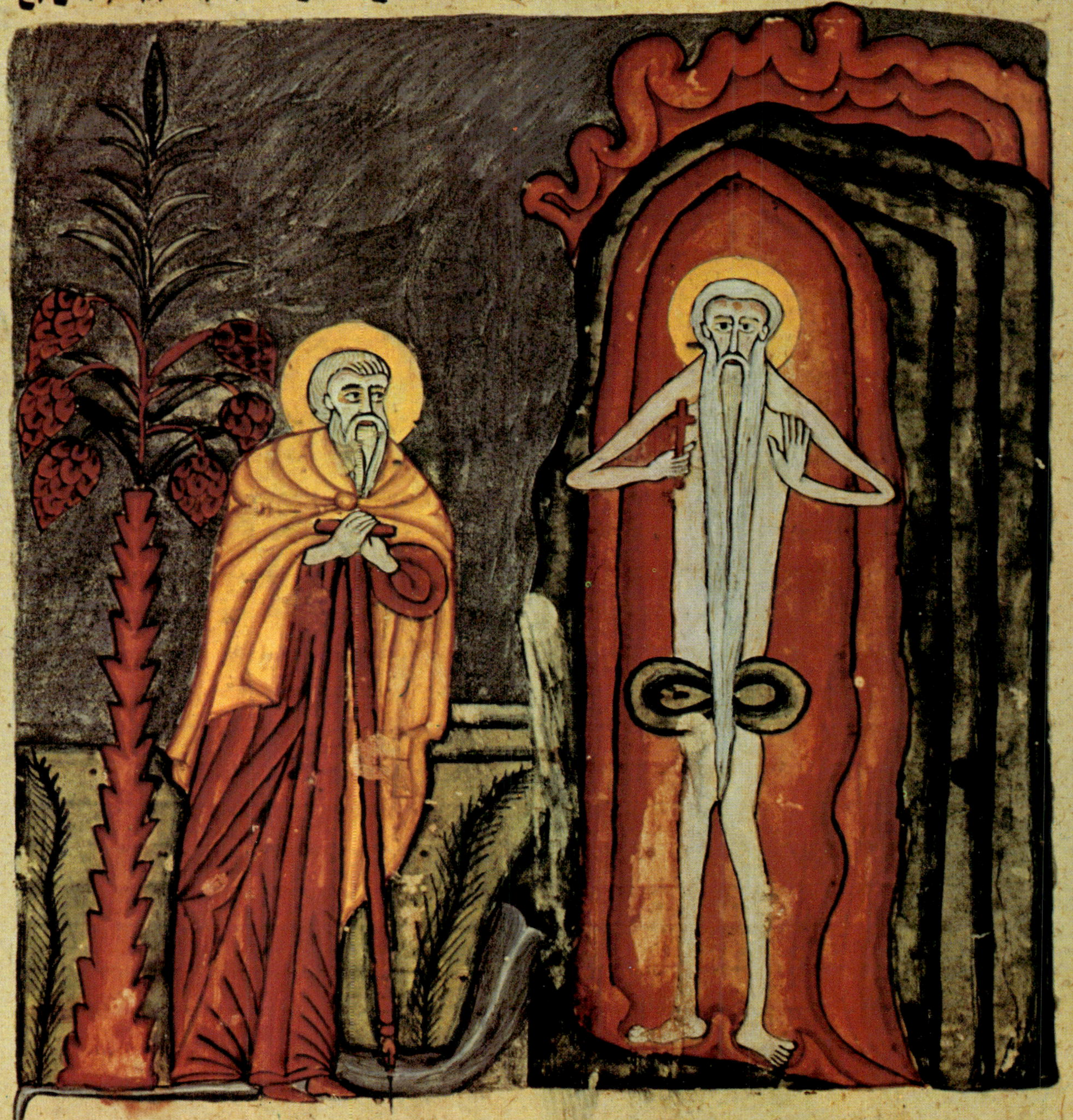

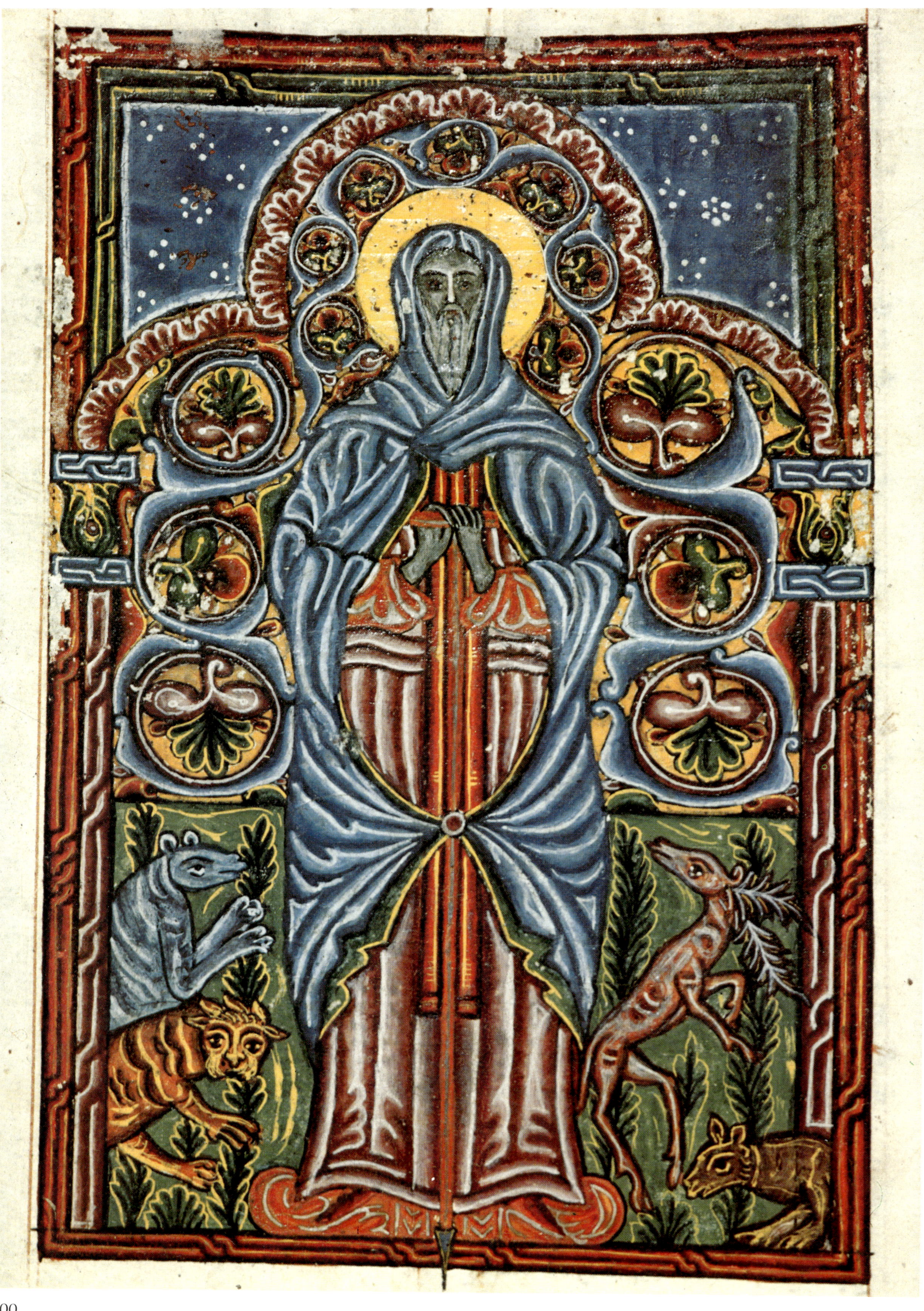

Figure 120: *St. Anthony and the beasts of the desert. Frontispiece to the 1623* Lives of the Fathers, *painted, perhaps in Jerusalem (ms. 971, fol. 16v).*

125

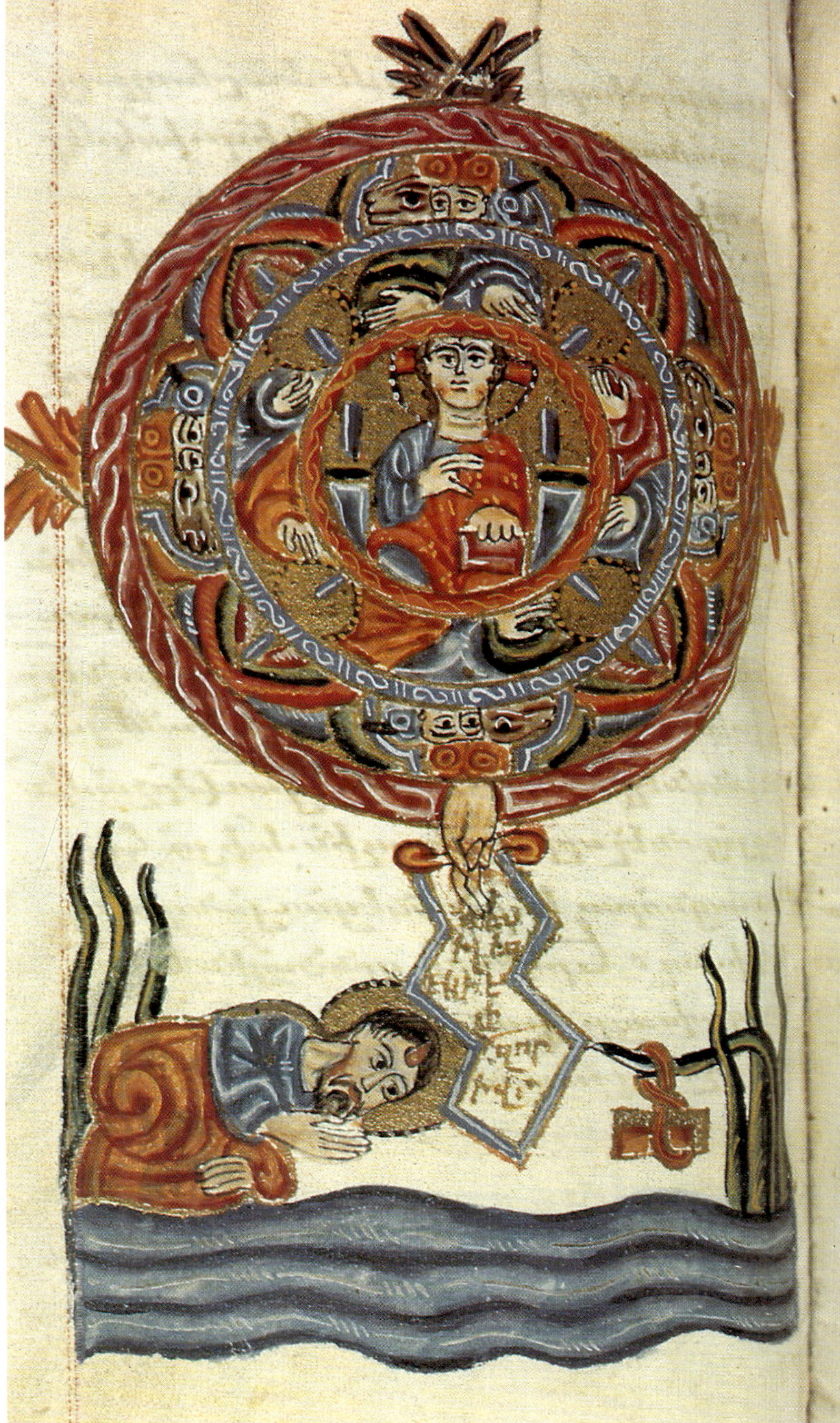

126

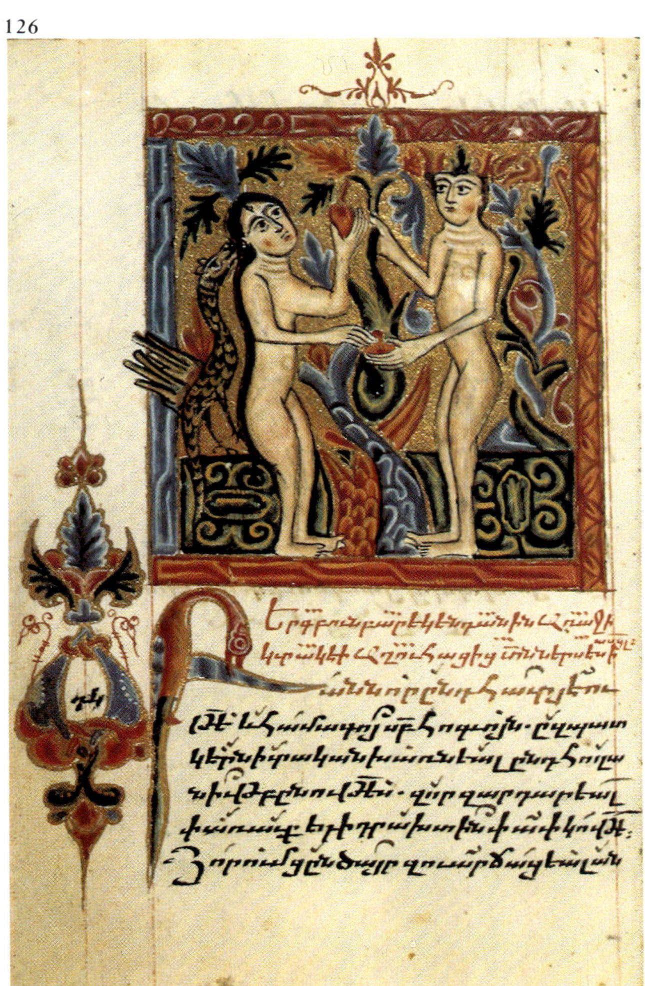

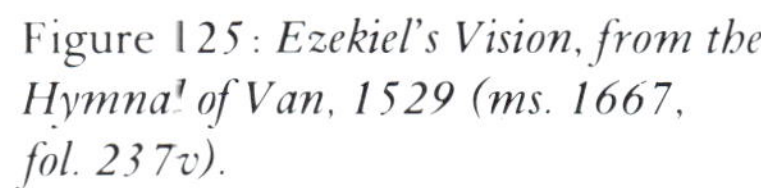

Figure 125: *Ezekiel's Vision, from the Hymnal of Van, 1529 (ms. 1667, fol. 237v).*

Figure 126: *The Temptation of Adam and Eve, from the Hymnal of Van, 1529 (ms. 1667, fol. 58v).*

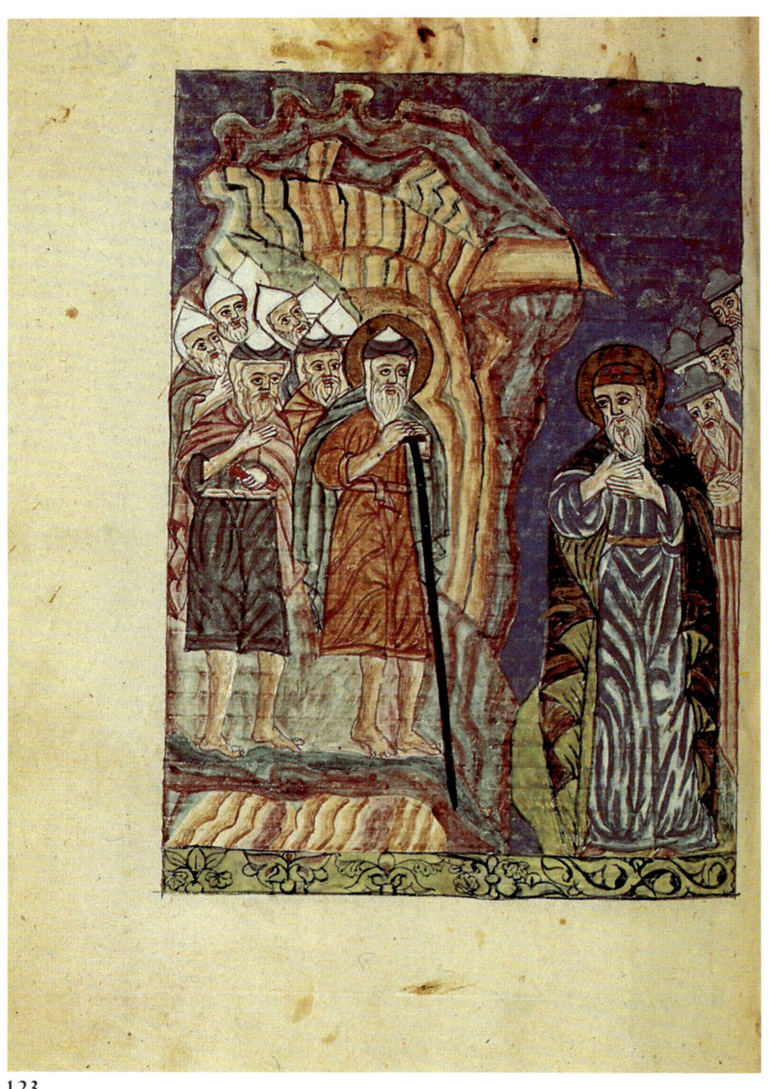

123

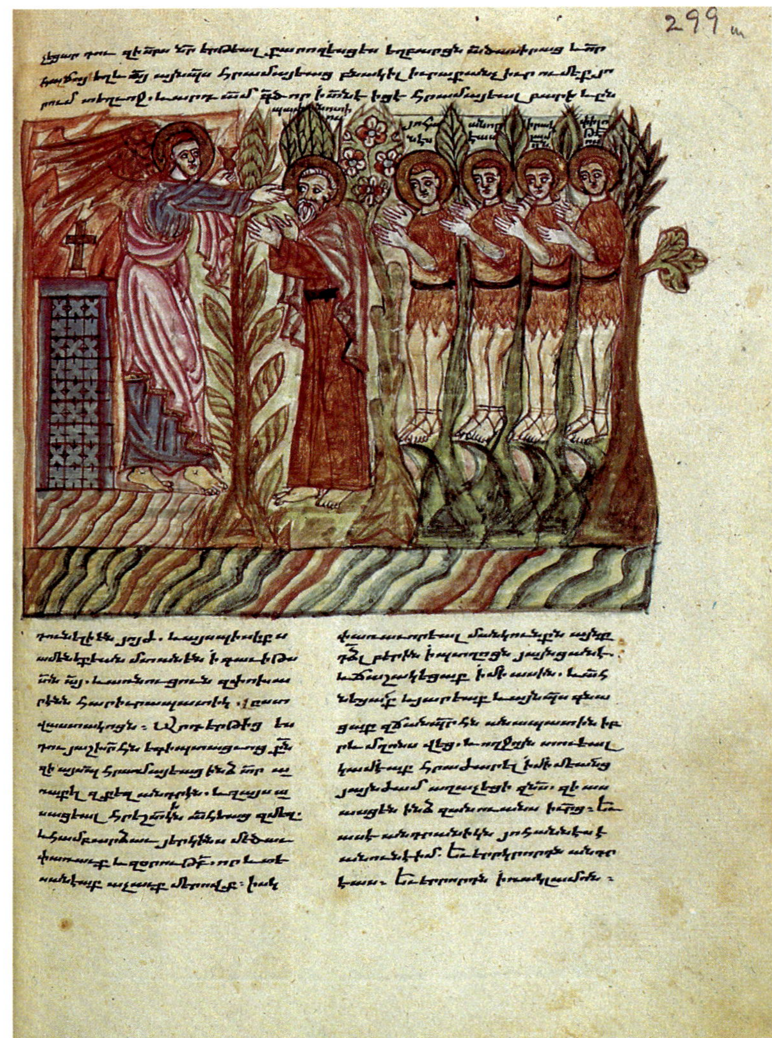

124

127

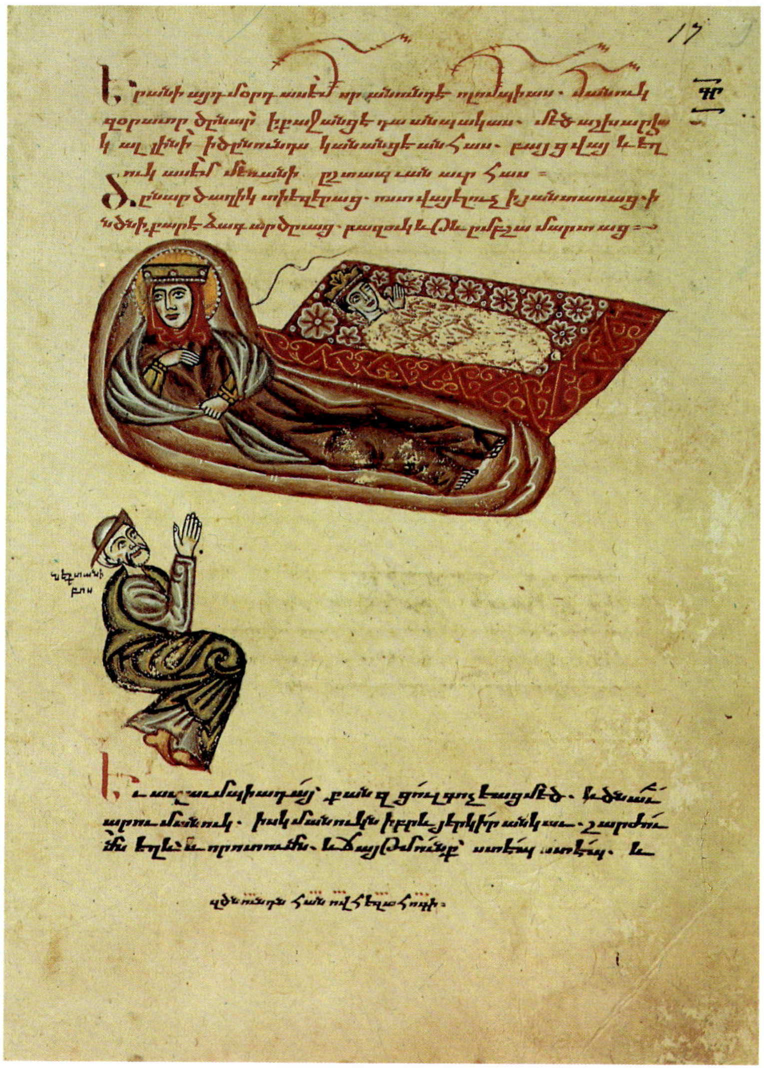

128

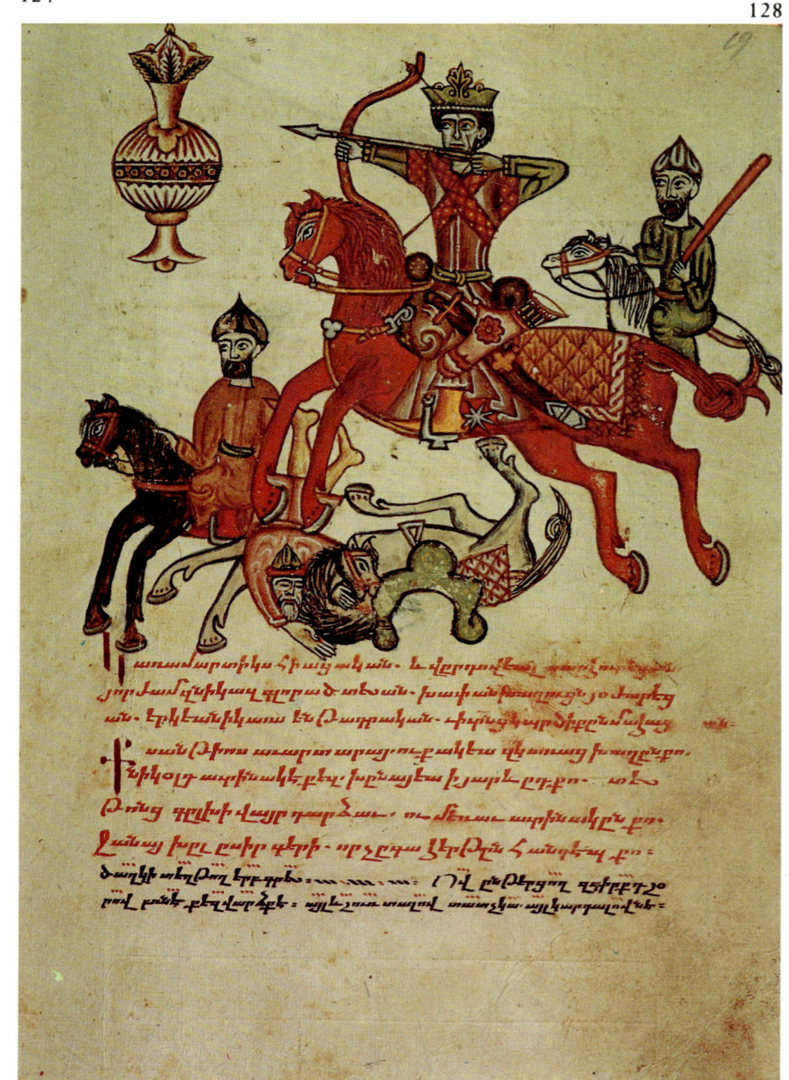

Figure 123: *Theophilus, Patriarch of Alexandria, meeting Father Pambo and his monks, from the* Lives of the Fathers, *Jerusalem, 1651 (ms. 228, fol. 276v).*

Figure 124: *St. Paphnutius receiving communion from an angel, from the* Lives of the Fathers, *Jerusalem, 1651 (ms. 228, fol. 299).*

Figure 127: *Nectanebos adoring the birth of Alexander, from the Alexander Romance, painted by Grigoris, Catholicos of Aghthamar, copied at Varag (ms. 473, fol. 17).*

Figure 128: *The death of Nicolaos, King of the Akarnanians, from the Alexander Romance, Varag and Aghthamar, 1535–36 (ms. 473, fol. 19).*

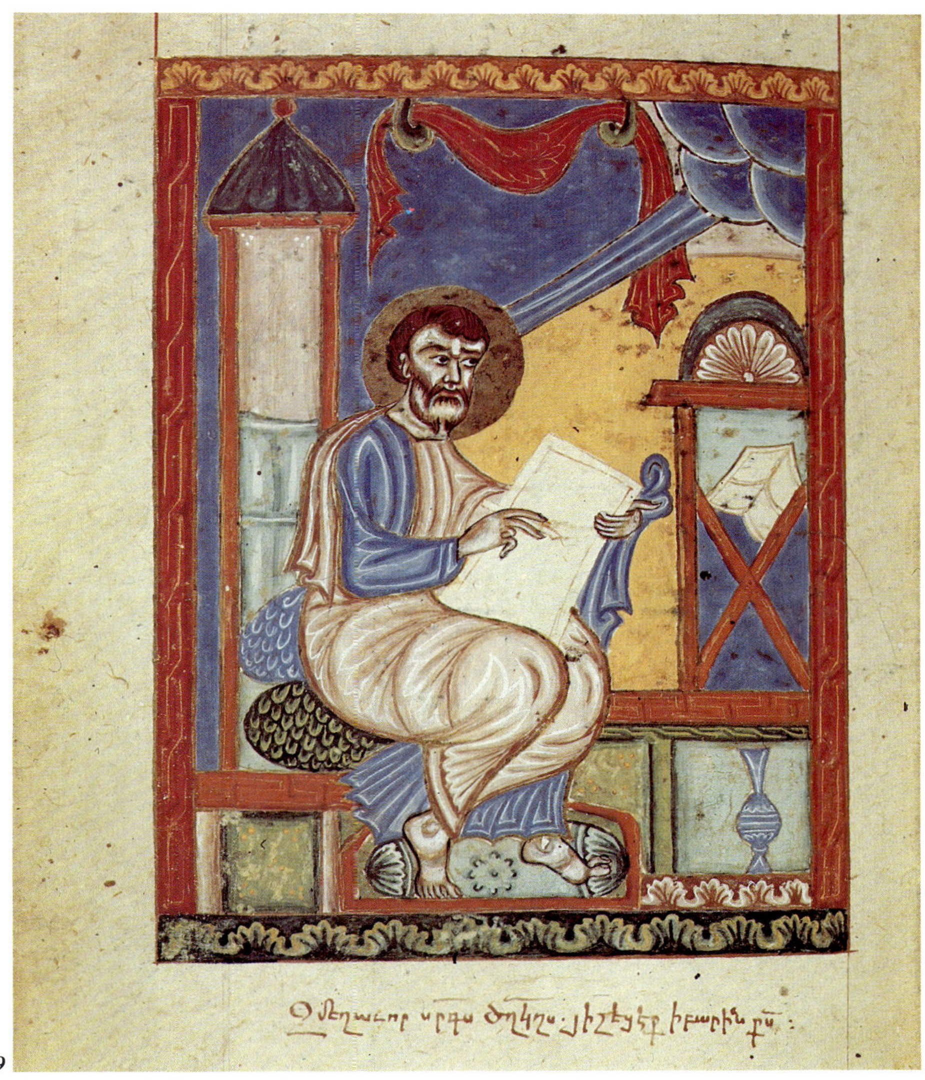

129

Figure 129: *St. Luke, from Sargis Khizantzi's Jerusalem Gospel, 1572 (ms. 868, fol. 141v).*

Figure 130: *Headpiece to the opening page of Sargis Khizantzi's Jerusalem Gospel, 1572 (ms. 868, fol. 13).*

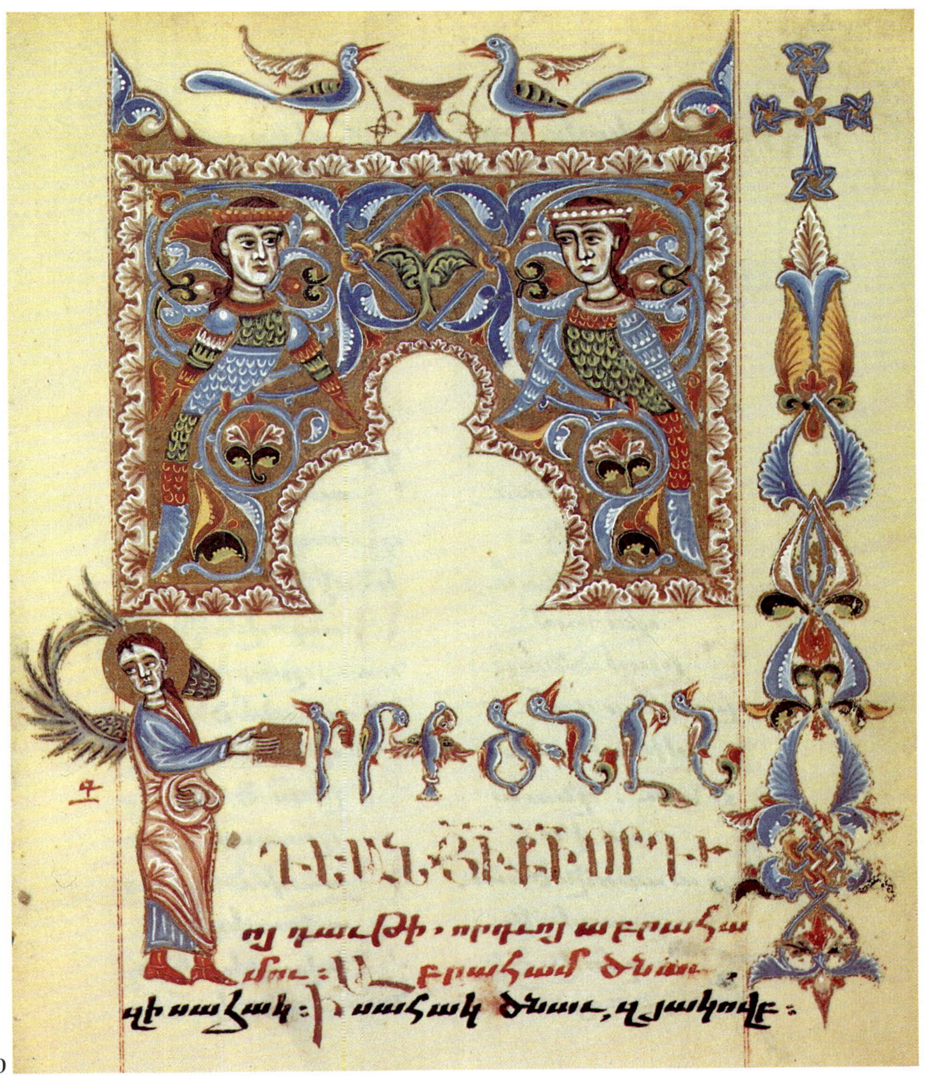

130

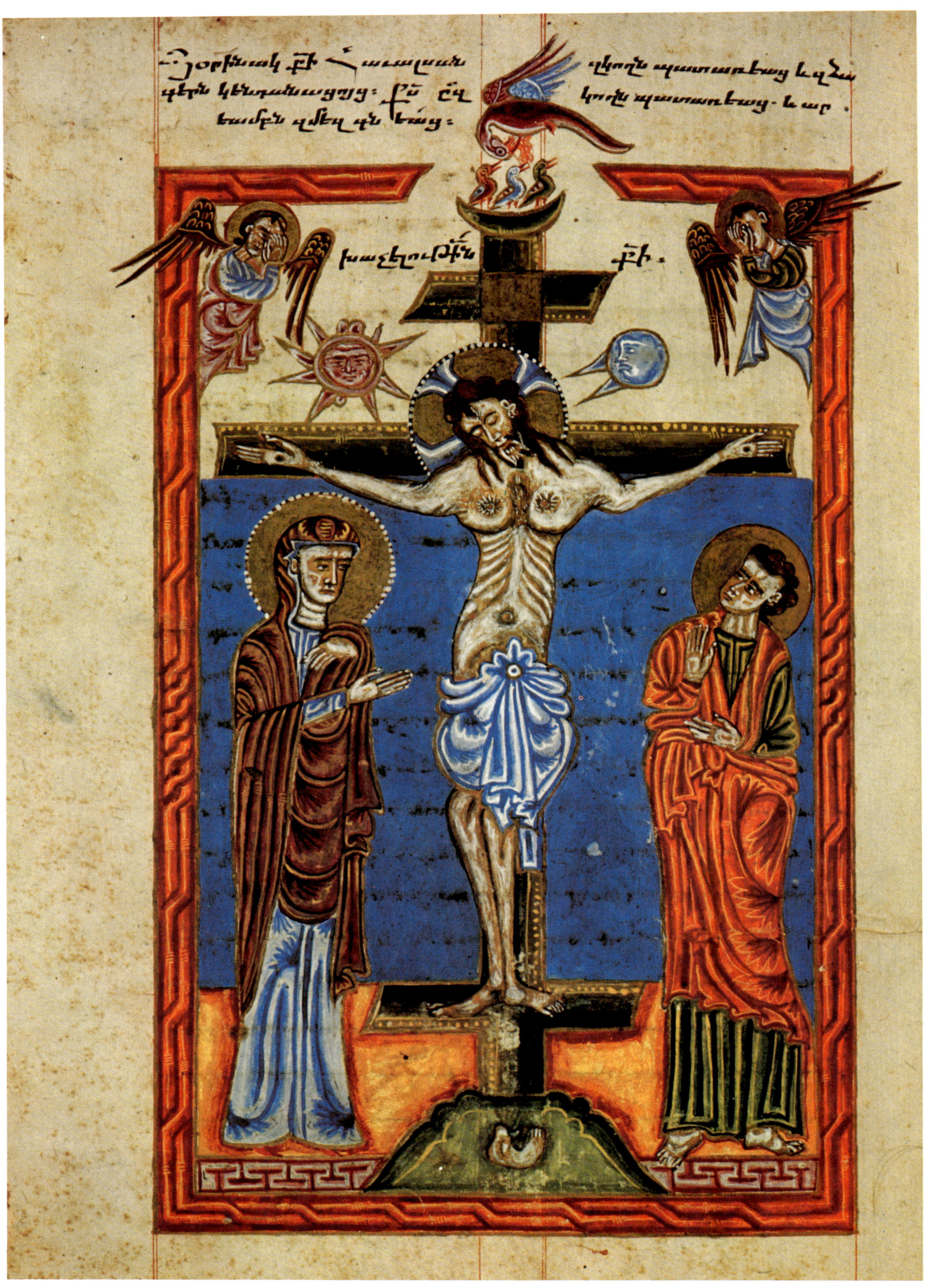

Figure 132: *Crucifixion from the earliest Martyros Khizantzi* Gantsaran *(religious poems), school of Khizan, 1575 (ms. 135, fol. 254v).*

Figure 133: *Dormition of the Virgin, from the earliest Martyros Khizantzi* Gantsaran, *school of Khizan, 1575 (ms. 135, fol. 394).*

Figure 134: *Dives, the rich man, tormented by thirst while being fried in hell, and Lazarus, the poor man to whom he did not give food, lying in Abraham's bosom in Paradise. From a Hymnal by Sargis Khizantzi the Younger, 1601 (ms. 1663, p. 193).*

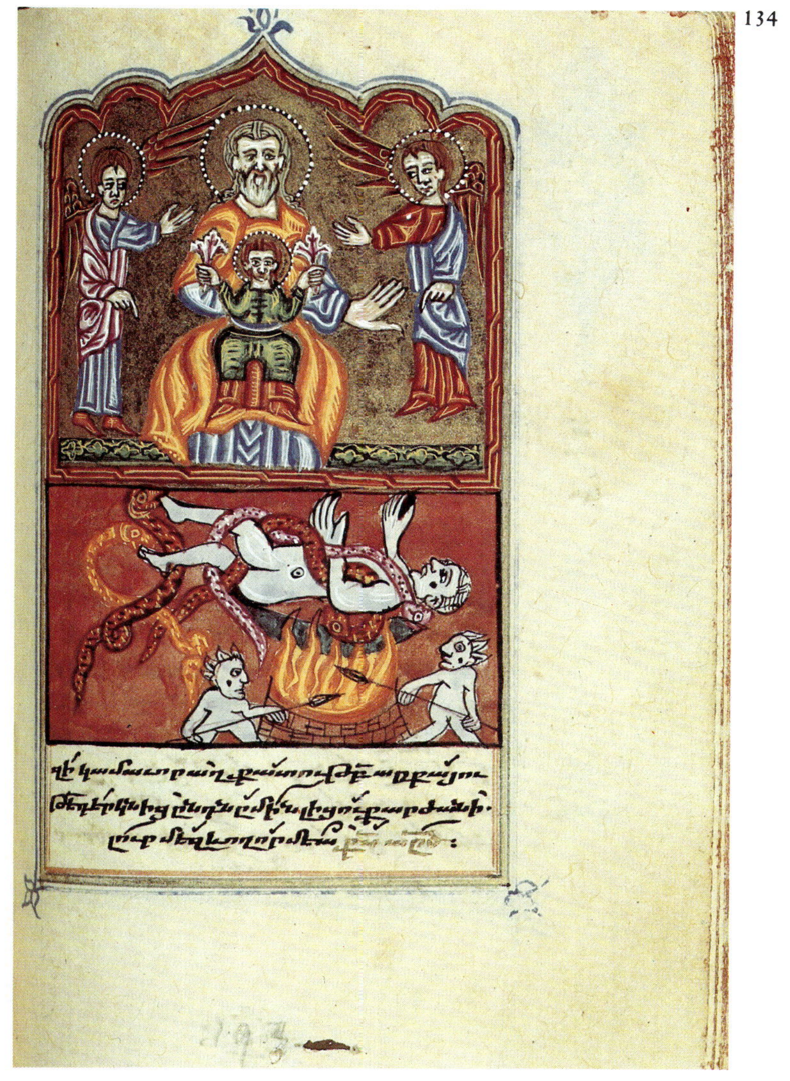

134

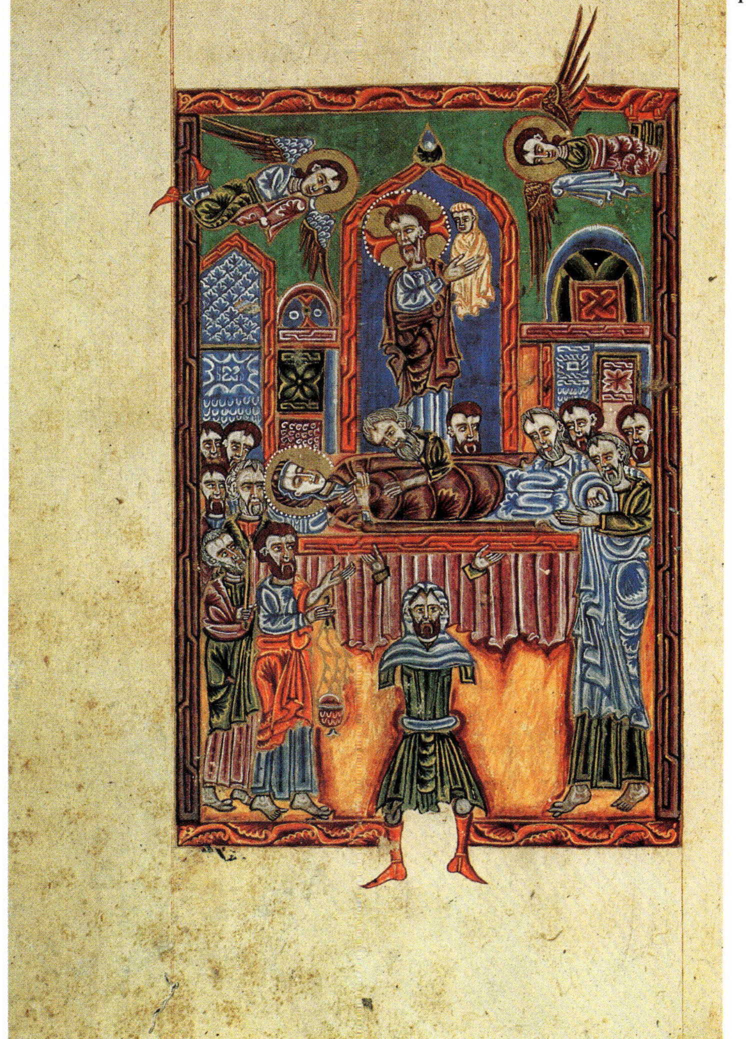

133

Figure 135 (page 106): *The Israelites crossing the Red Sea while the Egyptians are drowning and Pharaoh's crown and scepter fly up to heaven. From a Hymnal by Sargis Khizantzi the Younger, 1601 (ms. 1663, pp. 814–815).*

Figure 137 (page 106): *Descent of the Holy Spirit at Pentecost, from a Hymnal. The headpiece was decorated by Sargis Khizantzi the Elder and the panel painted by Kirakos, a pupil of his son, in 1623. See fig. 131. (ms. 1594, pp. 372–373).*

Figure 138 (page 107): *Nativity and Adoration of the Magi, from a menologium of 1591 from Jerusalem. The painter, Khatchatur of Khizan, copied it from the Queen Keran Gospel while he was in Jerusalem (ms. 1920, fol. 796).*

135

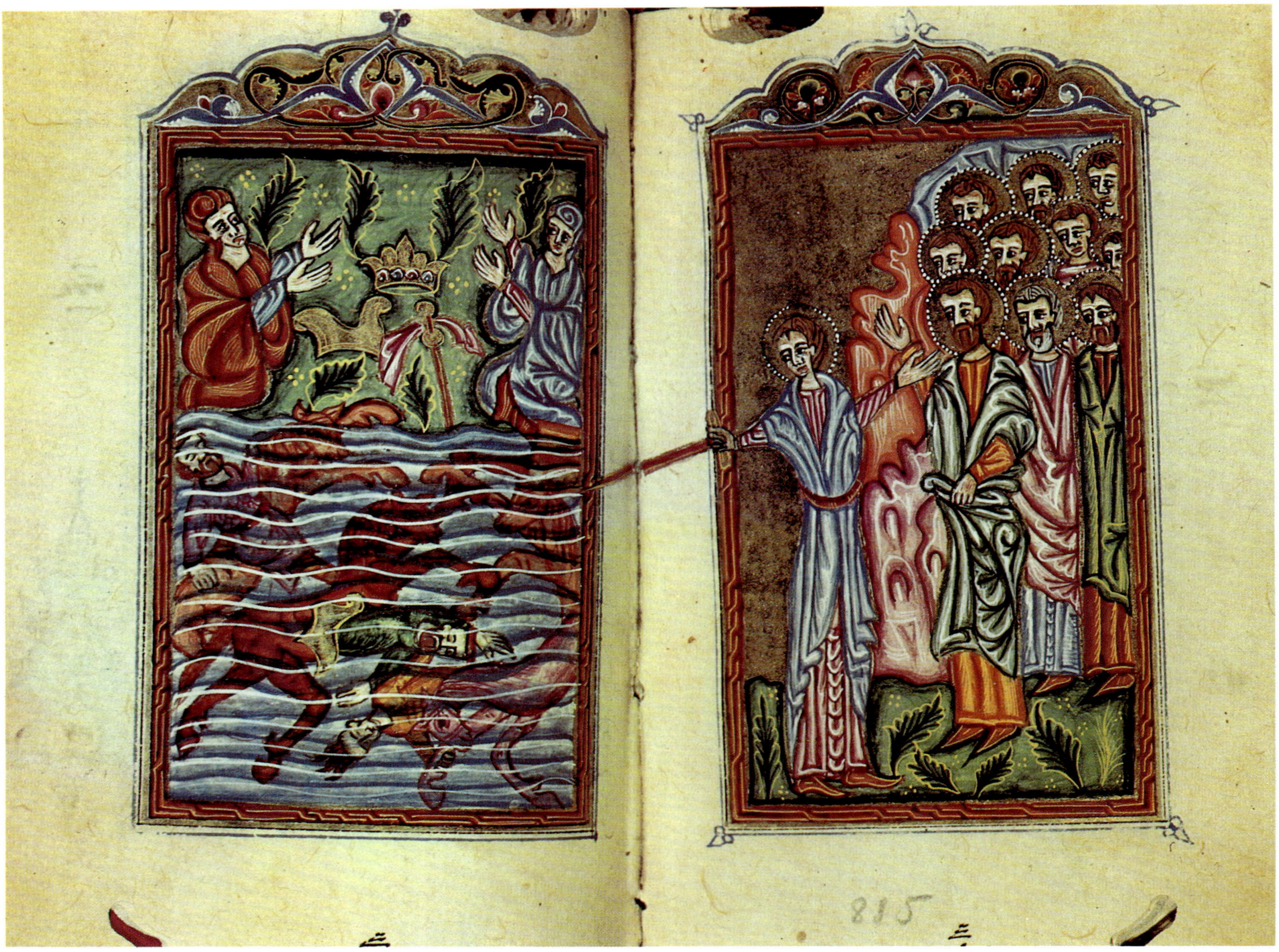

137

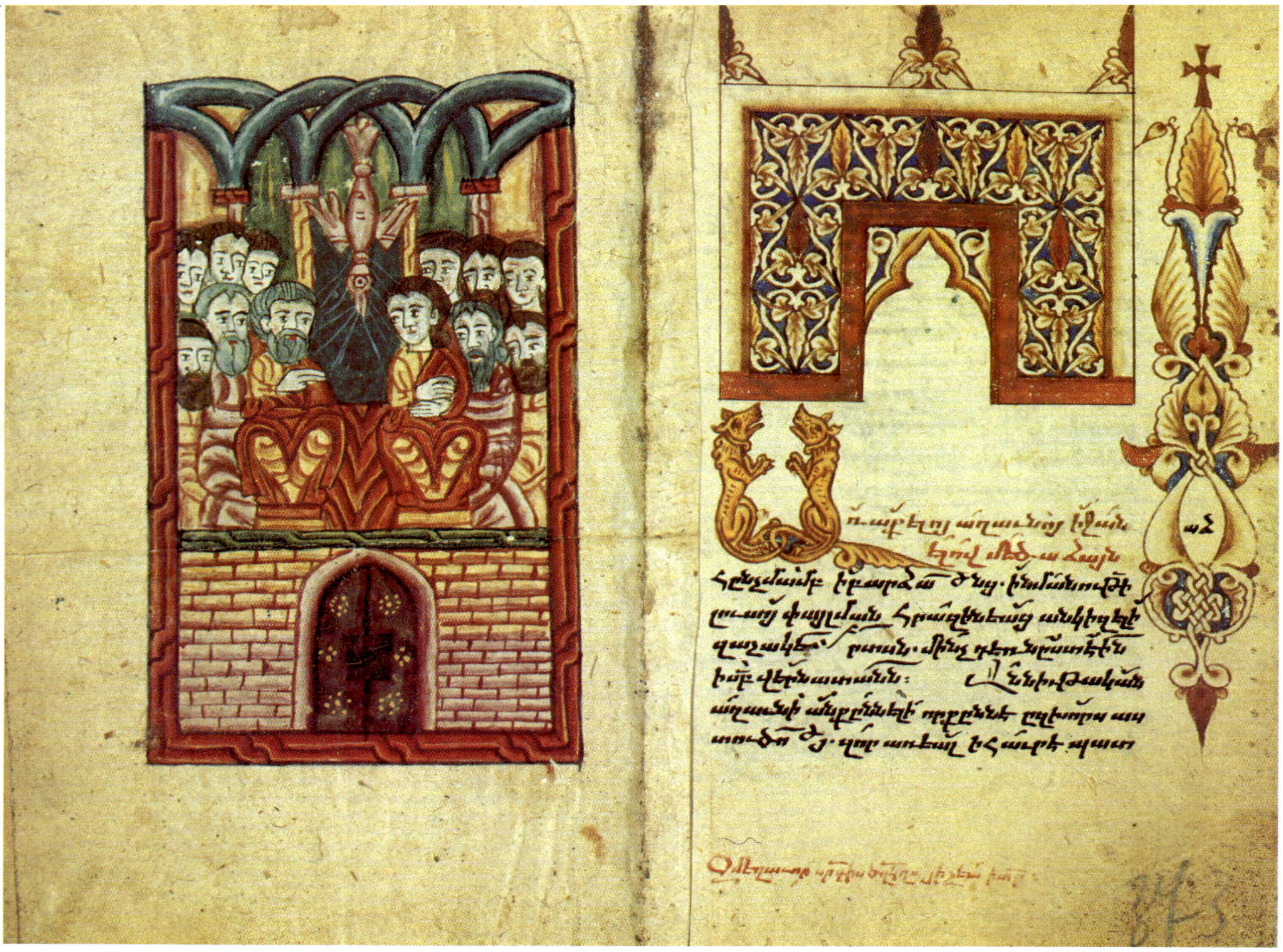

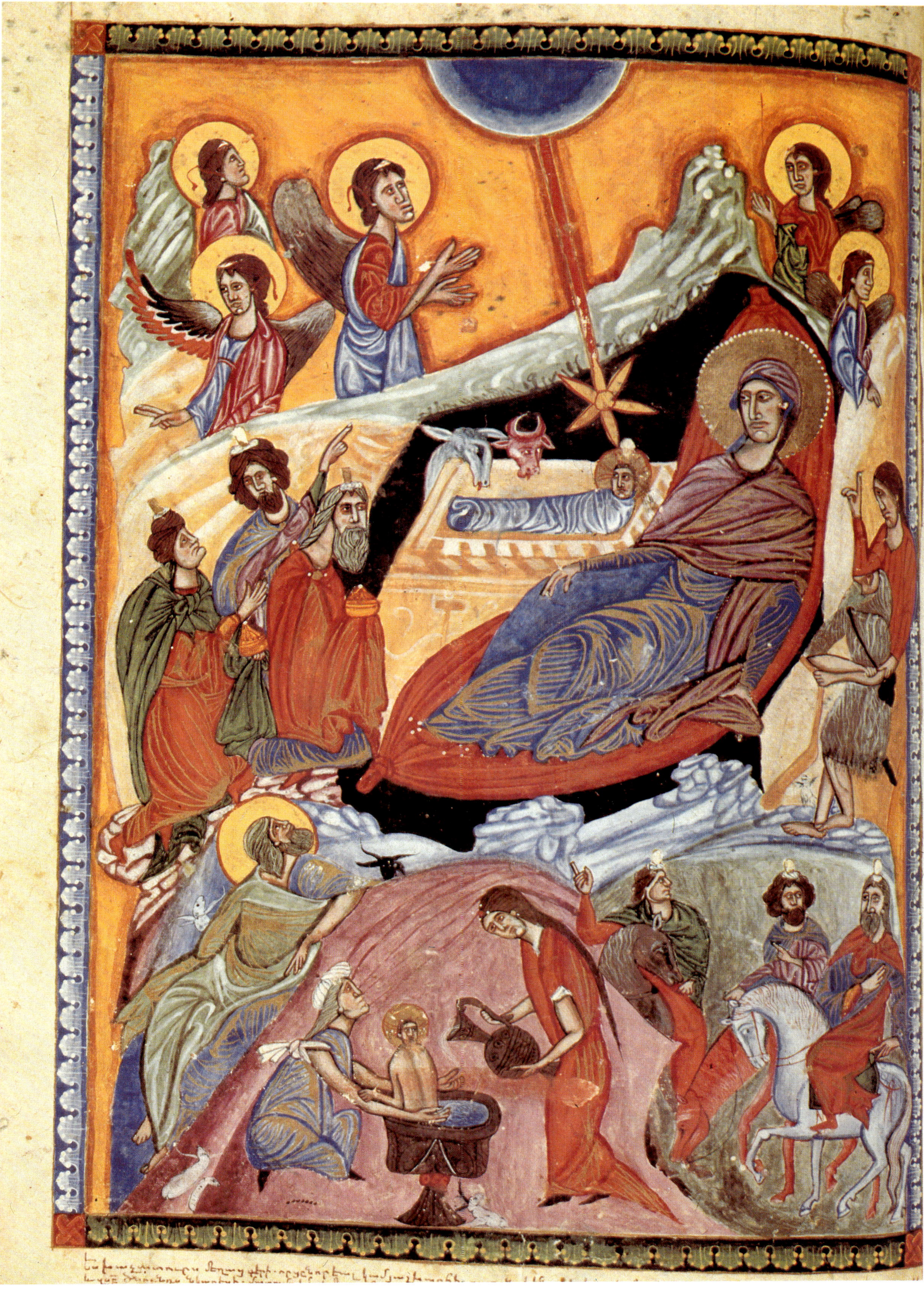

Figure 131: *Frontispiece and opening of a Hymnal from Pazentz. Headpiece decorated by Sargis Khizantzi in 1553, Joachim and Anne painted by Kirakos in 1623. See also fig. 137. (ms. 1594, pp. 6–7).*

Figure 136: *The Annunciation to Joachim and Anne, a frontispiece and a headpiece on the opening pages of a Hymnal by Sargis Khizantzi the Younger, 1602 (ms. 1460, pp. 10–11).*

136

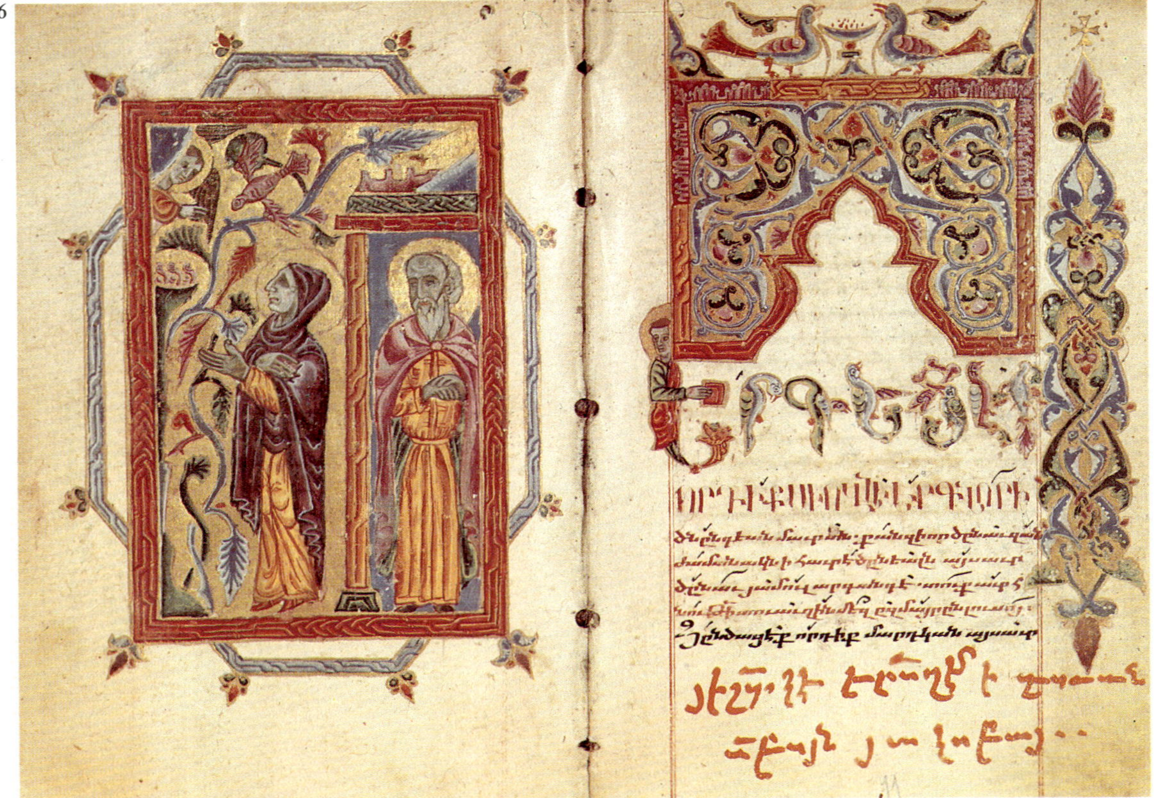

131

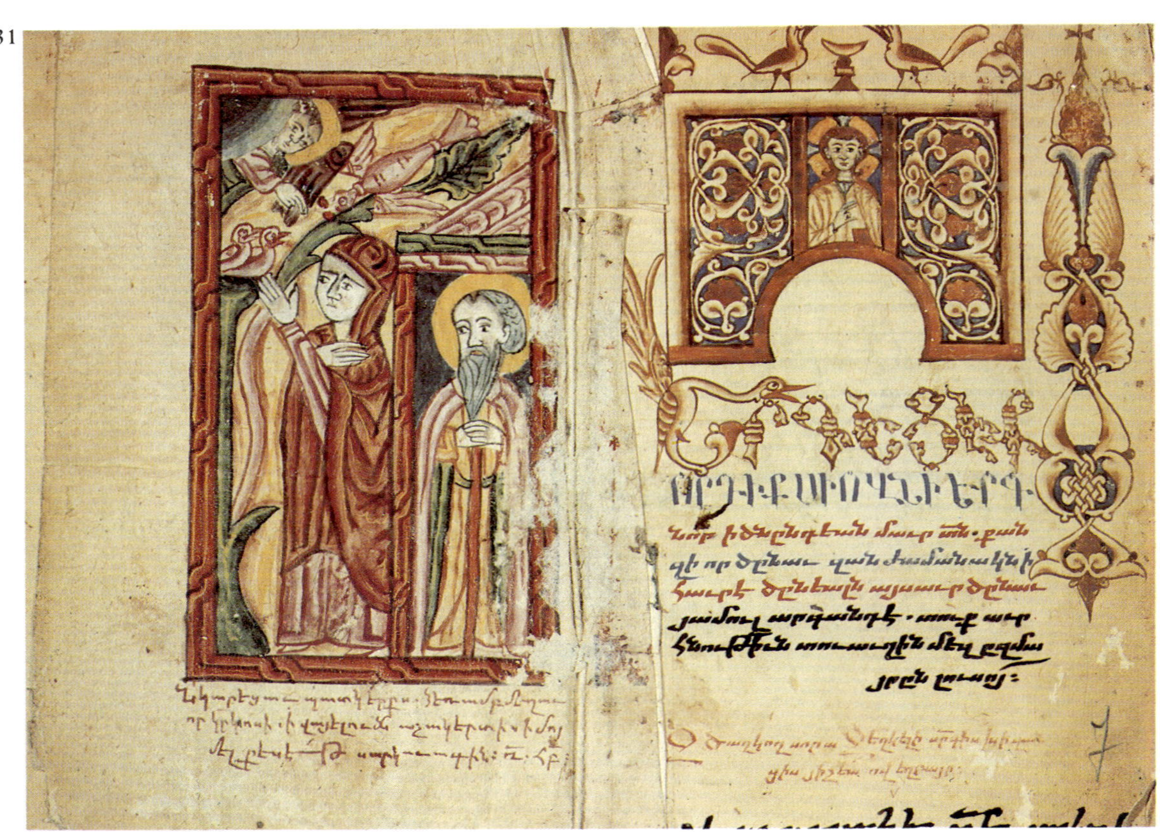

Figure 139: *God creating the world, the Creation of Eve and life in Paradise, the Fall, and Noah ordering the animals to go into the Ark. Full-page panel from the New Julfa Bible in the De Bry recension, Isfahan 1643–6 (ms. 1934, fol. 12v).*

Figure 140 (page 110): *Abraham and the three Angels, the Sacrifice of Isaac, Jacob's Dream, and the Israelites crossing the Red Sea. From the De Bry Recension Bible, Isfahan 1643–46 (ms. 1934, fol. 13).*

Figure 141 (page 111): *David rescuing a sheep from a lion, Saul enthroned, David and Goliath, and David sacrificing to stop the Plague. Panel from the De Bry Recension Bible (ms. 1934, fol. 425v).*

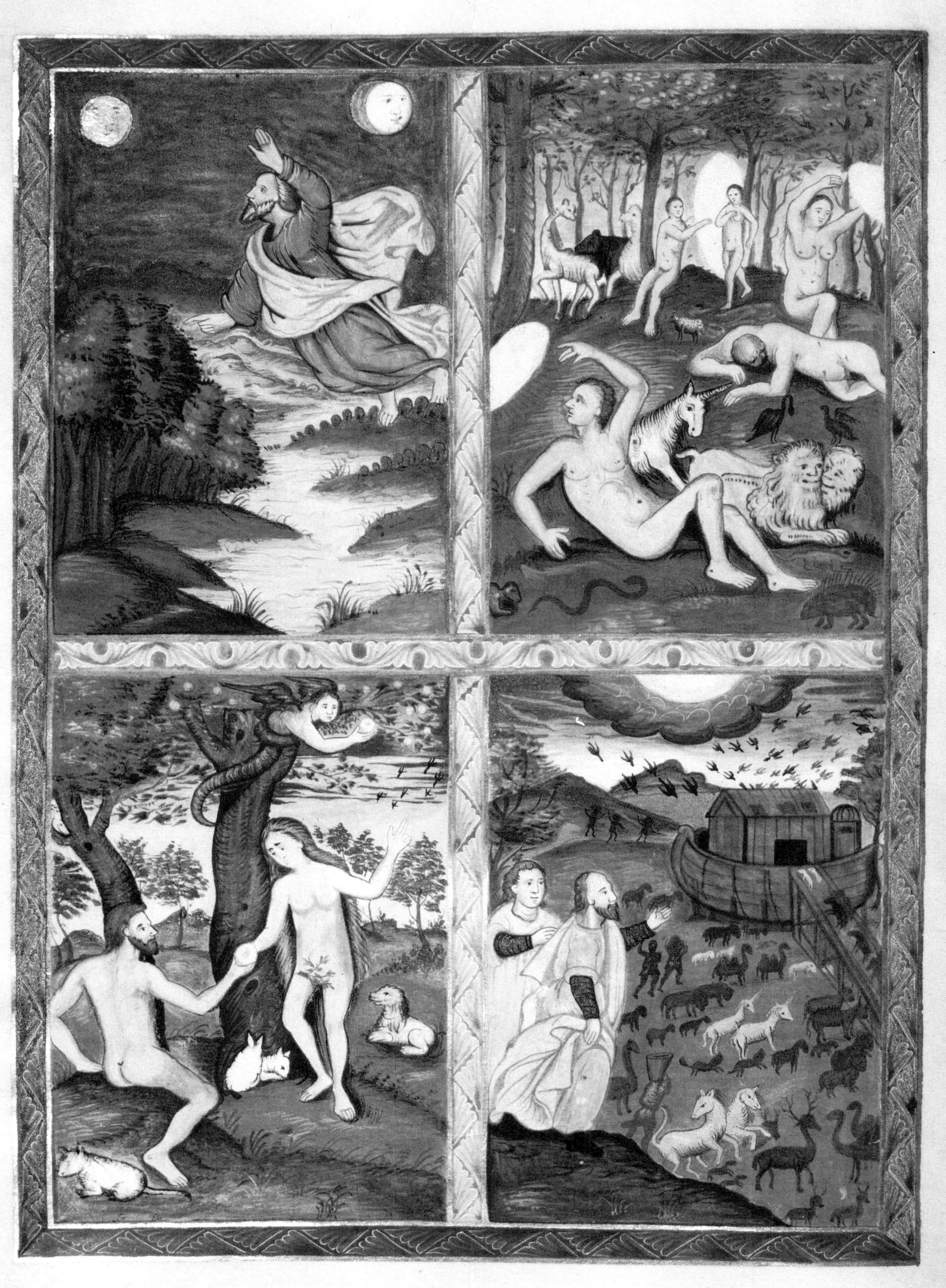

139

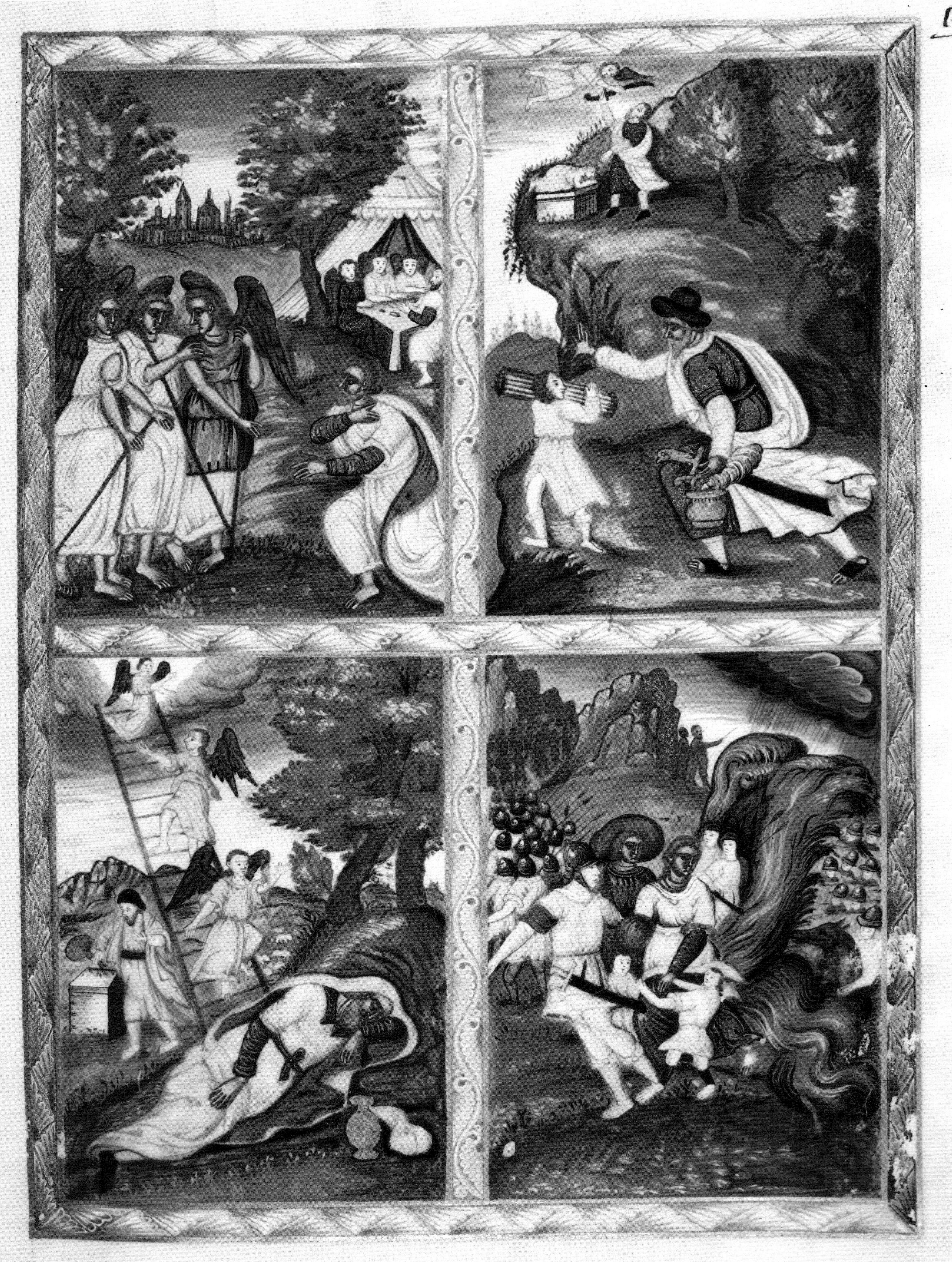

140

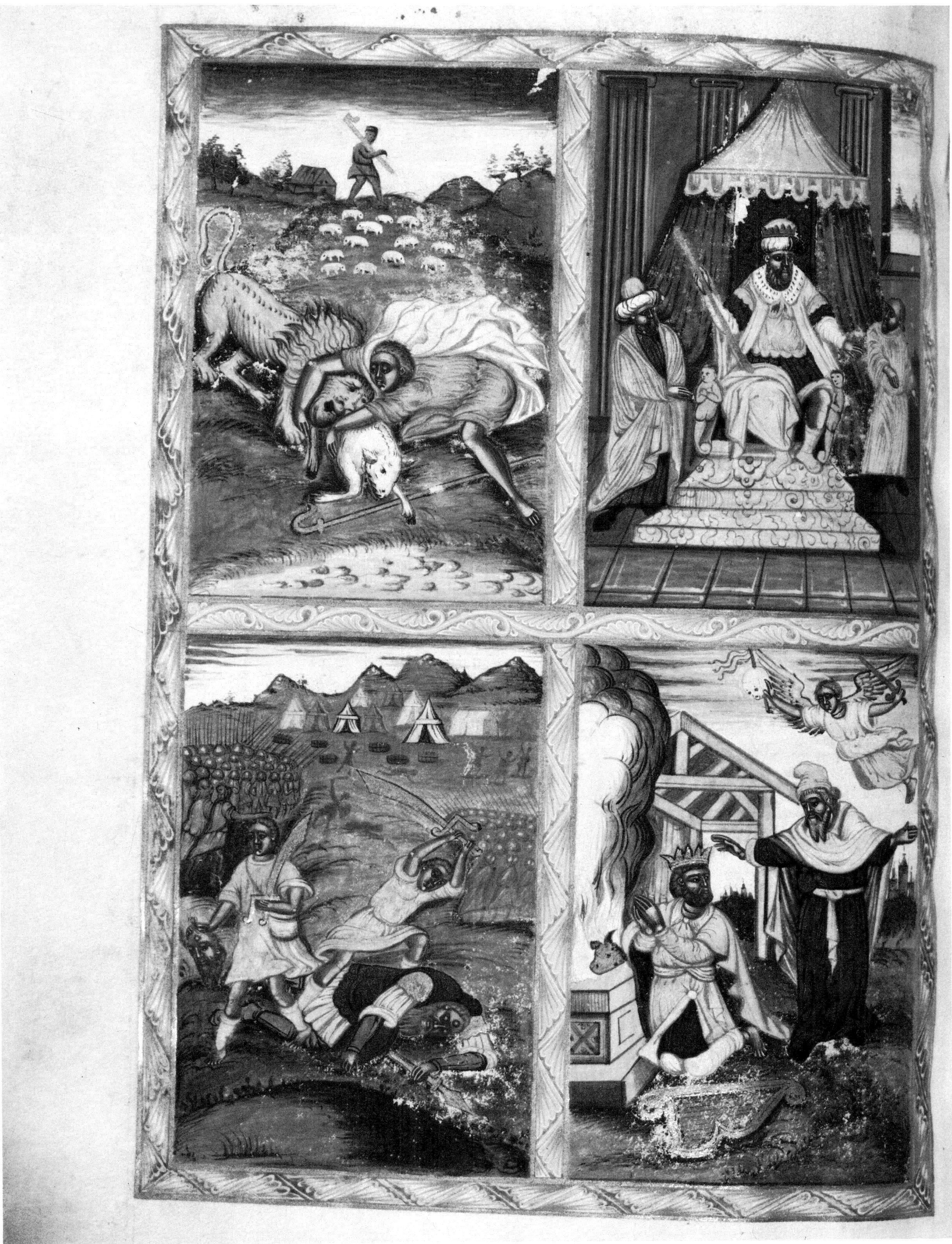

141

Figure 142: *The Seven Days of Creation, the Creation of Adam and Eve, the Fall and Expulsion from Paradise, the Twenty-Four Elders of the Apocalypse and Moses. Frontispiece and opening page of Genesis from a New Julfa Bible copied in Istanbul in 1626, illuminated by Khatchatur Isfahani (ms. 428, fols. 8v–9).*

Figure 143: *The Seven Days of Creation, the Creation of Adam and Eve, the Fall and Expulsion from Paradise, the Twenty-Four Elders of the Apocalypse, and Moses. Frontispiece and opening page of Genesis from a New Julfa Bible copied perhaps in Istanbul in 1640 (ms. 1932).*

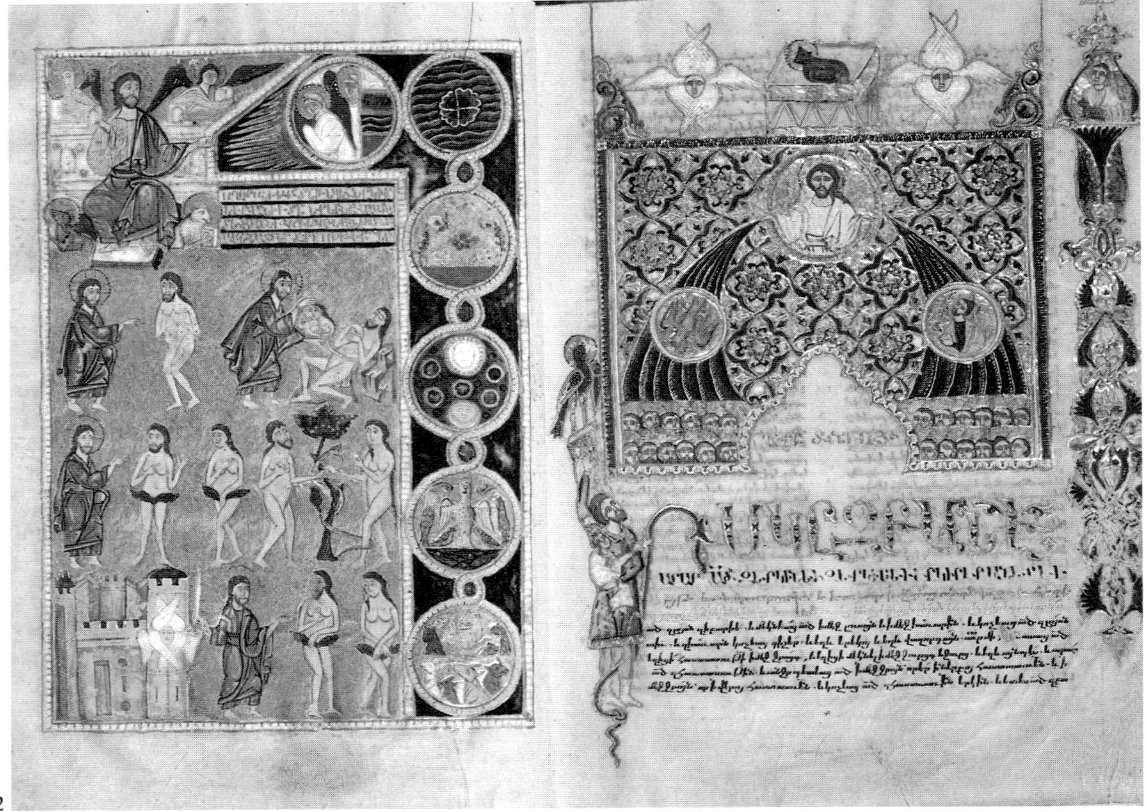

142

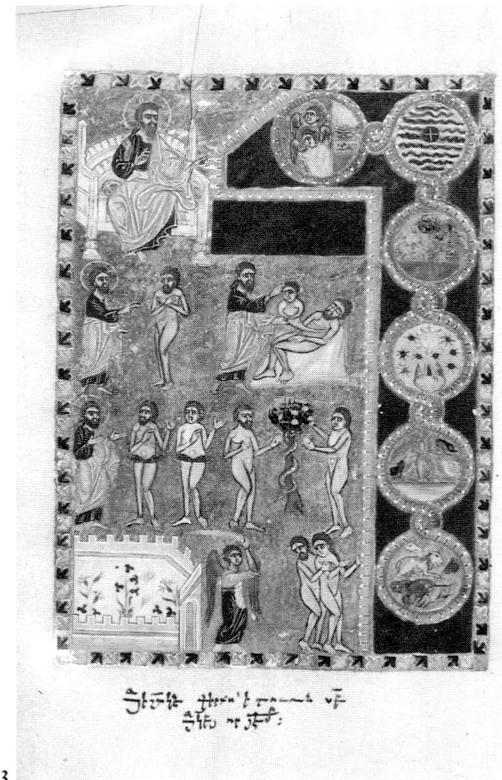

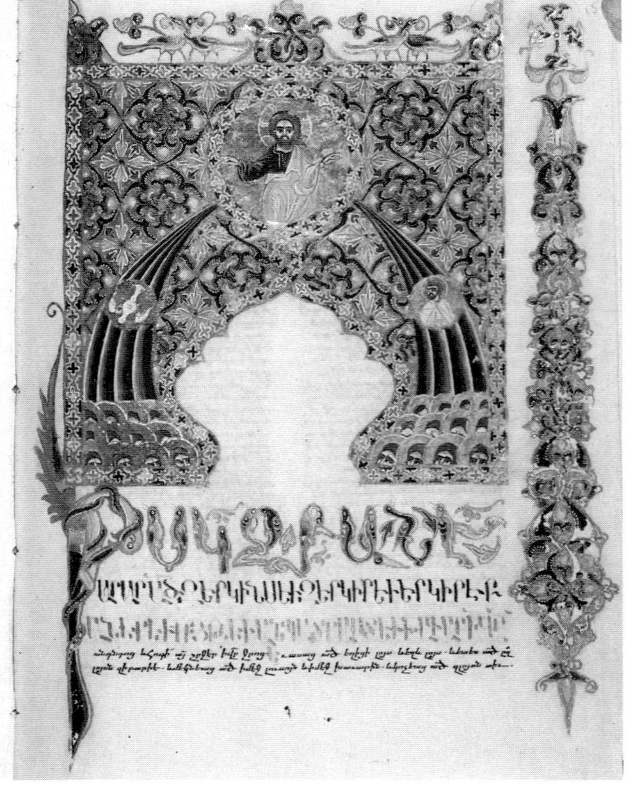

143

Figure 144: *Hannah sitting before Eli, a misbound full-page panel from a Bible of the seventeenth century copied in New Julfa or Istanbul (ms. 501, fol. 4v).*

Figure 145: *An angel showing St. John the Heavenly Jerusalem, from a New Julfa Bible of 1645 (ms. 1933, fol. 544).*

144

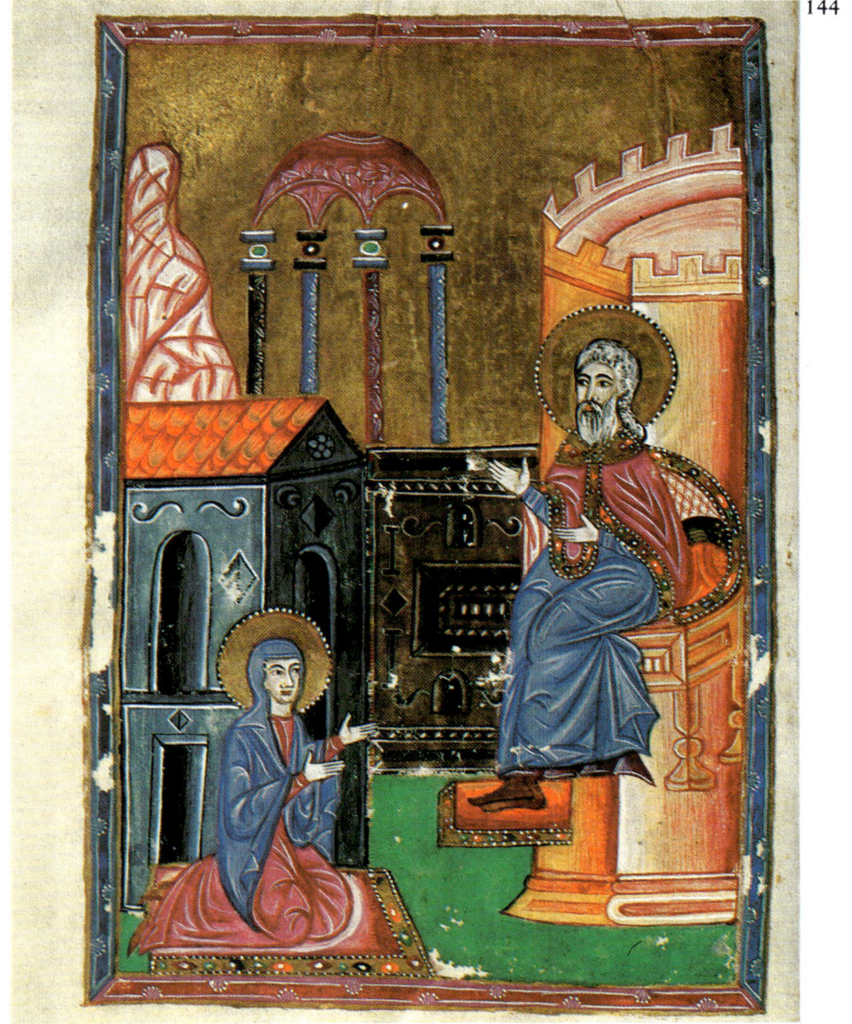

145

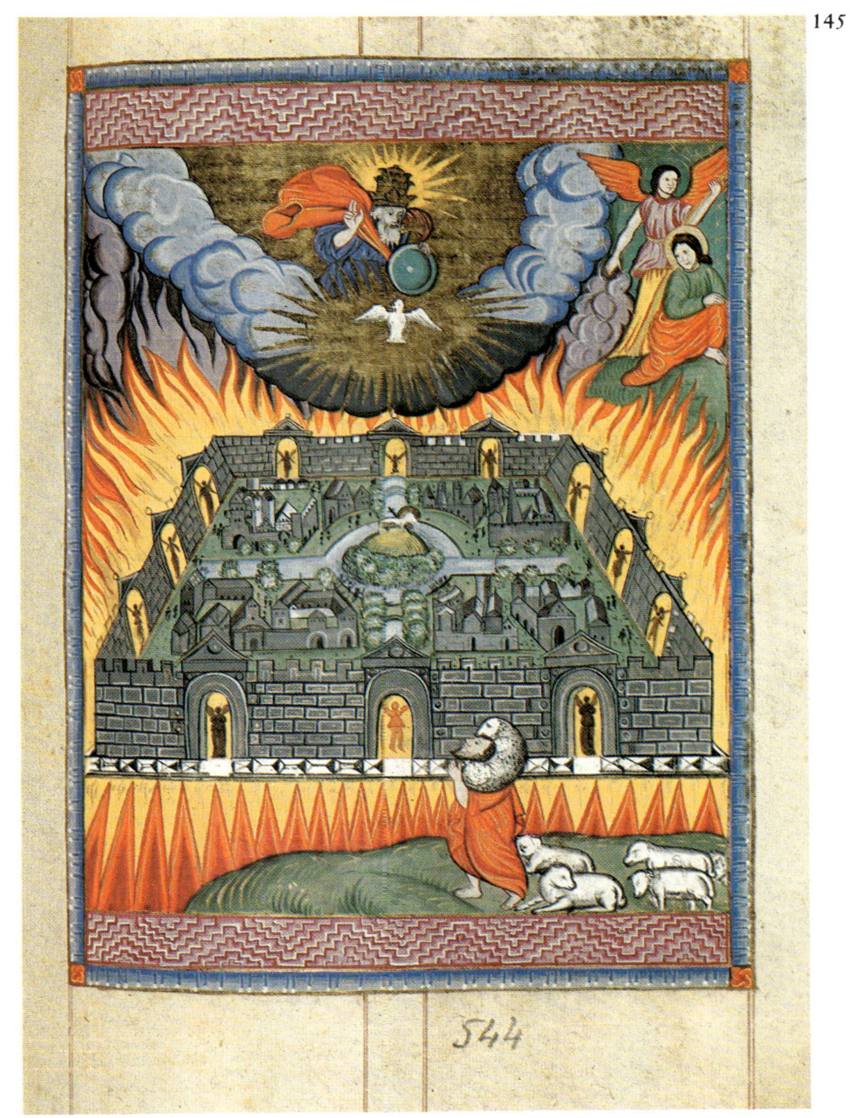

Figure 146: *The Twenty-Four Elders of the Apocalypse offering their crowns to God the Father. Woodcut by Christoffel van Sichem after Albrecht Dürer, from the Oskan Bible, Amsterdam, 1666, p. 700.*

Figure 147: *An angel showing St. John the Heavenly Jerusalem. Woodcut by van Sichem in the Oskan Bible, Amsterdam, 1666, p. 716.*

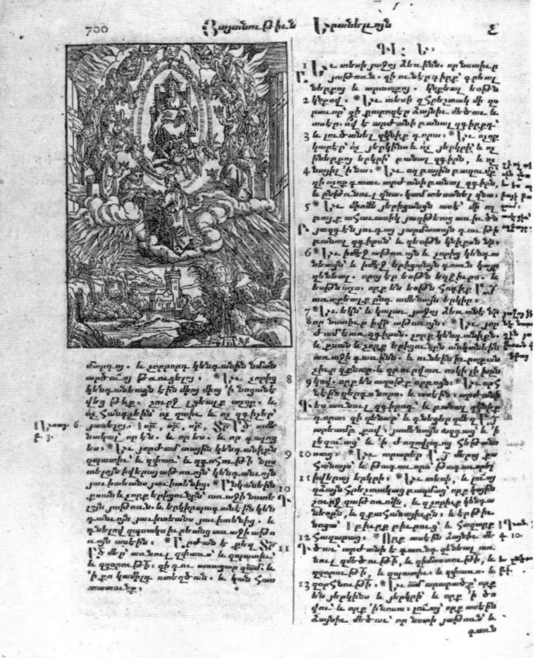

146

147

148

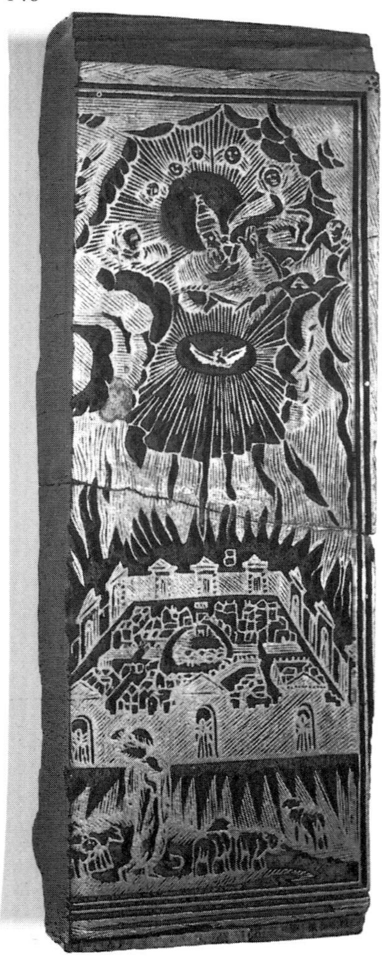

Figure 148: *The Heavenly Jerusalem, a wood block for printing, late seventeenth century.*

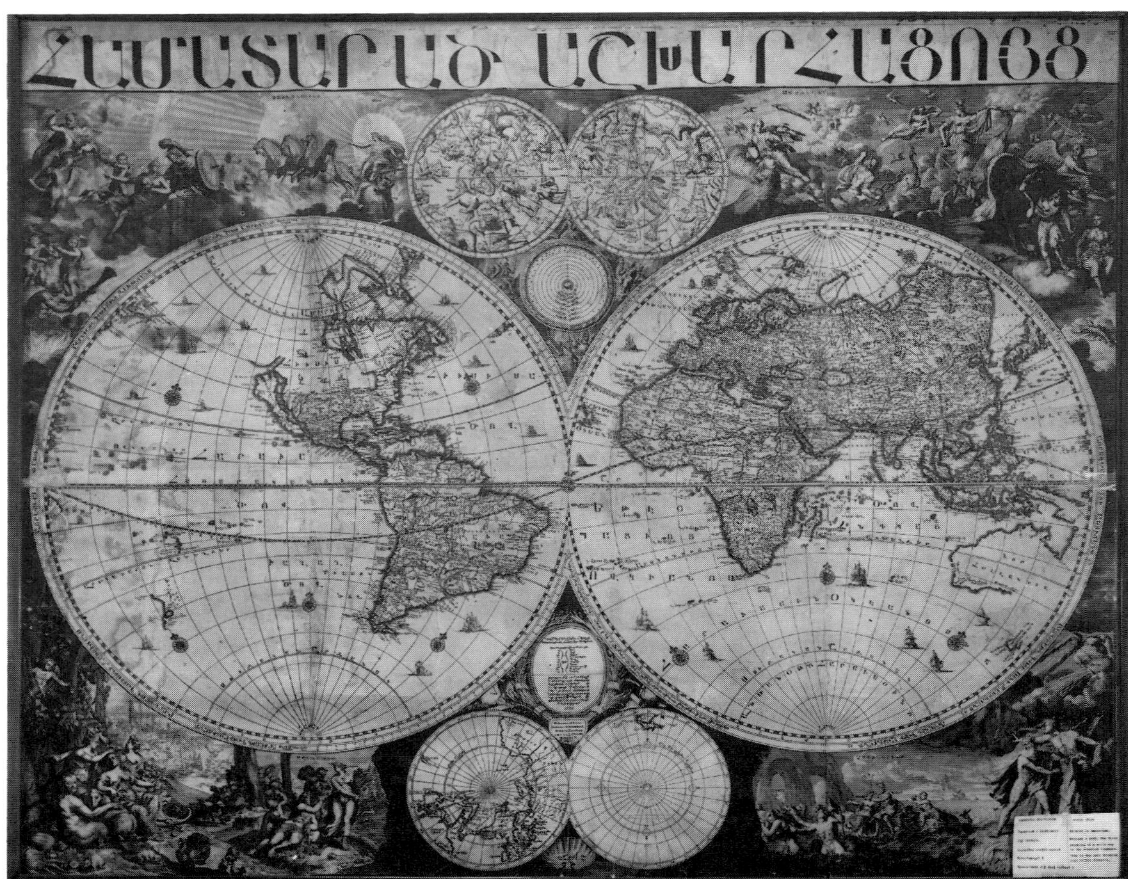

149

Figure 149: *The first map of the world with Armenian characters, printed by Hadrianus Schoonbeck in Amsterdam, 1695.*

Chapter Nine: Armenian Printed Books and Late Illumination

150

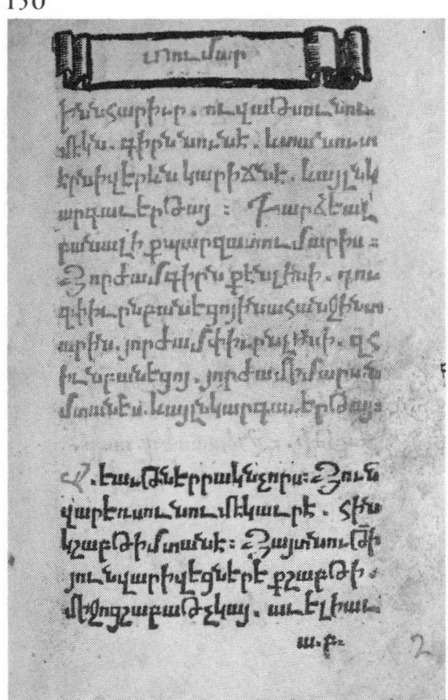

Figure 150: *Ecclesiastical Calendar, opening of the first Armenian printed book, Venice, 1512, p. 2.*

1. The Oskan Bible

The Heavenly Jerusalem together with other pictures of the Van Sichem Bible gained popularity in Armenian art, due mainly to the printer Oskan. He reproduced them with an Armenian text of the Bible in Amsterdam in 1666, as part of his activity in promoting Armenian printing in Italy and Holland.[1] His ambition to print a complete canonical Armenian Bible could not be fulfilled in Italy, since the Catholic canon differs from that of the Armenians. After a long delay Oskan succeeded in establishing a printing press in a church in Protestant Amsterdam, and acquired the rights to use the Van Sichem woodcuts to illustrate his Bible.

Some of Van Sichem's woodcuts were recut for the Oskan Bible, probably because they were damaged.[2] The new woodcutters, however, retained the signature of Christoffel Van Sichem, and those earlier artists he copied

The text of the Oskan Bible of 1666 was influenced to some extent by the Latin Vulgate, a situation which was altered in its 1703 edition printed in Istanbul. However the achievement of Oskan in printing a complete Armenian Bible, and its subsequent popularity, helped, no doubt, to spread the Van Sichem pictures in the entire Armenian diaspora. Among the illustrations to the Apocalypse, which are based on Dürer's woodcuts, is that of the Twenty- Four Elders offering their crowns to God the Father *fig. 146*. It bears both Van Sichem's and Dürer's signatures. However, the Heavenly Jerusalem of the Oskan Bible *fig. 147* is signed with the monogram of Van Sichem only, and its iconography resembles that of the New Julfa Bibles of 1643–6 and 1645.

This type of iconography was continuously used in other printed Armenian books, and wood blocks must have been cut several times copying many pictures. A section of such a carved wood block, which was in use in St. James' Printing Press in Jerusalem, still exists *fig. 148*. About a third of the block is lacking on the right, and the remnants of a wing indicate the missing figure of the angel and St. John, both standing on a cliff.

2. Other printed books

Illumination of Armenian books continued to be fashionable during the seventeenth and eighteenth

3. The Bibles of Istanbul

The fashion of illustrating complete manuscripts of the Bible, which has its origin in New Julfa at the beginning of the seventeenth century, spread rapidly throughout the Armenian diaspora, even after the first impression of the Oskan Bible in 1666. Western European printed Bibles had considerable influence on the plan of illustration and the iconography of these late Armenian illuminated manuscripts. Despite the hostilities between Turkey and Persia, there was an interchange of books and manuscripts between the Armenian communities in the two empires. It is therefore not surprising that New Julfa type of illuminated Bibles reached Istanbul and influenced the production of Bibles there. However, more interesting are the Istanbul Bibles which used other models. One Bible, illuminated by Lazar *mahdesi* in 1653, betrays the influence of the early New Julfa type of Bible illustration, as well as of other sources.[6] Its plan of illustration consists of three preliminary pages depicting scenes from the Creation of the World to the expulsion of Adam and Eve from Paradise *fig.152*. The text is illustrated in numerous places by full- and part-page panels, only a few of which are related to earlier New Julfa traditions of the Old and New Testaments. For example, Eli and Hannah are depicted in a similar way to the New Julfa Bibles *fig. 144*, but in the Istanbul Bible the figure of Samuel has been added sitting between them.[7] On the Adam and Eve page *fig.152* God the Father is shown resting on the seventh day, enthroned and flanked by adoring angels. In the second zone, on the left, are the three Persons of the Trinity, followed by the Fall and Expulsion of Adam and Eve from Paradise. The uncommon iconography is evident from the illustration of the New Testament as well. The panel with the portrait of St. Matthew depicts the angel of the Evangelist holding a scroll for him to copy, in addition to the anthropomorphic initial on the following page as the symbol of St. Matthew *fig.153*.[8]

4. A Menologium from Istanbul

Other illuminated manuscripts from Istanbul also appear to have special iconography. For instance, a Menologium of 1633[9] depicts on the opening page King Trdat kneeling and laying his crown at the feet of St. Gregory the Illuminator, with wild boars above *fig.154*. This picture illustrates the opening verse of the book, which refers to Gregory restoring King Trdat to human shape. As a pagan, King Trdat II persecuted the Christians in his kingdom (287–301), among them Gregory, the son of a prince, whom he tortured and cast into a pit, where he survived for fifteen years fed by a pious widow.[10] Trdat was afflicted by being turned into a wild boar. Advised by his sister, the king consulted Gregory, who healed him. Trdat was converted to Christianity, and declared it the state religion (301), thereby making Armenia the first officially Christian state. This picture differs from the opening pages of other menologia, which usually depict Gregory the Illuminator with John the Baptist, since the first chapter commemorates the latter's feast, but this innovation is not unique and is known from other menologia of the seventeenth century.[11] The text of the Menologium has illustrations for the usual feasts depicting relevant episodes from the life of Christ, such as the Nativity *fig.155*, which combines the washing of the Child, the Annunciation to the Shepherds, the Adoration of the Angels, and the Journey of the Magi. In style, the panels reveal well-proportioned figures within a landscape with accurate perspective.

Figure 152: *God resting on the seventh day, the Fall and Expulsion of Adam and Eve. From the Istanbul Bible of 1653 (ms. 1927, fol. 9v).*

Figure 153: *St. Matthew inspired by an angel, from the Istanbul Bible of 1653 (ms. 1927, fols. 387v–388).*

152

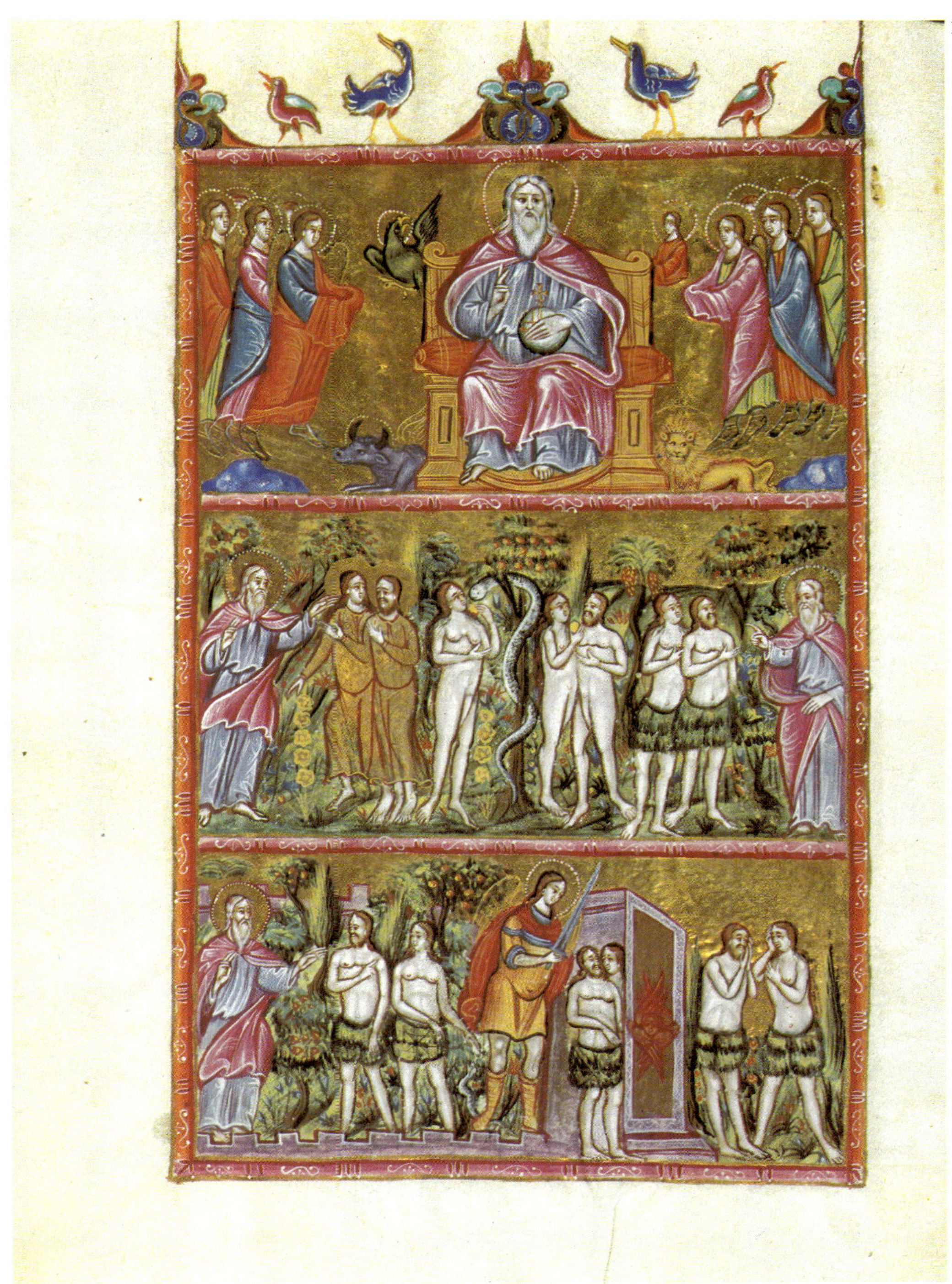

153

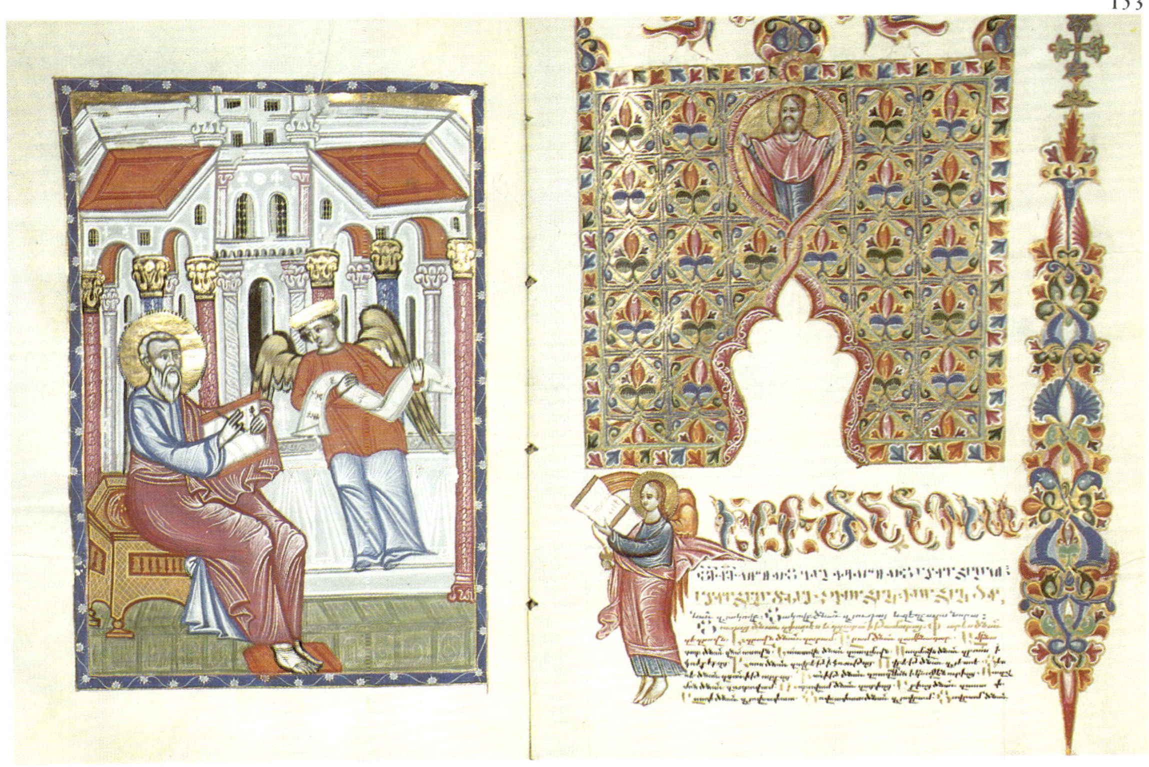

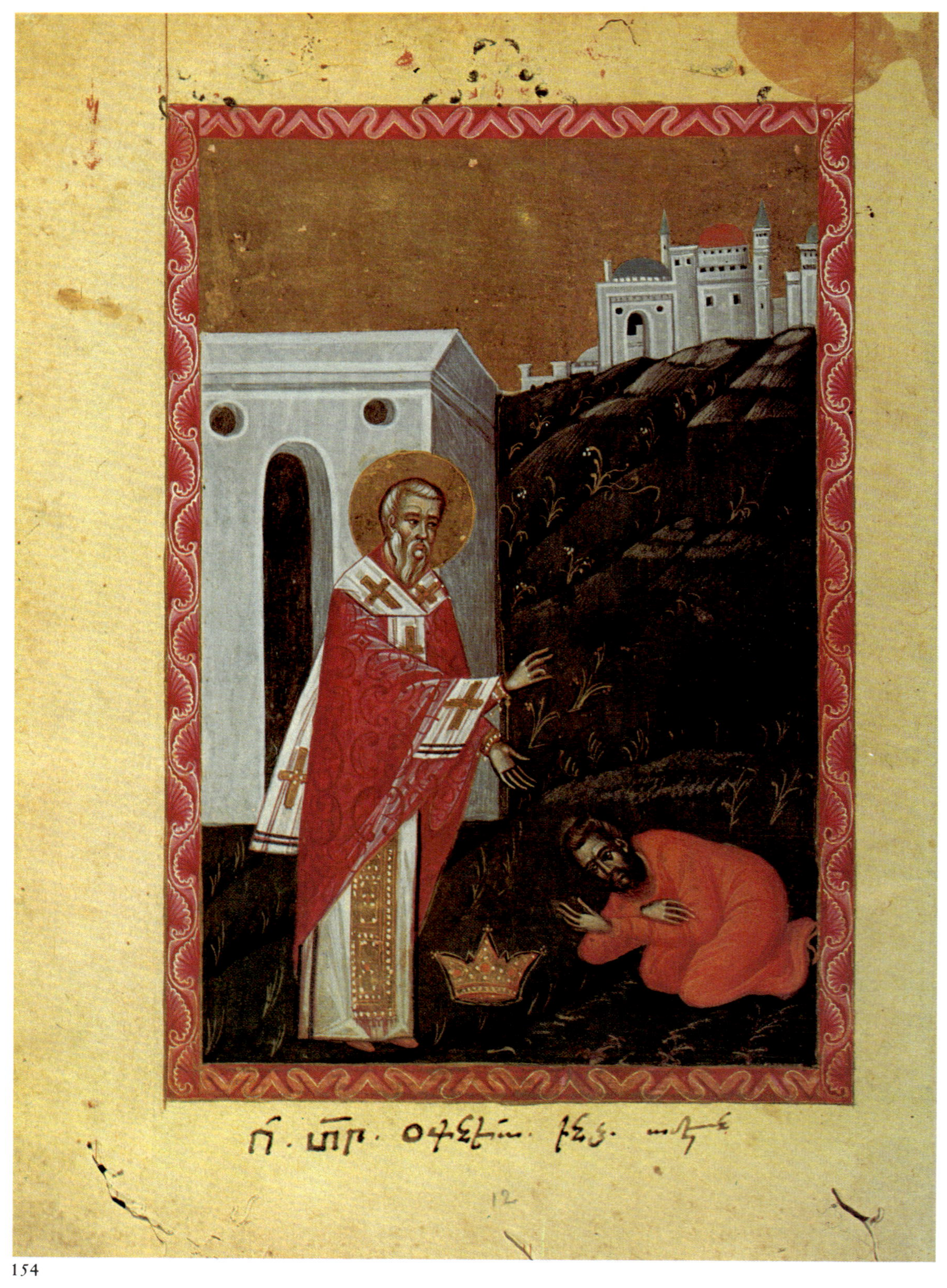

154

Figure 154: *King Trdat, after being changed back from a wild boar into human shape, kneeling before Gregory the Illuminator. Opening page of a Menologium, Istanbul, 1633 (ms. 66, p. 12).*

Figure 155: *The Nativity and Washing of the Child, together with the Annunciation to the Shepherds, the Adoration of the Angels, and the Journey of the Magi. From a Menologium, Istanbul 1633 (ms. 66, p. 500).*

Chapter Ten: St. James Cathedral and its Treasures

Figure 157: *Cathedral of St. James, view of the interior towards the apsis in the East, with part of the dome. Crusader architecture around 1160.*

At different periods throughout their history, the Armenian community in Jerusalem possessed and used different churches and monasteries.[1] After the Moslem conquest, many churches and monasteries were destroyed and abandoned, their monks dispersed, and buildings fell into decay for generations. Some of these were restored only at the time of the Crusaders.[2]

1. *The rebuilding of St. James*

The present Cathedral of St. James was built by the Armenians during the Crusader occupation of Jerusalem in the twelfth century, some time between 1142 and 1165 *fig.157*. When the Catholicos of all the Armenians Gregory Bahlavouni visited Jerusalem in 1142, on the occasion of the Second Council of Jerusalem in an attempt to unify the Christian Creed, the Cathedral did not have its present shape. Gregory Bahlavouni, who was received in Jerusalem with great pomp, was perhaps responsible for the enlargement of the Church of St. James, and the building of a hospice for Armenian pilgrims nearby.[3] However, the plausible suggestion has been made by Joshua Prawer that the building of St. James is due to the patronage of King Thoros II of Cilicia, who visited Jerusalem during the reign of King Amalrik I, in or about 1163 A.D.[4] What seems to be certain is that by 1165 the new Cathedral was in existence. The first evidence is by the pilgrim John of Würzburg who describes it as being a large church, inhabited by Armenian monks, with a large hospice in the same place.[5] Ever since then pilgrims to Jerusalem have attested that the Cathedral of St. James is Armenian and have praised its beauty. Fra Niccola da Poggibonsi in his *Voyage beyond the Seas* (1346–1350),[6] describes St. James as being

> *"a big beautiful church, with two small doors and at the entrance is a cistern: half way up the church there is in the wall an apse within which is enclosed a very beautiful altar; beneath the altar is a big stone of red marble, with a round hole four fingers wide and one palm high; and here was St. James beheaded, and here three lamps ever burn. The said place is held by the Armenians."*

Another pilgrim, John Poloner, says in his *Description of the Holy Land* (1422):[7]

> *"On our way (to David's Castle) we first come to the church of the Armenians. This church is round, with strong walls and exceeding powerful buttressed vaults, having four squared columns in the middle, and no window save one round glazed one at the top, but two hundred or more lamps. Indeed in my time one hundred and twenty lamps used to burn in this church in one chandelier, and I never saw or heard of such devotion of the people. On the left side of the church is shown the place where St. James the Great was beheaded."*

2. *The cult of St. James the Major*

Figure 157a: *Linen cloth depicting Virgin and Child.*

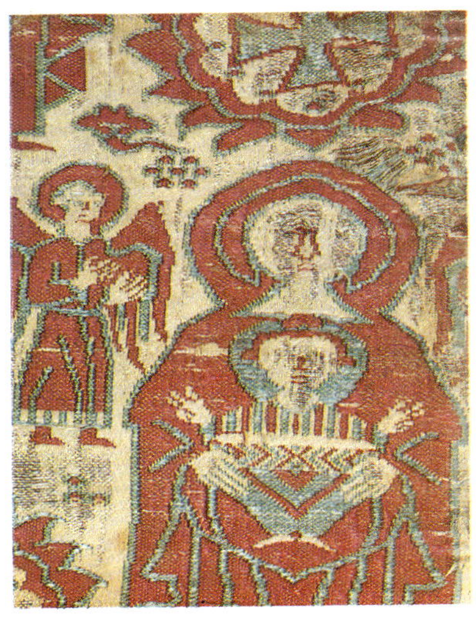

St. James the Major, son of Zebedee and brother of St. John, was with Peter and his brother one of the three closest disciples of Christ. They were all present at the Transfiguration of Christ, and followed Jesus to Gethsemane. James is regarded as the first Apostle to be martyred by Herod Agrippa I, in 44 A.D. It is not known when this spot was identified as the burial place of St. James. As is evident from the pilgrims' descriptions, it was considered by the Crusaders to be the burial place of his head.

From the seventh century, it was alleged that St. James the Apostle preached Christianity in Spain, and from the ninth century his body was supposed to have been miraculously transferred to Compostela in Galicia, North Western Spain, where his stone coffin emerged from the sea.[8] With this miracle established, Santiago (a corruption of St. James) de Compostela became one of the most popular pilgrimage centers of European Christianity during the Middle Ages. Nonetheless Jerusalem still holds supremacy as the place where St. James lived as a preacher to Judea and Samaria and where he was beheaded.

3. *The Crusader Cathedral of St. James*

The Church of St. James was built on a central plan, which was common in Armenia and Byzantium, but not in Western Europe *fig.157*.[9] The original Crusader church of St. James has a wide nave of 6.40 m. and two uneven aisles (2.50 and 4.15 m.) with a dome resting on four massive

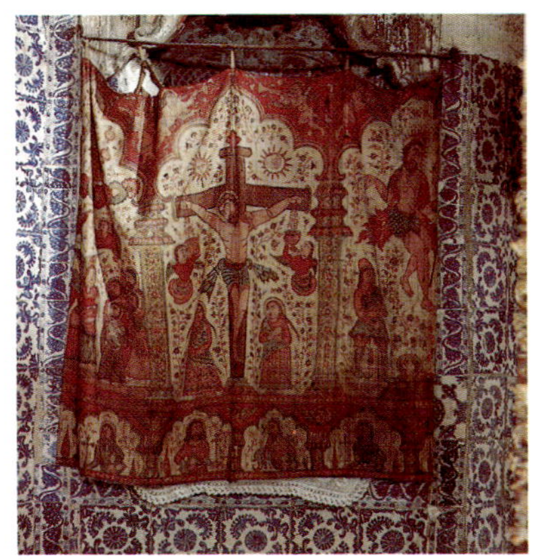

Figure 157b: *Painted cloth depicting a Crucifixion; on the right, the Risen Christ.*

pillars *fig.158*, all of which still exist, though covered with thick plaster and paintings. It had a major portal entrance on the south, which is now within the Etchmiadzin Chapel, and two minor doors in the west, the central one of which is still in use. The additions to the church were done at different periods. The three apsides in the east were built during the thirteenth or fourteenth century.[10] The Crusader narthex in the southern part of the church was walled in during 1666, in order to build the Etchmiadzin Chapel,[11] and the porch in the west was built by Gregory the Chainbearer in the eighteenth century.

Earlier edifices on the site are enclosed within the church on its northern side. These comprise the chapels of St. Menas[12] and St. Stephen[13] on the ground level, and the St. Apostles' Chapel above that of St. Menas.[14] The chapel of St. Menas is considered to be the oldest part of the building, allegedly a sixth century Byzantine chapel on the foundations of Lady Bassa's monastery. The Chapel of St. Stephen, the present sacristy, is also a later addition.[15]

Father H. Vincent in his study on the structure of the church compared it to other centralized churches of the Byzantine Empire, but mainly to the tenth century Armenian church of Haghbat, which is of a cruciform type and has a wide nave and narrow aisles.[16] Of Armenian origin may also be the dome in the center of the church, which has windows in the drum, the only source of light in the Cathedral *fig.157*. The dome is constructed with six crossing ribs, forming a decorative hexagon, with a raised lantern in the center.[17] It rests on the four pillars through mediating pendantives. An addition of the thirteenth century, this dome follows a construction known in Greater Armenia in the tenth century. The same church of Haghbat offers such an example of crossing ribs which construct the cupola,[18] but by contrast, these rest directly on the pillars. The type of decorative crossed ribs is also known from the south of France and northern Spain.[19] The incorporation of Armenian architectural forms on the one hand and of southern French on the other provides an example typical of sectarian Crusader art in Jerusalem and the Holy Land.[20]

158

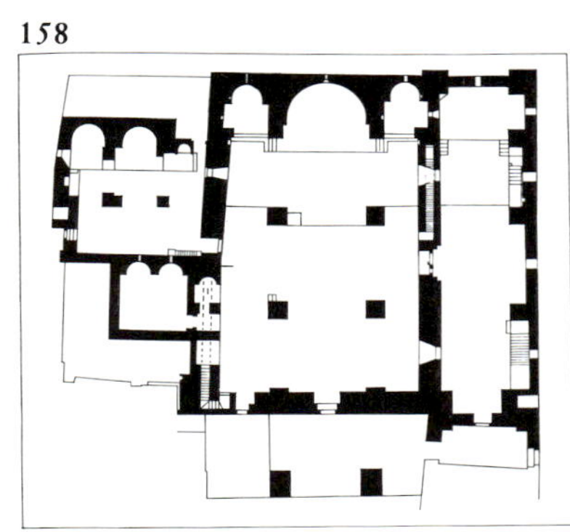

Figure 158: *Plan of the Cathedral of St. James with all its chapels and altars (after Vincent and Abel,* Jérusalem, *Vol. II, Plate LIV).*

4. *The Crusader decorations of St. James*

What remains of Crusader decorations of St. James are some capitals of the pillars *figs.159, 160, 161, 162* and the decorated southern doorway *fig.163*. Some of the round capitals protruding from the top of the pillar are of the acanthus type with two tiers of leaves and an enclosed bud in their flower part *figs.159, 160*. There are other Crusader capitals of this type in Jerusalem, some in the gallery of the Holy Sepulcher, and elsewhere, on the Temple Mount. Of these, some are made of two tiers of acanthus leaves, while others are of three. These capitals, based on the Late Antique Corinthian type, could have derived from local Byzantine capitals of the fifth century, but they may derive from southern French capitals. Similar are capitals of churches in Montmajour, Avalon, St. Trophime in Arles, and mainly from Les Saintes Maries-de-la-Mer.[21] The incorporation of three lambs within one of the Corinthian capitals *fig.162* is also indigenous to the same Provençal area.[22] The lower tier of the capital as well as the top leaves are similar to a two-tier acanthus capital next to it *fig.159* and the smooth, curved, style of the lambs resembles the figure style of St. Trophime and Saintes Maries-de-la-Mer.[23]

Most of the capitals on top of the pillars are square, and decorated with "tongue-leaves" *figs.157, 161*. This motif is common in Crusader art, though not usual in a square capital and not arranged in as dense a composition as that in the St. James capitals.

The original main entrance to the church, which is now the entrance to the Etchmiadzin Chapel from the south side of the Cathedral *fig.163* is decorated with a typical Crusader cushioned-gordons motif in the arch, and with tongue leaves in the round capitals. This kind of decoration developed in Jerusalem during the twelfth century, and became usual in arches of other buildings.[24] Even if the construction of the Church of St. James was done and augmented by Armenian architects and builders, the decorative capitals and portal were executed by one of the local southern French workshops of Jerusalem.

5. *Later decoration in St. James*

Armenian patronage continued in St. James throughout the following period. One of the most beautiful donations to the church is a carved wooden door, closing the secret passage to the chapels of Peter and Paul, which was built above the apsides in the fourteenth century *fig.164*. The carving has eight decorated interlacing crosses, surrounded by foliage scrolls. The carved Armenian inscription in the top part of the door gives the commissioners' names as Yovhannes and his son Thoros, who gave it to the church in the year 1371.[25]

The foliage decoration within the crosses and in the geometrical areas around is of palmette and bud motifs.[26]

Most of the other artistic additions to the Church are within the area of the main altar of St. James *fig.165*. This area, east of the two eastern pillars, is partly enclosed by a decorated wrought iron fence *fig.166* which was donated to the Cathedral in 1796. The floor of this area is decorated with geometric patterns made of marble segments in inlay technique, known as *opus sectile*, *fig.167*.[27]

Attached to the northeastern pillar of the church is the throne of St. James the Less *fig.168*, who is sometimes identified as the brother of Christ. St. James the Less, who is considered to have been the

Figure 159: *Crusader Corinthian capital on top of a pillar, in the Cathedral of St. James, ca. 1160.*

Figure 160: *Crusader Corinthian capital on top of a pillar in the Cathedral of St. James, ca. 1160.*

Figure 161: *Crusader capital of single tongue-leaves on top of a pillar in the Cathedral of St. James, ca. 1160.*

Figure 162: *Crusader capital with three lambs symmetrically exposed within the acanthus leaves, ca. 1160.*

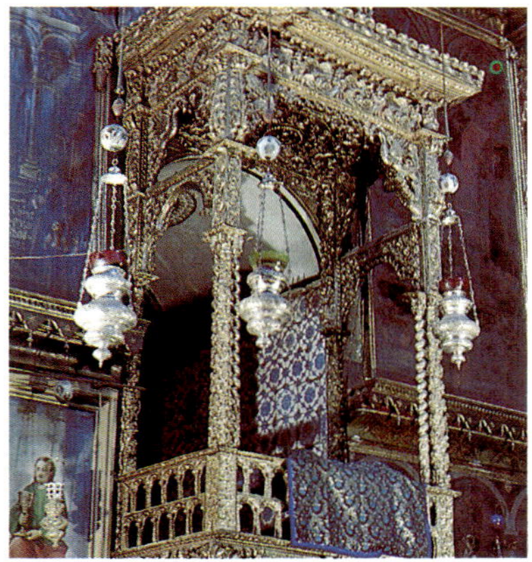

Figure 157c: *Balcony for lections, Cathedral of St. James.*

159

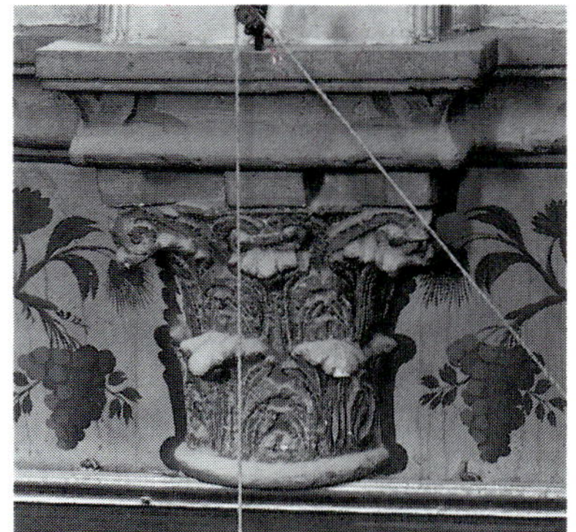

160

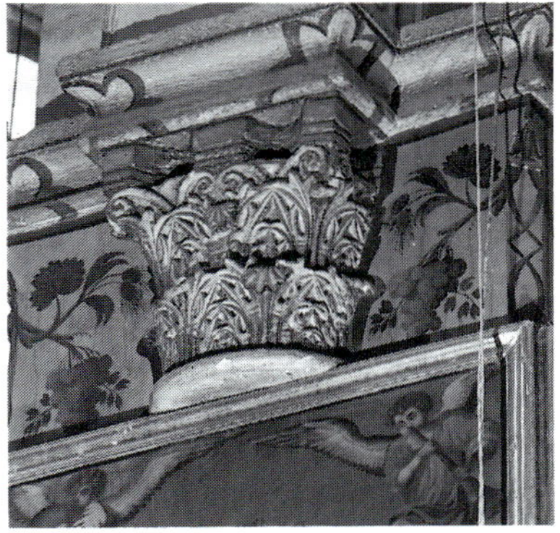

161

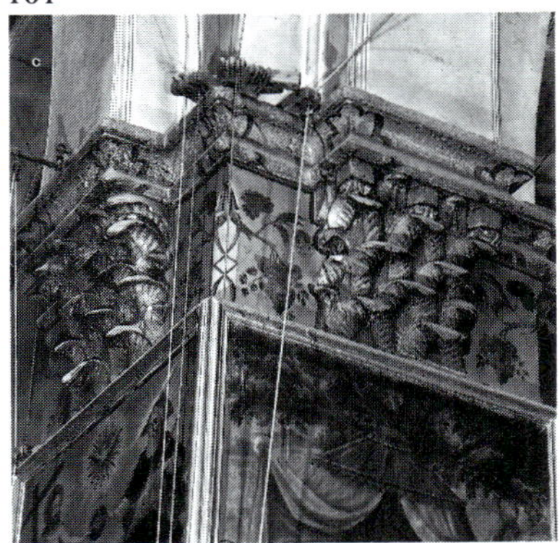

162

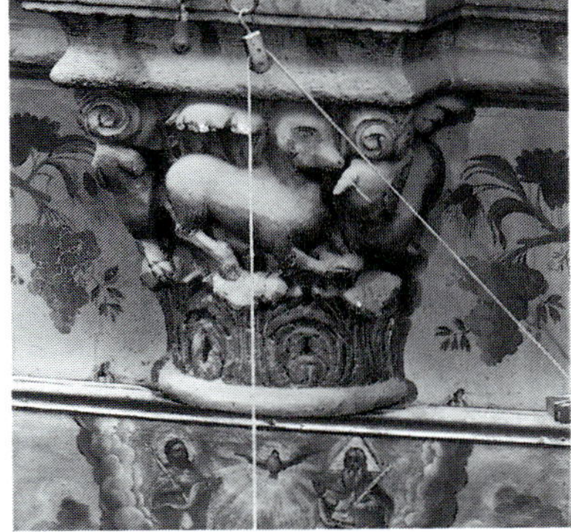

first Bishop of Jerusalem, was martyred in 60 A.D., and first buried in the Valley of Jehoshaphat. His remains were transferred, according to Eusebius, during the time of Cyril of Jerusalem to be interred in his house, which was traditionally on this spot. A low rounded fence, to the east of the throne, marks the place of his present burial, the floor of which is decorated in the technique of *opus sectile* as the rest of the floor, but with smaller, more ornate sections *fig.167*. The throne of St. James the Less is used once a year by the Armenian Patriarch of Jerusalem on the Saint's day. At other times, the Patriarch uses another throne, set next to this one. An impression of its beautiful workmanship, can be found in the description of the pilgrim, Henry Maundrell, who visited Jerusalem in 1697.[28]

> *"In the middle of the church is a pulpit made of tortoise-shell and mother-of-pearl, with a beautiful canopy or cupola over it, of the same fabric. The tortoise shell and mother-of-pearl are so exquisitely mingled and inlaid in each other that the work far exceeds the materials."*

The throne was donated to the Cathedral of St. James in 1656 during the Patriarchate of Eliezer, who also built the Etchmiadzin Chapel, by closing the Crusader narthex on the south side of the Cathedral. Preceding the description of the throne of St. James the Less, Henry Maundrell writes about the Cathedral:

> *"In this church are two altars set out with extraordinary splendour, being decked out with rich mitres, embroidered copes, crosses both silver and gold, crowns, chalices and other church utensils without number."*

One has to bear in mind that this description was written before the redecoration of the altars in the 1730's, during the Patriarchate of Gregory the Chainbearer. The main altar of St. James the Great is raised more than one meter above the floor and the wall is decorated with marble slabs, with reliefs of flowers issuing from vases *fig.169*. The beautifully carved wooden iconostasis of the altar is painted in gold and colors, decorated with Paradise scenes of human and animal figures, within foliage scrolls.

6. *The Chainbearer's activity in the Cathedral*

The embellishment of the Cathedral during the days of Gregory the Chainbearer was the most important and impressive since the days of the Crusaders. Through his dynamic and energetic character, he managed to draw the generosity of many ardent people to donate and dedicate to the building and embellishing of Armenian Jerusalem. The Cathedral of St. James became, through him, an intricate jewel of art objects to the glory of God. In style it is a mixture of Late European Baroque glory and the special Armenian sense and love of beauty.

The entrances to the different chapels in the northern wall of the Cathedral *fig.170* were each decorated individually during the Patriarchate of Gregory, with sumptuous doors, canopies, and domes. The doors to the shrine of the head of St. James *fig.171* are a remarkably intricate work of mother-of-pearl and tortoise shell inlaid in wood. The shrine is topped by a built dome and has a decorated canopy above it to enable the hanging of many lamps with eternal light.

For four long years (1717–1721), Gregory, the Patriarch of Jerusalem, stood at the entrance to the Church of the Holy Mother of God in Istanbul during feast days, wearing a heavy iron chain over his neck and swearing not to remove it until he could collect the sum of 800 purses of gold. He needed the money to pay the debts of the Armenian community in Jerusalem, and to remove the threat by Moslem creditors that they would seize the Cathedral of St. James and other churches and properties belonging to the Armenians in Jerusalem.

Gregory's fund-raising methods gained him the title "the Chainbearer", *Shghthayagir* in Armenian. The sum of money he succeeded in collecting not only enabled him to pay the church's heavy debts, but also to revive the Armenian community of Jerusalem, which had been dwindling in numbers and funds.

The restoration and decoration of churches, the construction of hostels for pilgrims, and the building of a wall around the Monastery of Jerusalem, began immediately after Gregory's arrival in Jerusalem on February 12, 1721. The most significant restoration work, however, was done after 1727, when a *firman* was obtained from the Turkish Government through the Patriarch of Istanbul, Yovhannes "*Kolot*" (i.e., "Midget"). Yovhannes considered the Holy Land as his private see since he had previously been a *locum tenens* in Jerusalem. In the interest of reviving the community, Yovhannes nominated Gregory as Patriarch of Jerusalem one day after his own election in Istanbul on September 16, 1715.

The *firman* gave permission to rebuild the Cathedral of St. James, and this was an impetus to restore and decorate many other churches, together with public and private buildings that were within the monastery. A detailed account of the extent of reconstruction is given by its main surveyor, the monk Elia *Vardapet*. In a colophon of a manuscript he copied in 1737, he lists all the work carried out during the ten years from 1727 to 1737.[29] The scribe Elia son of Yovasaph of Caesarea apparently took great pleasure in replastering and tiling the entire Cathedral of St. James, including all its chapels, St. Stephen in the north and St. Etchmiadzin along the entire southern side of the church.

Figure 165: *The Apsis of St. James Cathedral, with its altar, iconostasis, and the throne of St. James the Less, seventeenth or eighteenth century.*

Figure 169: *Marble slabs before the main altar of St. James Cathedral, carved in 1730 during the Patriarchate of Gregory the Chainbearer.*

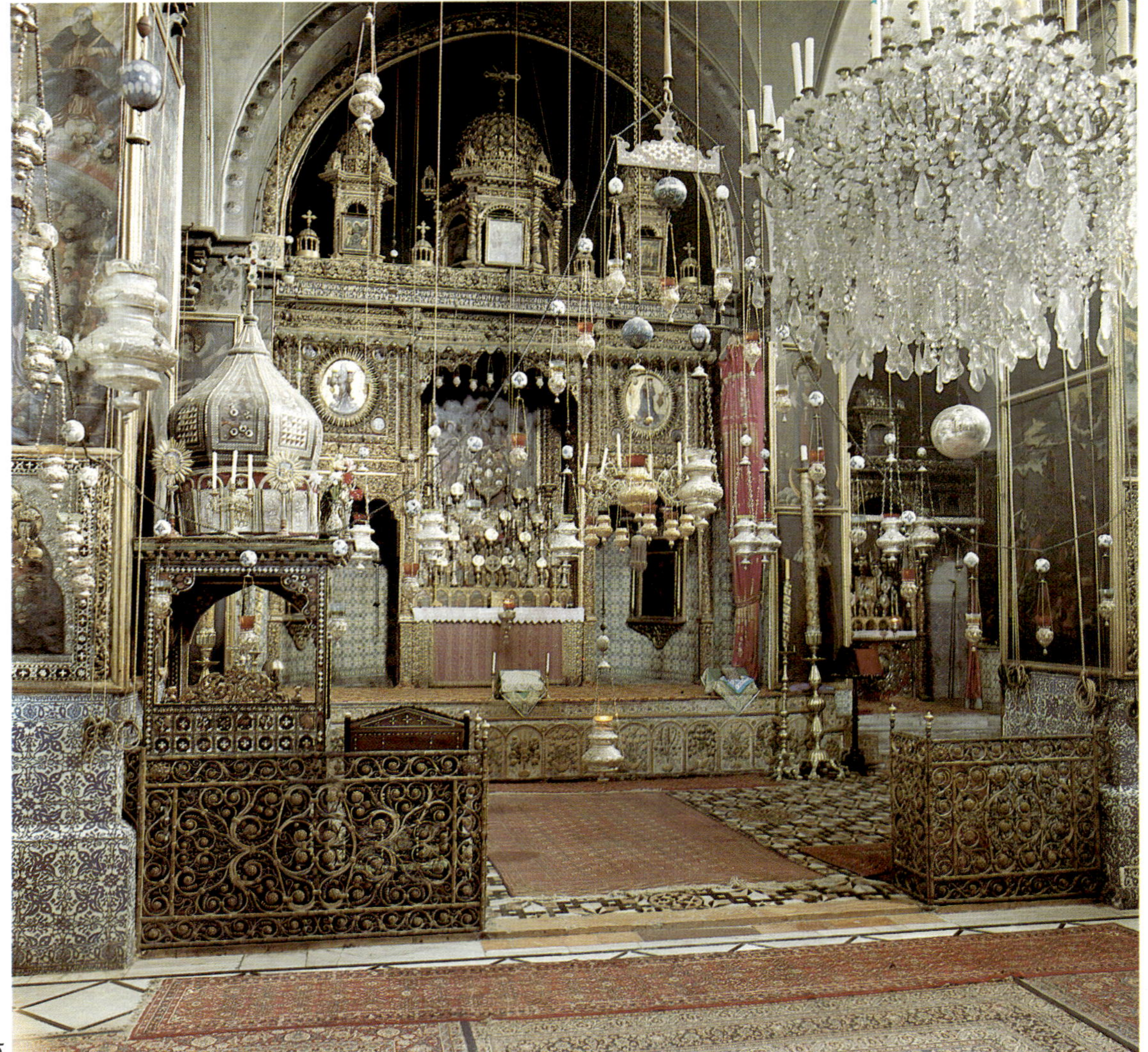

165

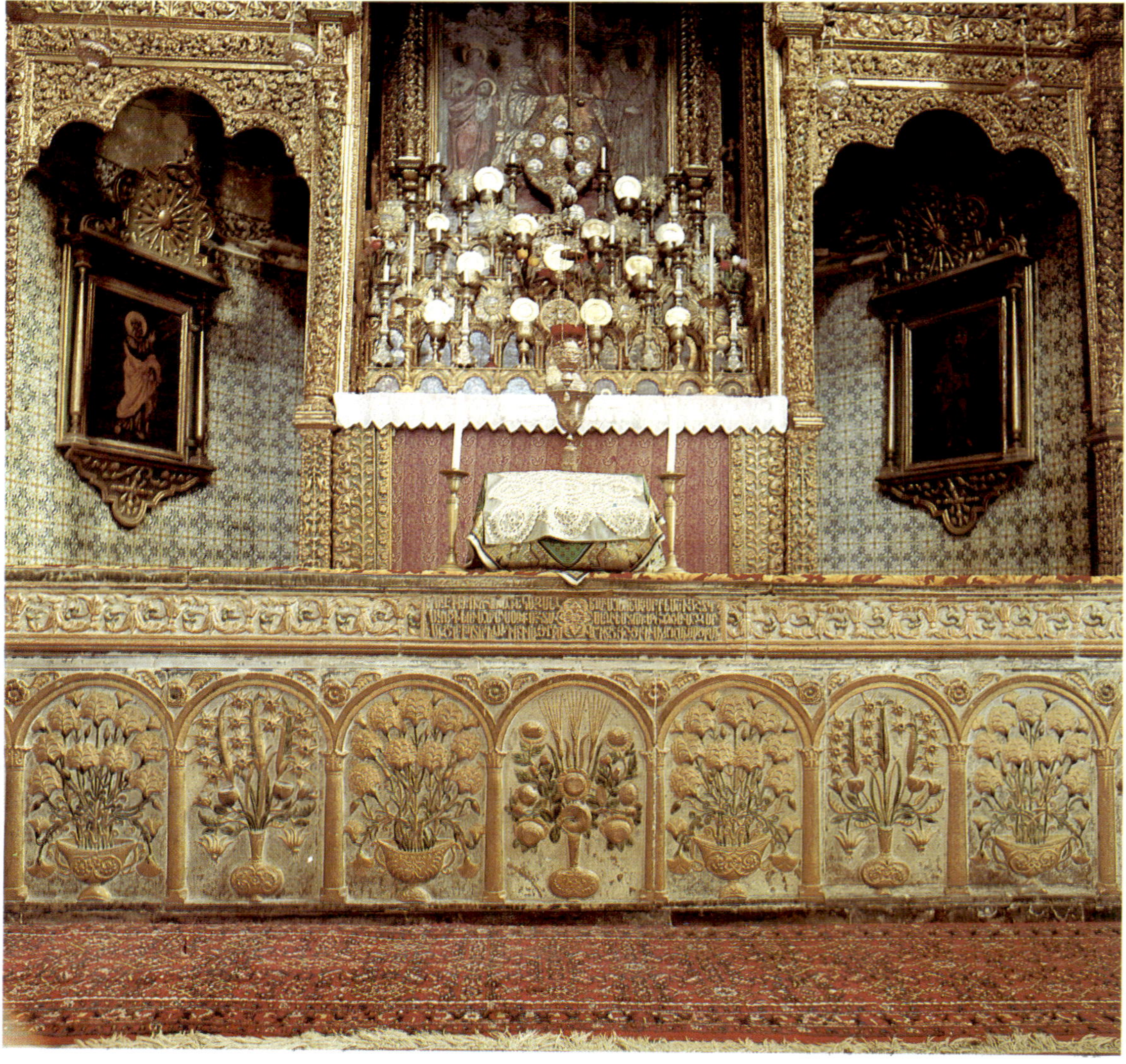

169

Figure 168: *Throne of St. James the Less, first bishop of Jerusalem. Made of wood inlaid with mother-of-pearl and tortoise shell in 1656, and used by the Patriarch once a year.*

Figure 170: *North wall of St. James Cathedral with entrances to the chapels of St. Menas, St. James' head, and St. Stephen.*

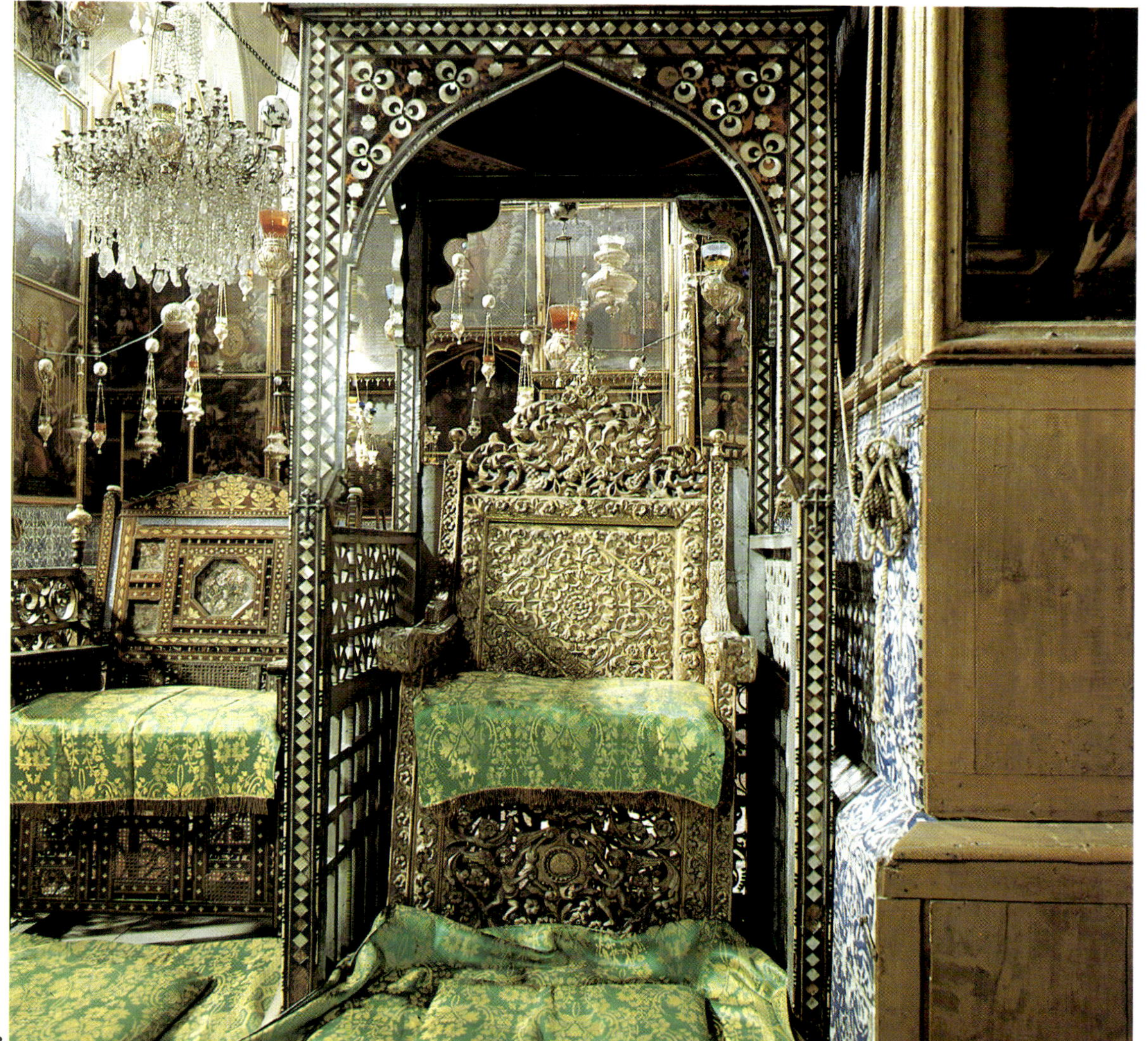

168

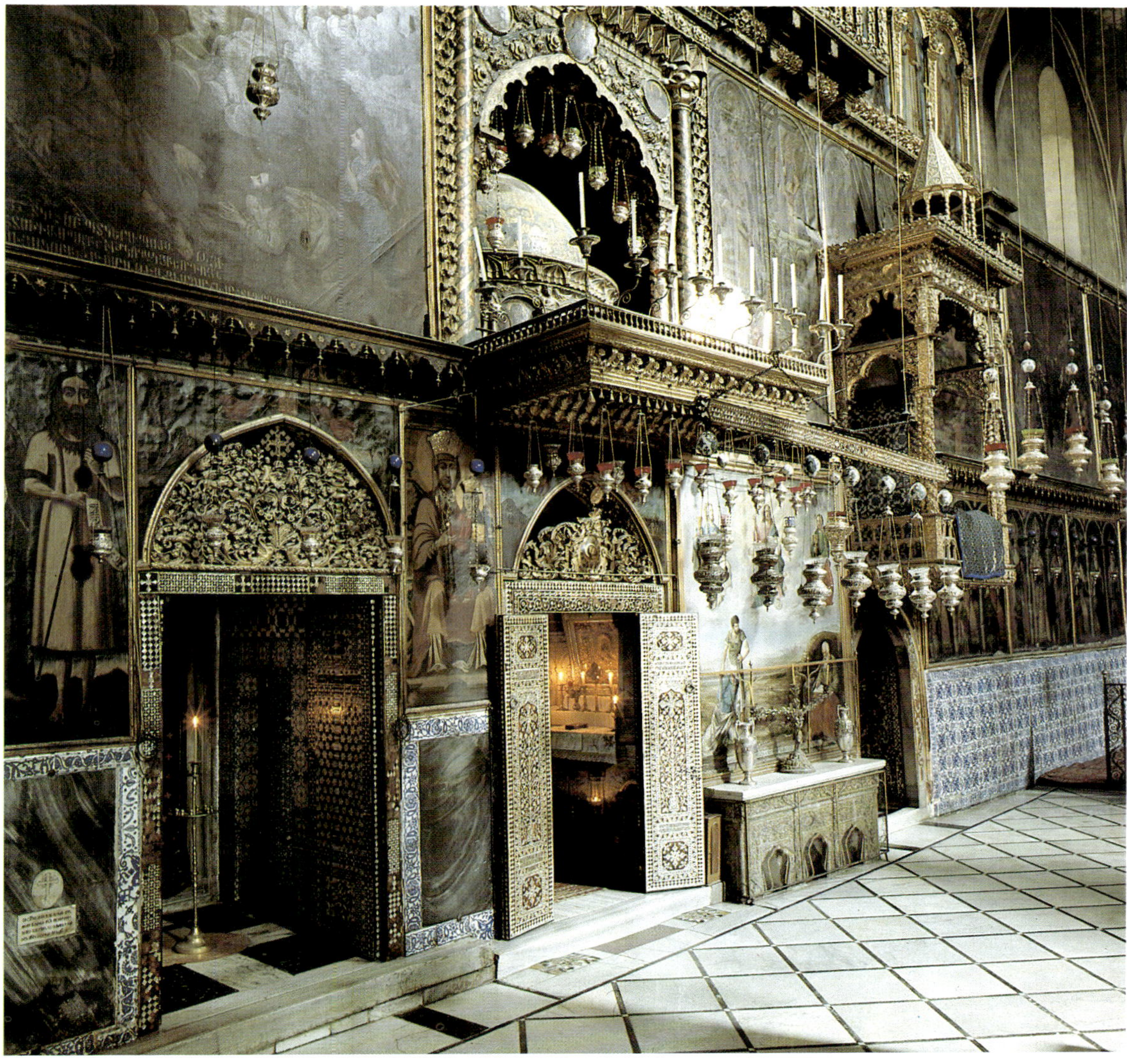

170

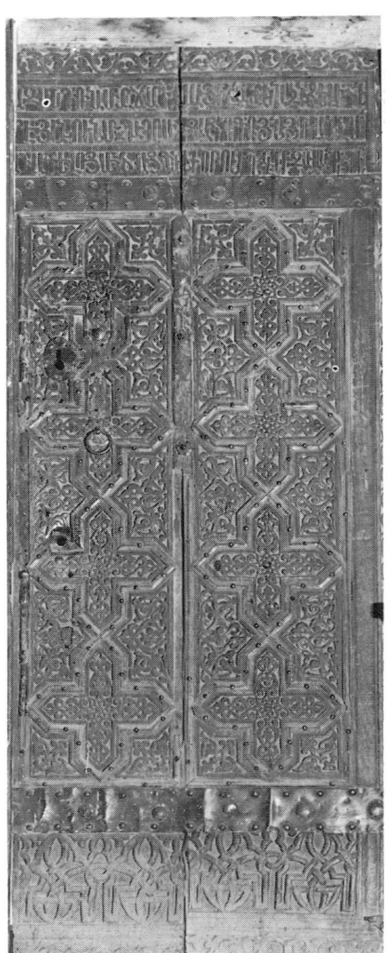

164

Figure 163: *The original Crusader entrance to St. James, from the south narthex. Now leading from the chapel of Etchmiadzin to St. James, ca. 1160. Coptic carving of 1371.*

Figure 164: *Carved wooden door closing the secret passage to the chapels of Sts. Peter and Paul, Egyptian.*

7. *The Etchmiadzin Chapel*

One of the most beautiful chapels of the Cathedral is the one erected in honor of the Catholicos of Etchmiadzin, which was also decorated anew during the Patriarchate of the Chainbearer *fig.172*, although walled-in earlier in 1666, during the Patriarchate of Eliezer. The Etchmiadzin Chapel has an apsis and an altar similar to the main ones of St. James, though smaller. The marble relief slabs in front of the altar are of 1732, two years later than those of St. James. The wooden engraved iconostasis, which is similar in shape and craftsmanship to the larger one, was made in 1753. The area of the apsis is fenced off by a decorated wrought iron rail, and encloses a throne under an elaborately decorated wrought iron canopy. To the right of the chapel, under a built dome, there are "three large rough stones, esteemed very precious, as being, one of them, the stone upon which Moses cast the two tables, when he broke them, in indignation at the Idolatry of the Israelites; the other two being brought, one from the place of our Lord's baptism, the other from that of his Transfiguration," as Henry Maundrell describes in 1697.

The most impressive decoration of the Etchmiadzin Chapel are the walls, covered by painted glazed ceramic tiles from Kütahya. Most of these were applied on the walls by the monk Elia, who was responsible for the redecoration of the Etchmiadzin Chapel after 1727.

The majority are decorative tiles, with floral and foliage motifs. Only a few contain pictures or are inscribed, which would enable the identification of their origin. The pictorial tiles were primarily assembled in the Etchmiadzin Chapel of St. James from other Chapels. The vertical pictorial tiles were applied by the monk Elia, whereas the horizontal ones were installed at different dates, as late as World War II.

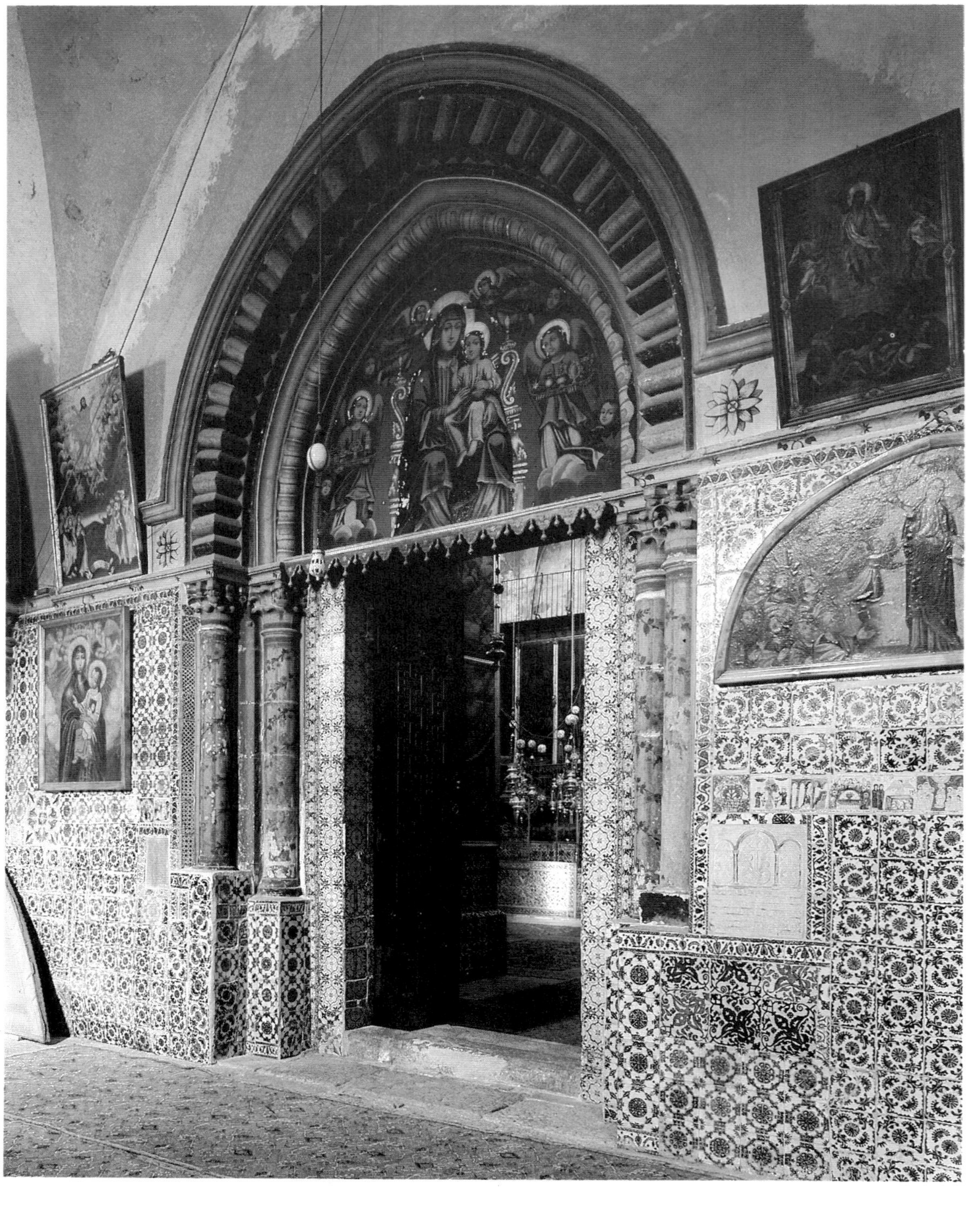

163

Figure 166: *Wrought-iron fence, enclosing the apsis and some chapels in St. James Cathedral, 1796.*

Figure 167: Opus sectile *floor in the apsis of St. James Cathedral, enclosed is the tomb of St. James the Less, in front of his throne.*

Figure 171: *Door of the chapel of St. James' head, wood with mother-of-pearl inlay, made by Yakob in 1731.*

166

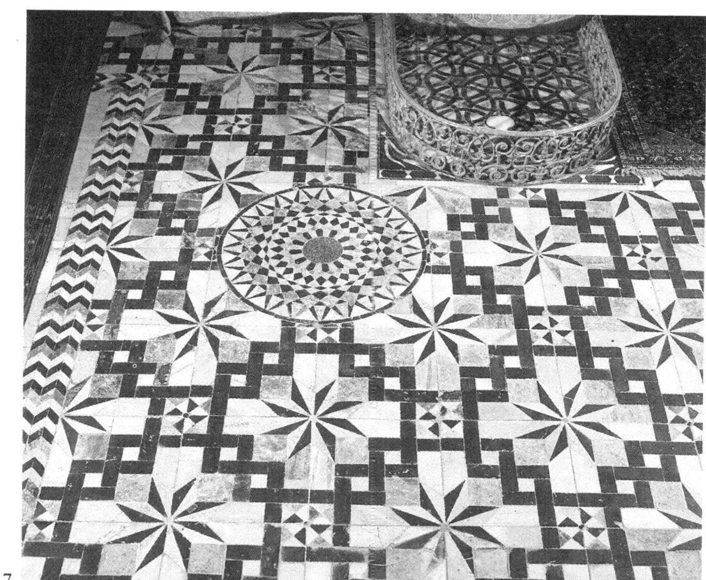

167

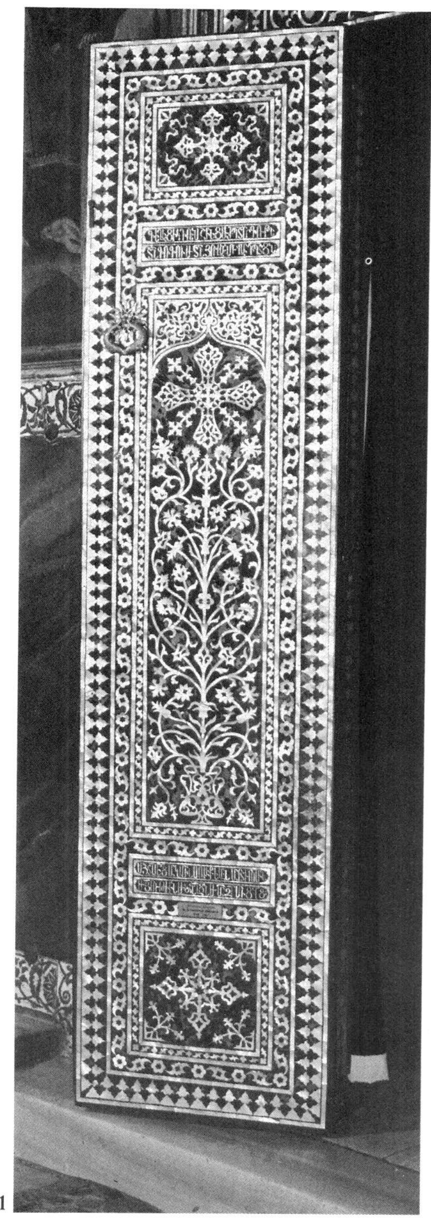

171

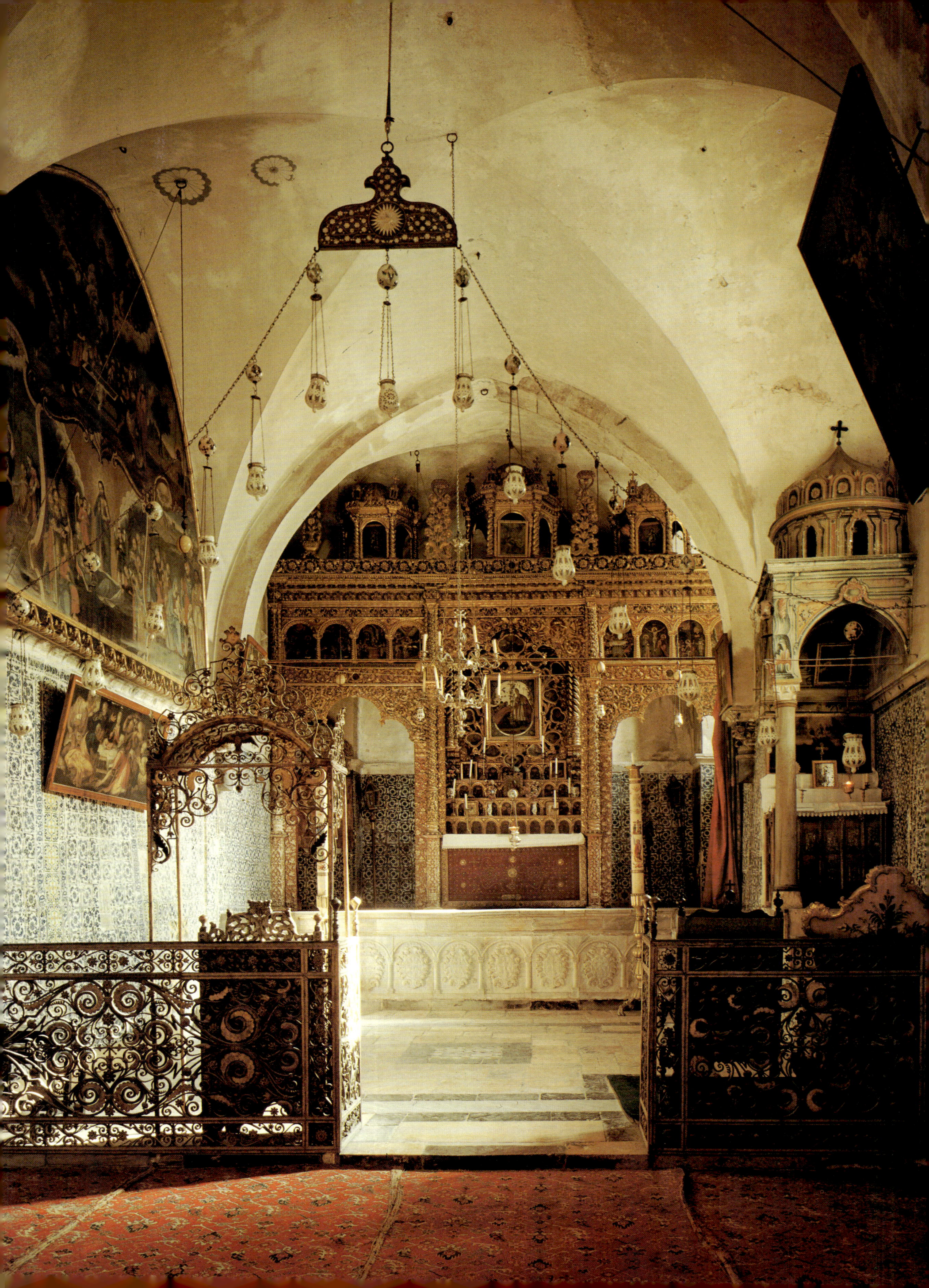

8. The Kütahya tiles

The pictorial tiles were produced with the intention of decorating the Holy Sepulcher, a plan which was to be a joint effort by the Greeks, Latins, and Armenians, in 1719. The plan was not carried out.[30] Strange as it may seem, these tiles contain the inscription concerning the Holy Sepulcher and are dated 1718–19, a date preceding the *firman* obtained by the Greeks and Latins to renovate the Sepulcher. It would seem that they were made previously for another purpose.[31] The name of Abraham *Vardapet*, the *Arajnord* of Thekirdag (East Thrace), mentioned in the pictorial tiles inscription, made his first visit to Jerusalem in 1719. He may have ordered some of these tiles as a gift to the Holy Sepulcher on the occasion of his pilgrimage. Other tiles were donated by individuals and families from Kütahya at about the same date, as their inscriptions imply. Most of these were executed by Christer Thoros, who is mentioned on some of the tiles as well as on various bowls of the same date.

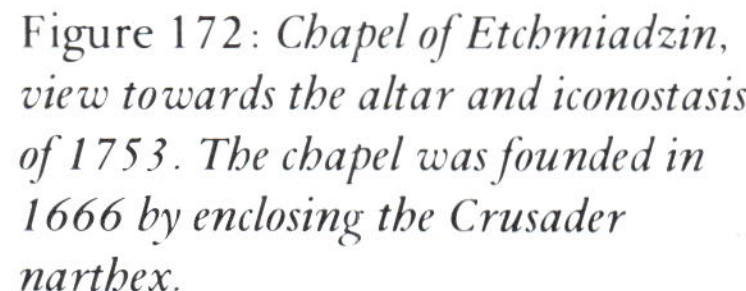

Figure 172: *Chapel of Etchmiadzin, view towards the altar and iconostasis, of 1753. The chapel was founded in 1666 by enclosing the Crusader narthex.*

In the Monastery of St. James in Jerusalem there are 45 pictorial tiles from Kütahya. Only a few are not in the Etchmiadzin Chapel: three are in Paris and some are missing. In his extensive book[32] on Kütahya tiles, John Carswell divides the pictorial tiles into three main groups according to subject and inscription. The first group of eight tiles has a continuous inscription in uncial script, *erkathagir*, depicting mainly Old Testament scenes. It starts with the picture, "the Prophet Isaiah Testifies" (Isaiah 7:14) *fig.173*.[33] There are also representations of Adam and Eve *fig.174*,[34] both fully dressed, flanking the Tree of Knowledge, the Sacrifice of Isaac,[35] Moses receiving the Tablets of the Law,[36] and the Devil leaving Saul's body as the king listens to David playing the harp.[37]

The second group has a continuous inscription in cursive script. It mentions the Patriarchs of Istanbul and Jerusalem and their deeds to restore the financial and spiritual state of the Jerusalem community. It also tells of their efforts to rebuild the Church of the Holy Mother of God, which was destroyed by the fire of 1719, in Istanbul. The tiles depict episodes from the New Testament,[38] from the Annunciation to the Virgin, through the Last Supper Passion *fig.175* and Resurrection of Christ *fig.176*. It also contains symbols of Evangelists with their books, saints and martyrs, the *Deisis*, angels, and dignitaries.

The third group, which was donated by families and individuals from Kütahya, contains scenes from the Old and New Testaments, and the Lives of Saints *fig.173*,[39] with various inscriptions, in no particular sequence. The artist Thoros, who executed most of the pictorial tiles, primarily used Byzantine iconography, though new, Western elements can be detected, possibly through printed books or Dutch biblical tiles.

In technique, the Kütahya tiles are close to the seventeenth-century Safavid Persian tiles. This is noticeable in the outlines and mainly in the use of yellow, a color unknown to the Isnik potters. Thoros' figures and composition seem rather crude, though they reveal a sure hand. He must have had a good knowledge of drawing and of ceramic technique. An artist working in ceramic cannot erase his drawing. Thoros seems to have the talent to bring animals to life with simple outlines, as St. Theodore's horse *fig.173*. His human figures are somewhat flat, specially noticeable in the faces and bare parts of the body. The scene usually fills up the entire space of the tile, and empty spaces were filled with red dots. Not all the tiles were done by Thoros. Some are markedly more primitive than his figures, such as the three archangels *fig.173*.[40] Others are more delicate and resemble engravings.

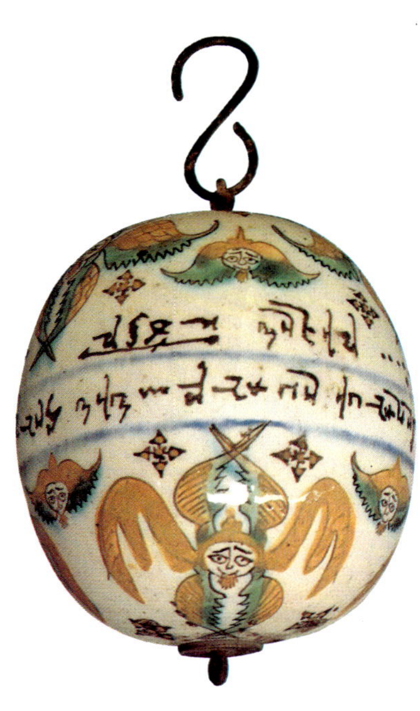

Figure 177: *Ceramic Kütahya "egg", used for suspending lamps in a church, made for the Church of the Archangels in 1740, now in the Patriarch's collection.*

Kütahya tiles became famous in the late seventeenth and early eighteenth century, and their production increased after the decline of the Isnik pottery industry. Kütahya took the place of Isnik (the classical Nicaea) which had been known for its pottery and tiles from the fourteenth until mid-seventeenth century.

Most of the late seventeenth- and eighteenth-century tiles in churches and mosques in the Turkish Empire were executed by Armenian craftsmen. There are documents showing that Armenians lived in Kütahya in the second part of the fourteenth century, and Armenians defined as potters (*brut*) from the middle of the fifteenth century. Actual Kütahya tiles exist from the beginning of the fifteenth century, but extant pottery with Armenian inscriptions appear to exist only from 1510 and 1529, corresponding to two vases in the Gulbenkian Collection – one a ewer, the other a water bottle.

The increase in production of Armenian Kütahya tiles and pottery during the eighteenth century is due mainly to a greater laxity in the attitude of the Turks toward the Christian minorities in general. During the last decade of the seventeenth century, a decree was issued against oppression of the Christians, abolishing the capitation tax, and allowing them to build new churches and restore old ones. As a result of the relaxation of financial restrictions the Armenian merchants and craftsmen grew richer, and the pious donated whole-heartedly toward the building and redecorating of their churches with tiles, gold, ritual objects, embroidered vestments, woodwork, and manuscripts. Consequently, the Kütahya tile industry flourished, and the Armenians became famous for their tile-making – a fame which continues to this very day.

9. Other Kütahya vessels

Not only tiles but also other ceramic vessels, for religious and secular use, were produced in the Armenian Kütahya workshops. One of the most popular vessels ever since the seventeenth century is the egg-like sphere used to prevent mice running down the chains from which lamps were suspended in the church.

An eighteenth-century sphere *fig.177*, one of a pair almost identical in ornaments, belongs to the Patriarchal collection. Evidently, it was donated by a pilgrim to the Church of the Archangel. There is no doubt that it was planned, designed, and executed in its country of origin especially for this purpose. Both the style and the special technique of these ceramic spheres point to their origin in a Kütahya workshop. Their decorations consist of six seraphim, each with six wings, and six other angel heads with double wings. They are painted in yellow, light blue, and green with black outlines on a white ground. Both spheres are glazed and painted in the Kütahya coloring technique. They are hollow and pierced at the top and bottom which enables the fastening of metal hooks through them for suspension. The spheres were intended for the church only, and are commonly used by other East-Christian denominations as hanging ornaments in their churches.

A ewer and a bowl also in the Patriarch's collection *fig.178*[41] was made for liturgical use in St. James Cathedral. The blue foliage decoration of the ewer and bowl is typical of Kütahya ware and tiles.

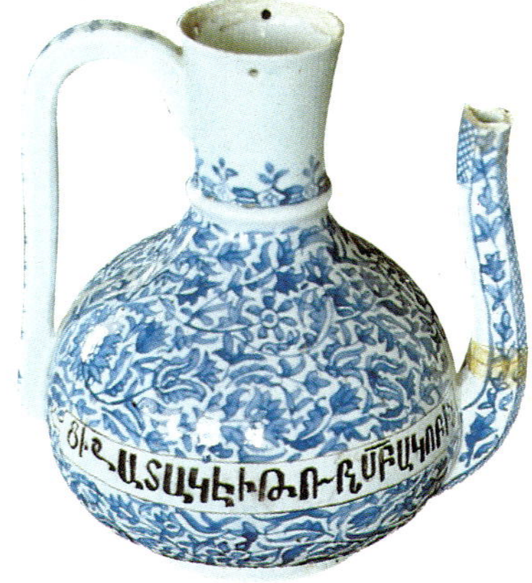

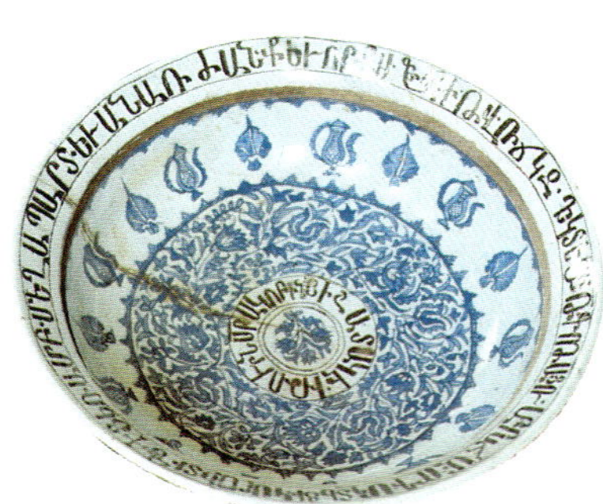

178

Figure 173: *Kütahya tiles from the chapel of St. Etchmiadzin depicting the Virgin and Child (dated 1719); Archangels Michael, Gabriel, and Uriel; St. Theodore and the Dragon (1719); the Prophet Isaiah.*

Figure 178: *Ewer and bowl for liturgical use, made by the craftsman George in 1716 for the pilgrim Karapet of Kütahya. Patriarch's collection.*

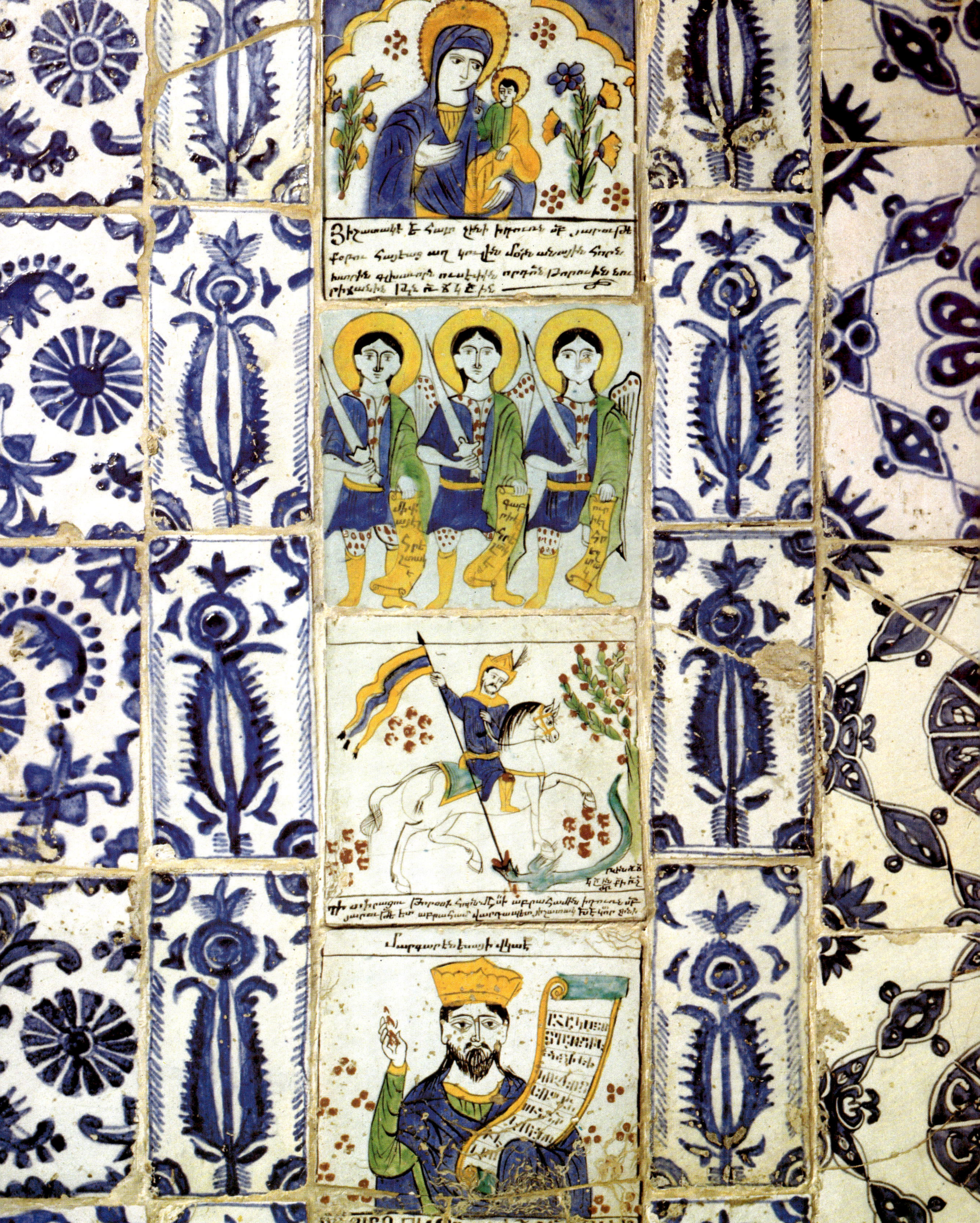

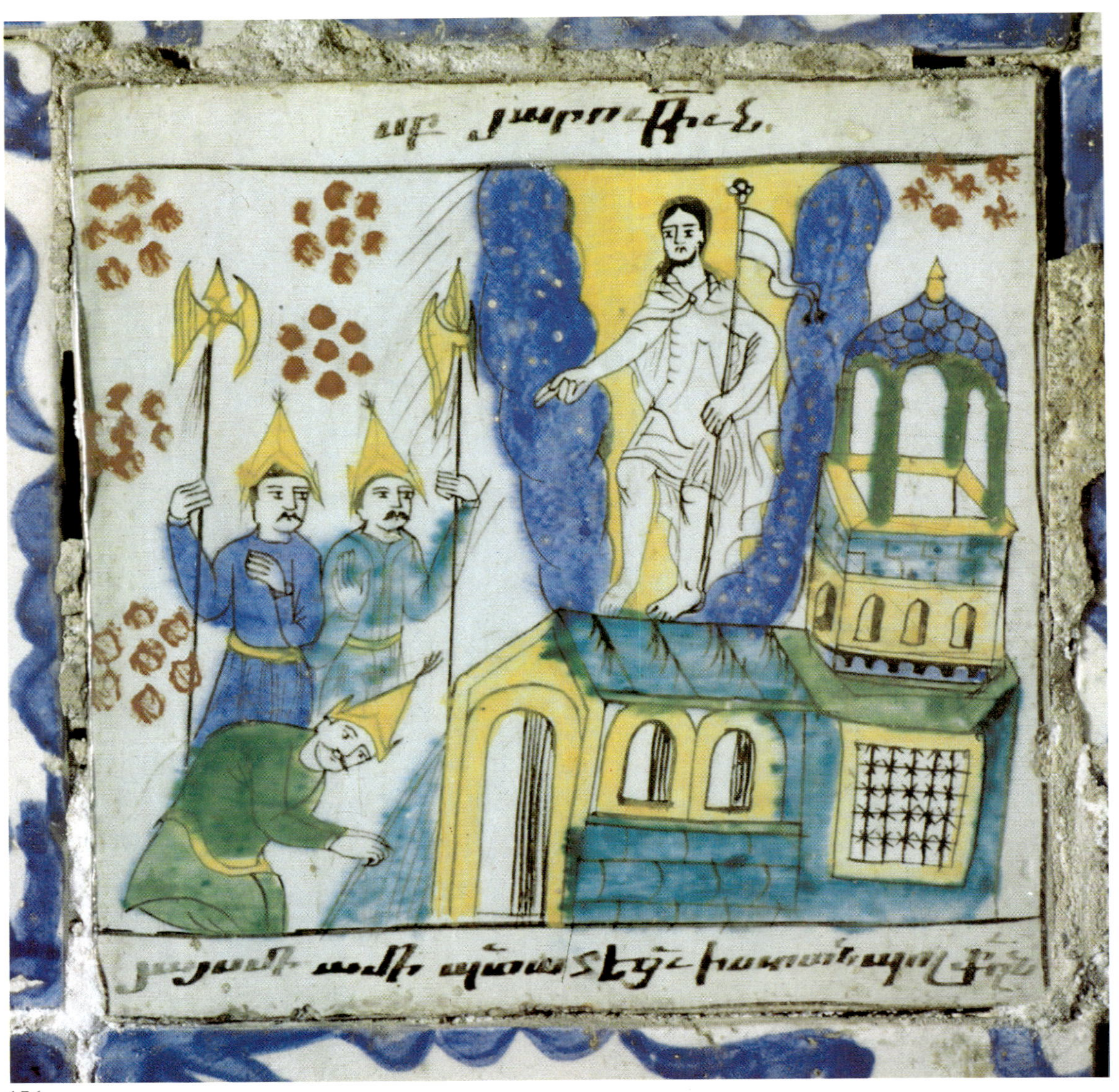

176

Figure 174: *Adam and Eve eating "of the forbidden tree", a Kütahya tile dedicated by Abraham* Vardapet *of Crete, ca. 1720, St. Etchmiadzin Chapel.*

Figure 175: *The Last Supper, with Christ feeding Judas, a Kütahya tile in the Etchmiadzin Chapel, ca. 1720.*

Figure 176: *The Resurrection of Christ, on top of the Holy Sepulcher, a Kütahya tile from the Etchmiadzin Chapel, ca. 1720.*

174

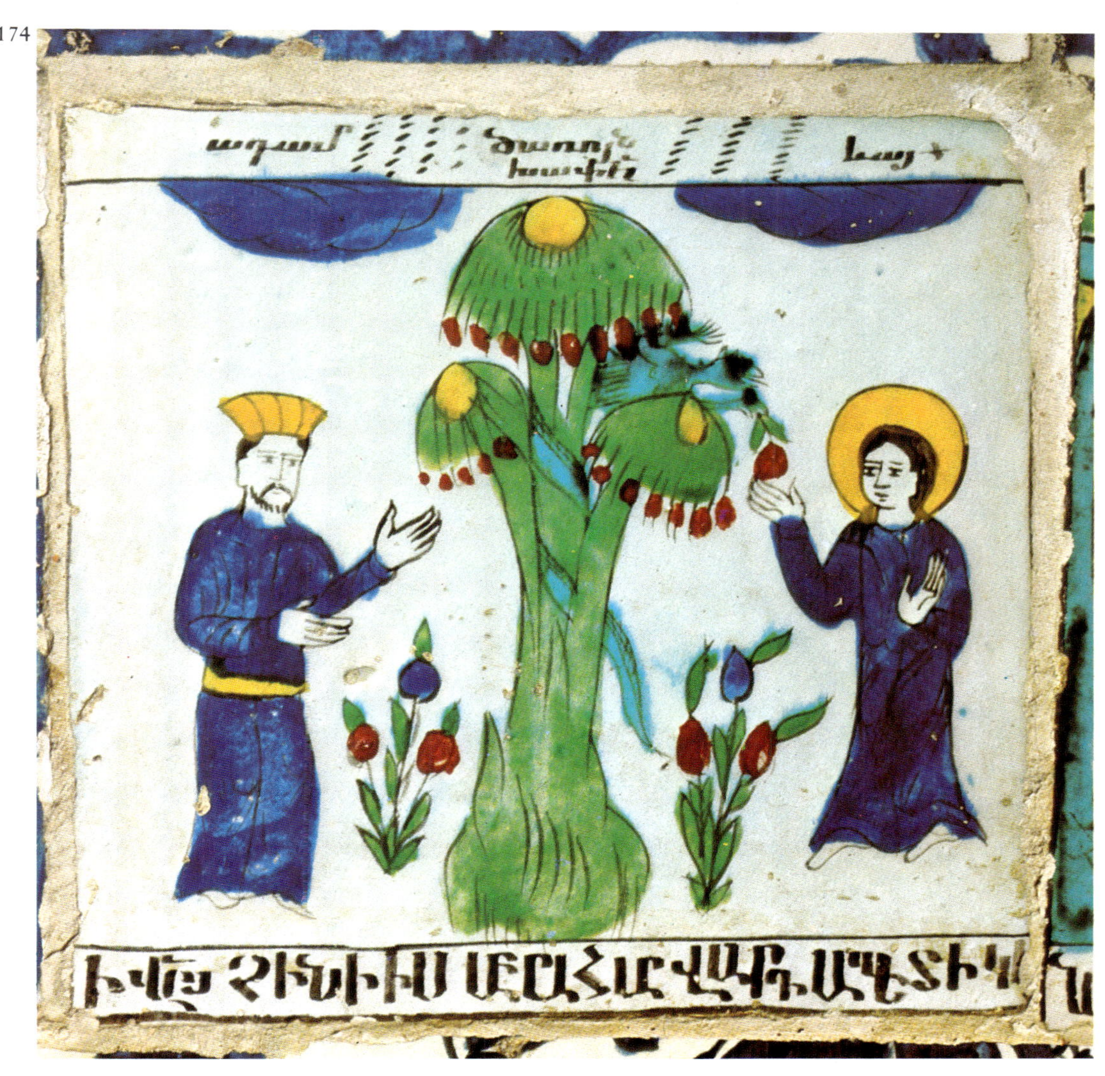

175

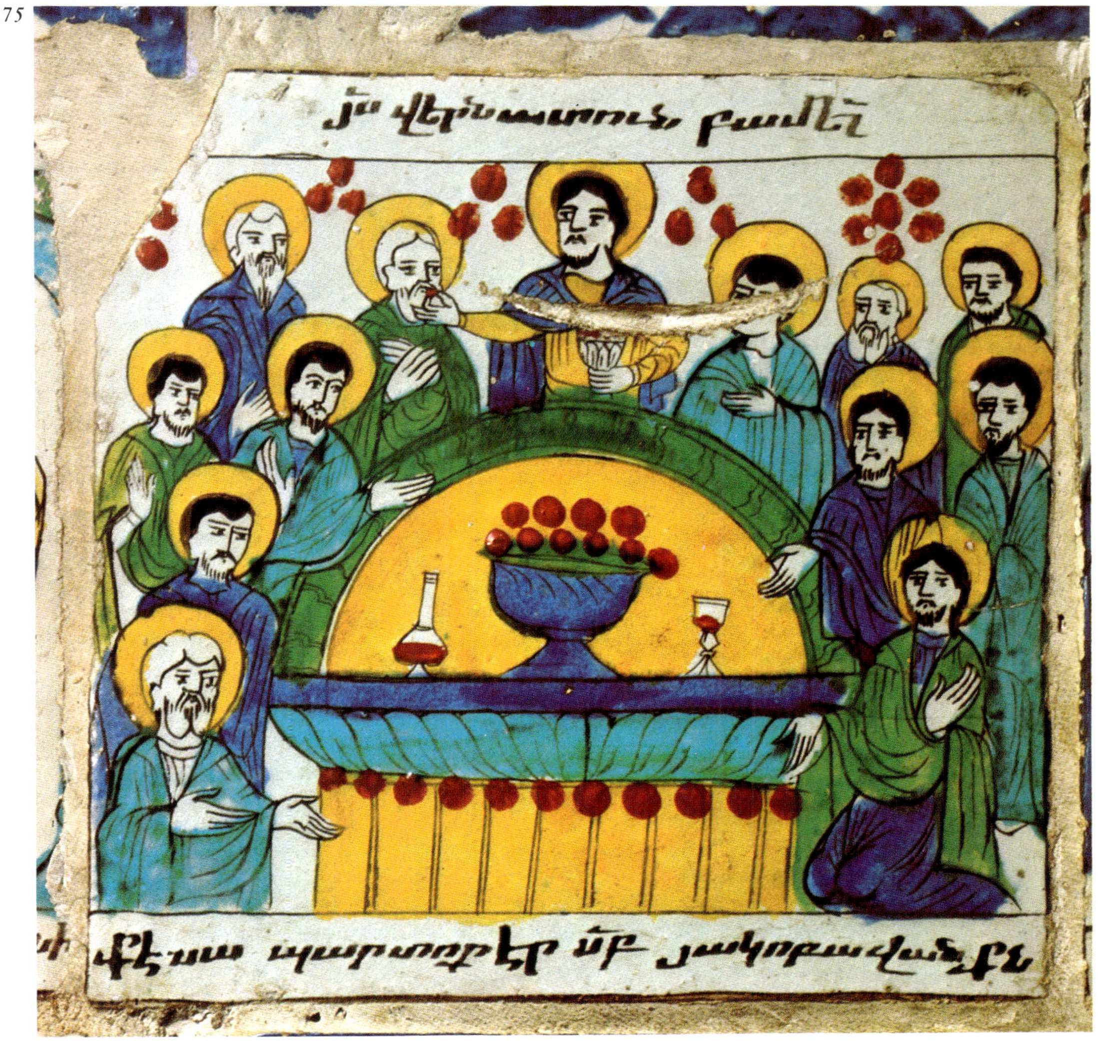

10. Some Church vestments

The Cathedral of St. James and its Treasury are especially rich in church vestments and ritual objects, which adorn the parts, the rites and the solemn celebrations of the church, for the glorification of God. Among these objects are some which embellish the altars and are used in the rites and others which are worn by the priests when officiating in the Church.

The custom of the Armenian church to have an altar-frontal change every Feast necessitates a collection of alternative frontals, which were traditionally embroidered from the seventeenth century. They are all stretched over a frame, which fits exactly the front of the altar. One of the most beautifully embroidered altar-frontals dates from 1619, and is used for the feast day of Sts. Peter, Paul, and the Apostles *fig.179*. The central picture depicts a hovering angel, who brings the head of St. James the Great to the enthroned Virgin. Witnessing it on the right are St. James the Less and St. John the Evangelist. This picture is surrounded by sixteen episodes from the Life and Passion of Christ. Starting with the Annunciation to the Virgin on the lower right-hand corner, and continuing with the Nativity to its right, it depicts many of the Church Feasts, and also narrative episodes.

Another impressive altar-frontal *fig.180* depicts the Last Supper as a central picture, surrounded on three sides by pictures of the Twelve Feasts of the church. This altar-frontal is partly made in patchwork, next to the embroidery. Other seventeenth and eighteenth century altar-frontals in the Cathedral's collection are made in different embroidery techniques using all kinds of materials. One depicting the Ancient of Days sitting in Glory surrounded by the sun, moon, and stars, is embroidered silk and cotton material using some metal threads *fig.181*. For important Feasts, a large embroidered curtain, which covers the entire iconostasis and altar, is hung above the podium of the altar. The workmanship of these curtains, which are traditionally the labor of love of pious women, is as elaborate as that of the altar-frontals, on a larger scale.

The most beautiful altar vessels are the chalices and some patterns for the celebration of Mass. They are mostly executed in gold, some with precious stones, others with added enamel and filigree work. Two chalices were dedicated to the Chainbearer in 1749, the year of his death, *figs.182*,[42] *183*, *184*.[43] Another magnificent altar vessel is a filigree Cross *fig.185*.

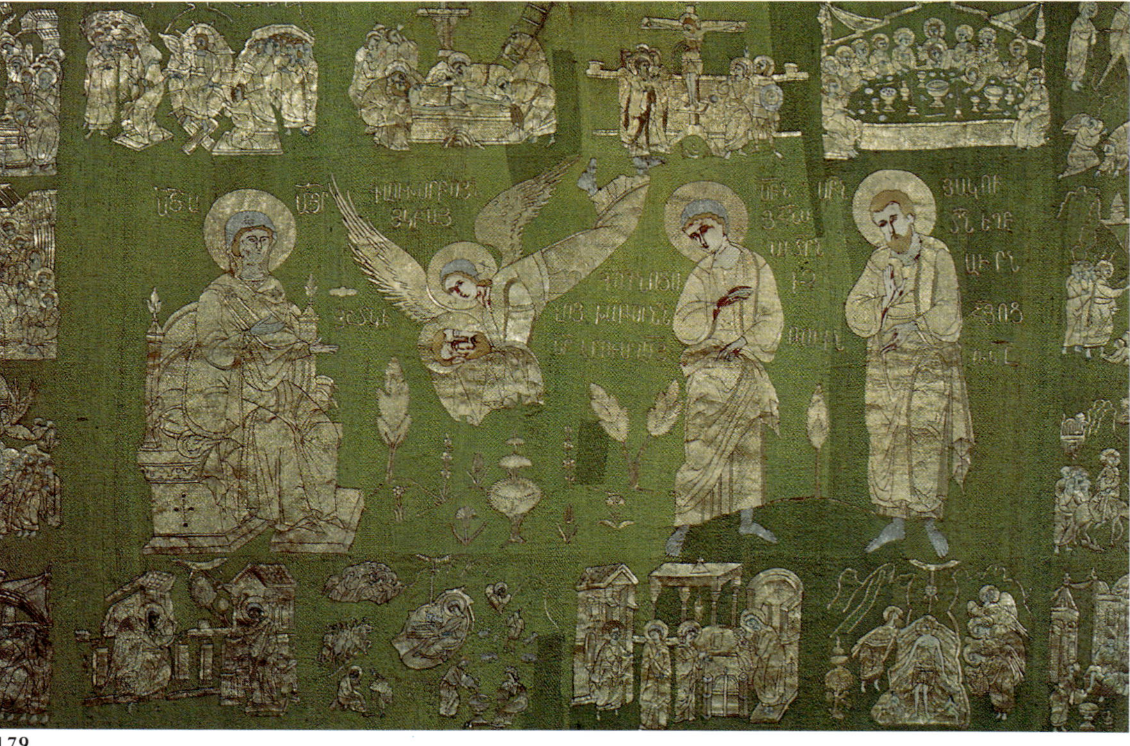

179

Figure 179: *Altar-frontal for the Feast-day of St. Peter and St. Paul depicting angel bringing the head of St. James to the Virgin, surrounded by Christological scenes, Constantinople, 1619.*

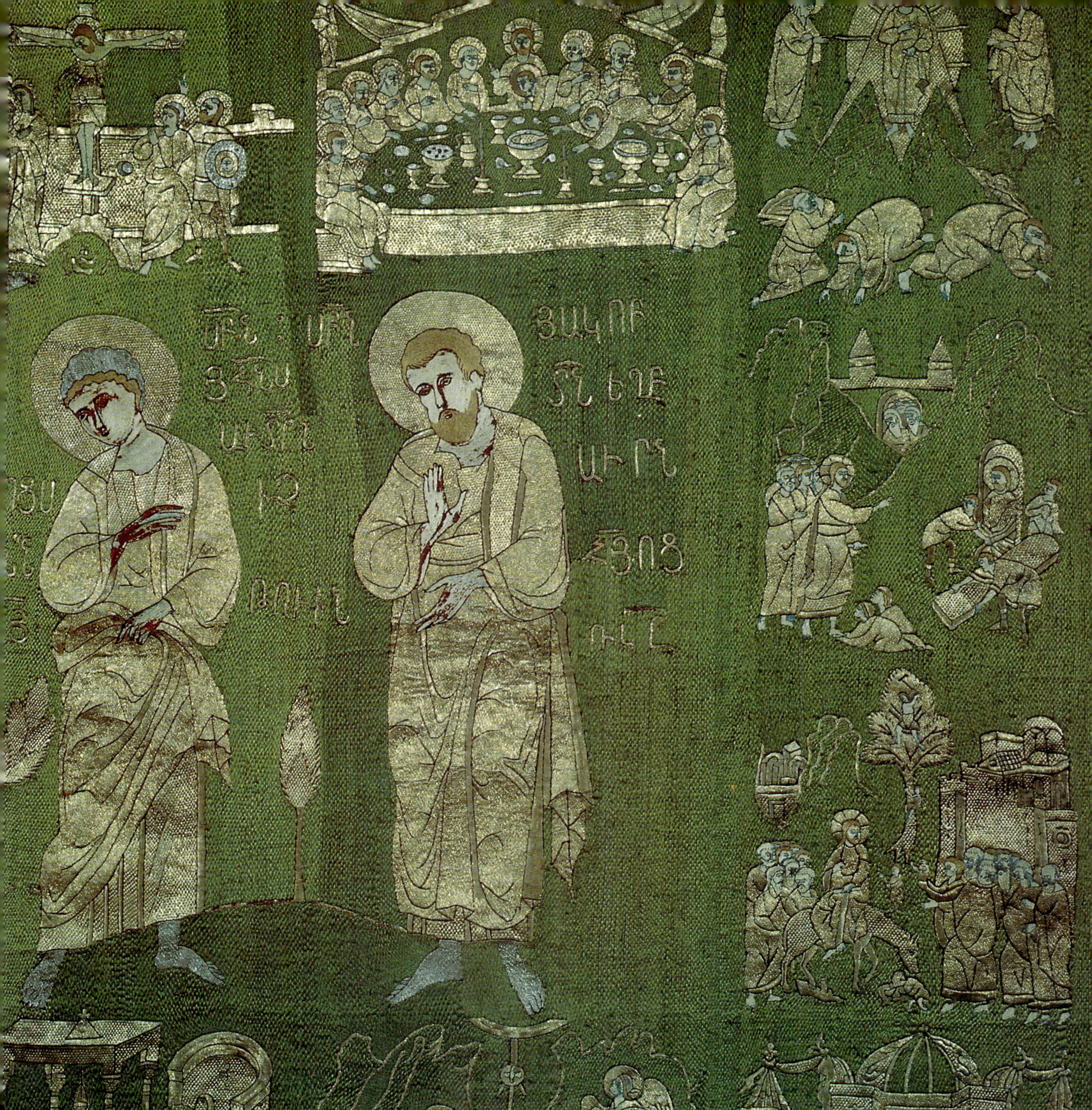

Detail

180

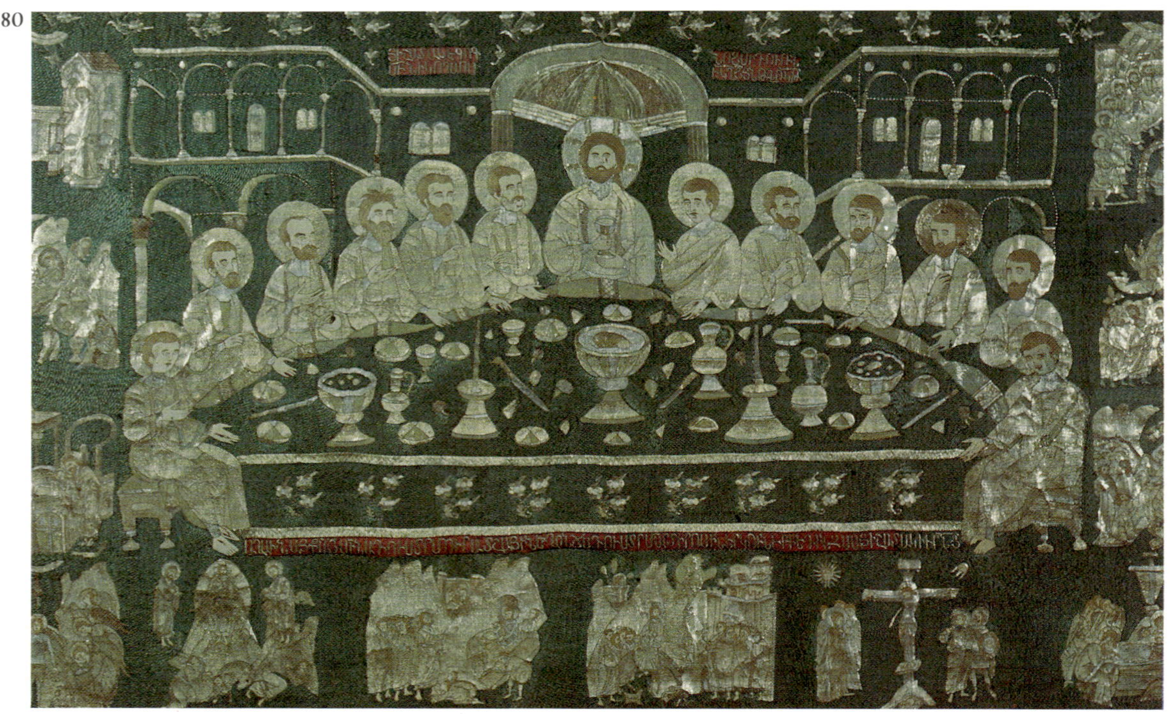

181

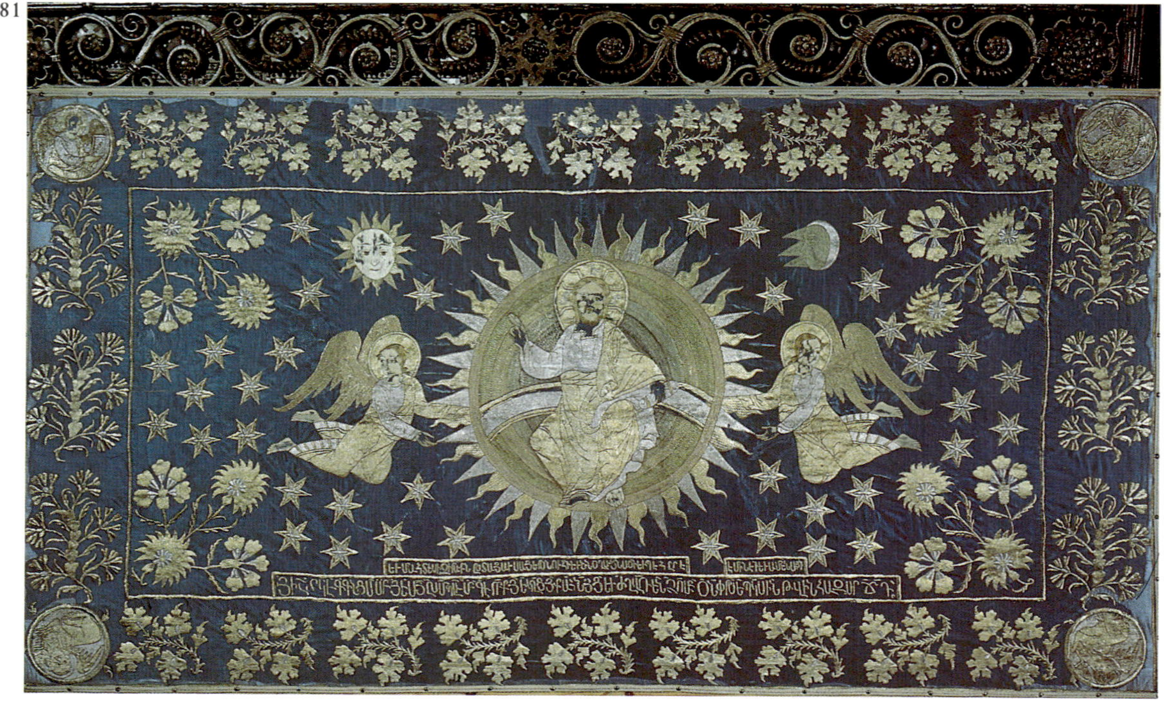

Figure 180: *Altar-frontal with the Last Supper, surrounded by the Twelve Feasts of the Church, Constantinople, 1620.*

Figure 181: *Altar-frontal with Christ in Majesty surrounded by sun, moon, and stars. Constantinople 1655.*

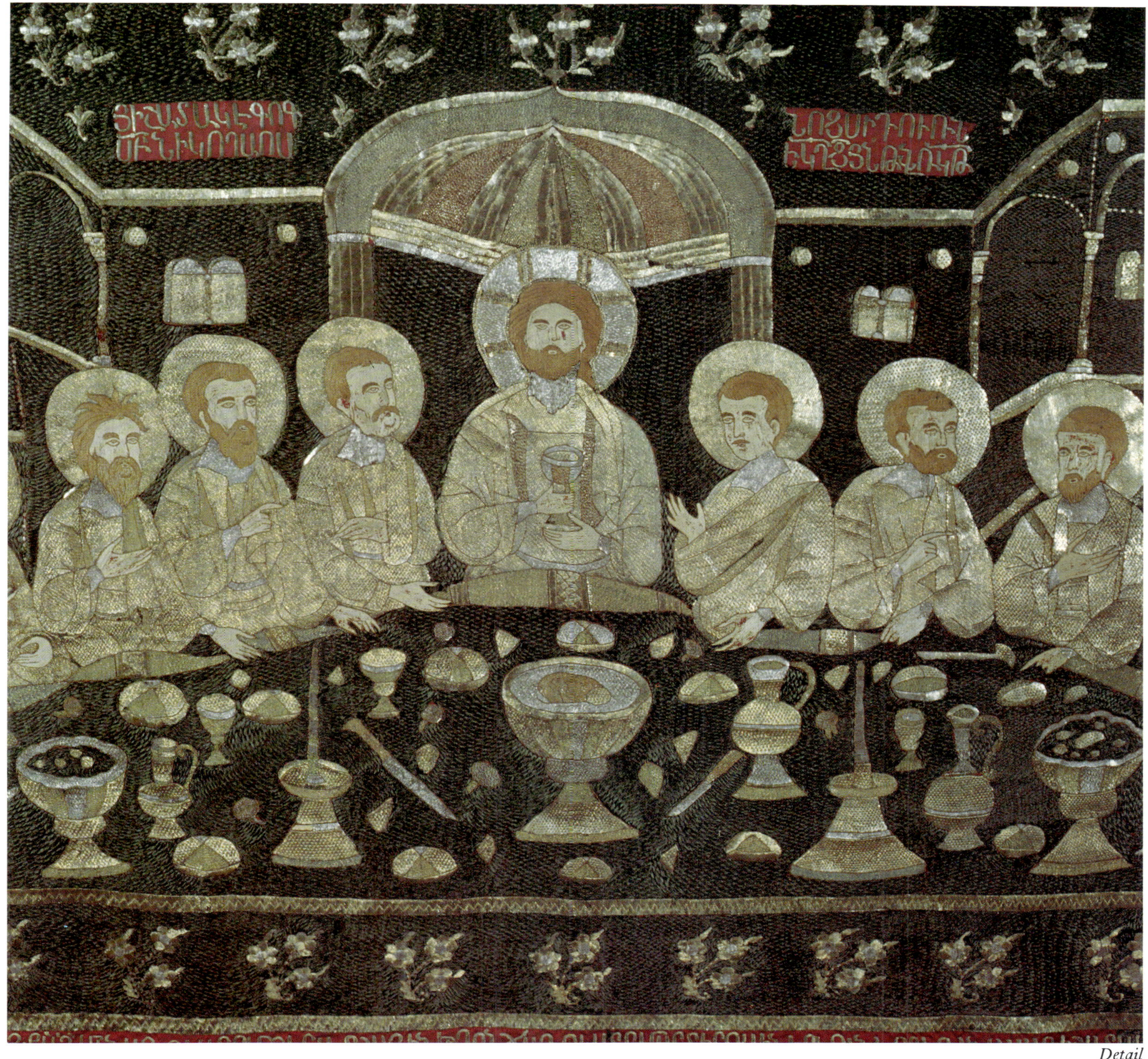

Detail

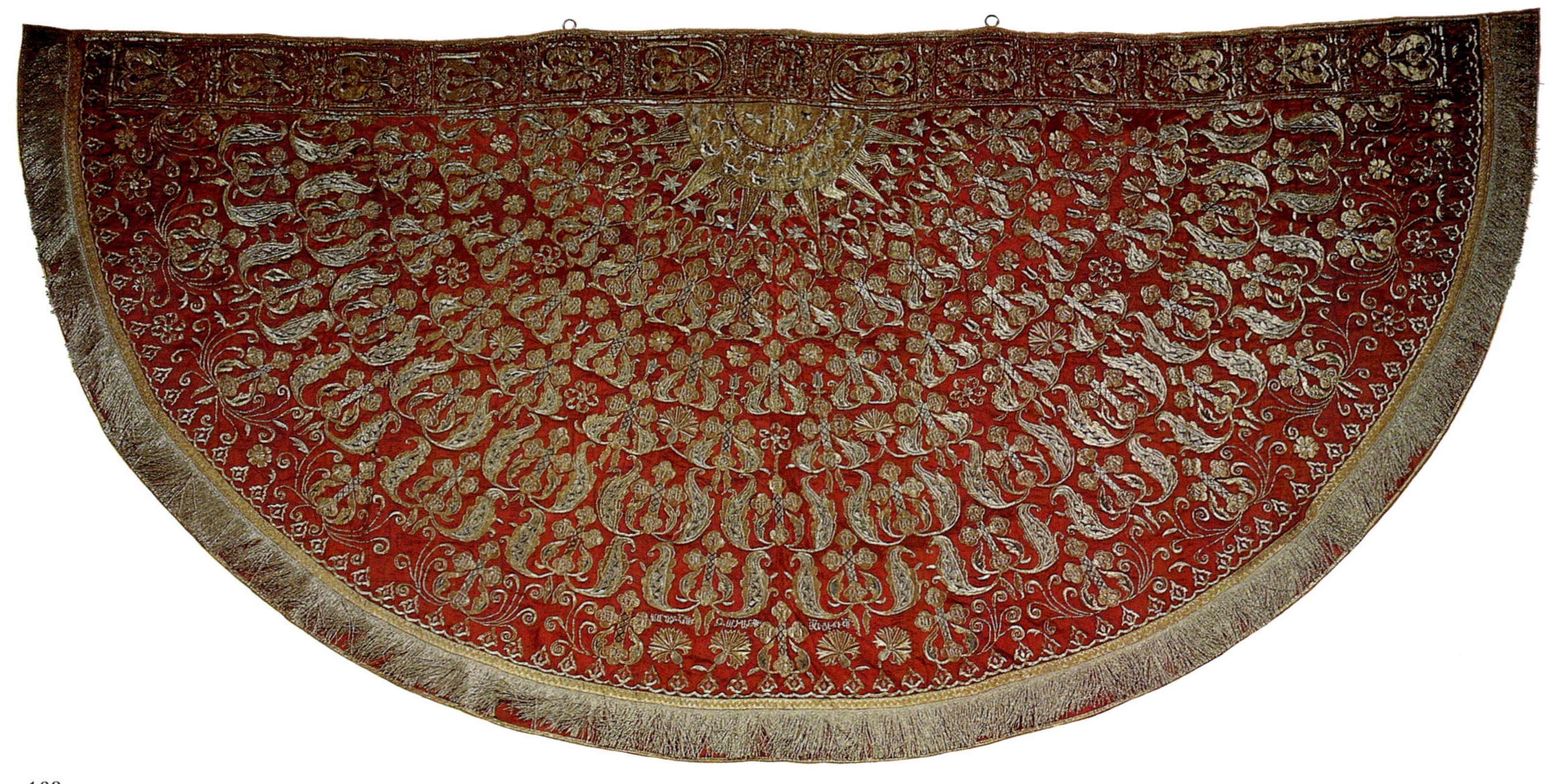

189

Figure 182: *Gold chalice inlaid with gems and precious stones, made for Gregory the Chainbearer in 1749 just before his death. Treasury of St. James.*

Figure 189: *Cope of Gregory Paronter, Patriarch of Jerusalem (1613 –1645)*

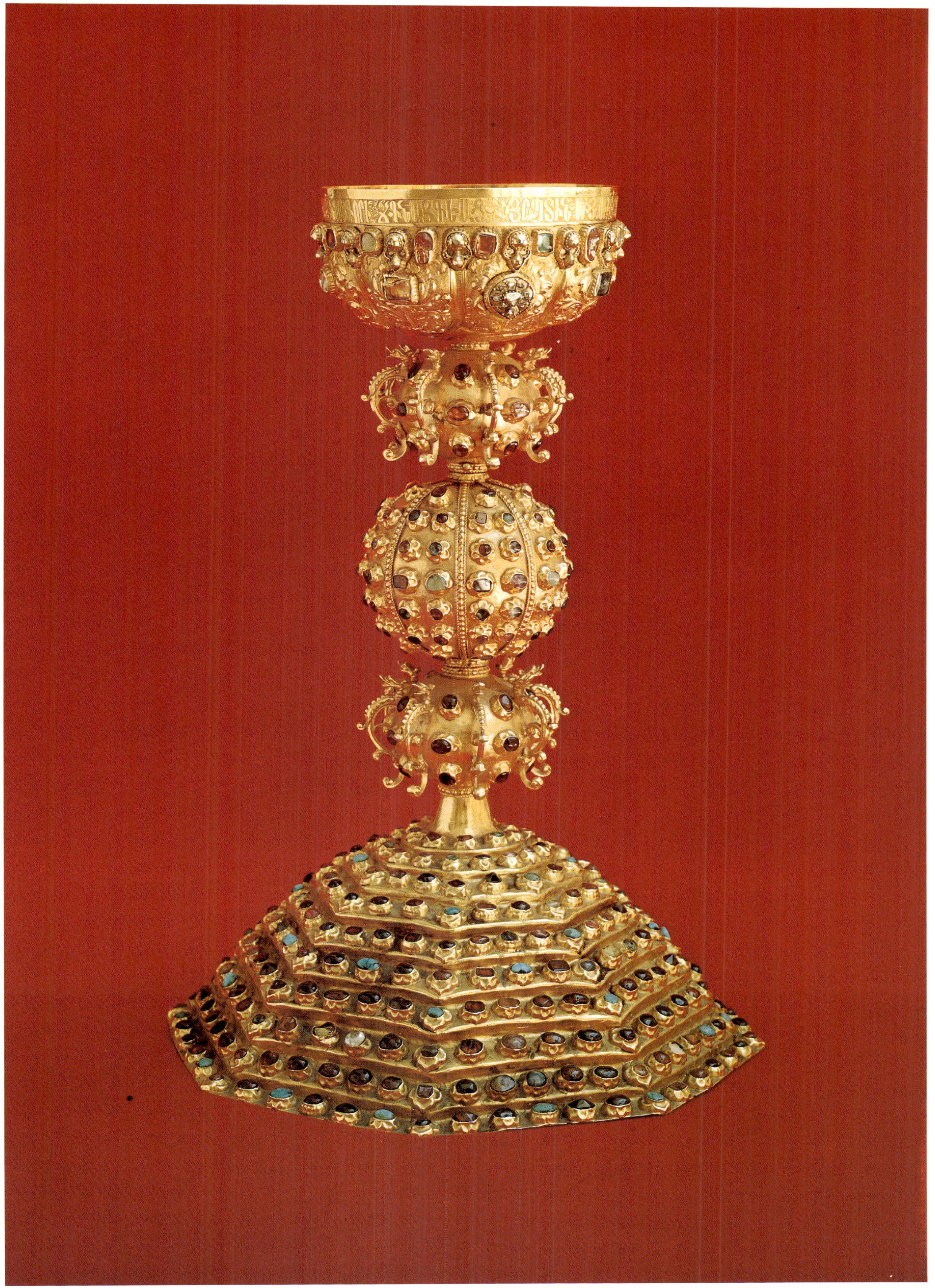

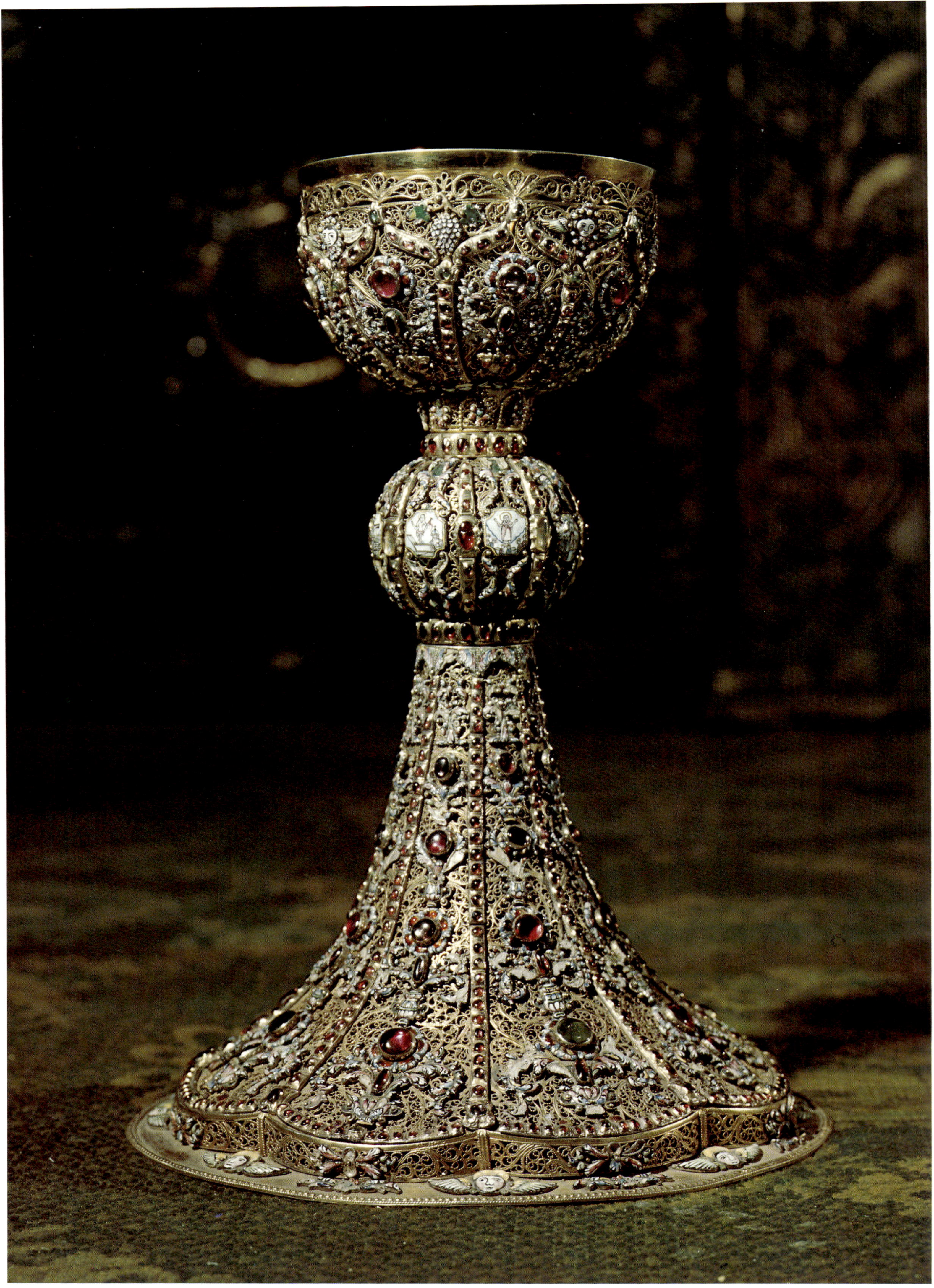

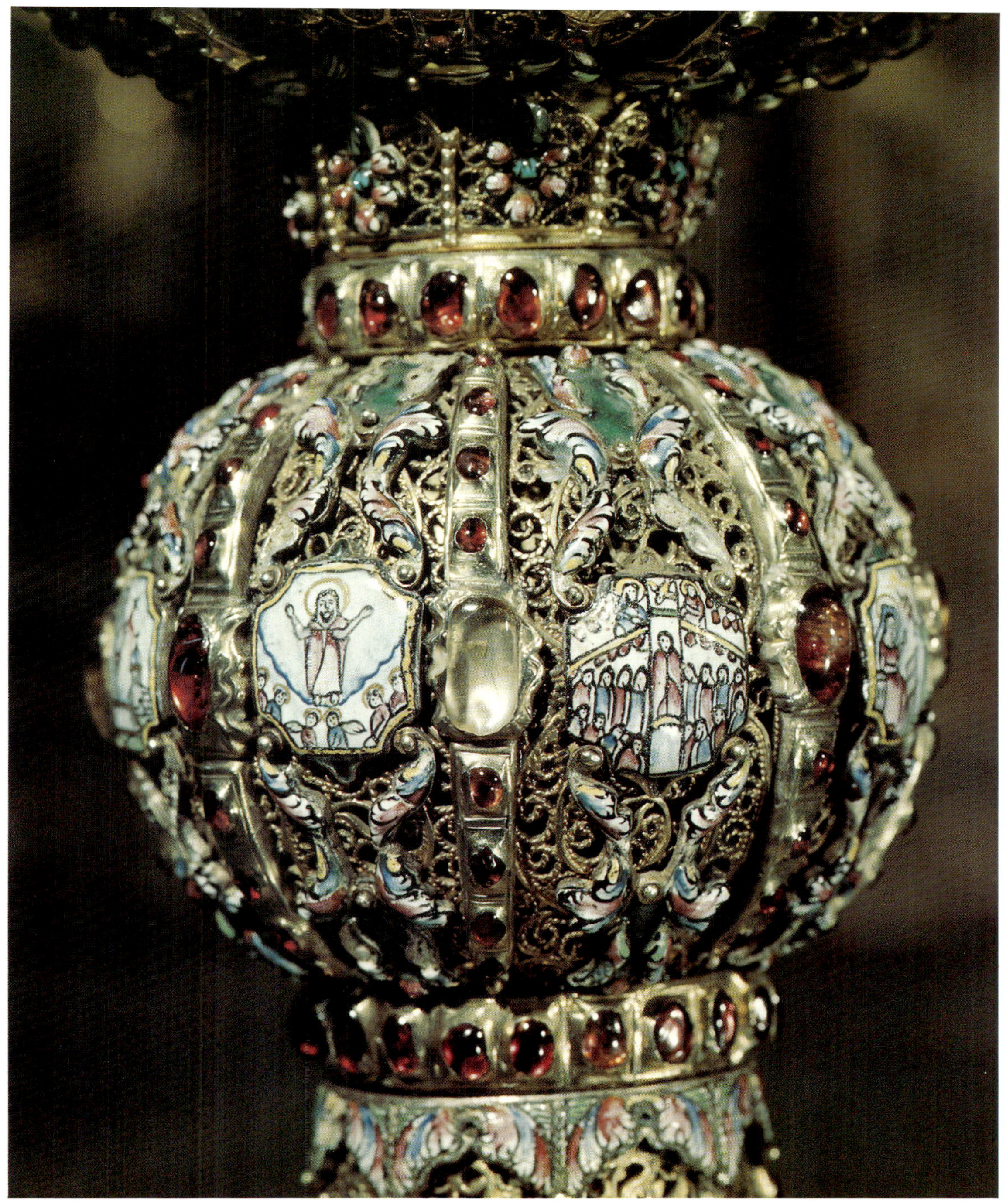

184

Figure 183: *Gold chalice with foliage and filigree work inlaid with gems and enamel medallions, made in memory of Gregory the Chainbearer in 1749 just after his death. Treasury of St. James.*

Figure 184: *Ascension of Christ and the Holy Spirit descending on the Apostles at Pentecost, enamel medallions from the chalice in memory of Gregory the Chainbearer, 1749.*

Figure 185: *Filigree Cross with enamel medallions, 1747. St. James Cathedral.*

Figure 186: *The crown of Gregory the Chainbearer, a gift of the baker Melkon and his family in Istanbul, 1747. Treasury of St. James.*

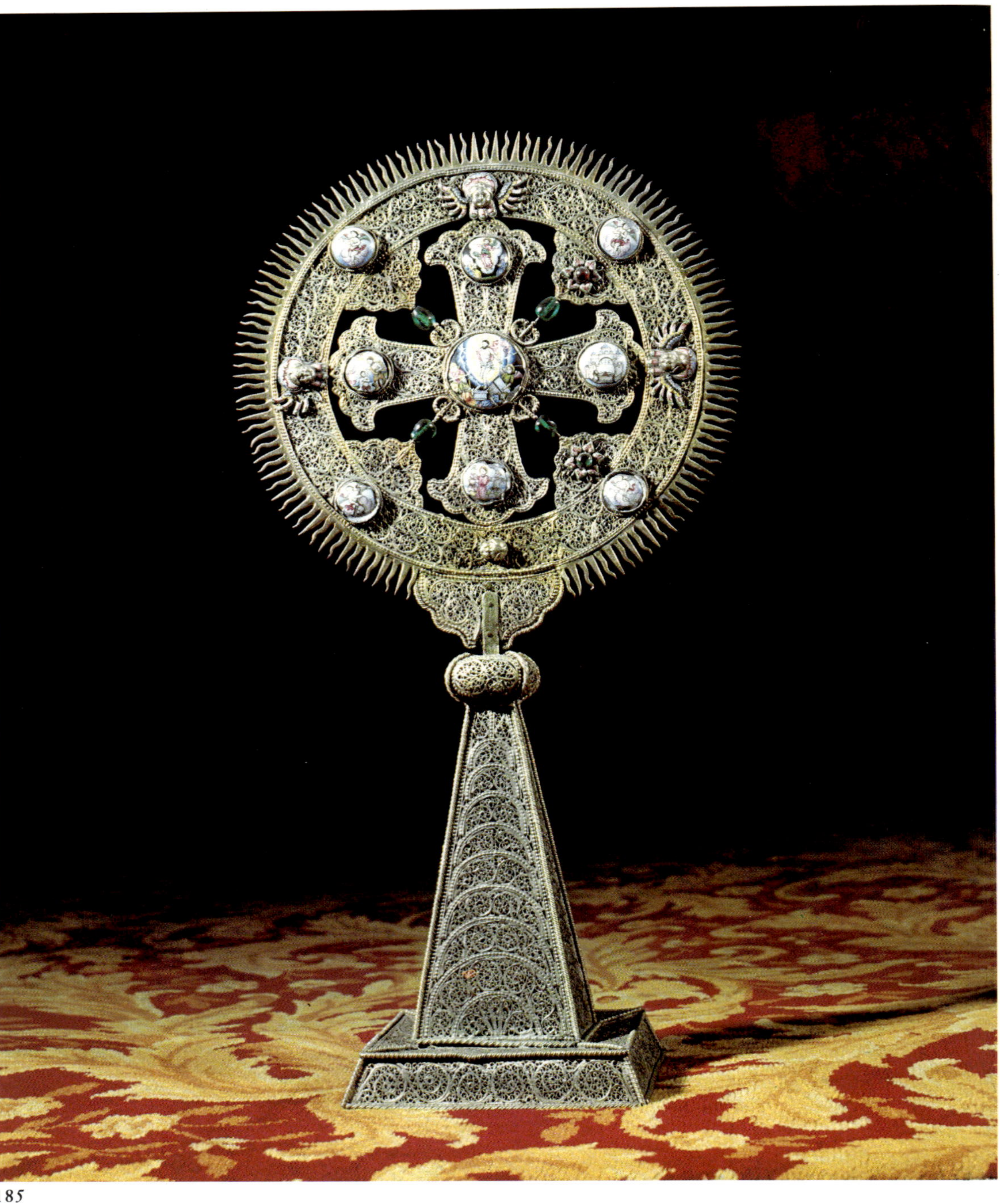

185

11. Some priestly vestments

It is hard to enumerate even part of the priestly vestments treasured in St. James. Here only very few of special interest can be reproduced. Very special in shape and use is a red tiara, a priestly crown, made for Patriarch Gregory the Chainbearer in 1747 at Constantinople, by an Armenian goldsmith and enamel forger *fig.186*.[44]

The miter of the Chainbearer is as richly decorated as the rest of his attire, *fig.187*. The miter was donated to Gregory in 1735, and the dedicatory inscription mentions Yovhannes Kolot the Patriarch of Constantinople, who came on pilgrimage to Jerusalem and may have brought a whole set of ecclesiastical clothes for his friend, the Chainbearer. The same date is mentioned on several vestments dedicated to Gregory. These include an embroidered belt with a large green enamel buckle with set rubies, a neck *horarium*, *fig.188*, and a large embroidered cope. The shoulder-piece mentions Yovhannes' pilgrimage to St. James and his gift to the See. All these vestments are executed in the same style, and in the same technique of outlining the scenes and decoration with pearls, on gold brocade, embroidered in very sublime colors of ocher, brown, red, blue, and lilac. They may have been made in the same workshop, possibly by Gabob *Verdapet*, who is mentioned on the neck-*horarium*, perhaps as the donor.

There are many bishops' copes in the Treasury of St. James, a number of which are very richly decorated and embroidered on brocade, some with elaborate episodes depicted on them. It is, however, befitting the Armenian sublime sense of beauty, to end this list of examples of church vestments, by reproducing a delicate cope, the earliest of the seventeenth century *fig.189*. Tradition says that it was the one most loved by Gregory Paronter (1613–1645). The entire cope is decorating by flowering crosses and interlace of foliage with crosses emerging from them. It is the most balanced and delicate cope in the collection and properly adorned for the Glory of the Lord.

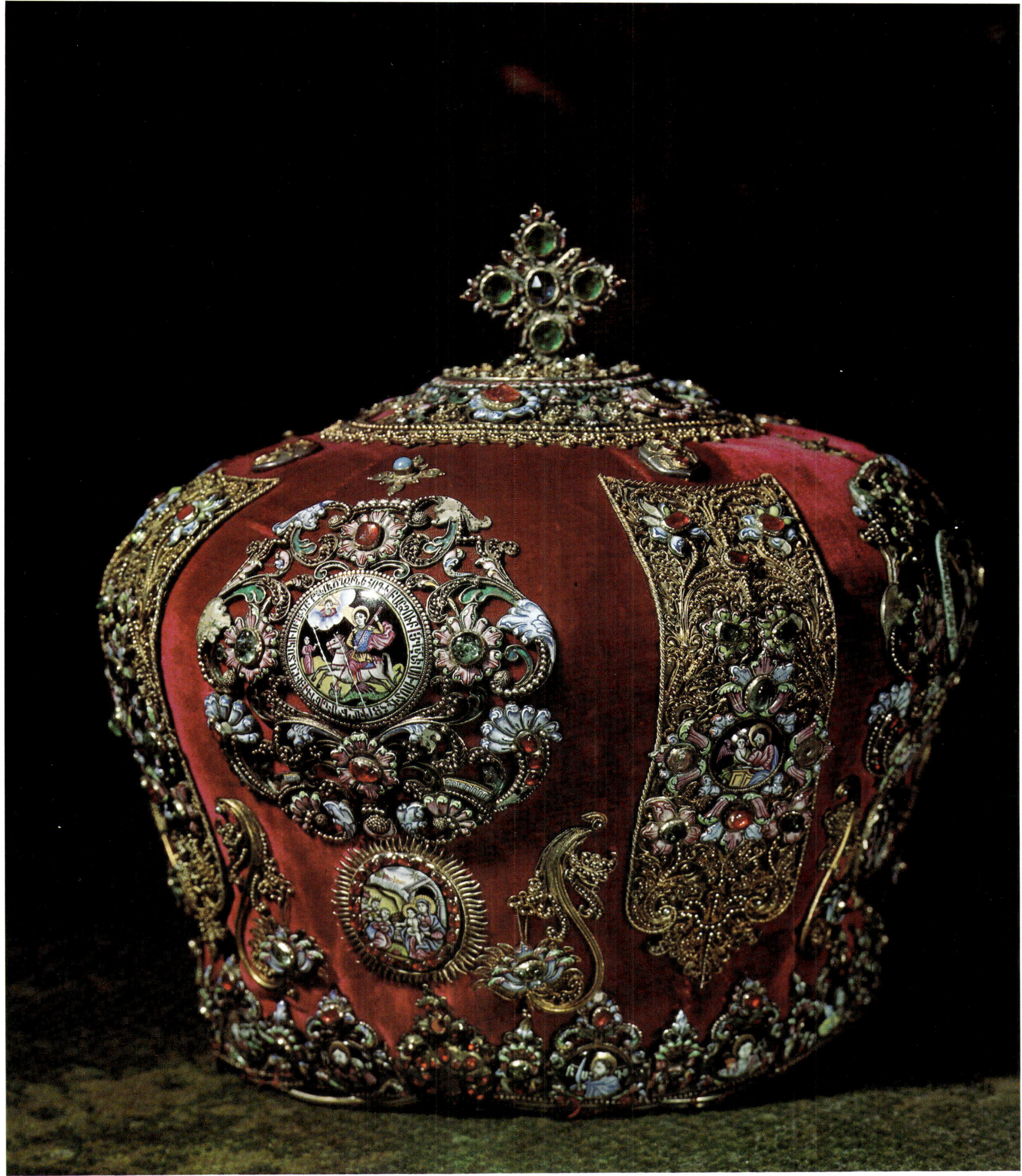

186

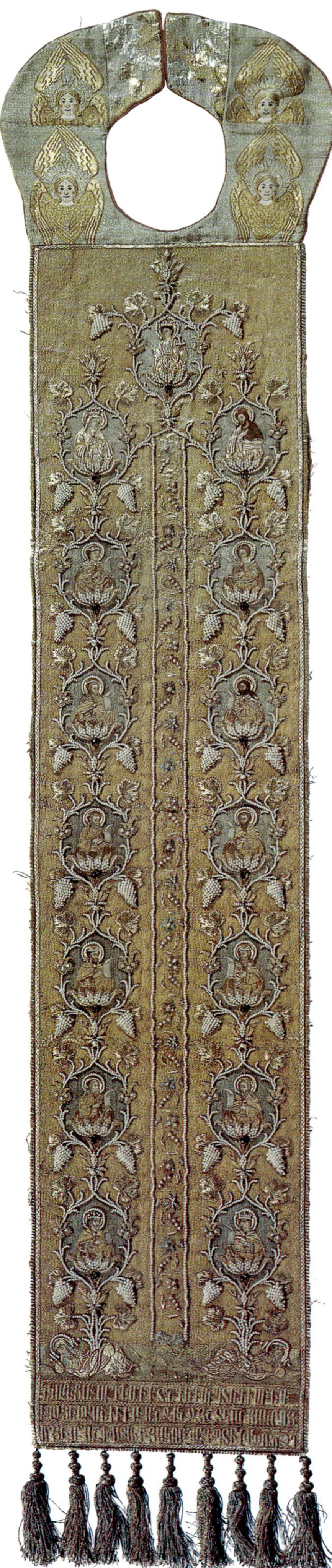

188

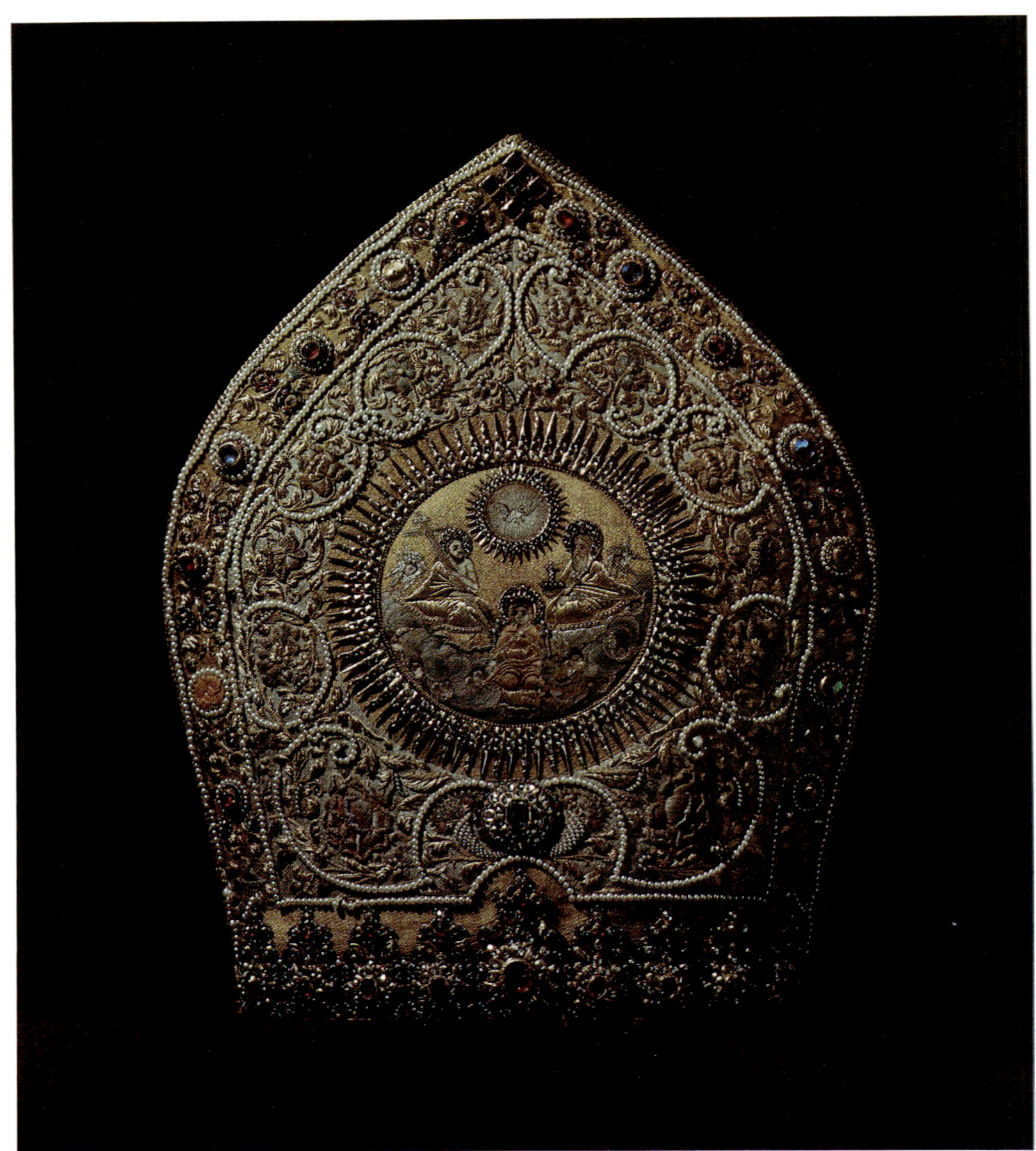

187

Figure 187: *The miter of the Chainbearer, given to him by Yovhannes Kolot, Patriarch of Constantinople, in 1735.*

Figure 188: *Neck-horarium of the Chainbearer, depicting the Tree of Jesse, Istanbul, 1735.*

Catalogue of Items

by Michael E. Stone

The Catalogue of Items is intended to supply a responsible and accurate description of the manuscripts and objects shown in the illustrations. Most of the objects are described here for the first time, while the manuscripts have been described anew, but only after careful consultation of Archbishop Norayr Bogharian's magistral *Grand Catalogue of St. James Manuscripts*, references to which are given throughout. I was unable to examine the items which appear as figs. 32–38 and 187 and the descriptions of them are the work of my colleague, Professor B. Narkiss. No attempt has been made to prepare a complete bibliographical listing for each item, but instead the reader should consult the relevant catalogue or other work of reference.

H.G. Archbishop Norayr Bogharian has been an unfailing source of help, inspiration and learning; I owe him a special debt of gratitude. His Beatitude, Elisha II, Patriarch of Jerusalem and H.G. Archbishop Shahe Ajamian have encouraged and aided me in every way they could. Professor B. Narkiss has made many helpful suggestions and the work has benefitted from the editorial skills of Dr. G. Wigoder.

The Armenian Communities of Jerusalem

Figure 1.
See figs. 39–40. Dedicatory inscription in mosaic pavement of the 6th century funerary chapel of St. Polyeuctos in the Musrara Quarter of Jerusalem.

Figure 2.
Firman attributed to the Prophet Muhammed, affirming the rights of the Armenians in the Holy Places. Paper on silk backing. 327 × 21 cm.

Figure 3
Firman attributed to the Caliph Omar Ibn-el-Qattab (634–644), affirming the rights of the Armenians in Jerusalem. Thick, yellowish parchment. 65 × 43 cm.

Figure 4
Firman attributed to the Caliph Ali (656–661), affirming the rights of the Armenians in Jerusalem. Parchment. 825 × 32.8 cm.

Figures 5, 6, 7
Firman of Saladin (1187–1188), affirming the rights of the Armenians in their possessions in Jerusalem. Parchment on green silk backing. 529 × 29 cm.

Figure 8
A *khatchkar* (stone cross) in the Church of the Archangels in a niche near old font. Inscription in uncial Armenian script: "Lord God, the year 811 (= 1362 A.D.)."

Figure 9
Main entrance to the Armenian Compound. In the center; a water fountain of 1900. Behind it an Arabic inscription of 1437 by the Mameluke Sultan A-Zaher Abu Sayad Chakmak, abolishing all taxes imposed on the Armenians by his predecessors. Opposite it is a copy of this inscription in Armenian, 1743.
Bibl. Hintlian, *Holy Land*, 51.

Figure 10
A *khatchk'ar* (stone cross) of the 11th century, set into the outer arch of St. James Cathedral in the 19th century.

Figures 11, 12
The scepter of King Hethum I of Cilicia (1215–1270). A solid staff of amber topped with gold chasing, extending 35.7 cm from the top. At the bottom is a gilt tip 12.7 cm long. The overall length is 133.5 cm. It has been suggested that the decoration was added to the amber rod in the 15th or 16th century.

Figure 13
Gregory Paronter (1613–1645) and Gregory the Chainbearer (1715–1749) in the Cathedral of St. James at the center of the north wall. Mid-18th century painting. Both panels 178 × 132 cm.

Figure 14
Portrait of Patriarch Esayi III Thalastzi (1865–1885). Sunprint (P.O.P.). 31 × 23 cm.

Figure 15
Letter addressed to Patriarch Gregory the Chainbearer by Cardinal de Fleury, Prime Minister of Louis XV, written in Versailles on 31 August, 1739, 8 pp. (5 written). Paper. 32 × 20 cm.

Figures 16, 17
Sunprints (P.O.P.) from about 1860–61, made by Esayi Thalastzi who later became Patriarch Esayi III (1865–1885).
Figure 16. The Church of the Holy Sepulcher from the south, 26 × 32 cm.
Figure 17. A group of Armenian priests, monks, and pilgrims at the entrance of the Cathedral of St. James. 26 × 20 cm.

Figure 18
Chalice,
Constantinople, 1733.
Silver gilt repoussé. The top bowl is decorated with angels holding the implements of the Passion. In the central sphere are eight Apostles holding books, seated under decorated arches. The base shows the four Evangelists with their symbols, and between them are busts of Solomon, horned Moses, crowned David, and perhaps Daniel with a flame on his head. Other figures are unidentifiable. Inscribed around the upper rim: "This chalice is a memorial for the soul of Nazar son of *Mahdesi* Arak'el and his wife *Mahdesi* Sarah for the Church of St. James in the year 1182 (= 1733)." Height: 39.5 cm, base: 26.6 cm, top: 12.1 cm. Treasury of St. James.

Figures 19, 20
The old Theological Seminary of 1857. Iron gates over heavy wood with bolts. A stylized eagle decorates the center of the wicket gate.

Figure 21
The new Theological Seminary, 1975. Benefaction of Alex and Marie Manoogian, Detroit.

Figure 22
"Prayer Book". First book in Armenian to be printed in Jerusalem, 1833, 48 pp. 14 × 9 cm.

Figure 23
Wooden printing block, hand carved, used for printing the title page of the first number of *Sion*, journal of the Armenian Patriarchate since 1866. This may have been a second use of these blocks. St. James Press.

Figure 24
Mashtotz ritual book printed in Jerusalem, 1843, by the St. James Press, 94 pp. 18 × 12 cm.

Figure 25
Concordance to the Bible, prepared by *Vardapet* Th. Astuadzaturian, printed and published by the St. James Press, 1895, 1573 pp. 50 × 23 cm.

Figure 26
History of Jerusalem, written in the 19th century by Bishop Tigran Sawalaniantz and printed in 1931 in a modern Armenian rendering by Abp. M. Nshanian, Jerusalem, St. James Press, 1931, 1387 pp. 23 × 15 cm.

Figure 27
Deux ans de séjour en Abyssinie by Bishop Sahak (Isaac) and the priest Timothy, dedicated to Queen Victoria, Jerusalem, St. James Press, 1871, 175 pp. 14 × 21 cm.

Figures 28, 29
The first issue of *Sion*, the scholarly journal of the Armenian Patriarchate of Jerusalem, 1866.

Figure 30
The seventh volume of the *Grand Catalogue of St. James Manuscripts* by Archbishop Norair Bogharian, Jerusalem, St. James Press, 1974, xxxii + 552 pp. This volume contains descriptions of manuscripts no. 2001–2365 in the Library of the Patriarchate. 27.5 × 19.5 cm.

Figure 31
(See Figures 16, 17). Sunprint of the south wall of St. James Cathedral with the three Crusader arches by Esayi Thalastzi (made in 1860). 22.5 × 16.5 cm.

The Armenian Treasures of Jerusalem

Chapter One: Mosaic Pavements

Figures 32, 33, 34
The Artavan Mosaic of the mid-5th century. From a funerary chapel on the Mount of Olives, now *in situ* in the Archaeological Museum of the Russian Convent. The inscription along the northern border states "This is the tomb of the blessed Susannah, mother of Artavan" and gives the date 18th *Hori*, with no mention of a year. The fragmentary extant section measures 6.70 × 4.00 m. It contains birds, fish, fruit, and a lamb within a heavily decorated border.
Bibliography: Hovsepian, *Mosaik*, 88–90; Guthe, *Mosaiken*, 51–53; Murray, *Damascus Gate*, 126–127; Vincent and Abel, *Jerusalem II*, pl. XLIII, 1; Avi-Yonah, *QDAP*, II, Nos. 118.

Figures 35, 36, 37, 38
The St. John Mosaics of the late 5th century. *In situ* in the chapel dedicated to the Head of St. John the Baptist within the Russian Convent on the Mount of Olives.
It is divided into three adjacent fields. The westernmost field, measuring 3.50 × 3.20 m., has a pattern of interwoven circles. To its east is a recess, 35 cm. in diameter, denoting the place of St. John's head. The middle field measures 3.45 × 2.65 m., and has interlaced roundels and squares enclosing many kinds of birds, fruit, and leaves, and a dog barking at a lamb. The third field, to the east, measuring 1.69 × 0.64 m., has an Armenian inscription, below a small field with a trellis pattern (61 × 28 cm.), reading: "This is the monument of the Lord Jacob, made at (his) request."
Bibliography: Avi-Yonah, *QDAP*, II, No. 117. Most of the literature is listed there. Vincent and Abel, *Jerusalem II*, pl. XLII, 2.

Figures 1, 39, 40
Musrara Mosaic, mid-6th century. Located close to the Damascus Gate, outside the walls of the Old City of Jerusalem, in the Musrara Quarter. It is housed in a rectangular room measuring 6.55 × 3.85 m. and was apparently part of the floor of a chapel. The inscription in its apse is one of the oldest examples of Armenian writing. It reads, "For the memorial and the salvation of all Armenians, whose names God knows." The design is of birds in 41 medallions formed by vines growing out of an amphora, flanked by two peacocks. The central column of medallions contains other motifs like a bird in a cage. The whole is surrounded by a decorative border.
Bibliography: Most of the early bibliography is to be found in: Murray, *Damascus Gate Mosaic*; cf. Sanjian, *Syria*, 315; Hjort, *L'Oiseau*, 21–32; Avi-Yonah, *QDAP*, II, No. 132.

Chapter Two: Early Illuminated Manuscripts

Figure 41
The Tyche Initial
Ms. 1949. The Tyche Initial and headpiece to the book of St. Mark is a single cropped leaf (fol. 390) from a fine uncial Gospel book of the late 10th century. It now forms part of the binding material of another Gospel from Taron of 1312 A.D., painted by Sargis Pidzak. According to one of the colophons (fol. 387v), it was rebound in Jerusalem in 1438, when this folio was probably inserted. 25 × 17 cm.

Figures 42, 43
The Second Etchmiadzin Gospel.
Four Gospels, western Armenian, late 10th or early 11th century.
Jerusalem, St. James ms. 2555.
General data: heavy vellum, 236 folios, 42 × 30 × 10 cm. Written in round *erkathagir* script in black ink which has faded in places, 20 lines in 2 columns. The text is incomplete in some places. 36 quires, usually of 10 folios. Bound in leather over wood, with nails in the front cover. The manuscript was apparently written in the western part of Armenia and is dated on palaeographic grounds to the end of the 10th or early 11th century. The names of the scribe and painter are unknown. Two fake colophons date the manuscript to the year 602 A.D. (fols. 7 and 91).
Decoration: full-page panels: fol. 1v, cross; fols. 2–6v, Eusebian letter and canon tables; fol. 7, Sanctuary of the Holy Sepulcher; fol. 7v, SS. Matthew and Mark; fol. 8, SS. Luke and John; fol. 8v, orant Virgin and Child, Sacrifice of Isaac.
Bibliography: Bogharian, *Grand Catalogue*, VIII (1977), 242–245; Mekhitarian, *Cat. Exh. Jerusalem 1969*, no. 1, p. 21; Strzygowski, *Ein Zweites Etchmiadzin*; Weitzmann, *Armenische Buchmalerei*, 16; Der Nersessian, *Etchmiadzin date* (1933), in *Studies*, 540; *Idem*, *L'Art Arménien*, 120–122; Garegin I Catholicos, *Yishatakarank' Jeragraez* (Antelias, 1951), 170; *Handes Amsorya*, 14 (1900), 353–386; ibid, 15 (1901), 33–45.

Figures 44–48
The King Gagik Gospel
Four Gospels, Kars, ca. 1050 A.D.
Jerusalem, ms. 2556, Treasury of St. James, No. 1.
General data: thick parchment, 481 folios, 46 × 35 × 16 cm. Written in large *erkathagir* script in black ink, usually 15 lines in two columns. Since the restoration of 1703 the manuscript has been well preserved, though due to deliberate prior mutilation, many miniatures and some text are missing.
Binding: the rebinding of 1703 was done by the priest Paul, executing the personal orders of Minas *Vardapet*, the Patriarch of Jerusalem. Many of the lost text pages were replaced by paper ones. In 1743 Patriarch Gregory the Chainbearer added, according to the inscription on the gold flap of the binding, a silver gilt cross on a red velvet background, and semi-precious stones.
Colophons: fols. 5v, 135, 135v, 222v, 371v, at the end of the dedication and each of the Gospels, mentioning Gagik, son of Abas, King of Kings, his wife Queen Gorandoukht and his daughter Marem. Since the main part of the colophon is lost (fol. 135), the place, date, and names of scribes and artists are not known. There may have been portraits of the royal family at the bottom of each of these folios, but only one (fol. 135v) survives, which was originally at the end of the manuscript.
History: the manuscript was mutilated at some time in its history, and many pages and parts of pages containing pictures were cut out.
Decoration: of the fragmentary opening section, the following pages are extant: fols. 5–5v, letter of Eusebius to Carpianus with a dedication to King Gagik of Kars written in gold; fols. 4, 4v, 8, 8v, canon tables (fols. 1–3v, 6–7v are blank). Each opening page of a Gospel is written in gold with a decorated headpiece (fols. 9,137, 223, 372). Of the many text illustrations, either within the text or at the bottom of pages, only a few have survived: fol. 18, first Temptation of Christ; fol. 18v, second Temptation (partly excised); fol. 19, third Temptation; fol. 21v, Christ choosing the Apostles, or the Sermon on the Mount; fol. 118, Christ in Gethsemane; fol. 125, Christ before Pilate; fol. 127, Roman soldiers mocking Christ (partly excised); fol. 132v, the Women at the Tomb; fol. 134v, Christ appearing to the Apostles,fol. 135v, King Gagik and his family; fol. 143v, the healing of the paralytic; fol. 206v, the Last Supper; fol. 214v, Peter in the High Priest's courtyard; fol. 222v, picture of the royal family (most of it excised); fol. 244, first Temptation of Christ; fol. 244v, second and third Temptations of Christ; fol. 330, Christ with the rich young ruler; fols. 332, 338, 340, drawing in the margins, copies of missing panels?; fol. 353v, Christ and the Pharisees (partly excised); fol. 419, the Pharisees talking to the blind youth who has been healed.
Most pages have marginal decorations of birds (300 according to Hovsepian's description), flowers, and small, highly decorated carpets (56).
Bibliography: Bogharian, *Grand Catalogue*, VIII (1977), 245ff.; Mekhitarian, *Cat. Exh. Jerusalem 1969*, No. 2, p. 20; Der Nersessian, *L'Art Arménien*, 109–114, figs. 75–77; Bogharian, in *Sion*, (1968), 70–72.

Figures 49–53
The Melitene Gospel of 1041
Four Gospels, Armenia 1041.
Jerusalem ms. 3624, Treasury of St. James 116
General data: medium vellum, 337 folios, 42.5 × 11 × 3.1 cm. Written in large *erkathagir* script in black ink, 19 lines in two columns. In a bad state of preservation. Bound in brown leather over wooden boards. On the front cover it is studded with many gold crosses, some with the crucified Christ; in the center a crucifixion flanked by Mary and John and surrounded by angels. Back cover with thin gold foil stamped with crucifixions, angels, and flowers round a large central rosette of filigree and enamel. Inscribed on the back cover with the date 1571, and on repoussé silver clasp with A.D. 1788.
Colophons: fol. 337: Copied by the married priest (*k'ahanay*) Samuel in 1041, during the reign of the Catholicos Petros I (1019–1054) and Michael (IV, the Byzantine Emperor), when John (Smbat III) died and was succeeded by his nephew Gagik (1042, sic!). No donor's name or painters are mentioned.
History: fol. 337: Undated note in *bolorgir* script states that it was rebound in Melitene in the village of Yamus by Gregory of Khrich.
fol. 71: A pencil note in the margin indicates that the manuscript was in Jerusalem by 1849.
Decoration: fully arcaded pages: fols. 1–1v, letter of Eusebius; fols. 2–5v, canon tables. Full-page Christological illustrations along the page, painted on the vellum ground with wash colors and thinly framed: fol. 6, Annunciation and Visitation; 6v, Nativity of Jesus and the Child being washed, Adoration of the angels and shepherds and of the Magi. 7, Presentation in the Temple and Baptism of Christ; 7v, Transfiguration and Raising of Lazarus; 8, Entry into Jerusalem; 8v, Last Supper; 9, Betrayal and Arrest of Christ; 9v, Crucifixion and Deposition; 10, Burial of Christ and Harrowing of Hell; 10v, Ascension; 11, Four standing Evangelists; 11v, monumental cross.
Bibliography: Izmailova, *L'Iconographie*; *idem*, *Localisation d'un groupe*; *idem*, *Tetraévangile de 1038*; Der Nersessian *Freer Gallery*, 1–6; *idem*, *Walters*, 1–5, pls. 1–11; *idem*, *L'Art Arménien*, 117–122, figs. 82–88.

Figures 54–56
The Shukhr Khandara Gospel
Four Gospels, Shukhr Khandara, Taurus Mountains, 1064.
Jerusalem ms. 1924.
General data: thick vellum, 282 folios, 37 × 29 × 10 cm. Written in large *erkathagir* script in faded black ink, 19 lines in two columns. In a good state of preservation.
Binding: blind-tooled leather binding on wooden boards, including a cross. Remains of silver ornaments.
Colophons: fols. 282–282v copied by Stephanos in Shukhr Khandara between 1064 and 1066, for the monks Yakob, Banereges, and Kyprianos.
History: fol. 281v: Renovated by Martiros of Baberd (no date known) and by Astuadzatur in 1587. Donated to Jerusalem by Arak'el S. Tatean on 10 September, 1880.
Decoration: fully arcaded pages: 1–1v, letter of Eusebius; fols. 2–5v, canon tables. Full-page illustrations along the page, painted on the vellum ground with wash colors, and framed: fol. 6, four standing Evangelists; 6v, Pentecost; 7, Crucifixion; 7v, four standing saints (Evangelists?); 8, monumental cross.
Bibliography: Izmailova, *L'Iconographie*; *idem*, *Localisation d'un groupe*; *idem*, *Tetraévangile de 1038*; Der Nersessian, *Freer Gallery*, 1–6; *idem*, *Walters*, 1–5, pls. 1–11; *idem*, *L'Art Arménien*, 117–122, figs. 82–88; Bogharian, *Grand Catalogue*, VI (1972), 397–401; Mekhitarian, *Cat. Exh. Jerusalem 1969*, No. 3.

Chapter Three: Illuminated Manuscripts in the Kingdom of Cilicia

Figures 57–60
The Theodore Gospel
Four Gospels, Hromkla?, Cilicia, end of the 12th century.
Jerusalem ms. 1796.
General data: vellum, 290 fols., 29 × 19 × 7 cm. Written in angular *erkathagir* script in black ink, 21 lines in two columns. In a good state of preservation.
Binding: blind-tooled leather on wooden boards, which once had silver decorations. Parchment fly-leaves at the end of the manuscript with the text of St. John in round *erkathagir*.
Colophons: fol. 287v (incomplete), scribes Matthew and possibly Vahan. fol. 5v, under the portrait of St. Matthew an elaborate signature of the painter Theodore. fol. 288v, the monk-patron Matthew donating the book to Christ.
History: fol. 2: A copy of an old colophon made in the year 1287. Donated to Jerusalem in 1866 (fol. 1).
Decoration: fully arcaded pages: fols. 2–3, letter of Eusebius; fols. 4v–5 canon tables. Full-page illustrations: portraits of the Four Evangelists, all seated except for St. John (fols. 5v, 91v SS. Peter and Mark, 142v, 225v); fol. 88v, the two Marys meeting an angel at the empty tomb, and meeting the Risen Christ; fol. 288v, Matthew the monk donating the Gospel to Christ. Opening pages of each Gospel decorated with headpiece, decorated initial, Evangelist's symbol and living cross (fols. 6, 92, 142 bis, 226).
Bibliography: Bogharian, *Grand Catalogue*, VI (1972), 145–150, Mekhitarian, *Cat. Exh. Jerusalem 1969*, No. 4; Der Nersessian, *Freer Gallery*, 10–17; *idem*, *L'Art Arménien*, 129f., figs. 90, 91.

Chapter Four: Thirteenth Century Illuminated Manuscripts in Cilicia

Figures 61–63
The Second Constantine Gospel,
Four Gospels, Hromkla, Cilicia, 1260
Jerusalem, ms. 251.
General data: fine vellum, 332 folios, 27 × 19 × 8 cm. Written in fine, regular *bolorgir* in black ink, 21 lines in two columns. The manuscript is in an excellent state of preservation.
Binding: fols. 300–300v: Colophon of binding: It was bound and restored early in the 18th century by Gregory of Constantinople and his son-in-law Jacob, who were sent to Jerusalem by Yovhannes Kolot, Patriarch of Constantinople, at the insistence of Gregory the Chainbearer, Patriarch of Jerusalem (1715–1749). A blind stamp is in the leather binding with the name of Gregory the Chainbearer.
Colophon: fols. 325–327: Copied and illuminated at Hromkla in 1260 by Thoros Roslin for the Catholicos Constantine I of Barjrabert (1221–1267).
History: fol. 13: The manuscript was donated to the Patriarchate of Jerusalem in the year 1540 by a merchant of Istanbul who redeemed it from captivity.
Decoration: fully arcaded pages: fols. 3v–4, letter of Eusebius; 5v–12 (confronting pages only, with blank pages on the reverse), canon tables; 13v, 14, dedication. Illustrations in the lunettes of the arches: 3v, Eusebius; 4, Carpianus; 7v, Micah; 8, Jeremiah; 9v, Daniel; 10, Isaiah; 11v, Zechariah; 12, Jonah; 13v, David; 14, *Deisis*. Four full-page panels as frontispieces to the Gospels, with Christological scenes: 15v, Nativity, Adoration of the Magi, Washing the Christ Child, and St. Matthew (lower left); 102v, St. Mark; 160v, St. Luke; 255v, St. John. Decorated headpieces, zoomorphic initials and marginal ornaments at the beginnings of books (16, 103, 161, 226).

Marginal illustrations: 18, Magi and Joseph's dream; 19, angel; 19v, Massacre of the Innocents; 20, St. John the Baptist; 21v, the Holy Spirit descending on Christ; 22, the devil leaving after the Temptation (Matt. 4:11); 23v, the Sermon on the Mount; 36v, two blind men; 37, Christ blessing; 81, Temple; 163v, angel of the Annunciation; 164, standing Virgin; 168v, Temple.

Sections are indicated by ornamental letters and two lines in gold. *Nomina sacra* and initials in gold.
Bibliography: Bogharian, *Grand Catalogue*, II (1967), 14–23, figs. 1–3; Mekhitarian, *Cat. Exh. Jerusalem 1969*, No. 5, figs. 5, 1–2.

Figures 64, 65
The Leo and Keran Gospel
Four Gospels, Hromkla, Cilicia, 1262.
Jerusalem, St. James ms. 2660, Treasury 105.
General data: vellum, 293 folios, 22 × 17.5 × 8 cm. Written in regular *bolorgir* script in black ink, 19 lines in two columns. In a good state of preservation.
Binding: a later leather binding on wood covered with red velvet with silver border and central cross, and four vellum fly-leaves written in *erkathagir* script.

Colophon: fols. 139, 285–286v, 288: Copied by the priest Avetis and illuminated by Thoros Roslin in the church of St. Saviour and Theotokos at Hromkla, completed in 1262 for the heir apparent Leo (later King Leo II) and his wife Keran, by the order of the Catholicos Constantine I of Barjrabert (1221–1267).
History: owner's colophon (fols. 289–290v) of 1312. Oshin, husband of Zabel and father of Stephan and Gregor.
Decoration: fully arcaded pages: fols. 1v–2, letter of Eusebius; 3v–10, canon tables, with illustrations next to them: standing prophets: 1v, Isaiah (on the left); 2, Micah (on the right), busts in the lunettes of the arches: 1v, Eusebius; 2, Carpianus; 3v, David; 4, Ezekiel; 5v, Jeremiah; 6, Zechariah; 7v, Habakkuk; 8, Jonah; 9v, Joel; 10, Hosea. Full-page panels: Evangelists' portraits: 11v, St. Matthew; 91v, St. Mark; 140v, St. Luke; 225v, St. John; 288, Prince Leo and his wife Keran. Decorated headpieces, zoomorphic initials and marginal ornaments at beginnings of books (12, 92, 141, 226). Marginal text illustrations: 15v, John the Baptist; 55, casting out a demon; 79, Apostles; 80, Last Supper: bread and lamb (Mt. 26:19–20); 107, head of St. John the Baptist; 144, Visitation; 255, the different sheep gathered by one shepherd (John 10:14–16); 260v, Entry into Jerusalem (John 12:12–13); 273v, Judas and soldiers.
Bibliography: Mekhitarian, *Cat. Exh. Jerusalem 1969*, 21, No. 6; Bogharian, *Grand Catalogue*, VIII (1977), 277.

Figures 66–72
The Lady Keran Gospel
Four Gospels, Hromkla, Cilicia, 1265.
Jerusalem, St. James ms. 1956.
General data: fine vellum, I–IV + 345 V–VIII folios, 23.5 × 15.5 × 7 cm. Written in a fine, regular *bolorgir* script in black ink, 19 lines in two columns. Initial letters and *nomina sacra* in gold. Ornamental script at the beginning of major sections. In an excellent state of preservation. Bound in stamped leather over wooden boards, possibly original. Fols. I–IV + V–VIII + fol. 13 are eight fly-leaves and a single leaf taken from a late 12th-century Gospel with a decorated opening page of the Gospel of Mark (Mk. 1:1–2:4) in a round, uncial script, and a full-page portrait of St. Mark (fol. 13v).
Colophon: fols. 342–343v: Copied and illuminated at Hromkla in 1265 A.D. by Thoros Roslin, for Lady Keran, daughter of Constantine of Lampron.
History: the colophon on fol. 344v has been tampered with. It implies that it was donated to Jerusalem in 1432 A.D.
Decoration: fully arcaded pages: fols. 1v–2, letter of Eusebius with, in the lunettes, busts of Eusebius (1v) and Carpianus (2); 3v–10, (confronting pages only, with blank pages on the reverse), canon tables with dedication to Christ (9v–10); 11v–12, dedication to the patrons. Illustrations: full-page, within the text, and marginal: 13v, 12th-century portrait, apparently of St. Mark; 14v, St. Matthew; 21, Baptism; 106v, Crucifixion; 110, Harrowing of Hell; 113v, St. Mark; 140v, Transfiguration; 150v, Entry into Jerusalem; 171, Deposition from the cross; 174v, St. Luke; 177v, margin, Archangel Gabriel; 178, margin, Virgin Mary; 183, lower margin, Presentation in the Temple; 270v, St. John; 310v, Raising of Lazarus.
Bibliography: Bogharian, *Grand Catalogue*, VI (1972), 526–530; Mekhitarian, *Cat. Exh. Jerusalem 1969*, No. 7, 22.

Figures 73–76
The Ritual of Thoros Roslin
Mashtotz (Ritual), Sis, Cilicia, 1266.
Jerusalem, ms. 2027.
General data: vellum, 275 folios third quire, fols. 28–39, unnumbered and on a different type of vellum), 23.5 × 17 × 6 cm. Written in regular *bolorgir* script in black ink, fifteen lines per page. Initials in brown or gold. The volume is well preserved, and restored in some places. Bound in leather over wooden boards, the inner side of the binding in colored linen. The fly-leaves are drawn from a vellum uncial Gospel.
Colophon: fols. 273–273v: Copied at Sis in 1266 by Awetik' *k'ahanay*, and painted by Thoros Roslin for Bishop Vardan Nesepnay.
History: donated to the Cathedral of St. James in 1766.
Decoration: full-page illustrations at major divisions: fol. 1v, Jonah being swallowed by the whale, and Jonah under the gourd; 4v, Crossing the Red Sea; 14v, three Hebrew youths in the fiery furnace; 131v, Baptism of Christ; 224v, burial of St. John the Evangelist. Large headpieces and initials in main sections: fols. 2, 15, 40, 87, 132, 157, 180, 204, 234; and some small ones: 5, 9v, 25v, 62. Some marginal decoration.
Bibliography: Bogharian, *Grand Catalogue*, VI (1974), 59–66.

Chapter Five: Later Thirteenth Century Cilician Illumination

Figures 77, 78
The Queen Keran Gospel
Four Gospels, Sis, Cilicia, 1272.
Jerusalem ms. 2563, Treasury of St. James, No. 8.
General data: medium vellum, 384 folios, 32.5 × 24 × 10 cm. Written in regular *bolorgir* script in black ink with colored capitals, 18 lines in two columns. Very fine state of preservation.
Binding: bound in Jerusalem in 1727 in gold repoussé work. The front cover represents the Crucifixion, and the back the Virgin and Child; on the clasps are the four Evangelists. The binding was made by Abraham in memory of the *vardapets* Gregory and Yovhannes (i.e., Gregory the Chainbearer and Yovhannes Kolot).
Colophons: the manuscript was perhaps written at Sis, in Cilicia in 1272 by the priest Avetis (the name of the painter is not preserved); commissioned by Queen Keran, who gave it to the monastery of Akner.
Decoration: fully arcaded pages: fols. 5v–6, letter of Eusebius; 7v–14, canon tables; 15v–16, dedication. Full- and half-page panels: 17v, St. Matthew; 21, Nativity; 25, Baptism; 69, Transfiguration; 166, Last Supper; 176, three women at the empty tomb; 180v, St. Luke; 184, Annunciation; 191, Presentation in the Temple; 286v, St. John; 333, Raising of Lazarus; 340v, Washing the disciples' feet; 349, Pentecost; 362v, Crucifixion; 368, Doubting Thomas; 380, King Leo II, Queen Keran and their three sons and two daughters; Many marginal illustrations. Decorated headpieces and initials to opening of books (fols. 18, 181, 286); many small decorated initials and marginal ornaments.
Bibliography: Mekhitarian, *Cat. Exh. Jerusalem 1969*, No. 11, pp. 23–24, figs. 11.1–2; Der Nersessian, *L'Art Arménien*, 144–150, figs. 104–107; Azarian, *Cilician Min.*, figs. 107–115.

Figures 79–83
The Second Prince Vasak Gospel
Four Gospels, Cilicia, 1268–1284.
Jerusalem ms. 2568, Treasury of St. James No. 13.
General data: fine vellum, 321 + 1 (fol. 152a) + 1 folios, 26 × 19 × 8 cm. Written in regular *bolorgir* script in black ink which has faded somewhat, 19 lines in two columns. Good state of preservation.
Binding: silver gilt, repoussé and giselé. Executed, according to the colophon (on paper fly-leaf, fol. 322), for *Mahdesi* Margar of Van, his wife Phebrikhan and his son Paul *vardapet* in 1640 A.D. The front cover depicts the Adoration of the Magi and the back cover, the Crucifixion.
Colophons: fol. 320 Dedicated to Prince Vasak (ca. 1240–1285), brother of King Hethum I of Cilicia, and his sons Kostandin and Hethum (born 1260), and revised by Vasak's elder brother, Archbishop John. The names of the scribe and painter are unknown. Executed after the death of Vasak's wife in 1268 and before his death in 1284; because the children depicted are young, it must have been copied closer to 1270. fol. 321v; At the end of the text the date 1537 is found: its import is unclear.
History: fols. 322–322v A second colophon records that one Biniath presented it to the church of St. George in the village of Achpadj in 1691 and that it was restored by one Moses *dpir* in 1695.
Decoration: fully arcaded pages: fols. 2v–3, canon tables. The full-page panels are all on separate, single folios painted on one side and sewn into the quires: 4v, St. Matthew; 8v, Nativity, 12v, Baptism; 88, Crucifixion; 91v, two women at the empty tomb; 94v, St. Mark; 151v, St. Luke; 152v, Annunciation; 159v, Presentation in the Temple; 247, Ascension; 248v, St. John and Prochoros; 295v, washing the disciples' feet; 320, Prince Vasak presented to Christ by the

Virgin. Decorated headpieces and initials at the opening of the Gospels (fols. 5, 95, 152, 249). Many marginal ornaments, some of them text illustrations: fols. 5, tree of Jesse; 154, Annunciation; 155, Visitation; 158 Annunciation to the Shepherds; 160, Simeon and Christ; 161v, Christ teaching in the Temple; 162, Temptation of Christ; 244, Christ and the two disciples on the road to Emmaus; 246, Christ giving thanks over dishes with breed and fishes; 250, Baptism, with the Trinity above.
Bibliography: Mekhitarian, *Cat. Exh. Jerusalem 1969*, 24, No. 12, figs. 12.1–2; Azarian, *Cilician Min.*, figs. 98–106; Der Nersessian, *L'Art Arménien*, 150–153, figs. 108–110.

Figures 84–86
The Erznka Bible
Old and New Testaments, Greater Armenia, Erznka, 1269.
Jerusalem ms. 1925.
General data: heavy paper, 603 folios, 37 × 27 × 13 cm. Written in regular *bolorgir* script in black ink with red capitals, generally 48 lines in two columns. The book is in a good state of preservation, with a few worm holes in the margins. It has been restored with great care.
Binding: blind-tooled leather over wooden boards, apparently of the 17th century, when it was donated to Jerusalem. It is the work of one Arak'el. Fly-leaves of parchment from an uncial Gospel.
Colophons: fols. 105v, 132v, 240v, 573 etc., 298v, 413v. Written at Erznka in 1269 A.D. by the monks Mkhithar, Yakob and Movses; painter unknown; paper made by Mkhithar, *dpir*. The manuscript was written for Sargis, archbishop of Erznka, and his son Yovhannes.
History: colophon fol. 536v and elsewhere. Donated to the Monastery of St. James in Jerusalem by Khodja Zirak of Van in 1626 A.D.
Decoration: thirty-five full- and part-page illustrations, at the opening of most books: fols. 8v, Moses receiving the Law; 9, Moses writing the initial of Genesis, with Christ giving a blessing in the panel; 106, Joshua and the angel; 119, Judges: Othniel, Gideon (seated), and Samson holding the skull of a donkey; 133, Samuel; 241, Job with his friends and wife; seated prophets: 277, Isaiah; 300, Jeremiah; 332, Hosea; 335, Amos; 337v, Micah; 339v, Joel; 341, Obadiah; 341v, Jonah; 342, Nahum; 343, Habakkuk; 344, Zephaniah; 345, Haggai; 346, Zechariah; 349, Malachi; 351v, Psalms: David with a zither-harp; 381, Proverbs, King Solomon; 404, Daniel, Susannah and the Elders; 414v, the Vision of Ezekiel; 415, Ezekiel; 459v, Eusebius; 460, Carpianus; 461v–468, canon tables; 470, St. Matthew; 485, St. Mark; 496, St. Luke; 508, St. John; 526, St. John on Patmos; 541, St. Paul; 575v, St. Luke. All books have decorated headpieces and initials. Some marginal painted and drawn decoration.
Bibliography: Bogharian, *Grand Catalogue*, VI, (1972), 401–416; Mekhitarian, *Cat. Exh. Jerusalem 1969*, No. 10, p. 23, figs. 10.1–2; Murad, *The Old Armenian Translation of the Revelation of John*, Jerusalem, St. James Press, 1905–1911, pp. [336–386] (in Armenian); Der Nersessian, *Bible d'Erznka* (1966), in *Studies*, 603–609, figs. 374–385; *idem, L'Art Arménien*, 218–220, fig. 166.

Chapter Six: Illuminated Manuscripts of the Thirteenth and Fourteenth Centuries in Greater Armenia

Figure 87
Miscellany of 1273
Religious Miscellany, Greater Armenia, Getkay Monastery, 1273.
Jerusalem ms. 1288.
General data: paper, 302 folios, 16.5 × 12 × 6 cm. Written in old *bolorgir* script in black ink, 28–30 lines per page. Well preserved, with some worm damage.
Binding: tooled leather over wooden boards. The parchment fly-leaves are in Greek minuscule script.
Colophons: fol. 300v Copied in Getkay Monastery in Greater Armenia in 1273 by Mekhithar.
History: fol. 302 Restored in 1624.
Decoration: full pages: fol. 1v, cross; fol. 142v, St. Anthony.
Bibliography: Bogharian, *Grand Catalogue*, IV (1969), 483–496.

Figure 88
St. Basil of 1298
St. Basil of Caesarea, *Lives of the Christian Fathers*, Gayl Monastery (E. Anatolia), 1298.
Jerusalem ms. 336.
General data: paper, 284 folios (foliated in two parts, 1–153 and from fol. 154:1–60), 25 × 18 × 6 cm. Written in regular *bolorgir* script in black ink which has faded to rust-color in the first part of the manuscript, generally one column and 20–24 lines per page. Well preserved after restoration.
Binding: tooled leather over wooden boards. Vellum fly-leaves.
Colophons: fols. 285, 287 Copied in the Gayl Monastery in eastern Anatolia in 1298 by the deacon Sargis, the monk Yovhannes, the pontiff (*hayrapet*) Markos, and Eutok's-Evthim, *k'ahanay*.
History: fol. 182 The manuscript was in Jerusalem by 1662 at the latest.
Decoration: fol. 2v One full-page illustration of St. Basil and the deacon-scribe Sargis. Decorated headpieces on fols. 3, 21, 158. Some red initials and capitals.
Bibliography: Bogharian, *Grand Catalogue*, III (1967), 217–221.

Figure 89
The Khatchen Gospel
Four Gospels, (north-east Armenia), Khatchen, 1326.
Jerusalem ms. 1794.
General Data: paper, 382 pages, 30 × 21× 7.5 cm. Written in an old *bolorgir* script, in black ink with first lines in red, 25 lines in two columns. After restoration the manuscript is in a fair state of preservation, having lost a few pages at the start.
Binding: tooled leather over wooden boards.
Colophon: pp. 378 ff. Copied in the land of Khatchen (north-eastern Armenia) in the year 1326 by the monk Thuma, son of Virapshah, for Vanakan *k'ahanay*.
History: the manuscript was brought to Jerusalem at an unknown date.
Decoration: three Evangelists' portraits on separate pages, that of St. Matthew being missing, since a few pages are lost from the first quire: p. 106, St. Mark; p. 176, St. Luke; p. 290, St. John.
Bibliography: Bogharian, *Grand Catalogue*, VI (1972), 140–144.

Figures 90–91
The Thoros of Taron Gospel
Four Gospels, Glatsor, 1321.
Jerusalem ms. 2360.
General data: parchment, 287 folios, 11 × 8.5 × 5.5 cm. Written in *bolorgir* script in black ink with red titles and gold initials and *nomina sacra*, 23 lines in two columns. Damaged by damp, the book has been restored.
Binding: tooled leather over cardboard.
Colophons: fols. 26, 90, 94v, 281v, et alia. Copied and illuminated by Thoros of Taron at the Monastery of Glatsor in 1321.
History: fols. 2v–3v, 283–283v, 284. It was rebound in 1585 by Bishop Karapet in the monastery of Sukhar (or Kharabast) in the canton of Kachperank' (north-east of Lake Van). No record of its subsequent history is preserved.
Decoration: fully arcaded pages: fols. 7v–8v, letter of Eusebius; 9–17v, canon tables. Full-page panels, including Evangelists' portraits, some wrongly bound: fol. 18v, St. Matthew; 21, Nativity; 26, Baptism; 90, Crucifixion; 93, women at the empty tomb; 98v, St. Mark; 119, Transfiguration; 127, Entry into Jerusalem; 146v, St. Luke; 149, Annunciation; 155v, Presentation in the Temple; 220v, St. John and Prochoros; 247v, Last Supper; 253, Raising of Lazarus; 264v, Descent of the Holy Ghost at Pentecost; 282v, Assumption of the Virgin.
Bibliography: Bogharian, *Grand Catalogue*, VII (1974), 510–514.

Figure 92
Isaiah Commentary of 1299
Commentary on Isaiah by George *vardapet* of Skewra (?1245–1301). Copied in Cilicia in 1299, illuminated at Glatsor (?) early 14th century.
Jerusalem ms. 365.
General data: paper, 476 pp., 24 × 17 × 4 cm. Written in regular *bolorgir* script in black ink, generally 33 lines per page. The book is in a good state of preservation.
Binding: blind-tooled leather over wooden boards, worn.
Colophons: pp. 243, 469 Copied, probably in Cilicia, by Vardan for Archbishop Tēr Kostandin.
History: p. 2 Sent to Esayi Ntchetzi in Glatsor by Constantine of Caesarea, and may have been illuminated there.
pp. 469–470 It was in Etchmiadzin in 1489, but its date of arrival in Jerusalem is not recorded.
Decoration: p. 2 One full-page panel of Esayi Nchetzi and his disciples; p. 3, one small headpiece.
Bibliography: Bogharian, *Grand Catalogue*, III (1969), 269–271.

Figures 93–99
The Thonrak Lectionary
Missal Lectionary, Thonrak (canton of Apahunik'), 1331.
Jerusalem ms. 95.
General data: paper, 559 folios, 32 × 24 × 12 cm. Written in regular *bolorgir* script in black ink, 30–31 lines in two columns. The book has been restored and is in a good state of preservation.
Binding: leather over wooden boards. Parchment fly-leaves from an uncial Gospel manuscript.
Colophons: fols. 174v, 228v, 556 Copied in the canton of Apahunik' in Greater Armenia in 1331 by Yovhannes *k'ahanay*, son of Tiratzu *k'ahanay*, for the monk Stephanos, and illuminated by Thoros, either Thoros of Taron, known to have been active in Apahunik' early in the 14th century (see Bogharian, *Grand Catalogue*, I, 297) or another.
History: fols. 3, 228v Restored by Stephanos *mahdesi* (undated). It was presented to Jerusalem by Khodja Shekhichan of Bitlis during the patriarchate of Gregory Paronter (1613–1645).
Decoration: three decorated headpieces (fols. 4, 229, 330). Numerous marginal line drawings illustrating the text, e.g., fols. 38v, Presentation in the Temple; 40v, John the Baptist; 43v, St. Basil; 45v, orant Virgin; 82v, St. George killing the dragon; 94v, St. Joseph; 121, Moses lifting up the Tablets of the Law; 123, the Forty Martyrs of Sebastia; 135v, St. Anthony; 137, the Holy Sepulcher; 142, Daniel's Vision; 172, the Sacrifice of Isaac; 305v, a child cutting down a branch for Christ's Entry into Jerusalem; 344v, two women at the tomb; 361, King Terdat; 423, the Dormition of the Virgin. Many grotesque and fantastic animals and birds in the margins. Ornamental letters drawn in dark red, colored capitals, and marginal ornaments at the beginning of new sections.
Bibliography: Bogharian, *Grand Catalogue*, I (1966), 289–301.

Chapter Seven: Cilician Illumination of the Fourteenth Century

Figures 41, 100, 101
Pidzak Gospel of 1312
Four Gospels, copied and partly decorated in Armenia, Taron, and illuminated by Sargis Pidzak in Cilicia, Sis, 1312.
Jerusalem ms. 1949.
General data: paper, 389 fols. 25 × 17 × 8.5 cm. Written in a regular *bolorgir* script, with capitals and first lines in red ink and the text in black ink, 19 lines in two columns. The book is in a fine state of preservation, having undergone restoration.
Binding: tooled leather over wooden boards. The fly-leaves at the beginning and end have been taken from an uncial Gospel manuscript of the late 10th century, which includes on fol. 390 the decorated Tyche initial and headpiece for the Gospel according to Mark (fig. 41), within which is an inscription in poor mediaeval Greek.
Colophons: fol. 383 Copied at the Monastery of Lazar in Taron in the year 1312 by the monk Arak'el for the monk Nerses, son of Shahinshah. The Evangelists' portraits were added by Sargis Pidzak at Sis, on separate, single vellum pages.
History: fol. 386 The manuscript was presented to Jerusalem in 1386 by a group of visiting priests.
fol. 387v It was rebound in Jerusalem in 1438.
Decoration: fully arcaded pages: fols. 2v–3, letter of Eusebius; 3v–7, canon tables. Full-page portraits of three of the Evangelists (fols. 10v, 116v, and 183v; St. John is missing). Decorated opening pages with headpieces and zoomorphic initials for the four Gospels (fols. 11, 117, 184, 297).
Bibliography: Bogharian, *Grand Catalogue*, VI (1972), 508–511.

Figure 102
Pidzak Bible of 1323
Bible (partial), Sis, Cilicia, 1323.
Jerusalem ms. 1930.
The incomplete Bible contains Psalms, Proverbs, Ecclesiastes, Song of Songs, Wisdom of Solomon, Job, major and minor prophets, and the complete New Testament, including the apocryphal Dormition of St. John. There is much prefatory and homiletic material included.
General data: parchment, 508 fols., 26 × 18 × 10 cm. Written in *bolorgir* script in black ink, 40 lines in two columns, with initials in red. The manuscript is in a fine state of preservation.
Binding: tooled leather over wooden boards; fly-leaves from an uncial manuscript of lives of saints.
Colophons: fol. 495v Copied at Sis in 1323 by Grigor *eretz*, and illuminated (fol. 6v) by Sargis Pidzak, for Bishop Stephanos of Drazark.
History: fol. 496 brought to Jerusalem by Gregory the Chainbearer, Patriarch of Jerusalem, in 1636.
Decoration: fully arcaded pages: fols. 275v–276, letter of Eusebius; 276v–277v, canon tables. Full-page Evangelists' portraits (fols. 279v, 305v, 324v, 352v). Decorated headpieces and capitals for the opening of books, some with illustrations: fol. 6v, David; 275, Eusebius and Carpianus; 437v, St. Paul with St. John the Less and Archbishop Stephanos, the donor. Marginal decoration in red pen-drawing at the opening of some books, some with biblical portraits: fol. 53, Solomon; 91, Job; 109, Isaiah; 148, Amos, 157v, Jonah emerging from the whale; 175, Jeremiah; 222, David; 237v, Ezekiel; 292, the Temple; 316, 318v, Palm Sunday; 320v, a cock; 377v, Pentecost.
Bibliography: Bogharian, *Grand Catalogue*, VI (1972), 433–439; Mekhitarian, *Cat. Exh. Jerusalem 1969*, No. 17, p. 25.

Figures 102a, 103–105
Pidzak Hymnal of 1322
Hymnal, Cilicia, Sis, 1322.
Jerusalem ms. 1644.
General data: parchment, 664 pp., 13 × 9 × 5 cm. Written in regular *bolorgir* script in black ink, 23 lines per page, with red and gold initial letters and first lines. The manuscript is in a good state of preservation.
Binding: tooled leather over boards; fly-leaves of parchment written in Ethiopia.
Colophons: pp. 637 ff. Copied and illuminated in the monastery of Drazark at Sis in 1322 by Sargis *k'ahanay* called *Pidzak* for Thoros *dpir*.
History: p. 656. In the possession of the Monastery of St. James in Jerusalem by 1663.
Decoration: decorated headpieces, pp. 3, 243. Some marginal illustrations and ornamental letters.
Bibliography: Bogharian, *Grand Catalogue*, V (1971), 462–465.

Figures 106, 107
Pidzak Hymnal of 1335
Hymnal, Cilicia, Sis, 1335.
Jerusalem ms. 1578.
General data: parchment, 357 fols., 14 × 10 × 6.5 cm. Written in *bolorgir* script in black ink, 23 lines per page, with red, blue and gold first lines and gold capitals. The book is in a good state of preservation.
Binding: tooled leather over boards. Fols. 335–357 are a later addition.

Colophons: fols. 48v, 93v, 287v, 329v. Copied and illuminated at Sis in 1335 by Sargis *k'ahanay* called *Pidzak*, son of Grigor *k'ahanay*, for Yovhannes, a celibate *k'ahanay*.
History: the date of its arrival in Jerusalem is not recorded.
Decoration: full-page panels: fol. 1v, Annunciation to Joachim and Anne; 120v, women at the empty tomb; 179, birth of John the Baptist. Sixteen marginal illustrations, and decorated initials and headpieces at the opening of each section.
Bibliography: Bogharian, *Grand Catalogue*, V (1971), 359–362; Mekhitarian, *Cat. Exh. Jerusalem 1969*, No. 19, p. 26.

Figures 108–111
Queen Mariun Gospel
Four Gospels, Cilicia, Sis, 1346
Jerusalem ms. 1973.
General data: paper, 276 fols., 17 × 12 × 6.5 cm. Written in *bolorgir* script in black ink with red initials, 23 lines in two columns. The book is in a fairly good state of preservation, with some worm damage on a few pages.
Binding: tooled leather over wooden boards. Fly leaves from an uncial Gospel manuscript.
Colophons: fol. 273 Copied at Sis in 1346 by Nerses, the scribe and donor, and (fols. 77v, 258) illuminated by the painter Sargis Pidzak as a gift for Mariun, Queen of the Armenians.
fol. 269v An older colophon recopied in this manuscript mentions its exemplar as being the copy of "Saint Sahak the Translator".
History: fol. 275 Restored by the cleric Leo in 1392; fol. 265, given to the Church of Golgotha in Jerusalem in 1396 by Awshin (Oshin).
Decoration: full-page panels on single vellum leaves depict: fol. 8v, Nativity; 77v, Crucifixion; 79v, Burial; 81, Resurrection; 106, Transfiguration; 114, Entry into Jerusalem; 134, Dormition of the Virgin; 208v, Ascension of Christ; 258v, Descent from the Cross. Four headpieces: fols. 9, 84, 132, 210.
Bibliography: Bogharian, *Grand Catalogue*, VI (1972), 553–557; Mekhitarian, *Cat. Exh. Jerusalem 1969*, No. 20, p. 26, figs. 20:1–2. Der Nersessian, *L'Art Arménien*, 161–2, figs. 118–9.

Chapter Eight: Later Armenian Manuscript Illumination

Figures 112, 113
The Thmok' Hymnal
Hymnal, Thmok' (North Armenia), 1426.
Jerusalem ms. 1534.
General data: paper, except for the first quire of parchment, XXXVI + 710 pp., 14 × 9 × 6 cm. Written in a regular *bolorgir* script in black ink, 21 lines per page, with red titles and red and gold first lines. The book is in a good state of preservation, although there is some worm damage, particularly in the margins.
Binding: tooled leather over boards; the back is split. Four fly-leaves of parchment, written in Latin (pp. XXIX–XXXII and 707–710).
Colophon: pp. 679ff. Copied in the fortress of Thmok' in 1426 by Yovhannes of Ani, a Bishop, and illuminated by the monk Yovhannes, for the monk Astuadzatur.
History: the date of its accession to the Monastery of St. James in Jerusalem is unknown.
Decoration: one full-page panel: p. 254, women at the tomb, and the Harrowing of Hell. Thirty-five marginal text illustrations and decorated initials. Two headpieces (pp. 1, 255).
Bibliography: Bogharian, *Grand Catalogue*, V (1971), 288–290.

Figure 114
The Epistles of 1399
Commentary on the Catholic Epistles by Sargis *vardapet* (1154), Jerusalem, 1399.
Jerusalem ms.7
General data: heavy paper, polished by Sahak *abeghay*, XII + 1126 pp.
42 × 30 × 13 cm. Written in large *bolorgir* script in black ink, 34 lines in two columns. The book is in a good state of preservation.
Binding: tooled leather over boards. The fly-leaves are from an angular *erkathagir* manuscript of the *Djarĕntir* (Collection of Homilies).
Colophon: pp. 1119ff. Copied in St. James, Jerusalem, in 1399 by its owner, Sargis, Bishop of Jerusalem (1393–1412).
History: the manuscript apparently remained in Jerusalem from 1399; other colophons testify that it was there from 1733 onwards.
Decoration: on p. II one full-page panel painting of Sargis *vardapet* wearing a cowl. P. 1, a major headpiece and ornamental title page; other headpieces and marginal ornaments.
Bibliography: Bogharian, *Grand Catalogue*, I (1966), 61–66.

Figures 115, 116
St. Saviour Gospel of 1475
Four Gospels, Jerusalem, 1475.
Jerusalem ms. 1943.
General data: paper, 688 pages, 26.5 × 18 × 7.5 cm. Written in a regular *bolorgir* script, in black ink, 19 lines in two columns, with red and blue first lines and red initials. The book is in a fairly good state of preservation.
Binding: leather over boards. The fly-leaves are parchment, from an *erkathagir* Gospel manuscript with some decoration.
Colophon: pp. 675 ff. Copied in St. Saviour's Church in Jerusalem in 1475 by the scribe Solomon *abeghay*, and illuminated by Yovhannes, for Mekhithar *abeghay* of Heshad.
History: the manuscript seems to have remained in Jerusalem.
Decoration: fully arcaded pages: pp. 12–13, Eusebius' letter, with bust portraits of Eusebius and Carpianus. pp. 16–17, 20–21, 24–25, 28–29, canon tables. Full-page panels: p. 38, Christ and Mekhithar *abeghay*; 40, St. Matthew; 218, St. Mark; 332, St. Luke; 522, St. John and Prochoros. Headpieces on pp. 41, 219, 333, 523.
Bibliography: Bogharian, *Grand Catalogue*, VI (1972), 488–491.

Figures 117–119
The Caffa Lives of the Fathers
Lives of the Fathers, Caffa (Crimea), Monastery of St. Anthony, 1430.
Jerusalem ms. 285.
General data: paper, 823 pp., 27 × 18 × 9 cm. Written in a transitional *bolorgir-notragir* script in black ink, with the titles and saints' names in red, 37 lines in two columns. The book is in a fairly good state of preservation. It has been repaired and there is still some worm damage.
Binding: leather over boards.
Colophons: pp. 757 ff. Compiled from different texts, copied and illuminated at the monastery of St. Anthony in Caffa (Crimea) in 1430 by Thaddeus *abeghay* Avramentz. No patron is mentioned. The paper was prepared by one Astuadzatur.
History: donated to the Church of St. Saviour in Jerusalem in 1443 by Lazar of Crimea. p. 823: Taken to Amida in 1615 to be copied and was repaired there (London, British Library Add. 27301), and subsequently returned to Jerusalem.
Decoration: 38 full- or part-page paintings from the lives of the various Fathers, some damaged. There are almost 500 small illustrations in the text, chiefly of busts of and episodes relating to the various saints; and one major headpiece on p. 15. Each section is marked by a small headpiece and a marginal ornament. This manuscript was the exemplar from which a number of copies of this work were made (see mss. 23, 228, 293, 971, and B.L. Add. 27301).
Bibliography: Bogharian, *Grand Catalogue*, II (1967), 107–112, figs. 8, 9; Conybeare, *Catalogue Bri. Mus.*, No. 88, ms. Add. 27301, pp. 209–215.

Figure 120
The 1623 Lives of the Fathers
Lives of the Fathers, Jerusalem?, 1623.
Jerusalem ms. 971.
General data: paper, 788 pp., 20 × 14 × 5 cm. Written in the *notragir* script in black ink with titles, initial lines and letters in red, 36 lines in two columns. The book is in a fair state of preservation.
Binding: tooled leather over boards by Daniel of Varag.
Colophons: Copied in 1623 (the name of the scribe and place of execution are not preserved) and illuminated by Kirakos, perhaps in Jerusalem, as it was commissioned by Gregory Paronter, Patriarch of Jerusalem, who donated it to the Monastery of St. James, Jerusalem.
Decoration: 36 full- and part-page panels, and about 260 marginal illustrations of some lives of saints. Pp. 11, 17, two headpieces; decorated letters and marginal ornaments at the beginning of each chapter.
Bibliography: Bogharian, *Grand Catalogue*, III (1968), 545–548, figs. 19–21.

Figures 121, 122
The Aleppo Lives of the Fathers
Lives of the Fathers, Aleppo, 1625.
Jerusalem ms. 23.
General data: paper, ii + 648 pp., 37 × 26 × 8 cm. Written in *notragir* script in black ink, with many words, chiefly *nomina sacra* and saints' names, in red, 39 lines in two columns. The book is moderately well-preserved; the beginning and a few middle pages have been lost.
Binding: leather over boards.
Colophons: pp. 641–646 Copied in Aleppo in 1625 by Mkrtich of Poland, son of Gregory, and illuminated by Vardan for *Paron* Sanos and his son *Paron* Sk'antar, who donated it to St. James in Jerusalem.
Decoration: 34 full- or part-page panels and about 500 marginal illustrations of the lives of the various saints. Decorated initials to openings of sections.
Bibliography: Bogharian, *Grand Catalogue*, I (1966), 116–125, figs. 10, 11.

Figures 123, 124
The 1651 Lives of the Fathers
Lives of the Fathers, Jerusalem 1651.
Jerusalem ms. 228.
General data: paper, 405 fols., 28 × 21 × 7 cm. Written in *bolorgir* with late characteristics, in black ink except for titles and some of the chapter headings and proper names, which are in red, 39 lines in two columns. The book is in a good state of preservation.
Binding: leather over wooden boards, with a cross tooled on it.
Colophons: fols. 402 ff. Copied in Jerusalem in 1651 by Yovhannes *k'ahanay* of Mokk', son of Melk'iseth; illuminated and bound by Yovhannes of Khizan; commissioned by the scribe's uncle, Yovhannes *abeghay* of Mokk', son of Basharath, and donated by him to the Monastery of St. James in Jerusalem.
History: a number of later colophons attest to its continued presence in Jerusalem.
Decoration: 35 full- or part-page panels, and numerous marginal illustrations of the lives of various saints. Fol. 5, decorated headpiece. Decorated initials at openings of sections.
Bibliography: Bogharian, *Grand Catalogue*, I (1966), 612–623, figs. 65, 66.

Figures 125, 126
Hymnal of Van, 1529
Hymnal, Van, 1529.
Jerusalem ms. 1667.
General data: parchment, 358 fols., 13 × 8 × 5.5 cm. Written in *bolorgir* script in black ink with rubrics in red and initial lines and letters in gold, 23 lines per page. The book is in a good state of preservation.
Binding: tooled leather over boards.
Colophon: fols. 337 ff. Copied at Van in 1529 by Zak'aria *eretz*. The name of the painter is not known; commissioned by Yovhannes *vardapet*.
History: the date of the accession to the Monastery of St. James in Jerusalem is unknown.
Decoration: two cycles of full-page panels are inserted next to the relevant text. The first comprises nine scenes and is original. The second was inserted at a later date and is painted on different, smaller vellum leaves. The first series is: fols. 3, Annunciation to Joachim and Anne; 37v, Presentation in the Temple; 58v, Adam and Eve; 130v, the women at the empty tomb; 165v, Ascension of Christ; 177v, Pentecost; 237v, Vision of Ezekiel; 259v, the Saints of Avarayr; 338, St. Nikolayos (?). The second series comprises: between fols. 15 and 16, the Nativity; 104–105, the Raising of Lazarus; 106–107, floral ornament; 115, the Last Supper; 128–129, The Entombment; 326v, Jesus Christ; 327, Mary Theotokos; 349v, Coronation of the Virgin. Decorated headpieces for the main sections (fols. 4, 131, 178, 221v); decorated letters and marginal decorations at the beginning of each canon.
Bibliography: Bogharian, *Grand Catalogue*, V (1971), 519–522.

Figures 127, 128
The Alexander Romance of 1536
Armenian translation of Pseudo-Callisthenes' *Alexander Romance*, with verses (*Kaffas*) by Grigoris, Catholicos of Aghthamar, followed by the *History of Abiqar*. Village of Varag, near Van, 1535–36.
Jerusalem ms. 473.
General data: heavy paper, 176 fols., 22.5 × 16 × 6 cm. Written in a regular *bolorgir* script in black ink, with red titles and verse and some red capitals, generally 29 lines per page. The book is in a good state of preservation.
Binding: leather over boards.
Colophons: copied in Varag in 1536 by Markarē *abeghay* of Ardjesh, and painted by Grigoris, Catholicos of Aghthamar.
History: the date of its accession to the Monastery of St. James is unknown.
Decoration: full- or part-page text illustrations: fols. 2, Nectanebos consulting the stars; 5v, a bird laying an egg in Philip's lap; 6v, Philip and Olympias; 7v, Philip and the dragon; 9, Olympias and Nectanebos; 10v, bull-headed Bucephalus, the mythical man-eating horse; 11, Nectanebos and Alexander; 12, Alexander smiting Nectanebos in the breast; 12v, Nectanebos in his coffin being buried by Alexander; 14, Aristotle and disciples; 16, Alexander riding a red horse; 17, Nectanebos adoring at the birth of Alexander (wrongly bound here); 19, Alexander killing Nicolaos, King of the Akarnanians; 19v, Alexander before Zeus Olympus; 21, Alexander embracing his reconciled parents; 22, Philip enthroned, and Darius; 23, Pausianos wounding Philip; 23v, Alexander killing Pausianos; 25v, Alexander being crowned; 29, building Alexandria; 31, Alexander praying in the Serapeum; 33, Alexander on horseback; 53, the singer Ismēnias before Alexander. Space has been left for other paintings, which were never executed. Fol. 1, decorated headpiece.
Bibliography: Bogharian, *Grand Catalogue*, II (1967), 460–66, figs. 24–26; Mekhitarian, *Cat. Exh. Jerusalem 1969*, No. 27, 28–29, figs. 27:1, 2; Der Nersessian, *Model II* (1969) in *Studies*, pp. 670–671, figs. 433, 434.

Figures 129, 130
Sargis of Khizan's Jerusalem Gospel
Four Gospels, Jerusalem, 1572
Jerusalem ms. 868
General data: paper, 285 fols., 20 × 14 × 7 cm. Written in a regular *bolorgir* script in black ink, with titles, initial lines and letters in red, 21 lines in two columns. The manuscript is in an excellent state of preservation.
Binding: tooled leather over boards.
Colophon: fols. 282–284 Copied and illuminated in the Monastery of St. James in Jerusalem in 1527 by Sargis *k'ahanay* of Khizan, son of Karapet *k'ahanay* for Herapet, celibate *k'ahanay*, son of Nerses.
History: the patron donated it to the Monastery of St. James, Jerusalem.
Decoration: fols. 2v–9, fully arcaded pages with the letter of Eusebius and ten canon tables; fol. 141v, a full-page panel of St. Luke; fols. 13, 91, 142, 223, four major headpieces. Decorated marginal ornaments and red pen-drawn ornamental letters at the opening of sections.
Bibliography: Bogharian, *Grand Catalogue*, III (1968), 366–368, figs. 7–9.

Figures 131, 137
Sargis and Kirakos Hymnal
Hymnal, copied and decorated in Pazentz (Khizan), 1553, panels painted in Khizan, 1623.
Jerusalem ms. 1594.
General data: paper, 764 pp., 14 × 9 × 7 cm. Written in *bolorgir* script in black ink, except for initial letters and lines in red, 22 lines per page. In a fair state of preservation, and has been restored.
Binding: tooled leather over boards.
Colophon: pp. 375 ff. Copied by Stephanos *k'ahanay* in the village of Pazentz in 1553, and decorated there by Sargis of Khizan, the father of the artist-scribes Martyros and Sargis, for Karapet *k'ahanay*. The full-page panels by Kirakos were added in 1623 (see p. 6, under the painting; Bogharian notes that they are on a different type of paper from the rest of the manuscript).
History: the date of accession to the Monastery of St. James is not recorded.
Decoration: two full-page paintings: p. 6, Joachim and Anne; p. 372, Pentecost. Three decorated headpieces (pp. 7, 275, 373). Initial words and marginal ornaments at the opening of canons.
Bibliography: Bogharian, *Grand Catalogue*, V (1971), 384–386, figs. 30, 31.

Figures 132, 133
The earliest Martyros Khizantzi Gantsaran
Gantsaran (religious poems), Khlath and Theghway, 1575.
Jerusalem ms. 135.
General data: paper, 475 fols., 30 × 20 × 13 cm. Written in a regular *bolorgir* script in black ink with initial letters and lines in red, 25 lines per page in two columns. In an excellent state of preservation.
Binding: tooled leather over wooden boards.

Colophons: fols. 470v ff. Copied partly in the village of Soghadz, Khlath, and partly in the monastery of Theghway Vank' in 1575 by Karapet of Soghadz; and (fol. 3v) illuminated by Martyros, probably the son of Sargis Khizantzi, for Martyros *abeghay*.
History: Donated to the Monastery of St. James in Jerusalem by the patron.
Decoration: eight full-page panels: fols. 3, sign of the cross; 228v, floral ornament; 254v, Crucifixion; 271v, Annunciation; 287v, Harrowing of Hell; 322v, Ascension; 379v, Transfiguration; 394v, Dormition of the Virgin. Twenty-three marginal text illustrations and eight headpieces (fols. 4, 79, 229, 279, 330, 380, 395, 417). Decorated initials and marginal ornaments.
Bibliography: Bogharian, *Grand Catalogue*, I (1966), 372–403, figs. 51–60.

Figures 134, 135
Sargis Khizantzi the Younger's Hymnal of 1601
Hymnal, Khizan, 1601.
Jerusalem ms. 1663.
General data: paper, 864 pp., 13 × 8.5 × 6 cm. Written in *bolorgir* script in black ink, rubrics lines in red, initial lines in gold and blue, initial letters and *nomina sacra* in gold, 21 lines per page. In a good state of preservation.
Binding: tooled leather over boards. The fly-leaves are parchment, drawn from an *erkathagir* Gospel manuscript.
Colophon: pp. 843 ff. Copied and illuminated in Khizan in 1601 by the scribe and illuminator, Sargis *k'ahanay* the Younger, son of Sargis Khizantzi, for Melk'izeth *k'ahanay*.
History: pp. 432–433 Presented to the Monastery of St. James in Jerusalem by Sargis, a monk, in 1609.
Decoration: 45 full-page panels: pp. 10, Annunciation to Joachim and Anne; 23, Virgin and Child; 26, Annunciation 35, Nativity; 39, Adoration of the Magi; 60, Tree of Jesse; 70, Circumcision; 72, Baptism; 87, Presentation in the Temple; 110, Jesus receiving the keys of the kingdom of heaven; 131, Jonah cast into the sea; 132, Jonah issuing from the sea monster; 138, temptation of Adam and Eve; 164, the three Children in the Fiery Furnace; 170, Noah after the Flood; 193, Dives, the rich man, and Lazarus, the beggar; 216, Temptation of Christ; 248, Ancient of Days supported by the Four Creatures; 263, Raising of Lazarus; 273, Adam and Eve in the Garden of Eden; 278, the Ten Virgins; 285, Jesus before Pilate; 287, washing the feet; 290, the Last Supper; 296, Peter's Denial; 297, the Betrayal; 317, the Entombment; 324, the women at the empty tomb; 342, Doubting Thomas; 405, Ascension; 434, Pentecost; 464, Visitation; 512, Transfiguration; 531, Dormition of the Virgin; 554, the Second Coming of Christ in the Sign of the Cross; 595, Ezekiel's Vision; 611, Massacre of the Innocents at Bethlehem; 615, the Heavenly Host; 628, Martyrdom of St. Ignatius; 648, Battle of Avarayr; 730, Saints; 739, Resurrection of the Dead; 797, the Risen Christ; 814, the Egyptians drowning; 815, the Israelites crossing the Red Sea. Four major decorated headpieces (pp. 11, 325, 435, 555), initials and marginal ornaments.
Bibliography: Bogharian, *Grand Catalogue*, V (1971), 508–513, figs. 49–52.

Figure 136
The Sargis and Kirakos Khizantzi Hymnal of 1602
Hymnal, Khizan, 1602.
Jerusalem ms. 1460.
General data: paper, 760 pp., 15 × 10 × 5.5 cm. Written in *bolorgir* script in black ink with red initials, rubrics and first lines, 23 lines per page. Fairly well preserved, with some worm damage.
Binding: tooled leather over boards. Fly-leaves from a small *erkathagir* Gospel in vellum.
Colophon: pp. 741 ff. Copied in Khizan in 1602 by the scribe, painter, and donor, Sargis *k'ahanay* Khizantzi the Younger; illuminated by Kirakos *k'ahanay* of Khizan.
History: the date of its accession to the Monastery of St. James is unknown.
Decoration: four full-page panels: pp. 10 Annunciation to Joachim and Anne; 278, Harrowing of Hell; 376, Pentecost; 484, Sign of the Cross. Four major headpieces (pp. 11, 279, 377, 485). Decorated letters and marginal ornaments.
Bibliography: Bogharian, *Grand Catalogue*, V (1971), 169–172, figs. 8–11.

Figure 138
Khatchatur Menologium of 1591
Menologium, Jerusalem, 1591.
Jerusalem ms. 1920.
General data: paper, 1212 pages, 37 × 27 × 15 cm. Written in *bolorgir* script in black ink, with titles and initial letters in red, 37 lines in two columns. In a fair state of preservation, having been restored.
Binding: tooled leather over wooden boards.
Colophon: Copied in the Cathedral of St. James, Jerusalem, in 1591 by Martiros *k'ahanay* of Khizan (first part), his brother, Sargis of Khizan (second part), and Khatchatur *k'ahanay* of Khizan (third part); and illuminated by the latter, for the monk Yakob and David, Archbishop and later Patriarch of Jerusalem.
History: pp. 1207–8 Restored a number of times, in Jerusalem.
Decoration: one full-page panel of the Nativity (p. 498), and some marginal text illustrations. P. 796, a sketch of the Risen Christ. Two major headpieces (pp. 5, 449). Decorated initials and marginal ornaments at the beginnings of sections.
Bibliography: Bogharian, *Grand Catalogue*, VI (1972), 376–383.

Figures 139–141
The New Julfa Bible with illustrations in the De Bry Recension
Old and New Testament and some apocryphal books, Isfahan, 1643–46.
Jerusalem ms. 1934.
General data: vellum, 907 fols., 25 × 18 × 15 cm. Written in a regular *bolorgir* script in black ink, with titles in red, within a red frame, and initial lines in gold and blue, 46 lines in two columns. In an excellent state of preservation.
Binding: tooled leather over boards. Restored in 1968.
Colophon: Copied in Isfahan in 1643–46 by Stephanos, son of Martiros and pupil of Khatchatur *vardapet*; and proof-read by Grigor *k'ahanay*, for Khodja Safar Amirasathentz of New Julfa. The name of the artist is not mentioned.
History: the date of accession to the Monastery of St. James in Jerusalem is not recorded.
Decoration: 27 full-page panels: fols. 11, title page; 12v, God creating the World, Adam and Eve in Paradise, the Fall, Noah sending animals into the Ark; 13, Abraham and the three Angels, the Sacrifice of Isaac, Jacob's Dream, Crossing the Red Sea; 14v, Moses receiving the Law, gathering manna and quails, marching round the walls of Jericho; 199v, Eli and Hannah; 425v, David rescuing a sheep from a lion, Saul enthroned, David and Goliath, David sacrificing to stop the plague; 552v, Jonah embarking, being thrown into the mouth of a whale, being spewed out by the whale, sitting under the gourd; 658v, Eusebius; 659, Carpianus; 668v, St. Matthew; 691v, St. Mark; 702v, St. Luke; 723v, St. John and Prochorus; 837, the Seven Candlesticks; 839, the Seven Churches; 839v, Twenty-four Elders; 840, the Four Horsemen; 841, Angels with trumpets; 841v, Third Trumpet and Falling of the Star; 842v, Angel with the Book; 843v, Dragon attempting to kill the woman's child; 844, Dragon and worshippers; 845v, Angels pouring out wrath; 846v, Babylon seated on the Beast; 848, Dragon in the Lake of Fire; 848v, Satan in the Abyss; 849, the Heavenly Jerusalem. Nine major headpieces. Ornamental and marginal letters at the beginning of chapters and decoration at the start of books.
Bibliography: Bogharian, *Grand Catalogue*, VI (1972), 461–469; Stone, *Testament of Levi*, 16–17.

Figure 142
The New Julfa Bible of 1620
Old and New Testaments, Istanbul, 1620.
Jerusalem ms. 428.
General data: vellum, 543 fols., 23 × 17 × 7 cm. Written in regular *bolorgir* script in black ink, 48 lines in two columns. The titles and capitals are in red ink, first lines in red and gold. The book is in an excellent state of preservation.
Binding: leather over boards.
Colophons: copied in Istanbul in 1620 by Yakob *dpir*, and illuminated by Khatchatur *abeghay* of Isfahan, who was invited to Istanbul by a patron whose name has been effaced.
History: the date of its transfer to Jerusalem is unknown.
Decoration: two full-page panels, fols. 8v, Creation cycle; 260v. Six decorated major headpieces, and at the beginning of each book there are decorated letters, small headpieces and marginal ornaments.
Bibliography: Bogharian, *Grand Catalogue*, II (1967), 382–387, figs. 21, 22, Stone, *Testament of Levi*, 14.

Figure 143
The New Julfa Bible of 1640
Old and New Testaments, Istanbul(?), 1640
Jerusalem ms. 1932

General data: parchment, 567 fols., 23 × 17 × 8.5 cm. Written in a small, regular *bolorgir* script in black ink, 50 lines in two columns. Titles are in red and first lines and initial letters usually in gold. The book is in an excellent state of preservation.
Binding: tooled leather over boards.
Colophons: copied perhaps in Istanbul, around 1640 by Mik'ayel, for Astuadzatur *vardapet*, son of Lukas. The name of the painter is unknown.
Decoration: 15 full- or part-page panels: fols. 11v, Moses; 14v, Creation cycle; 54v, Moses before the Lord; 65v, the Lord speaking with Moses; 98v, Joshua; 121, Eli and Hannah; 135, David and messenger; 147, David and Abishag; 161v, Ahaziah and the Soothsayers; 184v, God appearing to Solomon; 276v, David; 308v, Solomon the Wise; 445, Eusebius and Carpianus; 449v, the Four Evangelists; 530v, Paul. Fols. 445v–447, arcaded canon tables. Fols. 15, 450, two main headpieces. Marginal ornaments and decorated letters at the beginning of chapters.
Bibliography: Bogharian, *Grand Catalogue*, VI (1972), 444–448.

Figure 144
An Early Seventeenth-century New Julfa Bible
Old and New Testament with Apocryphal Books, Istanbul(?) or New Julfa (?), early 17th century.
Jerusalem ms. 501.
General data: vellum, 579 fols., 23 × 17 × 8 cm. Written in regular *bolorgir* script in black ink, with initial lines in gold uncial script and second lines in red, initials generally red, 48 lines in two columns. The book is in an excellent state of preservation.
Binding: leather over boards.
Colophon: the colophon has not survived. Perhaps copied and illuminated in New Julfa or in Istanbul in the early 17th century, since the manuscript is very similar to Jerusalem ms. 428 of 1620 (fig. 142) (see Bogharian below).
History: fol. 3 The manuscript was presented to the Monastery of St. James in 1804, having been brought from India.
Decoration: full- and part-page panels: fols. 4v, Eli and Hannah; 7v, Creation cycle; 47v, the drowning of the Egyptians in the Red Sea; 102v, Moses, Aaron and the Israelites; 156, David mourning Saul's death; 168v, King David; 207v, King Solomon; 233v, King Artaxerxes and Nehemiah; 449v, St. Matthew; 474v, St. Luke; 488, St. John and Prochoros. Some major and minor headpieces with decorated initials at the beginning of books and sections.
Bibliography: Bogharian, *Grand Catalogue*, II (1967), 495–496, fig. 27; Stone, *Testament of Levi*, 15.

Figure 145
The New Julfa Bible of 1645
Old and New Testaments with Apocryphal books. New Julfa, 1645.
Jerusalem ms. 1933.
General data: paper, 593 fols., 27 × 20 × 10 cm. Written in regular *bolorgir* script in black ink, with titles and chapter headings in red and initials in gold uncials, 50 lines in two columns. The book is in an excellent state of preservation.
Binding: tooled leather over boards, with a leather strap.
Colophon: fols. 587–590 Copied in New Julfa (Isfahan) in 1645 by Astuadzatur *dpir*, and illuminated by Hayrapet *dpir*, for Zohrab of Erevan and his son Nikoghayos, who donated it to the Monastery of St. James in 1661.
Decoration: 26 full-page panels: fols. 7v, Creation cycle; 116v, Eli and Hannah; 270v, Job, his wife and two friends; 281v, King David; 306v, King Solomon; 422v, Eusebius; 423, Carpianus; 428v, St. Matthew; 442v, St. Mark; 452v, St. Luke; 466v, St. John and Prochorus; 503v, Paul and Theophilus; Apocalypse cycle: 536, the Seven Candlesticks; 537, the Seven Churches; 537v, the Twenty-four Elders offering their crowns; 538, the Four Horsemen; 538v, Angels blowing trumpets; 539, the Third Trumpet and Falling Star; 539v, Angel opening the book; 540, the Dragon and the Woman; 540v, the Dragon with his worshippers; 541v, Angels with plates; 542, the Babylonian whore seated on the Dragon; 543, the Dragon in the Fiery Lake; 543v, Satan thrown into the Abyss; 544, the Heavenly Jerusalem. Decorated headpieces, ornamental letters and marginal ornaments at the beginning of each book.
Bibliography: Bogharian, *Grand Catalogue*, VI (1972), 448–461; Stone, *Testament of Levi*, 16.

Chapter Nine: Armenian Printed Books and Late Illumination

Figures 146, 147
The Oskan Bible
Old and New Testaments, Amsterdam, 1666.
Gulbenkian Library, Rare Book Room.
The first Bible printed in Armenian, edited by Oskan of Erevan, who printed it in Amsterdam at the St. Etchmiadzin and St. Sargis Press, 1666. VIII + 628 + 874 pp. The book is decorated with numerous engravings by the Dutch artist Christoffel van Sichem.
Bibliography: Anasian, *Early Armenian Printings*, No. 56. Special issues of the journals *Sion* and *Etchmiadzin* devoted to this edition were published in 1966.

Figure 148
The Heavenly Jerusalem
The Armenian Patriarchate Printing Press.
Wood block cut after the Oskan Bible of 1666, p. 716. 17th century. The Armenian Patriarchate Printing Press.

Figure 149
Armenian Map of the World
Amsterdam, 1695.
The Gulbenkian Library. 118 × 149 cm.
Earliest printing by Hadrianus Petrus Damianus Schoonbeck.

Figure 150
The First Book printed in Armenian
Venice, 1512.
The St. Thoros Library.
It was produced at the press of the otherwise unknown Yakob the Sinful in Venice in the year 1512, and contains an ecclesiastical calendar entitled *Parzatumar Hayotz*, the Psalms in verse form, and a prayer book.

Figure 151
Lectionary
Printed in Venice in 1686.
Gulbenkian Library, Rare Book Room.
Printed at the press of Khodja Sakrat of Julfa and Thaddeos *eretz* in 1686. VIII + 9–20 + 998 + 204 (= 1222) pp., 43 × 29 cm. Decorated by some full-page engravings, painted by hand.
Bibliography: Anasian, *Early Armenian Printings*, No. 139; A. Kalaydjian, "Catalogue and Colophons of Old Armenian Printed Books in the Gulbenkian Library, Jerusalem," *Sion* 41 (1967), 338–339, no. 51.

Figures 152, 153
The Istanbul Bible of 1653
Old and New Testaments with Apocryphal Books, Istanbul, 1653.
Jerusalem ms. 1927.
General data: vellum, 495 fols., 26 × 18 × 9 cm. Written in regular *bolorgir* script in black ink with red titles, red and gold initial lines, gold initial letters and *nomina sacra*, generally 53 lines in two columns. The manuscript is in a fine state of preservation.
Binding: tooled leather over wooden boards.
Colophon: fols. 491 ff. Copied in Istanbul in 1653 by Astuadzatur *dpir* and illuminated by Lazar *mahdesi*, for Khatchatur *vardapet* of Atish.
History: the date of its accession to the Monastery of St. James in Jerusalem is unknown.
Decoration: many full- and half-page panels: fols. 8v, 9, 9v, Creation cycle; 11v, Cain and Abel; 12v, 13v, Noah; 17, Sacrifice of Isaac; 19, Isaac and Esau; 19v, Isaac blessing Jacob; 22, Jacob wrestling with the Angel; 24v, Joseph and Potiphar's wife; 40v, Joseph and Asenath; 48v, Jacob and his sons going down to Egypt; 49, Moses and the Burning Bush; 49v, Moses' rod turning into a snake; 54v, Moses striking water from the rock; 64v, Moses and Aaron; 75v, God speaking to Moses; 80, the return of the Spies; 83v, the Brazen Serpent; 84v, Balaam; 90v, Moses receiving the Tables of the Law; 103v, Joshua, 105v Joshua, 107, Gibeonites coming to Joshua; 107v, hanging of the kings; 113v, Joshua talking to the Israelites; 119, Samson; 124v, Eli, Hannah, and Samuel;

143, Absalom hanging from the tree; 159, Elijah; 160, Ahab; 178v, Solomon; 207v, Nehemiah; 250, the afflicted Job praying; 258v, David, composer of the Psalms; 277v, the Judgment of Solomon; 293v, the Wisdom of Ben Sirach; 300, Isaiah; 316v, Hosea; 330v, Jeremiah; 350, the Judgment of Daniel on Susannah; 357v, Ezekiel; 376v–377, letter of Eusebius to Carpianus; 378v–384v, canon tables; 387v, St. Matthew; 399v, St. Mark; 407v, St. Luke; 419v, St. John; 449v, Vision of St. John, Christ and the Twenty-Four Elders of the Apocalypse; 460v, Paul. Many marginal text illustrations in the New Testament. Decorated headpieces and letters, with marginal ornamentation at the beginning of most books.
Bibliography: Bogharian, *Grand Catalogue*, VI (1972), 421–427; Stone, *Testament of Levi*, 15 f.; Der Nersessian, *Chester Beatty*, XLIII, 11.

Figures 154, 155
The Istanbul Menologium of 1633
Menologium, Istanbul, 1633.
Jerusalem ms. 66.
General data: paper, 1256 pp., 34 × 25 × 8 cm. Written in regular *bolorgir* script in black ink, 33 lines in two columns. Generally well preserved, with some worm damage in the margins.
Binding: leather over boards.
Colophons: pp. 1247–1252. Copied in 1633 by Avetis *eretz* and Yakob *dpir* for the pilgrim (*mahdesi*) Markos, who presented it to the Church of the Holy Sepulcher in Jerusalem. Name of painter is unknown.
Decoration: three full-page illustrations: pp. 12, St. Gregory the Illuminator and King Trdat; 500, Nativity; 826, Resurrection. A headpiece at the beginning of the readings for each month, and elaborate headpieces on pp. 13, 501, 827, with decorated letters and marginal ornaments.
Bibliography: Bogharian, *Grand Catalogue*, I (1966), 208–216, figs. 22–27.

Figure 156
Hemaiyl of 1709
Hemaiyl, charm scroll, Istanbul 1709.
Jerusalem, Archbishop Shahe Ajamian Collection.
Copied and illuminated by David. 300 × 15 cm.

Chapter Ten: St. James Cathedral and its Treasures

Figures 157–158, 165, 170
Cathedral of St. James
General view of interior towards the East. Built 1142–1165.
Seen are the main Altar of St. James with the Iconostasis, three of the four pillars, carrying the arches and the cross-ribbed dome on top of the pendentives. The capitals on top of the pillars are Crusader. Built in its present form either after the visits of Catholicos Pahlavouni in 1142 or that of King Thoros II of Cilicia around 1163. First described in 1165 by John of Würzburg. The many decorative additions to the Church cover most of the medieval Crusader building. On the left is seen the entrance to the chapel of the Head of St. James. Some of the hundreds of lamps which obstruct the view were there as early as the 15th century; they are mentioned by the pilgrim John Poloner in 1422.
Bibliography: Vincent and Abel, *Jerusalem II*, 522–546

Figure 157a
Linen cloth
Linen cloth depicting Virgin and Child, pasted inside binding of Jerusalem ms. 1272. Copied in Cilicia in 1290.

Figure 157b
Painted cloth
Church of St. Etchmiadzin, Cathedral of St. James.
This painted cloth covers a niche on the left of the altar. On it can be seen a Crucifixion, to the right of which is the Risen Christ. It was perhaps made in India.
Dimensions: 122 cms. wide × 114 cms. high.

Figure 157c
Balcony for lections
Cathedral of St. James.
This balcony is made of wood covered with plaster, painted gold, red and blue. It is entered through the Church of St. Step'anaos, in the north wall of the Cathedral of St. James.
Dimensions: 90 cms. deep × 157 cms. wide × circa 400 cms. high. It is 237 cms. up from the floor level of the Cathedral.

Figures 159–162
Crusader Capitals
Cathedral of St. James, 1142–1165
The capitals of the Crusader Period on top of pillars in the Cathedral of St. James are either of tongue-leaves or of acanthus motifs. One (fig. 162) has three symmetrical lambs within the acanthus leaves.

Figure 163
Crusader Doorway
Cathedral of St. James, between 1142 and 1165
The original Crusader main entrance to the Cathedral of St. James, from the south narthex, now leads from the Church of St. Etchmiadzin into the Cathedral of St. James. The arch is decorated with cushioned gadroons, resting on tongue-leaves capitals. At its narrowest, the opening measures 1.84 m. and at its widest, including the outermost pilasters, 2.75 m.
Bibliography: Vincent and Abel, *Jerusalem II*.

Figure 164
Carved Wooden Door
Cathedral of St. James, 1371
The door in the southern wall of the Cathedral closes a secret passage and a flight of steps, built into the width of the wall, leading up to the chapels of St. Paul and St. Peter. The door is carved over its front surface, with an uncial inscription above giving the name of the commissioners: Yovhannes and his son Thoros and the date of execution 1371. The door is, apparently, in its original site. The door is some height off the ground and is accessible by means of a ladder. It is in a good state of preservation, and is protected now by a plain wooden outer door.
Bibliography: Vincent and Abel, *Jerusalem II*, 585–6, fig. 225, pl. LVIII, 3; Kurdian, *Wood-Carving*, *Sion* 41 (1967), 45 pl. 25 (in Armenian); Mekhitarian *Cat. Exh. Jerusalem, 1969*, 43–44; Carswell, *Kütahya Tiles*, 3.

Figure 165 See entry for fig. 157.

Figure 166
Wrought-iron fence
Cathedral of St. James, 1796
These fences donated in 1796 during the Patriarchate of Petros (1793–1800) enclose the apses of the main church, that of St. Etchmiadzin Chapel and some of the chapels in the northern part of the main church. The decoration is of foliage scrolls and flowers.
Dimensions of each section: 121 cm. height, about 3 m. in length.

Figure 167
Opus Sectile floor
Cathedral of St. James, 18th century
In the entire area of the apses in the main church of St. James, each of the eastern pillars is paved with decorative geometric sections executed in an *opus sectile* technique of the 18th century.
Bibliography: Vincent and Abel, *Jerusalem II*, 556, pl. LVIII, 1.

Figure 168
Throne of St. James the Less
Canopy of Bishop's Throne, Cathedral of St. James, 1656
Made of wood, inlaid with mother-of-pearl and tortoise shell. Dated to the year 1656 during the Patriarchate of Eliezer.
Dimensions: 100 cm. broad × 111 cm. wide × 400 cm. high.

Figure 169
Marble Slabs before the Altar
Cathedral of St. James, 1730

The marble slabs before the main altar of St. James are decorated with flowers issuing from vases, symmetrically arranged within arcades. There are floral decorations in the spandrels and a framing band at top and sides with floral and foliage interlace. A dedicatory inscription at the center top states that it was dedicated by one Saraf *mahdesi* during the Patriarchates of Gregory the Chainbearer and Yovhannes Kolot of Constantinople, in 1730.
Dimensions: 105 × 880 cm.
Bibliography: T. Sawalaneantz, *History of Jerusalem* (1931), 1221 (in Armenian).

Figure 170
See entry for fig. 157.

Figure 171
Doors of the Chapel of St. James the Great
St. James Cathedral, 1731.
The pair of doors of the Chapel of St. James were made by Yakob of wood with mother-of-pearl inlay in 1731. The doors are decorated with crosses, surrounded by floral and geometric decoration with some oriental motifs. They lead from the Cathedral into the Chapel of St. James, where St. James' head is buried. The dedicatory inscription is also in mother-of-pearl inlay stating that it was made by Yakob during the patriarchate of Gregory the Chainbearer (1715–1749).
Dimensions: each 198.5 × 49 cm.
Bibliography: T. Sawalaneantz, *History of Jerusalem* (1931), 1222 (in Armenian).

Figure 172
Chapel of St. Ethmiadzin
Cathedral of St. James, 1666 and later
The chapel was founded by Patriarch Eliezer in 1666 by enclosing the Crusader narthex. The wrought-iron fence is of 1796, and the Iconostasis of 1753. The latter is a wooden structure with gesso (plaster) relief decoration, in gold, blue, red paint, depicting Paradise with animals and angels within foliage scrolls. Above the opening on the left-hand side is an inscription dating the structure to the year 1182 of the Armenian era (1753 A.D.). Above the right and left openings are series of eight icons, four on each side, depicting (from left to right): Annunciation, Nativity, Presentation in the Temple, Baptism, Last Supper, Crucifixion, Harrowing of Hell, Resurrection. The overall width is 6.35 m. The altar frontal used here in red velvet with copper decoration is dated 1758.

Figures 173–176
Kütahya Tiles
Chapel of St. Etchmiadzin, St. James Cathedral, ca. 1719
A display of Kütahya tiles in the Chapel of St. Etchmiadzin, originally made for repair of the Church of the Holy Sepulcher, and later collected by Elia son of Yovasaph of Caesarea into the Chapel between 1727 and 1737.

Figure 173
1. Virgin and Child (1719); 2. Archangels Michael, Gabriel, and Uriel; 3. S. Theodore and the dragon (1719).

Figure 174
Adam and Eve flanking the Tree of Knowledge

Figure 175
The Last Supper

Figure 176
The Resurrection of Christ.
Bibliography: Carswell, *Kütahya Tiles*, 25–67, pls. 1–15.

Figure 177
Ceramic "egg" 1740
Kütahya, 1740
Patriarch's Collection
The ceramic "egg" is used for suspending lamps in the church. This egg is of white pottery with figures of cherubs and an inscription in *notragir* script with many vulgar spellings and errors, reading: "This ball is a memorial of Stebanos, pilgrim (in the) church (of the) Archangels. In the year 1189 A.D. (1740)".
Dimensions: 12 cm. high, 32.5 cm. in diameter.
Bibliography: Carswell, *Kütahya Tiles*, 85, pl. 24a.b.c.

Figure 178
Ewer and bowl
Kütahya, 1716
Patriarch's Collection
The ewer and bowl for liturgical use in the church were especially done for the Cathedral of St. James in 1716 by the craftsman "George (of the church) of the Holy Prophets, for the pilgrim Karapet son of Abraham of Gotha (Kütahya)". The bowl was made on the 9th of December and the ewer on the 29th.
Dimensions: Ewer: 20 cm. high, 14.5 in diameter. Bowl: 8.2 cm high, 26 cm. in diameter.
Bibliography: Carswell, *Kütahya tiles*, 81–82, pl. 22a,b,c.

Figures 179–181
Altar-frontals
Constantinople, 1619, 1620, 1655
Treasury of St. James
The altar-frontals are used for decorating the altar on different festivals and saints' days. They were invented in the 17th century and traditionally embroidered by women.

Figure 179
For the Feast-Day of St. Peter and St. Paul, depicting the Virgin receiving the head of St. James, witnessed by St. James the Less and St. John the Evangelist. Surrounded by Christological scenes. Dated 1619.

Figure 180
The Last Supper, surrounded by the Twelve Feasts of the year. Dated 1620.

Figure 181
Christ in Majesty, surrounded by heavenly bodies. Dated 1655.

Figure 182
Gold Chalice.
Istanbul, 1741.
Treasury of St. James.
Gold chalice inlaid with gems, made at Istanbul in 1749 for Gregory the Chainbearer just before his death.
Dimensions: height, 35 cm, diameter of base, 22 cm.
Bibliography: Mekhitarian, *Cat. Exh. Jerusalem 1969*, 35, No. 50.

Figures 183–184
Gold Chalice with enamel
Istanbul, 1749
Treasury of St. James
Gold chalice, studded with precious stones and seven small enamel medallions showing scenes from the life of Christ. Dedicated to the memory of Gregory the Chainbearer, Patriarch of Jerusalem, who died in 1749.
Dimensions: height, 31 cm, base diameter, 22.5 cm., bowl diameter, 11.2 cm.
Bibliography: Mekhitarian, *Cat. Exh. Jerusalem, 1969*, 35, No. 49.

Figure 185
Filigree Cross
Cathedral of St. James, 1747
A filigree silvered metal cross on a square base. Into the cross are set two circles of enamel medallions on each side. On one, starting from the top and moving clockwise, they are – the inner circle: Ascension, the Holy Sepulcher, the Arrest of Christ, the Baptism; the outer circle: four medallions with angels carrying instruments of the Passion. At the center is the Resurrection. On the other side, in the same direction are the inner circle: St. Luke, Presentation in the Temple, Annunciation, Nativity. In the outer circle: two are missing, remaining are Matthew and Mark. Apparently some displacement and repair have taken place. In the center are the Virgin and Child. The dedicatory inscription inside the base records that it was donated by a pilgrim Lukas in memory of his parents Astuadzatur and Anna to the Church of the Archangels in the year 1747.
Dimensions: height, 52 cm., diameter, 27 cms.

Figure 186
The Red Tiara
A priest's crown. Constantinople, 1747.
St. James Treasury.
Made in Constantinople in 1747 probably for Patriarch Gregory the Chainbearer. Gift of the baker Melkon and his family. The crown is 27 cm. high, and has a diameter of 20–27 cm. On a background of dark red velvet, gold foliage and filigree work is studded with precious stones and enamel medallions with narrative scenes.

Depicted in the top and the largest of the four rows of enamel medallions are St. George killing the dragon, bishop, a deacon and bishops. The dedicatory inscription is written around the edges of this row of medallions. The second row is also composed of four medallions, mounted directly below the top row, depicting the Adoration of the Magi, Baptism, Resurrection, and Crucifixion. In the third row are the four Evangelists and in the fourth, around the lower edge, are the Apostles.

No indication of the identity of the Bishops or the Deacon in the first row is found, although identifications such as Gregory the Chainbearer, St. Stephen and Yovhannes Kolot respectively have been suggested.

The crown is surmounted by a cross, 5 cm. high, set in the center of a circular gold ornament, with precious stones set in it.
Bibliography: Mekhitarian, *Cat. Exh. Jerusalem, 1969*, 41, no. 78.

Figure 187
Miter of the Chainbearer
Constantinople, 1735
Treasury of St. James
The miter is embroidered and adorned with precious stones and pearls depicting the Adoration of the Magi on one side and the Baptism of Christ on the other. It was probably brought to Jerusalem by Yovhannes Kolot, Patriarch of Constantinople, on the occasion of his pilgrimage in 1735.
Dimensions: height, 43 cm., width, 30 cm.

Figure 188
Neck Horarium of the Chainbearer
Constantinople, 1735
Treasury of St. James
Neck horarium depicting the Tree of Jesse. Gold embroidery on brocade with pearls and precious stones. The rectangular strip, 123 × 23 cm., has a circular top 23 cm. high and has a maximum diameter of 34 cm. It was made for Patriarch Gregory the Chainbearer by Yakob *Vardapet* in 1735.

Figure 189
Cope of Patriarch Gregory Paronter
17th century.
Treasury of St. James
The cope is said to be of Patriarch Gregory Paronter (1613–1645), though no precise date is given and the provenance is unknown. It is of red velvet with gold embroidery.
Diameter: ca. 3 m.
Bibliography: Mekhitarian, *Cat. Exh. Jerusalem, 1969*, 40, no. 75.

Frontispiece
Silver Binding of the Gospels of the Sea
Crucifixion (front) and Nativity (back)
Executed by Yovhannes, deacon, Sis (Cilicia), 1334
Jerusalem ms. 2649, Treasury of St. James No. 94
This Gospel was copied by priest Grigor, and illuminated by Sargis Pidzak in 1332 at Sis (Cilicia). Its name "Gospel of the Sea" came because of its salvage from the sea. The Evangelists' portraits were damaged. The binding is the oldest metal binding preserved in the Patriarchate of Jerusalem. It is of beaten and engraved silver gilt. Executed by Yovhannes, deacon, in the year 1334. The front cover depicts the Crucifixion, framed by busts of the Twelve Apostles with St. Sargis and George in medallions. The back cover depicts the Nativity, with the adoration by the Magi and the Shepherds.

The manuscript is of vellum, 324 fols., 25.5 × 20 × 8 cm. Written in *bolorgir* script, in black ink, 12 lines in two columns, with colored capitals and decorated initials and marginal ornaments. Illuminated canon tables and portraits of the Evangelists.
Bibliography: Der Nersessian, *Mss. Arm. de Venice*, 139 notes 1, 2; Mekhitarian, *Cat. Exh. Jerusalem, 1969*, 25–26.

Front end-paper
Map of the Holy Land
Venice (?), 1746.
The Patriarchal Collection
Printed on paper, probably in Venice, in 1746. 39 × 49 cm.

Back end-paper
Map of Armenia
Venice, 1751.
The Patriarchal Collection.
Printed on paper in Venice, 1751. 38.5 × 51 cm.

Glossary

Apsis, Apse	projecting section in the eastern part of a church, usually semi-circular.
Arachnord	primate.
Bolorgir	a formal minuscule Armenian script which became prevalent from the 12th century.
Canon Tables	tables of concordance between the Four Gospels, composed by Eusebius in answer to a query from Carpianus.
Christological	concerning the life of Christ.
Colophon	note by the scribe, or other later person, written in a manuscript or on an object.
Cornucopia	animal horn filled with fruit and grain, used in art as a symbol of plenty.
Deisis	Christ implored by the Virgin Mary and John the Baptist.
Dionysios of Furna	16th century monk of Mt. Athos who wrote a manual for painters on scene illustrations.
Drum	cylindrical block supporting a dome.
Erkathagir	Armenian uncial (majuscule) script in predominant use between the fifth and twelfth centuries.
Eusebius to Carpianus, Letter of	letter in which Eusebius describes the organization and function of the Canon Tables, q.v.
Firman	order stating the rights or privileges issued by a Moslem ruler.
Folio	a leaf of a book or manuscript.
Hagiographical	having to do with the stories of the lives of saints.
Hieratic	frontal depiction of persons (derived from the depiction of priests and saints).
Iconoclastic Controversy	controversy in the eastern church in the eighth-ninth centuries on the veneration of icons.
Iconography	study of illustrations of a topic by visual representations.
Iconostasis	the screen which, in Byzantine churches, separates the sanctuary from the nave.
Illuminated Manuscripts	manuscripts decorated or illustrated by pictures or ornaments, illuminating the page.
kolot	"dwarf" – cognomen of Yovhannes, Patriarch of Constantinople in the 18th century.
Lantern	turret which crowns the dome and is broken up with windows or arcading.
Leaves	folios in a manuscript.
Lectionary	book containing the readings from Scripture used in the various services and festivals of the Church.
Living Cross	cross sprouting from a bush or tree or a cross of tree branches.
Mekhitarist Fathers	Armenian Catholic order with centers in Venice and Vienna.
Menologium	the lives of the saints provided for reading in Church.
Narthex	in the Byzantine Church, the antechamber to the nave.
Neck-horarium	frontal embroidered church vestment worn by priest during Passion Week.
Notragir	a semi-formal Armenian minuscule script used in non-Church manuscripts from the 14th century.
opus sectile	marble inlay where the pieces are cut into shapes which follow a pattern or picture.
Orant	personification of prayer, usually through a woman raising her arms on either side.
Pantocrator	bust of Christ as the ruler of the world, normally blessing with his right hand and holding book in left.
Pericope	portion of Bible read in public worship.
Pyxis	small ivory box for the Eucharistic wafer or church valuables.
Quinisext Councils	synods held in 692 by Eastern bishops to pass disciplinary canons.

Rabbula Gospel	illuminated Gospel copied by Rabbula, a 6th century Syrian priest, completed in 586 and now in the Biblioteca Laurenziana, Florence.
shghtayagir	"chainbearer", cognomen of Gregory, Patriarch of Jerusalem in the 18th century.
Sacristy	room adjoining church or chapel where sacred vessels and garments are kept.
Safavid	Persian dynasty founded in 1502.
Tempietto	small round classical temple-like edifice.
Tessera (pl. tesserae)	small piece of colored marble, tile etc. used in mosaic work.
Tiara	Patriarchal headdress.
Tyche	Greek goddess of chance or of a town.
Uncial	large capital letter, see *erkathagir*.
Vartaped	"doctor" or "teacher"; learned cleric, lately celibate priest.

Bibliography

Abu Salih, *Egypt 1168* — Abu Salih, *Al Armani, The Churches and Monasteries of Egypt and Neighbouring Countries (1168)*, Oxford, 1895, photocopy, London, 1969.

Aghawnuni, *Visitors* — M. Aghawnuni, *Miabank ew Aytseluk Hay Erusaghemi* (Armenian Monks and Visitors in Jerusalem), Jerusalem, 1929 (in Armenian).

Aghawnuni, *Monasteries* — M. Aghawnuni, *Haykakan Hin Vanker ew Ekeghetsiner Surb Erkrin mej* (Ancient Armenian Monasteries and Churches in the Holy Land), Jerusalem, 1931 (in Armenian).

Akinian, *Armenischer Alexanderroman* — P.N. Akinian, "Die handschriftliche Ueberlieferung der armenischen Uebersetzung des Alexanderromans von Pseudo-Kalisthenes", *Byzantion* 13 (1938), 201–206.

Akinian, *Skevra-Evangeliar 1197* — P. Nerses Akinian, *Das Skevra-Evangeliar vom Jahre 1197 aufbewahrt im Archive des Armenischen Erzbistums Lemberg*, Wien, Mechitharisten- Buchdruckerei, 1930 (in Armenian with German résumé).

Akopian, *Vaspuragan* — G.G. Akopian, *Vaspuragan Miniatures*, Erevan 1976 (in Armenian).

Alishan, *Anastas* — L. Alishan, "Anastas d'Armenie", *Archives de l'Orient Latin*, 2(1884), 395–399.

Alishan, *Monasteries* — Ghewond Alishan, *Vasn vanoreits or i Surb Kaghakn Herusaghem* (On the Monasteries in the Holy City of Jerusalem), Venice, 1896 (in Armenian).

Anasian, *Early Armenian Printing* — H.S. Anasian, *Catalogue of Early Armenian Printing 1512–1800*, Erevan, 1963.

Aubert, *L'Art Roman* — M. Aubert, *L'Art Roman en France*, Paris, 1961.

Avetysian, *Gladzor* — A.N. Avetysian, *The School of Gladzor*, Erevan, 1971 (in Armenian).

Avi-Yonah, *Mosaic* — M. Avi-Yonah, "Mosaic Pavements in Palestine", *QDAP*, 2(1932), 136–181; 3(1933), 26–73.

Avi-Yonah, *Nirim* — M. Avi-Yonah, "The Mosaic Pavement of Maon (Nirim) Synagogue", in *Eretz-Israel*, 6(1960) (in Hebrew), 86–93, fig. 1, pls. 17–22.

Azarian, *Cilician Min.* — L.R. Azarian, *Cilician Miniature Painting, XII–XIII centuries*, Erevan, 1964 (in Armenian).

Azarian, *Drazark* — L.R. Azarian, "The Significance of Drazark in Cilician Miniature Painting" (in Armenian), *Akad. Nauk Arm. S.S.R. Izvestiia*, 1957, facs. 5, pp. 95–106, figs. 4, 6.

Azarian, *The Narek of 1173* — L.R. Azarian, "The 'Narek' copied in 1173 and the School of Miniaturists of Skevra" (in Armenian), *Bauber Matenadarani* 4(1958), 83–110, figs. 1–15.

Bagatti, *Uccelli* — B. Bagatti, "Uccelli nei Pavimenti Musivi delle Cappelle Funerarie Palestinesi", *Revista di Archeologia Christiana*, vol. 28/29 (1952–53), 207–214.

Bahat, *Beth Shean* — D. Bahat, "The Synagogue at Beth Shean, Preliminary Report", *Qadmoniot*, 18(1972) (in Hebrew), 55–58.

Bain, *Anastas* — Nisbet Bain, "Armenian Description of the Holy Places in the 7th century", *Palestine Exploration Fund* (1896), 346–349.

Biblia, De Bry 1609 — *Biblia Sacra vulgatæ ed. Sixti V. Pont. Max. jussu recognita et Clementis VII autoritate ed., nunc autem 90 figuris noviter inventis et in æs incisis illustrata a Johann Theodor De Bry*, Moguntiæ, 1609.

Biblia Sacra 1607 — *Sacra Biblia vulgatæ, editionis Sixti Quinti Pont. Max. iussu recognita autque edita*, Venetiis, 1607.

Bogharian, *Grand Catalogue* — N. Bogharian, *Grand Catalogue of St. James' Manuscripts*, Jerusalem, Armenian Convent Printing Press, vol. I, 1966, vol. II, 1967, vol. III, 1968, vol. IV, 1972, vol. V, 1971, vol. VI, 1973, vol. VII, 1974, vol. VIII, 1977.

Borg, *Provence* — A. Borg, *Architectural Sculpture in Romanesque Provence*, Oxford, 1972.

Brassinne, *De Bry* — J. Brassinne, *Le Trois Thiry de Bry*, Liège, 1906.

Buchthal, *Latin Kingdom* — H. Buchthal, *Miniature Painting in the Latin Kingdom of Jerusalem*, Oxford, 1957.

Buchthal, *Paris Psalter* — H. Buchthal, *The Miniatures of the Paris Psalter*, London, 1938.

Buchthal and Kurz, *Hand List* — H. Buchthal and O. Kurz, *A Hand List of Illuminated Oriental Christian Manuscripts*, London, 1942.

Buschhausen, *Wien* — H. und H. Buschhausen, E. Zimmermann, *Die Illuminierten Armenischen Handschriften der Mechitharisten-Congregation in Wien*, Wien, 1976.

Butler, *Lausiac History* — C. Butler, *The Lausiac History of Palladius II*, Cambridge, 1904, 2 vols.

Carswell, *Kütahya* — J. Carswell, *Kütahya Tiles and Pottery from the Armenian Cathedral of St. James*, Jerusalem, 1972. Vol. I, *Pictorial Tiles and Other Vessels;* Vol. II, *A Historical Survey of the Küttachia Industry and a Catalogue of the Decorative Tiles*.

Catergian, *Ephesianal* — J. Catergian, *Ecclesiae Ephesianae de obitu Joannis apost. narratio ex versione armeniaca saeculi V.*, Wien, 1877.

Charanis, *Armenians in Byz.* — P. Charanis, *The Armenians in the Byzantine Empire*, Lisbon, 1963.

Clermont-Ganneau, *Palestine 1873–4* — Fr. Clermont-Ganneau, *Archaeological Researches in Palestine in the Years 1873–4*, Paris, 1875.

Codices e Vaticani Selecti, 8 — *Codices e Vaticani Selecti 8, Il Menologio de Basilio II*, Turin, 1907.

Conybeare, *Catalogue Br. Mus.* — F.C. Conybeare, *A Catalogue of the Armenian Manuscripts in the British Museum*, London, 1913.

Cramer, *Koptische Buchmalerei* — M. Cramer, *Koptische Buchmalerei*, Recklinghausen, 1964.

Crowfoot, *Early Churches* — J.W. Crowfoot, *Early Churches in Palestine*, London, 1941.

Cust, *Status Quo* — L.G.A. Cust, *The Status Quo in the Holy Places, With an Annex on "The Status Quo in the Church of the Nativity, Bethlehem"*, by Abdulla Effendi Kardus. Printed for the Government of Palestine by His Majesty's Stationery Office, 1929.

Dashian, *ZDPV* — J. Dashian, "Anhang" to J. Strzygowski, "Neue Angefundene Orpheus Mosaic in Jerusalem", 39–165. *Zeitschrift des Deutschen Palästina-Vereins*, 24 (1901), 165–71.

Der Nersessian, *Aght'amar* — S. Der Nersessian, *Aght'amar, Church of the Holy Cross*, Cambridge, Mass., 1956.

Der Nersessian, *Armenia & Byzantium* — S. Der Nersessian, *Armenia and the Byzantine Empire*, Cambridge, Mass., 1945.

Der Nersessian, *L'Art Arménien* — S. Der Nersessian, *L'Art Arménien*, Paris, 1977.

Der Nersessian, *Chester Beatty* — S. Der Nersessian, *The Chester Beatty Library, A Catalogue of the Armenian Manuscripts*, I, II, Dublin, 1958.

Der Nersessian, *Freer Gallery* — S. Der Nersessian, *Armenian Manuscripts in the Freer Gallery of Art*, Washington, 1963.

Der Nersessian, *MSS. Arm. de Venise* — S. Der Nersessian, *Manuscrits Arméniens illustrés des XIIe, XIIIe et XIVe siècles, de la Bibliothèque des Pères Mekhitaristes de Venise*, Paris, 1937, I, text; II, album.

Der Nersessian, *Psautiers Grecs II* — S. Der Nersessian, *Illustration de Psautiers Grecs du Moyen Age*, II, Londres, Add. 19352. Paris, 1970.

Der Nersessian, *Studies* — S. Der Nersessian, *Byzantine and Armenian Studies, Etudes Byzantines et Arméniennes*, 2 vols., Louvain, 1973. The collected works are cited by page number of the *Studies*, mentioning year of original appearance.

Der Nersessian, *Apologie des Images (1944–45)* — "Un Apologie des Images du septième siècle", I, 379–403.

Der Nersessian, *Bible d'Erznka (1966)* — "La Bible d'Erznka de l'an 1269: Jerusalem no. 1925", I, 603–609; II, figs. 374–385.

Der Nersessian, *Boston Gospel (1950)* — "An Armenian Gospel of the Fifteenth Century", I, 683–694; II, figs. 444–456.

Der Nersessian, *Etchmiadzin (1964)* — "La Peinture Arménienne au VII siècle et les Miniatures de l'Evangile d'Etchmiadzin", I, 525–532.

Der Nersessian, *Etchmiadzin date (1933)* — "The Date of the Initial Miniatures of the Etchmiadzin Gospel", I, 533–558.

Der Nersessian, *Evangile de Zeytoun (1952)* — "T'oros Roslin et l'Evangile de Zeytoun", I, 559–562, II, figs. 315–317.

Der Nersessian, *Hartford's Taronatsi (1929)* — "An Illustrated Armenian Gospel of the XIVth Century", I, 632–635; II, figs. 389–391.

Der Nersessian, *Image Worship (1946)* — "Image Worship in Armenian and its Opponents", I, 405–415.

Der Nersessian, *The Kingdom of Cilician Armenia (1969)* — "The Kingdom of Cilician Armenia", I, 329–352.

Der Nersessian, *Min. Ciliciennes (1969)* — "Miniatures Ciliciennes", I, 509–515; II, figs. 234–261.

Der Nersessian, *Model I (1969)* — "Le Carnet de Modèles d'un Miniaturiste Arménien", I, 665–672; II, figs. 418–434.

Der Nersessian, *Model II (1968)* — "Copies de Peintures Byzantines dans un Carnet Arménien de Modèles", I, 673–681; II, figs. 435–443.

Der Nersessian, *Morgan 803 (1954)* — "An Armenian Lectionary of the Fourteenth Century", I, 653–659; II, figs. 411–417.

Der Nersessian, *Synaxaire (1950)* — "Le Synaxaire Arménien de Grégoire VII d'Anazarbe", I, 417–435.

Der Nersessian, *Vienna 278 (1961)* — "Un Evangile Cilicien Illustré", I, 577–583, II, figs. 352–365.

Der Nersessian, *Vierge de Miséricorde (1970)* — "Deux Exemples Arméniens de la Vierge de Miséricorde", I, 585–596; II, figs. 366–371.

Der Nersessian, *Walters* — *Armenian Manuscripts in the Walters Art Gallery*, Baltimore, 1973.

Didron, *Christian Iconography* — A.N. Didron, *Christian Iconography*, 2 vols., London, 1886.

Dufrenne, *Psautiers Grecs* (1) — Suzy Dufrenne, *L'Illustration de Psautiers Grecs du Moyen Age*, I, Pantocrator 61, Paris grec 20, British Museum 40731. Paris, 1966.

Durnovo, *Arm. Miniatures* — Lydia A. Durnovo, *Armenische Miniaturen*, Köln, 1960; *Armenian Miniatures*, London, 1960; *Miniatures Arméniennes*, Paris, 1960.

Ebersolt, *Miniature Byzantine* — J. Ebersolt, *La Miniature Byzantine*, Paris et Bruxelles, 1926.

Ettinghausen, *Arab Painting* — R. Ettinghausen, *Arab Painting*, Genève: Skira, 1962.

Fitzgerald, *Beth-Shean* — G.M. Fitzgerald, *A Sixth Century Monastery at Beth-Shean*, Philadelphia, 1939.

Friend, *Evangelists* — A.M. Friend, "Portraits of Evangelists in Greek and Latin Manuscripts", *Art Studies*, 1929, part I, 115–149, part II, 3–29.

Gevorkian, *Leo III Gospel* — A. Gevorkian, "The Gospels of King Leo III" (in Armenian), *Banber Matenadarani*, 8 (1967), 143–156.

Grabar *Byzantium, Theodosius to Islam* — A. Grabar, *Byzantium from the Death of Theodosius to the Rise of Islam*, London, 1966.

Grabar, *Eglise de Quartamin* — A. Grabar, "Quelques observations sur le décor de l'Eglise de Quartamin" (1956), in *L'Art de la fin de l'Antiquité et du Moyen Age*, vol. II, Paris (1968), 637–644.

Grabar, *Formation de l'Est* — A. Grabar, "Le tiers monde de l'Antiquité à l'Ecole de l'Art Classique et son rôle dans la Formation de l'Art du Moyen Age", *Revue de l'Art*, 1972, No. 18, 9–24.

Grabar, *Iconography* — A. Grabar, *Christian Iconography, a Study of its Origins*, Princeton, 1968.

Guthe, *Mosaiken* — H. Guthe, "Mosaiken mit Armenischer Inschrift auf dem Ölberge", *ZDP* (1895), 51–53.

Hakobian, *Vaspouragan* — H.H. Hakobian, *The Miniatures of Vaspouragan*, I (in Armenian), Erevan, 1976.

Hanne, *Jerusalem 1782* — Yovhannes Vardapet Hanne, *Girk' patmutian srboy ew metsi Kaghakin Astutsoy Erusaghemi, ew srbots tnorinakanats teghiats* (History of the Holy and Great City of God, Jerusalem, and of the Holy Dominical Places). 3rd printing. Constantinople, 1782 (in Armenian).

Hazard, *Crusader Art* — Harry W. Hazard, ed., *The Art and Architecture of the Crusader States* in the series: *A History of the Crusades*, Kenneth M. Setton, General ed., Vol. IV, Wisconsin–London, 1977.

Hemmer, *Evangiles Apocryphes* — H. Hemmer and P. Lejay (ed.), *Evangiles Apocryphes*, Paris, I(1911) and II(1914).

Henry, *Kells* — F. Henry, *The Book of Kells*, London, 1974.

Hintlian, *History Jerusalem 1976* — K. Hintlian, *History of the Armenians in the Holy Land*, Jerusalem, 1976.

Hjort, *L'Oiseau* — O. Hjort, "L'Oiseau dans la cage", *Cahiers Archaéologiques*, 18(1968), 21–32.

Hollstein, *Dutch and Flemish Etchings* — F.W.H. Hollstein, *Dutch and Flemish Etchings, Engravings and Woodcuts, ca. 1450–1700*, Amsterdam, 1949.

Hollstein, *German Engravings* — F.W.H. Hollstein, *German Engravings, Etchings and Woodcuts, ca. 1400–1700*, Amsterdam.

Hovsepian, *Colophons* — G. Hovsepian, *Colophons of Manuscripts* (in Armenian), Antilias, 1951.

Hovsepian, *Khizan* — G. Hovsepian, "A page from the Artistic History of Khizan", *Hayastanyaitz Yeghe*, New York, VI(1944), 7–27.

Hovsepian, *Mosaik* — G. Hovsepian, "Mosaik mit armenischer Inschrift in norden Jerusalem", *ZDPV*, 18(1895), 88–90.

Hovsepian, *Patriarchs* — Barnabas Hovsepian, *Hajordutiun patriarkatsn Erusaghemi* (Chronology of the Patriarchs of Jerusalem). Constantinople, 1872 (in Armenian).

Hutter, *Corpus Byz. Min. Oxford* — I. Hutter, *Corpus der Byzantinischen Miniaturenhandschriften*, I, *Oxford, Bodleian Library*, Stuttgart, 1977.

IEJ — *Israel Exploration Journal.*

Izmailova, *L'Iconographie* — T.A. Izmailova, "L'Iconographie du Cycle des Fêtes d'un groupe de Codex Arméniens d'Asie Mineure", *Revue des Etudes Arméniennes*, N.S. IV (1967), 125–166, figs. 1–37.

Izmailova, *Localisation d'un groupe* — T.A. Izmailova, "Localisation d'un groupe de manuscrits arméniens enluminés du XIe siècle d'après leurs colophons", *Lraber*, 9 (1966), 280.

Izmailova, *Tetraévangile de 1038* — T.A. Izmailova, "Le Tetraévangile illustré arménien de 1038: Matenadaran no 6201", *Revue des Etudes Arméniennes*, N.S. VII (1970), 203–240.

Izmailova, *Tetraévangile de Mougna* — T.A. Izmailova, "Le Cycle des Fêtes du Tetraévangile de Mougna", *Revue des Etudes Arméniennes*, N.S. VI(1969), 105–139, XV pls.

Janaskian, *San Lazzaro* — Mesrop Janaskian, *Armenian Miniature Paintings of the Monastic Library at San Lazzaro*, I, Venice 1966.

Jarphanion, *Cappadoce* — G. Jarphanion, *Les Eglises Rupestres de Cappadoce*, Paris, 1925.

John of Würzburg — John of Würzburg, *Description of the Holy Land (1165)*, *PPTS*, Vol. 3.

John Poloner — John Poloner, *Description of the Holy Land* (1422), *PPTS*, Vol. 6.

Kalaydjian, *Early Printing* — A. Kalaydjian, *Catalogue and Colophons of Early Armenian Printings in the Gulbenkian Library, Jerusalem* published serially in *Sion*, 1967–70.

Kitzinger, *S. Cuthbert's Coffin* — E. Kitzinger, "The Coffin-Reliquary", *The Relics of S. Cuthbert*, Oxford (1956), 203–304.

Kleinschmidt, *Anna* — P.B. Kleinschmidt, *Die Heilige Anna*, Düsseldorf, 1930.

Kondakoff, *Bogomateri* — N.P. Kondakoff, *Ikonografia Bogomateri*, 2 vols., Saint Petersburg, 1915 (in Russian).

Korxmazyan, *Crimea* — Emma M. Korxmazyan, *The Armenian Miniatures of Crimea (XIV–XVII centuries)*, Erevan, 1978 (in Armenian).

Lafontaine-Dosogne, *Nouvelles Cappadociennes* — J. Lafontaine-Dosogne, "Nouvelles Notes Cappadociennes", *Byzantion*, 33(1963), 121–183.

Lafontaine-Dosogne, *Review of Thierry* — J. Lafontaine-Dosogne, Review of Thierry, *Nouvelles Eglises* in *Byzantinische Zeitschrift*, 58(1965), 131–136.

Lafontaine-Dosogne, *Vierge* — J. Lafontaine-Dosogne, *Iconographie de l'Enfance de la Vierge dans l'Empire Byzantine et en Occident*, 2 vols., Bruxelles, 1964, 1965.

Lauer, *Sancta Sanctorum* — P. Lauer, "Les Fouilles du Sancta Sanctorum au Latéran", *Mélanges d'Archéologie et d'Histoire* (Ecole Française de Rome), 1900, XX, 251–287, pls. VI–XII.

Leroy, *Mss. Syriaques* — J. Leroy, *Les Manuscrits Syriaques à Peintures conservés dans les Bibliothèques d'Europe et d'Orient*, Paris, 1964.

Levi, *Antioch* — D. Levi, *Antioch Mosaic Pavements*, 2 vols., Princeton University Press, 1947.

Loukianoff, *Musée russe* — E. Loukianoff, "Le musée du Couvent russe du Mont des Oliviers à Jérusalem.", *Bulletin de l'Institut d'Egypt*, 13(1930–31), 100ff.

Macler, *Documents* — F. Macler, *Documents d'Art Arméniens*, 2 vols., Paris, 1924.

Macler, *Livres d'Amsterdam* — F. Macler, "Les Livres Imprimés Arméniens de la Bibliothèque de l'Université d'Amsterdam", *Revue des Etudes Arméniennes*, VI (1926), 71–148.

Macler, *Min. Arm.* — F. Macler, *Miniatures Arméniennes, Vie du Christ*, Paris, 1913.

Macler, *Reliure d'Oskan* — F. Macler, "La Reliure de la Bible Arménienne d'Oskan", *Revue des Etudes Arméniennes*, VIII(1928), 7–17, figs. 1–5.

Macler, *Syrie* — Frédéric Macler, *Les Arméniennes en Syrie et en Palestine*, Marseilles, 1919.

Markosian, *Jerusalem 1883* — Mambre Markosian, *Surb Erusaghemi Hayots azgayin vanuts teghekutiunner* (Information Concerning the Armenian Monastery in Holy Jerusalem), Rostov, 1883 (in Armenian).

Maundrell, *Jerusalem 1697* — Henry Maundrell, *A Journey from Aleppo to Jerusalem in 1697*, Beirut, 1963.

Mekhitarian, *Cat. Exh. Jerusalem 1969* — A. Mekhitarian, *Treasures of the Armenian Patriarchate of Jerusalem, Catalogue No. 1*, Jerusalem, 1969.

Milik, *Topographie* — J.T. Milik, "La Topographie de Jérusalem vers la fin de l'Epoque Byzantine", *Mélanges offerts au Père René Mouterd (Mélange de l'Université Saint-Joseph)*, Beyrouth, XXXVII, 1960, Cat. 127–189.

Millet, *L'Iconographie* — G. Millet, *Recherches sur l'Iconographie de l'Evangile aux XIV–XVI siècles etc.*, Paris, 1916.

Mkhitarian, *Jerusalem 1867* — Khoren Mkhitarian, *Hamarot patmutium Erusaghemi ew storagrutium srbazan teghiats* (A Brief History of Jerusalem and Description of the Holy Places), Jerusalem, 1867 (in Armenian).

Morey, *East Christian Miniatures* — C.R. Morey, "Notes on East Christian Miniatures", *Art Bulletin*, 1929, XI, 1.

Muñoz, *Rossano* — A. Muñoz, *Il Codice purpureo di Rossano e il Fragmento Sinopense*, Rome, 1907.

Murray, *Damascus Gate Mosaic* — A. S. Murray, "The Mosaic with Armenian Inscription from near Damascus Gate, Jerusalem", *PEFQ* (April 1898), 126–127.

Nagler, *Künstler Lexikon* — G.K. Nagler, *Künstler Lexikon*, Leipzig 1835–1852.

Narkiss, *Relation* — B. Narkiss, "The Relation between the Author, Scribe, Massorator and Illuminator in Mediaeval Manuscripts", *La Paléographie Hébraïque Médiévale* (Cologne, 11–13 September 1972), Paris, CNRS. (1974), 79–86, pls. LXXVIII–XCVI.

Nersessian, *Armenian Studies* — V. Nersessian, *An Index of Articles on Armenian Studies in Western Journals*, (London, Luzac & Co., 1975), 82–90: Architecture, Archaeology, Arts, Miniatures, Music.

Neumüller, *Millenarius* — W. Neumüller and K. Holder, *Der Codex Millenarius*, Graz, 1959.

Neuss, *Ezechiel* — W. Neuss, *Das Buch Ezechiel in Theologie und Kunst*, Münster in Westf., 1912.

Niccolo da Poggibonsi — Niccolo of Poggibonsi, *A Voyage beyond the Seas* (1346–1350), translated by T. Bellorini and E. Honde, Jerusalem, Stadium Biblicum Franciscanum, 2, 1945.

Nordenfalk *Kanontafeln* — C. Nordenfalk, *Die Spätantiken Kanontafeln*, Göteborg, 1938.

Nordenfolk, *Zierbuchstaben* — C. Nordenfalk, *Die Spätantiken Zierbuchstaben*, Stockholm, 1970.

O'Leary, *The Saints of Egypt* — De Lacy O'Leary, *The Saints of Egypt*, London–New York, 1937.

Omont, *BN MSS. Grecs* — H. Omont, *Miniatures des plus anciens Manuscrits Grecs*, I, texte, II, planches, Paris, 1929.

Omont, *Grec 74* — H. Omont, *Evangiles avec Peintures Byzantines du XIe siècle, Reproduction des 361 Miniatures du ms. grec 74 de la Bibliothèque Nationale*, I, II, Paris (no date).

Ormanian, *Jerusalem 1931* — Maghakia Ormanian, *Haykakan Erusaghem: Nkaragir atoroy srbots Hakobiants* (Armenian Jerusalem: Description of the See of St. James). Jerusalem, 1931 (in Armenian).

Oskan, Etchmiadzin — *Etchmiadzin*, vol. XXIII (1966)
Oskan, Sion — *Sion* vol. XL (New Series) (1966).

Ovadia, *Gaza* — A. Ovadia, "The Synagogue at Gaza", *Qadmoniot*, 44(1968) (in Hebrew), 124–127, color pls. between 144–145.

PEFQ — *Palestine Exploration Fund Quarterly.*

PG — *Patrologia Graeca.*

PL — *Patrologia Latina.*

PO — *Patrologia Orientalis.*

PPTS — *Palestine Pilgrims' Text Society.*

Paleografica Vaticana — *Collezione Paleografica Vaticana*, fasc. I, *Miniature della Bibbia Cod. Vat. Reg. Greco 1 e del Salterio Cod. Vat. Palat. greco 381*, Milano, 1905.

Pelekanidis, *Treasures of Mount Athos* — S.M. Pelekanidis, P.C. Christou, Ch. Tsioumis and S.N. Kadas, *The Treasures of Mount Athos, Illuminated Manuscripts*, I, Athens, 1974.

Prawer, *Armenians in Jerusalem* — J. Prawer, "The Armenians in Jerusalem under the Crusaders", *Armenian and Biblical Studies*, edited by M.E. Stone, Jerusalem (1976), 222–235.

QDAP — *Quarterly of the Department of Antiquities in Palestine*.

Renoux, *Cod. Arm. 121* — Athanase Renoux, *Le Codex Arménien Jérusalem 121* (Patrologia Orientalis, Vols. XXXV–XXXVI, nos. 163, 168), Turnhout, Belgium, 1969–1971.

Restle, *Asia Minor* — M. Restle, *Byzantinische Wandmalerei in Kleinasien*, I–III, Recklinghausen, 1967.

Rhodes, *List of Arm. N.T.* — Erroll F. Rhodes, *An Annotated List of Armenian New Testament Manuscripts*, Tokyo, 1959.

Riess, *Ölberg* — Riess, "Reste eines alten armenischen Klosters auf dem Ölberg und die daselbot aufgefundene Inschriften", *ZDPV*, 8(1885), 155–161.

Sanjian, *Anastas* — A.K. Sanjian, "Anastas Vardapet's List of Armenian Monasteries in Seventh-Century Jerusalem; A Critical Examination", *Le Muséon*, 82(1968), 265–292.

Sanjian, *Syria* — A.K. Sanjian, *The Armenian Communities in Syria under Ottoman Dominion*, Cambridge Mass., 1965.

Sawalaniants, *Jerusalem 1931* — Tigran Sawalaniants, *Patmutiun Erusaghemi* (History of Jerusalem), 2 vols., Jerusalem, 1931 (in Armenian).

Schellenberg, *Dürers Apokalypse* — Carl Schellenberg, *Dürers Apokalypse*, München, 1923.

Schut, Historien 1659 — *Historien den Ouden en Nieuwen Testaments* afgebeelt door P.H. Schut, uytgegeven door N. Visscher anno 1659.

Simaika Pacha, *Musée Copte* — Marcus H. Simaika Pacha, *Guide Sommaire du Musée Copte et des Principales Eglises du Caire*, Le Caire, 1937.

Sotiriou *Mont Sinaï* — G. et M. Sotiriou, *Icones du Mont Sinaï* I, Athens, 1956 (in Greek).

Steger, *David Rex* — H. Steger, *David Rex et Propheta*, Nürnberg, 1961.

Steger, *Philologia Musica* — H. Steger, *Philologia Musica*, München, 1971.

Stone, *Testament of Levi* — M.E. Stone, *The Testament of Levi*, Jerusalem, 1969.

Stornajolo, *Giacomo Monaco* — C. Stornajolo, *Miniature delle Omilie di Giacomo Monaco (Cod. Vat. gr. 1162) e dell'Evangeliario greco Urbinate (Cod. Vat. Urbin. gr. 2)*, Roma, 1910.

Strzygowski, *Ein Zweites Etschmiadzin* — J. Strzygowski, "Ein Zweites Etschmiadzin-Evangeliar", *Huschardzan-Festschrift aus Anlass des 100-jährigen Bestandes des Mechitaristen-Kongregation in Wien (1811–1911)*, Vienna (1911), 344–352, pls. I–III.

Strzygowski, *Etschmiadzin* — J. Strzygowski, *Das Etschmiadzin-Evangeliar, Beiträge zur Geschichte der Armenischen, Ravennatischen und Syro-ägyptischen Kunst, Byzantinische Denkmäler*, Bd. I, Vienna, 1891.

Strzygowski *Kleinarmenische Min.* — J. Strzygowski, "Kleinarmenische Miniaturen-malerei, Die Miniaturen des Tübinger Evangeliars Ma. XIII. 1 vom J. 1113 bzw. 893 n. Chr.", *Atlas zum Katalog der Armenischen Handschriften*, Tübingen (1907), 19–43, Taf. VII–X, Abb. 1–12.

Strzygowski, *Koptische Kunst* — J. Strzygowski, *Koptische Kunst, Catalogue Général du Musée du Caire*, Vienna, 1904.

Strzygowski, *Serbischen Psalters* — J. Strzygowski, *Die Miniaturen des Serbischen Psalters... in München*, Wien, 1906.

Ter-Hovhannesiants, *Jerusalem 1890* — A. Ter-Hovhannesiants, *Zhamanakagrakan patmutiun S. Erusaghemi* (Chronological History of Holy Jerusalem), 2 vols., Jerusalem, 1890 (in Armenian).

Ter-Movsisian, *MSS. Arm. Kings* — Mesrop Ter Movsisian, "Armenian Miniatures, Manuscripts written for the Armenian Kings of Cilicia and for the Catholicos Constantine I, *Azgagrakan Handes* (1913), 61–82 (in Armenian).

Thierry, *Nouvelles Eglises* — N.M. Thierry, *Nouvelles Eglises Rupestres de Cappadoce*, Paris, 1963.

Tsafrir, *Zion* — Y. Tsafrir, *Zion – The South-Western Hill of Jerusalem, and its place in the urban development of the city in the Byzantine Period*, thesis submitted for the degree of Doctor of Philosophy at the Hebrew University of Jerusalem, September 1975 (in Hebrew, with English Abstract).

Trapp, *Sir Thomas More* — J.B. Trapp and H. Schulte Herbrüggen, *The King's Good Servant, Sir Thomas More, 1477–1535*, Catalogue of an Exhibition at the National Portrait Gallery, London, 1977.

Trendall, *Shellal* — A.D. Trendall, *The Shellal Mosaic*, Canberra, 1957.

Underwood, *Fountain of Life* — P.A. Underwood, "The Fountain of Life in Manuscripts of the Gospels", *Dumbarton Oaks Papers*, 5(1950), 43–158.

Underwood, *Kariye Djami* — P.A. Underwood, *The Kariye Djami*, 3 vols., New York, 1966.

Van Sichem,
Biblia Sacra
Biblia Sacra, Dat is de Geheele heylighe Schrifture Bedeylt in't Out en Nieu Testament schoone figuren gesneden door Christoffel van Sichem, eerst T'Antwerpen by Ian van Moerentorf, en nu herdruckt by Pieter Jacopsz Paetz, 1657.

Velmans,
Fontaine de Vie
T. Velmans, "L'Iconographie de la 'Fontaine de Vie' dans la tradition Byzantine à la fin du Moyen Age", *Synthronon*, II, Paris (1968), 119–134.

Vincent and Abel,
Jerusalem II
H. Vincent et F.M. Abel, *Jérusalem* T. II; *Jérusalem Nouvelle*, Paris, 1922, 1926.

Volbach,
Early Christian Art
W.F. Volbach, *Early Christian Art*, London, 1958; *Frühchristliche Kunst*, München, 1958.

Volbach,
Elfenbeinarbeiten
W.F. Volbach, *Elfenbeinarbeiten der Spätantike und des Frühen Mittelalters*, Mainz, 1916.

Voskan,
see *Oskan*.

Waller,
Nederlandsche Graveurs
F.G. Waller, *Biographisch Woordenboek van Noord Nederlandsche Graveurs*, 's-Gravenhage, 1938.

Weitzmann,
Armenische Buchmalerei
K. Weitzmann, "Die Armenische Buchmalerei des 10. und Beginnens des 11. Jhs.", *Istanbuler Forschungen*, 4, Bamberg (1933), 1–85, figs. 1–51.

Weitzmann,
Athos
K. Weitzmann, *Aus der Bibliotheken des Athos*, Hamburg, 1963.

Weitzmann,
Byz. Buchmalerei 9–10. Jhds.
K. Weitzmann, *Die Byzantinische Buchmalerei des 9. und 10. Jahrhunderts*, Berlin, 1935.

Weitzmann,
Byz. Mins. and Icons
K. Weitzmann, "Byzantine Miniatures and Icon Painting", *Studies in Classical and Byzantine Manuscript Illumination*, Chicago (1971), 271–313.

Weitzmann,
Ill. MSS. at St. Catherine
K. Weitzmann, *Illuminated Manuscripts at St. Catherine's Monastery on Mount Sinai*, Collegeville, Minnesota, 1973.

Weitzmann,
Joshua
K. Weitzmann, *The Joshua Roll*, Princeton, 1948.

Weitzmann,
Lectionary of Dionysiou
K. Weitzmann, "An Imperial Lectionary in the Monastery of Dionysiou on Mount Athos, its Origin and its Wanderings", *Revue des Etudes sud-est Européennes*, 7(1969), 239–253.

Weitzmann,
Narrative and Liturgical
K. Weitzmann, "The Narrative and Liturgical Gospel Illustrations", *Studies in Classical and Byzantine Manuscript Illumination*, Chicago and London (1971), 246–270.

Weitzmann,
Sinai Icons
K. Weitzmann, *Icons from South Eastern Europe and Sinai*, London, 1968.

Wessel,
Koptische Kunst
K. Wessel, *Koptische Kunst*, Recklinghausen, 1963.

Wolohojian,
Armenian Alexander
A.M. Wolohojian, *The Romance of Alexander The Great by Pseudo-Callisthenes*, New York–London, 1969.

Wormald,
St. Augustine's Gospels
F. Wormald, *The Miniatures in the Gospels of St. Augustine, Corpus Christi College ms. 286*, Cambridge, 1954.

ZDPV
Zeitschrift des Deutschen Palästina-Vereins.

Zimmermann,
Vorkarolingische Min.
E.H. Zimmermann, *Vorkarolingische Miniaturen*, Berlin, 1966.

Notes

The Armenian Treasures of Jerusalem

Chapter One pages 21–28

1 Avi-Yonah, *QDAP* II, 4 (Jerusalem, 1932), nos. 117, 118, 119, 120, 123, 124, 132; III, 2 (1933), no. 374c. Most of the Armenian mosaic pavements were uncovered during the latter half of the 19th century, unrelated to any existing building. Those on the Mt. of Olives were found during the building of the Russian convent between 1870 and 1887, see Riess, *Ölberg*, 155–161.

2 Kenyon, *Jerusalem*, 273–4, figs. 29, 36, pl. 113, 114.

3 Dashian, *ZDPV*, 167–168; Avi-Yonah, *QDAP* II, Nos. 117–120, 132. M.E. Stone is of the view that the script of the Musrara mosaic, at least, is to be dated on palaeographic grounds no later than the 6th century.

4 See note 1 above.

5 See note 2 above.

6 Hovsepian, *Mosaik*, 88–90; Guthe, *Mosaiken*, 51–53. Murray, *Damascus Gate Mosaic*, 126–127, sums up the previous discussion on the identity of Artavan, stressing that he must have been a well-known person. He agrees with the identification with Artabanes, a general in Africa during the mid-6th century. Vincent and Abel, *Jerusalem II*, pl. XLIII, 1. Avi-Yonah, *QDAP* II, no. 118.

7 E. Loukianoff, "Le musée du Couvent russe du Mont des Oliviers à Jérusalem", *Bulletin de l'Institut d'Egypte*, 13 (1930–1), 100ff., pls. VI, VII.

8 Grabar, *Byzantium, Theodosius to Islam*, fig. 113; Levi, *Antioch*, I, 351–355; II, pls. LXXXIII, CXXXIV–V.

9 Avi-Yonah, *Nirim*, 86–93, fig. 1, pls. 17–22.

10 Avi-Yonah, *QDAP*, II, no. 117. It should perhaps be identified with the Armenian convent of St. John on Mt. of Olives, mentioned by Anastas as being in the convent of Pantaleon (see note 1 above) and by the *Commemoratorium de Casis Dei* of ca. 808, cf. Clermont-Ganneau, in *Archaeological Researches in Palestine in the Years 1873–4*, (Paris 1875), 333; Vincent and Abel, *Jerusalem II*, pl. XLIII, 2.

11 Ovadia, *Gaza*, 125, 144 (in Hebrew).

12 See note 1 above, and Avi-Yonah, *QDAP*, II, No. 132; Murray, *Damascus Gate*, 126.

13 For similar motifs and composition in 6th century synagogue and church mosaics, see Bahat, *Beth Shean* 56 pl. 4; Ovadia, *Gaza*, 124–127, pls. between 144–145; Avi-Yonah, *Nirim*, 86–93, fig. 1, pls. 17–22; M.S. Briggs in *The Burlington Magazine*, 32 (1918), 185–189; Trenall, *Shellal*; G.M. Fitzgerald, *A Sixth Century Monastery at Beth Shean*, (Philadelphia, 1939).

14 Hjort, *L'Oiseau*, 21–32.

15 Room L. See Crowfoot, *Early Churches*, pl. XX.

Chapter Two pages 29–40

1 The most significant collections are the Matenadaran in Erevan, the Mekhitarist Libraries in Vienna and Venice, and that in the All-Savior Cathedral in New Julfa. The small collections in the Walters Art Gallery in Baltimore and the Freer Gallery of Art in Washington, among others, contain important illuminated mss. Archbishop Norair Bogharian is at present completing a descriptive catalogue of the Jerusalem collection. Sirarpie Der Nersessian, to whose studies we owe most of our knowledge of Armenian art, has catalogued a number of the collections in Europe and U.S. For details, see the Bibliography at the end of this book under Der Nersessian, Bogharian, Janashian and Buschhausen. For a survey of chief collections and the status of cataloguing see M.E. Stone, "The Study of Armenian Manuscripts", *Armenian and Biblical Studies*, Jerusalem (1976), 283–294. On the history of the Jerusalem library, see M.E. Stone "The Manuscript Library of the Armenian Patriarchate in Jerusalem", *IEJ* 19 (1969), 20–43.

2 Ms. 1144, Der Nersessian, *L'Art Arménien*, 82–85, figs. 76, 77; Janashian, *San Lazzaro*, I, 20–28, pls. 1–11; Weitzmann, *Armenische Buchmalerei*, 4–8; Nordenfalk, *Kanontafeln*, Taf. 34–35.

3 Ms. 2374, formerly in the Library of the See of Etchmiadzin ms. 229. Strzygowski, *Etschmiadzin*; *idem*, *Ein Zweites Etschmiadzin*, 250; Durnovo, *Arm. Miniatures*, 27–41; Der Nersessian, *Etchmiadzin* (1964) in *Studies*, 525–558; *idem*, *L'Art Arménien*, 75–79, 91–93.

4 Der Nersessian, *Etchmiadzin date* (1933), in *Studies*, 554–557; *idem*, *Etchmiadzin* (1964) in *Studies*, 525–532; *idem*, *Apologie des Images* (1944–5) in *Studies*, 385.

5 *Idem*, *Apologie des Images* (1944–5) in *Studies*, 386, 393.

6 *Idem*, *The Armenians*, 35–39.

7 Ms. 1949, Bogharian, *Grand Catalogue*, VI (1972), 509.

8 ***ΤΟΥ ΓΕΟΡΓΕΟΣ ΤΟΥ ΚΑΛΟΥΓΡΑΦΗΣ ΚΑΤ ΑΒΑΝΚΕΑΗ ΤΟΥ ΜΑΡΚΟΣ.***

9 For an example of a Greek manuscript, see Weitzmann, *Byz. Buchmalerei*, 9–10 Jht., 76, fig. 519.

10 E.g. fols. 6–8.

11 Fol. 7v, Durnovo, *Arm. Miniatures*, 31.

12 Strzygowski, *Ein Zweites Etschmiadzin*; Bogharian, *Grand Catalogue*, VIII (1977), 242–245; Mekhitarian, *Cat. Exh. Jerusalem* (1969), No. 1; Der Nersessian, *Etchmiadzin date* (1933), in *Studies*, 540, considered it to be the 9th century, but in her recent *L'Art Arménien*, 120–122, she assumes it to be 11th century.

13 Fols. 7v and 8. Durnovo, *Arm. Miniatures*, 31 and 29 respectively.

14 E.g., Matenadaran ms 7735 of 986, fol. 7, and ms. 288 of 1099, fol. 4v.; Jerusalem ms. 3624 of 1041, fol. 11v., and ms. 1924 of 1064, fol. 8; Walters Art Gallery ms. 537 of 966, fol. 3, see Der Nersessian, *Walters*, pl. 5. For Syriac full-page crosses, see Leroy, *MSS. Syriaques*, pls. 2–7.

15 K. Weitzmann added to this recension the fragmentary Gospel of Vienna, Mekhitarist Monastery Lod. 697, see Weitzmann, *Armenische Buchmalerei*, 16; Buschhausen, *Wien*, 17–19, pls. 1–13. S. Der Nersessian added two other Gospels with similar iconography. The Dsghruth of 974 and the Walters Art Gallery of 966, Ms. W. 537, see Der Nersessian, *Walters*, 1–9, pls. B, 1–11; for the Dsghruth Gospel see pl. 3.

16 Kondakoff, *Bogomateri*, II, fig. 91. It recalls many other orant women without a child in Early Christian catacombs and on sarcophagi, gold glasses, and ampullae. *Ibid.*, figs. 45–49, 55–67, 73–76, 92. This may also be the origin of the standing, orant Virgin Blachernitissa carrying the Christ Child in an aureole on her breast, cf. *ibid.*, I, figs. 38–48.

17 Kondakoff, *Bogomateri*, I, 316–356, figs. 177–202, II, pp. 267–319, figs. 180–213. For some exceptions see e.g., Kondakoff, *ibid.*, vol. I, figs. 31 (Venice, St. Mark), 33 (Byzantine cross), 34–39 (Byzantine coins), 196 (the 12th century English Landsdowne Psalter, B.L. Lands. 383, fol. 105), vol. II, 92 (an ampulla), 93 (the Etchmiadzin Gospel).

18 Kondakoff, *ibid.*, I, fig. 200.

19 This has in fact been lost from the Munich manuscript and survives only in the copy in Belgrade, fol. 259, cf. Strzygowski, *Serbische Psalters*, No. 144, p. 82, Taf. LVII. He gives other examples from Athos and interprets the scene according to the Byzantine Painter's manual by Dionysios of Fourna, Didron, *Christian Iconography*, Appendix II, vol. II, 350.

20 T. Velmans. *Fontaine de Vie*, 127–134, figs. 7–11.

21 Staatliche Museen, Volbach, *Early Christian Art*, pl. 95, p. 62; cf. Volbach, *Elfenbeinarbeiten*, No. 162, Taf. 53 for a similar representation in Trier. These iconographical traditions do not continue in the Vienna Gospel (ms. 697). The orant Virgin does not appear and in the Sacrifice of Isaac the altar is built in steps, Buschhausen, *Wien*, fig. 12.

22 Cod. 697.

23 See note 3 above.

24 Der Nersessian, *L'Art Arménien*, 82–93, figs. 53, 54, 58–61; *idem*, *Aghthamar*; *idem*, *Etchmiadzin date* (1933) in *Studies*, 553–554, figs. 313–314.

25 Thierry, *Nouvelles Eglises*, 73–87, figs. 15–19, pls. 40–43; Restle, *Asia Minor*, I, 69–71, 172; III, No. LV, figs. 488–492.

26 Restle, *Asia Minor*, III, Annunciation, fig. 489; Apostles, fig. 488.

27 Other Cappadocian painted churches of the 9th–11th centuries have the same geometrical, decorative style, e.g., Göreme, Chapel 1, *El Nazar* (Restle, *Asia Minor*, I, 101–103; II, figs. 1–20); Chapel 6 (*ibid.*, I, 109 ff., II, figs. 53–56); Chapel 7, *Tokali Kilise*, vestibule and New Church (*ibid.*, I, 111–116, II, figs. 61–123); Chapel 9, Theotokos, John the Baptist and George (*ibid.*, I, 117–119, III, figs. 124–133). Outside Göreme is the *Tavsanli Kilise* (Church with the Hare) *ibid.*, I, 152 ff., III, figs. 388–402). This style developed in Cappadocia during the Iconoclastic Period, when the program of decoration was changed from narrative to symbolic.

28 Lafontaine-Dosogne, *Nouvelles Cappadociennes*, 171–172; *idem*, *Review of Thierry*, 135; Restle, *Asia Minor*, I, 67–74.

29 Der Nersessian, *L'Art Arménien*, 117; Grabar, *Formation de l'art*.

30 In Armenia during the 9th to 11th centuries, the sumptuous Queen Mlk'ē, the Etchmiadzin, Gagik and Trebizond (Venice, Mekhitarist Monastery of San Lazzaro, ms. 1400 of ca. 1000, see Weitzmann, *Armenische Buchmalerei*, 19–23, figs.

36–50, Janashian, *San Lazzaro*, 2–3, 23–27, pls. XII–XXIII) Gospel books, were executed concurrently with the more geometrical Gospels of the Walters (ms. W. 537), the Second Etchmiadzin, the Vienna (cod. 697), and that of Mougna (Matenadaran ms. 7736, see Durnovo, *Arm. Miniatures*, 50–59; Izmailova, *Tetraévangile de Mougna*). In Byzantium the refined and classicizing style of the Leo Bible (Vat. Reg. 1, see *Paleografica Vaticana*, 1–14, pls. 1–18), the Paris Psalter (Paris, Bib. Nat. gr. 139 see Buchthal, *Paris Psalter*) and the Menologium of Basil II (Vat. gr. 1613, see *Codices e Vaticani Selecti*, 8, (Turin, 1907), and many other 11th century manuscripts exist side by side with some pen-drawn, decorated Greek manuscripts, crudely outlined and filled with wash colors. Examples are some Gospel books in the Bib. Nat. in Paris, mss. gr. 62, gr. 63, gr. 277 (see Ebersolt, *Miniature Byzantine*, pls. XVII–XX; Weitzmann, *Byz. Buchmalerei 9–10 Jhds*, figs. 415–439). Some motifs in the Armenian illumination reflect Sassanian art (e.g. St. Catherine in Sinai, ms. 213, see Weitzmann, *Ill. Mss. at St. Catherine*, 10, fig. 5) Coptic (e.g. St. Catherine ms. 417, see Weitzmann, *ibid.*, 11, figs. 6, 7). Some manuscripts have both contrasting (?) styles, as in the Adrianople Gospel of 1007 (Venice, *San Lazzaro*, ms. 887, see Weitzmann, *Armenische Buchmalerei*, 17–19, figs. 30–35; Janashian *San Lazarro*, 3, 28–30, pls. XXXIV–XLI), where all the figural illustrations are classicizing in style, whereas the Eusebian tables and the two crosses are decorative and colorful in style.

31 Jerusalem, ms. 2556, Treasury of St. James, no. 1. Bogharian, *Grand Catalogue*, VIII (1977), 245 ff.; Der Nersessian, *L'Art Arménien*, 109–114, figs. 75–77.

32 Such as the Gospel in Paris, Bib. Nat. ins. gr. 74, see Omont, *Grec 74* and the Imperial Lectionary in Mt. Athos, Dionysou ms. 587.

33 Fols. 18, 18v, 19.

34 Fols. 135v, 222v, 317v, with remnants of a frame below the inscription on fol. 222v, which indicates that a large panel has been cut out. The inscription at the end of St. John has not survived, since the last ten folios, 471–481 are paper replacements.

35 Another short dedicatory inscription mentioning Gagik alone is written in gold at the end of Eusebius' letter to Carpianus on fol. 5v., Bogharian, *Grand Catalogue*, VIII (1977), 245 ff. For the use of Gagik's Gospel as a model of a good text, see Bogharian, *Zion*, (1968), 70–72 (in Armenian). Bogharian assumes that the Trebizond Gospel (Venice, San Lazzaro ms. 1400/108, Janashian, *San Lazzaro*, 23–27) was copied from Gagik's Gospel by the famous scribe Grigor Morghanetsy on the orders of the Catholicos Grigoris (1066–1105). He lists seven manuscripts which were copied from the model of Grigor between 1144 and 1342.

36 Monastery of Dionysiou, ms. 587, Der Nersessian, *L'Art Arménien*, 110. Some reproductions of Dionysiou ms. 587 are in K. Weitzmann, *Narrative and Liturgical*, figs. 216, 239, 241, 246, 248, 251–253; for color plates, see Pelekanides, *Treasures of Mount Athos*, I, 434–446, figs. 189–277; and K. Weitzmann, *Aus der Bibliotheken des Athos* (Hamburg, 1963), figs. 12–15. The most thorough discussion is in Weitzmann, *Lectionary of Dionysiou*, 239–253. The resemblance lies in the program of the text illustrations, and in the style. There are however some iconographic differences between the lectionary and the Gagik Gospel, such as the scene of the Last Supper, see e.g. Dionisiou ms. 587, fol. 53, Pelekanides, *Treasures of Mount Athos*, I, fig. 224.

37 *Codices e Vaticani selecti* 8, *Il menologio de Basilio II* (Turin, 1907).

38 Not as suggested by Janashian, *San Lazzaro*, I, 10, during his reign in Asia Minor 1064–1081. cf. Der Nersessian, *Armenian Byzantium*, 118 ff.

39 Der Nersessian, *Freer Gallery*, 1–6, with all the literature up to 1963; see also Der Nersessian, *L'Art Arménien*, 117–122, figs. 82–88; Izmailova, *L'Iconographie*, 129–166; Izmailova, *Tetraévangile de 1038*, 203–240; Der Nersessian, *Walters*, 1–5, pls. 1–11.
The list of ten manuscripts comprises:
1 Matenadaran ms. 7739 of late 10th or early 11th century. Only one canon table and the Annunciation are left. Not included in the group by Der Nersessian or by Izmailova.
2 Matenadaran ms. 4804 of 1018 from Talash. Four Evangelists and the indications of the Twelve Apostles remain.
3 Matenadaran ms. 283 of 1033. Contains canon tables, Evangelists, the Baptism, Adoration of the Magi, and the Shepherds.
4 Matenadaran ms. 6201 of 1038. Contains Eusebius' letter and canon tables, the Nativity, Baptism, Transfiguration, Entry into Jerusalem, Last Supper, Crucifixion, Women at the Sepulcher with the Risen Christ, and the Evangelists.
5 Jerusalem ms. 3624 of 1041. Contains the largest cycle, almost identical with Matenadaran 3784 of 1057.
6 Matenadaran ms. 3723 of 1045, contains the entry into Jerusalem, the Last Supper, Entombment and Harrowing of Hell, and the Evangelists.
7 Matenadaran ms. 974, of no exact date in the 11th century, but closely related to Jerusalem ms. 3624 of 1041 and Matenadaran 3784 of 1057. It contains a reversed cycle starting with the Evangelists, Entombment and Harrowing of Hell, Crucifixion, Betrayal, Transfiguration and Raising of Lazarus, Presentation and Baptism.
8 Matenadaran ms. 3784 of 1057 from Melitene. Contains an identical choice of scenes to Jerusalem 3624 of 1041, although it differs somewhat in iconography and may be closer to the original model.
9 Jerusalem ms. 1924 of 1064 from Shukhr Khandaria.
10 Freer Art Gallery mss. 33.5, 47.2–4. Fragmentary Gospel of no exact date in the 11th century, related in style and iconography to Jerusalem ms. 1924 of 1064. Contains canon tables and the Evangelists.

40 Ms. 3624.

41 Ms. 3784.

42 Fols. 11v, the foliation in both manuscripts is identical.

43 Fols. 2–5v.

44 Fols. 6–10v.

45 Fol. 11v.

46 In the tenth century Matenadaran Gospel, ms. 7739, there is only one illustration depicting the Annunciation, see Durnovo, *Arm. Miniatures*, p. 25. It has some elements which are of Islamic origin. Firstly, the illustration is executed along the width of the page, which must be turned sideways to view it. This creates a horizontally elongated format, as the Koran manuscripts of the period; and secondly it has a stylized foliage motif on the right which is common in carpet pages and title panels of Koran manuscripts. See Ettinghausen, *Arab Painting*, 167–170, 191. In the Matenadaran 4804 of 1018 and the Freer ms. 335, 47.2–4 Gospels, only the Evangelists remain. This may mean either that part of their full cycle is lost or that they belong to a short cycle recension. For instance, the Gospel of 1045 (Matenadaran 3723) must have had a fuller cycle which was lost. Each of the two remaining leaves has successive scenes which correspond to a full cycle. The Entry into Jerusalem (fol. 1) is followed by the Last Supper (fol. 1v). The Descent into Hell and the Entombment (fol. 2) are followed by the Four Evangelists (fol. 2v).

47 For instance, the most original artist of the 1038 Gospel (Matenadaran 6201) made a very peculiar choice of scenes and iconography (see Izmailova, *Tetraévangile de 1038*, figs. 9–16), starting with the Nativity (fol. 5), introducing four Magi, continuing with the Baptism (fol. 5v), Transfiguration conflated with the Raising of Lazarus (fol. 6), Entry into Jerusalem in uncommon fashion from right to left (fol. 6v), the Last Supper near a square table (fol. 7), Crucifixion depicting the two crucified robbers flanking Christ (fol. 7v), the three women at the empty tomb, on which two angels are seated, and the Risen Christ appearing to Peter and John (fol. 8), and the Evangelists (fol. 8v). The artist of the 1045 Gospel (Matenadaran 3723) omitted the scene of the Ascension of Christ, which should have come between the Descent into Hell (fol. 2) and the Evangelists (fol. 2v).
A similarly cut cycle appears in the undated Gospel of the Matenadaran ms. 974. As Izmailova has proved (*L'Iconographie*, 128), it is not wrongly bound and was probably copied from the Syriac cycle which is read from right to left, and therefore originally ended with the Evangelists (fol. 1), and started with the Presentation in the Temple (fol. 3v). Here, too, the Ascension was never depicted, nor was the Deposition. Two folios are missing: one which depicted the Annunciation with the Visitation on the recto and the Nativity on the verso; the second had the Entry into Jerusalem on the recto and the Last Supper on the verso.

48 See Sotiriou, *Mont Sinai*, figs. 17, 39–40, 57; Weitzmann, *Sinai Icons*, I, pl. 45.

49 Ms. 6201, fol. 8.

50 The Dormition of the Virgin, which appears at the end of the more conventional feast cycle in Byzantine icons, from the 11th century onwards, instead of the Women and the Risen Christ (e.g., St. Catherine icon No. 529 of the 11th century,

Sotiriou, *Mont Sinai*, I, fig. 57 and also fig. 42) does not appear in any of the Armenian Melitene group Gospels.

51 As well as in the Gospels of 1038, fol. 7 and of 1045, fol. 2v, see Izmailova, *L'Iconographie*; Durnovo, *Arm. Miniatures*, 49.

52 As well as in the Gospel Matenadaran ms. 974, fol. 2v, Durnovo, *op. cit.*, 61.

53 As well as in the Gospel of 1057, fol. 10, Izmailova, *L'Iconographie*.

54 Izmailova, *L'Iconographie*, 126. She includes only four manuscripts in the group: Jerusalem 3624, Matenadaran 3723, 3784, and 974.

55 Restle, *Asia Minor*, I, 111–116 (the Vestibule of the Tokali); II, figs. 61–123; and Kiliçclar Kilise, I, 131–134, II, figs. 251–278.

56 Izmailova, *L'Iconographie*, 129–131, figs. 1, 2; Restle, *Asia Minor*, II, figs. 110 (repainted) and 262, cf. Chapel 9, fig. 125, and Chapel 16, fig. 156, of the 10th and 11th centuries respectively.

57 Izmailova, *L'Iconographie*, *ibid.*; Restle, *Asia Minor*, II, figs. 64, 263, cf. figs. 125, 156. It also appears in the so-called Armenian Mougna Gospel of the 11th century (Matenadaran ms. 7736, fol. 11); Durnovo, *Arm. Miniatures*, 55; Izmailova, *Tetraévangile de Mougna*, fig. 1. The maiden holding a curtain in the Visitation as well as in the Annunciation also appears in western art of the Early Middle Ages. A well-known example is the Genoels-Elderen ivory diptych at the Royal Museum of Art and History, Brussels, a Rhine-Meuse work of the 8th century. See *Art Chrétien, Catalogue*, ed. A Jansen (Bruxelles, 1964), No. 265, fig. 261. This certainly indicates that the Early Christian model was known in the West at this early stage.

58 Izmailova, *L'Iconographie*, 137–140, figs. 7–9; Restle, *Asia Minor*, II, figs. 70, 257.

59 Izmailova, *L'Iconographie*, 142–143, figs 13–15; Restle, *Asia Minor*, II, figs. 91, 257.

60 Izmailova, *L'Iconographie*, 145–148, figs. 21–23; Restle, *Asia Minor*, II, figs. 73, 272, cf. fig. 107.

61 Izmailova, *L'Iconographie*, 157–160, figs. 32–34; Restle, *Asia Minor*, II, fig. 95.

62 Examples are the standing Virgin in the Annunciation, and the maiden holding the curtain in the Visitation, both in the apse mosaic of the basilica of Poreč, mid-6th century; Grabar, *Iconography*, fig. 316. The Baptism of Christ, the Last Supper and the Ascension also have their origin in Early Christian iconography.

63 Izmailova, *L'Iconographie*, 131–137, 140–145, 148–157, 160–166, figs. 5–20, 24–37, and her references to Millet, *l'Iconographie*, and Der Nersessian, *Manuscrits arméniens des XIIe et XIVe s.*, (Paris, 1937).

64 Other examples are the mounted Magi in the Nativity in the Gospel of 1057, pl. 6v and in the Greek Gospel, Paris, Bib. Nat.

65 London, Brit. Lib. Add. 7167, fol. 13v, see Leroy, *MSS Syriaques*, I, 350 ff., II, pl. 124:1. The Pentecost in the Syriac Rabbula Gospels of 586 also has the standing Apostles, but the Virgin is in the center with a dove above her. Florence, Laurentiana, Plut. I. 56, fol. 14v; see Leroy, *ibid.*, II, pl. 34; cf. Restle, *Asia Minor*, III, fig. 404.

66 For example, the artist of Chapel 28 in Göreme of ca. 1071 used white background to his paintings. Restle, *Asia Minor*, II, figs. 245–250.

67 P. Charanis, *The Armenians in the Byzantine Empire*, (Lisbon, 1963), 30–34.

68 Izmailova, *Localisation d'un groupe*, suggested as place of origin Sebastia (Sivas), further north from Melitene, well into the Cappadocian region.

Chapter Three pages 41–46

1 For a detailed historical analysis of the kingdom of Cilicia, see Der Nersessian, *The Kingdom of Cilician Armenia*, (1969), in *Studies*, 329–352.

2 Weitzmann, *Narrative and Liturgical*, 247–270. All the relevant bibliography there.

3 Ms. 1796 fol. 5v. Bogharian, *Grand Catalogue*. VI (1972), 146, fig. 18. The colophon on fol. 287v is not complete.

4 Der Nersessian, *L'Art Arménien*, 129f, figs. 90, 91. Bogharian, *ibid.*, 149, fig. 20. The other inscription is based on Isaiah 43:25.

5 Millet, *L'Iconographie*, 517 ff., 540 ff., figs. 566–571, 584–588.

6 As in the Gospels of Queen Mlk'ē and Etchmiadzin, although there the illustrations are not attached to the texts.

7 The manuscripts of the group are listed with bibliography by Der Nersessian, *Freer Gallery*, 10–17. The dated manuscripts are: 1) Matenadaran 7347, from Hromkla, 1166; 2) Matenadaran 1568, from Skevra, 1173; 3) a Gospel book formerly in Toakat, now lost, from Hromkla, 1173; 4) Walters Art Gallery 538, probably also from Hromkla, 1193; 5) Venice, Mekhitarist ms. 1635, from Skevra, 1197. The undated manuscripts are: 7) Freer Gallery of Art 50.3; 8) the Theodore Gospel, Jerusalem 1796; 9) Venice 888; and 10) Venice 141. Moreover, Grigor, the scribe of "the Narek" collection of prayers, who states in a colophon of another manuscript that he copied it in 1173, while he was a guest of Skevra, is known to have come from Hromkla. Der Nersessian, *Freer*, 11–12; Azarian, *The Narek of 1173*, 85–110, figs. 1–6; Hovespian, *Colophons*, 445–8. A fragment of another 12th century Gospel is inserted in Thoros Roslin's Lady Keran Gospel of 1265, Jerusalem ms. 1956, fols. I–IV, 13 (see Catalogue below). It contains the full-page portrait of St. Mark (fol. 13v) and a gold decorated frame with headpiece to St. Mark (fol Iv). The painting of the Evangelist's portrait was apparently not completed. I am grateful to Prof. H. Buchthal for helping me date this fragment. See Theophylact, *Enarrationes in quattuor Evangelistas*, Byzantine 12th century, Oxford, Corpus Christi College ms. 30; F. 3.7, cf. J.3. Trapp, *Sir Thomas More*, National Portrait Gallery, London (1977), No. 91, p. 57.

8 Ms. 141, Janashian, *San Lazzaro*, 34–36, pls. XLVIII–L; and ms. 888, Janashian, *ibid.*, 36–39, pls. LI–LV; Der Nersessian, *Manuscrits Arm. de Venise*, figs. 69–85.

9 Ms. 50.3, Der Nersessian, *Freer*, figs. 9–32.

10 Der Nersessian, *Freer*, 12–13.

11 Ma. XIII, 1, Strzygowski *Kleinarmenische min.* pls. VIII–X; Azarian, *Cilician Min.*, 17 ff. figs. 5–7.

12 Ms. 7737, Azarian, *Cilician Min.*, 17 ff, figs. 2–4.

13 Durnovo, *Arm. Miniatures*, 65; Azarian, *Cilician Min.*, figs. 9, 10.

14 The rare occasions in the 10th century where Evangelists' symbols can be seen in a Greek Gospel book are represented within medallions in margins of the Gospels of Mount Athos, Stauronikita ms. 43. Weitzmann, *Byz. Buchmalerei 9–10 Jhds.*, 24. An example of zoomorphic Evangelists' symbols can be found in the 10th century Gospels in the Vatican, gr. 2138, fols. 35, 37, 39v, see Weitzmann, *ibid.*, figs. 581–583. Half-figures of symbols in the head panel of each book exist in Constantinopolitan Gospels from the beginning of the 12th century, e.g., Oxford, Bodleian Library ms. Auct. T. Inf. 1.3, fols. 7, 51, 89, 153; see Hutter, *Corpus Byz. Min. Oxford*, I, 76, figs. 279, 282–284, see also figs. 407, 409, 411, 413. Full and half-figures of Evangelists' symbols, at times with wings and books, appear, however, in Early Christian representations, e.g., ivory diptych in Milan, wall mosaic of Hosias David in Thessaloniki, Archbishop's Chapel and San Vitale in Ravenna, and others, see Volbach, *Early Christian Art* (London, 1961), figs. 100, 101, 134, 148, 160.

15 Neuss, *Ezechiel*, 167.

16 E.g., St. Augustine's Gospel, cf. Wormald *St. Augustine's Gospels*, pl. II; The Lindisfarne Gospels, cf. Zimmermann, *Vorkarolingische Min.*, Tafs. 223–226; Kitzinger, *St. Cuthbert's Coffin*, 229–230; Codex Millenarius of ca. 800 in the Kremsmünster Stiftsbibliothek, Cim. 1, Neumüller, *Millenarius*, 78–112; see also the insular Cuthbert Gospels of the 8th century, Vienna, Nat. Bibl. Cod. Lat. 1224, *idem*, figs. 9, 10, 21, 22, 50–53. There are many others.

17 Cambridge, Corpus Christi ms. 286, fol. 78, the symbol of St. Mark; Wormald, *op. cit.*, pl. X.

18 Munich, Staatsbibliothek, Cod. Lat. 6224, fols. 12, 81v, 82v, Zimmermann, *Vorkarolingische Min.*, Tafs. 5, 6, 7.

19 Neumüller, *Millenarius*, fig. 53. Symbols as zoomorphic initials are also known from western Europe, e.g., a sacramentary from Gellone, Paris, Bibl. Nat. Lat. 12048, fols. 42, 42v, 115v; see Zimmermann, *Vorkarolingische Min.*, Tafs. 154–155.

20 Der Nersessian, *Freer*, 9, and figs. 13, 14.

21 Janashian, *San Lazzaro*, 34–36, pls. XLVIII–L.

22 Ms. 1635, Der Nersessian, *Manuscrits Arm. de Venise*, figs. 38–68, cf. especially figs. 46, 48, 50, 52.

23 Bogharian compares it with some notes of 1095 written in angular *bolorgir* script on fols. 117v, and 242v, of a manuscript by Nemesius, *The Nature of Man*, copied in 1047, possibly at Ani (Jerusalem ms. 1862), cf. Bogharian, *Grand Catalogue*, VI (1972), 255–257. This does not accord with the style of the illustrations. Moreover the slanting, angular *erkathagir* script, which was modern in the 11th century, continued to be used in the 12th century and later, cf. the Lectionary from Meshkevor copied in 1192 (Jerusalem ms. 121). A Gospel book of the same period (Jerusalem ms. 1795) used interlacing motifs in the decorative panels, similar in design and color to the 1192 Lectionary. The juxtaposition in the Khatchadur Gospel of the slanting, angular *erkathagir* script in one column

and the formal *bolorgir* script in the other is also typical of this period (Bogharian, *Grand Catalogue*, VI (1972), 144–146, figs. 16, 17).

Chapter Four pages 47–62

1 Der Nersessian, *The Kingdom of Cilician Armenia*, pp. 345–349.
2 Istanbul, Armenian Patriarchate, see Der Nersessian, *Evangile de Zeytoun*, 559–562.
3 Jerusalem, ms. 251.
4 Baltimore, Walters Art Gallery, ms. 539.
5 Jerusalem, ms. 2660.
6 Jerusalem, ms. 1956.
7 Jerusalem, ms. 2027.
8 Formerly, Jerusalem, ms. 3627, treasury no. 119; now in the Matenadaran ms. 10675, see Der Nersessian, *L'Art Arménien*, 136–138, figs. 93, 97; other pictures in *idem*, *Freer Gallery*, figs. 361–363; *idem*, *The Armenians*, pl 68.
9 Der Nersessian, Freer Gallery, 26–54, figs. 53–181. Matenadaran, mss. 5458 from Hromkla of 1266 and ms. 8321 of 1236, formerly at Nov Nakhitchevan, ms. 14, see Der Nersessian, *Chester Beatty*, 29; Tchobanian, *Roseraie Arm.*, II, 26; Ter Movsisian, *MSS Arm. Kings*, 14–16; Der Nersessian, *Walters Gallery*, 15; Gevorkian, *Leo III Gospel*; Der Nersessian, *L'Art Arménien*, 148.
10 See for example Durnovo, *Arm. Miniatures*, 112–138, who attributes to him three manuscripts in the Matenadaran, ms. 197, a Gospel of 1287, an undated Gospel ms. 9422, and ms. 979, a lectionary of 1288. For these, see Buschhausen, *Wien*, 52–55.
11 Der Nersessian, *Chester Beatty*, 28–29.
12 Kirakos was a very prolific scribe whose work is known from 1239 to about 1267. Der Nersessian, in *ibid.*, 28–30, lists eight manuscripts. The Nov Narkhitchevan ms. 14 in her list is now Matenadaran ms. 8321, which was illuminated by Thoros Roslin, see note 9 above.
13 Yovhannes is known to have copied two manuscripts for Constantine I. See Der Nersessian, *Freer Gallery*, pp. 18–25, cf. Buschhausen, *Wien*, pp. 43–44, fig. 20.
14 Der Nersessian, in *Chester Beatty*, 29. no. 3, lists five manuscripts by Konstandin.
15 See also Lady Keran Gospel of 1265, Jerusalem ms. 1956, fol. 6; Walters 539, fol. 6, Gospel of 1262, cf. Der Nersessian, *Walters*, fig. 48; and the Yovhannes Gospel of 1253, Freer 44.17, fol. 7, cf. Der Nersessian, *Freer Gallery*, fig. 38.
16 Der Nersessian, *Mss. Arm. de Venise*, 58–60. 12th century manuscripts are e.g. Matenadaran ms. 7347 of 1166, see Azarian, *Cilician Min.*, figs. 41–46; the Narek of 1173, Matenadaran 1568, *ibid.*, figs. 12–13; Walters 538 of 1193, Der Nersessian, *Walters*, figs. 23–34; Venice 1635 of 1193, Der Nersessian, *MSS. Arm. de Venise*, figs. 38–51; Lvov (Lemberg), Archbishop's Lib. of 1197, Akinian, *Skevra-Evangeliar* 1197, figs, 1–7, 10, 13; Freer ms. 50.3, Der Nersessian *Freer Gallery*, figs. 9–12, 15–32. The program of the Freer and Lvov Gospels as well as details antedate those of Yovhannes and Thoros Roslin.
17 Venice 1400, Janashian, *San Lazzaro*, pls. 12–17.
18 Matenadaran 7736, Durnovo, *Arm. Miniatures*, 51.
19 Matenadaran 311, Durnovo, *ibid.*, 65; Azarian, *ibid.*, figs. 9–10.
20 Nordenfalk, *Kanontafeln*, Tafs. 1–83, 130–148.
21 See Weitzmann, *Armenische Buchmalerei*, 19f., Abb. 11, fig. 37, on the origins of the Trebizond Gospel. Cf. Weitzmann, *Byz. Buchmalerei 9–10 Jhds.*, 25–26, Abb. 194–195; Vat. gr. 364 and Florence, Laurentiana, Conv. Soppr. 159. See also Oxford, Bodleian Lib. Auct. T. Inf. 1.10. Hutter, *Corpus Byz. Min. Oxford*, I, 59–67, Abb. 227–235. Mount Athos, Monastery of Dionysiou, ms. 4, Pelekanidis, *Treasures of Mount Athos*, I, figs. 17–21.
22 E.g., Oxford, Bodleian Lib. Auct. T. inf. 1.10, fol. 16v. Hutter, *Corpus Byz. Min. Oxford*, I, fig. 225. These standing types were based on eastern Early Christian models, such as the standing Ammonius and Eusebius in the Rabbula Gospel, see Leroy, *MSS. Syriaques*, pl. 21.2. Busts of authors other than Eusebius and Carpianus, were used in the arches of Early Christian canon tables, as the Apostles' medallions of the 7th century Greek canon tables in the British Lib. Add. 5111. Nordenfalk, *Kanontafeln*, Taf. 1–4. Evangelists and Apostles can be found in the 8th century Trier Gospel, Dombibl. 61/134, cf. *ibid.*, Taf. 74–83. These portraits in lunettes go back to late classical art, as in the Roman Calendar of 354, and others, cf. Der Nersessian, *MSS. Arm. de Venise*, 57–58.
23 Ms. 1635 fols. 1v–2, Der Nersessian, *MSS. Arm de Venise*, figs. 38, 39. And Akinian, *Skevra-Evangeliar 1197*, fig. 1.
24 For the lists of prophets in the Jerusalem manuscripts, see Catalogue entries below. For the Walters Gospel, see Der Nersessian, *Walters*, 12, 27–28, figs. 47, 48, 51, 52.
25 E.g. Freer Gospel 32.18, pp. 43, 452, 516, 535; see Der Nersessian, *Freer Gallery*, 44–45, figs. 66, 147, 160, 165; Walters Gospel, fol. 174, cf. *idem*, *Walters*, 13, fig. 97; *idem*, *L'Art Arménien*, 138–141, fig. 98.
26 In the Rabbula Gospel (see Leroy, *MSS. Syriaques*, pls. 22–27), prophets and kings, some holding rolled scrolls, stand flanking the arches of the canon tables, and although they do not display any texts, their presence there must be typological. In the Greek Codex Rosannensis, prophets and kings indicating New Testament scenes appear below the Gospel illustrations, see Muñoz, *Rossano*, Tav. I–VIII, XI, XII. These hold open scrolls inscribed with biblical verses which refer to the Old Testament typological prefigurations of the Gospel scenes. A later representation of this kind is David depicted as a prefigural type in some 11th century Byzantine monastic psalters, such as the Pantocrator 61 on Mount Athos, see Dufrenne, *Psautiers grecs*, I, e.g. fols. 24v, 26v, 55v, pls. 3, 4, 8,. However, these portraits, like those of the Rosannensis, are not related to the canon tables.
27 E.g. the Apostles in the Trier Gospel Dombibl. Cod. 61/134, Nordenfalk, *ibid.*, Taf. 75–83.
28 An 11th century example is in the Parma Gospels (Bibl. Palatina ms. gr. 5, fol. 5), where David and Isaiah flank Christ in Glory. Later Byzantine typological images of prophets next to New Testament scenes are numerous, e.g. the Homilies on the Virgin by Jacobus Kokkinobaphos, Vat. gr. 1162, fols. 2v, 41 cf. Stornajolo, *Giacomo Monaco*, pls. 1, 15; and in the Riccardiana Psalter, Florence, Bibl. Riccardiana ms. 323, fol. 14v, cf. Buchthal, *Latin Kingdom*, pl. 52a and pl. 144a from another Kokkinobaphos manuscript in Princeton Univ. Libr. I am grateful to my teacher, Prof. Hugo Buchthal, for letting me use the examples he gave in his lecture at Dumbarton Oaks, on the 11th May, 1978, during the Symposium on the Mosaics of San Marco and their Byzantine antecedents.
29 E.g. a twelfth-century Gospel from the Monastery of St. Panteleimon on Mount Athos, ms. 25, cf. Pelekanidis, *Treasures of Mount Athos*, II, figs. 323–326; a late 11th century Gospel in Oxford, Bodl. Clark 10, and a 12th century one, Bodl. Auct. T. inf. 1.10, cf. Hutter, *Corpus Byz. Min. Oxford*, figs. 214, 216, 218, 220, 236–239.
30 For the Walters Gospel of 1262, see Der Nersessian, *Walters*, figs. 55, 56, 88, 89, 105, 106, 122, 123. For the Freer Gospel ms. 32.18, see Der Nersessian, *Freer Gallery*, figs. 53, 132, 167. The Evangelists' portraits are missing from the latter manuscript and may never have been included.
31 Matenadaran ms. 311.
32 Der Nersessian, *Freer Gallery*, figs. 46, 47, 49, 51.
33 Der Nersessian, *Walters*, 10–30, figs. 57–133. Rich in text illustrations is also the Freer Gospel ms. 32.18 (Der Nersessian, *Freer Gallery*, 26–54, figs. 54–176).
34 Der Nersessian, *Freer Gallery*, 49.
35 Fol. 15v, Mekhitarian, *Cat. Exh. Jerusalem 1969*, fig. 5.2.
36 I am indebted to Archbishop Bogharian for pointing this out to me. Cf. Azarian, *Cilician Min.*, p. 115, fig. 69; Der Nersessian, *Min. Ciliciennes*, 512, fig. 249.
37 Examples can be found in the Walters Gospel, fol. 208v, Der Nersessian, *Walters*, fig. 110, pl. D; in the Freer Gospel, Der Nersessian, *Freer Gallery*, fig. 60; in Thoros' last Gospel of 1268, Matenadaran 10675, fol. 23, *ibid.*, fig. 362, and Der Nersessian, *The Armenians*, pl. 68.
38 Cf. *idem*, *Freer Gallery*, fig. 59.
39 Fol. 22, cf. *ibid.*, figs. 65, 136; cf. *idem*, *Walters*, figs. 62, 90, with no devil.
40 Fol. 36v, cf. *idem*, *Freer Gallery*, figs. 71, 90; *idem*, *Walters*, fig. 78.
41 Jerusalem ms. 2660, fol. 288. Der Nersessian, *The Armenians*, pl. 74.
42 Cf. Jerusalem ms. 251, fol. 20.
43 Cf. Der Nersessian, *Freer Gallery*, figs. 64, 72, 84, 117; *idem*, *Walters*, fig. 66.
44 For similar rendering of the standing Apostles, see *idem*, *Freer Gallery*, figs. 73, 76, 124; *idem*, *Walters*, figs. 74, 94.
45 *Ibid.*, fig. 97. I am grateful to Dr. V. Nersessian of the British Library for helping me to identify these scenes.
46 Cf. for similarity in rendering sheep and goats *ibidem*, figs. 111, 120. I am indebted to Mrs. Aliza Cohen for the identification of this scene.
47 Jerusalem ms. 1956.
48 Der Nersessian, *L'Art Arménien*, 141, 143, figs. 99, 100.
49 Der Nersessian, *L'Art Arménien*, 137–138, fig. 94.
50 *Idem*, *Walters*, fig. 97.
51 *Idem*, *Freer Gallery*, fig. 93. In Thoros' illumination there are even briefer representations of

the Entry into Jerusalem. In the Freer Gospels (*ibid.* fig. 153), only the back of the ass entering the gate and the procession of the disciples are seen as an illustration to St. Luke; and in the Leo and Keran Gospel of 1262 (Jerusalem 2660, fol. 260v) three men in front of a palm tree illustrate St. John's version.

52 Der Nersessian, *Walters*, 16, fig. 84; cf. the *Freer Gallery* (p. 46, fig. 126) version of both Joseph and Nicodemus on ladders, as in Byzantine iconography.
53 *Idem, Walters*, fig. 112.
54 Matenadaran ms. 10675, fol. 172. *Idem, Freer Gallery*, fig. 361.
55 *Idem, L'Art Arménien*, 134.
56 *Idem, Walters*, 19.
57 E.g. inhabitants of Nineveh coming out of their city can be found in the tenth century Paris Psalter, Paris, B.N. gr. 139, fol. 431v.
58 Matenadaran ms. 7739, fol. 1v, Der Nersessian, *L'Art Arménien*, 138, fig. 95.
59 E.g. on the doors of Santa Sabina in Rome, and in the 9th century Chludov Psalter in Moscow, fol. 270v.
60 Der Nersessian, *L'Art Arménien*, 138, fig. 96.
61 E.g. the Catacomb of Priscilla in Rome, which has a bird above the three youths.
62 E.g. in the Paris Gregory of the late 9th century, Paris, B.N. gr. 510, fol. 535v; cf. the Theodore Psalter of 1066, in the British Library Add. 19352, fol. 202; Der Nersessian, *Psautiers Grecs*, II, fig. 318.
63 J. Catergion, *Ecclesiae Ephesianae de obitu Joannis apost. narratio ex versione armeniaca saeculi V*, Wien 1877.
64 Der Nersessian, *Freer Gallery*, p. 67, who points out that this is a confusion with James the brother of Jesus, who was the first Bishop of Jerusalem.
65 E.g. St. Gregory Nazianzus in the Paris B.N. gr. 510, fol. 452, and St. Athanasius in gr. 550, fol. 209, see Omont, *B.N. Mss. grecs*, pls. LX, CXIII.
66 Washington, Freer Gallery, ms. 56.11, fol. 7, see Der Nersessian, *Freer Gallery*, 66–67, fig. 194, who mentions another Gospel copied for Bishop John in 1287, which has the same scene (Matenadaran ms. 197, fol. 311v).
67 P. Lauer, "Les Fouilles du Sanctorum au Latéran", *Mélanges d'Archéologie et d'Histoire*, (Ecole Française de Rome), XX (1900), 262, pl. VI.
68 Stuttgart, Württembergische Landesbibliothek, Cod. His. Fol. 415, fol. 83, see K. Löffler, *Schwäbische Buchmalerei in Romanischer Zeit*, Augsburg 1928, 56, pl. 33.
69 E.g. the Paris Gregory gr. 510, fol. 32v, Omont, *B.N. Mss. Grecs*, pl. XXII, cf. Der Nersessian, *Freer Gallery*, 67, note. 168.
70 Der Nersessian, *Freer Gallery*, 66.
71 In the Freer Gallery ms. 56.11, see Der Nersessian, *Freer Gallery*, 55–72, figs. 183–256. The decoration of the Gospel copied at Mamistra in 1275–6, by the Deacon Astuatsatur, surnamed Gaznuk follows Roslin's motifs and iconography in great detail. Jerusalem ms. 3628.
72 Washington, Freer Gallery ms. 36.15, Der Nersessian, *Freer Gallery*, 89–101, figs. 318–344.

Chapter Five pages 63–74

1 For suggested lists of manuscripts and literature, see Der Nersessian, *L'Art Arménien*, 143–162, figs. 101–117; *idem, Freer Gallery*, 58–62; *idem, Chester Beatty*, 29; Durnovo, *Arm. Miniatures*, 96–139; Azarian, *Cilician Min.*, figs. 28–39, 58–65, 95–134; Buschhausen, *Wien*, 54–55.
2 E.g. the Lectionary of King Hethum II, of 1286–88, Matenadaran ms. 979, see Durnovo, *Arm. Miniatures*, 128–139; Der Nersessian, *L'Art Arménien*, 156–157, figs. 114, 116; Azarian, *Cilician Min.*, figs. 130–134, pl. VIII.
3 Ms. 2563, Der Nersessian, *ibid.*, 144–150, figs. 104–107; Azarian, *ibid.*, figs. 107–115. Mekhitarian, *Cat. Exh. Jerusalem 1969*, No. 11, figs. 11.1–2.
4 Jerusalem ms. 2660, fol. 288. Der Nersessian, *The Armenians*. pl. 74.
5 Der Nersessian, *L'Art Arménien*, 148, fig. 104.
6 Jerusalem (ms. 2568). Der Nersessian, *ibid.*, 150–153, figs. 108–110; Azarian, *Cilician Min.*, figs. 98–106; Mekhitarian, *Cat. Exh. Jerusalem 1969*, No. 12, figs. 12.1–2. The first Vasak Gospel is the Freer Gallery ms. 32.18, cf. Der Nersessian, *Freer Gallery*, 31–32.
7 Der Nersessian, *L'Art Arménien*, 151; Buschhausen, *Wien*, 54.
8 Der Nersessian, *Vierge de Miséricorde* (1970) in *Studies*, 585–596, refers to another Armenian example with a seated Madonna and Child, and traces its type to Duccio's Virgin of the Franciscans in the Pinacotheca in Sienna.
9 Buschhausen, *Wien*, 54. The inscription under the picture mentions his sons Constantine and Hethum as well as Bishop John, Vasak's brother, who revised the text of the manuscript.
10 Azarian, *ibid.*, fig. 102.
11 Fol. 5, Der Nersessian, *L'Art Arménien*, fig. 110; and fols. 95, 152, 249.
12 Mekhitarian, *Cat. Exh. Jerusalem 1969*, fig. 5.2.
13 Matenadaran ms. 979. Der Nersessian, *ibid.*, 156–160, figs. 114, 116. Azarian, *ibid.*, figs. 130–134; Durnovo, *Arm. Miniatures*, 128–139.
14 Der Nersessian, *Vienna Gospel* (1961), in *Studies*, 577–583, figs. 352–354, 358–363, 365; Buschhausen, *Wien*, ms. 278, 45–55, Abb. 70–88.
15 Jerusalem ms. 1925, Der Nersessian, *Bible d'Erznka* (1966), in *Studies*, 603–609, figs. 374–385; Mekhitarian, *Cat. Exh. Jerusalem, 1969*, No. 10, figs. 10.1–2; Der Nersessian, *L'Art Arménien*, 218–220, fig. 166.
16 Matenadaran ms. 1746. Der Nersessian, *Bible d'Erznka*, 604.
17 E.g. Syriac Bible of the 6th–7th century, Paris, Bib. Nat. Syr. 341. Leroy, *MSS. Syriaques*, I, 208–219, II, pls. 43–48.
18 Fol. 8v, Der Nersessian, *Bible d'Erznka*, fig. 375.
19 K. Weitzmann, *Ancient Book Illumination*, (Harvard, 1959), 116–127.
20 F. Macler, *L'Evangile Arménien, Edition Photocopique du ms. 299 de la Bibliothèque d'Etchmiadzin*, (Paris, 1920), e.g. fols. 211v, 221v.
21 Bibl. Nat. Syr. 341, fol. 52v, and also in the Rabbula Gospel, fol. 4, as well as in the Cambridge U.L. 001.002, fol. 63v, Leroy, *MSS. Syriaques*, pls. 44.1, 22.2, 62.1.
22 Weitzmann, *Joshua*, figs. 13–15.
23 Grabar, *Eglise de Quartamin*, 638.
24 Volbach, *Early Christian Art*, fig. 134.
25 Neuss, *Ezechiel*, fig. 11.
26 *Ibid.*, figs. 35 and 39 respectively.
27 *Ibid.*, figs. 27, 28; Wessel, *Koptisch Kunst*, figs. 99, 100, pl. VII; Grabar, *Iconography*, pl. 134, notes that the figure of Ezekiel appears among the Apostles in Chapel 17, fig. 323.
28 *Ibid.*, fig. 10.
29 Neuss, *Ezechiel*, fig. 58. In the Gebhard Bible the angel turns towards Christ and away from the reclining Ezekiel, *ibid.*, fig. 55; in the English Winchester Bible, there is no angel next to Ezekiel, *ibid.*, fig. 44.
30 Matenadaran ms. 2743, Durnovo, *Armenian Miniatures*, 88–95; Der Nersessian, *L'Art Arménien*, 218, fig. 167.
31 E.g. the Evangelists' portraits in Matenadaran ms. 7644 and ms. 7690 of 1249, see Durnovo, *Armenian Miniatures*, 98, 99, 102.
32 Der Nersessian, *L'Art Arménien*, 219.
33 One of the Cilician artists reached Czips in Cyprus, where he produced a tinted drawn manuscript of Psalms and Canticles in 1306. Jerusalem ms. 1033. Bogharian, *Grand Catalogue*, IV (1969), 45–49, figs. 1–4.

Chapter Six pages 75–80

1 Matenadaran ms. 7729, Der Nersessian, *L'Art Arménien*, 211–212, fig. 163, now ascertained as being from Avag vanthk'.
2 Matendaran ms. 6288, *ibid.*, 214–215, 218, figs. 164, 165; Durnovo, *Armenian Miniatures*, 82–83.
3 For Moslem examples, see the illuminated Arabic Galen on Electuaries of the first half of the 13th century, Vienna, Nat. Lib. ms. A.F. 10, fol. 12v, Arnold-Grohmann, *Islamic Book*, pl. 33.
4 Jerusalem, ms. 1288 fol. 142v; Bogharian, *Grand Catalogue*, IV (1969), 483–496.
5 Cf. the priests standing to the right of the canon table in the Haghbat Gospel, Der Nersessian, *ibid.*, fig. 164, and see Arnold-Grohmann, *ibid.*, pls. 32–34.
6 Jerusalem ms. 336, fol. 2v; Bogharian, *Grand Catalogue*, III (1967), 217–221.
7 Jerusalem ms. 1794, Bogharian, *Grand Catalogue*, VI (1972), 140–144.
8 Examples of a similar type are the late 12th century Gospel of Hromkla in the Matenadaran (ms. 7737, Durnovo, *ibid.*, 77), and the Gospel of 1224 of Princess Vaneni (Matenadaran ms. 4823, Durnovo, *ibid.*, 85).
9 Ms. 1917, Der Nersessian, *MSS. Arm. de Venise*, 110–112, figs. 118–145.
10 Matenadaran ms. 2187. I am most grateful to Prof. Thomas Mathews for providing me with a list of 22 manuscripts which he compiled together with Prof. Sirarpie Der Nersessian. I hope that these will be published with the monograph on one of Thoros' richest Gospels at the University of California, Los Angeles, which Prof. Mathews is working on. See also Der Nersessian, *Chester Beatty*, I, p. XXIX note 3.
11 Jerusalem ms. 2360 and ms. 95 respectively.
12 Jerusalem ms. 365.
13 E.g., Matenadaran ms. 2743, Durnovo, *Arm. Miniatures*, 88–95.

14 See Der Nersessian, *MSS. Arm. de Venise*, 134–136.
15 Jerusalem ms. 365, Bogharian, *Grand Catalogue*, III (1969), 269–271.
16 *Ibid.*, 270.
17 Venice, ms. 1971, Der Nersessian, *MSS. Arm. de Venise*, cf. figs. 116, 120, where the facial features are most similar to those of Esayi and his disciples.
18 *Ibid.*, 133, fig. 119.
19 Four miniatures on two folios were in the Rosenberg Collection, Macler, *Documents*, I, 59–62, figs. 251–254; and later belonged to the Hazarian Collection in New York. Two are in the Chester Beatty Collection in Dublin, ms. 559. One is in the Garret Collection of Princeton University. One belonged to Mr. Kurdian, see Der Nersessian, *Chester Beatty*, pp. XXX–XXXI, 31–33, and colored frontispiece, both reproduced in Macler, *ibid.*, figs. 255, 256; and the second now in *The Christian Orient*, Catalogue of an exhibition at the British Library, London 1978, No. 117, pl. 14. The date of 1311 and the fact that it formerly belonged to the church of Theotokos in Tabriz (ms. 1) were established by H. Kurdian in *The Princeton University Library Chronicle*, IV (1943), 109–112. Der Nersessian, (*ibid.*, p. XXX) added four more panels from the B. Berenson Collection, now in I Tatti in Florence, cf. *idem*, *L'Art Arménien*, 224, fig. 168.
20 *Chester Beatty*, p. XXX.
21 E.g. *ibid.*, frontispiece; *idem*, *L'Art Arménien*, fig. 168; Macler, *Documents*, figs. 253–256.
22 Der Nersessian, *L'Art Arménien*, fig 168.
23 Macler, *Documents*, figs. 253, 254.
24 Jerusalem ms. 95, Bogharian, *Grand Catalogue*, I (1966), 289–301, figs. 37–47.
25 *Ibid.*, 297.
26 Ms. 278, Buschhausen, *Wien*, 45–55, figs. 70–88.
27 See Chapter V, note 33 the Czips Psalter.
28 Der Nersessian, *Vienna Gospel* (1961), in *Studies*, 579, enumerates other manuscripts of this period with a similar technique.
29 Another Lectionary from Berdak of 1334 in P. Morgan Lib. ms. 803 must have had a similar model. In Chester Beatty ms. 599, the artist used a similar model for his iconography of the Vision of Daniel (p. 217) and the Sacrifice of Isaac (p. 266). See *idem*, *Chester Beatty*, I, 147–152, II pls. 30–32, especially pls. 31b and 32a.
30 In the Morgan 803 Lectionary the angel and Abraham's knife are also missing.
31 It is somewhat differently composed in the Morgan Lectionary of 1334, fol. 102v, cf. *ibid.* fig. 413.

Chapter Seven pages 81–88

1 Other artists were active in other centers, e.g. a Gospel copied and illuminated in Tarsus in 1316 for Bishop Stephanos by the scribe and artist Leo Lazartsi, Jerusalem ms. 1950, see Bogharian, *Grand Catalogue*, VI (1972), 512–516; Der Nersessian, *L'Art Arménien*, 160–161 fig. 117; *idem*, *Studies*, II, fig. 356. In composition and style this manuscript preserves traditional Cilician art of the late 13th century.
2 Matenadaran ms. 2566, Der Nersessian, *MSS. Arm. de Venise*, 137–138.
3 *Ibid.*, 138–141. To the fifteen manuscripts (eleven of them signed and dated) which Der Nersessian lists should be added a further eighteen (fourteen of which are signed and dated), which she published in *Chester Beatty*, 37, note 2.
4 E.g., three in 1319, 1325 and in 1338, two in 1331.
5 Der Nersessian, *MSS. Arm. de Venise*, 137.
6 E.g. Jerusalem ms. 1949, the Gospel of 1312, and ms. 1973, Queen Mariun Gospel.
7 Jerusalem ms. 2649, Treasury of St. James No. 94. See Der Nersessian, *ibid.*, 139.
8 New York, Pierpont Morgan ms. 622, see Der Nersessian, *Synaxaire* (1950) in *Studies*, I, 417–435.
9 Venice ms. 107, Der Nersessian, *MSS. Arm. de Venise*, 138–139.
10 Jerusalem ms. 1949.
11 Fols. 11, 117, 184, 297.
12 Fols. 10v, 116v, 183v.
13 *Idem*, *Chester Beatty*, pl. 20.
14 Ms. 16, *idem*, *MSS. Arm. de Venise*, figs. 146–213; and of course the other ones, such as the Chester Beatty Gospel of 1342, ms. 614, *idem*, *Chester Beatty*, pls. 21–23.
15 Jerusalem ms. 1930, Bogharian, *ibid.*, vol. 6 (1972), 433–439, figs. 49–50.
16 On fol. 320v. Cf. the 1331 Gospel in Venice, ms. 16, *idem*, *MSS. Arm. de Venise*, figs. 165, 182.
17 Venice, ms. 1508, fol. 214, see *ibid.*, fig. 217.
18 Jerusalem, ms. 2649. The Evangelists' portraits by Pidzak in this Gospel are in a bad state and therefore do not merit reproduction here. The binding of 1334 is the earliest Armenian silver binding known, and is reproduced here (see frontispiece). See Mekhitarian, *Cat. Exh. Jerusalem 1969*, figs. 18:1–2.
19 Jerusalem ms. 1644, p. 243, Bogharian, *Grand Catalogue*, V (1971), 462–465, fig. 42.
20 Der Nersessian, *ibid.*, figs. 173, 175, 178.
21 Jerusalem ms. 1578, Bogharian, *Grand Catalogue*, V (1971), 359–362, figs. 25–28; Mekhitarian, *Cat. Exh. Jerusalem 1969*, No. 19, p. 26.
22 See C. Michel, "Pseudo-Matthieu" in H. Hemmer & P. Lejoy (ed.), *Evangiles Apocryphes*, I, (Paris, 1911), 62–64.
23 See P. Peeters, "Evangile de l'Enfance, Rédactions Syriaques, Arabes et Arméniennes", in *ibid.*, II (Paris, 1914), 69–71.
24 Der Nersessian, *Freer Gallery*, 84.
25 E.g. two 16th century hymnals, Vienna ms. 189, fol. Cv, and ms. 1270, p. 4, see Buschhausen, *Wien*, 80–81, 85, figs. 151, 181; Chester Beatty ms. 592 of 1588, see Der Nersessian, *Chester Beatty*, 135; Freer Gallery ms. 37.19 of 1651–52, see *idem*, *Freer Gallery*, 83–84, fig. 273. Many such hymnals exist in Jerusalem; some will be discussed later; see Bogharian, *Grand Catalogue*, V (1971), Nos. 1460, 1594, 2358. In the Armenian model book in Venice, ms. 1434, this picture appears in a similar way to Sargis', though without a snake, see Der Nersessian, *Model I*, (1969) in *Studies*, 668, figs. 428, 429. Byzantine representations of Anne's prayer are found in the Kariye Djami Church in Istanbul (1315–1320), see Underwood, *Kariye Djami*, No. 85, vol. 2, pls. 92–95. For other contemporary representations, see Lafontaine-Dosogne, *Vierge*, I, 44–51; in none of them does the serpent appear, nor does Joachim stand behind Anne at the door.
26 Vat. gr. 1162, fol. 16, *ibid.*, figs, 42, 43, pp. 37–44; see also the icon of Zarzma (1010–1020), fig. 41, and St. Clement in Ochrid, of 1295, fig. 19. The Early Christian ivory panel in Leningrad has a standing angel in front of Anne and a tree with birds, fig. 40.

Chapter Eight pages 89–114

1 Jerusalem, ms. 1534, Bogharian, *Grand Catalogue*, V (1971), 288–290, figs. 16–18.
2 Jerusalem, ms. 7, Bogharian, *Grand Catalogue*, I (1966), 61–66, fig. 6.
3 See Der Nersessian, *Chester Beatty*, ms. 599, a Lectionary of 1414, XXXV, note 6, 147–152, pls. 30–32.
4 E.g. figs. 141, 142, 150, 151, 152, 153, 154, 155, 156.
5 *Ibid.*, XXXIII, XXXVII–XL.
6 *Idem*, *Chester Beatty*, XXXIII f.
7 Ms. 543, *ibid.*, XXXIV f.; *idem*, *Walters*, pls. E, F, figs. 138–190; Gospel of 1434, in Jerusalem, ms. 2784, see *ibid.*, figs. 191–194.
8 *Idem*, *L'Art Arménien*, 233, 236–7, figs. 178–182, *idem*, *Chester Beatty*, XL–XLI
9 E.g. Bible of 1645 in Jerusalem, ms. 1983, the De Bry Bible of 1643–6 in Jerusalem, ms. 1934, figs. 139, 140, 141 below.
10 The later text was printed in Isfahan in 1632. The earlier text was printed in Venice in 1855. See Butler, *Lausiac History*, I, 97–106; Conybeare, *Catalogue Br. Mus.*, 209. Both texts are based on the Greek Lives of the Fathers, cf. Rosweyde, *Vita Patrum*, 1615; *PL*. vols, 73–74.
11 Jerusalem ms. 285, Bogharian, *Grand Catalogue*, II (1967), 107–112, figs. 8, 9. The best known illuminated Lives of the Fathers are in Jerusalem ms. 971 from Van, 1623; ms. 23 Aleppo 1623; ms. 228, Jerusalem 1651; ms. 293, Istanbul 1652, four of which will be discussed here. Others are in Venice, Mekhitarist Library mss. 1922, 1947, and one in the British Library, ms. Add. 27301; cf. Der Nersessian, *Chester Beatty*, 6, note 5; Conybeare, *Catalogue Br. Mus.*, No. 88, pp. 209–215.
12 A Miscellany manuscript, which perhaps dates from 1359 in Jerusalem, ms. 773, has a full-page opening panel (fol. 4v) with Nerses the Graceful, which may point to such origins in the local school. Cf. Bogharian, *ibid.*, III (1968), 218–222, fig. 5.
13 *Pa-fnuti* in Coptic means "my God". Paphnutias was called *Cephalas* (= wise head), his life as a hermit also earned him the nickname *Bubali* (= Buffalo). See J. Cassian, *Collationes*, III, 1; XVIII, 15. *PL* vol. 49, cols. 559, 1116; cf. Bibliotheca Sanctorum, X (1968) cols. 26–29.
14 De Lacy O'Leary, *The Saints of Egypt*, London, New York (1937), 219–220.
15 Our ms. reached Jerusalem by 1443. Another colophon of 1615 states that it was taken to Hamith (Amida) to be copied in the church of St. Sargis. British Library Add. ms. 27301 of 1615 is indeed the copy made by Yovhannes, who also restored our manuscript before returning it to Jerusalem. Conybeare, *Catalogue Br. Mus.*, 213–214.
16 Jerusalem ms. 228, Bogharian, *ibid.*, I (1966), 612–623, figs. 65, 66.

17 Jerusalem ms. 971, *ibid.*, III (1968), 545–548, figs. 19–21.
18 Jerusalem ms. 23, *ibid.*, I (1966), 116–125, figs. 10, 11.
19 *PL*, 73, cols. 213 f. I am most grateful to Dr. V. Nersessian of the British Library for helping me to identify some of the episodes in the Lives of the Fathers, and to Aliza Cohen for her help in identifying the appropriate texts.
20 Der Nersessian, in *Chester Beatty*, 6, quotes an iconographical example of how the depiction of the upright rivers of the Garden of Eden, in the episode of the six monks who went to look for the Earthly Paradise in the *Lives of the Fathers*, helped to fashion the representation of the garden in the abridged Bibles of the 17th century.
21 Der Nersessian, *Chester Beatty*, XXXIII; *idem*, *Boston Gospel* (1950) in *Studies*, 683–694, figs. 444–459; *idem*, *L'Art Arménien*, 230, fig. 176, of Jerusalem ms. 3815 of 1455.
22 Jerusalem ms. 1667. Bogharian, *ibid.*, V (1971), 519–522, figs. 53–56.
23 Der Nersessian, *Bataille de Vardaniens* (1952) in *Studies*, 701–704, figs. 460–462; Buschhausen, *Wien*, cod. 189, pp. 80–82, figs. 169–170.
24 Cf. Buschhausen, *Wien*, figs. 156, 171.
25 E.g. Buschhausen, *Wien*, figs. 168, 185. This also appeared in later Gospel books, see e.g. Der Nersessian, *Chester Beatty*, pls. 51a, 54a.
26 Jerusalem ms. 473. Bogharian, *Grand Catalogue*, II (1967), 460–466, figs. 24–26; Der Nersessian, *L'Art Arménien*, 230–233, fig. 177; *idem*, *Chester Beatty*, 65.

27 Narkiss, *Relation*, 79–86, pls. LXXVIII–XLVI.
28 Akinian, *Armenischer Alexanderroman*, 201–296, groups the text into three recensions, with illustrated examples only in the first group.
29 See Bogharian in *Sion*, (1953), pp. 133–135.
30 Fol. 100: "Oh pitiful village of ours! Besides sour milk mixed with water and dry bread, there is nothing else." Bogharian, *Grand Catalogue*, vol. II (1964), 454. I am most grateful to Archbishop Bogharian for pointing out to me some of the most interesting inscriptions.
31 E.g. fol. 156: "Here I forgot to copy the king's word from Grigor the Catholicos' text, and used the old text instead."
32 Wolohojian, *Armenian Alexander*, 32–33.
33 Wolohojian, *Armenian Alexander*, 41.
34 Der Nersessian, *L'Art Arménien*, 233.
35 Bucephalus, the bull-headed, man-eating horse, was copied from our ms. (fol. 10v) onto an Armenian model book, see Der Nersessian, *Model II* (1969) in *Studies*, 670–671, figs. 433, 434.
36 Der Nersessian, *Chester Beatty*, XXXIV–XL.
37 E.g. Jerusalem ms. 2784 of 1434, cf. *ibid.*, XXXV, XXXVII; and ms. 566 of 1451, 50–57, pls. 34–37; and ms. 543 at Walters Art Gallery of 1455, cf. *idem*, *Walters*, 31–44, pls. E, F, 86–127.
38 *Idem*, *Chester Beatty*, XXXVI, pls. 34b.
39 *Ibid.*, XXXV.
40 *Ibid.*, XXXVIII–XXXIX, 79–80; Hovsepian, *Khizan*.
41 Jerusalem ms. 868, Bogharian, *ibid.*, III (1968), 366–368, figs. 7–9.
42 Jerusalem ms. 1594, *ibid.*, V (1971), 384–386, figs. 30, 31.
43 Der Nersessian, *ibid.*, 79–80.
44 Jerusalem ms. 135, Bogharian, *ibid.*, I (1966), 372–403, figs. 51–60
45 Jerusalem ms. 2569. Bogharian, *ibid.*, VIII (1977), 264.
46 M. Aghavnuni, *Monks and Visitors of Armenian Jerusalem*, Jerusalem (1929), 266 (in Armenian).
47 Jerusalem, ms. 1920. Bogharian, *ibid.*, VI (1972), 376–383, figs. 39–40.
48 Jerusalem, ms. 397. Bogharian, *ibid.*, II (1967), 324–326.
49 Ms. 573. Der Nersessian, *ibid.*, 76–81, pl. 46, 47.

50 Jerusalem, ms. 420. Bogharian, *ibid.*, II (1967), 370–372, fig. 20.
51 For other itinerant artists, such as Sargis of Mokhs, see *ibid.*, 136–138.
52 Jerusalem, ms. 340. Bogharian, *ibid.*, III (1968), 321–326.
53 Der Nersessian, *ibid.*, XXXIX, 79.
54 *Ibid.*, 137, notes 7 and 8.
55 Jerusalem, ms. 1663. Bogharian, *ibid.*, V (1971), 508–513, figs. 49–51.
56 E.g. ms. 2663 of 1414; ms. 2569 of 1577–79; ms. 2670 of 1640–43; and in the Chester Beatty Collection ms. 547 of the 17th century; cf. Der Nersessian, *ibid.*, p. 85.
57 Jerusalem, ms. 1460. Bogharian, *ibid.*, V (1971), 169–172, figs. 8–11.
58 See note 42 above.
59 Der Nersessian, *ibid.*, 136–137; Bogharian, *ibid.*, I (1966), ms. 234 of 1601, pp. 644–647.
60 Jerusalem, ms. 1920. Bogharian, *ibid.*, VI (1972), 376–383.
61 Der Nersessian. *ibid.*, XXXIX.
62 See Der Nersessian, *ibid.*, p. XL.
63 See M. Stone, *The Testament of Levi*, Jerusalem. 1969.
64 Jerusalem, ms. 1934. Bogharian, *ibid.*, VI (1972), 461–469.
65 Son of Theodor de Bry. *Thieme-Becker*, V. 162, cf. Brassinne, *De Bry*, I, 13–17.
66 *Biblia De Bry*, 1609. Not mentioned in Thieme-Becker, nor in Hollstein, *Engravings*, IV, 27–52.
67 Jerusalem, ms. 428. Bogharian, *ibid.*, II (1967), 382–387, figs. 21–22.
68 E.g. Jerusalem, ms. 1933 of 1645, cf. Der Nersessian, *L'Art Arménien*, 233–236, figs. 178–179.
69 Jerusalem, ms. 1932, fol. 14v. Bogharian, *ibid.*, VI (1972), 444–448, figs. 51, 52.
70 Jerusalem, ms. 501. Bogharian, *ibid.*, II (1967), 495–496, fig. 27.
71 Jerusalem, ms. 1933. Bogharian, *ibid.* VI (1972), 448–461, figs. 53–55.
72 Der Nersessian, *L'Art Arménien*, fig. 178.
73 This picture which exists also in the New Julfa Bible of 1643–5 (Jerusalem ms. 1934), is missing from the De Bry Bible, though it exists in other intermediary Bibles which J.T. De Bry used as models, like the Plantin Bible of 1572, which was engraved by Godefoid Ballain, see M. Rooses, *Het Oud en het Nieuw Testament*, Antwerpen 1911, II, 177; and woodcuts of Lucas Cranach the Elder, see J. Jahn, *1472–1553 Lucas Cranach I. A.*, Munich 1972, 740, and the Venice Bible of 1607 which was not used by De Bry (*Editiones Sixti Quinti Pont. Max.*, 635). However in these earlier representations of square Jerusalem God the Father, the dove and the shepherd are missing. Of the 14 illustrations in the New Julfa Bibles only 10 depend on the De Bry Bible of 1609, the other four must have had a different origin. All these Apocalypse illustrations depend ultimately on Albrecht Dürer's 14 woodcuts of 1496–98, with the exception of the Heavenly Jerusalem, see Schellenberg, *Dürers Apokalypse*.
74 Basle 1582–Amsterdam 1658, son of the engraver Christoffel the First, and father of the third. See Waller, *Nederlandsche Graveurs*, 300; *Thieme-Becker*, XXX, 586; Nagler, *Künstler Lexikon*, XVIII, 362–365.
75 Sichem, *Biblia Sacra*, II, 453. Another edition of 1657 from Amsterdam has similar woodcuts.
76 All of Van Sichem's woodcuts are signed with his initials CVS. To the woodcuts which he copied from others, he added their monogram to his. For instance the Passion pictures have the initials HG of his Dutch teacher Hendrik Goltzius, see Hollstein, *Dutch and Flemish Etchings*, VIII, 10–11, whereas most of the Apocalypse scenes have Dürer's monogram AD, see Hollstein, *German Engravings*, VII, 135–143. The Heavenly Jerusalem in the Van Sichem Bible (p. 453), the last in the book, is of inferior quality, lacking Dürer's monogram. The penultimate picture (p. 452) repeats the last scene of Dürer's version, and carries his monogram.
77 Ms. 1933, fols. 7v, 8; see Der Nersessian, *L'Art Arménien*, figs. 178–179. Other pictures which belong to the original manuscript are Hannah and Eli (fol. 116v) and David at prayer (fol. 281v). To the later style belongs the story of Job (fol. 270v).

Chapter Nine pages 115–120

1 See Macler, *Livres d'Amsterdam*, 71–84; *idem*, *Reliure d'Oskan*, 7–17; and special issues dedicated to the Oskan Bible of the periodicals *Sion* and *Etchmiadzin* were published in 1966. I am grateful to Dr. V. Nersessian, for helping in the Oskan Bible. I regret I was unable to see his forthcoming book on Armenian Printing due to be published by the British Museum.
2 There are slight size variations from both the Antwerp 1646 and Amsterdam 1657 editions of the Van Sichem Bible.
3 By Hadrianus Petrus Damianus Schoonbeck, an engraver and printer, Amsterdam 1658–Moscow 1705. Cf. Nagler, *Künstler Lexikon*, XVII, 503–504.
4 E.g. Hollstein, *German Engravings*, VII, 15, 111.
5 Nagler, *Künstler Lexikon*, XVIII, 363.
6 Jerusalem ms. 1927. Bogharian, *Grand Catalogue*, VI (1972), 421–427; Der Nersessian, *Chester Beatty*, XLIII, 11.
7 Fol. 124v, full-page. Cf. Der Nersessian, *Chester Beatty*, XLIII, 11.
8 For a similar Bible, see London, British Library ms. Or. 8833.
9 Jerusalem ms. 66. Bogharian, *Grand Catalogue*, I (1966), 208–215, figs. 22–27.
10 Der Nersessian, *The Armenians*, 75.
11 E.g. Chester Beatty ms. 606, *idem*, *Chester Beatty*, 169.

Chapter Ten pages 121–144

1 For the seventy churches said to have belonged to the Armenians prior to the Persian conquest, see the first part of this book "The Armenian Communities of Jerusalem".
2 Prawer, *Armenians in Jerusalem*, 229–230.
3 Prawer, *ibid.*, 230; Vincent and Abel, *Jerusalem II*, 522.
4 Prawer, *ibid.*, *230–231*.
5 *John of Würzburg*, *PPTS*, Vol. 3, 45; Hintlian, *History*, 54; Vincent and Abel, *ibid.*, 522.
6 *Nicolo da Poggibonsi*, 29, Hintlian. *History*, 55.
7 *John Poloner*, *PPTS*, Vol. 6, 15.
8 Prawer, *ibid.*, 231; Vincent and Abel, *ibid.*, 522–524.
9 Vincent and Abel, *ibid.*, 529–541; R. Krautheimer, *Early Christian and Byzantine Architecture* (London, 1965), 201–213.
10 *Ibid.*, 532.
11 *Ibid.*, 541–542; Hintlian, *History*, 54.
12 Vincent and Abel, *ibid.*, 544–546.
13 *Ibid.* 542–544.
14 *Ibid.*, 544–546.
15 Prawer, *ibid.*, 229–233.
16 Vincent and Abel, *ibid.*, 531–532, fig. 198.
17 *Ibid.*, figs. 203–205.
18 *Ibid.*, 536–538, fig. 206.
19 E.g. the cupola in the Church of Hopital Saint-Blaise in the Pyrenees; see M. Aubert, *L'Art Roman en France*, (Paris, 1961), 241; Vincent and Abel, *ibid.*, 538.
20 *Ibid.*, pl. XIX, 4, 6.
21 Borg, *Provence*, figs. 141, 142. I am grateful to Dr. Bianca Kühnel for suggesting these examples to me.
22 Human heads within the leaves are very common in Provence, see Borg, *ibid.*, figs. 145–148; but there are also some scenes, see *ibid.*, fig. 140. cf. Vincent and Abel, *ibid.*, pl. XVIII.
23 See *Congres Archéologique de France*, 121 (1963), 21, 155.
24 Vincent and Abel, *ibid.*, pls. XXI, XXIV, XXVI, LXII, LXXIII.
25 Vincent and Abel, *Jerusalem II*, 555 556, fig. 225, pl. LVIII, 3. Mekhitarian, *Cat. Exh. Jerusalem* (1969), 43–44, Kurdian, *Wood-Carving*, 45, pl. 25.
26 Cf. an iconostasis in the Coptic Church of Aboul Sefein. See M.H. Simaika Pacha, *Guide Sommaire du Musée Copte*, (Cairo, 1937), pl CXL.
27 Vincent and Abel, *ibid.*, 556, pl. LVII, 1.
28 H. Maundrell, *A Journey from Aleppo to Jerusalem in 1697*, (Beirut, 1963), 163.
29 Jerusalem, ms. 154, Bogharian, *Grand Catalogue*, I (1966), 429–466.
30 Carswell, *Kütahya Tiles*, 12–26.
31 Abraham *Vardapet*, the *Arajnord* of Thekirdag (East Thrace) mentioned in the pictorial tiles inscription, made his first visit to Jerusalem in 1719. On this occasion, he may have ordered some of these tiles as a gift to the Holy Sepulcher. Other tiles were donated by individuals and families from Kütahya at about the same date, as their inscriptions imply.
32 Carswell, *ibid.*, 2 volumes, 1972.
33 *Ibid.*, 29–30, pl. 1, A1.
34 *Ibid.*, 31, pl. 1, A3.
35 *Ibid.*, 31–32, pl. 1, A4.
36 *Ibid.*, 33, pl. 2, A7.
37 *Ibid.*, 33–34, pl. 2, A8.
38 *Ibid.*, 34–49, pls. 3–9.
39 *Ibid.*, 50–52, pl. 10, C1.
40 *Ibid.*, 54, pl. 11, C6.
41 *Ibid.*, 81–83, pl. 22 a–c.
42 Mekhitarian, *Cat. Exh. Jerusalem*, 1969, 35, no. 50.
43 *Ibid.*, No. 49.
44 *Ibid.*, 41, No. 78.

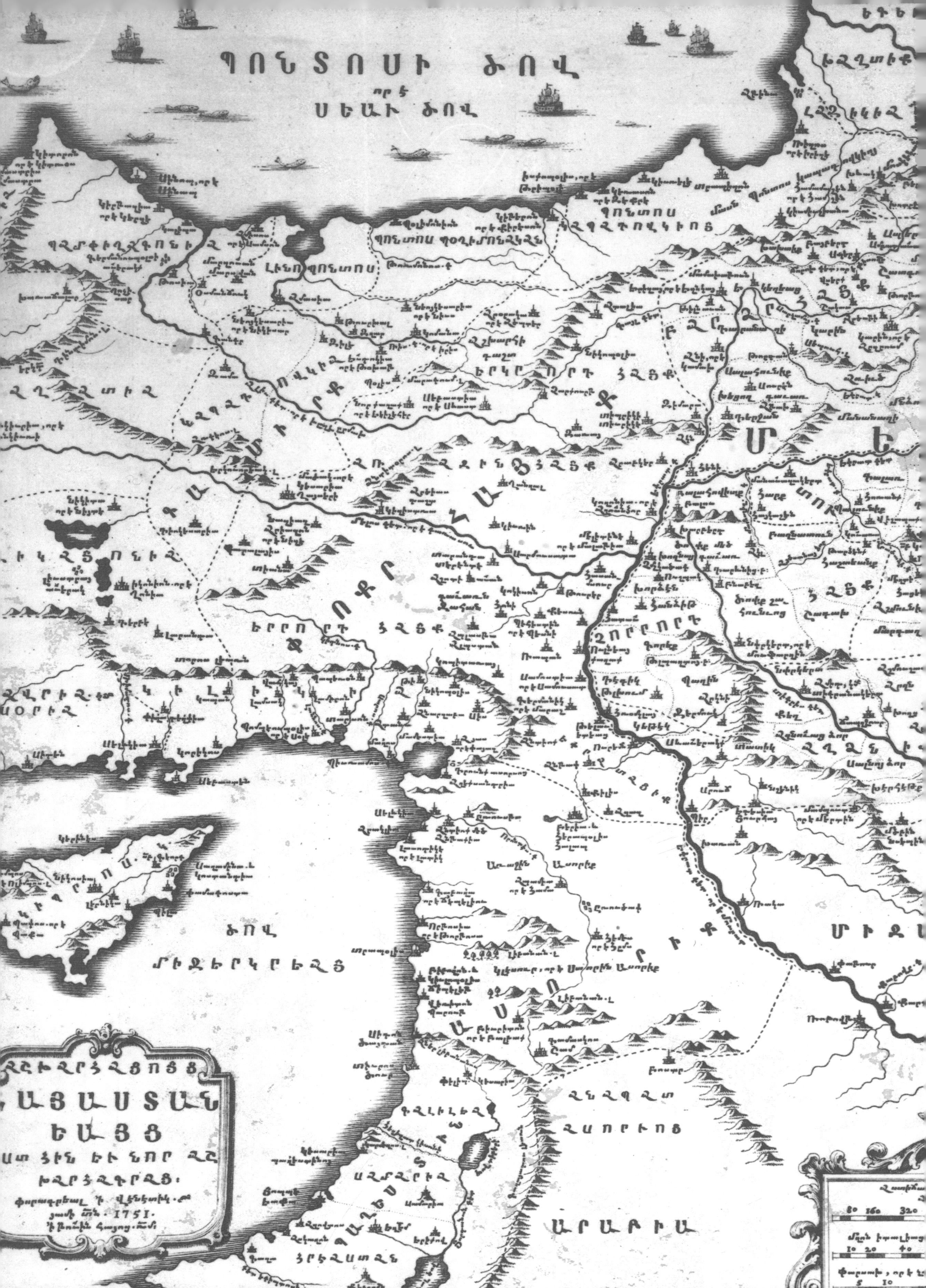

ՊՈՆՏՈՍԻ ԾՈՎ
որ է
ՍԵԱՒ ԾՈՎ
ԾՈՎ
ՄԻՋԵՐԿՐԵԱՅՑ
ԱՐԱԲԻԱ
1751
80 160 320
10 20 40
5 10